Contributions to Economics

For further volumes:
http://www.springer.com/series/1262

Marcel Wiedmann

Money, Stock Prices and Central Banks

A Cointegrated VAR Analysis

Physica-Verlag

Marcel Wiedmann
McKinsey and Company
Birkenwaldstraße 149
70191 Stuttgart
Germany
marcel_wiedmann@mckinsey.com

ISSN 1431-1933
ISBN 978-3-7908-2646-3 e-ISBN 978-3-7908-2647-0
DOI 10.1007/978-3-7908-2647-0
Springer Heidelberg Dordrecht London New York

Library of Congress Control Number: 2011925994

Cover design: WMXDesign GmbH, Heidelberg

Printed on acid-free paper

Physica-Verlag is a brand of Springer-Verlag Berlin Heidelberg
Springer-Verlag is a part of Springer Science+Business Media (www.springer.com)

Acknowledgements

This book presents the results of my doctoral study. It would not have been possible without the encouragement, guidance and support of my dissertation supervisor Professor Dr. Ansgar Belke. I would also like to thank him for all the lively discussions related to the thesis and to current events. Our work together has always been a pleasure. I am also grateful to Professor Dr. Gerhard Wagenhals, who acted as my secondary advisor and Professor Dr. Hans-Peter Burghof for serving on my PhD committee.

I am indebted to Professor Dr. Katarina Juselius and Professor Dr. Soren Johansen for hosting the Summer School in Econometrics at the University of Copenhagen. These three very intense weeks enabled me to apply the cointegrated VAR model to my data in a meaningful way and have buttressed my results. Thank you again, Katarina, for your enduring patience in responding to my follow-up questions, even long after the course had ended.

My heartfelt gratitude also goes out to my friend Denise Möbius for lending me her organizational skills, which included, among others, the tedious but necessary tasks of creating the bibliography and ensuring proper formatting. You were an invaluable help. I also owe thanks to my friend Alexander Krieg for insightful discussions, Latex tutoring and providing the necessary distractions during the course of this project.

On a more personal level, I wish to thank my parents for their support. Your being there makes everything so much easier. Most importantly, I want to thank Margarita for improving the flow of my thesis and, especially, for loving me and taking care of our little family. You have enabled me to accomplish this. Thank you.

Lastly, I wish to thank all of those who have supported me in any respect during the completion of this project. "No man is an island unto himself", John Donne (1624).

Stuttgart
October 2010

Marcel Wiedmann

Contents

List of Figures

List of Tables

List of Abbreviations

Δ	Change (first difference)
ADF	Augmented Dickey–Fuller
ASEAN	Association of Southeast Asian Nations
BIS	Bank for International Settlements
BoE	Bank of England
BoJ	Bank of Japan
BoK	Bank of Korea
BoP	Balance of Payments
BoT	Bank of Thailand
CI	Cointegration
CVAR	Cointegrated Vector AutoRegressive
DGF	Degrees of Freedom
ECB	European Central Bank
ecm	Error-correction Mechanism
EMU	Economic and Monetary Union
EUR	Euro
Fed	Federal Reserve System of the United States of America
G7	Group of Seven (industrialized nations)
GDP	Gross Domestic Product
i.i.d.	Independently and Identically Distributed
IFS	International Financial Statistics
IMF	International Monetary Fund
log	Logarithm
LR	Likelihood Ratio
LTCM	Long Term Capital Management
JPY	Japanese Yen
MA	Moving-Average
NBER	National Bureau of Economic Research
NSA	Not Seasonally Adjusted
NYSE	New York Stock Exchange

OECD	Organisation for Economic Co-operation and Development
PP	Phillips–Perron
PPP	Purchasing Power Parity
RBoA	Reserve Bank of Australia
SA	Seasonally Adjusted
UK	United Kingdom (of Great Britain and Northern Ireland)
US	United States of America
USD	US Dollar
WSJ	Wall Street Journal
VAR	Vector AutoRegressive

Chapter 1
Introduction

1.1 Context, Motivation and Objectives

Starting with the 'Great Moderation' in the mid-1980s, five phenomena have influenced and characterized economic conditions and financial markets, especially in developed markets:

- Low and constant inflation rates.[1]
- Strong and persistent money growth and the unprecedented access companies, financial investment firms and ordinary people have to borrowing and foreign exchange.[2]
- Massive increases in world trade, financial globalization and international capital flows.[3]
- Large asset price swings and an increased number of financial crises.[4]
- Reduced output volatility.[5]

Many economic observers point to globalization and the resulting pricing-to-market of companies to explain low inflation rates. They hypothesize that, contrary to conventional theory, abundant liquidity in the system has not led to goods price

[1] For an overview, see, for example, The Economist (2007, p. 4), which shows the reduced median and variation for inflation across 13 industrialized countries.

[2] Rees (2009, p. 1) calculated that between 1980 and 2007 global liquidity increased tenfold while nominal gross domestic product (GDP) 'only' grew sixfold. Accordingly, excess liquidity accounts for 65% of economic output.

[3] Evans and Hnatkovska (2005, p. 1) point out that gross capital flows between developed economies rose by 300% during the 1990s alone compared to a 63% increase in trade flows and 26% for real GDP. See also Hau and Rey (2004, p. 126), who find that gross cross-border flows based on bond and equity transactions in the United States of America (US) were equivalent to only 4% of GDP in 1975, 100% in the early 1990s and increased to 245% by 2000.

[4] Bordo et al. (2001, pp. 56–57) show that the chance of suffering a currency crisis, banking crisis or twin crisis in a given year has more than doubled for the period 1973 to 1997 compared to during the Bretton Woods and the gold standard periods.

[5] See Kohn (2008, p. 5).

M. Wiedmann, *Money, Stock Prices and Central Banks*, Contributions to Economics,
DOI 10.1007/978-3-7908-2647-0_1, © Springer-Verlag Berlin Heidelberg 2011

increases. Instead it is the antecedent to excessive asset price rises and increased volatility, such as in housing, commodities and stocks (Rogoff 2006, p. 2).

Price increases in real goods and services usually lead to reduced demand and substitution. This is not true of asset prices. For example, rising share prices are regarded as a sign of confidence and breed optimism. Thus, ordinary people invest more money when prices go up and less when prices go down.

Abundant liquidity can exacerbate this. It is easier and cheaper for people, hedge funds and companies to borrow under conditions of ample liquidity. If portions of these additional funds are invested, prices are pushed up further and optimism spreads. Herding behavior and rational speculation are signs of this process. After all, even if prices depart from justified long-run levels, it is still lucrative to bet on rising prices if stocks can be sold at a higher level before the market corrects itself. Thus, irrationally high levels on the stock market can result from rational speculation and people's perception that they are smarter than others and able to get out of the market before it turns. This type of thinking and rational speculation increase with ample monetary liquidity, which, in turn, also increases market liquidity. As a result, there always seems to be a ready buyer.

Additionally, confidence and optimism are also boosted because owners of assets feel richer when house or share prices increase. This, in turn, results in increased spending on goods and assets. The former helps companies increase profits and, consequently, also leads to increases in share prices and the valuation of bonds, which justifies previous purchases ex post.[6] The number of defaults decreases and lenders want to lend more to participate in the upswing, thereby intensifying it.

The same mechanisms apply once markets turn sour. When prices decline, previous overconfidence turns into paralyzing uncertainty and lenders demand that borrowers hold more collateral. At the same time, falling asset prices decrease the amount of collateral, forcing borrowers to sell assets. This drives prices down further.

Whereas the above described play of optimism, confidence and asset prices evolves independent of liquidity conditions, there is a strong case that high liquidity levels reinforce this process. The procyclicality of credit markets influences the business cycle, heightens stock market ups and exacerbates downs.

In conclusion, rising asset prices, abundant credit and liquidity conditions, optimism, confidence and rational speculation all feed into each other and amplify the normal behavior of stock markets. By this token, the same mechanisms apply in a downturn. This reasoning indicates a long-run relationship between liquidity/ 'excess liquidity' and stock market levels with a potential inclusion of economic activity or other macro variables.[7] Four testable hypotheses can be derived from the above discussion:

---

[6] Farmer (2009, pp. 14–17) provides a methodological description of the self-fulfilling behavior of stock markets in the context of a labor market model.

[7] It could be argued that these connections are especially strong during bubbles. However, it might only be the intensity that varies. In addition, stock market behavior over the last 25 years is characterized by long boom and bust phases.

- H_1 – Market agents' behavior (herding, rational speculation, contagious confidence and optimism) leads to strong persistence in stock market developments, i.e., shocks to the stock market have positive long-run effects on future developments.
- H_2 – Long-run equilibria exist between stock prices and liquidity conditions.
- H_3 – Liquidity conditions influence stock prices positively in the long run.
- H_4 – Liquidity conditions influence stock prices positively in the short run.

Liquidity conditions can be described via the quantity of money, either the total level or the amount in excess of demand and via the price of money, i.e., the short-term interest rate.

The high level of integration of the international financial markets points to the importance of cross-country capital flows for domestic developments. Strong economic activity and rising stock markets attract foreign investments, which, in turn, enforce market trends. In addition, if a stock market boom is built on foreign money, the withdrawal of external financing often leads to a reversal of the direction of the market. Hence, the influence of international capital flows on stock markets might be especially intense at market turning points. In addition, inflation and markets seem to be strongly driven not only by national circumstances, but also by global trends and sentiment. The substantial growth of international capital flows and the cross-border holdings of financial assets and liabilities are indicative of this (Lane and Milesi-Ferretti 2006, pp. 12–14, 33–34). This has led to the growing influence of foreign portfolio decisions on domestic stock markets. International capital flows also influence the above mentioned liquidity conditions. This suggests the inclusion of the following testable hypotheses:

- H_5 – International capital flows have a positive long-run impact on the stock market behavior of individual countries.
- H_6 – International capital flows have a positive short-run impact on the stock market behavior of individual countries.

The above described mechanisms have led to ever larger swings in asset prices, with a potentially harmful effect on the real economy, as exemplified by the global financial crisis that started in July 2007.[8] But, even before this severe financial crisis, economists began asking whether or not central banks should include asset prices in monetary policy setting or target them directly. The issue is still under discussion. Moreover, the ability to target asset prices in a manner which influences stock prices is unclear. Notwithstanding this lack of knowledge of central bank abilities, equity prices play a major role in various theories of the monetary transmission mechanism. This leads to the following questions, which must be answered empirically:

- Q_1 – Are central banks able to influence stock prices in the long run?
- Q_2 – Are central banks able to influence stock prices in the short run?

[8] See also Reinhart and Rogoff (2009, pp. 4–10) and Helbling and Terrones (2003, pp. 69–70) for consequences of stock market and real estate busts for the real economy.

Consequently, the analysis also sheds light on the monetary transmission mechanism, especially the asset price channel, which is advocated by the Monetarist perspective. However, not only the asset price channel, but also other transmission mechanism theories, such as the balance sheet channel and the liquidity effects view, incorporate the effect of expansive monetary policy on equity valuation and its subsequent impact on the real economy.[9] It is surprising that although a large part of transmission mechanism theory relies on the connection between stock prices and the real economy, the effect that monetary policy has on stock market prices is still questioned. Mishkin (2001, p. 16) expresses this conundrum as follows:

> "The linkage between monetary policy and stock prices, although an important part of the transmission mechanism, is still nevertheless, a weak one. Most fluctuations in stock prices occur for reasons unrelated to monetary policy, either reflecting real fundamentals or animal spirit."

The above described market forces might interact differently across countries because economic development, financial market depth[10] and institutional circumstances differ. In addition, some countries are lenders and others borrowers of international capital. As a result, the above described interrelations should be analyzed on a country basis instead of a global level. This allows for the analysis of monetary policy's effectiveness and the abilities of central banks to influence macroeconomic variables across their respective currency areas. Comparative country analyses can help to answer the following questions:

- Q_3 – Do country-specific characteristics influence the relationship between liquidity conditions and the stock market?
- Q_4 – Do central banks' ability to target stock markets depend on the respective country-specific conditions?

The objective of this contribution is to empirically analyze hypotheses $H_1 - H_5$ and answer questions $Q_1 - Q_4$. The empirical analyses focus on five developed economies and three emerging markets, namely the US, the euro area, Japan, the United Kingdom (UK), Australia, South Korea, Thailand and Brazil. The goal of the country comparisons is to distinguish features that may influence the above described relationships.

Since cointegration between non-stationary data series represents the statistical expression of the economic notion of a long-run economic relation, the above outlined issues are analyzed applying the parametric approach of the Cointegrated Vector Autoregressive (CVAR) model. The classification of the data generating process into stationary and non-stationary parts enables the distinction between long-run equilibria and short-run dynamic adjustment. In addition, common trends that push the variables and determine the long-run impact of shocks to the variables can be identified. The usefulness of the CVAR model depends on the ability to

[9] For an overview of the transmission mechanism theories, which include equity prices, see Mishkin (1995, pp. 5–9).

[10] In this case, financial market depth means the ratio of a country's financial assets to its GDP.

identify relevant economic structures within the statistical model. Hence, for a valid application of the CVAR approach it is crucial to carefully choose the variables that should enter the analysis. To achieve this, first, the underlying economic theory and data series possibilities are discussed. Then the above stated hypotheses are tested.

However, once the economic theory is derived and the necessary variables are identified the focus is on the variation and covariation of the data without applying prior untestable restrictions (as is the case in most economic models). This is reasonable because economic policy makers also base their decisions on observable changes in the relevant macro variables (Johansen and Juselius 1994, p. 10). In conclusion, information from economic theory models is used to derive additional testable hypotheses and to determine the relevant variables. However, the objectives of this contribution do not include testing the models themselves.

Although a plethora of papers on macroeconomic variables and stock market behavior already exist, the scope of previous research has so far been lopsided in favor of the US market and focused mainly on the short-run impact of variables. The above hypotheses and questions still remain unsolved and are timelier than ever since the current global financial crisis has once again proven the destructive consequences of large asset price swings. Consequently, the objectives of this contribution are worth exploring, especially in the framework of the CVAR model.[11] In addition, the CVAR methodology enables empirical testing of additional theoretical hypotheses, which describe the interrelations between the included variables, such as, among others, the term structure of interest rates, the Fisher hypothesis and the relationship between stock markets and economic activity. A further objective of this contribution is to obtain an enhanced picture of stock market behavior across different countries.

The following section gives an overview of the structure of the contribution, paying heed to the necessity to first find the ideal variables based on economic theory, then to define a valid statistical model and finally, to test the economic hypotheses as parametric restrictions in a well-specified statistical model.

1.2 Structure

Figure 1.1 provides an overview of the structure of this contribution. Chapters 2–5 cover the preparation phase to ensure a valid statistical analysis. Chapter 6 presents the detailed statistical investigation of the eight country analyses. Finally, Chaps. 7 and 8 focus on the interpretation of the findings, derive policy recommendations and discuss limitations of the analysis herein in order to derive further research opportunities.

The objectives of the preparation chapters are, first, to clearly state the hypotheses, second, to validate the hypotheses by economic theory, third, to identify the

[11] See, for example, Adalid and Detken (2007, p. 6).

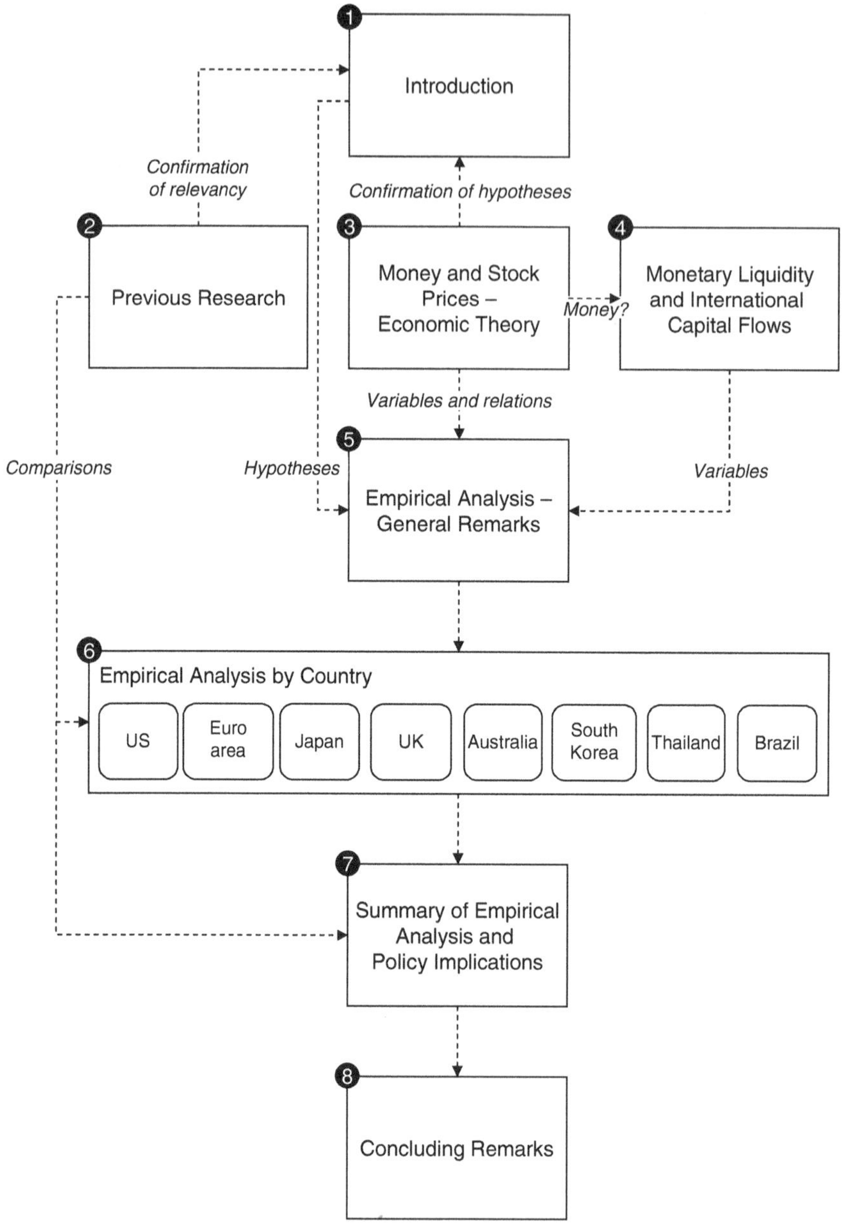

Fig. 1.1 Structure of the dissertation

necessary variables for the analysis and, fourth, to introduce the statistical method. To achieve this, Chap. 2 gives an overview of previous research in the field, identifying main findings and shortcomings of previous analyses. This chapter confirms the necessity of the investigation in this contribution and enables comparisons between the findings of this contribution with previous research. Chapter 3 introduces various theories that connect the development between money and stock prices. These theories confirm the hypotheses, which are stated in the introduction. In addition, variables, which are helpful to analyze the main hypotheses, are identified. Since Chap. 3 discusses the relationship between the stock market and monetary aggregates as well as interest rates in a general way, Chap. 4 analyzes in more detail, which monetary variables to focus on. In addition, it introduces international capital flows as a proxy for international monetary developments that have the potential to affect domestic stock market developments. Lastly, Chap. 5 introduces the statistical methodology of this contribution, which is the CVAR model. Additionally, it restates the main hypotheses and summarizes the variables, which are included in the system. Moreover, it presents further theoretical aspects, which outline potential economic long-run relations between the system variables. These additional long-run relations are also tested in the CVAR framework.

Execution of the empirical analysis is the focus of Chap. 6. The main structure is organized by country. As such, a complete country analysis is conducted (long-run equilibria, short-run dynamic adjustments and long-run impact) before moving on to the next country. The structure of the different country analyses is the same. All start with a presentation of the data and model specifications that guarantee a statistically well-specified model. Once a well-specified model is obtained, the cointegration rank is determined based on several criteria. Afterwards, the focus is on the identification of the long-run structure. This starts with a first inspection of the unrestricted Π matrix and some preliminary hypotheses testing before turning to the final identified long-run structure. Once an overidentified long-run structure is tested and fixed, short-run dynamics are analyzed in a structural error-correction model. Significant short-run effects are tested by applying the full information maximum likelihood estimator in simultaneous equation modeling. Finally, the last part of the analysis focuses on the common trends and the permanent impact of shocks to the variables. Each country analysis has its own country-specific conclusion section.

Chapter 7 summarizes the findings of the main hypotheses across the analyzed economies, thereby, pointing out similarities and differences. It shows whether or not the impact of liquidity on stock markets depends on country characteristics, such as monetary policy, openness or development grade. In addition to the main hypotheses of this contribution, other questions of economic interest are also discussed with a focus on determinants of stock market developments. Based on these findings, the chapter derives policy implications. These include a case for central banks to pay more attention to asset prices and instruments, other than the policy rate, which may influence asset prices. Chapter 8 concludes and describes research opportunities that would help, on the one hand, improve understanding of stock market developments and, on the other hand, focus on liquidity conditions and their potential impact on assets aside from stocks. Detailed descriptions of the data and supporting material for the various analyses are given in the appendix.

Chapter 2
Previous Research

2.1 Money and Stock Prices

2.1.1 Historical Overview

Sprinkel (1964) pioneered the investigation of the relationship between the amount of money and the stock market. He justifies his approach with the monetary portfolio model.[1] His findings are based on a graphical inspection of money growth and stock market turning points. His main conclusion is that stock prices lag behind changes in the growth rate of money supply. Applying this finding to the market, Sprinkel (1964, p. 149) formulates an investment rule, which states that "[a]ll funds were invested in stocks until monetary growth had declined 15 months, and then all funds were invested in bonds until monetary growth had risen two months." This rule is based on the finding that for the period under investigation between 1918 and 1960 a bear market in stock prices was predicted 15 months after each peak in monetary growth, and that a bull market was predicted two months after each trough of monetary growth. One downside of Sprinkel's analysis is the ex-post identification of peaks and troughs, because he uses data which is only available several quarters after the peaks and troughs. Hence, it is difficult to apply his rule in real time. The reason for this is that he identifies peaks and troughs not only numerically but also pays attention to business cycle peaks as identified by the National Bureau of Economic Research (NBER). The information from the NBER, however, is only available several quarters after the turning points (Rozeff 1974, p. 288).

In his follow-up book, Sprinkel (1971) finds that the relationship no longer holds true and, therefore, can no longer be used to gain excess returns. His explanation for this is that too many investors focus on money growth as a leading indicator and, as a result, price differences are immediately diminished. Modigliani (1971, p. 21) takes the same line when summarizing his discussion of the determination of the market value of corporate equity with the following statement: "[w]e still cannot

[1] See Sect. 3.2.1.1 for a description of the monetary portfolio model and the derivations for the relationship between money and asset prices.

M. Wiedmann, *Money, Stock Prices and Central Banks*, Contributions to Economics,
DOI 10.1007/978-3-7908-2647-0_2, © Springer-Verlag Berlin Heidelberg 2011

see any direct mechanism through which the rate of change of money could affect market values – except possibly because operators take that variable as an indicator of things to come. But even this explanation is hardly credible except, perhaps, in the last couple of years, when watching every wiggle of the money supply has suddenly become so fashionable."

This view is opposed by, for example, Hamburger and Kochin (1972, pp. 236–242), who find ample support for the hypothesis that money supply changes have an important impact on the stock market in the short run, independent of the influence money has on interest rates and expected corporate earnings.

In general, the relationship between money supply and stock prices was widely studied in the 1970s with mixed results. On the one hand, Homa and Jaffee (1971, quarterly data from 1954 to 1969, S&P 500, regression analysis), Keran (1971, quarterly data from 1956 to 1970, S&P 500, regression analysis) and Hamburger and Kochin (1972, quarterly data for three periods, 1956–1970, 1953–1960 and 1961–1970, S&P 500, regression analysis) find a positive significant relationship between money supply and stock prices. In their studies, money leads stock prices. The implication of their results is that investors can earn excess profits if they follow a trading strategy, which is based on the observed behavior of the money stock. Their findings show that the effect of money on stock prices is mostly indirect. As such, Keran (1971, p. 31) notes that "[a]ccording to this analysis, changes in nominal money stock have little direct impact on the stock price, but a major indirect influence on stock prices through their effect on inflation and corporate earnings expectations."

On the other hand, Rozeff (1974, monthly data, several subperiods ranging from 1916 to 1970, S&P 500, regression analysis), Pesando (1974, quarterly data from 1956 to 1970, S&P 500, regression analysis), Cooper (1974, monthly, quarterly and annual data from 1947 to 1970, S&P 500, regression analysis) and Rogalski and Vinso (1977, monthly data from 1963 to 1974, four US stock market indices, Granger causality of mixed autoregressive-moving average processes) find evidence that past money changes do not contain predictive information for stock prices. They point out that their findings are consistent with the efficient market hypothesis as documented by Fama (1970). Current stock prices incorporate all information, which is contained in past money supply data and even seem to anticipate future money supply changes. Consequently, they deny the existence of lags and profitable trading rules. It is important to note, though, that these authors do not deny a relationship between money and stock prices. Instead, "monetary variables may have a consistent effect on stock returns in an efficient market without opportunities for excess profit arising" (Rozeff 1974, p. 247).

In the 1980s, the focus shifted a bit to the relationship between macroeconomic factors and stock returns. The main reason for this was the development of the Arbitrage Pricing Theory by Ross (1976) in the second half of the 1970s. This framework is used to address the question of whether risk, which is associated with certain macroeconomic variables, is reflected in expected asset returns. It is the main finding of Chen et al. (1986) that macro variables have a systematic effect on stock returns. In their view, economic forces affect the discount rate, the ability of firms to generate cash flows and future dividend payments.[2] This approach was applied in many studies.[3]

In addition, the 1980s also introduced studies that focused on the relationship between anticipated and unanticipated changes of money supply and stock prices. For example, Pearce and Roley (1983, weekly data from September 1977 to January 1982, Dow Jones Industrial Average, regression analysis) investigate the response of stock prices to weekly money announcements. They apply survey data on market participants' forecasts to distinguish expected from actual changes in money. Their results are in line with the efficient market hypothesis because only unanticipated changes have a significant effect on stock prices. The distinguished relationship is negative, which they justify with the increase in expected inflation associated with an unanticipated rise in money supply.[4]

In contrast, Hashemzadeh and Taylor (1988, p. 1608, weekly data from January 1980 to July 1986, S&P 500, regression analysis) find bidirectional causality between money supply and stock prices in the US. They find that both variables react to each other. Consequently, they characterize the relationship between money supply and stock prices as a feedback system, which reminds one of a cointegration relation. Moreover, Friedman (1988, quarterly data from 1961 to 1986, S&P 500, regression analysis) finds that real stock prices are positively correlated with the velocity of money three quarters ahead. Darrat (1987, quarterly data from 1960 to 1982, UK and West Germany, regression analysis) focuses his regression analyses on West Germany and the UK. Lagged anticipated as well as unanticipated money growth is statistically significant for stock returns in both countries.

The preferred research methodology to analyze the relationship between money and stock prices in the 1990s was the vector autoregressive (VAR) model. Lee (1992, monthly data from 1947 to 1987, New York Stock Exchange (NYSE), VAR analysis), Marshall (1992, quarterly data from 1959 to 1990, NYSE, VAR analysis), Dhakal et al. (1993, monthly data from 1973 to 1991, S&P 400 industrials, VAR analysis) and Abdullah and Hayworth (1993, monthly data from 1980 to 1988, S&P 500, VAR analysis) apply a VAR model to analyze the relationship between share prices and the macro economy. Since the multivariate VAR model allows for the inclusion of several endogenous variables, these investigations did not focus solely on the relationship between stocks and money but included a broad set of macro indicators and are, therefore, closer to the analysis in this contribution. Marshall (1992, p. 1335), Dhakal et al. (1993, p. 71) and Abdullah and Hayworth (1993, p. 58) find a significant causal impact of money supply changes on share price changes. In addition, Lastrapes (1998) analyzes the reaction of real equity returns to money supply shocks across the Group of Seven (G7) countries and the Netherlands for

[2] See Sect. 3.2.2.2 for theoretical considerations of the discount factor for stock prices as well as Sect. 3.2.3.1 for theoretical aspects of the relationship between dividends and stock prices.

[3] For non-US analyses, see, for example, Cheng (1995) for the UK and Cheng (1996) for international analyses.

[4] See Sect. 3.2.1.2 for theoretical considerations of the relationship between inflation and stock prices.

post-war data. His results, based on a VAR in first differences, show that, with the exception of France and the UK, "real equity prices respond positively, persistently and significantly" to nominal money supply shocks (Lastrapes 1998, p. 394).

The research presented above is characterized by a strong focus on US markets. While more recent research still has a bias in favor of US markets, newer studies also incorporate international and global perspectives. Two of the first important studies to do so are Conover et al. (1999) and Baks and Kramer (1999). While Conover et al. focus on developments across 16 countries,[5] Baks and Kramer are the first to introduce the concept of global liquidity and its potential impact on aggregated global stock markets.

2.1.2 Recent Research

Baks and Kramer (1999) pioneered the analysis of the impact of global liquidity on asset prices in a scientific context. Preceding their research, the notion that global excess liquidity exists and that it influences global capital markets, e.g., by compressing risk premia before the 1998 Russian debt crisis and the collapse of Long Term Capital Management (LTCM), was mainly advocated in research conducted by investment banks or newspapers.[6]

Baks and Kramer (1999) assess the empirical influence of global excess liquidity on asset prices utilizing three different aggregation methods for money growth, namely, a weighted growth rate series (by GDP in US Dollars (USD)), a simple sum USD aggregate and a Divisia index. All three aggregation methods are applied to narrow and broad money. Their global measures are based on the G7 countries. Excess liquidity is derived by subtracting weighted average nominal GDP growth rates from money growth rates.[7]

Based on quarterly data between 1971 and 1998, Baks and Kramer (1999) derive three main conclusions from their empirical research. First, higher liquidity growth rates are consistent with higher real stock returns. Second, an increase in liquidity growth rates leads to a reduction in real interest rates. And third, liquidity spillovers exist. This means that increased liquidity growth in one country is consistent with the first two results in other countries.[8]

[5] The analysis of Conover et al. (1999, monthly data from 1956 to 1995, national stock markets, regression analysis) focuses more on the monetary policy stance and stock prices instead of money supply developments.

[6] See, for example, Williams (1999), Montgomery (1999) and The Economist (1997, pp. 77–78).

[7] However, this measure of excess liquidity has a crucial underlying assumption. It assumes that the velocity of money remains constant over time, which is far from certain (Becker 2007, p. 6).

[8] A study that closely follows the systematic of Baks and Kramer (1999) is the one from Borja and Goyeau (2005). They apply quarterly data between 1995 and 2005 to determine whether or not international liquidity affects asset prices in the US, the euro area and the ASEAN[9] region. The findings of their regression analyses can be summarized by the fact that liquidity spillover effects

Rapach (2001) uses a structural VAR model to analyze the effects of macro factors on a broad index of US stock prices in real terms. His findings, which are based on quarterly data between 1959 and 1999, indicate that money supply shocks have a positive short-run effect on real stock prices.

Gouteron and Szpiro (2005) analyze a set of excess liquidity measures and their effect on stock, bond and housing prices in the US and the euro area for the time period 1980–2004.[10] They do not find causality (Granger causality) from any of the excess liquidity measures to asset prices. Instead, causality runs from assets to money, which they rationalize with the 'flight to quality' effects after the market turmoil at the beginning of the millennium.

Congdon (2005) limits his analysis of money and asset prices to major boom-bust phases in the UK, the US and Japan. He also investigates sectoral money holdings during boom-bust cycles in the UK. His main conclusions are that it is broad money instead of narrow money, which is important for asset prices. In his view, causality runs from money to asset prices and inflation.

Pepper and Oliver (2006) analyze the interplay of monetary developments and the stock market for different boom-bust periods in the UK and in the US. Based on a fact-based approach, they find ample evidence of the positive influence of monetary forces on investors and the stock market. They admit, though, that their findings can not be replicated econometrically. Their main point is that 'liquidity' is not the sole factor explaining stock market behavior; but, it is important for deviations from market fundamentals.

Adalid and Detken (2007) focus on the relationship between developments in money and credit aggregates and asset price developments. They, too, limit their analysis to phases of asset price booms, which are followed by a bust. They identify 42 boom-bust episodes across 18 OECD (Organisation for Economic Co-operation and Development) countries since the beginning of the 1970s. Their findings are that money growth shocks during the boom and pre-boom phases and real residential property prices during the boom and in the post-boom period partly explain the depth of the recessions following the boom. While two liquidity measures are applied, namely a broad monetary aggregate and private credit growth, the results are mainly based on the former. The latter does not include much informational content. In addition, Adalid and Detken (2007) show that the positive relationship between liquidity conditions and asset price developments are stronger during boom-bust periods. If the whole sample (boom and non-boom periods) is used for the analysis their results show a much weaker relationship.

While Adalid and Detken (2007) analyze the interplay of money and asset prices during phases of asset price booms, Bruggeman (2007) focuses on periods of sustained excess liquidity and investigates how often these periods are followed by an asset price boom. In doing so, the author allows for non-linearities in the relationship

exist, which play a role for US and European asset returns, but not for asset returns in the ASEAN region.

[10] Since their paper is only available in French, this overview is based on the description in Clerc (2007, pp. 19–22).

between liquidity and asset prices. The first main finding is that only about a third (14 out of 40) of sustained excess liquidity periods are followed by a boom (Bruggeman 2007, p. 21). Hence, Bruggeman warns against a naive type of monetary analysis with respect to asset prices. The other main finding is that the inclusion of other variables, such as inflation and real GDP growth helps to forecast asset price booms. In particular, periods of strong real money growth in combination with low interest rates, high economic growth and low inflation increase the risk of being followed by an asset price boom (Bruggeman 2007, p. 21).

Giese and Tuxen (2007, 2008) analyze the impact of global liquidity on asset prices in a CVAR framework. Their findings show that money supply has exceeded money demand since the beginning of this millennium. Excess liquidity is defined as deviations from the long-run money demand relation. The identified excess liquidity contributed, among other factors, to rising asset prices. Their analyses focuses on aggregated quarterly data between 1982 and 2006 for France, Germany, Italy, Japan, the UK and the US.

Belke et al. (2008) pursue a related analysis estimating a variety of VAR models on a global level. They utilize aggregated data for a wide range of countries, which together account for 72.2% of global GDP (in 2006). The impulse responses, which are based on quarterly observations between 1984 and 2006, show that a positive shock leads to increases in global house prices but not to higher stock prices. These results are confirmed by Belke and Rees (2009, p. 18), who analyze how global shocks affect global aggregates as well as national variables to determine central banks' action span with respect to international spillovers. Their findings show that global liquidity shocks do not have a positive effect on global stock prices.[11]

2.1.3 Research of Money and Stock Prices in Cointegrated VAR Models on a National Level

The following scientific contributions come closest to the analysis in this contribution. First, because they focus on national stock markets and domestic macro variables. Second, because they apply the same econometric methodology as in this contribution, the CVAR model.

Mukherjee and Naka (1995) focus their cointegration analysis on the Japanese stock market. They base their findings on monthly observations between 1971 and

[11] Other recent studies investigate the consequences of global excess liquidity. Since their focus is more on output and inflation than on the stock market, they are not described in detail. For example, Rüffer and Stracca (2006) analyze the consequences of global excess liquidity and liquidity spillovers on domestic variables in the US, the euro area and Japan in a VAR analysis for quarterly data between 1981 and 2004. Sousa and Zaghini (2004) estimate a structural VAR model to analyze the effects of global liquidity on euro area money stock, prices and output. In addition to academic contributions, the analysis of global liquidity and its consequences is on the radar of many investment banks and economic think tanks. See, for example, Heise et al. (2005), Financial Markets Center (2005, 2006), Sachs (2006) and BCA Research (2007).

1990 for the stock market and six macro variables. They find that money supply, among other variables, enters a relation with the stock market. However, since they do not interpret or show the adjustment coefficients towards this long-run relation, it is unclear whether or not the stock market reacts to the variables or only affects them.

Cheung and Ng (1998) apply cointegration analysis to country-specific economic real variables and the stock market. They analyze quarterly data for Canada, Germany, Italy, Japan and the US. The time periods differ but roughly cover the time between 1960 and 1990. They identify a negative relationship between the stock market and oil in four of the five countries and a positive relationship between consumption and the stock market in all countries. Results for real money and economic activity are ambiguous. Since they do not restrict the cointegration vectors, no t-values are reported. Consequently, the above results have to be interpreted with caution because it is unclear which of the variables form a statistically significant relationship.

Kwon and Shin (1999) analyze the relationship between macroeconomic variables and stock returns in Korea. They apply monthly data of the value-weighted Korea Composite Stock Price Index and the Small-Size Stock Price Index from 1980 to 1992. The macro variables included are industrial production and narrow money supply (M1) as well as the trade balance and the exchange rate; they account for the openness of the Korean economy and the importance of international trade. Their empirical analysis of cointegration and short-run adjustment shows that cointegration exists between the stock market and the macro variables. In addition, the macro variables cause the stock market, but not the other way round. Unfortunately, the cointegration analysis does not test for restrictions of the identified long-run structure and includes insignificant coefficients. Since the cointegration relation is normalized on the stock market variable, the significance of the stock market is unclear. Consequently, their results have to be interpreted with caution.[12]

Chaudhuri and Smiles (2004) analyze the relationship between the stock market and macroeconomic variables for Australia. They identify one cointegration relationship using quarterly data between 1960 and 1998. However, they do not provide information on the cointegration vector. Instead, their impulse response analysis shows that shocks to real GDP, real money and the real oil price have a negative effect on stock prices.

Ratanapakorn and Sharma (2007) focus their analysis on the US stock market (S&P 500) and investigate the relationship between stock prices and six macro variables. Their main finding is that all variables affect the stock market in the long run

[12] Maysami and Koh (2000) apply cointegration analysis to the Singapore stock market. They focus on a relatively short period of monthly data between 1988 and 1995. They identify a cointegration relationship between the stock market and the macro variables. However, no restrictions are tested. In addition, analysis of the adjustment coefficients shows that the stock market does not react to the long-run disequilibrium. Consequently, the derived results seem questionable and are not reported here. The same applies for analyses conducted by Wong et al. (2006) who perform cointegration analyses on the Singapore and US stock market.

but not in the short run. However, they admit that stock prices are relatively exogenous because 87% of stock market variance can be explained by shocks to the stock market, even after 24 months. They base their findings on monthly data between 1975 and 1999. They detect a clear positive relationship between the money supply and stock prices. However, they do not test restrictions of the long-run structure. Instead, they test whether variables can be excluded from the cointegration space (see test in Sect. 6.2.2.2). This test, however, only shows whether or not the variables react to or influence the system. The test does not provide information on the question of whether or not the stock market reacts to the variables included in the cointegration vector. In addition, the significance of the coefficients in the 'untested' long-run relation remains unclear. Hence, their results have to be viewed with caution as well.

Humpe and Macmillan (2009) compare the behavior of potential relationships between the stock market and a set of macro variables between the US and Japan. They apply monthly data from 1965 to 2005. For the US, they find that the S&P 500 forms a long-run relationship with real industrial production, consumer price inflation and the real 10-year bond yield. Industrial production influences the stock market positively, inflation and the long rate negatively. Real money (M1) does not play a role in the US stock market. The findings for Japan are different. While industrial production also plays a positive role for the Nikkei 225, the money supply and the stock market form a negative relationship. Unfortunately, Humpe and Macmillan do not provide any tests on parameter constancy. It seems questionable that the parameters of the cointegration relations and the adjustment coefficients are constant over the analyzed 40-year time span, which includes oil price shocks and high inflation in the seventies, the stock market and real estate boom-bust in the 1980s in Japan and different monetary regimes, at least in the US.

2.2 Academic Void

The foregoing discussion of the literature, which is related to the subject of this thesis, shows the existence of a wide array of angles in approaching the topic of money and stock prices. It also shows that over the last 50 years many authors have tried to prove that there is a relationship between money and stock prices. At the same time, many others have tried to show that this relationship does not exist or that it can not be exploited to gain excess returns. Some focus on anticipated effects, others on surprise effects. Obviously, this is not an exhaustive overview, simply because the amount of literature is too vast. Instead, the focus is on empirical investigations, which are close to the study at hand and have received considerable attention in the scientific community. Nevertheless many more exist.[13]

[13] As an example, Flannery and Protopapadakis (2002) estimate a generalized autoregressive conditional heteroskedasticity (GARCH) model based on daily equity returns between 1980 and 1996. They include announcements of 17 macroeconomic series and find that nominal money supply

This summary of the main literature shows that most studies focus solely on the US market. While empirical methods have changed over the course of the years, the main result has remained the same: it is mixed. Some authors find a significant and causal relationship between money and stock prices, others show that the relationship does not exist at all and a third group shows that causality runs from stocks to money.

More recent research increased the focus from US analyses to global developments. Here, too, results differ. However, most observers agree that global liquidity is related to the most recent housing boom, which took place in many countries across the world. While some of the global studies focus on spillover effects onto national stock markets, none of them includes international capital flows.[14] Capital flows, however, can directly measure how much 'additional' money flows in and out of a specific currency area.

For the most part, recent publications that focus on national stock markets and domestic macro variables apply cointegration analysis. Unfortunately, the interpretation of the results remains questionable since important information on the behavior of the variables in the system is ignored or not provided. For example, many analyses do not restrict the cointegration space, which enables empirical testing of the cointegration relations and provides information on the significance of the coefficients. In addition, the analysis of the short-run adjustment structure is widely ignored. This, however, is essential to determine whether or not the stock market reacts to the variables in the system.

The main conclusion that can be drawn from this discussion is that economists still argue over whether or not a relationship exists, and if it does exist, how important it is and in which direction causality runs. In addition, the discussion suggests that many important issues concerning stock price fluctuations are still open to empirical investigation.

Room for improvement exists via a full and correct analysis of liquidity conditions and stock market behavior in a CVAR framework, which includes long-run equilibria as well as short-run dynamics and the long-run impact of shocks to the variables. In addition, the application of the same approach to several countries enables the comparison of results and the determination of country-specific characteristics that might influence the interplay between money and stocks. Moreover, the inclusion of international capital flows in the analysis enables one to analyze domestic developments without ignoring the global factor. This is especially important for

affects the level and volatility of equity returns positively. Even though their study is related to the subject at hand, it differs in its objective and approach.

[14] The studies that investigate capital flows mostly focus on the determinants of international capital flows (see, for example, van Wincoop and Tille (2007), Reinhart and Rogoff (2004), and Taylor and Sarno (1997)). Sometimes they include implications on economic growth but rarely in relationship to the stock market. An exception is the literature on the Asian financial crisis, where capital flow reversals ('hot money') are often scapegoated for triggering the crisis (see, for example, Mishkin (1999) and Sarno and Taylor (1999)). This, however, is only a point analysis without a focus on the overall role of capital flows.

monetary policy since central banks need to understand how macroeconomic variables interact in their respective currency areas. As a result, the analysis in this contribution adds new insights to the following fields of research:

- The relationship between stock market developments and monetary conditions.
- The impact of international capital flows on stock markets.
- Comparisons of stock market behavior across a broad range of countries.
- The analysis of central banks' ability to influence the stock market.
- The interaction of domestic macro variables with each other in an endogenous system.

Chapter 3
Money and Stock Prices: Economic Theory

3.1 Chapter Overview

This chapter delivers theoretical aspects, which form the underlying basis for the empirical investigation of the relationship between liquidity conditions and the stock market. The chapter is divided into three parts. The main part covers theoretical considerations of why money might affect stock prices (Sect. 3.2). Since it is unclear from the outset whether causality runs from money to stocks or from stocks to money, the second part of this chapter presents theories that describe the role of stocks for money demand (Sect. 3.3). Last, Sect. 3.4 derives the variables, which should be included in the empirical analysis based on the theoretical findings in this chapter.

The first part is divided into three sections. First, Sect. 3.2.1 focuses on changes in the quantity of money and its effect on stocks. Second, Sect. 3.2.2 shows how changes in the price of money affect stock prices. Finally, Sect. 3.2.3 describes how stock prices are influenced by changes in either price or quantity of money.

One theory that describes the linkage between changes in the quantity of money and the stock market is the portfolio-balance effect, which represents the Monetarist view (Sect. 3.2.1.1). It shows that increased money supply leads to a portfolio rebalancing towards other assets, such as stocks. This asset reallocation results in upward pressure on stock prices, which, in turn, enables a new equilibrium level between money holdings and other assets in investors' portfolios. Higher money supply may also have a negative effect on stock prices, which results from increases in expected inflation (Sect. 3.2.1.2). Inflation uncertainty rises with the absolute level of inflation and can have adverse consequences on the stock market.

In addition to the quantity of money available, liquidity can also be measured via the price of money, which is the short-term interest rate.[1] Interest rate movements affect stock market prices mainly in three ways: one is via the relative attractiveness of the investment alternatives bonds and stocks (Sect. 3.2.2.1). The other two can be rationalized via the standard present-value evaluation principle. First,

[1] Of course, both measures are interconnected (see Sect. 4.3).

M. Wiedmann, *Money, Stock Prices and Central Banks*, Contributions to Economics,
DOI 10.1007/978-3-7908-2647-0_3,

a decreasing interest rate reduces the discount factor with which future dividend payments are transferred to the present value (Sect. 3.2.2.2). Second, lower interest rates might exert a positive effect on aggregate output, which, in turn, increases economic prospects and dividends and, thus, also increases the present value of equity investments.

The connection between dividends and the stock market is part of the third section because dividend changes can result from variability in either the quantity or the price of money (Sect. 3.2.3.1). In addition, Sect. 3.2.3.2 describes the interplay of liquidity conditions and investors' behavior on the stock market. It shows that optimism and confidence of investors are important determinants of stock prices. The resulting herding behavior and rational speculation allows stock markets to deviate from fundamental levels. Liquidity conditions intensify this process.

Often, the influence of monetary policy on asset prices is taken as a given because it is part of the monetary transmission mechanism and stamped as the traditional view (Bordo and Wheelock 2004, p. 2). However, no space is devoted to the actual theoretical connections between the two. This gap is filled in this chapter.

The second part provides a brief overview of the role of stock prices in money demand relations. After the outline of general money demand theory considerations (Sect. 3.3.1), the focus lies on the impact of stocks on money demand (Sect. 3.3.2). Theoretical considerations distinguish between positive aspects, such as the wealth effect, the transaction effect and the risk-spreading effect and negative relations, which are based on the substitution effect.

3.2 Effects of Money on Stock Prices

3.2.1 Effects Initiated by Changes in the Quantity of Money

3.2.1.1 Portfolio-Balance Effect

This effect is based on the Monetarist view and serves as one explanation for equity price changes in transmission mechanism theory. The 'portfolio-balance effect', also termed 'monetary portfolio model' (Rogalski and Vinso 1977, p. 1017; Rozeff 1975, p. 20), refers to the consequences of a money supply increase, which unbalances private agents' desired money holdings (Brunner 1961, pp. 52–53). They perceive that they have too much money in comparison to their spending patterns. As a result, private agents can respond to a money supply shock in three different ways. They either reduce money holdings by, first, increasing their spending on consumer goods, second, by substituting between money and other assets or third, a mixture of the two. Whereas the second has a direct effect on relative prices, the first has an indirect effect. While individuals can reduce their money holdings through purchasing additional goods, the society as a whole can not (Fisher 1912, p. 244). Therefore, in the short term, more money will flow into equities or other investment alternatives. In the long term, the boost in spending increases demand. Consequently, prices of the demanded goods and assets adjust upwards to restore the equilibrium between holdings of money, assets and spending patterns (Mishkin 1996, pp. 6–7). In other words, relative prices change to enable a new equilibrium with a higher level of money holdings.

More formally, a monetary shock results in changes in the stock of money relative to the stocks of other domestic and foreign assets combined with changes in their relative marginal utility and the utility of consumption (Meltzer 1995, p. 52; Sprinkel 1964, pp. 11–12). The former is a result of the fact that the different assets are imperfect substitutes in investors' portfolios (Brand et al. 2003, p. 12; Kuttner and Mosser 2002, p. 17). The latter can be derived from the fact that money is a good, and, as such, it is subject to the law of diminishing marginal utility (Belke and Polleit 2009, p. 4). Money holders try to restore their equilibrium levels by equating the ratios of the marginal utilities to the relative prices of all assets and current production and consumption.

It is important to realize that the monetary shock does not have to be induced by the central bank but can also be a result of market agents' behavior. Pepper and Oliver (2006, pp. 1–2) point to the example of a debt-financed takeover transaction. For example, at the end of a recession stocks are perceived as cheap, which encourages one company to make a cash bid for another corporation. Where it finances the takeover via bank borrowing two effects lead to rising stock prices. First, the takeover announcement effect. Second, on the day of the transaction the sellers of the stock receive bank deposits. Most likely they will want to reinvest the proceeds in the stock market, which then drives prices up further. As mentioned above, this only reduces individual money holdings but not money in society as a whole. To bring the aggregated portfolio structure back to levels that reflect personal preferences, comparable to prior to the positive money supply effect, stock prices have to increase. In Pepper and Oliver's view, liquidity positively influences asset prices because excess liquidity increases the demand for a fixed supply of assets. They put further emphasis on liquidity conditions because they affect the underlying motivation of investment transactions. Many investment transactions are a result of the need to either raise or invest cash ('liquidity transactions') (Pepper and Oliver 2006, p. 12; Pepper 1994, p. XVIII). Often tendencies of these liquidity transactions persist across the market. These tendencies affect market sentiment through the movement of prices and, as a result, the market reacts biased to news (Sutthirat 2006, p. 45).

In conclusion, this effect points to a positive impact of money on stocks as well as other assets, such as bonds. If the demand for fixed income securities increases, nominal returns fall with higher bond prices. This has an additional positive effect on the stock market because stocks become more competitive as substitute investments (see Sect. 3.2.2.1).

3.2.1.2 Increased Inflation Expectations

The quantity theory of money states that, in the long run, the level of prices varies with the quantity of money in circulation, assuming that money velocity remains unchanged (see also Sect. 5.2). If this holds, economic agents expect inflation to rise after an increase in money supply growth. Increased inflation expectations have primarily negative but also positive (relative to other assets) effects on the stock market.

It seems intuitive that deflation is negative for stock markets. The question, however, of why inflation is also bad for the stock market is less clear. At first thought, the opposite seems to be true. After all, stocks are claims to the productive capital of the real economy and should, thus, "be usable as hedges against inflation" (Bakshi and Chen 1996, p. 243; see also Bernanke and Kuttner 2005, p. 1253; Sellin 2001, p. 508; Graham et al. 1962, p. 61).[2] In addition, if material prices rise, companies are expected to increase their sales prices as well. Nominal profits will rise with inflation. As a result, inflation does not undermine real values of stocks (contrary to the real value of nominal bonds, see below).

Nevertheless, history paints a different picture. During the high-inflation years of the early 1970s and 1980s the average price-earnings ratio of shares dropped heavily below long-term averages (Feldstein 1980, p. 839). In addition, several studies show that stocks perform poorly during relatively higher inflation phases (see, for example, Ely and Robinson (1992) and the mentioned literature). Marshall (1992, p. 1317) shows that for postwar U.S. data real equity returns and inflation are negatively correlated.[3]

Part of the argument behind this observation are some smaller problems, which are inherent to inflation. These include 'menu costs', such as additional price negotiations, continuous adjustments in marketing and hedging. More importantly, there is one major negative effect, which arises from an increase in uncertainty and a worsening of price transparency (ECB 2004, p. 42). This increase in uncertainty stems from the fact that inflation's volatility increases with its absolute value (Ball and Cecchetti 1990, p. 215; Taylor 1981, pp. 59–71; Okun 1971, pp. 493–497). Unanticipated changes in the inflation rate redistribute wealth because many assets are denominated in nominal terms. Consequently, increased inflation variability leads to higher uncertainty and lowers welfare (Romer 1996, p. 431). For corporations, this translates into greater difficulty assessing purchasing costs, production (labor) costs and sales prices. As a result, companies increase risk premia in profitability calculations to avoid mistakes in decision making. Risk premia rise in other areas, too, e.g., bond investors request higher real returns to offset inflation surprises. Stock investors face the same dilemma as corporations because they are uncertain about market price signals. Thus, uncertainty and changing relative prices result in resource misallocation.

Fama (1981, p. 563) provides an alternative view to the relationship between stock returns and inflation. In his opinion, the negative correlation between stock

---

[2] It has to be noted, though, that increased inflation decreases real after-tax profits because inventory and depreciation charges are not inflation-indexed, which tends to depress stock prices (Feldstein 1980, p. 840). Modigliani and Cohn (1979, p. 24), on the other hand, point out that shareholders gain from inflation because the real value of corporate liabilities depreciates.

[3] However, other studies exist that show that inflation does not have a negative impact on stock returns (see, for example, Lee (2008, pp. 127–129)).

returns and inflation is not a causal relation. Instead, it can be associated with a positive relation between stock returns and real activity and a negative relation between real activity and inflation.

Contrary to the negative effects described above, higher inflationary expectations improve the relative position of equity investments. In particular, this results from the negative effect on two main investment alternatives, namely money and bonds. For the former, inflation acts as a tax on money holdings with negative effects on the exchange value of money (Belke and Polleit 2009, p. 382). Thus, investors hold lower real balances of money and switch from money to non-nominal assets. The latter is a result of investors' subsequent demand for higher nominal bond returns as a reaction to higher expected inflation. Investors who want to hold nominal assets over the longer term demand an 'inflation risk premium' to compensate them for the risks involved (ECB 2004, p. 42; Altug and Labadie 1995, pp. 219–222).[4] As a result, the price of bonds is expected to fall and stocks become a more attractive alternative for bond investors. If the outlined effects are stronger than the above mentioned negative effects on stocks, the stocks competitiveness for investors' funds then increases. However, stocks are not the only alternative. Real investments in houses or durable goods might also be considered if inflation is expected to be high and persistent (Meltzer 1995, p. 61). Therefore, this 'relatively' positive effect should be small compared to the negative effect of increased uncertainty.

3.2.2 *Effects Initiated by Changes in the Price of Money*

3.2.2.1 Relative Attractiveness of Stocks and Bonds

If the term structure theory of interest rates can be taken as given (see also Sect. 5.2.2), lower short-term interest rates translate through the system and reduce long-term interest rates. Consequently, bond investments become less attractive compared to equity investments and the demand for stocks increases (Mishkin 2001, p. 2).[5] Eventually this leads to higher stock prices. This reasoning is based

[4] Otherwise inflation would lead to a redistribution of wealth from creditors to debtors (Belke and Polleit 2009, p. 382).

[5] It has to be noted that this is not contrary to the remarks at the end of the previous section. There, expectations of higher nominal bond yields are associated with expectations of lower bond prices. In the short run, investors sell bonds and shift into equity investments to avoid price deterioration. In the long run, the higher nominal bond yields are in line with previous real yields because of higher inflation. As a result, bond investments do not become more attractive compared to equity investments. The situation in this section is different. Lower long-term yields are a consequence of changes in short-term interest rates. If inflation expectations remain unchanged, this leads to a reduction in real long-term yields, which is a comparative disadvantage of bond investments compared to equity investments. Nevertheless, in the transition phase, expectations of lower long-term yields might lead to a temporary increase in demand for bonds. As long as interest rates are decreasing, bond investors can participate in positive price movements. However, in the long run,

on the observation that bond yields and earnings yields, which is the reciprocal of the price-earnings-ratio, tend to move together. Hence, if bond yields are reduced, stocks become relatively more attractive and the increased demand leads to higher prices for stocks, thereby reducing the earnings yield of stocks and realigning bond and earnings yields. In other words, arbitrage should ensure that, in equilibrium, the yield on all assets, adjusted for risk, is the same (Ross 1987, pp. 29–34).

This follows the assumption that many investors constantly make the decision whether to invest in stocks as opposed to bonds and that funds are channeled towards the more attractive investment (Campbell and Vuolteennaho 2004, p. 19; Graham et al. 1962, p. 510). This holds true for the individual investor as well as for professional money managers, especially those from insurance companies and pension funds. If the promised rate of return to clients is higher than the matching long-term bond rate (and expectations are that low rates will persist), they have no choice but to increase risk and divest into alternative assets, such as stocks (Rajan 2006, p. 2).

3.2.2.2 The Discount Factor

Lower interest rates affect the valuation of equities through the discount factor. A decreased discount factor results in higher net present values of corporations' future income streams and, therefore, higher stock prices (Sellin 2001, p. 492; Baks and Kramer 1999, p. 5). The discounted cash flow model is mostly applied to determine the fundamental value of stocks. This type of model relates the price of a stock with its expected future cash flows, which are discounted to the present (Campbell et al. 1997, p. 253). Future cash flows are represented by the dividends. Rapach (2001, pp. 11, 21) utilizes the following present-value equity valuation model:

$$S_t = E_t \sum_{i=1}^{\infty} \frac{D_{t+1}}{\prod_{j=1}^{i}(1 + R_{t+j})}, \tag{3.1}$$

where S_t is the real price of equities, E_t is the expectations operator conditional on information available at time t, R_t is the real rate at which cash flows are discounted and D_t is the real dividend. It becomes clear from (3.1) that either a reduced discount rate or improved dividend expectations (see Sect. 3.2.3.1) increase the valuation of stocks.[6]

lower real yields will lead to a shift from bond investments to equity investments. These portfolio reallocations lead to price adjustments, which realign bond and equity yields. In conclusion, the main discrepancy between the two sections comes from different causal effects (changes in inflation vs. changes in the short-term interest rate) on real bond yields.

[6] An alternative description of the present-value model is the classical Gordon growth model (Gordon 1962, pp. 56–66; see also Shiller 2007, p. 15): $P = \frac{D}{R-g}$, where P is the price of the share today, D is the expected dividend of next year, R is the real rate at which cash flows are discounted and g is the expected growth rate of dividends. Since both models describe the same mechanisms, they also result in the same conclusions. It has to be noted, though, that the present value model

For instance, if the central bank lowers the short-term interest rate then the actual stock price is lower than the 'new' fundamental value; thus, the stock is undervalued. If, in turn, market agents buy the stock to achieve a capital gain, the increased demand leads to higher prices for the stock, thereby, aligning the actual with the fundamental value.[7] The present value-based relationship of the discount rate and the stock market is the main argument for the stock market channel of monetary policy transmission (Ehrmann and Fratzscher 2004, p. 719).

Economic theory argues in favor of focusing on real instead of nominal rates because payouts (dividends or rents) supposedly grow with the inflation rate (Shiller 2007, p. 5). However, two bases justify the usage of either real or nominal rates. One is the close connection between the two rates. A decrease in the short-term nominal interest rate results in lower short-term real interest rates (Fisher hypothesis) and also in lower long-term real interest rates, due to the expectations hypothesis of the term structure (Mishkin 1996, p. 3; Taylor 1995, p. 18).[8] The other is the concept of 'money illusion,' which states that market participants may neglect inflation and may use nominal rates to discount future dividends into today's price (Modigliani and Cohn 1979, p. 25; Fisher 1928, pp. 13–15).[9]

3.2.3 Effects Initiated by Changes in Either Quantity or Price of Money

3.2.3.1 Monetary Effects on Stock Prices via Economic Growth

Theories on the monetary transmission mechanism state that both increased money supply and reduced short-term interest rates have positive effects on economic prospects. These, in turn, can also lead to increases in stock prices.

A money supply-driven increase in aggregate demand on goods markets leads to an increase in the quantity provided. However, the quantitative increase does not have to go in hand with rising goods prices because of sticky prices in the medium-run. Sticky prices can result from, for example, global competition and resulting

---

can only be an "approximate guide to an empirical analysis" (Borio et al. 1994, p. 20). Both the ex ante required rate of return (the discount factor) and (expectations of) future income streams are neither observable nor explained by the model.

[7] In addition, discounted cash flows also increase after interest rate reductions because lower interest rates enable companies to reduce interest payments on debt (Belke and Polleit 2009, p. 285, 587).

[8] The term structure argument holds for real and nominal interest rates. The shocks that drive the term structure of interest rates differ, however. While the real term structure is driven by technological shocks, the nominal term structure is driven by monetary shocks (Bakshi and Chen 1996, pp. 261–266).

[9] For an empirical analysis that supports the view that stock markets suffer from money illusion, see Cohen et al. (2005).

pricing-to-market instead of mark-up pricing. The higher quantity of goods on offer can result from additional imports from global goods markets and/or an expansion of national capacities, which, thereby, increases real GDP.[10] This, in turn, leads to improved economic prospects, higher expected dividends and again higher stock prices.

The Keynesian perspective arrives at the same result, albeit via a different road. Reduced interest rates make investments more profitable and, thereby, increase firms' investment and, in the end, economic activity. "Experience and common sense tell us that [. . .] ordering materials and hiring workers [. . .] will look like a better deal if the prime rate is 6% instead of 8%. . ." (Tobin 1991, p. 14). If the market lending rate decreases below the natural rate of interest[11] more investment projects become profitable and will be financed (Adalid and Detken 2007, p. 12; White 2006, p. 9). Additional investment projects will result in higher business volume and ultimately, higher profits and dividends (Bodurtha et al. 1989, p. 25). Higher dividend expectations enter positively into the stock market valuation model and raise today's stock prices (see Sect. 3.2.2.2).[12] In addition, lower interest rates raise the value of durable assets and, thus, households' resources and consumption appetite increases (Kuttner and Mosser 2002, p. 16).

3.2.3.2 Confidence, Optimism and Bubbles

Price increases in real goods and services usually lead to reduced demand and substitution with relatively cheaper goods. This is not the case for asset prices. Rising share prices, for instance, are regarded as a sign of confidence among investors and breed optimism. As a result, market agents tend to invest more heavily when prices go up and reduce investment spending, when prices go down.

Abundant liquidity can exacerbate this (Borio et al. 1994, p. 67). Ample liquidity makes it easier and cheaper for people, hedge funds and companies to borrow. If borrowed funds are channeled towards the stock market, prices are pushed up further and optimism spreads (Allen and Gale 2000, p. 239). Crowd behavior, for example in the form of herding, and rational speculation are signs of this process and lead to market exaggerations (Pepper 1994, pp. 24–28).[13] After all, even if prices departed from justified long-run levels it is still lucrative to bet on rising prices if the stocks can be sold at a higher level before a potential bubble bursts. Thus, irrationally high levels on the stock market may result from rational speculation and people's perception that they are smarter than others and able to get out before the

---

[10] Instead of increasing capacities, the increase in domestic output can also result from a higher utilization of existing capacities.

[11] The real rate that ensures price stability in the long run (BIS 2004, p. 71).

[12] See Semmler (2006, pp. 90–95) for a theoretical dynamic macro model that derives conditions for excess demand for stocks and shows the positive relationship between output and stock prices.

[13] Investment managers also have an incentive to herd to avoid underperforming in comparison to their peers (Rajan 2005, p. 3).

market turns (Campbell et al. 1997, p. 258).[14] This is contrary to the idea that in a market, in which information is processed efficiently, the actual value of stocks corresponds to the fundamental value (see Sect. 3.2.2.2). However, as Keynes (1936, p. 156) already pointed out in 1936, stock market levels do not necessarily reflect fundamental values. Instead, they reflect average expectations of what other market participants expect the market to do (on average). His reasoning led him to compare stock market price setting with betting on the outcome of a beauty contest, where the bet that is closest to the average preferences of all participants wins. As with the stock market, it does not depend on what one thinks is the most beautiful contestant (or the best-performing firm) but how one anticipates all other participants' expectations of what all participants' concept of beauty is. The Keynesian investor buys when prices rise and sells when they fall, that is, adopts positive feedback investment strategies (English 2001, p. 121). This further exacerbates stock price inefficiencies.

Additionally, confidence and optimism are also boosted because owners of assets feel richer if house or share prices increase. This results in increased spending on goods and assets (Kuttner and Mosser 2002, p. 16). The former helps companies increase profits and, thus, also leads to increases in share prices and the valuation of bonds (Borio et al. 1994, pp. 22–23). As a result, the number of defaults decreases and lenders want to lend more to participate in the upswing, thereby, further perpetuating it. In addition to healthier balance sheets, due to less defaults, banks are also directly influenced by rising asset prices. Adrian and Shin (2007, pp. 2–4) point out that banks, which actively target their leverage ratio, react to rising or falling asset prices.[15] Asset price increases lead to stronger balance sheets and a higher net worth for banks. Higher net worth means lower leverage as leverage is inversely related to total assets. To keep the leverage ratio constant and at target level, banks engage in additional borrowing and invest the proceeds into more assets. As a result, leverage is procyclical, amplifying the already existent spiral between asset prices and money.[16] The additional borrowing might show up in broad monetary aggregates.

[14] See also the influential study of Brunnermeier and Nagel (2004) for an analysis of hedge funds behavior during the dot-com bubble. Their findings show that it is reasonable (and profitable) to ride a bubble instead of leaning against it. Consequently, even if a bubble is recognized, it does not mean that rational investors will instantly try to prick it. Instead, these investors ride the bubble or wait at the sidelines until a majority is formed that is ready to bring stock prices back to fundamental values. This, of course, is contrary to what the efficient market hypothesis would expect. Brunnermeier and Nagel's argument is based on the observation that the rational investors can not agree to bet against the bubble. If they did, they could make big profits. However, if coordination is impossible, it is too risky for the individual investor to bet against a bubble.

[15] The same is of course true for other players, such as hedge funds or private equity funds, which apply high levels of leverage.

[16] For a theoretical study on how credit constraints, which are based on asset prices, interact with economic activity, see Kiyotaki and Moore (1997). Kiyotaki and Moore (1997, p. 212) find that the relationship between credit limits and asset prices amplifies shocks and makes them more persistent.

This additional 'monetary' liquidity also improves 'market' liquidity.[17] Market liquidity, in turn, increases rational speculation further as there always seems to be a ready buyer.[18] Easier financing also enables executives to launch share buyback schemes, which at the same time increases stock prices and market liquidity.[19]

The same self-reinforcing mechanism applies once markets turn sour. When prices decline, previous overconfidence turns into crippling uncertainty and lenders demand that borrowers hold more collateral. At the same time, falling asset prices decrease the amount of collateral, forcing borrowers to sell assets. This drives prices down further. In addition, forced selling leads to inefficient asset liquidation, which is associated with additional costs (Allen and Gale 2002, p. 35).[20] If banks have to write off loans in a market downturn their equity capital ratio might drop under a critical level of capital requirements set by the authorities. This leaves banks with two options (Belke and Polleit 2009, p. 37): dispose of risky assets and/or issue new equity. Whereas the latter is difficult in times of market distress and painful for existing share holders, the former lowers asset valuations and with it increases banks' capital losses further (Allen and Gale 2000, p. 253). The above described downward spiral is aggravated further because investors' concern rises and funding costs increase.

Whereas the above described play of optimism, confidence and asset prices evolves independent of liquidity conditions, there is a strong case that high (or low) liquidity levels reinforce this process. The procyclicality of credit markets influences the business cycle, heightens stock market ups and exacerbates downs.[21]

---

[17] Brunnermeier and Pedersen (2007, pp. 35–37) find that market liquidity and funding liquidity are mutually reinforcing, which can lead to liquidity spirals. This also means that central banks can influence market liquidity by affecting funding liquidity. Funding liquidity also has an impact on contagion effects between hedge funds returns. Boyson et al. (2008, p. 2) find that hedge fund contagion is highest when funding liquidity is low. Stronger contagion effects exacerbate market ups and downs.

[18] This is in line with the well-documented finding that market illiquidity raises expected future stock returns (Amihud et al. 2005, pp. 305–322; Amihud 2002, p. 52). In this case, stock prices decline to make the expected return rise. Hence, higher market liquidity leads to higher stock price levels and lower expected returns.

[19] Since most executive pay includes share options, share buybacks become increasingly popular with executives and equity owners alike.

[20] Brunnermeier and Pedersen (2004, pp. 2–6) analyze the impact of predatory trading, which further exacerbates the consequences of forced selling. If, for example, a hedge fund is nearing margin calls and needs to liquidate and other traders know about this, then these 'predatory' traders initially trade in the same direction to trigger the margin calls. Consequently, they withdraw the much needed liquidity, which increases liquidation costs and leads to price overshooting. The predatory traders buy back the asset at the lower cost, thereby, profiting from triggering another trader's crisis. This can also have spillover effects across traders and markets.

[21] Procyclicality means that cyclical deviations from the potential total output are further amplified. Applied to the banking industry, this means that banks increase their risk weighting in a financial downturn and, thus, decrease their borrowing (Lowe 2002, p. 2; ECB 2001a, p. 71). Procyclicality of the banking system is exacerbated further by the application of Basel II (Catarineu-Rabell et al. 2003, pp. 10–11; Estrella 2001, pp. 1489–1490).

The described effects are intensified by the prevailing incentive structure of professional money managers (Rajan 2006, pp. 2–5). For example, hedge funds managers' compensation usually depends on a percentage value of assets under management plus a share of annual returns in excess of a minimum nominal return. The problem starts when risk-free returns are low.[22] Low risk-free returns can be a result of abundant liquidity and low interest rates. For fund managers to achieve desired compensation levels, they have to increase risk as abundant liquidity makes it more difficult to create 'alpha'.[23] However, there are only a few sources of 'alpha'. They range from fund managers' special abilities to spot undervalued assets over activist investor behavior to liquidity provision (Rajan 2006, pp. 3–4). While the first two depend on special skills, which are probably rare, the latter depends on illiquid investment opportunities. However, when monetary policy is loose and more and more funds enter the market, they compete away potential returns from liquidity provision. Consequently, to keep returns on a high level, fund managers have to bet on market beta and by doing that, they increase risk. In addition, they can increase returns (and risk) by taking on more leverage, which is also easier if borrowing costs are low. As a result, the compensation structure of fund managers adds momentum to the play of liquidity, optimism and confidence. This is especially the case if interest rates are low and ample liquidity is available (Rajan 2006, p. 7).

In conclusion, rising asset prices, abundant credit and liquidity conditions, optimism, confidence and rational speculation all feed into each other and amplify the normal behavior of stock markets. Since the same mechanisms apply in a downturn there should be a long-run relationship between liquidity and stock market levels.

3.3 Effects of Stock Prices on Money Demand

3.3.1 Money Demand

Many theories on money demand exist.[24] They are usually based on the main functions of money, which are money as a medium of exchange, as a common unit of account, as a standard of deferred payment and as a store of value. Money is a generally accepted means of payment for the delivery of goods or the settlement of debt.

[22] If risk-free returns are high, the fund does not have to take on additional risk to be well compensated.

[23] Here, 'alpha' is referred to as returns due to the skills and experience of the investment manager. On the other hand, 'market beta' refers to increased returns by taking on more risk and, hence, depends more on market conditions.

[24] The objective of this section is not to provide details on general money demand theory. The focus lies on the effect of stock market behavior on money demand. For an extensive overview of money demand theories see Belke and Polleit (2009, pp. 91–122) or Serletis (2007, pp. 89–121). See also Sriram and Adams (1999) for an overview of the different demand theories combined with empirical analyses that focus on vector error-correction models.

Hence, it is the medium of exchange that facilitates transactions in an economy. It also serves as a unit of account, enabling relative prices to be easily compared. This, in turn, reduces transaction costs and increases productivity. Money also acts as a standard of deferred payment, enabling payments to be made in the future rather than today. Finally, to some extent, money can act as a store of value over time, although the value of money is eroded by inflation.

Most money demand theories have in common that real money demand depends on the amount of transactions market agents wish to undertake (means of payment).[25] This suggests that money demand depends on the level of income. In addition, money is held as a store of value. Hence, it reacts positively to interest paid on money holdings and negatively to interest paid on other assets, which is the opportunity cost of holding money (Boyle 1990, p. 1050).

Money demand relations describe the relationship between the money stock willingly held at any particular point in time and other economic variables, such as prices, output, wealth and the yield on alternative assets (ECB 1999a, p. 30). A simplified equilibrium in the money market requires that the supply of real money balances equals real money demand[26]:

$$\frac{M}{\overline{P}} = D(Y, i, b), \tag{3.2}$$

where M is the nominal money supply and $\overline{P}$ is the fixed price level. $D(\cdot)$ is the demand for real money. Y denotes total output, i is a short-term interest rate (e.g., the deposit rate) and b is a long-term interest rate. The left hand side of (3.2) is the supply of real money balances. The right hand side, real money demand, varies positively with income, $D_Y > 0$, reflecting that a rise in income leads to more transactions. Money demand also varies positively with the return on money holdings, $D_i > 0$, but negatively with the long-term bond rate, $D_b < 0$, because higher long-term interest rates increase the opportunity cost of holding money.[27]

To accommodate for the long run, prices are allowed flexible and have to enter the money demand relation as well, here in the form of the inflation rate, π.[28] The partial derivative is $D_\pi < 0$, because inflation decreases the real value of money holdings and, thus, increases the opportunity costs of cash holdings. In other words, inflation

[25] For example, the only difference between the Keynesian and Monetarist view on this point is that Keynesians focus on current income while Monetarists focus on permanent income.

[26] Nominal demand for money is expected to be positively related to the price level. The assumption here is that market agents want to hold a certain stock of real money instead of nominal money. Hence, an increase in the price level leads to rising demand for nominal money.

[27] Some studies apply the 3-months interest rate as a proxy for opportunity costs. However, if the focus is on a broad aggregate, such as M3, then this aggregate includes short-term securities, which bear interest. Hence, the long-term interest rate is superior to represent opportunity costs (Brüggemann and Lütkepohl 2006, p. 686).

[28] There is still debate on whether or not to include inflation in money demand functions. For an overview of the main arguments, see Coenen and Vega (1999, p. 3), who conclude that it is valid to include the inflation rate.

measures the yield foregone on physical assets, which appreciate with inflation. Hence, holders of physical capital are compensated by higher prices, but money holders are not (Dhakal et al. 1993, p. 55). The focus of the following section is to determine how stock market developments affect money demand.

3.3.2 *Money Demand Augmented with Stock Prices*

In theory, the question of whether stock market developments exert a positive or a negative effect on money demand depends on the strength of different opposing effects. The influence of stock prices on money is theoretically ambiguous and, consequently, has to be determined empirically. The literature on the role of stock prices for money demand identifies three positive effects and one effect that explains a negative relation.[29] The positive effects are: first, the wealth effect, second, the transaction effect and third, the risk-spreading effect. The negative effect is termed the substitution effect.

The wealth effect is based on the fact that nominal wealth increases with rising stock prices. This results in a higher wealth-to-income ratio, which, in turn, translates into a higher money-to-income ratio because individuals want to align their money holdings with the increased perceived wealth (Friedman 1988, pp. 222–223). Therefore, stock prices affect the money demand function positively. Another, albeit potentially smaller, positive effect is the transaction effect. Higher stock prices may result in bigger transactions. If higher money balances are needed to carry out these transactions, the demand for money increases. The risk-spreading effect results from the assumption that higher equity prices and higher expected excess returns on equity reflect higher risk. Consequently, investors might substitute equity for assets with lower risk perceptions, such as money (Friedman 1988, p. 223).

The substitution effect explains negative consequences of stock market advances for money demand. Unlike the influence of the level of asset prices, the rate of change of asset prices, which can be regarded as a proxy for their rate of return, is expected to have a negative impact on money demand. If the yield on alternative assets (to money) rises, the quantity of money demanded decreases. This is termed the substitution effect. In other words, rising stock prices lead to rising return expectations, which, in turn, make equity investments relatively more attractive in comparison to money holdings (Deutsche Bundesbank 2007, p. 19). Contrary to the risk-spreading effect in the previous section, the substitution effect assumes that investors switch their money holdings into equity investments (due to increased return expectations) and the demand for money declines.

[29] For empirical studies that investigate the importance of stock markets for money demand (with differing conclusions), see, for example, Friedman (1988), Choudhry (1996), Carpenter and Lange (2003), Bruggeman et al. (2003), Carstensen (2004), and Caruso (2006).

3.4 Conclusion

The theories outlined in this chapter suggest including the following variables in the empirical analysis:

- A monetary aggregate.
- A measure for the inflation rate.
- A short-term interest rate.
- A long-term interest rate.
- A measure for economic activity (representing dividends).

Monetary aggregates can be used to analyze the portfolio-balance effect and, together with inflation, whether higher inflation has a negative relationship with the stock market can be tested. On the basis of the present value formula, a discount rate and a measure of the income from stocks should be included. GDP might be used as a proxy for the latter, indicating changes in dividends. The long-term interest rate can proxy the yield on alternative assets. The advantages of including a short and a long-term interest rate also stem from the different determining factors of the two interest rates. While the short-term interest rate is significantly influenced by central bank actions, the long-term rate is associated with expectations of future macroeconomic developments (Deutsche Bundesbank 2006, p. 15). Since an indicator of optimism and confidence is difficult to measure, it is assumed to be implicitly included in price movements of stocks. Consequently, a long-run relationship between liquidity conditions and the stock market is hypothesized.

The question of which monetary aggregate to include and which interest rates to choose for the analysis is the focus of the next chapter. In addition, it raises the question of whether domestic money is sufficient for the analysis or if global factors have to be taken into account.

Chapter 4
Monetary Liquidity and International Capital Flows

4.1 Chapter Overview

The concept of liquidity can be interpreted in many different ways and liquidity measures differ widely. However, as this chapter shows, there is no best liquidity measure that fulfills all purposes. Instead, the important point is to choose a measure that is in line with the objectives of the study. Therefore, the aim of this chapter is to derive a bundle of liquidity measures, which cover stock market relevant monetary aspects. This chapter is structured as follows.

Section 4.2 distinguishes monetary liquidity from market liquidity. As could be seen in Chap. 3, quantities and prices of money play a role in asset price determination. To better understand the close relationship between quantity and price, Sect. 4.3 depicts the interconnection between them.

After this general discussion, the remaining sections focus on the different measures of liquidity. First, in Sect. 4.4 monetary aggregates are discussed. To facilitate this discussion, standard theory on money creation is presented (Sect. 4.4.1). The main distinctions of monetary aggregates are between narrow and broad money (Sect. 4.4.2) and between the overall level of liquidity and measures of excess liquidity (Sect. 4.4.3). Second, Sect. 4.5 analyzes which interest rates to include in the analysis. Third, Sect. 4.6 discusses whether to focus on global or national money developments. Section 4.6.1 shows the importance of global monetary developments. How best to incorporate international information is debated. Aggregation issues associated with empirical analyses of global conditions are discussed in Sect. 4.6.2. It is shown that for country-based analyses global monetary liquidity conditions can best be captured via international capital flows. Finally, Sect. 4.6.3 derives the methodology of how to calculate international capital flows. The objective for this methodology is to measure liquidity entering and exiting a country. Section 4.7 concludes and states the variables to include in the empirical analysis.

M. Wiedmann, *Money, Stock Prices and Central Banks*, Contributions to Economics,
DOI 10.1007/978-3-7908-2647-0_4,

4.2 Monetary Liquidity Versus Market Liquidity

In principle, two liquidity concepts can be differentiated: first, monetary liquidity, based on macroeconomic variables, such as monetary aggregates and short-term interest rates and, second, market liquidity, which is based on the transaction volume of a specific financial product and, thereby, determined by supply and demand conditions.

The idea behind market liquidity lies in the ability to quickly buy or sell large quantities of an asset at low cost and without affecting the market price. Put in other words, the liquidity of an asset is the ease with which it can be converted into cash without loss. Market illiquidity, on the other hand, occurs if asset transactions can only take place under massive price movements, thus, incurring high transaction costs. Several sources of illiquidity exist, e.g., direct costs, such as brokerage fees or order-processing costs, but also indirect costs, such as demand pressure, inventory risk or private information in the hands of the counterparty (Amihud et al. 2005, pp. 270–271). Market depth is associated with market liquidity. It is measured as the units bought or sold for a given transaction cost.[1] Examples of market liquidity proxies are the bid-ask spread, transaction-by-transaction market impact, trading volume or the turnover rate, which is the number of shares traded as a fraction of the number of shares outstanding (Huang and Wang 2008, p. 3; Amihud 2002, p. 32). Many theorems in finance rely on investors' abilities to buy or sell assets without affecting the price. In reality, however, trading costs, circuit brakers, short sale restrictions and other frictions exist (Chordia et al. 2001, p. 1).

Monetary and market liquidity are interrelated. Since monetary aggregates include short to medium-term bank liabilities, which can be used for funding and underwriting in securities markets, higher levels of monetary liquidity lower the cost of funding and support market making and, hence, increase market liquidity (Baks and Kramer 1999, p. 4).[2] However, market liquidity focuses on the market microstructure, whereas the objective of this contribution is to analyze macroeconomic influences on stock prices. Consequently, the focus is on monetary liquidity.

4.3 The Connection Between Money Stock and Interest Rates

Monetary authorities have to decide whether to try to control the supply of money or an interest rate. Thus, they can either focus on the quantity or the price of base money. Money which originates from commercial banks can only be created

[1] The market depth referred to in this section differs from financial market depth as used in the introduction. There it is defined as the ratio of a country's financial assets to its GDP.

[2] In addition, both liquidity measures behave consistently in the business cycle. They rise in upswings because money demand rises and risk aversion is reduced, which in turn increases market depth (Becker 2007, p. 4.)

if commercial banks possess required amounts of base money. In targeting base money supply central banks give up control of the interest rate and vice versa. Nowadays, almost all monetary authorities prefer to steer monetary policy via short-term interest rates instead of limiting the supply of base money.[3] Nevertheless, the two measures are closely related.

Many empirical studies have shown the 'liquidity effect', which says that the interest rate falls in the short run after an expansionary money supply shock (see, for instance, Rapach 2001, pp. 9–10; Galí 1992, pp. 726–728; McKibbin and Sachs 1991, pp. 80–89). Intuitively, one could also expect interest rates to rise after an expansive monetary policy shock as a consequence of the expected inflation effect (Neri 2004, p. 17; Ohanian and Stockman 1995, p. 3). However, strong agreement exists in the literature that, at least in the short run and for short-term interest rates, the liquidity effect of a money supply shock is stronger than the anticipated inflation effect (Lastrapes 1998, p. 377; Christiano and Eichenbaum 1995, pp. 1125–1132; Gordon and Leeper 1994, pp. 1238–1241; Christiano and Eichenbaum 1992, pp. 351–352).[4]

In theory, one potential depiction of the liquidity effect is via the traditional IS/LM/AS model with sticky prices.[5] Assuming market clearing in production and labor markets, the (neo-classical) aggregate supply curve (AS) is vertical and the aggregate demand curve (AD) has a negative slope in the price level-output-space. Figure 4.1 shows that an increase in money supply shifts the LM curve to the right (LM') and the aggregate demand curve (AD) upwards (AD'). With the price level p unchanged, aggregate demand exceeds aggregate supply. If prices were flexible, the price level would adjust to p' and the LM curve would shift back to its original level $\left(\frac{M}{p} = \frac{M+\Delta M}{p'}\right)$. However, in the short run, goods prices are assumed

[3] See Poole (1970, pp. 203–208) for advantages and disadvantages of monetary targeting compared to interest rate targeting. His main results are that monetary targeting is preferable if the economy is subject to goods demand and supply side shocks. Interest rate targeting on the other hand, is superior if money demand shocks are more frequent.

[4] However, the liquidity effect is not limited to the short run. See Benassy (2007, pp. 54–56) for possible persistence of the liquidity effect in a dynamic stochastic general equilibrium model. He shows that the negative effect on the interest rate is not only present in the period of the positive monetary innovation but also in all subsequent periods.

[5] Many other but related theoretical explanations of the liquidity effect can be found in the literature: Fuerst (1992, pp. 7–22) and Christiano (1991, pp. 17–23) provide a theoretical explanation of the liquidity effect via 'limited participation' channels; Ohanian and Stockman (1995, pp. 4–24) analyze the liquidity effect using sticky price, representative agent and cash-in advance models. Keynes (1936, pp. 165–174) bases his argument on heterogeneous investors with diverse opinions on the true state of the nominal interest rate. In his opinion, at any interest rate, two groups of people exist. Those who fear capital losses hold money and those who expect capital gains hold bonds. The equilibrium interest rate exists where fears and positive expectations meet. Thus, an increase in money supply leads to lower interest rates because lower rates increases the share of 'fearers' and with it the willingness to hold the new money. For problems with proving the liquidity effect empirically, see Pagan and Robertson (1995, pp. 35–50), who point out that results depend strongly on estimation methods, use of different money variables and restrictions in the models.

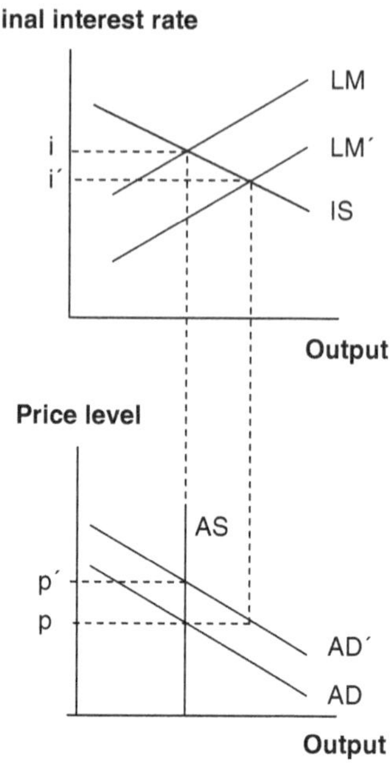

Fig. 4.1 Liquidity effect in the IS/LM/AD model with sticky prices

sticky. Consequently, output rises and interest rates fall (from i to i') (Romer 1996, pp. 394–395). This fall represents the 'liquidity effect'.

Causality also works in the other direction. If central banks decide to increase the overnight rate and this rise affects other interest rates, such as the deposit rate, money demand increases (see also Sect. 3.3.1). The reduced opportunity cost of money can lead to increases in the money stock. However, this argument is weakened if the yield spread is stationary and the term structure argument of interest rates holds, such that an increase in short-term interest rates affects long-term interest rates in the same way. In that case, the opportunity cost of money compared to bonds remains the same. Nevertheless, compared to other assets, such as stocks, money has become more attractive and its demand should rise. This shows the interrelationship between short-term interest rates and monetary aggregates.

4.4 Monetary Aggregates

4.4.1 Monetary Liquidity Creation

Central bank money (also referred to as 'high-powered money' or 'base money') is a central bank liability. It is the narrowest measure of money supply, defined by the sum of the cash amount (coins and notes) outstanding and sight deposits of commercial banks held with the central bank (ECB 1999a, p. 30). However, money supply does not only consist of notes and coins but also of money that can be withdrawn from the banking system upon demand. Commercial bank money is issued by commercial banks and consists of 'non-banks' deposits held with commercial banks. Hence, wider money supply measures exist and the line between 'money' and 'non-money' is often a thin one. A well-accepted definition of 'one' money supply measure does not exist in monetary theory or in central bank policy (Donnery 2003, p. 77). The classification problem results from the fact that, aside from the perfect means of payments assets (money and sight deposits), a number of other assets also qualify for the function of payment and the means of storing wealth, such as time and savings deposits, money market funds and other securities.[6] These assets are commonly referred to as money substitutes.

Whereas both the central bank and commercial banks have the ability to create money, the ability of the latter depends on the actions of the former. Commercial banks need central bank issued base money to create commercial bank money. Central banks can create base money by either purchasing assets from or issuing credit to banks or non-banks (Belke and Polleit 2009, p. 19). The importance of the monetary base stems from the fact that increases in the supply of monetary base money may lead to multiple increases of commercial bank money.

Operation procedures of the commercial banking system show the link between central bank-controlled base money and the other money supply measures. In a simplified view, banks make money by taking deposits from the public and lending these funds. The (demand) deposits qualify as a form of money because people can transfer money holdings to each other. Bankers know that, at any point in time, depositors only wish to withdraw a proportion of their deposits in cash.[7] Consequently, parts of an initial deposit can be used by banks to create loans, which, in turn, end up as deposits at the same bank or at a different bank.[8] Commercial banks rely on base money for three main reasons (Belke and Polleit 2009, p. 29): first, to process payments between banks. Second, to meet the above mentioned cash withdrawals of non-banks. And third, they must hold base money with the central bank to fulfill minimum reserve requirements (ECB 1999a, p. 30). The 'minimum reserve' is a ratio of cash reserves to deposits that the central bank requires commercial banks to hold. The link between the monetary base and the money supply is given by the money multiplier, which depends negatively on non-banks' preferences for cash holdings and minimum reserve requirements for commercial banks. It describes the maximum money creation potential of the banking sector based on a fixed stock of base money.

To influence the money supply, monetary authorities can either change the supply of base money or influence the money multiplier. The monetary base, on the one

---

[6] Money only acts as a store of wealth in nominal terms. The purchasing power of money may change due to inflation.

[7] This rule holds as long as depositors believe in the solvency of the bank. It does not hold for situations of distress, which may end up in bank runs.

[8] This is based on the valid assumption, that the customer, who takes out the loan, does not store the cash outside of the banking system.

hand, can be reduced via contractionary open market operations, e.g., selling treasury bills in the money market, thereby, reducing public cash holdings and with it decreasing commercial banks' ability to create money. On the other hand, the money multiplier can be influenced in two ways: either by raising reserve requirements or by raising the central bank lending rate. The central bank lending rate is the interest rate that the central bank charges commercial banks that want or need to borrow money. If commercial banks pass on interest rate changes, this will alter non-banks' preferences for cash holdings.

In addition to base money, minimum reserve requirements and the public's desire for cash holdings, the commercial banks' ability to create money is also limited by regulatory requirements, which are independent of central banks. Governments demand that banks own equity capital to engage in credit transactions or other risky positions that affect banks' balance sheets. Based on the 1988 Basle Accord (International Convergence of Capital Measurements and Capital Standards, commonly referred to as Basle I), supervisors require banks to hold minimum capital to mitigate against credit and market risk.[9] As a result, banks credit creation is limited by the amount of equity capital and their risk exposure. This is especially crucial during economic downturns when banks have to deal with defaulting loans. These write-offs affect banks' equity capital ratio and can force banks to sell assets to keep the capital ratio above the minimum requirement, thereby, worsening the current economic situation. This inflexible approach to equity capital ratios leads to procyclicality of credit markets. This means that credit creation is higher in economic upswings and lower in economic downturns. As can be seen with the current global financial crisis, this can worsen the situation for the real economy and significantly lengthen recessions.[10]

4.4.2 *Narrow Versus Broad Money*

Money supply measures (monetary aggregates) include different liabilities of banks and are segregated by their 'moneyness', which is the degree of liquidity. As mentioned in the previous section there is no one money supply measure. Instead, definitions of monetary aggregates depend on the liabilities included. A common definition of which liabilities to include in the various money supply measures

[9] Basle II (A Revised Framework on International Convergence of Capital Measurement and Capital Standards) succeeds Basle I and tries to align capital requirements with actual risk, based on past observations and institutional circumstances. Thus, it covers new approaches to credit risk, adapts to the securitization of bank assets and incorporates market-based surveillance and regulation. Its roll-out across a wider range of countries is still ongoing.

[10] For an investigation of the consequences of an economic downturn and the duration of recovery phases see Cerra and Saxena (2007, pp. 7–12). They find that economic contractions are not followed by offsetting fast recoveries. This finding increases the importance of avoiding crises, which may lead to real output contractions.

Table 4.1 Monetary aggregates definitions of the ECB (ECB 2008a, p. 1)

M1	Narrow money	Currency in circulation + overnight deposits
M2	Intermediate money	M1 + deposits with an agreed maturity up to 2 years + deposits redeemable at a period of notice up to 3 months
M3	Broad money	M2 + repurchase agreements + money market fund shares + debt securities issued with a maturity of up to 2 years

does not exist internationally. The European Central Bank (ECB), for example, distinguishes the money aggregates M1, M2 and M3 as defined in Table 4.1.

For the analysis at hand it is important to determine whether to use a narrow or a broad money supply measure.[11]

The usage of narrow money has the advantage that it is more closely influenced by the central bank compared to wider measures (see previous section).[12] Hence, it is preferable if the focus lies on the analysis of central banks' abilities to influence macro variables. Additionally, since narrow money generally comprises banknotes, coins and highly liquid deposits such as overnight deposits, it is more homogeneous across countries (ECB 2006b, p. 27). This enhances comparability between the various country analysis.

On the flip side are its higher volatility, its domination by transactions demand and its small share in respect to monetary and credit aggregates of the economy, which are usually used to explain aggregate demand for goods. The higher volatility results from non-banks' cash holding preferences. For example, nowadays, people tend to hold less money (compared to their incomes) due to financial innovations, which are an alternative to balance payments. In addition, if people switch their time deposits to savings deposits, the narrow money measure is reduced by that amount while a broader measure includes both positions and, hence, remains stable. Narrow money is more sensitive to portfolio decisions.

On the other hand, broad money has the advantage that it covers narrow money plus money substitutes which can easily be transferred into cash and, therefore, can easily be used to purchase assets, such as stocks. The broader measure includes all the liquidity inside a country and, as such, determines non-financial agents' spending capacity. Hence, it has more influence on stock market variability than narrow

[11] Narrow and broad money, as defined by central banks, are usually simple sum aggregates in which all components enter with the same weight. A further alternative can be found in divisia or currency equivalent indices. These indices are based on microeconomic theory and stem from the observation that instruments in monetary aggregates are imperfect substitutes (Stracca 2001, pp. 9–10). They differ from simple sum indices in that the individual components enter the aggregate with different weights, depending on expenditure share or return (Serletis 2006, pp. 23–24, 73–75; Reimers 2002, pp. 3–5). However, these alternative indices are not available for a broad range of economies. In addition, the German central bank, the Bundesbank, has used simple sum M3 as its primary target. Consequently, this contribution focuses on simple sum aggregates as well.

[12] It has to be pointed out, though, that even though a clear connection between base money and narrow money exists, the money multiplier is far from constant over time. For an overview of money multipliers in the US see Belke and Polleit (2009, pp. 35–36).

money. Congdon (2005, pp. 78–85) points to the importance of the behavior of (non-bank) financial institutions for the determination of asset prices and the superiority of broad money over the traditional Monetarist focus on narrow money. Pepper and Oliver (2006, p. 125) confirm the higher relevance of broad money for the behavior of asset prices.

In addition, volatility is lower than for narrow money and the broad aggregate probably reflects a more accurate picture of monetary growth (ECB 2006b, p. 27). Financial innovation along with the liberalization of international capital markets and deregulation of financial markets created a variety of substitutes for financial assets, which are only included in broad monetary aggregates. Consequently, it is more likely to find a stable money demand relation for broad money than for narrow money (ECB 1999b, p. 48). Since this is a prerequisite to calculate excess liquidity in the system, broad money is superior to narrow money for the analysis at hand.

The use of a broad money aggregate also brings shortfalls. If non-residents sold domestic stocks and shifted the proceeds into money market funds, this would increase broad monetary aggregates.[13] In that case, the impact on stocks would be negative, since it is a sign of risk aversion. Consequently, some form of international capital transactions must be included in the analysis to account for it. The influence of portfolio shifts on broad monetary aggregates is the main reason why it is difficult to interpret shocks in broad money as a monetary policy shock (Adalid and Detken 2007, p. 21).

In conclusion, the ideal analysis should include two measures, one that is broad and includes all monetary liquidity that could potentially be used to drive asset prices and one that is narrow enough to be quasi-controlled by the monetary authorities. However, since it is common procedure today for central banks to focus on interest rate setting instead of trying to control money supply growth, a narrow money supply measure only makes sense for central bank regimes in which money supply growth plays a key role. For all other countries the narrow monetary aggregate should be replaced by a short-term interest rate (see also Sect. 4.5).

4.4.3 Total Liquidity Versus Excess Liquidity

Based on Friedman's famous dictum that 'inflation is always and everywhere a monetary phenomenon' most economists point out that excess liquidity is responsible for driving inflation and asset prices. Excess liquidity can be associated with the money overhang. Simply put, excess liquidity exists if money supply grows faster than money demand and, hence, deviates from the equilibrium level. Unfortunately, money demand is not easy to measure and parameters often change over time. One problem that persists with most measures of liquidity is the development of the

[13] For an example of the influence of capital flows on domestic liquidity see ECB (2005c, pp. 19–22), in which four periods of capital flows with different characteristics and implications are presented for the euro area between 2001 and 2005.

velocity of money. The velocity of money is often assumed to be constant. However, many empirical studies have shown that this is not the case. The change or trend in the velocity of money can be measured via long-run money demand relations. A prerequisite to achieving this is determining a money demand relation, which is stable over time.

Various excess liquidity measures exist, which have in common that they try to identify the deviation of the actual money stock from an estimated long-run equilibrium level (ECB 2001b, p. 48). The most prominent ones are the following four measures: the 'price gap', the 'real money gap', the 'nominal money gap' and the 'money overhang'.[14] The first three, however, apply externally calculated equilibrium or target levels. Hence, they can not be applied in cointegration analysis because predefined target levels are not part of the system. This leaves the money overhang, which also describes the deviation of actual money stock from an equilibrium level. Unlike the other measures, the equilibrium level is based on other macro variables instead of predefined target or equilibrium levels of money stock (Borja and Goyeau 2005, pp. 5–6). These macro variables mostly include a transaction variable (such as real output) and various interest rates, which can enter the system of the cointegration analyses. As a result, actual money stock and money demand equilibrium values can be identified simultaneously. If a stable cointegration relationship exists between money and its demand determinants, the residuals describe the monetary overhang, which then is a stationary variable (Belke and Polleit 2009, p. 686). This enables one to determine short-run adjustment processes that describe the development of actual money holdings towards their equilibrium level. Cointegration analyses can also show whether the stock market or inflation react to a disequilibrium or behave independently of it.

Therefore, in the empirical part of this contribution, the relationship between excess liquidity and the stock market is only analyzed if an empirically stable long-run money demand relationship and with it the monetary overhang (or, if negative, the monetary shortfall) can be identified. The total level of liquidity in the system will of course always be considered. Hence, influences of money on stock prices that are not captured via deviations from the money demand relation can also be identified.

4.5 Interest Rates

Financial market prices, such as short-term interest rates, bond yields and exchange rates, are often used in theoretical models and empirical applications. Often, short-term interest rates instead of monetary aggregates are applied to capture

[14] A detailed overview of the measures of excess liquidity is provided by Polleit and Gerdesmeier (2005, pp. 7–15).

the monetary policy stance (Brand et al. 2003, p. 8).[15] One major reason for this is the reliability of the measure and its data availability. Financial market quantities on the other hand are often subject to changes due to technology, regulation or simply definition changes and, thus, are not as reliable.[16]

The follow-up question is, which financial prices to use. The focus in empirical applications usually lies on one short-term market rate (e.g., the 'fed funds' rate in the US) and one long-term interest rate with constant maturity (e.g., 10-year government bonds). The decision which particular interest rates to include is mainly one based on empirical judgment.

For the analysis in this contribution, it seems reasonable to include two interest rates: first, a short-term interest rate that can be directly influenced by the central bank, such as the overnight interbank rate. This enables one to analyze central banks' abilities since the money market rate is the preferred monetary policy operational target of central banks around the globe (King 2003, p. 85). Since central banks have a monopolistic supply position they can directly influence the price of holding base money, i.e., the short-term market interest rate (ECB 1999a, p. 30). Consequently, they must take responsibility for effects or the absence of desired effects associated with changes in the short-term market rate. By setting a target for the overnight rate central banks try to achieve two objectives. On the one hand, they want to ensure a functioning money market so that commercial banks can meet their liquidity needs on a daily basis. On the other hand, central bankers want to signal their current attitudes towards monetary policy. This is done by altering the conditions under which central banks engage in transactions with commercial banks.

The second interest rate that should be included is a long-term government bond yield that represents a competitive asset alternative to stocks and also covers information on expected inflation. In addition, the short-term interest rate can be used as a proxy for the interest paid on money holdings. This is obviously not the average interest payment, which is paid on the securities of a broad monetary aggregate. However, both measures are expected to move closely together, so that a change in the overnight rate also affects, e.g., deposit rates. For this contribution, the analysis of central banks' abilities is more important than the exact nominal interest paid on the securities of the broad monetary aggregate. In addition, to keep the number of variables in the model manageable, only one short-term interest rate shall be included.

[15] For the opposite view, namely that monetary aggregates are superior to interest rates in determining the direction of monetary policy, see Brunner and Meltzer (1968, p. 8).

[16] Another example of circumstances where monetary aggregates might be misleading is in times of inverted yield curves, i.e., when long-term rates are lower than short-term rates. This can lead to strongly growing monetary aggregates because agents shift their portfolios towards shorter securities. However, this rise in the monetary aggregate does not reflect an increase in bank lending and, as such, money creation dynamics might be overstated (Belke and Polleit 2009, p. 74).

4.6 National Versus Global Focus

4.6.1 International Economic and Financial Integration

Capital mobility between countries, the switch from fixed to floating exchange rates, monetary spillovers and the extent of price links between different countries are characteristics that have increased tremendously over the last 40 years. Global financial integration has experienced a tremendous increase. The huge growth of international capital flows and the cross-border holdings of financial assets and liabilities are indicative of this (Papademos 2007, p. 6; Lane and Milesi-Ferretti 2006, pp. 12–14, 33–34). However, even today, some countries still have capital controls in place and others pro-actively influence exchange rate movements and trade flows. This means that conditions across countries are different and raises the question: should the focus of the analysis be on global conditions or on a country basis?

Up until the global financial crisis that started in July 2007 financial markets were dominated by a few characteristic trends, which emphasize the importance of the global picture[17]:

- Growth and deepening of global capital markets. Old and new investors (oil-exporting nations, Asian Central Banks, hedge funds and private equity boutiques) poured money into equities, debt securities, bank deposits and other assets ('global search for yield').
- Soaring growth of financial markets in emerging economies and growing ties between financial markets in developed and developing countries.
- Huge increases in global financial assets, cross-border holdings and international capital flows.

In addition, the extent of global economic integration could be observed after the Asian financial crisis, the collapse of LTCM, the burst of the dot-com bubble and amid the current financial crisis. Financial integration, liberalization of international capital flows, the need to fund the US' external trade deficit and the spread of multinationals resulted in widespread waves of the crisis, which could be felt in most regions of the world (Walter 2003, p. 76). Whether the above mentioned trends are going to persist is questionable. By now it is clear, that all trends experienced a big dent during the current crisis.[18] Most likely, though, the trends will continue following the normalization of global circumstances, albeit potentially with lower trend growth.

The role of China and other Asian countries in the global liquidity creation process has increased considerably over the last years (Becker 2007, pp. 5–6). This

[17] For a detailed overview of global capital markets developments, see McKinsey Global Institute (2008, pp. 9–16).

[18] In example, according to the latest report of the McKinsey Global Institute (2009, pp. 8, 14)) global financial assets declined by 8% from 194 trillion USD in 2007 to 178 trillion USD in 2008. In addition, cross-border capital flows dropped by more than 80% in 2008.

increase is based on the Asian central banks' accumulation of high USD reserves through market interventions in their effort to prevent their currencies from appreciating too fast or too far.[19] Despite high trade surpluses, Asian currencies have not appreciated much against a basket of USD, euro (EUR) and Japanese Yen (JPY). One consequence is low long-term interest rates in the US due to purchases of dollar-denominated assets, such as US Treasury bonds (Warnock and Warnock 2006, pp. 13–16; The Economist 2005, p. 23).[20] In addition, the zero-interest rate and 'quantitative easing' policy of the Bank of Japan has led to a sharp increase in global 'narrow' money supply (ECB 2006b, p. 28). This has drawn investors from all over the world to borrow money in Japan and invest in higher-interest regions such as the US, the euro area and especially Australia and New Zealand (carry trades). Baks and Kramer (1999, p. 3) show that excess liquidity in one country can influence liquidity conditions in other regions. These spillover effects can result from, for example, the above mentioned carry trades.

As a result, and a sign, of the increased integration of global capital markets, easier access to foreign financial markets has changed the international pattern of asset ownership. For example, investors have diversified their portfolios internationally to reduce portfolio risk. These developments highlight the importance of global liquidity conditions for the world as a whole and for individual countries. The global surge of cross-border capital flows has increased the potential impact of capital flows as a channel for the transmission of external shocks (Anderton et al. 2004, p. 40). Consequently, the high degree of openness of individual economies gives rise to the need for central banks to pay special attention to the implications of external transactions. This is further strengthened by empirical findings of Ciccarelli and Mojon (2005), who show that the inflation rate in developed economies is mainly determined by common driving forces. A single global factor can explain the trend component of inflation and also fluctuations at business cycle frequencies. According to their research, this global factor alone accounts for about 70% of the overall variance of the inflation rates in 22 OECD countries. In addition, Belke and Rees (2009, pp. 20–26, 34–36) show the importance of global shocks for national macro variables empirically and discuss the implications for central bank policy with respect to international spillovers.

[19] Aizenman and Lee (2005, pp. 1–4) provide an alternative explanation of international reserve hoarding by developing countries. In their view international reserves accumulation is a result of precautionary demand. This precautionary demand reflects self-insurance against sudden stops and reversals of capital flows associated with costly output contractions. This also touches the discussion over whether low long-term yields and low risk premia are a result of global excess liquidity (i.e., monetary shocks) or the global savings glut (i.e., preference shocks) (Bracke and Fidora 2008, pp. 6–7; Bernanke 2005). In their empirical investigation of the US and Emerging Asia, Bracke and Fidora (2008, p. 23) conclude that monetary shocks play a greater role than preference shocks.

[20] This, however, is not the only explanation for low long-term yields. Over the last decade demand for long-term securities has also been strong due to the increase in pension commitments and the growing weight of institutional investors, such as insurance and pension funds, which tend to favor long-term securities (Bini Smaghi 2007, p. 9).

4.6.2 *Aggregation Issues and Importance of Country-Level Analysis*

As argued above, globalization compels one to focus on global liquidity rather than national measures. However, to determine global measures national quantities must be aggregated. This brings about technical difficulties inherent to international aggregation.

First is the choice of an appropriate exchange rate measure. National series have to be converted into a common unit of account to arrive at a global measure. Different exchange rate possibilities exist, which can be used to achieve that. Among them are rates defined by Purchasing Power Parity (PPP), a fixed rate of a base year or completely flexible actual exchange rates (Brüggemann and Lütkepohl 2006, pp. 683–684). Flexible exchange rates might lead to a volatile global aggregate. Volatility can be reduced by using a moving average. If volatility needs to be reduced further the usage of relative PPP exchange rates is preferable. They are advantageous because they take price levels of different countries into account and are less volatile.

Second is the issue of which weights to use for aggregation. Several options exist for the weights, such as GDP, money stock, market capitalization or financial depth. Hence, exchange rate and weighting choices offer many possibilities with potentially different outcomes and implications.[21]

Third is the challenge related to the definitions of monetary aggregates, which vary across countries. If one country includes a wider array of financial instruments in its broad money supply measure as compared to another country, then the first country's monetary development has a stronger influence on the global aggregate than the second country's monetary conditions.[22]

In conclusion, several global liquidity indices can be created with potentially different outcomes and conclusions in empirical analyses. The most commonly used measure is a GDP-weighted aggregation using PPP exchange rates because this reflects the most stable measure of worldwide liquidity in the long run.[23]

In addition, the question remains, which countries should be included in the global measure. Analysis of the ECB (2006b, p. 28) shows that the global measure can be improved by including emerging market economies, especially for recent years. However, this is problematic for comparisons across time since meaningful historical time series do not exist for many of the emerging economies. This, however, would be crucial for the analysis at hand.

---

[21] For a discussion on the impact of the choice of GDP-weights based on different exchange rate measures on world growth rates, see ECB (2006a, pp. 13–15).

[22] This point can be circumvented by weighting growth rates instead of absolute values of money stock (Giese and Tuxen 2007, pp. 12–13).

[23] For an extensive discussion of cross-country aggregation issues based on euro area experience see Bruggeman et al. (2003, pp. 10–12), Beyer et al. (2001) and Fagan and Henry (1998, pp. 486–487, 503–505).

Whereas a global liquidity measure can still be a useful complement to national liquidity measures, the focus of stock markets should be on national (or single currency area) indices and not on global aggregates for the following reasons: first, to understand if central banks have the ability to influence asset prices, the focus must be on the stock indices of their geographical region. If transmission mechanisms are asymmetric, this can not be achieved with a global measure. Second, the aggregation of national stock markets might create misleading results for the relationship between global liquidity and stock markets, because different stock market performances may cancel each other out. Since some countries are net exporters and others are net importers of capital, their stock market indices might behave differently.[24] These differences in country-behavior can only be explored by analyzing national measures.

Ultimately, though, the question of whether to apply a global or national focus can only be answered subject to the specific objectives of the analysis. For economics as a whole, the focus must lie on both. Important findings can be obtained from a purely global analysis, especially to explore the opportunities of global cooperation between central banks and financial authorities. For the analysis at hand the focus is on the country level for the above outlined reasons. International capital flows are included to take account of global monetary developments.

4.6.3 International Capital Flows

An alternative to the rather blunt measure of aggregated global liquidity is to focus on the country-relevant portion of worldwide liquidity. Meaning, independent of liquidity conditions outside one country, the amount of liquidity that arrives in and leaves a particular country is crucial to the country itself.[25] This draws attention to international capital flows. Strong capital inflows can generate a strong increase in money supply and exert pressure on national currency appreciation, thereby, fueling the overheating of an economy and increasing its vulnerability to crises.

The channels through which capital flows impact domestic conditions depend on the type of capital inflows, the way the central bank reacts to inflows and outflows and the specific banking and non-banking sector behavior and preferences. Various measures of international capital flows are possible and none of them are perfect,

---

[24] Between 2000 and 2008 the US, UK, Ireland and Spain borrowed 40%, 20%, 20% and 50% of their 2007 GDP, respectively, from abroad (The Economist 2009b, p. 4). At the same time countries such as Japan, China and oil-exporting countries provided relatively cheap credit for different reasons of their own.

[25] This, however, neglects the consequences of ample liquidity conditions in foreign countries and their potential influence on foreign economic conditions, stock markets and sentiment. These effects from positive conditions abroad are not fully covered in cross-border capital flows.

Table 4.2 Overview of Balance of Payments credit and debit items

Credit	Debit
Exports of goods and services	Imports of goods and services
Income receivable from abroad	Income payable abroad
Transfers from abroad	Transfers to abroad
Increases in external liabilities	Decreases in external liabilities
Decreases in external assets	Increases in external assets

because data availability and reliability is limited.[26] In addition, due to restrictions in the data, the impact of capital flows on national liquidity measures (such as M3) can not be pinpointed. Nevertheless, the advantages dominate the disadvantages. International capital flows include all investments of new global players (such as sovereign wealth funds) and most forms of investment, such as the increasingly popular carry trades, direct and portfolio investment. In addition, there are no aggregation issues because the flows do not have to be weighted and can be measured in domestic currency. The following sections introduce measurement alternatives for international capital flows with different upsides and downsides for the empirical analysis.

4.6.3.1 The Balance of Payments

The Balance of Payments (BoP) covers all transactions one country makes with the rest of the world. It is a statistical statement that summarizes the money-value of cross-border flows, such as goods, services, factor income and current transfers an economy receives from or provides to the rest of the world for a specific period. Additionally, it records all capital transfers and changes in an economy's external financial claims and liabilities. The BoP has a net balance of zero as it uses a double-entry accounting system. Therefore, every transaction has a credit and a debit entry. Credits denote a reduction in assets or an increase in liabilities and debits denote an increase in assets or a reduction in liabilities (see Table 4.2). Therefore, the credit side describes transactions associated with money inflows and the debit side is associated with money outflows.

The BoP consists of four main positions: first, the 'current account', which is comprised of exports and imports, receivable/payable income and receivable/payable current transfers. Second, the 'financial account', which contains changes in financial assets and liabilities and in official reserves. Third, the 'capital account', which covers long-term transfers. Last, 'net errors and omissions', which is a position of statistical discrepancies to net out the BoP. The first two divide the bulk of international transactions between them, the latter are relatively

[26] For problems with the reliability of US Balance of Payments data, see the analyses of, for example, Lane and Milesi-Ferretti (2008) and Gros (2006a, 2006b).

minor positions. All BoP data is expressed in USD. Consequently, to use it for the empirical analysis, the data has to be converted into local currency.

The biggest problem with using BoP data for financial analysis lies in its double-entry system. All financial transactions enter the financial account twice, once on the credit side and once on the debit side. This means that, by definition, financial transactions alone always have a net balance of zero. Consequently, the 'financial and capital account' balance mirrors the 'current account' balance. Accordingly, net flows in the BoP only depend on the net amount of goods and services traded and the net income and net current transfers.[27] While it is true that this is the amount of money flowing into or out of the country, it is not a complete measure of transactions that actually affect the money stock. If foreigners buy stocks and bonds of domestic companies from residents, this also increases the domestic money stock. In addition, the amount of financial transactions is sometimes larger than that of real transactions. However, these 'financial' effects are not included in the net BoP and, thus, the net balance is an inferior liquidity measure with regard to overall liquidity conditions in a country and the analysis of stock price movements.

4.6.3.2 The Monetary Presentation of the Balance of Payments

To solve this dilemma the ECB created the 'Monetary Presentation of the Euro Area Balance of Payments' and began reporting it in June 2003 (ECB 2003, p. 15). It has been developed to highlight the effects of international transactions on monetary developments.[28] The underlying idea is the fact that money and banking statistics (i.e., the consolidated balance sheet of the domestic banking system) and BoP data are derived from a coherent methodological framework. As a result, the change in the net external position of the domestic banking sector can be presented as the mirror image of the external transactions of the banking system in the BoP, which in turn is the same (with the opposite sign) as the external transactions of non-bank residents in the BoP. Several identities can be set up to retrieve this result.[29]

One starting point is the consolidated balance sheet of the monetary sector, including monetary authorities, as depicted in a simplified version in Table 4.3:

The liability side of the consolidated balance sheet of the domestic banking sector shows all of the monetary holdings of residents and non-residents. In particular, the relatively short-term assets of non-financial agents, which represent the broad monetary aggregate, in this example M3. Most broad monetary aggregates consist of currency in circulation, liquid deposits, repurchase agreements, money

[27] One other factor is the accumulation of official reserves. This means that countries with current account surpluses can also have net capital inflows if central banks accumulate official reserves (Jara and Tovar 2008, pp. 9–10).

[28] For the importance of developments in net external assets for monetary policy, see also Trichet (2005, p. 9).

[29] The derivation of the capital flows time series, as outlined here, closely follows IMF (2008, pp. 335–336), Be Duc et al. (2008, pp. 12–16) and Bank of England (2006, pp. 13–18).

Table 4.3 Consolidated balance sheet of the domestic banking sector

Assets	Liabilities
	M3
Loans to domestic non-banks	Longer-term financial liabilities
Claims on non-residents (external assets)	Financial liabilities to non-residents (external liabilities)
Other assets (including fixed assets)	Other liabilities (including deposits by central government)

Table 4.4 Counterparts of M3

M3 =	Credit to domestic residents
+	Net external assets
+	Other counterparts
−	Longer-term financial liabilities

market fund shares/units and debt securities with a limited maturity, albeit vary across countries (see also Sect. 4.4). The liability side of the balance sheet also includes the banking sector's longer-term financial liabilities, which are not part of the monetary aggregate because they are of a non-monetary nature. This position includes deposits and loans with an agreed maturity (usually more than two years) and deposits redeemable at a period of notice of over three months. In addition, it includes capital, reserves and provisions. The next position is financial liabilities to non-residents, which includes deposits and received loans from non-residents plus the counterparts of special drawing rights. Other liabilities include deposits made by the government.

The asset side, on the other hand, represents the main methods of money creation. The biggest position comprises credit to non-bank residents. In addition, the asset side includes external assets, which are claims on non-residents and other assets, which also include fixed assets. The domestic banking sector balance sheet is called 'consolidated' because inter-bank positions are netted out.

Given the balance sheet identity (total assets equal to total liabilities), the sum of the broad monetary aggregate components can be expressed by the sum of other balance sheet items, i.e., its counterparts. The loans extended to domestic residents as well as securities issued by domestic residents account for the most significant counterparts of money supply. However, international transactions also play a role. Net external assets, which result from the difference between claims on the 'rest of the world' (on the asset side) and deposits of the 'rest of the world' (on the liability side) also need to be taken into account. The counterparts of M3 can be derived from Table 4.3 and are depicted in Table 4.4. The domestic banking sector's net assets and net liabilities vis-à-vis non-residents (net external assets) form the external counterpart of M3 (see also ECB (2007, p. 34)):

Since the focus here is on flows, the accounting identity of Table 4.4 in the form of transactions, Δ, becomes:

$$\Delta M3 = \Delta DC + NET^{\text{Banks}} + OTR\,, \tag{4.1}$$

where DC = domestic credit, NET^{Banks} = net external transactions of banks and OTR = other net transactions with non-bank residents. As such, the domestic banking balance sheet accounting framework associates developments in money stock to changes in net external assets of the banking system (ECB 2005c, p. 18).[30]

Assuming similar compilation procedures, changes in external assets and liabilities of the consolidated balance sheet of the banking sector should, in principle, be consistent with the external transactions of the banking sector in the BoP (ECB 2008c, p. 1)[31]:

$$NET^{\text{Banks}}_{\text{Balance Sheet}} = NET^{\text{Banks}}_{\text{BoP}}\,, \tag{4.2}$$

where $NET^{\text{Banks}}_{\text{BoP}}$ equals financial and non-financial external transactions of the banking sector recorded in the BoP.

In addition, when external payments of non-financial agents are channeled through the banking system, the offsetting entry appears in the banking sector within the BoP. This is a result of the fact that, by definition, the sum of BoP transactions is equal to zero. This means that, to a large extent, BoP transactions of the domestic banking sector are a balancing record of cross-border transactions of non-bank residents, leading to[32]:

$$NET^{\text{Banks}}_{\text{BoP}} + NET^{\text{Non-Banks}}_{\text{BoP}} = 0\,, \tag{4.3}$$

where $NET^{\text{Non-Banks}}_{\text{BoP}}$ equals non-financial BoP transactions and transactions in foreign assets and liabilities of the non-banking sector as stated in the BoP.[33] Rearranging (4.3):

$$NET^{\text{Banks}}_{\text{BoP}} = -NET^{\text{Non-Banks}}_{\text{BoP}} \tag{4.4}$$

---

[30] However, whether or not changes in the net external assets of the banking system affect domestic money stock also depends on how residents finance their transactions with the rest of the world (ECB 2007, p. 35). The impact on M3 can be ambiguous. For example, if purchases of foreign assets are financed, on the one hand, via deposits in a domestic bank account the broad monetary aggregate will decline. If, on the other hand, the transaction is financed by a loan granted to the resident, then there is no impact on M3.

[31] Changes in net external assets of the banking sector have to be corrected for non-transaction related changes, such as revaluations due to asset price and exchange rate changes and other reclassifications.

[32] In the BoP, the non-bank resident sector is comprised of the positions 'general government' and 'other sectors', which includes other financial intermediaries, non-financial companies and households (IMF 1993, pp. 37–50).

[33] For this identity to hold in practice, transactions in foreign assets between residents (and, as such, not BoP transactions) need to be recorded as well. Most likely, transactions in financial assets are derived from data that does not distinguish between residents and non-residents and, thus, fulfill the above prerequisite (IMF 2008, p. 37).

and inserting (4.4) into (4.1), based on the conceptual identity of (4.2), results in:

$$\Delta M3 = \Delta DC - NET_{\text{BoP}}^{\text{Non-Banks}} + OTR\,. \tag{4.5}$$

Equation (4.5) states the relationship between external transactions of resident non-banks and the transactions in money ($\Delta M3$) held by resident non-banks. Ergo, this link establishes the impact of international capital flows on the money stock. Put in a different way, since the 'net external assets of the domestic banking sector' position is a counterpart of domestic M3 (see Tables 4.4 and 4.3), this is one way of dividing M3 into a domestic component and an international component. It takes account of non-bank BoP transactions, which are channeled through the banking system. These transactions are reflected in the current and capital account and the non-bank part of the financial account of the BoP. Thus, a statistical link between the external transactions of the money-holding sector and developments in monetary aggregates can be established.

As an example of the above mentioned transactions, consider the sale of a bond security by a domestic resident to a non-resident. If the non-resident pays for the bond via money transfer from an account with a domestic bank, which is not included in the money stock, to the bank account of the resident household, which is included in the money stock, then the domestic money stock increases (ECB 2005b, p. 22). At the same time, the net external asset position of the domestic banking sector increases because the balance of the non-resident bank account falls and the non-resident bank account is an external liability of the bank.[34] This is the major difference to a transaction between two residents, where the same transaction in the bond security has no impact on the overall money stock (ECB 2005b, pp. 21–22). It is only a circulation of money among the money-holding sector.

Another example would be a non-resident importer buying a product from a domestic exporter and settling this purchase by debiting his non-resident bank account in favor of the bank account of the resident exporter. Again, money supply increases accompanying a reduction in external liabilities (which is an increase in net external assets) of the resident bank, in this case vis-à-vis the bank of the non-resident importer.[35] However, if the transactions are not settled via resident banks, there is no effect in the balance sheet of the domestic banking system and there are opposing effects in the BoP (a credit and debit entry in the non-bank sector).

Unfortunately, the concept of the 'monetary presentation of the balance of payments' also comes with a few limitations. First, external transactions may not have an impact on the monetary aggregate. Second, the data consistency between banking balance sheet data and BoP data is sometimes limited. Third, the distinction between BoP transactions by banks and non-banks is not always straight forward.

[34] The same result occurs if the non-resident is debiting his bank account with a foreign bank. In which case it is equal to a fall in external liabilities of the resident bank vis-à-vis the bank of the non-resident buyer.

[35] For further examples see Annexes 1 and 2 in Be Duc et al. (2008, pp. 26–28).

The first issue refers to external transactions of non-banks, which do not impact banking statistics. This could result from the fact that they do not give rise to counterpart payments (such as mergers and acquisitions settled in shares[36]), from transactions, which may be netted out without a cash payment (such as intra-group transactions) or from transactions, which are settled via accounts of foreign banks (Be Duc et al. 2008, p. 11).

The second issue, methodological (in-)consistency between the BoP and the consolidated domestic banking balance sheet, arises from the practical application of data compiling. Different sources may be used to account for external transactions. Whereas for the BoP banks report the actual transactions; the 'transactions' derived from the balance sheet of the domestic banking system are calculated as differences in stock data (ECB 2003, p. 15).[37] Additionally, the timing of the reporting might differ. For example, in the euro area BoP, data is provided within 30 working days, whereas monetary data is provided within 15 working days (Be Duc et al. 2008, p. 15).

The third constraint arises from limited options to distinguish between BoP transactions by banks and non-banks. Be Duc et al. (2008, p. 16) name the following transactions, which can not be split into bank or non-bank transactions (this is specific for the euro area BoP and might differ between countries):

- Current and capital account transactions.
- Foreign direct investment in resident banks in the form of equity and reinvested earnings.
- Financial derivatives transactions of the banking sector.
- Transactions in equity and long-term debt securities of the portfolio investment liabilities position of the banking sector.

Even though these transactions clearly play a role, their impact is probably a minor one. In addition, one part of the BoP data is 'errors and omissions' due to overlapping or incomplete coverage, inconsistent times of recording, non-uniform valuation and other data compilation problems. That means that the sources of changes in the external counterpart of M3 are not always clear cut (ECB 2008c, p. 3).

Notwithstanding these limitations, the change in net external assets of the banking system, measured as the BoP transactions of the non-banking sector, is the best measure for the analysis in this contribution. The main reason for this is the direct impact of international transactions on the domestic money stock (IMF 2008, p. 336). As a result, the measure is in line with the leading hypothesis of this contribution that liquidity conditions affect stock market behavior. This can not be achieved with any other measure of international capital flows.[38] Appendix A

[36] An example is the takeover of Mannesmann by Vodafone in February 2000, where the offsetting entry of this acquisition appears in portfolio investment, since the deal was financed by a stock swap.

[37] Adjusted for exchange rate and asset price changes as well as reclassifications.

[38] Other measures of international liquidity exist, which are inferior for the objectives of this contribution. For example, Barbosa Filho (2001) defines 'international liquidity' as the ratio of

provides exact details and examples on the construction of the 'capital flows' time series.

Unfortunately, the details of the available information in the BoP are limited for some countries and do not completely suffice to calculate the monetary presentation of the BoP. In these cases, the changes in net external assets of the banking system present an alternative, which can be used as a proxy for capital flows that affect money supply. However, as these are calculated as differences in stock data because data on flows is not available, the measure is distorted by exchange rate changes and adjustments due to revaluations.

In conclusion, for each country one must determine whether to focus on capital flows based on the monetary presentation or based on changes in net external assets of the banking system.[39] The former data series might be affected by a lack of data in the sub-series (see Appendix A, Table A.1 for details on the sub-series included). The latter time series is affected by exchange rate changes and asset price revaluations. As a result, neither time series is optimal from a theoretical point of view but both are superior for the analyses in this contribution as compared to the standard capital flows measure – the net BoP – which only represents trade flows.[40]

4.7 Conclusion

This chapter shows that the following variables can be helpful in determining the relationship between monetary liquidity conditions and national stock markets:

- A broad monetary aggregate.
- A short-term interest rate.
- A long-term interest rate.
- A measure for international capital flows, which influence the money stock.

---

a country's net foreign reserves to net foreign debt, which is derived from the liquidity ratios used in the corporate sector. As a result, he determines a critical liquidity ratio at which the underlying country is prone to speculative attacks.

[39] For the country analyses in Chap. 6, changes in net external assets of the banking system are only used in the US analysis.

[40] In example, Walter (2003) analyzes the impact of external transactions on euro area monetary growth. Her findings show that international economic activity of non-residents resulted in an outflow of EUR 150 billion between 1999 and 2002 while real economic transactions only summed up to EUR 1.5 billion (Walter 2003, p. 81). Since the BoP data is further categorized into, e.g., direct investment, equity and bond transactions, loans and options and the focus of this analysis is on stock markets, an alternative measure could be to solely use equity flows. However, it is hard to say beforehand, which source of funding could lead to movements or exaggerations on capital markets. During the Asian crisis 10 years ago, for example, the sudden stop of international bank lending triggered the crisis. Although the massive withdrawal of equity investments made the crisis more severe, it did not trigger it. Consequently, a complete picture of international transactions (included in a broad measure, such as net external assets of the banking system) is needed.

Broad instead of narrow money is chosen to avoid the influence of portfolio allocations of money holdings in the private sector on the monetary aggregate. In addition, the instruments included in broad money reflect the readily available liquidity position, which can be used for stock market investments. Broad money is also less volatile than narrow money.

Interest rates are included for several reasons. First, they describe the price of money.[41] Second, the short-term interest rate can be associated with a proxy for the interest paid on money. Moreover, and more importantly, it can be used to analyze the abilities of central banks, since the short-term interest rate is their preferred policy instrument. Third, the long-term interest rate, in the form of the 10-year government bond rate, represents a competitive investment alternative.

To account for the fact that capital is increasingly mobile and can be readily deployed internationally, capital flows are included in the analysis. The capital flow proxy applied here measures the flows that affect the money stock and, hence, liquidity conditions in the respective country. Capital flows are also included to allow for changes in monetary conditions in one country, which may affect monetary and financial conditions in other countries.

[41] The inclusion of not only a quantity measure but also of a price indicator of money, is in line with the reasoning of the IMF, because an easing of liquidity conditions tends to show up in both an extending stock of money and lower interest rates (IMF 1999, pp. 118–121).

Chapter 5
Empirical Analysis: General Remarks

5.1 Econometric Approach: The Cointegrated VAR Framework

5.1.1 Methodological Motivation

Since cointegration between non-stationary data series represents the statistical expression of the economic notion of a long-run economic relation, the objectives of this contribution are analyzed by applying the parametric approach of the CVAR model. The classification of the data generating process into stationary and non-stationary parts enables the distinction between long-run equilibria and short-run dynamic adjustment. In addition, common trends that push the variables and determine the long-run impact of shocks to the variables can be identified.

Many empirical analyses, which are based on macroeconomic variables, use the VAR model as a starting point. The variables in these analyses are usually assumed to be stationary or allowed to be non-stationary, even though stationarity is a necessary and sufficient condition for valid statistical inference (Johansen 1995, p. 11).[1] However, economic processes in real world macro analysis are often characterized by non-stationary behavior. Non-stationarity means that time series do not show a tendency to return to or fluctuate around a constant mean or a linear trend. Instead, in a non-stationary unit root process shocks accumulate and form a stochastic trend, which can be associated with a permanent, non-deterministic shift in the mean (Hoover et al. 2008, p. 253). Exogenous shocks influence the behavior of macroeconomic variables. As a consequence, the variables move away from a given equilibrium of the economy. These disturbances then activate adjustment forces pulling the system gradually back to a new equilibrium position.

---

[1] See Johansen (2007, pp. 5–8) for a discussion of spurious correlations and the interpretation of correlation and regression in non-stationary economic time series. This view is confronted by Sims et al. (1990, pp. 136–137), who show that in a VAR analysis of non-stationary variables the ordinary least square estimates of the coefficients are consistent for a broad set of circumstances.

M. Wiedmann, *Money, Stock Prices and Central Banks*, Contributions to Economics,
DOI 10.1007/978-3-7908-2647-0_5,

To allow for non-stationarity in the data and to be able to determine long-run equilibria as well as the above mentioned adjustment forces a CVAR model with Gaussian errors is applied. The idea is to formulate a well-specified statistical model and then apply the principle of maximum likelihood to estimate the parameters. This parametric approach allows for a formal check of the model specification and for testing of economic hypotheses. In addition to allowing for non-stationary data series, the CVAR model has many other advantages for the analysis of money and the stock market. First, the CVAR model is a system of multiple equations and is capable of modeling the interdependence and feedback effects that are likely to be present among the variables in the system. Therefore, the findings of the analysis exceed the relationship between money and stocks because the behavior of stocks with other variables and with the long-run equilibria will be analyzed at the same time.

Second, since the unrestricted CVAR model is a simple representation of the covariances in the data it allows for the dynamic structure in the data and if modeling is done carefully, it usually provides an adequate fit of the data. The advantage is the ability to 'let the data speak' without imposing a priori assumptions based on economic theory (which have not been formally tested). The modeling approach here starts by building a statistical model that describes the fluctuations of the data. A highly over-parameterized system is formulated and economic hypotheses are tested as parametric restrictions in order to obtain an economically identified model. This is the principle of 'general-to-specific' modeling (Hendry and Mizon 1993).

On the flip side, however, the CVAR approach is highly dependent on data quality and the results may be vulnerable to measurement errors, changes in statistics and other data inherent problems. In addition, the lack of a theoretical economic structure implies that economic explanations must be provided to support the results. It is often argued that the generality of the reduced form VAR comes at the cost of a lack of structure. However, if the model is well-specified and an identified long-run structure is imposed and tested, the model may be characterized as structural. The distinguishing feature of this approach is that the assumptions are tested formally.

Whereas the above is the motivation from a statistical point of view, there are also advantages of the CVAR model from an economic perspective. Due to uncountable influences, short-run movements of stocks strongly fluctuate and, therefore, are difficult to model and predict. However, it has previously been shown that the direction can be predicted in the long-run (Campbell and Shiller 2001, pp. 7–13; Campbell and Shiller 1988, pp. 671–674). This is where cointegration analysis picks up. Co-integration analysis enables one to check for various long-run relations in the data that can help to improve the understanding of the relationship between money and stock prices, such as:

- A money demand function and, consequently, the impact of excess liquidity on stock prices.
- A direct long-run relationship between money and stock prices.
- A direct long-run relationship between international capital flows and stock prices.

In addition, the CVAR methodology enables empirical testing of additional theoretical hypothesis, which describe the interrelations between the included variables, such as, among others, the term structure of interest rates, the Fisher hypothesis and the relationship between stock markets and economic activity. As a result, an enhanced picture of stock market behavior across different countries can be obtained. In sum, based on the variable characteristics and the objectives of this contribution, the CVAR model is a good choice for the statistical model to perform the empirical analysis.

In addition to being able to impose long-run economic structure on the unrestricted cointegration relations, the short-run adjustment dynamics can be analyzed by imposing short-run structure on the equations of the differenced process. However, the short-run identification is guided less by economic theory (in contrast to the long run) and more by restricting insignificant coefficients to zero. Hence, the result is a parsimonious system of equations where all included regressors are significant. This is in line with the notion that economic theory is not as informative of short-run dynamics (Garratt et al. 2003). The short-run dynamics are modeled conditional on the deletion of statistically irrelevant short-run parameters. This enables one to determine the short-run impact on stocks from:

- Money
- Interest rates
- International capital flows
- Excess money (residuals of the money demand equation)
- Other deviations of long-run equilibria.

5.1.2 *The Cointegrated VAR Model*

This section introduces the econometric methodology of the CVAR model.[2] Consider the p-dimensional VAR(k) model,

$$x_t = \Pi_1 x_{t-1} + \ldots + \Pi_k x_{t-k} + \Phi D_t + \epsilon_t, \quad t = 1, \ldots, T, \tag{5.1}$$

where x_t is a $(p \times 1)$ vector of endogenous variables and ϵ_t is an error term, which is assumed to be independently and identically distributed (i.i.d.) multivariate normal with constant variance: $\epsilon_t \sim i.i.d.\ N_p\ (0, \Omega)$, where Ω is a $(p \times p)$ covariance matrix. $(\Pi_1, \ldots, \Pi_k)$ is a $(p \times p)$ matrix of unrestricted parameters, D_t is a vector of general deterministic terms, such as a constant, a linear term, seasonal dummies and intervention dummies and Φ is the corresponding vector of unrestricted parameters.[3]

[2] For a detailed presentation and discussion see Juselius (2006) and Johansen (1995).

[3] Seasonal dummies are included because throughout the whole contribution seasonally unadjusted data is applied where available. Seasonal adjustment procedures are problematic if the underlying time series is subject to structural shifts (Brüggemann and Lütkepohl 2006, p. 685).

The error-correction version of the VAR (k) model is used to account for non-stationarity in the data and to facilitate the economic interpretation. The vector equilibrium-correction model reformulates the VAR model in terms of differences, lagged differences and levels of the process. It is obtained from a reparametrization of (5.1):

$$\Delta x_t = \Pi x_{t-1} + \sum_{i=1}^{k-1} \Gamma_i \Delta x_{t-1} + \Phi D_t + \epsilon_t, \quad t = 1, \dots, T, \tag{5.2}$$

where $\Pi = \sum_{i=1}^{k} \Pi_i - I_p$ and $\Gamma_i = -\sum_{j=i+1}^{k} \Pi_j$.

The properties of x_t can be investigated by solving the characteristic polynomial associated with (5.2):

$$\Pi(z) = (1-z)I_p - \Pi z - (1-z)\sum_{i=1}^{k-1} \Gamma_i z^i \tag{5.3}$$

with determinant $|\Pi(z)|$. If $\Pi(z)$ has a unit root, $z = 1$, i.e., $|\Pi(1)| = 0$, then $-\Pi(1) = \Pi$ is of reduced rank $r < p$, and Π can be decomposed into $\Pi = \alpha\beta'$ where α and β are $(p \times r)$ of rank r. The presence of a unit root in the VAR model corresponds to non-stationary stochastic behavior, which can be accounted for by a reduced rank restriction of the long-run levels matrix $\Pi = \alpha\beta'$. By substituting $\Pi = \alpha\beta'$ into (5.2) an expression for the CVAR model, which is the reduced form error-correction model, is obtained:

$$\Delta x_t = \alpha\beta' x_{t-1} + \sum_{i=1}^{k-1} \Gamma_i \Delta x_{t-1} + \Phi D_t + \epsilon_t, \tag{5.4}$$

where the parameters $(\alpha, \beta, \Gamma_1, \dots, \Gamma_{k-1}, \Phi, \Omega)$ vary freely. The necessary and sufficient conditions for the solution of (5.2) to be a cointegrated $I(1)$[4] process are:

$$|\Pi(z)| = 0 \;\Rightarrow\; |z| > 1 \;\vee\; z = 1 \tag{5.5}$$

and

$$|\alpha'_\perp \Gamma \beta_\perp| \neq 0, \tag{5.6}$$

[4] If the underlying series are integrated of order 1, they are denoted as I(1), i.e., non-stationary with stationary differences (Johansen 1995, p. 5). A stationary process is a process for which the distribution of $X_{t_1}, \dots, X_{t_m}$ is the same as the distribution of $X_{t_1+h}, \dots, X_{t_m+h}$ for any $h = 1, 2, \dots$. Or, in other words, stationary means that the mean and variance of a stochastic process are constant over time and the covariance between two periods only depends on the lag but not on the actual time of the periods (Hendry and Juselius 1999, p. 1).

where Γ is defined as $\Gamma = I_p - \sum_{i=1}^{k-1} \Gamma_i$ and the orthogonal complement of α and β, $\alpha_\perp$ and $\beta_\perp$, are both of dimension $(p \times (p-r))$, such that $\alpha' \alpha_\perp = 0$ and $\beta' \beta_\perp = 0$. Condition (5.5) guarantees that all characteristic roots are on or outside the unit circle. This rules out seasonal or explosive roots. Equation (5.6) excludes variables integrated of order $d > 1$ and is equivalent to $\Pi(z)$ having exactly $p - r$ unit roots at $z = 1$, that is, $rank(\alpha_\perp' \Gamma \beta_\perp) = p - r$.

Note, however, if $r = p$ then $x_t \sim I(0)$, i.e., p cointegrating relations exist and the process is already stationary. This implies that all variables are stationary by themselves and standard inference applies. The other borderline case, $r = 0$, means that p autonomous trends in x_t exist. Thus, each variable is non-stationary with its own individual trend. In this case, the vector process is driven by p different stochastic trends and it is not possible to obtain stationary cointegration relations between the levels of the variables. If, however, $p > r > 0$ then r directions exist into which the process can be made stationary by linear combinations. Hence, the cointegration rank of the system is equal to the number of 'stable' economic long-run relations between the 'unstable' economic data.

The primary result of cointegration analysis is that even though x_t is non-stationary, linear combinations, $\beta' x_t$, exist, which are stationary (Granger 1986, p. 215; Granger 1981, p. 128). That means that there can be stationary relations between non-stationary variables. The reason for this is that the linear combinations eliminate the common trends, which represent the non-stationary part and push the process. As a result, the cointegrating relations can be interpreted as long-run economic equilibria. If the system is shocked out of the steady state, there will be forces reacting to the deviations from the equilibrium level, potentially in an error-correcting manner, as represented by the adjustment coefficient α. This can be interpreted as agents' reaction to the disequilibrium error. Additional short-run dynamics are contained in Γ_i.

The main advantage of modeling non-stationary data is being able to focus on two economic aspects. On the one hand are the stable economic relations between the variables and the related adjustment dynamics. On the other are the cumulated disturbances, referred to as common trends, which lead to the non-stationary behavior in the data (Johansen 1995, p. 34). The latter are analyzed via the moving-average (MA) representation and can be used to determine the long-run impact of shocks to the levels of the variables. The MA representation can be derived from (5.4) using Granger's representation theorem (see Johansen 1995, Theorem 4.2, p. 49).

If (5.5) and (5.6) are satisfied and $\Pi(z)$ has some unit roots, that is, $rank(\Pi) = r < p$, then $\Delta x_t - E(\Delta x_t)$ and $\beta' x_t - E(\beta' x_t)$ can be given initial distributions such that they become $I(0)$, and the solution of (5.4), x_t, has the representation:

$$x_t = C \sum_{i=1}^{t} (\epsilon_i + \Phi D_i) + \sum_{i=0}^{\infty} C_i^* (\epsilon_{t-i} + \Phi D_t) + A, \tag{5.7}$$

where

$$\Pi^{-1}(z)(1-z) = C(z) = C(1) + C^*(z)(1-z) \tag{5.8}$$

and $C_i^* = \alpha(\beta'\alpha)^{-1}(I_r + \beta'\alpha)^i\beta'$ captures the transitory impact of shocks. A is a stationary process that depends on the initial value of the process, such that $\beta' A = 0$ and the long-run impact matrix, C, is given by:

$$C = C(1) = \beta_\perp(\alpha_\perp'\Gamma\beta_\perp)^{-1}\alpha_\perp'. \tag{5.9}$$

By expressing (5.9) as $C = \tilde{\beta}_\perp\alpha_\perp'$ with $\tilde{\beta}_\perp = \beta_\perp(\alpha_\perp'\Gamma\beta_\perp)^{-1}$ one can recognize that the decomposition of the C-matrix is similar to that of $\Pi = \alpha\beta'$. The difference between the two decompositions is that in the error-correction representation, (5.4), β determines the common long-run relations and α the loadings, whereas in the moving average representation, (5.7), $\alpha_\perp'$ determines the common stochastic trends that push the system out of equilibrium and $\tilde{\beta}_\perp$ provides the loadings of the common trends to each variable in the system. For an $I(1)$ process the number of unit roots equals $p - r$, which is the same as the number of common stochastic trends. The common stochastic trends describe the long-run movements of the series and are described by the $p-r$ dimensional vector $\alpha_\perp'\sum_{i=1}^{t}\epsilon_i$. They are combinations of the cumulated residuals of each variable. Put in a different way, cointegrated variables share the same stochastic trend. As such they can not drift too far apart. As a result, cointegration and common trends are two sides of the same coin. One discrepancy between the two, however, is the different behavior when the information set is increased. While the cointegration relations are not affected, the common trends are (Johansen 1995, p. 42).

The CVAR model also provides the starting point to the analysis of short-run dynamics. For this, the reduced form representation of (5.4) is transformed to the structural form representation by pre-multiplying with a non-singular $p \times p$-matrix A_0, resulting in:

$$A_0\Delta x_t = A_1\Delta x_{t-1} + a\beta' x_{t-1} + \tilde{\Phi}D_t + v_t \text{ with } v_t \sim IN(0,\Sigma), \tag{5.10}$$

where $A_1 = A_0\Gamma_1$, $a = A_0\alpha$, $\tilde{\Phi} = A_0\Phi$, $v_t = A_0\epsilon_t$ and $\Sigma = A_0\Omega A_0'$. Equation (5.10) formulates stationary equations for each of the variables in the system. Hence, the analysis focuses on the dynamic short-run adjustment of each variable to the past and the other simultaneous variables in the system (Johansen 1995, p. 79). The long-run equilibria (the cointegration relations) are uniquely identified in the reduced form error-correction model and are fixed accordingly (with no restrictions on the short-run parameters). As a result, the variables in differences and the residuals of the equilibrium errors (the regressors in the short-run analysis) are stationary and the usual regression analysis can be applied. In this case, this is done by applying the full information maximum likelihood estimator in simultaneous equation modeling, using PcGive in OxMetrics (Doornik 2007).

The starting point is estimating the multivariate dynamic equilibrium-correction model for the whole system. Identification of the p short-run equations requires at least $p - 1$ just-identifying restrictions on each equation (Juselius 2006, p. 208). This is achieved by restricting current effects between the variables to zero.[5] In addition, insignificant coefficients are removed from each single equation based on a likelihood ratio (LR) test, which results in overidentified equations for each variable. Since the VAR model is usually overparameterized, and particularly so for short-run parameters, imposing zero restrictions allows a reduction in the number of model parameters (Juselius 1999, p. 284). The result is a parsimonious stationary model with significant coefficients that describe short-run dynamics.[6]

Further details on the statistical methods applied are given in the empirical analysis where appropriate. Before starting the analysis it is useful, however, to look at potential long-run relations based on economic theory (which are cointegrating relations in the statistical model). These are tested in all of the empirical analyses and are, therefore, introduced beforehand in the next section.

5.2 Introduction to Potential Long-Run Relations Between the Economic Variables

5.2.1 Necessary Economic Variables

Using the CVAR model means 'letting the data speak'. Thus, a theory model is not directly estimated in the empirical model. However, some macro relations that are often assumed to explain the economy are helpful in statistically testing for stationary relationships in the data. The ideas from theoretical economic models can be expressed as statistical concepts. In this case 'economical' long-run steady-state relations can be interpreted as cointegrating relations in the statistical model. The underlying theoretical relationships are outlined in this section and used as guidance to identify the long-run structure in the empirical analysis. Neoclassical, Keynesian and Monetarist views are presented in order to avoid restrictions from the outset. To focus on those relationships, which are relevant to improving the understanding of the questions raised in this contribution, the main hypotheses and necessary economic variables needed for the analysis are re-stated at this point. The hypotheses to be tested and questions to be answered to achieve the objectives of this contribution, as stated in the introduction, are:

---

[5] Since, at the outset, current effects are restricted to zero and, hence, left in the residuals, potentially important simultaneous effects might be ignored. Whereas correlation between the residuals is not problematic for the long-run relations, identification of the short-run structural equations requires uncorrelated residuals (Juselius 2006, p. 229). Consequently, in the empirical analysis the residual covariance matrix is analyzed, in which large elements can be an indication of significant current effects between the system variables. If this is the case, current effects are introduced in a second step. Comparison of the results improves the analysis of the short run.

[6] For more details on simultaneous equations modeling, see Doornik and Hendry (2006b, pp. 76–87).

- H_1 – Market agents' behavior (herding, rational speculation, contagious confidence and optimism) leads to strong persistence in stock market developments, i.e., shocks to the stock market have positive long-run effects on future developments.
- H_2 – Long-run equilibria exist between stock prices and liquidity conditions.
- H_3 – Liquidity conditions influence stock prices positively in the long run.
- H_4 – Liquidity conditions influence stock prices positively in the short run.
- H_5 – International capital flows have a positive long-run impact on the stock market behavior of individual countries.
- H_6 – International capital flows have a positive short-run impact on the stock market behavior of individual countries.
- Q_1 – Are central banks able to influence stock prices in the long run?
- Q_2 – Are central banks able to influence stock prices in the short run?
- Q_3 – Do country-specific characteristics influence the relationship between liquidity conditions and the stock market?
- Q_4 – Do central banks' ability to target stock markets depend on the respective country-specific conditions?

Chapters 3 and 4 show that the following variables are needed in the analysis to test these hypotheses empirically in a multivariate system:

- A proxy for the quantity of money in the form of a broad monetary aggregate (see Sects. 3.2.1, 3.2.3 and 4.4.2).
- A proxy for national stock market levels, which incorporates dividend payments (see Sect. 4.6.2).
- A proxy for economic activity (GDP for quarterly data, industrial production for monthly data, see Sect. 3.2.3.1).
- A proxy for the inflation rate (see Sect. 3.2.1.2).
- A proxy for the price of money in the form of a short-term interest rate (overnight interbank rate, see Sects. 3.2.2, 3.2.3 and 4.5).
- A proxy for competitive financial assets in the form of a long-term bond rate (10-year government bond rate, see Sects. 3.2.2.1 and 4.5).
- A proxy for international capital flows (see Sect. 4.6).

5.2.2 Potential Long-Run Relations Between the Economic Variables

The IS-LM framework represents the Keynesian perspective. In theory, the point where the IS and LM curve intersect represents simultaneous equilibrium on the goods and money market, thereby, defining the output level and interest rates (Blanchard 2009, p. 115). However, the IS-LM model is static and the relations are without a time index. For the empirical analysis dynamics have to be considered and time indices introduced. In addition, the IS-LM model focuses on the short run with fixed prices and, thus, may not directly be used to identify long-run steady-state relations. Including the neoclassical interpretation and allowing prices to be flexible enables this simplification to capture basic theoretical connections. These can be amended to distinguish potential long-run relationships. Consequently, the IS-LM framework serves as a good starting point.

Aggregate Demand for Goods

The IS-relation represents an equilibrium in the goods market and requires the aggregate demand for goods to be equal to total output (Blanchard 2009, pp. 110–111):

$$Y = C(Y - T) + I(Y, r) + G, \tag{5.11}$$

where Y denotes total output, $C(\cdot)$ is the consumption function, $I(\cdot)$ is an investment function and G represents government spending. T denotes total tax payment and, hence, $Y - T$ is current disposable income. The nominal interest rate, r, could either be the nominal short-term interest rate, i, or the nominal long-term interest rate, b, and is equal to the real interest rate in this specific case since expected inflation equals zero (fixed prices in the short run). The signs of the partial derivatives are $0 < C_{Y-T} < 1$, $I_Y > 0$ and $I_r < 0$. Although this model is designed to depict short-run developments, long-run equilibria may exist between interest rates and output in the form stated above. However, the focus should then be on real interest rates. Using the logarithm (log) the aggregate demand relation becomes[7]:

$$y_r = y_r^p + \delta_1 (r - \pi), \tag{5.12}$$

where y_r^p denotes potential output and $\delta_1 < 0$, such that real output reacts negatively to a rise in the real interest rate (either short or long-term).[8] By allowing prices to vary over the medium to long run, the AD curve can be obtained from the IS LM relations, which relates output and prices for given levels of nominal money, M, government spending and taxes (Blanchard 2009, pp. 160–169). Hence, $Y = Y(M/P, G, T)$, where output is an increasing function of the real money stock, $Y_{M/P} > 0$. As a result, the aggregate demand curve is downward sloping in the (Y, P)-space. A higher price level is associated with lower aggregate demand for output.[9] The aggregate demand relationship of (5.12) becomes:

---

[7] All long-run relations are directly reported in log-linear functional form for variables in levels and percentages for inflation, interest rates and capital flows since multiplicative effects are assumed to exist. This is also the specification used in the empirical analysis.

[8] Since no variable is included to represent consumption or taxes, (5.12) focuses on deviations of potential output induced by changes in interest rates.

[9] For a given level of nominal money an increase in the price level leads to decreasing real balances, which, in turn, increases interest rates, decreases investment demand and, ultimately, decreases aggregate spending. Inflation can have a positive effect on economic activity as well. For this to hold though, the concept of 'money illusion' has to be applied to wage negotiations of workers.

$$y_r = y_r^p + \delta_1(r - \pi) + \delta_2\pi + \delta_3 m_r, \tag{5.13}$$

where π represents the inflation rate with $\delta_2 < 0$ and m_r is real money with $\delta_3 > 0$.

In addition, stock prices may enter the aggregate demand relation. Rising stock prices have a positive effect on aggregate demand for goods through four main channels. The first channel is based on Tobin's 'q'-theory (Tobin 1969, pp. 19–29; Caballero 1997, p. 5). The 'q'-theory of investment states that the firm's demand for new capital goods, as captured by its investment expenditures, increases if the value of the firm is high relative to the replacement cost of its stock of capital. Consequently, high share prices enable companies to finance investments with relatively small issues of new shares. Higher investment spending leads to increased aggregate demand and output.

The second channel, as suggested by Modigliani (1971, pp. 19–34), operates through the impact of wealth on consumption, where higher stock prices increase the propensity to spend (Disyatat 2005, p. 5; Schwert 1990, p. 1237). The main idea behind this is that in an intertemporal framework consumers are expected to smooth consumption over time. Accordingly, higher permanent income based on permanent stock market increases leads to higher current and future consumption, which, in turn, increases aggregate demand for goods (Farmer 2009, pp. 15–16).

The third channel is based on consumers expectations of financial distress. Higher asset prices reduce the potential for individuals to enter phases of financial distress. As a result, they reduce their holdings of liquid assets and increase expenditures on durables, again, with a positive effect on aggregate demand (Cassola and Morana 2002, p. 8).

The last main channel, also termed the 'financial accelerator', operates through firms' balance sheets (see inter alia Bernanke and Gertler (1999)). Higher asset prices increase the collateral companies can offer to gain access to credit. Since information in credit markets is asymmetric, higher collateral reduces adverse selection and moral hazard and, consequently, enables firms to borrow and invest more (Mishkin 1995, p. 8). The term 'accelerator' stems from the self-reinforcing potential. If, for example, higher credit lines are used to purchase assets, this leads to further price increases (see also Sect. 3.2.3.2).[10] Summing up, (5.13) can be further extended to:

As a result, supply of labor depends on nominal wages while demand is a function of real wages. If this is the case, then inflation lowers real wages and, hence, increases the demand for workers, which, in turn, leads to increases in employment and output.

[10] Aside from these four main channels other views exist. For example, the stock market's importance for economic activity can be derived from its facilitation of the efficient allocation of investment resources. If stock prices reflect fundamental values, firms with high profitability are valued higher, which, in turn, lowers their cost of capital. Hence, funds are better allocated. Using the stock price index as a measure of an active stock market, Agrawalla and Tuteja (2008, p. 138) conclude that stock prices affect economic activity positively. Farmer (2009, pp. 16–17) describes the impact of the stock market on real economic activity with the Keynesian self-fulfilling effect of stock markets. He points out, that in Keynes view, individuals buy and sell shares because they expect other individuals to value the shares higher or lower at a later point in time, and, hence, be able to make a profit. In Farmer's opinion, persistent pessimism leads households to reduce

$$y_r = y_r^p + \delta_1(r - \pi) + \delta_2\pi + \delta_3 m_r + \delta_4 s_r, \tag{5.14}$$

where s_r is the log of the real stock market level and $\delta_4 > 0$.

Money Demand

The LM relation represents the corresponding equilibrium in the money market and requires that the supply of real money balances equals real money demand (Blanchard 2009, pp. 112–114):

$$\frac{M}{\overline{P}} = D(Y, i, b), \tag{5.15}$$

where M is the nominal money supply and $\overline{P}$ is the fixed price level. $D(\cdot)$ is the demand for real money and i is a short-term interest rate (e.g., the deposit rate). The left hand side of (5.15) is the supply of real money balances. The right hand side, real money demand, varies positively with income, $D_Y > 0$, reflecting that a rise in income leads to more transactions (see also Sect. 3.3.1). Money demand also varies positively with the return on money holdings, $D_i > 0$, but negatively with the long-term bond rate, $D_b < 0$, because higher long-term interest rates increase the opportunity cost of holding money.

The question, whether the monetary aggregate is supply or demand driven, is ultimately an empirical one. This can be investigated by trying to identify a long-run money demand relation. If a stable long-run money demand relation is found in the data this is a sign for demand-determined broad money and, thus, the markets determination of the money stock. On the other hand, if M3 is exogenous to the system, i.e., supply-determined, this is a sign of central banks' ability to influence broad money.

To incorporate the Monetarist perspective and to accommodate for the long run, prices are flexible and have to enter the money demand relation as well, here in the form of the inflation rate, π. The partial derivative is $D_\pi < 0$, because inflation decreases the real value of money holdings, which increases the opportunity costs of cash holdings. In log form the long-run money demand relation becomes:

$$m_r^d = \rho_1 y_r + \rho_2\pi + \rho_3(b - i), \tag{5.16}$$

where $\rho_1 > 0$, $\rho_2 < 0$ and $\rho_3 < 0$. Consequently, excess liquidity can be described by the positive deviation of the real money equilibrium, m_r^s from m_r^d (see also Sect. 4.4.3). Section 3.3.2 describes the influence of changing stock prices on the

purchases of consumption goods, which eventually leads to lower economic activity, thereby, confirming the self-fulfilling effect of the stock market. For additional theories that link stock returns and output growth, see Mauro (2000, pp. 5–6).

demand for money. Accordingly, (5.16) can be augmented with a role for stock prices:

$$m_r^d = \rho_1 y_r + \rho_2 \pi + \rho_3 (b - i) + \rho_4 s_r, \tag{5.17}$$

where s_r denotes stock prices and either $\rho_4 > 0$ or $\rho_4 < 0$, depending on which effect (wealth vs. substitution) is stronger. Consequently, (5.17) describes a money demand equation in which agents' demand for money consists of transactions as well as precautionary and speculative demand for money.

Money and Prices

The long-run relationship between money and prices can be formalized via the quantity theory of money, which represents the Monetarist view. The quantity theory of money is based on a statement in the form of a mathematical equation, covering all transactions during a certain time period and in a certain economic area ($PY = MV$, where V represents velocity of money). If neo-classical assumptions hold, i.e., money velocity and the output level are constant (i.e., are in long-run equilibrium), it can be proven that, in the long run, the level of prices varies with the quantity of money in circulation. This can be formalized by the equation of exchange[11]:

$$P = M \frac{\overline{V}}{\overline{Y}}, \tag{5.18}$$

where equilibrium values are indicated by the bar. The link can be weakened by allowing for output growth and changes in velocity if these changes (growth rates) are relatively stable or predictable over time. The result is that excess money supply growth (corrected for long-run growth in output and velocity) determines the inflation rate but is neutral for long-run levels of economic activity:

$$\pi = \lambda_1 (m_r^s - m_r^d), \tag{5.19}$$

where $\lambda_1 > 0$.

Interest Rates and Inflation: The Fisher Parity

A crucial component in the determination of interest rates is the expected rate of inflation. The nominal interest rate can be divided into two components, the real

[11] The quantity of money equations are identity or definition equations, and, as such, do not provide information on causality (Issing 2007, p. 153). The quantity theory, however, states a clear causality from money to the price level.

interest rate plus the expected inflation rate (Fisher 1930, p. 438).[12] The real interest rate can be understood as the additional quantity of goods and services that an individual expects to be able to purchase at the end of the period if the individual invests at the beginning of the period, expressed in annual percentage terms. The Fisher parity defines the ex ante real interest rate (with k-periods to maturity), $r_{r,k}$, as:

$$r_{r,k} = r_{n,k} - \pi_k^e, \tag{5.20}$$

where $r_{n,k}$ is the nominal interest rate with the same maturity and $\pi_k^e = (P_k^e - P)/kP$ is the expected (average) inflation rate over the next k periods. The Fisher hypothesis states that, in the long run, the real interest rate is independent of monetary measures.[13] While the real interest rate is stationary and fluctuates around a constant mean, nominal interest rates are determined by inflation expectations. As it is not easy to observe the expected rate of inflation, it is common practice to use current inflation as a substitute. Deducting the current rate of inflation from the current nominal interest rate gives an approximation of the current real interest rate. Here, too, only actual variables will enter the empirical analysis.

Term Structure of Interest Rates: The Expectations Hypothesis

This is the key relationship between short and long-term interest rates. The pure expectations theory, which can be tracked back to Fisher (1896, pp. 26–29), says that the long-term bond rate, b, is given by the expected weighted average of future short-term interest rates, i^e, appropriate to the maturity k of the long bond:

$$b_k = \frac{1}{k} \sum_{j=1}^{k} i_{j-1}^e. \tag{5.21}$$

In the real world, however, uncertainty over future short-term interest rates exists. According to the 'liquidity preference theory', investors of long-term securities are risk averse and demand a risk premium for holding long-term bonds (Pilbeam 2005, p. 89). Thus, the yield on long-term bonds will not only reflect market expectations but also an (il-)liquidity premium.[14] Nevertheless, because the liquidity premium is

[12] A risk premium reflecting inflation uncertainty could also be included but is very hard to quantify. This is one of the reasons why many central banks have adopted a numerical inflation target, thereby, reducing inflation uncertainty and, ultimately, the risk premium.

[13] This is also the basis for the hypothesis that changes in the money supply have no long-run effect on real economic activity because aggregate demand for goods depends on real interest rates instead of nominal interest rates (see (5.12)).

[14] The 'preferred habitat theory' is contrary to the 'liquidity preference theory' in that the liquidity premium does not have to rise uniformly with the maturity of the security. Instead, it states that investors have specific objectives to meet for their investments and this leads to preferred time horizons (habitats) for their investment (Pilbeam 2005, pp. 89–90).

assumed to be relatively constant over time, the spread of interest rates is supposed to be stationary:

$$b = \eta i, \tag{5.22}$$

where $\eta = 1$ implies that a change in the short-term rate is associated with a similar change in the long rate.[15]

Monetary Policy Rules

To understand central banks' ability to target asset prices it is helpful to formalize their current reaction functions. Taylor (1993, pp. 199–203) suggests that the complex monetary policy process can be summarized with a simple rule: the central bank adjusts the short-term interest rate in reaction to deviations of inflation from its policy target and deviations of output from potential output. It can be specified as:

$$i = \bar{i}_r + \pi + k\mu_1(\pi - \pi^*) + (1-k)\mu_2(y_r - y_r^*), \tag{5.23}$$

where $\bar{i}_r$ reflects the real interest rate in the long-run equilibrium[16] and π and π^* denote the inflation rate and the monetary policy inflation target rate, respectively. Equivalently, y_r is real output and y_r^* is the target for real output. The inflation rate is added to ensure comparability of the Taylor interest rate with the prevailing nominal interest rate. Policy makers choose the parameter k, depending on the monetary policy targets of the respective central bank.[17] A stabilizing rule would indicate $\mu_1 > 0$ and $\mu_2 > 0$ such that the short-term interest rate is changed every time inflation and/or output deviate from their targets. This reflects the belief that considerable price increases and extensive capacity utilization need to be countered by increases in the short-term interest rate (Deutsche Bundesbank 1999, pp. 48–49).

If central banks decide to pay attention to asset price misalignments, the policy rule (5.23) has to be modified to:

$$i = \bar{i}_r + \pi + k_1\mu_1(\pi - \pi^*) + k_2\mu_2(y_r - y_r^*) + k_3\mu_3(s_r - s_r^*), \quad \sum_{i=1}^{3} k_i = 1, \tag{5.24}$$

---

[15] Other hypotheses on the term structure of interest rates exist. For an overview see Belke and Polleit (2009, pp. 263–267). These include the market segmentation hypothesis or the term structure with time-variying risk. They do not change the relevant implications for the empirical analysis. An influential analysis is Cox et al. (1985), which relates the term structure argument to rational expectations.

[16] The equilibrium real interest rate can be defined by the real interest rate level that persists if the desired inflation rate is realized, the economy runs at full capacity and this long-run equilibrium is not affected by monetary policy (Deutsche Bundesbank 1999, p. 49).

[17] Since Taylor specified this rule for the US Federal Reserve System (Fed), it has to be adjusted to the targets of the respective central bank. If a central bank only targets the inflation rate (and not economic growth) then the 'central bank-specific' Taylor rule has to reflect that and ignore output deviations ($k = 1$).

where $\mu_3 > 0$, such that positive deviations from the fundamental value of stock prices, s_r^*, lead to a rise in the policy rate.

Demand for Stocks

Considering the theoretical remarks of Sect. 3.2, a demand equation for asset prices could be the following:

$$s_r = \kappa_1 m_r + \kappa_2 (y_r^e - y_r^p) + \kappa_3 (i - \pi) + \kappa_4 (b - \pi), \tag{5.25}$$

where $\kappa_1 > 0$, $\kappa_2 > 0$, $\kappa_3 < 0$ and $\kappa_4 < 0$. Real stock prices are positively related to real money and the future output gap and negatively to the current short and long-term real interest rates (Disyatat 2005, p. 5).[18]

The idea that capital flows affect stock prices can be rationalized via 'push' and 'pull' channels of the international transmission of monetary developments.

First, if money stock rises strongly in one country and this causes capital flows to foreign asset markets (a 'push' of liquidity out of the country), one would expect upward pressure on foreign asset prices (Borja and Goyeau 2005, p. 4; Baks and Kramer 1999, p. 6). Thus, capital outflows are favorable for the country that receives the capital, which are capital inflows from the view of the receiving country. As a result, the theory of the push channel delivers a positive connection between capital inflows and the stock market.

Second, spillover effects could occur through the 'pull' channel. If domestic money stock increases lead to higher domestic asset prices and foreign investors are attracted by these asset price increases, then this would lead to capital inflows from abroad (a 'pull' of capital from abroad) (Baks and Kramer 1999, p. 6). These inflows drive domestic asset price inflation further.

In conclusion, the consequences of capital flows on stock market performance are the same, independent of whether the 'push' or 'pull' channel of international monetary transmission dominates. In either case, capital inflows are positive for domestic stock markets and capital outflows are negative or neutral. As such, (5.25) can be amended by a variable associated with foreign liquidity, in this case reflected by international capital flows:

$$s_r = \kappa_1 m_r + \kappa_2 (y_r^e - y_r^p) + \kappa_3 (i - \pi) + \kappa_4 (b - \pi) + \kappa_5 cf, \tag{5.26}$$

where $\kappa_5 > 0$.

[18] Section 3.2 shows that the focus does not have to be on real interest rates. Instead, changes in nominal interest rates may affect stock prices in the same direction as changes in real rates. Hence, the empirical tests are conducted for real as well as nominal rates.

Table 5.1 Summary of potential long-run relations

Name	Based on	Stationary relation
Demand for goods	(5.14) with	$y_{r,t} + \delta_1(r_t - \pi_t) + \delta_2\pi_t + \delta_3 m_{r,t} + \delta_4 s_{r,t} \sim I(0)$ $\delta_1 > 0, \delta_2 > 0, \delta_3 < 0, \delta_4 < 0$
Money demand	(5.17) with	$m_{r,t} + \rho_1 y_{r,t} + \rho_2\pi_t + \rho_3(b_t - i_t) + \rho_4 s_{r,t} \sim I(0)$ $\rho_1 < 0, \rho_2 > 0, \rho_3 > 0, \rho_4 > or < 0$
Inflation	(5.19) with	$\pi_t + \lambda_1(m_{r,t} - y_{r,t}) \sim I(0)$ $\lambda_1 < 0$
Fisher parity	(5.20) with	$i_t + \psi_1\pi_t \sim I(0)\, itand/or\, b_t + \psi_2\pi_t \sim I(0)$ $\psi_1 = -1, \psi_2 = -1$
Expectations hypothesis	(5.22) with	$b_t + \eta_1 i_t \sim I(0)$ $\eta_1 = -1$
Policy rules	(5.24) with	$i_t + \mu_1(\pi_t - \pi^*) + \mu_2(y_{r,t} - y_r^*) + \mu_3(s_{r,t} - s_r^*) \sim I(0)$ $\mu_1 < 0, \mu_2 < 0, \mu_3 < 0$
Demand for stocks	(5.26) with	$s_{r,t} + \kappa_1 m_r + \kappa_2(y_{r,t} - trend_t) + \kappa_3(i_t - \pi_t) + \kappa_4(b_t - \pi_t) + \kappa_5 cf \sim I(0)$ $\kappa_1 < 0, \kappa_2 < 0, \kappa_3 > 0, \kappa_4 > 0, \kappa_5 < 0$

5.2.3 Summary of Potential Cointegration Relations

Table 5.1 summarizes the above stated relationships between the variables. They are in the form of the empirical analysis, indicating that the linear combinations of the variables represent stationary long-run relations. In addition, a time index, t, is added.

One should recognize that the relations in Table 5.1 are abstract theoretical items. In general, they have to be modified to qualify for empirical modeling. Moreover, the theoretical model does not provide information on the dynamics from one steady state to another or the stochastic time series properties of the data (Juselius 1996, p. 797). The relations in Table 5.1 are translated into testable hypotheses in the CVAR framework. They are tested individually in the country analyses in the section 'preliminary testing' to improve the identification procedure of an economically and statistically identified long-run structure. Since subelements of the relations might be stationary, these also have to be tested to arrive at a complete picture. The hypotheses are of the form:

$$\beta = (H\phi\psi), \tag{5.27}$$

where H is the design matrix, ϕ contains the restricted parameters and ψ is a vector of parameters which are freely estimated. Thus, the hypotheses test restrictions on a single vector but leave the other vectors unrestricted (Johansen and Juselius 1992, pp. 233–236). The idea is to analyze whether stable relationships between the economic variables can be identified by linear relations.

Table 5.2 demonstrates the necessary linear restrictions for the hypotheses to be testable. It is not sorted the same as Table 5.1 in order to reflect the importance of the individual hypotheses. It starts with the main hypotheses, to focus on the objectives of this contribution and continues with supporting hypotheses,

Table 5.2 Overview of testable single cointegration relations

	Involved variables	Based on	m_r	s_r	y_r	π	i	b	cf	*Trend*	Restrictions
Demand for stocks											
H_1	Stock market and real money	Liquidity conditions hypothesis	$-y$	1	0	0	0	0	0	y	5
H_2	Stock market and real short-term interest rate	Discount factor and relative attractiveness	0	1	0	$-x$	x	0	0	y	5
H_3	Stock market and real long-term interest rate	Discount factor and relative attractiveness	0	1	0	$-x$	0	x	0	y	5
H_4	Stock market and nominal short-term interest rate	Liquidity conditions hypothesis	0	1	0	0	y	0	0	y	5
H_5	Stock market and nominal long-term interest rate	Relative attractiveness and money illusion	0	1	0	0	0	$+y$	0	y	5
H_6	Stock market and real output minus trend	Economic activity, dividend expectations	0	1	$-y$	0	0	0	0	$+y$	5
H_7	Stock market and capital flows	Liquidity conditions hypothesis	0	1	0	0	0	0	$-y$	y	5
H_8	Stock market, real money and capital flows	Liquidity conditions hypothesis	$-y$	1	0	0	0	0	$-y$	y	4
Money demand											
H_9	Liquidity relation	Transactions effect	1	0	-1	0	0	0	0	y	6
H_{10}	Real money and the interest rate spread	Opportunity costs of holding money	1	0	0	0	$-x$	$+x$	0	y	5
H_{11}	Real money, real output and interest rates	Combinations of the above	1	0	$-y$	0	$-y$	y	0	y	3
H_{12}	Real money, real output and inflation	Transactions effect amended by inflation	1	0	$-y$	$+y$	0	0	0	y	4
H_{13}	Real money and the stock market	Wealth effect vs. substitution effect	1	$+-y$	0	0	0	0	0	y	5
H_{14}	Real money, stock market and yield spread	Combinations of the above	1	$+-y$	0	0	$-x$	$+x$	0	y	4
H_{15}	Liquidity relation, stock market	Combinations of the above	1	$+-y$	-1	0	0	0	0	y	5
H_{16}	Liquidity relation, yield spread, stock market	Combinations of the above	1	$+-y$	-1	0	$-x$	$+x$	0	y	4

(continued)

Table 5.2 (Continued)

	Involved variables	Based on	m_r	s_r	y_r	π	i	b	cf	*Trend*	Restrictions
Policy rules											
H_{17}	Policy instrument and inflation	Taylor rule	0	0	0	$-y$	1	0	0	0	6
H_{18}	Policy instrument and real output	Taylor rule	0	0	$-y$	0	1	0	0	$+y$	5
H_{19}	Policy instrument and the stock market	Taylor rule	0	$-y$	0	0	1	0	0	$+y$	5
Demand for goods											
H_{20}	Real output and the short-term real interest rate	IS-LM model	0	0	1	$-x$	$+x$	0	0	y	5
H_{21}	Real output and the long-term real interest rate	IS-LM model	0	0	1	$-x$	0	$+x$	0	y	5
H_{22}	Real output and real money	Expansive monetary policy effect	$-y$	0	1	0	0	0	0	y	5
H_{23}	Real output, real money and the stock market	Mon. policy amended with wealth effects	$-y$	$-y$	1	0	0	0	0	y	4
Inflation and interest rates											
H_{24}	Inflation and excess liquidity	Quantity theory of money	$-x$	0	x	1	0	0	0	0	6
H_{25}	Real money and nominal bonds	Expected inflation effect	$-x$	0	0	0	0	1	0	y	7
H_{26}	Real short-term interest rate	Fisher hypothesis	0	0	0	-1	1	0	0	0	7
H_{27}	Real long-term interest rate	Fisher hypothesis	0	0	0	-1	0	1	0	0	7
H_{28}	Inflation and short-term interest rate	Weakened Fisher hypothesis	0	0	0	$-y$	1	0	0	0	6
H_{29}	Inflation and long-term interest rate	Weakened Fisher hypothesis	0	0	0	$-y$	0	1	0	0	6
H_{30}	Yield spread	Term structure of interest rates	0	0	0	0	-1	1	0	0	7
H_{31}	Yield spread	Weakened term structure	0	0	0	0	$-y$	1	0	0	6
H_{32}	Inflation and interest rates	Homogeneity of inflation and interest rates	0	0	0	-1	1	$-y$	0	0	6
H_{33}	Inflation and yield spread	Actual and expected inflation	0	0	0	$-y$	-1	1	0	0	6

necessary for the identification of the long run. The first section describes relations between the stock market and the other variables as outlined in Chap. 3. The next part focuses on stable long-run money demand relations. If such a relationship is found, the impact of excess liquidity on stock markets can be analyzed. The third part provides suggestions for how to test for monetary policy rules. The subsequent parts describe potential long-run behavior of the remaining variables, focusing on aggregate demand for goods as well as inflation and interest rates.

Free parameters are represented by 1 or y, where 1 is the normalization variable. The signs of y describe the relationship, which is suggested by economic theory. Restrictions are either in the form of 0 or by positive or negative homogeneity, 1 and -1 or x and $-x$.

It is important to realize that some of the relations can be interpreted in different ways. For example, a closer look at hypothesis H_6 reveals that it can also be interpreted as an aggregate demand for goods relation, reflecting wealth and balance sheet effects. Therefore, for a successful preliminary testing it is crucial to investigate the adjustment coefficients, α, to understand which of the variables show error-correcting behavior and, hence, whether it indicates a 'demand for stocks'- or 'demand for goods'-relationship or both (Juselius 1998, p. 462). The variables, which have significant α-coefficients, are reported in the respective tables in the empirical country analyses as well.

In addition, one should note that the hypotheses in Table 5.2 are not exhaustive. Instead, many combinations of these linear restrictions are imaginable and other not-reported relationships might exist. As a result, the final overidentified long-run structure does not have to be based on these relations. Rather, the idea is to understand the behavior of the economy better. The long-run structure is restricted and tested based on this information, the additional information from the preliminary hypotheses section and further testing.

Chapter 6
Empirical Analysis by Country

6.1 Chapter Overview

This chapter covers the empirical analysis. It is structured as follows. It is organized primarily by country. Each country analysis is conducted completely (long-run equilibria, short-run dynamic adjustments and long-run impact) before moving on to the next economic region. The structure of each country analysis is the same. They all begin with a presentation of the data and model specifications that guarantee a statistically well-specified model. To achieve this, the variables of the system are defined and deterministic terms and the lag length are specified and tested. Once a well-specified model is obtained, the cointegration rank is determined.[1]

Afterwards, the focus is on the identification of the long-run structure. This starts with a first inspection of the unrestricted Π-matrix and some preliminary hypotheses testing before turning to the final identified long-run structure. Once an overidentified long-run structure is tested and fixed, short-run dynamics are analyzed in a structural error-correction model. Significant short-run effects are tested by applying the full information maximum likelihood estimator in simultaneous equation modeling. To be able to understand short-run adjustments of the variables an economically valid short-run structure is identified and tested. Since the long-run structure is fixed, the equations of the system variables in first differences can include the stationary equilibrium errors of the cointegration relations. Finally, the last part of the analysis focuses on the common trends and the permanent impact of shocks to the variables.

All calculations are conducted either using CATS in RATS (long-run analysis), version 2 (Dennis et al. 2005) or PcGive (short-run analysis), version 12 in OxMetrics, version 5 (Doornik 2007).[2] Cross-country comparisons of the different analyses are the focus of Chap. 7.

[1] It may seem like a lot of attention is given to diagnostic testing. The reason for this is that statistical inference in the CVAR model only makes sense in a well-specified probability model (Hoover et al. 2008, p. 253).

[2] Statistical explanations are mostly provided in the US analysis and only selectively repeated in the other country analyses to avoid repetition and in order to focus on the main findings.

M. Wiedmann, *Money, Stock Prices and Central Banks*, Contributions to Economics,
DOI 10.1007/978-3-7908-2647-0_6, © Springer-Verlag Berlin Heidelberg 2011

6.2 United States of America: Quarterly Data

6.2.1 Model Specification

6.2.1.1 Data Overview, Deterministic Components and Lag Length

As outlined in Sect. 5.2.1, the data vector consists of the following variables:

$$x_t' = [m_r, s_r, y_r, \Delta p, ff, b10, cf]_t, \tag{6.1}$$

where m_r is the log of real money (M3[3]), s_r is the log of real stock market levels (total market including dividends) and y_r is the log of real GDP. Real variables are transformed from nominal variables using the consumer price index, p, and, hence, Δp is the inflation rate.[4] Short and long-term interest rates are represented by the overnight interbank rate (fed funds rate), *ff*, and the 10-year Treasury bond yield, $b10$. All interest rates have been converted to quarterly rates and divided by 100 to achieve comparability with the inflation rate (logarithmic quarterly changes).[5] The changes in net external assets of the banking system represent capital flows, cf, and are calculated in percent as a share of the total money stock M3.[6] All time series are obtained either from Datastream or the IMF International Financial Statistics (IFS) database and detailed information on specific sources of the data are provided in Appendix B.1.1.

The data used for the analysis covers the last 25 years and consists of quarterly observations from 1983:3 to 2008:3.[7] The motivation for starting the sample period in 1983 was to ensure a constant parameter regime. Therefore, the volatile and high-inflation periods of the 1970s and the beginning of the 1980s are excluded.

---

[3] The Fed stopped reporting values for M3 at the end of 2005. Economists at the Fed believe that the analysis of the broad money stock developments is not useful in an inflation-targeting regime because it is distorted by offshore holdings and the increasing shift from traditional bank lending to securitization. To account for that, the time series M3 used here is constructed by applying growth rates of M2 from 2006 onwards.

[4] The consumer price index was chosen for the empirical analysis instead of the GDP deflator for two main reasons. First, to capture monetary policy aspects consumer price inflation is superior to the GDP deflator because central banks focus on consumer price developments. Second, within the scope of money demand analysis a cost-of-living index is preferable to the GDP deflator because it is a more important determinant of transaction balances (Muscatelli and Spinelli 2000, p. 722).

[5] See Juselius and Toro (2005, p. 515).

[6] The usage of a percentage value of a variable included in the system does not lead to any problems of statistical inference. It is important, though, that the model is well specified.

[7] Throughout the whole contribution, ex-post revised data is used. This has the consequence that the effect of publications of real-time data can not be measured. However, the focus of the analysis is on the underlying fundamentals, not on announcement effects. Consequently, revised data is closer to the actual behavior of the economy. In addition, studies at the Deutsche Bundesbank by Döpke et al. (2006a, 2006b) show that predictions of stock returns and volatility based on real-time macro data do not differ much from hypothetical predictions, which are based on revised data.

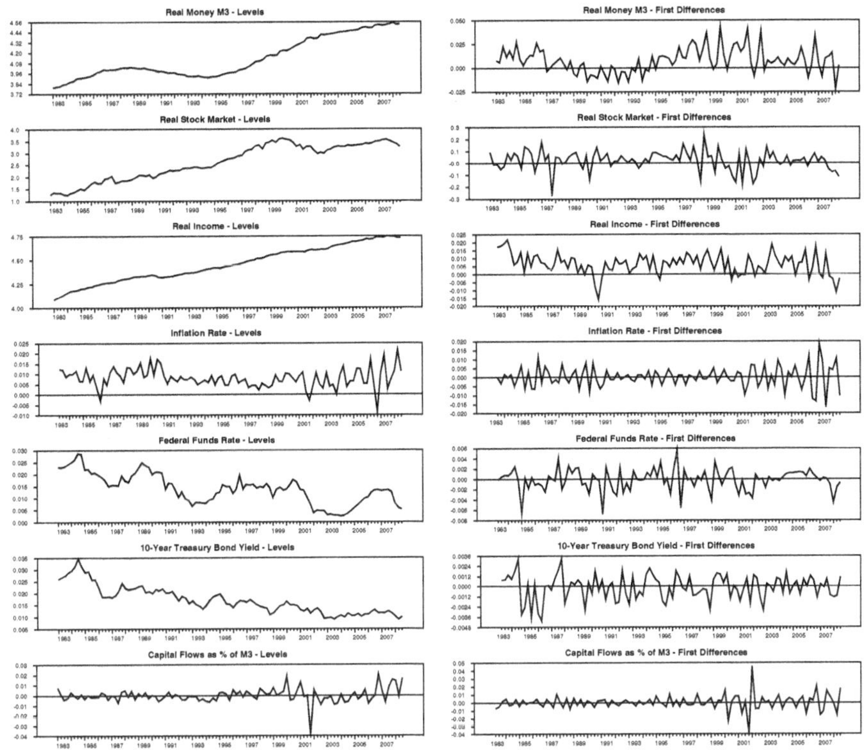

Fig. 6.1 US quarterly data in levels and first differences

In addition, the starting point was chosen to follow the Fed's decision to abandon targeting the money supply in favor of setting a target for the fed funds rate. As a result, during the whole period under investigation the Fed has used the fed funds rate as an instrument to achieve its objectives and, hence, the monetary regime did not change. Thus, it is possible to analyze whether monetary conditions have influenced real stock prices during the last quarter century and whether the Fed was able to influence stock prices.[8] Figure 6.1 displays the time pattern of all variables in levels and first differences.

Aside from the time series that represents capital flows the data series in levels do not look stationary. However, in first differences all time series seem to be mean-reverting and, therefore, stationary. Further characteristics of the data are that real money, real stock prices and real GDP seem to follow a trend. Thus, a deterministic

[8] Moreover, 1983 also coincides with a general increase in international capital flows due to the abolition of previous control measures in many western economies and with the beginning of more efficient electronic transmission technologies.

(non-stochastic) trend should be allowed for in the model.[9] In addition, it seems that variability was higher at the beginning (the aftermath of the oil price shocks and fighting double-digit inflation), at around 2000 (during the dot-com bubble) and at the end (global financial crisis) of the sample. This might need to be accounted for by including dummy variables to ensure valid statistical inference.

Deterministic Components

As can be seen in Fig. 6.1, money, output and stock prices seem to follow a linear deterministic trend. To allow for a deterministic trend in the levels, an unrestricted constant, μ_0, will be included in the model. The consequences of including a constant in the model are twofold, because the constant serves not only as a constant in the equations for first differences but also cumulates into a linear trend for the variables in levels. In addition, since the deterministic trends might not cancel out in the cointegration relations, a trend, which is restricted to the cointegration relations, μ_1, is also included in the model. The CVAR model from (5.4) then becomes

$$\Delta x_t = \alpha\beta' x_{t-1} + \sum_{i=1}^{k-1} \Gamma_i \Delta x_{t-1} + \Phi D_t + \mu_0 + \mu_1 + \epsilon_t, \tag{6.2}$$

where $\mu_0 = \alpha\rho_0 + \gamma_0$ and $\mu_1 = \alpha\rho_1 + \gamma_1$, such that the parameters μ_0 and μ_1 are decomposed in the direction of α and $\alpha_\perp$. Consequently, (6.2) can also be expressed as:

$$\Delta x_t = \alpha[\beta', \rho_0, \rho_1] \begin{bmatrix} x_{t-1} \\ 1 \\ t \end{bmatrix} + \sum_{i=1}^{k-1} \Gamma_i \Delta x_{t-1} + \Phi D_t + \gamma_0 + \gamma_1 + \epsilon_t. \tag{6.3}$$

The constant, μ_0, is unrestricted. The trend, μ_1, however, is restricted to the cointegration space. Hence, $\gamma_1 = 0$ and $(\gamma_0, \rho_0, \rho_1) \neq 0$.[10] With an unrestricted constant and a trend restricted to the cointegration space, linear trends ($\gamma_0 \neq 0$), but not quadratic trends ($\gamma_1 \neq 0$), are allowed for in the data. This specification ensures similarity in the rank test procedure because the trend might not cancel in the cointegration relations (Nielsen and Rahbek 2000, pp. 12–15). If $\rho_1 \neq 0$, the linear trend in the variables does not cancel in the cointegration relations, which will be formally tested in the model in Sect. 6.2.2.2, Table 6.9. If the trend is included in the cointegration relations it represents a stationary process plus a deterministic trend, i.e., a

---

[9] Linear stochastic and deterministic trends differ in that the increments of stochastic trends are random while those of deterministic trends are constant over time (Hendry and Juselius 1999, p. 5).

[10] These specifications correspond to case 4 in Juselius (2006, pp. 99–100) and model $H^*(r)$ in Johansen (1995, Equation (5.14), p. 81). In CATS it is processed via the use of det = cidrift.

Table 6.1 US quarterly data: intervention dummies

Dummy variable	Motivation	Impact on
$dum8602_t$	Sharply falling energy prices[a]	Inflation and bond rate
$dum8704_p$	Black Friday stock market crash in October	Real stock market
$dum9004_p$	First Gulf War, high oil prices, severe recession	Real income
$dum0104_p$	The aftermath of September 11, 2001[b]	Capital flows
$dum0604_p$	Sharply falling energy prices	Inflation and capital flows

[a] See, for example, Homer and Sylla (2005, pp. 386–387). When the cartel of the Organization of the Petroleum Exporting Countries became looser in December 1985, oil prices collapsed. That, along with a more moderate rate of economic expansion, helped to make the 1986 inflation rate the lowest in two decades.

[b] The high residual might also have been a consequence of an additive outlier because the IMF IFS database combined several other databases at this point, which might have systematically changed the level of net external assets of the banking system. However, it is impossible to correct this from the outside. In addition it coincides with the repercussions of the 9/11 attacks, which might have led to capital flight. In conclusion, it seemed more reasonable to correct this outlier with a permanent dummy variable instead of from the outset in the original data. This way information is still contained in the lagged variables.

trend-stationary process. The intercept of the cointegrating relations, ρ_0 is allowed to be $\neq 0$, thus, the equilibrium mean can be different from zero.

Dummy Variables

Two kinds of dummies are used in the model. First, centered seasonal dummies are included to account for seasonality in the data.[11] Second, intervention dummies are used to account for significant political or institutional events and reforms. These interventions frequently show up as extraordinarily large shocks in the VAR analysis, which violate the normality assumption.

Misspecification testing shows that normality is rejected with a p-value of 0.000.[12] To ensure normality, dummies are included based on the economic calendar and the graphs of the standardized residuals, which have revealed some large outliers. Table 6.1 provides an overview.

In general, three forms of intervention dummies are possible: first, shift dummies of the form $[0, \ldots, 0, 0, 1, 1, \ldots, 1]$, denoted by $dumyyqq_s$, second, permanent blip dummies, denoted by $dumyyqq_p$, with the form of $[0, \ldots, 0, 1, 0, \ldots, 0]$ and, finally, transitory blip dummies of the form $[0, \ldots, 0, 1, -1, 0, \ldots, 0]$, denoted by $dumyyqq_t$ at time $19yyqq$ or $20yyqq$.

[11] Centered seasonal dummies have the advantage that they sum up to zero over a year as they are orthogonalized on the constant term (Johansen 1995, p. 84).

[12] The test is not reported here at this stage. Instead, misspecification tests are reported for the specified model in Sect. 6.2.1.2.

Since the CVAR model contains differences and levels of the variables the above mentioned dummies enter both.[13] Consequently, an unrestricted shift dummy represents a mean shift in first differences and cumulates to a broken trend in the levels. An unrestricted permanent blip dummy cumulates to a level shift and an unrestricted transitory dummy is equal to two consecutive blips of opposite sign in first differences, which cumulates to a single blip in the levels (Juselius 2006, p. 106). If dummy variables should not cumulate in the levels, they need to be restricted to the cointegration space. The analysis of US quarterly data requires one transitory and four permanent blip dummies.

Determination of the Lag Length

To guarantee valid statistical inference, it is crucial to test for the satisfaction of the assumptions underlying the model. This includes the determination of lag length as well as tests to exclude serial correlation, conditional heteroscedasticity and deviations from Gaussian white noise, which is the focus of the next section.

The maximum likelihood value is used to assess the satisfactoriness of the VAR specification and the preferred lag length, k. It is given by (Johansen 1995, p. 18):

$$-(2/T)\ln L_{\max} = \ln\left|\hat{\Omega}\right| + constant\ terms, \qquad (6.4)$$

where T denotes the effective sample length (in contrast to the full sample length $T+k$). Various test procedures exist to determine the optimal lag length. Table 6.2 reports the two information criteria 'Schwartz' (SC) and 'Hannan–Quinn' (H–Q) and the Lagrange multiplier (LM) test for autocorrelation. Both information criteria are based on the maximum value of the likelihood function and include a penalizing factor based on the number of estimated parameters. Avoiding too many lags is important because the larger the lag length the more parameters have to be estimated. The criteria compromise between lag length and the number of parameters and are defined by (6.5) and (6.6), respectively (Juselius 2006, p. 71):

$$SC = \ln\left|\hat{\Omega}\right| + (p^2k)\frac{\ln T}{T}, \qquad (6.5)$$

$$H--Q = \ln\left|\hat{\Omega}\right| + (p^2k)\frac{2\ln T}{T}. \qquad (6.6)$$

[13] Whereas in a static regression model a dummy cancels out the observation and the information is lost, a dummy in a dynamic model (such as the CVAR) does not cancel the information in the observation. Instead, it only cancels the unexpected part of the shock. The information, however, is still included in the lags. This reflects people's reaction to unexpected shocks; these shocks happen and then people use the information as a basis for further actions. For more information on dummy variables see Doornik and Hendry (2006a, p. 122) and Juselius (2006, pp. 104–112).

Table 6.2 US quarterly data: information to determine lag length

Model	k	T	Regressive	Log-Likelihood	SC	H–Q	LM(1)	LM(k)
VAR(5)	5	98	45	3,889.758	−64.645	−69.593	0.425	0.052
VAR(4)	4	98	38	3,843.589	−65.996	−70.174	0.883	0.190
VAR(3)	3	98	31	3,801.242	−67.424	−70.833	**0.378**	**0.698**
VAR(2)	2	98	24	3,755.404	−68.781	−71.420	0.050	0.026
VAR(1)	1	98	17	3,701.569	**−69.975**	**−71.844**	0.001	0.001

The two criteria differ with respect to the strength of the penalty, which is associated with the increased number of parameters that result from an increase in lag length. The test criteria are calculated for different values of lag length, k, where the smallest result suggests the ideal lag length. The last two columns in Table 6.2 report the LM test for autocorrelation of order 1 and k. Numbers in bold indicate the suggested lag length of the respective test.

Whereas both the Hannan–Quinn criterion and the Schwartz criterion suggest one lag, the LM test shows that there is left-over residual autocorrelation if only one or two lags are applied. To avoid autocorrelation, a lag length of $k = 3$ is used for the analysis.[14]

The discussion in this section on lag length, deterministic components and dummy variables results in the following VAR(3) model (in error-correction form) for US quarterly data:

$$\Delta x_t = \alpha \tilde{\beta}' \tilde{x}_{t-1} + \Gamma_1 \Delta x_{t-1} + \Gamma_2 \Delta x_{t-2} + \Phi D_t + \mu_0 + \epsilon_t, \qquad (6.7)$$

where $x_t' = [m_r, s_r, y_r, \Delta p, ff, b10, cf]_t$ and $\tilde{x}_t = \left[x_t', 1, trend\right]$ is a $((7+2) \times 1)$ data vector containing the p variables, a constant and a trend. The cointegration vectors are represented by $\tilde{\beta} = \left[\beta', \rho_0, \rho_1\right]'$, which is a $((7+2) \times r)$ matrix with rank r. The analysis is based on 7×98 observations and conditions on the initial values (data points for 1983:3 to 1984:1). The dummy variables are contained in the vector

$D_t = \left[dum8602_t, dum8704_p, dum9004_p, dum0104_p, dum0604_p\right]$.

6.2.1.2 Misspecification Tests

Before one is able to determine the reduced rank of the model, the model must be well specified. Tables 6.3 and 6.4 report multivariate and univariate misspecification tests, respectively. The multivariate LM test shows no sign of autocorrelation in the

[14] It is an empirical finding that two lags are mostly adequate to model the dynamics of the CVAR model (Johansen 1995, p. 4, see also the other country analyses). However, since autocorrelation results in invalid statistical inference, a lag length of $k = 3$ is a sensible choice.

Table 6.3 US quarterly data: multivariate misspecification tests (p-values in brackets)

Test for no autocorrelation			
LM(1):	$\chi^2(49)$	=	51.446 [0.378]
LM(2):	$\chi^2(49)$	=	46.747 [0.565]
LM(3):	$\chi^2(49)$	=	43.429 [0.698]
LM(4):	$\chi^2(49)$	=	60.186 [0.131]
Test for normality	$\chi^2(14)$	=	10.870 [0.696]
Test for no ARCH effects			
LM(1):	$\chi^2(784)$	=	747.540 [0.821]
LM(2):	$\chi^2(1568)$	=	1643.718 [0.090]
LM(3):	$\chi^2(2352)$	=	2451.963 [0.074]
LM(4):	$\chi^2(3136)$	=	2744.000 [1.000]

first 4 lags (the null of the test is 'no autocorrelation'). It is asymptotically distributed as χ^2 with p^2 degrees of freedom (Johansen 1995, p. 22).

The normality tests are based on skewness (the third moment around the mean) and kurtosis (the fourth moment around the mean).[15] They are asymptotically χ^2-distributed, with $2p$ degrees of freedom in the multivariate and 2 degrees of freedom in the univariate case. The null of the tests is normally distributed errors, which means that skewness and kurtosis of the residuals, ϵ_i, are asymptotically normal with the following mean and variance:

$$Skewness: \quad \sqrt{T}(skewness_i - 0) \overset{a}{\sim} N(0,6)\ and \tag{6.8}$$

$$Kurtosis: \quad \sqrt{T}(kurtosis_i - 3) \overset{a}{\sim} N(0,24), \tag{6.9}$$

where T denotes the number of observations in the effective sample. As can be seen from (6.8) and (6.9) the variance of kurtosis is bigger than the one of skewness. Hence, the normality tests are more sensitive to deviations from normality due to skewness, which often results from outliers, than to deviations from kurtosis, which results from thick tails or too many small residuals close to the mean. Tables 6.3 and 6.4 show that normality is accepted for the multivariate case and for the univariate case.

Additionally, tests for multivariate AutoRegressive Conditional Heteroskedasticity (ARCH) of order q (with $q = 1, \ldots, 4$) and univariate second order ARCH effects are reported. The multivariate test statistic is approximately distributed as χ^2 with $\frac{q}{4}p^2(p+1)^2$ degrees of freedom. The univariate test is approximately distributed as χ^2 with k degrees of freedom (Dennis 2006, pp. 179–180). ARCH in the data means that the variances of the residuals will not be constant and this could make

[15] The reported normality tests were developed by Doornik and Hansen (2008) and build on previous work of Shenton and Bowman (1977).

Table 6.4 US quarterly data: univariate misspecification tests (p-values in brackets)

	ARCH(2)	Normality	Skewness	Kurtosis
Δm_r	3.768 [0.288]	0.020 [0.990]	0.026	2.742
Δs_r	3.895 [0.273]	0.768 [0.681]	0.171	3.042
Δy_r	4.018 [0.259]	2.239 [0.327]	0.292	2.651
$\Delta^2 p$	6.284 [0.099]	0.675 [0.714]	−0.157	2.650
Δff	6.420 [0.093]	0.770 [0.680]	0.110	3.113
$\Delta b10$	1.134 [0.769]	2.865 [0.239]	0.136	3.529
Δcf	5.181 [0.159]	3.089 [0.213]	0.381	3.442

the cointegration estimates inefficient. Both tests show no signs of ARCH effects. Since all test statistics are accepted, the model describes the data well.

6.2.1.3 Rank Determination

The hypothesis that the system has reduced rank (see Sect. 5.1.2) is the same as the hypothesis that cointegration vectors exist. Hence, the characteristic feature of the cointegration rank is its division of the data into r linearly independent cointegrating relations and $p - r$ common driving trends.[16] The cointegrating relations are interpreted as equilibria (steady-state relations), to which the process is adjusting. The common trends, on the other hand, are the non-stationary parts of the system, which are pushing the process. Consequently, the determination of cointegration rank is crucial to the underlying analysis and is likely to influence all further inference. Since the number of variables is greater than two, there might be more than one cointegration relation (Engle and Granger 1987, p. 254). Unfortunately, the distinction between stationary and non-stationary directions of the vector process is not always straightforward and several formal and informal procedures exist to determine the rank (Juselius 2006, p. 142):

- Trace test (formal LR test).
- Modulus of the roots of the companion matrix.
- Significance of the α-coefficients.
- Graphical inspection of the recursively calculated trace test statistics.
- Graphical inspection of the stationarity of the cointegration relations.

Trace Test

The test for cointegration between the variables is calculated by looking at the rank of the Π-matrix via its eigenvalues. The rank of a matrix is equal to the number of

[16] The space spanned by the cointegration relations is the cointegrating space (Johansen 1995, Definition 3.4, p. 36).

its characteristic roots (eigenvalues) that are different from zero. To calculate the LR test for cointegration rank the reduced form ('R-form') is used. For the R-form all short-run dynamics have been concentrated out of the model.[17] Thus, the eigenvalues, α_i $(i = 1, \ldots, p)$, are the solutions to the eigenvalue problem of the R-form. The magnitude of the eigenvalues, λ_i, is a measure of the stationarity of the corresponding cointegration relation.[18] If $\lambda_i = 0$ then the relation is a unit root process and if $\lambda_i > 0$ then the process is stationary.

The trace test can be calculated based on the eigenvalues $1 > \hat{\lambda}_1 > \ldots > \hat{\lambda}_p > 0$ and tests the following hypotheses:

- $H^0(r) : rank = r$, i.e., $p - r$ unit roots, r cointegration relations and x_t is non-stationary.
- $H^1(p) : rank = p$, i.e., no unit roots and x_t is stationary.

This means, that the LR-test procedure tests the maximum of the likelihood function under the null hypothesis against the alternative, which gives the test statistic (Juselius 2006, p. 133; Johansen 1995, p. 93):

$$-2\ln Q(H_r|H_p) = -T \sum_{i=r+1}^{p} \ln(1 - \hat{\lambda}_i). \tag{6.10}$$

The null hypothesis $(rank(\Pi) = r)$ is rejected if one of the estimated $p - r$ eigenvalues is larger than zero. Consequently, the asymptotically most correct procedure is to test the most restricted model, $H^0(r = 0)$, against the alternative, $H^1(p)$ (Juselius 2006, pp. 133–134). If the test statistic, $Q_{r=0}$, is larger than the critical value, $C^{95\%}_{r=0}$, the null hypothesis is rejected. This means that less than $p - r$ unit roots exist. The next step is, thus, to test $H^0(r = 1)$ against the alternative, $H^1(p)$. This sequence continues until the test is accepted. The asymptotic distribution of the rank test also depends on the deterministic components included in the model.

In addition, (5.6) in Sect. 5.1.2 shows that, as a prerequisite for valid statistical inference, the variables can be integrated of first but not of higher order. Hence, it is important to ensure that no $I(2)$ variables are part of the data set. The time series for prices in levels and nominal money appear to contain an $I(2)$ trend. In the above stated data vector (6.1) it is implicitly assumed that the nominal-to-real transformation holds, such that a system of nominal variables can be transformed into a system of real money, real stock prices and real GDP (Kongsted 2005, pp. 206–207). Including the inflation rate enables tracking of the $I(2)$ trend (Coenen and Vega 1999, p. 3). Valid nominal-to-real transformation is identical to the assumption of long-run price

[17] The short-run transitory effects are concentrated out based on the Frisch–Waugh theorem (Juselius 2006, p. 116).

[18] It is important to see that $\lambda = 1 - \rho$, where ρ denotes the roots of the companion matrix. Hence, $\lambda_i = 0$ corresponds to $\rho = 1$, which implies that the relation is a unit root process. Note that the roots, ρ, are the inverses of the roots, z, of the characteristic polynomial, which was defined in Sect. 5.1.2, (5.3).

homogeneity, which means that nominal money and prices share the same stochastic $I(2)$ trend. In most analyses this is assumed without testing or tested but ignored.[19] However, if long-run price homogeneity is violated and real transformations are imposed nevertheless, the data may contain a small $I(2)$ component. As a result, inference might be affected and the existence of the $I(2)$ trend has to be weighed (Kongsted 2005, pp. 211–212; Juselius and Toro 2005, pp. 518–520). For the period under investigation, long-run price homogeneity is rejected because nominal money has grown faster than prices. This does not come as a surprise as one hypothesis of this contribution is that excess money has not led to increased inflation but to increased asset prices, such as housing and stocks. However, these prices are not part of the goods in the inflation basket. Therefore, by including a stock price index in the analysis, this can be empirically tested. It is important to rule out remaining I(2)-trends in the data. Various criteria can be analyzed to investigate if I(2)-ness persists (Juselius 2006, pp. 297–302; Juselius and Toro 2005, p. 520):

- Compare the trace test (Q_r) to the Bartlett corrected trace test (Q_r^{Bart}) (see Table 6.5): if divided, the result should be between 1 and 1.2, but not greater than 1.5.
- Roots of the companion matrix (see Table 6.6): if the first root that is not restricted always jumps up close to one it is a sign for I(2)-ness in the data.
- Graphical inspection of the cointegration relations (not reported): if the included variables of the analysis are I(1), then the graphs of the R-form ($\beta' R_{1t}$) and the Z-form ($\beta' y_t$) should look alike. If the variables are I(2), they look very different.

Applying these criteria to US quarterly data shows that no $I(2)$-trends exist in the data. Therefore, even though nominal-to-real transformation was formally rejected, it is still valid to carry out the analysis.[20]

---

19 For examples, see Humpe and Macmillan (2009, p. 115), Giese and Tuxen (2007, p. 15), Juselius (2001, p. 348), Nasseh and Strauss (2000, pp. 234–235), Cheung and Ng (1998, p. 283), Ericsson (1998, p. 297), Juselius (1998, pp. 466–468), Juselius (1996, pp. 799–800), Friedman and Kuttner (1992, pp. 487–490) and Baba et al. (1992, pp. 31, 38).

20 Because univariate unit root tests are used in most analyses, they are conducted as well, in spite of their many limitations in the multivariate setting. The Augmented Dickey–Fuller (ADF) test and the Phillips–Perron (PP) test fail to reject the null hypothesis of the existence of a unit root at the 5% level for all variables in levels aside from the time series representing capital flows. The PP test is also rejected for inflation. In contrast, both tests reject the null hypothesis for the variables in first-differenced form of the series. Consequently, the variables are at most integrated of order one. The appropriate lags for the ADF test are selected based on the Schwartz Criterion and the Akaike Information Criterion. The truncation point for the Newey–West adjustment, required for calculating the PP statistic, is determined by using the smallest integer greater than or equal to the sample size, T, to the power of $\frac{1}{4}$ (Greene 2003, p. 267). The test results are not reported here because of the questionable usefulness of univariate tests in a multivariate setting. Rao (2007, p. 1624) points out that these tests lack power and combinations of the many options of the tests almost always enable one to prove that the variables are I(1) in levels. Additionally, Muscatelli and Spinelli (2000, p. 724) refer to difficulties in using unit root tests as pre-tests if regime shifts are inherent to the model. For these and other reasons, Juselius (2006, p. 136) does not even discuss univariate unit root testing in her textbook on cointegration analysis. Instead, the stationarity of

Table 6.5 US quarterly data: trace test of cointegration rank

$p-r$	r	λ_i	Q_r	Q_r^{Bart}	$C_r^{95\%}$	p-value	p-value*
7	0	0.532	219.577	171.662	150.348	0	0.002
6	1	0.379	145.200	115.238	117.451	0	**0.069**
5	2	0.260	98.442	79.452	88.554	0.007	0.195
4	3	0.254	68.874	56.754	63.659	0.016	0.172
3	4	0.203	40.180	32.454	42.770	**0.091**	0.370
2	5	0.124	17.932	15.010	25.731	0.356	0.580
1	6	0.049	4.939	3.870	12.448	0.612	0.758

Table 6.5 provides an overview of the trace test results. It reports the estimated eigenvalues, λ_i, the trace test, Q_r, the small sample Bartlett corrected trace test (Johansen 2002, pp. 1932–1940), Q_r^{Bart}, and the 95% quintile from the asymptotic distribution corrected for deterministic components, $C_r^{95\%}$. In addition, the table reports the p-value of the test statistic and the p-value of the Bartlett small sample corrections, p-value*, respectively. In this case, the Bartlett small sample corrections are probably irrelevant because the analysis is based on an effective sample of 98 observations.

The trace test accepts the null of $p-r = 3$ unit roots and, therefore, $r = 4$.[21] These test results are a first indication for rank $r = 4$. However, it is important to include the other information criteria mentioned above.

Roots of the Companion Matrix

The analysis of the modulus of the roots of the companion form matrix, as depicted in Table 6.6, shows that for $r = 4$ the modulus of the largest unrestricted root drops to 0.757 and, thus, far away from a unit root.[22] Hence, Table 6.6 also indicates rank $r = 4$.

a variable is easily tested inside the multivariate model as a restriction on β (see Table 6.10 in Sect. 6.2.2.2). The advantage of the multivariate analysis is to define a well-specified model first and then test for stationarity. With univariate unit root tests, stationarity is tested before guaranteeing i.i.d. error terms, constant parameters and the absence of ARCH effects and before determining cointegration rank. The results of the ADF and PP tests are available on request.

[21] As a sensitivity analysis the trace test is performed with the intervention dummies excluded. The results are $r = 3$ for the standard trace test. The additional rank of the trace test with dummies included is due to the stationarity of the capital flows time series. Including the dummy variables leads to the capital flows process being $I(0)$. This is equal to an additional cointegration relation.

[22] The rule of thumb is a value smaller than 0.85 for quarterly and 0.90 for monthly data. Nevertheless, the discussion of the roots is only indicative because they are reported without confidence bands.

Table 6.6 US quarterly data: modulus of the seven largest eigenvalue roots

$r = 7$	$r = 6$	$r = 5$	$r = 4$	$r = 3$	$r = 2$	$r = 1$	$r = 0$
0.974	1	1	1	1	1	1	1
0.974	**0.938**	1	1	1	1	1	1
0.893	0.883	**0.912**	1	1	1	1	1
0.893	0.883	0.912	**0.757**	1	1	1	1
0.754	0.783	0.730	0.757	**0.821**	1	1	1
0.754	0.783	0.730	0.736	0.821	**0.706**	1	1
0.725	0.704	0.677	0.736	0.649	0.699	**0.736**	1

Table 6.7 US quarterly data: t-values of the α-coefficients

	α						
	Alpha(1)	Alpha(2)	Alpha(3)	Alpha(4)	Alpha(5)	Alpha(6)	Alpha(7)
Δm_r	(0.276)	(2.019)	(0.068)	(−1.842)	(−2.023)	(1.311)	(−1.657)
Δs_r	(−0.698)	(0.544)	(−1.572)	(−0.493)	**(2.835)**	(−1.354)	(−1.523)
Δy_r	(2.241)	**(2.705)**	(−1.416)	(−0.756)	(2.529)	(2.523)	(−0.468)
$\Delta^2 p$	**(−6.557)**	(−0.931)	(2.584)	**(2.770)**	(0.204)	(−0.861)	(0.782)
Δff	(1.768)	**(−6.510)**	(0.694)	(0.844)	(0.780)	(1.420)	(−0.550)
$\Delta b10$	**(4.291)**	(−0.644)	(1.011)	**(5.139)**	(−0.091)	(−0.262)	(−0.056)
Δcf	**(3.189)**	(0.406)	**(4.603)**	(−2.540)	(−0.341)	(−0.307)	(−0.664)

Significance of Adjustment Coefficients α

The t-values of the α-coefficients indicate the significance of the equilibrium adjustment behavior of the relative variables. They are derived from the unrestricted estimates and can be used to identify the cointegration rank. As can be seen from Table 6.7, adjustment behavior to the first four relations is stronger and involves several variables, whereas for the fifth relation only one variable (with a lower t-value) and none for the sixth and seventh equation show significant t-values.[23] Therefore, the investigation of the adjustment coefficients' significance again points to a rank of $r = 4$.

The Recursive Graphs of the Trace Statistic

Figure 6.2 shows the forward and backward recursively calculated graphs for the trace statistic. The plots are normalized to the 5% significance level, represented by the horizontal line.

[23] The t-values of a given relation are no longer Student's t distributed if the relation is nonstationary. Instead, it is better to compare the t-values to the Dickey–Fuller distribution, where the critical values are larger. As a rule of thumb, the t-values should be close to 3.0 for the relation to still qualify as adjusting.

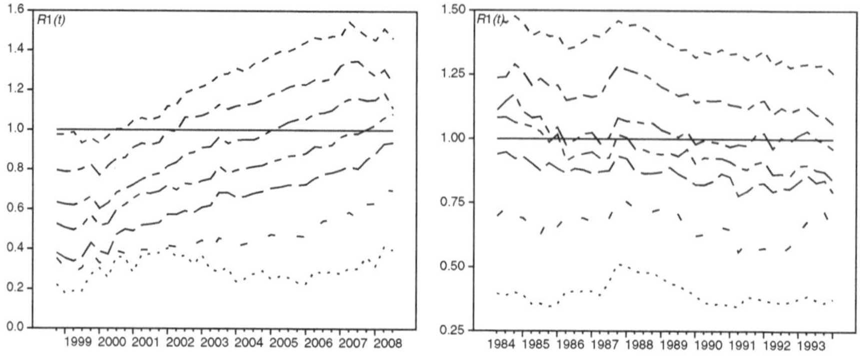

Fig. 6.2 US quarterly data: recursively calculated trace test statistics (forward, base sample 1984:02 to 1998:04, depicted left; backward, base sample 2008:03 to 1994:01, depicted right)

If $\lambda_i \neq 0$, the recursively calculated components of the trace statistic should grow linearly for $i = 1, \ldots, r$ because they are functions of non-zero eigenvalues. On the other hand, they should stay constant for $i = r + 1, \ldots, p$ because they are functions of zero eigenvalues (Juselius 2006, p. 142). Since four of the graphs show linear growth and are above or cross the 1-line (5% critical value), this also indicates a rank of $r = 4$. The dents in the graphs in the years 1987, 2000 and 2007 indicate a regime change due to the 1987 stock market crash, the burst of the dot-com bubble and the global financial crisis, respectively. One reason for this could be a change in the way market participants perceive risk. One may account for them with shift dummies. Another explanation is the strong influence of the stock market, which turns out to be weakly exogenous. Since the model is already well specified, no additional dummies are included.

Graphical Analysis of the Cointegration Relations

Finally, Appendix B.1.2 depicts the graphs of the cointegrating relations of the unrestricted model. The graphs of the fifth, sixth and seventh relation show persistent behavior and do not strongly suggest mean-reversion behavior, whereas the first four graphs looks fairly stationary. As a result, this indicator points to a rank of $r = 4$.

In sum, the various information criteria used to determine the rank of the model all point to a rank of $r = 4$ and this is chosen for the subsequent analysis of the long-run equilibria. That also means that $p - r = 3$ common trends exist, which is also valid from an economic point of view since it is reasonable for a real, monetary and financial trend to exist. In addition, recursive tests show that the data describes a constant parameter regime. Figure 6.3 depicts the recursively calculated log-likelihood. For both, the forward and the backward recursive test, the graph with short-run effects concentrated out, (R1(t)), stays under or drops below the line early on. The line represents the 5% critical value. Thus, constancy of the overall

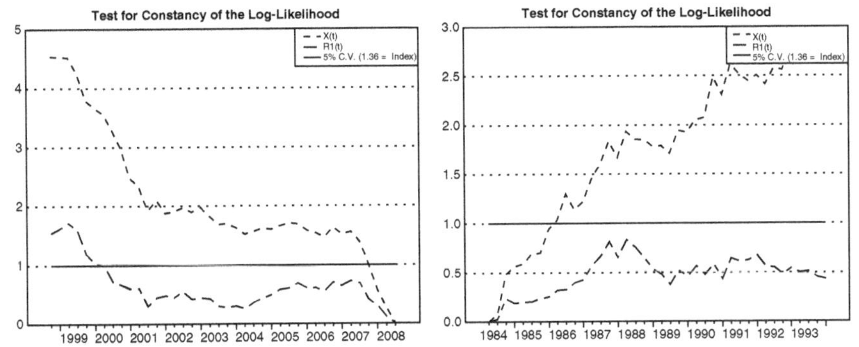

Fig. 6.3 US quarterly data: recursively calculated test of log-likelihood (forward, base sample 1984:02 to 1998:04, depicted left; backward, base sample 2008:03 to 1994:01, depicted right)

model is accepted. Appendix B.1.3 provides further information on parameter constancy, such as the eigenvalues λ_i, the eigenvalue fluctuation test, the max test of β constancy and the test of β_t equals a known β.[24] All confirm a constant parameter regime. As a result, the assumption of constant parameters, which is important for valid identification of the long-run structure, is fulfilled.

6.2.2 *Identification of the Long-Run Structure*

6.2.2.1 Assessment of the Unrestricted Π-Matrix

To help facilitate the identification of an empirically acceptable long-run structure, the unrestricted Π is tentatively interpreted. However, the cointegration space can be rotated by taking proper linear combinations of the equations and, consequently, the final identified long-run structure does not have to reflect the initial suggestions from the unrestricted system. Also, the unrestricted Π-matrix may not be economically interpretable. Nevertheless, a rough indication of the long-run information in the data can be obtained. Basically, these estimates measure the combined effect of the cointegration relations in each of the equations (Johansen and Juselius 1992, p. 223).

The unrestricted Π-matrix for the chosen rank $r = 4$ is depicted in Table 6.8. The fact that the signs on the diagonal are negative for all variables but money and the stock market shows that these equations exhibit error-correction behavior. However, the signs for the real money and the real stock market equations are positive. This suggests that these two variables are driving the system but are not reacting to it, i.e., are weakly exogenous. In addition, the stock market is not significantly related to

[24] For an overview and explanations of the various tests, see Juselius (2006, pp. 151–167).

Table 6.8 US quarterly data: the unrestricted Π-matrix for a rank of 4 (t-values in brackets)

	Π							
	m_r	s_r	y_r	Δp	ff	$b10$	cf	*Trend*
Δm_r	**0.027**	**0.009**	−0.172	−0.280	0.412	0.205	−0.380	0.001
	[1.999]	[2.484]	[−1.771]	[−0.516]	[1.123]	[0.339]	[−1.290]	[1.734]
Δs_r	0.110	0.025	−0.646	−1.611	−0.824	2.025	2.654	0.002
	[1.015]	[0.879]	[−0.827]	[−0.369]	[−0.280]	[0.417]	[1.122]	[0.735]
Δy_r	**0.021**	**0.006**	**−0.186**	0.478	**0.428**	−0.488	−0.222	**0.001**
	[2.773]	[3.135]	[−3.316]	[1.527]	[2.023]	[−1.400]	[−1.308]	[3.357]
$\Delta^2 p$	−0.008	**−0.006**	**0.118**	**−1.144**	−0.063	0.112	**0.330**	**−0.001**
	[−1.614]	[−4.564]	[3.509]	[−6.083]	[−0.493]	[0.535]	[3.233]	[−3.710]
Δff	**−0.014**	**−0.003**	**0.088**	**0.288**	**−0.283**	0.184	0.030	**−0.000**
	[−6.459]	[−4.901]	[5.499]	[3.225]	[−4.690]	[1.850]	[0.611]	[−5.327]
$\Delta b10$	−0.003	**−0.001**	−0.002	**0.294**	**0.111**	**−0.395**	−0.056	0.000
	[−1.719]	[−2.678]	[−0.198]	[4.417]	[2.471]	[−5.336]	[−1.567]	[0.581]
Δcf	−0.006	0.002	0.023	0.309	0.255	0.132	**−0.852**	−0.000
	[−0.868]	[1.321]	[0.483]	[1.161]	[1.420]	[0.446]	[−5.907]	[−0.240]

any of the variables in the system and real money is only related to the stock market. This also points to weak exogeneity.[25]

The equation for real output shows an aggregate demand relation that is positively related to real money and the stock market and shows a positive deterministic trend. Real output is also positively related to the fed funds rate. The latter seems surprising as higher short-term interest rates are expected to be negative for output. This is an indication of the importance of long-term rates for investment decisions. In addition, it might be a sign for the Fed's reaction to output growth, which leads to similar movements of output and the fed funds rate.

Inflation is negatively related to the stock market and reacts positively to deviations of real output and capital inflows. The fed funds rate equation already indicates a monetary policy reaction function. It reacts positively to real output and inflation but reacts negatively to real money and the stock market. The negative relation with real money is an indication of the liquidity effect. Since the fed funds rate reacts to so many variables it shows strong adjusting behavior. The bond rate equation follows text book theory as it is negatively related to the stock market (competition between stocks and bonds) and positively to inflation (expected inflation effect) and the fed funds rate (term structure of interest rates). Finally, the last equation shows that capital flows only show error-correction behavior to deviations of their own mean. It turns out that capital flows are stationary by themselves. As a result, this equation already describes one cointegrating relation with only one variable.

Table B.2 in Appendix B.1.4 shows the α- and β'-matrices of the partitioned unrestricted Π-matrix. The α-coefficients can indicate which variables are strongly adjusting to long-run equilibria and, which variables are more on the pushing side. The estimated α-matrix suggests that the cointegration relations might consist of an

[25] Weak exogeneity means that the variables do not react to equilibria inside the system. Nevertheless, they can still add information to the explanation of the long-run behavior of the variables. Weak exogeneity is formally tested in the next section and again for the identified long-run structure.

Table 6.9 US quarterly data: test of variable exclusion (p-values in brackets)

			Test of exclusion							
r	DGF	5% C.V.	m_r	s_r	y_r	Δp	ff	$b10$	cf	*Trend*
4	4	9.488	17.461 [0.002]	**6.209** [0.184]	23.444 [0.000]	46.201 [0.000]	20.017 [0.000]	16.439 [0.002]	26.775 [0.000]	25.082 [0.000]

inflation or monetary policy rule relation, an aggregate demand for goods relation, stationary capital flows and a bond rate relation since these variables show the most significant adjustment behavior in the respective relations.

The following section outlines preliminary tests for purposes of assessment structure and to provide additional information.

6.2.2.2 Preliminary Hypotheses Testing

This section is divided into preliminary tests for β' and α. Automated tests on β' include the possibility to exclude variables from the long-run relations and stationarity of individual variables. The α-matrix is formally analyzed for weak exogeneity and unit vectors. Afterwards, single cointegration tests are conducted. This is to test for potential long-run equilibria as outlined in the section on long-run economic relations (5.2).[26] This helps facilitate the final identification of the long-run structure and provides additional insight on information contained in the data set.

Table 6.9 provides LR tests for the exclusion of any variable from the cointegration relations. If the test is accepted, the variable can be excluded from the cointegration space. Thus, a zero restriction can be imposed on the coefficient of the variable in all cointegration relations. The table shows that the stock market is long-run excludable. However, since this test only tests one variable at a time it might be misleading if multicollinearity exists between the variables. Therefore, if this test is accepted it is advisable to perform a plausibility check. The above analysis of the unrestricted Π-matrix shows that the stock market does not react to the other variables in the system but some other variables react to the stock market. In addition, since the stock market is the focus of the analysis and it is valid from an economic point of view to include it in the analysis, it is part of the data set and the long-run structure.

Table 6.10 reports tests for long-run stationarity. It tests for stationary and trend-stationary variables. Stationarity for capital flows is strongly accepted and, thus, capital flows may represent a cointegrating vector of their own. Stationarity is also accepted for the stock market, real output and the bond rate, however, with very low t-values. Nevertheless, this is a surprising result. The identification of the long-run

[26] All test statistics on α and β are asymptotically distributed as χ^2 because the asymptotic distribution is mixed Gaussian (Johansen 1995, pp. 177–178). As a result, the usual statistical inference can be applied (Johansen and Juselius 1994, p. 16).

Table 6.10 US quarterly data: test of variable stationarity (p-values in brackets)

Test of stationarity									
r	DGF	5% C.V.	m_r	s_r	y_r	Δp	ff	$b10$	cf
4	4	9.488	15.226 [0.004]	**8.898** [0.064]	11.316 [0.023]	10.212 [0.037]	12.519 [0.014]	**6.675** [0.154]	**3.199** [0.525]
Restricted trend included in the cointegrating relation(s)									
4	3	7.815	13.064 [0.004]	**7.523** [0.057]	**7.493** [0.058]	10.123 [0.018]	12.235 [0.007]	**4.762** [0.190]	**3.069** [0.381]

Table 6.11 US quarterly data: test of weak exogeneity (p-values in brackets)

Test of weak exogeneity									
r	DGF	5% C.V.	m_r	s_r	y_r	Δp	ff	$b10$	cf
4	4	9.488	**4.291** [0.368]	**1.586** [0.811]	**8.324** [0.080]	28.981 [0.000]	23.547 [0.000]	15.793 [0.003]	12.432 [0.014]

Table 6.12 US quarterly data: test for a unit vector in the α-matrix (p-values in brackets)

Test of unit vector in alpha									
r	DGF	5% C.V.	m_r	s_r	y_r	Δp	ff	$b10$	cf
4	3.000	7.815	15.169 [0.002]	16.102 [0.001]	11.454 [0.010]	**2.818** [0.421]	**7.039** [0.071]	**1.796** [0.616]	**1.016** [0.797]

structure shows that this does not hold. Only capital flows can be included in the long-run structure as a cointegrating vector.

Tables 6.11 and 6.12 test restrictions on α. The test of weak exogeneity is equivalent to testing a zero row in the α-matrix. This means that a variable is not error-correcting but can be considered weakly exogenous for the long-run parameters β'. If the test is accepted, this also means that the sum of the cumulated empirical shocks to the variable in question defines one common driving trend. Table 6.11 shows that, when tested separately, weak exogeneity is strongly accepted for real money and real stock market levels as well as borderline accepted for real output. The combined test is also accepted with a p-value of 0.267 ($\chi^2(12) = 14.557$), pointing, again, towards a monetary, financial and real trend pushing the system. This can be tested again in combination with the identified long-run structure of the β'-vectors. The test of a unit vector in α tests for the opposite, namely if a variable is exclusively adjusting, i.e., it does react to long-run disequilibria but does not affect the other variables in the long run. If the unit vector test is accepted, the properties of the relevant variable are that its shocks have no permanent effect on any of the other variables in the system and it can be regarded as endogenous. The transitory shocks do not cumulate into trends, instead they die out over time. Consequently, together the two tests of α can identify the pulling and pushing forces of the system. Table 6.12 shows the complement to Table 6.11 since shocks to inflation, fed funds, the bond rate and capital flows only have transitory effects. Table 6.12 also indicates that the Fed might not have had any long-run impact on the inflation rate or on stock market behavior.

In addition to the above tests on single variables, the focus of the remaining preliminary tests is on single cointegration relations. The idea is to analyze whether stable relationships between the economic variables can be identified by linear relations. Testing follows the theoretical connections outlined in Chap. 3 and Sect. 5.2, summarized in Table 5.1. The hypotheses are of the form:

$$\beta = (H\phi, \psi_1, \psi_2, \psi_3), \tag{6.11}$$

where H is the design matrix, ϕ contains the restricted parameters and ψ_i is a vector of parameters which are freely estimated. It is important to note that each hypothesis in Table 6.13 tests restrictions on a single vector but leaves the other cointegration vectors unrestricted (Johansen and Juselius 1992, pp. 233–236).

Table 6.13 furnishes an overview of the single cointegration test results. It is structured the same as Table 5.2. However, since the rank is set to $r = 4$, a minimum of 4 restrictions has to be set to formally test for cointegration. The reason for this is the $\chi^2(v)$-distribution of the single cointegration test with v being the number of degrees of freedom. The degrees of freedom are derived from the decrease in the number of free parameters. They are calculated as $v = no.of restr. - rank + 1$. As a result, the number of restrictions has to be a minimum of four to obtain one degree of freedom and, thus, have testable results.[27] Therefore, only those theoretical relations of Table 5.2, which restrict at least four of the parameters (all but H_{11} do), can be formally tested.

In addition, because capital flows are found to be inherently stationary and, hence, are integrated of order 0, the variable can not be part of another cointegration relation or adjust to a non-stationary variable (Juselius 2001, p. 343). The test results are still shown for purposes of comparison, because each country analysis utilizes the same preliminary tests and to keep the final long-run structure open. However, for relations including capital flows, one must keep in mind that stationarity may be a result of the already stationary capital flows rather than the linear combination of the variables.

Hypotheses H_1 to H_8 test for cointegration between stocks and the other variables. Even though stationarity is accepted for hypotheses H_3 to H_8, the stock market variable does not exhibit significant adjustment behavior to any of the stationary relations. Cointegration by itself does not indicate the direction of causality between the variables. Instead, the test results have to be jointly evaluated with the α-matrix. The last column shows that real output, inflation and both interest rates react to the respective relations.

H_9 to H_{16} test monetary relations. The test for a stationary liquidity relation (H_7) is rejected. If amended with the yield spread (H_{13}) the liquidity relation becomes stationary. However, this is probably due to a stationary yield-spread (see H_{30} and H_{31}). In addition, as with the stock market relations, real money does not show

[27] Put in a different way, one can always impose $r-1$ restrictions without changing the value of the likelihood function. Then the system is just identified. However, only over-identified systems can be formally tested (Juselius 2006, p. 215). Hence, more than $r-1$ restrictions must be imposed.

Table 6.13 US quarterly data: testing the stationarity of single relations

	m_r	s_r	y_r	Δp	ff	$b10$	cf	*Trend*	$\chi^2(v)$	p-value	$sign.\alpha$
					Demand for stocks						
H_1	0.865	1	0	0	0	0	0	−0.02	6.1 (2)	0.048	
H_2	0	1	0	−80.38	80.38	0	0	−0.001	6.6 (2)	0.038	
H_3	**0**	**1**	**0**	**1,267**	**0**	**−1,267**	**0**	**−0.137**	**3.6 (2)**	**0.166**	$\Delta p, b10$
H_4	**0**	**1**	**0**	**0**	**39.28**	**0**	**0**	**−0.007**	**5.9 (2)**	**0.053**	ff
H_5	**0**	**1**	**0**	**0**	**0**	**345.2**	**0**	**0.019**	**4.4 (2)**	**0.112**	$b10$
H_6	**0**	**1**	**13.54**	**0**	**0**	**0**	**0**	**−0.086**	**4.6 (2)**	**0.100**	y_r
H_7	**0**	**0.001**	**0**	**0**	**0**	**0**	**1**	**0**	**3.0 (2)**	**0.223**	$y_r, b10, cf$
H_8	**0.731**	**1**	**0**	**0**	**0**	**0**	**644.4**	**−0.03**	**3.0 (1)**	**0.082**	$y_r, b10, cf$
					Money demand						
H_9	1	0	−1	0	0	0	0	−0.039	13.1 (3)	0.005	
H_{10}	**0.002**	**0**	**0**	**0**	**−1**	**1**	**0**	**0**	**4.8 (2)**	**0.093**	$ff, b10$
H_{11}	1	0	−8.449	0	45.25	−85.36	0	0.037	(0)		$ff, b10$
H_{12}	**1**	**0**	**−40.78**	**383.0**	**0**	**0**	**0**	**0.221**	**2.2 (1)**	**0.139**	Δp
H_{13}	1	1.157	0	0	0	0	0	−0.023	6.1 (2)	0.048	
H_{14}	**1**	**1.882**	**0**	**0**	**288.1**	**−288.1**	**0**	**−0.02**	**3.7 (1)**	**0.054**	$\Delta p, ff, b10$
H_{15}	1	1.134	−1	0	0	0	0	−0.017	6.3 (2)	0.042	
H_{16}	**1**	**1.615**	**−1**	**0**	**242.3**	**−242.3**	**0**	**−0.013**	**3.7 (1)**	**0.054**	$\Delta p, ff, b10$

(continued)

Table 6.13 (Continued)

	m_r	s_r	y_r	Δp	ff	$b10$	cf	$Trend$	$\chi^2(v)$	p-value	$sign.\alpha$
					Policy rules						
H_{17}	0	0	0	−16.82	1	0	0	0	10 (3)	0.017	
H_{18}	0	0	−0.446	0	1	0	0	0.002	7.1 (2)	0.028	
H_{19}	**0**	**0.025**	**0**	**0**	**1**	**0**	**0**	**0**	**5.9 (2)**	**0.053**	ff
					Demand for goods						
H_{20}	0	0	1	−6.773	6.773	0	0	0.00	7.0 (2)	0.030	
H_{21}	**0**	**0**	**1**	**−22.04**	**0**	**22.04**	**0**	**−0.003**	**2.8 (2)**	**0.249**	$y_r, \Delta p, b10$
H_{22}	**−0.116**	**0**	**1**	**0**	**0**	**0**	**0**	**−0.005**	**2.7 (2)**	**0.258**	y_r
H_{23}	**−0.137**	**−0.026**	**1**	**0**	**0**	**0**	**0**	**−0.004**	**2.3 (1)**	**0.130**	y_r
					Inflation and interest rates						
H_{24}	**−0.009**	**0**	**0.009**	**1**	**0**	**0**	**0**	**0**	**6.4 (3)**	**0.094**	Δp
H_{25}	**−0.004**	**0**	**0**	**0**	**0**	**1**	**0**	**0.000**	**4.5 (2)**	**0.107**	$y_r, b10$
H_{26}	0	0	0	−1	1	0	0	0	14 (4)	0.007	
H_{27}	**0**	**0**	**0**	**−1**	**0**	**1**	**0**	**0**	**6.6 (4)**	**0.160**	$y_r, \Delta p, b10$
H_{28}	0	0	0	−16.82	1	0	0	0	10 (3)	0.017	
H_{29}	**0**	**0**	**0**	**−1.178**	**0**	**1**	**0**	**0**	**6.7 (3)**	**0.081**	$y_r, \Delta p, b10$
H_{30}	0	0	0	0	−1	1	0	0	9.6 (4)	0.047	
H_{31}	**0**	**0**	**0**	**0**	**−0.628**	**1**	**0**	**0**	**1.8 (3)**	**0.618**	$ff, b10$
H_{32}	**0**	**0**	**0**	**0.924**	**1**	**−1.924**	**0**	**0**	**2.9 (3)**	**0.415**	$\Delta p, ff, b10$
H_{33}	**0**	**0**	**0**	**1.504**	**−1**	**1**	**0**	**0**	**4.3 (3)**	**0.229**	$\Delta p, ff$

error-correcting behavior to any of the stationary relations. This is another sign that real money is weakly exogenous to the system and that the hypotheses H_9 to H_{16} do not qualify as money demand relations. This also means that the implications of excess liquidity can only be analyzed via the often used simple form of real money increases in excess of advances in real income. Normally, though, a stable money demand function would be required to determine excess liquidity as supply of money being in excess of demand (see Sect. 4.4.3).

'Policy rules' (H_{17} to H_{19}) are harder to test for because the monetary policy target is unknown. Hence, deviations from the target inflation rate, the target output level or the target stock market level are uncertain and cannot be measured directly. One possibility is to test for monetary policy reactions to changes in the inflation rate (independent of a target level) and to deviations of real output and real stock market levels from their trend. As can be seen in Table 6.13 only cointegration between the stock market and the short-term interest rate is borderline accepted ($p - value = 0.053$). However, as recognized during the assessment of the unrestricted Π, the real stock market exhibits the wrong sign, indicating a short-term interest rate increase as a reaction to stock market drops. Thus, the usefulness of this relation is questionable from an economic point of view and should be regarded with caution.

Hypotheses H_{20} to H_{23} focus on potential stationary aggregate demand for goods relations. H_{21} shows that output reacts negatively to deviations in the real bond rate. Hence, H_{21} indicates an IS-type relation in the long-run structure. H_{22} and H_{23} are also accepted, showing the reaction of output to expansive monetary policy and stock market performance (wealth and balance sheet effects).

Under the headline 'Inflation and interest rates' cointegration between inflation and the nominal interest rates ('Fisher parity') as well as between the interest rates themselves ('expectations hypothesis') is tested. Additionally, H_{24} tests the Monetarist explanation of price inflation, which states that monetary growth in excess of real productive growth in the economy leads to inflation. This hypothesis is accepted and inflation shows adjustment behavior towards this steady-state relation. The 'Fisher parity'-hypothesis is accepted for the real long-term interest rate in the strong form (H_{27}, i.e., with proportionality imposed) and the weak form (H_{29}, i.e., free parameters). Stationarity of the yield spread is accepted in a weakened form with a β-coefficient of -0.628 instead of -1.

Additionally, for the combinations of inflation and interest rates ($H_{32} - H_{33}$) stationarity is also accepted. This shows that these three variables are 'bound', i.e., tied together, in an economically interpretable way. In this case, the homogeneous relation of interest rates and inflation in H_{32} can be interpreted, such that the yield spread and the long-term real interest rate are cointegrating. H_{33} can, in general, be interpreted as the relationship between actual and expected inflation (Berk 1998, pp. 306–307). However, for this to make sense economically, the sign of the inflation-coefficient must be negative. Since this is not the case, this relationship is not useful for the long-run structure.

In conclusion, the preliminary tests suggest that an over-identified long-run structure consists of real output, inflation and interest rate relations but not of money or stock market demand relations. Additionally, capital flows might be a stationary relation by themselves and represent one of the four cointegration vectors.

6.2.2.3 Identification of the Long-Run Cointegrating Relations

The identification procedure is based on the outlined economic theory and the preliminary testing of the econometric model in the previous section. By imposing different linear restrictions on the cointegrating relations an empirically and economically uniquely identified long-run structure can be obtained.

In this case, the joint hypotheses of H_{23}, H_{24} and H_{31} in addition to capital flows being $I(0)$ are tested to identify the full cointegration structure. The restrictions on the identified long-run structure are accepted with a p-value of 0.35 ($\chi^2(10) = 11.097$). This shows that the imposed restrictions describe the data well. The structure is formally and empirically identified because all β-coefficients are strongly significant (Juselius and MacDonald 2004, p. 18). Appendix B.1.5 shows that the rank conditions are accepted for the full cointegration space. This means that the four cointegration relations are linearly independent and, as such, can not be replaced by each other.

The graphs of the cointegrating relations are displayed in Appendix B.1.6 with the deterministic terms and short-term parameters concentrated out. This removes the seasonal fluctuations and outliers, which can be observed in the raw series and, thus, provides a clearer picture (Brüggemann and Lütkepohl 2006, p. 692).[28] In addition, graphical overviews of forward and backward recursive tests of parameter constancy in Appendix B.1.7 show that parameter constancy for α_i and β_i ($i = 1, \dots, 4$) is given.

The structural representation of the cointegration space is depicted in Table 6.14 with the estimated eigenvectors β and the weights α. Table B.4 in Appendix B.1.8 shows the identified long-run structure with weak exogeneity imposed on real money and the stock market. It turns out that the coefficients and the significance of the results remain the same. This long-run structure is accepted with a slightly higher p-value of 0.38.

The first cointegrating relation describes liquidity, wealth and balance sheet effects on aggregate demand for goods:

$$y_{r,t} - 0.123 m_{r,t} - 0.027 s_{r,t} - 0.004\,trend \sim I(0), \tag{6.12}$$

where real activity is positively related to real money and the stock market. The α-coefficients show that output is significantly adjusting to this relation and that it takes approximately five quarters to reestablish equilibrium after innovations in real

[28] See also Sect. 6.2.1.3.

Table 6.14 US quarterly data: the identified long-run structure (t-values in brackets)

β'

	m_r	s_r	y_r	Δp	ff	$b10$	cf	$Trend$
Beta(1)	**−0.123** [−9.124]	**−0.027** [−4.303]	**1.000** [NA]	0.000 [NA]	0.000 [NA]	0.000 [NA]	0.000 [NA]	**−0.004** [−19.21]
Beta(2)	**−0.011** [−5.135]	0.000 [NA]	**0.011** [5.135]	**1.000** [NA]	0.000 [NA]	0.000 [NA]	0.000 [NA]	**0.000** [5.874]
Beta(3)	0.000 [NA]	0.000 [NA]	0.000 [NA]	**−0.348** [−6.152]	**−0.652** [−11.55]	**1.000** [NA]	0.000 [NA]	0.000 [NA]
Beta(4)	0.000 [NA]	0.000 [NA]	0.000 [NA]	0.000 [NA]	0.000 [NA]	0.000 [NA]	**1.000** [NA]	0.000 [NA]

α

	Alpha(1)	Alpha(2)	Alpha(3)	Alpha(4)
Δm_r	−0.138 [−1.404]	−0.034 [−0.067]	−0.369 [−0.680]	−0.113 [−0.403]
Δs_r	−0.693 [−0.911]	−1.478 [−0.377]	4.210 [1.003]	2.087 [0.962]
Δy_r	**−0.203** [−3.807]	0.045 [0.164]	−0.440 [−1.496]	−0.276 [−1.817]
$\Delta^2 p$	**0.123** [3.659]	**−1.009** [−5.821]	0.196 [1.056]	**0.334** [3.478]
Δff	**0.076** [4.517]	**0.258** [2.972]	**0.306** [3.284]	−0.033 [−0.696]
$\Delta b10$	−0.012 [−0.961]	**0.135** [2.087]	**−0.268** [−3.870]	**−0.102** [−2.855]
Δcf	0.038 [0.786]	0.474 [1.899]	−0.168 [−0.628]	**−0.729** [−5.267]

money or the stock market.[29] In addition, deviations from the long-run steady state between real output, real money and the stock market push inflation and the short-term interest rate. The positive reaction of the inflation rate can be interpreted in the framework of the short-run Phillips curve, where inflation increases with excess aggregate demand for goods (Juselius 2001, p. 344).

The second long-run relation describes a relationship between 'excess liquidity' (in its weak form) and inflation:

$$\Delta p_t - 0.011(m_{r,t} - y_{r,t}) + 0.000\, trend \sim I(0), \tag{6.13}$$

where inflation is driven by money advances exceeding increases in transactions. It has to be stressed that this is a very simple form of excess liquidity for two main reasons. First, transactions are measured by economic activity and the velocity of money is assumed to be constant. Second, since this relation does not describe a money demand relation, because real money does not react to it, it is only a calculated form of excess liquidity based on the quantity theory of money and constant velocity. Ergo, it does not reflect actual excess supply over demand for money. Nevertheless, this cointegration relation demonstrates the inflationary effects of money

[29] The positive relation between the stock market and economic activity has been documented by several studies, for an overview see Mauro (2000, p. 3).

in the long run, which is confirmed by the analysis of the long-run impact (see Sect. 6.2.4).

The inflation rate strongly reacts to this relationship and the α-coefficient of -1 indicates that inflation corrects disequilibria over the course of one quarter. In addition, the analysis of the α-coefficients shows that both interest rates are pushed by deviations from this equilibrium. This is a sign that the Fed reacts to advances in the inflation rate and the bond rate reacts to higher expected inflation.

The third β'-vector describes a homogeneous relationship (i.e., the coefficients sum to zero) between the short and long-term interest rate as well as inflation:

$$b10_t - 0.652ff_t - 0.348\Delta p_t \sim I(0). \tag{6.14}$$

Both interest rates show dynamic adjustment behavior towards this relationship. This indicates that it can be interpreted either as a bond rate relation or a fed funds rate relation. Economically, it is more reasonable to regard it as a bond rate relation because it shows that the bond rate is positively related to the fed funds rate (term structure hypothesis) and inflation (expected inflation effect). The bond rate takes approximately four quarters to restore the long-run equilibrium.

In addition, using the homogeneity property of relation 6.14, it can be restated to reflect cointegration between the yield spread and the long-term real interest rate:

$$(b10_t - ff_t) + 0.534(b10_t - \Delta p_t) \sim I(0). \tag{6.15}$$

This shows that the interest rate spread and the real interest rate form a stable long-run relationship. Cointegration between both interest rates and the inflation rate suggests that a single nominal trend drives all three processes (Cassola and Morana 2002, p. 22).

The last cointegrating relation consists of the capital flows variable, which is found to be stationary on its own:

$$cf_t \sim I(0). \tag{6.16}$$

The α-coefficient shows that capital flows error correct with high significance and take less than two quarters to reverse towards equilibrium. Additional analysis of the last column in the α-matrix shows that capital inflows increase inflation and reduce long-term interest rates. This is in line with previous findings that inflationary spillover effects exist between countries and that large capital inflows suppress long-term yields in the US.

To find out if the cumulated shocks to a variable have any long-run impact on other variables, Sect. 6.2.4 analyzes the unrestricted C-matrix. The focus there will also be on the controllability of stock markets.

6.2.3 Short-Run Dynamics

Whereas the previous section focused on stable long-run economic relations, this section applies a structural error-correction model and formulates stationary equations for each of the variables in the system. Hence, the analysis focuses on the dynamic short-run adjustment of each variable to the past and the other simultaneous variables in the system (Johansen 1995, p. 79). First, the long-run equilibria (the cointegration relations) are uniquely identified in the reduced form error-correction model and are fixed according to the prior analysis (with no restrictions on the short-run parameters). As a result, the variables in differences and the residuals of the equilibrium errors (the regressors in the short-run analysis) are stationary and the usual regression analysis can be applied. In this case, this is done by applying the full information maximum likelihood estimator in simultaneous equation modeling, using PcGive in OxMetrics.

Theoretical hypotheses for the behavior of macro variables are researched and postulated much more for the long run than for short-run behavior. As a result, identification for the short run is different from the long-run relations. Instead of focusing on well-specified economic hypotheses, the objective is to determine a parsimonious system of equations where all included regressors are significant (Boschi and Girardi 2007, p. 12). Additionally, it is important to realize that the identification of the short-run structure, as applied here, does not allow for the interpretation of the residuals as structural shocks to the variables. For this to be valid, the residuals would need to be invariant and, as such, not subject to additional explanation when increasing the information set. However, adding variables to a stochastic and interdependent macroeconomic system will most likely change the VAR residuals, and with it the estimated shocks.[30]

The starting point is estimating the multivariate dynamic equilibrium-correction model for the whole system. Identification of the p short-run equations requires at least $p-1$ just-identifying restrictions on each equation (Juselius 2006, p. 208). This is achieved by restricting current effects between the variables to zero. In addition, insignificant coefficients are removed from each single equation based on an LR test, which results in overidentified equations for each variable. Since the VAR model is usually overparameterized, and particularly so for short-run parameters, imposing zero restrictions allows a reduction in the number of model parameters (Juselius 1999, p. 284).

The result is the parsimonious model shown in Table 6.15. The dependent variables can be found in the top row as the column headings of each of the model equations. The row headings, on the other hand, indicate the conditioning variables. The 123 zero restrictions of insignificant coefficients are accepted based on an LR test of over-identifying restrictions $\chi^2(123) = 130.64$ with a p-value of 0.30.

---

[30] For a deeper discussion of the interpretation of shocks in VAR models see Juselius (2006, pp. 231–232) and Rapach (2001, pp. 6–9).

Table 6.15 US quarterly data: short-run dynamics (t-values in brackets)

	Δm_r	Δs_r	Δy_r	$\Delta^2 p$	Δff	$\Delta b10$	Δcf
$\Delta m_{r,t}$	**1**	0	0	0	0	0	0
$\Delta s_{r,t}$	0	**1**	0	0	0	0	0
$\Delta y_{r,t}$	0	0	**1**	0	0	0	0
$\Delta^2 p_t$	0	0	0	**1**	0	0	0
Δff_t	0	0	0	0	**1**	0	0
$\Delta b10_t$	0	0	0	0	0	**1**	0
Δcf_t	0	0	0	0	0	0	**1**
$\Delta m_{r,t-1}$	**0.308**						
	[3.96]						
$\Delta m_{r,t-2}$	**0.230**		y	**−0.079**			
	[2.77]			[−3.31]			
$\Delta s_{r,t-1}$	**−0.024**						
	[−2.47]						
$\Delta s_{r,t-2}$							
$\Delta y_{r,t-1}$						**0.117**	
						[5.07]	
$\Delta y_{r,t-2}$			**0.235**		**0.070**		
			[3.31]		[2.11]		
$\Delta^2 p_{t-1}$							
$\Delta^2 p_{t-2}$							
Δff_{t-1}							
Δff_{t-2}	**1.210**						
	[3.05]						
$\Delta b10_{t-1}$				**0.501**	**−0.246**		
				[2.93]	[−2.31]		
$\Delta b10_{t-2}$							
Δcf_{t-1}				**−0.130**			**−0.331**
				[−3.41]			[−3.49]
Δcf_{t-2}							**−0.285**
							[−3.96]
$ecm1_{t-1}$			**−0.093**	**0.072**	**0.085**		
			[−2.63]	[3.64]	[5.61]		
$ecm2_{t-1}$				**−0.964**	**0.199**	**0.085**	
				[−15.5]	[3.96]	[2.31]	
$ecm3_{t-1}$					**0.369**	**−0.135**	
					[4.92]	[−3.23]	
$ecm4_{t-1}$				**0.187**		**−0.048**	**−0.590**
				[3.68]		[−2.77]	[−5.24]
$dum8602_{t,t}$				**−0.005**		**−0.002**	
				[−3.08]		[−2.55]	
$dum8704_{p,t}$		**−0.332**			**0.004**	**0.003**	
		[−4.65]			[2.83]	[3.00]	
$dum9004_{p,t}$	**−0.020**		**−0.024**	**0.007**			
	[−2.30]		[−4.78]	[2.32]			
$dum0104_{p,t}$				**−0.005**			**−0.043**
				[−1.99]			[−9.65]
$dum0604_{p,t}$	**0.018**		**0.012**	**−0.015**			**0.023**
	[1.98]		[2.26]	[−4.99]			[4.87]

The analysis of the short-run dynamics shows that real money reacts positively to lagged values of itself and the fed funds rate. The latter suggests increased money demand as a result of higher short-term interest rates. In addition, lagged values of the stock market have a negative effect on real money. This shows that the 'substitution effect' is stronger than the 'wealth effect'.

The stock market only reacts to the dummy variable that covers the 1987 crash, but not to any of the other variables in the system. The result is that the stock market is strongly exogenous to the system. To understand stock market behavior better, the information set needs to be expanded, e.g., with additional domestic variables, such as the unemployment rate or global variables. Neither the stock market nor real money react to the residuals of any cointegration relation (error-correction mechanism (ecm)), confirming the results of the previous sections.

In addition, Table 6.15 shows that real output is positively related to lagged values of itself and shows error-correcting behavior to the first ecm, which is the aggregate demand for goods relation.

The short-run dynamics of the inflation rate are not clear cut. The short-run impact of the residuals of the cointegration relations confirms the findings of the long-run analysis, namely that inflation is pushed by innovations in the level of aggregate demand for goods, capital flows and excess liquidity. However, Table 6.15 also shows that the growth rates of real money and capital flows have a negative short-run effect on inflation. Consequently, levels and first differences of real money and capital flows have different effects on inflation. The analysis of the short-run behavior of inflation might be distorted due to the high correlation between inflation and real money as well as between inflation and real output (see Table 6.16 and remarks further below). Accordingly, greater weight should be put on the dynamic adjustment associated with the long-run structure because there inference is not affected by residual correlation. In conclusion, rationality requires an interpretation of real money and capital flows as having a positive effect on inflation. Furthermore, inflation reacts positively to the bond rate. The latter is an indication of the cost-push effect of higher financing costs or higher expected inflation (Juselius and MacDonald 2004, p. 23).

The fed funds rate is influenced by real output and the bond rate and react towards the third cointegration relation, which is the homogeneous interest rate-inflation relation. In addition, the residuals of the first and second cointegration relation push

Table 6.16 US quarterly data: correlation of structural residuals (standard deviations on diagonal)

	Δm_r	Δs_r	Δy_r	$\Delta^2 p$	Δff	$\Delta b10$	Δcf
Δm_r	*0.009*						
Δs_r	0.16	*0.075*					
Δy_r	0.31	0.34	*0.005*				
$\Delta^2 p$	**−0.56**	−0.28	**−0.59**	*0.003*			
Δff	−0.10	0.03	0.19	−0.08	*0.002*		
$\Delta b10$	−0.33	−0.14	−0.07	0.23	0.34	*0.001*	
Δcf	0.32	−0.13	−0.10	−0.09	0.03	−0.08	*0.005*

the overnight rate. Accordingly, the fed funds rate reacts to advances of aggregate demand for goods and inflation, which is in line with expectations from monetary policy following a Taylor rule.

The bond rate only reacts to lagged values of the growth rate of real output. This is in line with the simple valuation model that is often used to assess whether bonds are fairly priced (Becker 2007, p. 9). It assumes that the nominal yield of a risk-free bond should equal the yield of the underlying economy as a whole. To wit, over the long run, government bond yields should be the same as nominal GDP growth rates. Moreover, the bond rate error corrects to the third cointegration relation, which is the bond rate relation. The residuals of the second cointegration relation affect the bond rate positively, which is associated with the expected inflation effect. The negative impact of *ecm*4 indicates that the bond rate drops as a result of excess capital inflows, in line with the recent behavior of treasury bills. Yields on treasury bills have been low as a consequence of the huge investments made by Asian Central Banks in their effort to prevent their currencies from appreciating.[31]

Capital flows only react negatively to themselves and show strong adjustment behavior to the fourth cointegration relation, which is the capital flows relation. This is another clear sign that deviations from the mean are quickly corrected and capital flow behavior can not be explained by the other domestic macroeconomic variables.

Table 6.15 shows that most of the autoregressive coefficients are insignificant and, thus, restricted to zero. The bulk of explanatory power in the short run is based on the inclusion of the ecms. The coefficients of the ecms are mostly highly significant, indicating the potential loss of information if the VAR model had only been estimated in first differences.

One downside of the above equations is that current effects are not modeled. Instead they are left in the residuals. However, simultaneous effects have potential importance. Whereas correlation between the residuals is not problematic for the long-run relations of the previous section, identification of the short-run structural equations requires uncorrelated residuals (Juselius 2006, p. 229). Table 6.16 shows the residual covariance matrix, in which large off-diagonal elements can be an indication of significant current effects between the system variables. The high values between real money and inflation and between real output and inflation must be critically recognized. High residual correlation can result from the aggregation of the data over time, inadequately modeled expectations or omitted variables (Juselius 2006, pp. 239–240).

---

[31] This, however, is not the only explanation for low long-term yields. Over the last decade demand for long-term securities has also been strong due to the increase in pension commitments and the growing weight of institutional investors, such as insurance and pension funds, which tend to favor long-term securities (Bini Smaghi 2007, p. 9). This was further exacerbated by the efforts of some European countries to reduce debt growth levels and, especially, the widespread use of international financial reporting standards by English and American pension funds, which has inspired them to improve their maturity mismatch risk and better back their liabilities with long-term assets.

One way to reduce residual correlation is to introduce current effects between the variables into the short-run structure. Unfortunately, for the US analysis, current effects between the variables do not reduce the high correlation coefficients. This does not render the above results useless. However, the inability to fully explore the short-run dynamics based on the available dataset must be acknowledged and more attention should be paid to the information included in the α-coefficients of the previous section.[32]

6.2.4 The Long-Run Impact of the Common Trends

The C-matrix provides the key to understanding the long-run implications of the model. It contains information on the overall effects of the stochastic driving forces in the system. The Fed can only influence the stock market in the long run if a shock to a monetary instrument has a significant impact on the stock market. Hence, when evaluating the effectiveness of monetary policy the long-run impact of shocks to money stock and the short-term interest rate (i.e., the fed funds rate) on the stock market is of particular interest. An alternative method of influencing stock markets is using monetary instruments to control an intermediate target, such as the (real) long-term bond rate, if the intermediate target has a long-run impact on stocks. However, for this to be manageable, cointegration between the policy instrument and the intermediate target is a necessity.

The residual $\epsilon_{i,t}$ is interpreted as an estimate of the unanticipated shock to variable x_i. The estimated long-run impact of these cumulated shocks is reported in Table 6.17 and is calculated from the estimates of the restricted VAR model as

$$C = \tilde{\beta}_\perp \alpha'_\perp \tag{6.17}$$

where $\tilde{\beta}_\perp = \beta_\perp(\alpha'_\perp \beta_\perp)^{-1}$ and $\alpha_\perp, \beta_\perp$ are the $(p \times p - r)$ orthogonal compliments of α and β (Johansen 1995, pp. 49–50). Since C has reduced rank, only $p - r = 3$ linear combinations of the $p = 7$ innovations, ϵ_t, have permanent effects.

The C-matrix can be read column or row-wise. The columns show the long-run impact of a shock to a variable on each of the variables in the system and the rows show which of the shocks have a long-run impact on the particular variable.

---

[32] The only way to eliminate residual correlation would be to apply the Cholesky decomposition of the covariance matrix. The result is that A_0 (see (5.10) in Sect. 5.1.2) is an upper triangular matrix. This leads to uncorrelated errors by construction (Juselius 2006, pp. 240–242). However, to achieve this, the triangular system must be based on a specific ordering of the variables. Hence, causality between the variables is assumed but not tested and different assumptions often lead to different results (Abdullah and Hayworth 1993, p. 55). Since the objective of this contribution is to determine causality empirically and not to set causality from the outset, this approach will not be followed here.

Table 6.17 US quarterly data: the long-run impact matrix (t-values in brackets)

The long-run impact matrix, C							
	$\hat{\epsilon}_{m_r}$	$\hat{\epsilon}_{s_r}$	$\hat{\epsilon}_{y_r}$	$\hat{\epsilon}_{\Delta p}$	$\hat{\epsilon}_{ff}$	$\hat{\epsilon}_{b10}$	$\hat{\epsilon}_{cf}$
m_r	**2.681** [4.060]	−0.036 [−0.585]	0.705 [0.486]	1.195 [0.836]	5.109 [1.717]	1.735 [0.563]	−0.717 [−0.696]
s_r	0.533 [0.210]	**1.216** [5.119]	−7.149 [−1.278]	0.684 [0.124]	−6.821 [−0.595]	20.39 [1.718]	3.875 [0.978]
y_r	**0.343** [3.453]	**0.028** [3.047]	−0.106 [−0.484]	0.165 [0.767]	0.443 [0.990]	0.761 [1.641]	0.016 [0.106]
Δp	**0.027** [3.951]	−0.001 [−1.165]	0.009 [0.623]	0.012 [0.804]	0.053 [1.750]	0.011 [0.353]	−0.008 [−0.795]
ff	−0.029 [−0.417]	0.011 [1.683]	0.295 [1.897]	0.210 [1.371]	**0.660** [2.071]	**0.704** [2.135]	−0.108 [−0.983]
$b10$	−0.010 [−0.214]	0.007 [1.616]	0.196 [1.921]	0.141 [1.406]	**0.449** [2.151]	**0.463** [2.144]	−0.074 [−1.020]
cf	0.000 [*NA*]	0.000 [*NA*]	0.000 [*NA*]	0.000 [*NA*]	0.000 [*NA*]	0.000 [*NA*]	0.000 [*NA*]

The C-matrix in Table 6.17 confirms the exogeneity of real money and real stock market levels.[33] Both variables are only influenced by themselves in the long run. This indicates the procyclical behavior of the money stock due to credit expansion in good economic times and credit constraints during economic downturns. For the stock market, this confirms the herding and trend-following behavior of economic agents. The C-matrix also shows that for the period under investigation, the Fed was unable to influence stock market developments in the long run, which confirms findings of Durham (2003, p. 2).[34]

Aside from that, the C-matrix shows that shocks to both, real money and the stock market, have positive long-run effects on the level of economic activity. The positive reaction of real output to shocks to the stock market confirms previous findings. Based on a multivariate VAR-analysis Lee (1992, p. 1602) finds that shocks to stock returns help to explain a substantial fraction of the variance in real output for postwar monthly data.[35]

---

[33] Real money and the stock market can also be restricted to be weakly exogenous. This restriction is accepted with a p-value of 0.38 ($\chi^2(18) = 19.2$). However, this does not change the implications of the long-run impact matrix (see Table B.5 in Appendix B.1.9). Restrictions of real money, the stock market and real output to be weakly exogenous, as suggested by the preliminary tests, were rejected with a p-value of 0.037 ($\chi^2(22) = 35.2$).

[34] Bernanke and Kuttner (2005, p. 1223) point out, however, that financial markets are forward looking, in the sense that asset prices reflect expectations of future changes in the discount factor and income streams. As a result, current changes of the fed funds rate might only influence stock markets if the rate change comes as a surprise to markets. Nevertheless, since the C-matrix incorporates cumulated shocks to the fed funds rate, the long-run outcome should not be influenced by the question of whether or not the shock was anticipated. Rigobon and Sack (2004, pp. 1565–1568) identify an asset price response to changes in monetary policy. They analyze the variance of policy shocks that occur on days of FOMC meetings and of the Chairman's semi-annual monetary policy testimony before Congress. Based on their analysis, an increase in the short-term interest rate leads to a decline in stock prices. In addition, Chen (2007, p. 669) finds that contractionary monetary policy in the US depresses stock returns.

[35] See also Dhakal et al. (1993, p. 71) for similar findings.

In addition, shocks to real money translate into higher inflation. This means that the Fed's decision to disregard broad monetary developments and to stop reporting M3 must be seen as a mistake. Another interesting finding is the non-existent long-term impact of the fed funds rate on inflation, which indicates that the Fed was unable to control inflation over the past 25 years. This result is confirmed by cointegration analyses conducted by Moller Christensen and Bohn Nielsen (2003) and Johansen and Juselius (2001). Both analyses utilize monthly data and focus on subsample periods of this contribution. This also indicates that inflation has become a global phenomenon, determined more by global competition than by domestic monetary policy.

Table 6.17 also exhibits the positive long-run impact of the fed funds rate and the bond rate on each other. This confirms the importance of the term structure of interest rates. However, all four positive coefficients are only borderline accepted.

6.2.5 Conclusion

The introduction stated that confidence and optimism of market participants are important factors for the development of stock prices. In addition, one objective of this contribution is to test whether or not abundant liquidity amplifies the upward and downward spirals of stock prices. Whereas, with regard to the first statement, the self-reinforcing and trend-following behavior of stock markets is apparent from the data, the latter hypothesis does not hold for the US and the timeframe under consideration. The analysis of the variables in levels and in first differences shows that the stock market behaves strongly exogenous and is not influenced by any of the other variables, neither in the long run nor in the short run. One potential explanation, which is not tested herein, for the non-existent link between money and stocks is that excess liquidity has not been invested in stocks but in housing, leading to a real estate boom at the beginning of the 1990s and culminating in the biggest housing boom in American history in the first years of the new millennium. The analysis by Greiber and Setzer (2007, pp. 15–17), which focuses on the US as well as analyses focusing on global conditions by Belke et al. (2008, pp. 416–420) and Giese and Tuxen (2007, pp. 22–24), support this point.

Table 6.18 shows that the results of the econometric analysis do not confirm the main hypotheses. Instead, the strong exogeneity of real stock market levels rules out any influence of monetary factors on stock markets. However, the stock market forms a stable long-run relationship with real money and real output. Hence, the three variables are pushed by a common stochastic trend, which could be interpreted as the self-reinforcing behavior of market agents. This confirms the interplay of optimism and confidence on stock markets and the procyclicality of credit markets, which exacerbate business cycles. Nevertheless, neither real money nor the stock market react to this relationship, which was the expectation underlying the original hypotheses. Analysis of the short-run adjustment behavior towards this long-run cointegrating relation shows that goods demand reacts positively to stock market

Table 6.18 US quarterly data: results of main hypotheses

	Hypotheses/Questions	Result
H_1	US stock market behavior shows strong persistence, i.e., shocks to the stock market have positive long-run effects on future developments	Yes
H_2	Long-run equilibria exist between stock prices and liquidity conditions	(Yes)
H_3	Liquidity conditions influence stock prices positively in the long run	No
H_4	Liquidity conditions influence stock prices positively in the short run	No
H_5	International capital flows have a positive long-run impact on the stock market behavior in the US	No
H_6	International capital flows have a positive short-run impact on the stock market behavior in the US	No
Q_1	Is the Fed able to influence stock prices in the long run?	No
Q_2	Is the Fed able to influence stock prices in the short run?	No

and real money developments, but not the other way round. When regarded from this angle, the Fed's efforts to revive the economy after the recent crises were successful.

Nevertheless, by rapidly lowering short-term interest rates in connection with a strong increase in money supply, the Fed is playing a dangerous game; because, in the end, the accumulated excess liquidity needs to go somewhere. First, the analysis of the long-run impact matrix showed that shocks to real money translate into higher inflation in the long run. Second, other asset prices, such as housing or commodities have not been included in the analysis. Although not researched here, these asset classes might have been recipients of the additional money. This, in turn, also puts pressure on the inflation rate in the long run and increases the chances of severe price distortions and with it the susceptibility to crises.

In addition, the above results also put our current understanding of the monetary transmission mechanism into question. The asset price channel, the balance sheet channel and the liquidity effects view are all theories that are based on the connection between monetary policy and equity markets. If this causality is non-existent, the first link in the transmission mechanism is broken and, consequently, the theory does not hold. On the other hand, the second part of the transmission mechanism, the link between equity prices and economic activity, was confirmed by the empirical analyses.

The above analysis also sheds light on a few other aspects of economic interest, mainly as follows:

- Real money is weakly exogenous in the long run but shocks to real money have a positive long-run impact on itself, which demonstrates the procyclicality of credit supply. In addition, the short-run analysis shows that real money is positively influenced by itself and the short-term interest rate and reacts negatively to stock market advances. This indicates that money demand decreases with higher stock prices (substitution effect) and increases with the short-term interest rate, which can be regarded as a proxy for income on money holdings (reduced opportunity costs of holding money).
- Real aggregate demand for goods is pushed by real money and real stock market developments in the long run and shows adjusting behavior to the same variables

in the short run. This shows two things: first, expansive real money growth has a positive long-term effect on real activity. This confirms the end result of monetary transmission mechanism theory. Second, stock market increases have a positive impact on real activity.[36] This confirms that certain links in monetary transmission theory hold. In addition, lagged values of real output have a significant positive short-run effect on real output.

- The analysis illustrates that inflation is influenced by developments in the amount of money. Inflation reacts positively to excess liquidity (measured by money growth in excess of transactions growth) and forms a stable steady-state relation with excess liquidity in the long run. Further, the cumulated shocks to real money have a positive long-run impact on inflation. In addition, positive deviations from the goods demand relation and capital flows have a positive and significant effect on inflation. The positive reaction of the inflation rate can be interpreted in the framework of the short-run Phillips curve, where inflation increases with excess aggregate demand for goods. These findings indicate that inflation is mainly, but not exclusively, a monetary phenomenon and that it is a mistake to ignore developments in monetary aggregates.[37] The Fed abandoned reporting M3 because of the belief that factors outside the scope of monetary policy influence this broad monetary aggregate. It seems that it would make more sense to try to understand M3 better and to identify ways of influencing M3. The empirical findings also show that liquidity spillovers from other countries can play an important role for domestic inflation. Policy makers should, therefore, take global liquidity conditions into account. This finding should also be a warning of future US inflation and with it global inflation. Even though inflation rates are currently suppressed due to the global economic downturn associated with the global financial crisis, one can expect inflation to rise above desired levels in the years to come. This means that the Fed has to start collecting the previously injected money as soon as possible to avoid permanent inflationary pressures.
- The fed funds rate reacts positively to output growth and the bond rate in the long and short run. This suggests that the Fed's focus is on the business cycle and it pays more attention to expected inflation (included in the bond rate) as compared to actual inflation (The fed funds rate is, in point of fact, negatively related to actual inflation). However, the fed funds rate does not affect the inflation rate. As such, the low and stable inflation environment of the last 25 years was probably more a result of global economic forces than of central bank policy. The fed funds rate only has a long-run impact on the bond rate, confirming the expectations

[36] This finding confirms previous analyses by Estrella and Mishkin (1995, pp. 11–13), Dhakal et al. (1993, p. 71) and Lee (1992, p. 1602). As a result, the relationship between the stock market and real activity as suggested by Fama (1981, p. 563), holds.

[37] This does not mean that it is necessarily useful to reinstate a monetary growth objective since no stable money demand relation could be found for the US. It does say, however, that the attention US central bankers currently pay to monetary aggregates is too limited. For a historical perspective and the limited current role of monetary aggregates in US monetary policy, see Bernanke (2006, p. 3).

hypothesis of the term structure of interest rates. In addition, the long-run impact matrix shows that the reaction of the Fed towards the stock market is insignificant. This is in line with previous findings, for example, by Dupor and Conley (2004, pp. 26–27) but contrary to results from Laopodis (2006, p. 540).

- The bond rate shows dynamic adjustment behavior towards inflation and the fed funds rate, reflecting expected inflation and term structure effects. In addition, real output has a significant positive short-run effect on the bond rate, which shows the importance of economic growth for long-term yields. Capital flows on the other hand, have a negative impact on the long-term interest rate, which indicates that bond rates drop as a result of excess capital inflows, in line with the recent behavior of treasury bills. One argument for this is that yields on treasury bills have been low as a consequence of the huge investments made by Asian Central Banks in their effort to prevent their currencies from appreciating (see also Sect. 4.6.1).
- The time series for capital flows is identified as stationary on its own. As such, it is not subject to a common trend and shocks to the other variables can not have a permanent impact on capital flows. The analysis of the short-run shows that capital flows do not react to any of the other macro variables. In addition, they do not affect the stock market. They are, however, important for the short-run behavior of the inflation rate and the bond rate.

To understand whether the above findings are country-specific or represent a universal phenomenon, the above analyses are also conducted for other regions. The next section focuses on the relatively new economy of euro area countries, combined under a common central bank, the ECB.

6.3 Euro Area: Monthly Data

6.3.1 Model Specification

6.3.1.1 Data Overview, Deterministic Components and Lag Length

As outlined in Sect. 5.2.1, the data vector for the euro area analysis consists of the following variables:

$$x_t' = [m_r, s_r, y_r, \Delta p, or, b10, cf]_t \,, \qquad (6.18)$$

where m_r is the log of real money (M3), s_r is the log of the real stock market level (top 600 listed companies in the euro area, including dividends) and y_r is the log of real industrial production (IP). Real variables are transformed from nominal variables using the consumer price index, p. Hence, Δp is the inflation rate.[38] Interest rates are represented by the overnight interbank rate, or, and the 10-year government bond yield, $b10$.[39] All interest rates have been converted to monthly rates and divided by 100 to achieve comparability with the inflation rate. Transactions in the external counterpart of M3 (as provided by the ECB), cf, represent the proxy for international capital flows and enter the analysis as a percentage share of the total money stock, i.e., M3.[40] All time series are obtained from Datastream. Detailed information on the sources of the data can be found in Appendix B.2.1.

The data used for the analysis starts with the launch of stage three of the European Economic and Monetary Union (EMU) on January 1, 1999 and consists of monthly observations from 1999:1 to 2008:9, thus, the complete era of the common European currency up to now.[41] With the introduction of the irrevocably-fixed euro exchange rates on December 31, 1998, eleven countries of the European Union entered a new monetary union. Since then, monetary policy for these countries is set by the ECB. Figure 6.4 displays the time pattern of all variables in levels and first differences. Aside from the graphs for inflation and capital flows, the data series in levels do not look stationary. The differenced series, however, look very stationary for all variables. In addition, real money and real income appear to be trending. Thus, an unrestricted constant and a restricted trend are included in the model.[42] The graph depicting capital flows in Fig. 6.4 shows that, at the beginning of the sample period, capital outflows dominated due to the new-economy boom in the US. Starting in 2001 inflows were bigger than outflows for a few years, reflecting the often

[38] The time series for industrial production is compiled as a 'fixed base year Laspeyres type volume-index' and, thus, only available in real terms and not additionally transformed.

[39] The overnight market interest rate is represented by the Euro OverNight Index Average (EONIA). It is an effective overnight rate computed as a weighted average of all overnight uncollateralized lending transactions in the interbank market. The bond rate is an average of national long-term government bond yields according to the Maastricht definition.

[40] Since capital flows are positive and negative they cannot enter the analysis in log linear form.

[41] For monthly observations, 10 years of data should be sufficient. An alternative would be to use synthetic data, constructing aggregates of the individual member countries. This, however, has many shortcomings, especially methodological and comparability aspects, which reflect the "fundamental problem that it is only from 1999 onwards that a single currency has been in place" (ECB 1999a, p. 36). See, e.g., Bruggeman et al. (2003, pp. 10–12) for aggregation issues and Angelini and Marcellino (2007, pp. 18–23) for different outcomes of econometric analyses dependent on the method of backdating time series. Brüggemann and Lütkepohl (2006, p. 684) point out that additional aggregation problems arise from the Maastricht criteria. The resulting adjustment and convergence processes might be associated with changes in economic systems, which hinder the construction of valid time series data for the pre-euro period. According to Beyer et al. (2001, p. F.102) another problem arises if the underlying variables contain unit roots and structural breaks, which is the case here because the variables are in levels. Belke and Polleit (2007, pp. 2197–2198) add that structural stability in the transition period of shifting power from national central banks to the ECB is highly questionable. In addition, from a monetary policy perspective it is highly unlikely that national central banks followed a consistent strategy (on average), which is comparable to the strategy of the ECB. For an overview of the advocates of the validity of synthetic data, see the literature overview in Girardi and Paesani (2004, p. 1).

[42] For a discussion of deterministic components in the model, see Sect. 6.2.1.1.

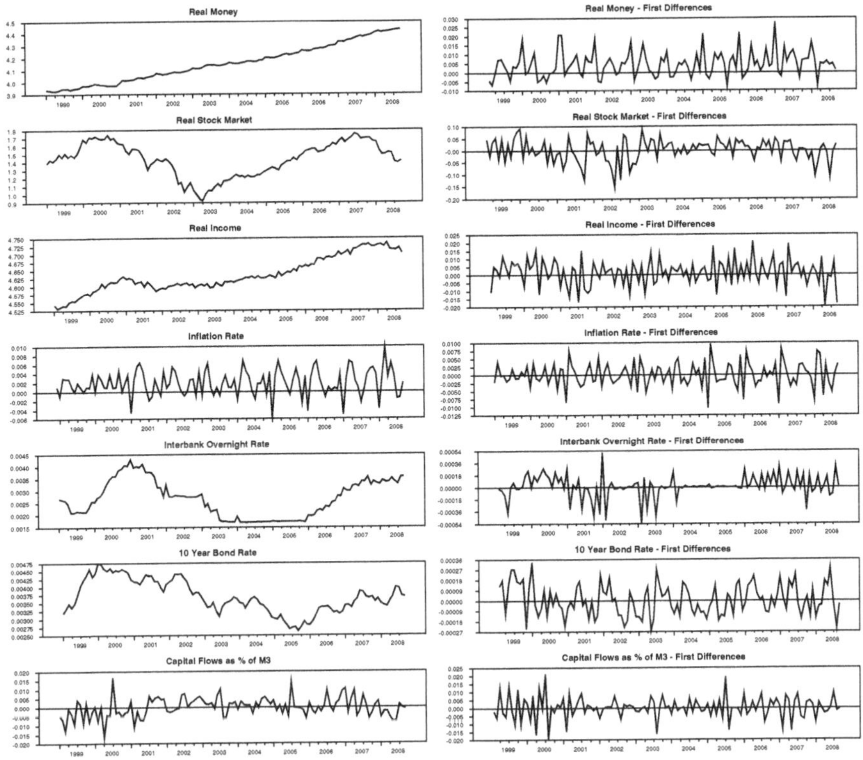

Fig. 6.4 Euro area monthly data in levels and first differences

mentioned 'flight to safety' after the burst of the dot com bubble (ECB 2008b, p. 74; Deutsche Bundesbank 2007, p. 17; ECB 2005b, pp. 20–22; ECB 2005c, pp. 18–21).

Dummy Variables

Misspecification testing shows that normality is rejected.[43] To ensure normality and rule out correlation and ARCH effects, dummy variables are included. They are based on the economic calendar and the graphs of the standardized residuals, which have revealed some large outliers. Table 6.19 provides an overview.

The analysis of the euro area monthly data requires three permanent blip dummies in the form of $[0, \ldots, 0, 1, 0, \ldots, 0]$.[44]

[43] The test is not reported here at this stage. Instead, misspecification tests are reported for the specified model in Sect. 6.3.1.2.

[44] For the different forms of intervention dummies, see Sect. 6.2.1.1.

Table 6.19 Euro area monthly data: intervention dummies

Dummy variable	Motivation	Impact on
$dum0004_p$	Peak of the dot-com bubble	Capital Flows
$dum0102_p$	Narrowing interest rate spread between euro area and US[a]	Real money
$dum0201_p$	Introduction of Euro banknotes and coins[b]	Overnight rate

[a] Walter (2003, p. 83) mentions the reverse of the euro carry trade and the downturn of the global economy as reasons for high capital inflows and their effect on broad real money.
[b] The cash change-over in January 2002 led to turbulence on the money market at the end of 2001 and during 2002 (Nautz 2008, pp. 30–31).

Table 6.20 Euro area monthly data: information to determine lag length

Model	k	T	Regressive	Log-Likelihood	SC	H–Q	LM(1)	LM(k)
VAR(5)	5	112	51	5220.36	−78.18	−83.33	0.37	0.44
VAR(4)	4	112	44	5165.28	−79.26	−83.70	0.06	0.34
VAR(3)	3	112	37	5109.32	−80.33	−84.06	0.07	0.52
VAR(2)	2	112	30	5070.46	−81.70	−84.73	**0.39**	**0.35**
VAR(1)	1	112	23	5005.55	**−82.60**	**−84.92**	0.00	0.00

Determination of the Lag Length

The two information criteria SC and H–Q are reported in Table 6.20 and are calculated for different values of lag length, k, where the smallest result suggests the ideal lag length.[45] The last two columns in Table 6.20 report the LM test for autocorrelation of order 1 and k. Numbers in bold indicate the suggested lag length of the respective test.
Whereas both the SC and the H–Q criterion suggest only one lag, the LM test shows that the hypothesis of no residual autocorrelation can not be accepted with only one lag. Thus, a lag length of $k = 2$ is more appropriate for a valid inference of the statistical model.

The discussion in this section on lag length, deterministic components and dummy variables results in the following VAR(2) model (in error-correction form) for euro area monthly data:

$$\Delta x_t = \alpha \tilde{\beta}' \tilde{x}_{t-1} + \Gamma_1 \Delta x_{t-1} + \Phi D_t + \mu_0 + \epsilon_t, \tag{6.19}$$

where $x_t' = [m_r, s_r, y_r, \Delta p, or, b10, cf]_t$ and $\tilde{x}_t = \left[x_t', 1, trend\right]$ is a $((7+2) \times 1)$ data vector containing the p variables, a constant and a trend. The cointegration vectors are represented by $\tilde{\beta} = \left[\beta', \rho_0, \rho_1\right]'$, which is a $((7+2) \times r)$ matrix with rank r. The dummy variables are contained in the vector $D_t = \left[dum0004_p,\ dum0102_p,\ dum0201_p\right]$. The discussion is based on 7×115 observations and conditions on the initial values (data points for 1999:1 to 1999:2).

[45] For additional information, see Sect. 6.2.1.1.

Table 6.21 Euro area monthly data: multivariate misspecification tests (p-values in brackets)

Test for no autocorrelation			
LM(1):	$\chi^2(49)$	=	52.965 [0.324]
LM(2):	$\chi^2(49)$	=	54.085 [0.286]
LM(3):	$\chi^2(49)$	=	51.468 [0.377]
LM(4):	$\chi^2(49)$	=	58.236 [0.172]
Test for normality	$\chi^2(14)$	=	14.457 [0.416]
Test for no ARCH effects			
LM(1):	$\chi^2(784)$	=	839.804 [0.082]
LM(2):	$\chi^2(1568)$	=	1606.582 [0.243]
LM(3):	$\chi^2(2352)$	=	2435.278 [0.113]
LM(4):	$\chi^2(3136)$	=	3220.000 [0.145]

Table 6.22 Euro area monthly data: univariate misspecification tests (p-values in brackets)

	ARCH(2)	Normality	Skewness	Kurtosis
Δm_r	2.318 [0.314]	0.072 [0.965]	0.057	2.826
Δs_r	0.597 [0.742]	2.417 [0.299]	−0.340	3.173
Δy_r	2.315 [0.314]	0.481 [0.786]	−0.087	3.042
$\Delta^2 p$	0.318 [0.853]	0.116 [0.944]	0.074	2.820
Δor	1.041 [0.594]	3.253 [0.197]	−0.266	3.539
$\Delta b10$	1.850 [0.396]	1.300 [0.522]	−0.110	3.245
Δcf	0.223 [0.894]	2.560 [0.278]	0.332	2.860

6.3.1.2 Misspecification Tests

This section shows test results for the specification of the model. The model has to be well specified to guarantee valid statistical inference. Tables 6.21 and 6.22 report multivariate and univariate misspecification tests, respectively. The multivariate LM test shows no sign of autocorrelation in the first 4 lags (the null of the test is 'no autocorrelation').

The multivariate and univariate normality tests, which are based on skewness and kurtosis, show that the null of the tests, normally distributed errors, is accepted. Additionally, tests for multivariate ARCH effects of order q (with $q = 1, \ldots, 4$) and univariate second order ARCH effects are reported. Again, the multivariate and univariate test statistics show no signs of ARCH. Since all test statistics are accepted, the model describes the data well.

6.3.1.3 Rank Determination

As outlined in Sect. 6.2.1.3 the following five test procedures are analyzed to determine the number of cointegrating relations, which is equal to the cointegration rank of the system.

- Trace test (formal LR test).
- Modulus of the roots of the companion matrix.
- Significance of the α-coefficients.
- Graphical inspection of the recursively calculated trace test statistics.
- Graphical inspection of the stationarity of the cointegration relations.

Trace Test

Table 6.23 shows the results of the trace test. It reports the estimated eigenvalues, λ_i, the trace test, Q_r, the small sample Bartlett corrected trace test (Johansen 2002, pp. 1932–1940), Q_r^{Bart}, and the 95% quintile from the asymptotic distribution corrected for deterministic components, $C_r^{95\%}$. In addition, the table reports the p-value of the test statistic and the p-value of the Bartlett small sample corrections, p-value*, respectively. In this case, the effective sample is based on 115 observations. Hence, the Bartlett small sample corrections are not needed, but are reported for informational purposes.[46]

Whereas the trace test excepts the null of $p-r = 2$ unit roots and, therefore, $r = 5$, the Bartlett small sample trace test borderline accepts the null of $p - r = 4$ unit roots and, therefore, $r = 3$.

[46] Equation (5.6) in Sect. 5.1.2 shows that, as a prerequisite for valid statistical inference, the variables can be integrated of first but not of higher order. Hence, it is important to ensure that no $I(2)$ variables are part of the data set. As outlined in Sect. 6.2.1.3 different criteria exist to analyze if $I(2)$-ness persists. Applying these criteria to euro area data shows that no $I(2)$-trends exist in the data. Because univariate unit root tests are used in most analyses, they are conducted as well, in spite of their many limitations in the multivariate setting. The ADF test and the PP test fail to reject the null hypothesis of the existence of a unit root at the 5% level for all variables in levels aside from the time series representing inflation and capital flows. In contrast, both tests reject the null hypothesis for the variables in first-differenced form of the series. Consequently, the variables are at most integrated of order one. The appropriate lags for the ADF test are selected based on the Schwartz Criterion and the Akaike Information Criterion. The truncation point for the Newey–West adjustment, required for calculating the PP statistic, is determined by using the smallest integer greater than or equal to the sample size, T, to the power of $\frac{1}{4}$ (Greene 2003, p. 267). The test results are not reported here because of the questionable usefulness of univariate tests in a multivariate setting. Rao (2007, p. 1624) points out that these tests lack power and combinations of the many options of the tests almost always enable one to prove that the variables are I(1) in levels. Additionally, Muscatelli and Spinelli (2000, p. 724) refer to difficulties in using unit root tests as pre-tests if regime shifts are inherent to the model. For these and other reasons, Juselius (2006, p. 136) does not even discuss univariate unit root testing in her textbook on cointegration analysis. Instead, the stationarity of a variable is easily tested inside the multivariate model as a restriction on β (see Table 6.28 in Sect. 6.3.2.2). The advantage of the multivariate analysis is to define a well-specified model first and then test for stationarity. With univariate unit root tests, stationarity is tested before guaranteeing i.i.d. error terms, constant parameters and the absence of ARCH effects and before determining cointegration rank. The results of the ADF and PP tests are available on request.

Table 6.23 Euro area monthly data: trace test of cointegration rank

$p-r$	r	λ_i	Q_r	Q_r^{Bart}	$C_r^{95\%}$	p-value	p-value*
7	0	0.540	281.171	257.225	150.348	0	0
6	1	0.423	191.993	174.322	117.451	0	0
5	2	0.359	128.669	116.356	88.554	0	0
4	3	0.241	77.453	63.404	63.659	0.002	**0.053**
3	4	0.195	45.688	39.695	42.770	0.024	0.101
2	5	0.121	20.734	18.377	25.731	**0.194**	0.326
1	6	0.050	5.936	4.945	12.448	0.479	0.611

Table 6.24 Euro area monthly data: modulus of the seven largest eigenvalue roots

$r=7$	$r=6$	$r=5$	$r=4$	$r=3$	$r=2$	$r=1$
0.960	1	1	1	1	1	1
0.960	**0.965**	1	1	1	1	1
0.954	0.965	**0.937**	1	1	1	1
0.942	0.871	0.937	**0.927**	1	1	1
0.686	0.695	0.705	0.927	**0.884**	1	1
0.686	0.695	0.705	0.487	0.488	**0.581**	1
0.486	0.483	0.481	0.487	0.488	0.474	**0.547**

Roots of the Companion Matrix

The modulus of the roots of the companion form matrix in Table 6.24 show that for $r = 5, 4, 3$ the modulus of the largest unrestricted root only drops to 0.94, 0.93 and 0.88, all still fairly close to 1.[47] Thus, it is hard to discriminate cointegration rank based on this information. However, as 0.88 is below 0.90 (the critical value for monthly data), Table 6.24 indicates a rank of $r = 3$.

Significance of Adjustment Coefficients α

The t-values of the α-coefficients are presented in Table 6.25 and give an indication of the significance of the equilibrium adjustment of the relative variables. They are derived from the unrestricted estimates and can be used to identify the cointegration rank. Table 6.25 substantiates that several variables show adjusting behavior up to the fifth relation.[48] Therefore, the investigation of the adjustment coefficients' significance points to a rank of $r = 5$.

[47] However, the discussion of the roots is only indicative because they are reported without confidence bands.

[48] As a rule of thumb the t-values should be close to 3.0 for the relation to still qualify as adjusting because the t-values of a given relation are no longer Student's t distributed if the relation is non-stationary. Instead, it is better to compare the t-values to the Dickey–Fuller distribution, where the critical values are larger.

Table 6.25 Euro area monthly data: t-values of the α-coefficients

	α						
	Alpha(1)	Alpha(2)	Alpha(3)	Alpha(4)	Alpha(5)	Alpha(6)	Alpha(7)
Δm_r	(−1.541)	(−1.498)	(−1.038)	(−1.802)	(−1.145)	(−1.534)	(−1.996)
Δs_r	(−1.800)	(−2.361)	(−0.679)	**(−2.578)**	(−2.012)	(−1.861)	(−1.474)
Δy_r	(−0.357)	(−1.076)	(−0.185)	**(−4.010)**	**(−3.748)**	(−0.542)	(−0.371)
$\Delta^2 p$	**(−6.209)**	(−0.622)	**(−5.186)**	(−0.106)	(−1.749)	(−0.103)	(−1.052)
Δor	**(−8.330)**	(−1.209)	**(−5.336)**	(−0.601)	(−0.365)	(−0.272)	(−0.206)
$\Delta b10$	(−1.343)	**(−2.888)**	(−0.426)	(−1.888)	**(−3.147)**	**(−2.607)**	(−0.104)
Δcf	(−1.522)	**(−7.260)**	(−1.483)	(−1.284)	(−0.448)	(−1.349)	(−0.978)

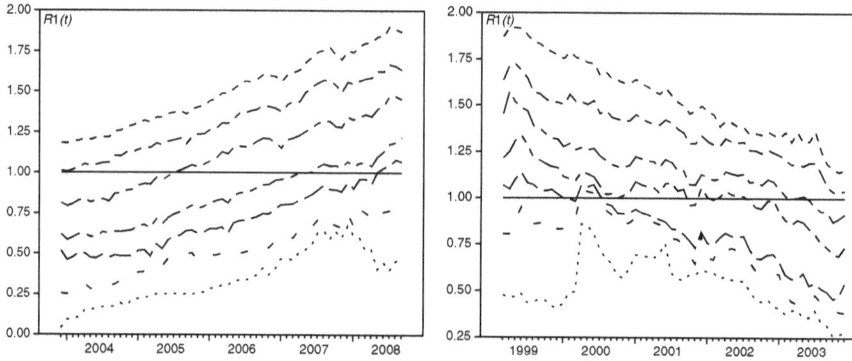

Fig. 6.5 Euro area monthly data: recursively calculated trace test statistics (forward, base sample 1999:03 to 2003:12, depicted left; backward, base sample 2008:09 to 2003:12, depicted right)

The Recursive Graphs of the Trace Statistic

Figure 6.5 shows the forward and backward recursively calculated graphs for the trace statistic.

If $\lambda_i \neq 0$, the recursively calculated components of the trace statistic should grow linearly for $i = 1, \ldots, r$, but stay constant for $i = r + 1, \ldots, p$ (Juselius 2006, p. 142). Since five of the graphs show linear growth and are above or cross the 1-line (5% critical value), this also indicates a rank of $r = 5$. Since there are no major dents in the graphs, it seems that the time frame of the analysis exhibited a constant parameter regime and, hence, no shift dummies need to be included.

Graphical Analysis of the Cointegration Relations

Finally, Appendix B.2.2 graphs the cointegrating relations of the unrestricted model. The graphs of the sixth and seventh relation clearly show persistent behavior and do not strongly suggest stationarity. However, for the fourth and fifth cointegration relations the picture is not painted as clearly. They still appear rather stationary, albeit with some persistence, especially in the fourth relation.

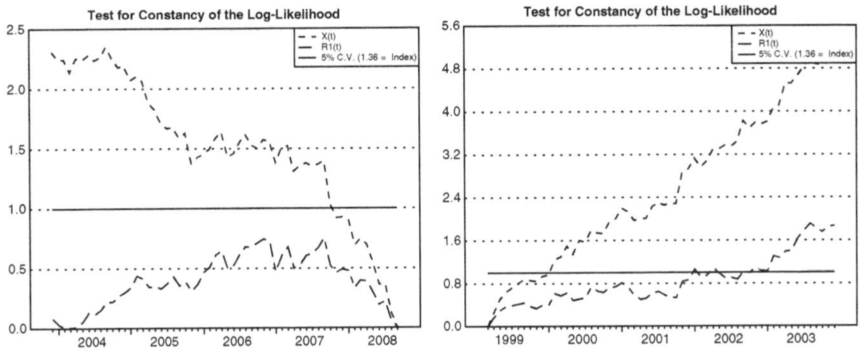

Fig. 6.6 Euro area monthly data: recursively calculated test of log-likelihood (forward, base sample 1999:03 to 2003:12, depicted left; backward, base sample 2008:09 to 2003:12, depicted right)

To conclude, the various information criteria used to determine the rank of the model support different possibilities. However, because the formal trace test, the graphical inspection of the trace test, the α-coefficients and, to a certain extent, the graphs of the cointegration relations all suggest a rank of $r = 5$ and only the roots of the companion matrix indicate otherwise, a rank of $r = 5$ is chosen for the analysis. This also means that $p - r = 2$ common trends exist. This is also valid from an economic point of view as it is reasonable for a real and a monetary trend to exist. In addition, recursive tests of the parameters with rank $r = 5$ imposed, show that the data describes a constant parameter regime. Figure 6.6 depicts the recursively calculated log-likelihood. For both the forward and the recursive test, the graph with short-run effects concentrated out, (R1(t)), stays under or drops below the line early on. The line represents the 5% critical value. Thus, constancy of the overall model is accepted. Appendix B.2.3 provides further information on parameter constancy, such as the eigenvalues λ_i, the eigenvalue fluctuation test, the max test of β constancy and the test of β_t equals a known β. All confirm a constant parameter regime. As a result, the assumption of constant parameters, which is important for valid identification of the long-run structure, is fulfilled.

6.3.2 *Identification of the Long-Run Structure*

6.3.2.1 Assessment of the Unrestricted Π-Matrix

As a starting point of the identification of an empirically acceptable long-run structure, the unrestricted VAR is tentatively interpreted.[49] The unrestricted Π-matrix for

[49] Tentatively, because the cointegration space can be rotated by taking proper linear combinations of the equations. Consequently, the final identified long-run structure does not have to reflect the

Table 6.26 Euro area monthly data: the unrestricted Π-matrix (*t*-values in brackets)

	Π							
	m_r	s_r	y_r	Δp	or	$b10$	cf	*Trend*
Δm_r	−0.011 [−0.657]	−0.000 [−0.067]	0.048 [0.902]	−0.221 [−0.749]	−0.688 [−0.731]	1.090 [1.116]	0.167 [1.741]	0.000 [0.040]
Δs_r	**0.680** [3.507]	−0.006 [−0.181]	**1.285** [2.154]	−4.738 [−1.417]	**−29.88** [−2.804]	**−32.38** [−2.928]	1.316 [1.210]	**−0.005** [−3.215]
Δy_r	−0.025 [−0.829]	**0.026** [5.400]	**−0.322** [−3.462]	0.065 [0.125]	−0.371 [−0.223]	2.207 [1.279]	0.239 [1.410]	**0.001** [2.213]
$\Delta^2 p$	0.012 [1.594]	**−0.003** [−2.156]	**0.054** [2.354]	**−0.991** [−7.716]	−0.436 [−1.065]	−0.488 [−1.148]	−0.033 [−0.786]	−0.000 [−1.956]
Δor	−0.001 [−1.353]	0.000 [0.373]	**0.009** [5.164]	−0.018 [−1.925]	**−0.231** [−7.753]	**0.110** [3.558]	**−0.006** [−2.039]	−0.000 [−1.679]
$\Delta b10$	**0.003** [4.550]	−0.000 [−1.207]	**0.004** [2.334]	0.015 [1.517]	**−0.066** [−2.106]	**−0.143** [−4.420]	0.006 [1.944]	**−0.000** [−4.020]
Δcf	**−0.061** [−3.643]	0.000 [0.062]	−0.093 [−1.805]	−0.386 [−1.334]	1.193 [1.295]	**2.986** [3.123]	**−0.694** [−7.379]	**0.000** [3.049]

the chosen rank $r = 5$ is depicted in Table 6.26. The fact that the signs of all coefficients on the diagonal are negative shows that all variables exhibit error-correction behavior. However, for both real money and the stock market, the effect is not significant. As none of the coefficients in the real money equation are significant, this in itself indicates the weakly exogenous behavior of this variable.

The equation for real stock market levels is positively related to real money and real output and negatively to the two interest rates; this represents standard textbook behavior. The equation for output shows that it is positively related to the stock market, indicating positive wealth effects for the economy. Inflation is negatively related to the stock market and positively related to real output. The overnight rate is positively related to real output and the bond rate and negatively related to capital flows. The long-term interest rate is positively related to real money and real output, but negatively related to the overnight rate, which is surprising as they are assumed to move together. Finally, the last equation shows that international capital flows are positively related to the bond rate and negatively to real money.
Table B.7 in Appendix B.2.4 shows the α- and β'-matrices of the unrestricted Π-matrix. The α-coefficients can indicate which variables are strongly adjusting to long-run equilibria and which variables are more on the pushing side. The estimated α-matrix shows that all variables, except real money, exhibit error-correcting behavior (significant t-values). Another sign that real money might be weakly exogenous.

The following section outlines preliminary tests for purposes of assessment structure and to provide additional information.

initial suggestions from the unrestricted system. Also, the unrestricted Π-matrix may not be economically interpretable. Nevertheless, a rough overview of the long-run information in the data can be used for further identification.

Table 6.27 Euro area monthly data: test of variable exclusion (p-values in brackets)

			Test of exclusion							
r	DGF	5% C.V.	m_r	s_r	y_r	Δp	ff	$b10$	cf	*Trend*
5	5	11.070	16.844 [0.005]	**10.086** [0.073]	28.445 [0.000]	56.100 [0.000]	37.430 [0.000]	22.703 [0.000]	45.259 [0.000]	21.782 [0.001]

6.3.2.2 Preliminary Hypotheses Testing

This section is divided into preliminary tests for β and α and single cointegration relation tests. Automated tests on β include the possibility to exclude variables from the long-run relations and stationarity of individual variables. The α-matrix is formally analyzed for weak exogeneity and unit vectors. The single cointegration tests are conducted to test for potential long-run equilibria as shown in Sect. 5.2. This will help facilitate the final identification of the long-run structure in the next section.

Table 6.27 provides LR tests for the exclusion of any variable from the cointegration relations.[50] The table shows that the stock market variable is borderline excludable. However, since the stock market is the focus of discussion and the p-value is very low, the stock market variable has not be excluded. Nevertheless, this may indicate that the stock market is pushing the system instead of strongly reacting to it.

Table 6.28 reports the tests for long-run stationarity. As already indicated by the graphical analysis of the time series in levels and first differences, stationarity for the inflation rate and capital flows is accepted with p-values of 0.31 and 0.36, respectively.[51] Therefore, two of the five cointegration relations could be single variable relations with the inflation rate and capital flows reacting to themselves. This also means that the two variables are not part of the other cointegrating relations because $I(0)$ and $I(1)$ variables can not cointegrate with each other. In addition, they are not pushed by the common trends and, therefore, do not react to the cumulated residuals of the other variables in the system. An argument in favor of leaving out the inflation rate and capital flows is that they do not enrich the long-run understanding of the variables. However, it is important to allow the components of a vector process to be integrated of different orders. After all, the variables are chosen for their economic importance, not for their statistical properties.[52] In addition, analyzing $I(0)$ and $I(1)$ variables in the same model enables a focus on long-run relations and short-run influences. The analysis in Sect. 6.3.3 determines how the inflation rate and capital flows influence the stock market in the short run.

[50] If the test is accepted, the variable can be excluded from the cointegration space, thus, a zero restriction can be imposed on the coefficient of the variable in all cointegration relations.

[51] Trend-stationarity is also accepted for both variables.

[52] Adding a stationary variable to the data vector x_t is the equivalent of adding an additional cointegrating vector and, thus, an extra dimension to the cointegrating space (Johansen 1995, p. 74).

Table 6.28 Euro area monthly data: test of variable stationarity (p-values in brackets)

Test of stationarity									
r	DGF	5% C.V.	m_r	s_r	y_r	Δp	ff	$b10$	cf
5	3	7.815	17.434 [0.001]	12.502 [0.006]	13.910 [0.003]	**3.594** [0.309]	13.187 [0.004]	19.115 [0.000]	**3.204** [0.361]
Restricted trend included in the cointegrating relation(s)									
5	2	5.991	15.044 [0.001]	9.990 [0.007]	9.349 [0.009]	**0.435** [0.805]	9.688 [0.008]	7.757 [0.021]	**2.564** [0.277]

Table 6.29 Euro area monthly data: test of weak exogeneity (p-values in brackets)

Test of weak exogeneity									
r	DGF	5% C.V.	m_r	s_r	y_r	Δp	ff	$b10$	cf
5	5	11.070	**7.690** [0.174]	12.962 [0.024]	13.779 [0.017]	46.336 [0.000]	57.437 [0.000]	12.359 [0.030]	38.417 [0.000]

Table 6.30 Euro area monthly data: test for a unit vector in the α-matrix (p-values in brackets)

Test of unit vector in alpha									
r	DGF	5% C.V.	m_r	s_r	y_r	Δp	ff	$b10$	cf
5	2.000	5.991	10.441 [0.005]	11.416 [0.003]	**0.686** [0.710]	**3.202** [0.202]	**1.649** [0.439]	6.049 [0.049]	**5.260** [0.072]

Table 6.29 tests for weak exogeneity, which is equivalent to testing a zero row in the α-matrix. It means that a variable is not error-correcting but can be considered weakly exogenous for the long-run parameters β. If the test is accepted, this also means that the sum of the cumulated empirical shocks to the variable in question define one common driving trend. Table 6.29 shows that the test is accepted for real money, which confirms the above mentioned indications.

The test of a unit vector in α tests if a variable is exclusively adjusting. If the unit vector test is accepted, the properties of the relevant variable are that its shocks have only transitory effects on the other variables in the system and it can be regarded as endogenous. Thus, the two tests of α can identify the pulling and pushing forces of the system. Table 6.30 shows that shocks to real output, the inflation rate, the overnight rate and to capital flows only have transitory effects. This is an indication that the ECB did not have a long-run impact on the inflation rate or on the performance of the stock market by influencing the overnight rate. It is also a sign that real money, the stock market and the long-term bond rate are driving the system. The joint test of four unit vectors for output, inflation, the overnight rate and capital flows is borderline accepted with a p-value of 0.124 ($\chi^2(8) = 12.66$).

In addition to the above tests on single variables, the focus of the remaining preliminary tests is on single cointegration relations. The idea is to understand how strongly cointegration is present for the theoretical connections outlined in Sect. 5.2 and summarized in Table 5.1. The hypotheses are of the form:

$$\beta = (H\phi, \psi_1, \psi_2, \psi_3, \psi_4), \qquad (6.20)$$

where H is the design matrix, ϕ contains the restricted parameters and ψ_i is a vector of parameters which are freely estimated. It is important to note that each hypothesis in Table 6.31 tests restrictions on a single vector but leaves the other cointegration vectors unrestricted (Johansen and Juselius 1992, pp. 233–236).

Table 6.31 presents an overview of the single cointegration test results. It follows the structure of Table 5.2. However, since the rank is set to $r = 5$, a minimum of 5 restrictions has to be set to formally test for cointegration. The reason for this is the $\chi^2(v)$-distribution of the single cointegration test with v being the number of degrees of freedom. The degrees of freedom are derived from the decrease in the number of free parameters. They are calculated as $v = no.ofrestr. - rank + 1$. As a result, the number of restrictions has to be a minimum of five to obtain one degree of freedom, and, thus, have testable results. Therefore, only those theoretical relations of Table 5.2 can be formally tested, which restrict at least five of the parameters. In addition, the inflation rate and capital flows can not be part of another cointegration relation or adjust to a non-stationary variable because they are found to be inherently stationary (integrated of order zero) (Juselius 2001, p. 343). As a result, some cointegration relations in Table 6.31 can not be tested or include a stationary variable but are still presented for informational purposes, i.e. to analyze parameter signs and values and to keep the final long-run structure open.

Hypotheses H_1 to H_8 test for stationary relations between real stock market values and the other variables. Even though stationarity is accepted for some of the hypotheses (H_2 to H_4, H_6 and H_7) the stock market variable only exhibits significant adjustment behavior to H_3 and H_6. The relation for stock markets and the real long-term interest rate (H_3) shows extremely high coefficients for inflation and the bond rate and should, therefore, not be interpreted as a stock demand relation. H_6 on the other hand shows valid coefficients for a relationship between the stock market and aggregate real output, where both variables error correct to this long-run equilibrium. No stationary relationship between the amount of money (M3 or capital flows) and the stock market can be found.

H_9 to H_{16} test for a stable money demand relation. All hypotheses are rejected or can not be formally tested. Since real money qualifies as weakly exogenous, identifying a valid money demand relation is unlikely. This also means, that implications of excess liquidity can not be tested.

All tests on 'Policy rules' (H_{17} to H_{19}) are accepted. However, inflation exhibits the wrong sign, indicating a short-term interest rate increase as a reaction to reduced inflation. As a result, the usefulness of this relation is questionable from an economic point of view and should be regarded with caution.

Hypotheses H_{20} to H_{23} focus on potential stationary goods demand relations. H_{21} shows that output reacts positively to deviations in the real bond rate. Hence, H_{21} indicates an IS-type relation in the long-run structure, albeit with an unrealistically high coefficient. H_{20} is also accepted, but the coefficients have implausible signs.

Under the headline 'Inflation and interest rates' cointegration between inflation and the nominal interest rates ('Fisher parity') as well as between the interest rates themselves ('expectations hypothesis') is tested. Inflation and excess liquidity (H_{24})

Table 6.31 Euro area monthly data: testing the stationarity of single relations

	m_r	s_r	y_r	Δp	*ff*	$b10$	cf	*Trend*	$\chi^2(v)$	p-value	*sign.* α
					Demand for stocks						
H_1	−2.918	1	0	0	0	0	0	0.016	10.3 (1)	0.001	
H_2	**0**	**1**	**0**	**408.3**	**−408.3**	**0**	**0**	**−0.007**	**0.0 (1)**	**0.852**	or
H_3	**0**	**1**	**0**	**−5,672**	**0**	**5,672**	**0**	**0.137**	**1.6 (1)**	**0.209**	$s_r, b10$
H_4	**0**	**1**	**0**	**0**	**−310.6**	**0**	**0**	**−0.002**	**0.6 (1)**	**0.446**	or
H_5	0	1	0	0	0	1,135	0	0.021	7.5 (1)	0.006	
H_6	**0**	**1**	**−14.32**	**0**	**0**	**0**	**0**	**0.018**	**0.1 (1)**	**0.813**	$s_r, y_r, \Delta p, or, b10$
H_7	**0**	**1**	**0**	**0**	**0**	**0**	**169.8**	**0.004**	**0.1 (1)**	**0.709**	or, cf
H_8	2.711	1	0	0	0	0	183.8	−0.008		no test	
					Money demand						
H_9	1	0	−1	0	0	0	0	−0.004	12.8 (2)	0.002	
H_{10}	1	0	0	0	53.73	−53.73	0	−0.004	9.0 (1)	0.003	
H_{11}	1	0	9.936	0	−250.9	8.424	0	−0.018		no test	$or, b10$
H_{12}	1	0	1.764	−320.6	0	0	0	−0.003		no test	Δp
H_{13}	1	−0.343	0	0	0	0	0	−0.005	10.3 (1)	0.001	
H_{14}	1	−0.301	0	0	95.97	−95.97	0	−0.005		no test	or
H_{15}	1	−0.102	−1	0	0	0	0	−0.004	11.4 (1)	0.001	
H_{16}	1	−0.206	−1	0	89.18	−89.18	0	−0.004		no test	$or, b10$

(continued)

Table 6.31 (Continued)

	m_r	s_r	y_r	Δp	ff	$b10$	cf	*Trend*	$\chi^2(v)$	p-value	*sign.* α
					Policy rules						
H_{17}	**0**	**0**	**0**	**5.840**	**1**	**0**	**0**	**0**	**3.1 (2)**	**0.207**	$s_r, \Delta p, or$
H_{18}	**0**	**0**	**−0.043**	**0**	**1**	**0**	**0**	**0**	**1.5 (1)**	**0.221**	$s_r, or, b10$
H_{19}	**0**	**−0.003**	**0**	**0**	**1**	**0**	**0**	**0**	**0.6 (1)**	**0.446**	$or, b10$
					Demand for goods						
H_{20}	**0**	**0**	**1**	**30.05**	**−30.05**	**0**	**0**	**0.000**	**0.0 (1)**	**0.863**	or
H_{21}	**0**	**0**	**1**	**−469.1**	**0**	**469.1**	**0**	**0.010**	**1.6 (1)**	**0.209**	$s_r, b10$
H_{22}	−0.278	0	1	0	0	0	0	0	8.9 (1)	0.003	
H_{23}	−0.021	−0.070	1	0	0	0	0	−0.001		no test	s_r, y_r
					Inflation and interest rates						
H_{24}	**−0.003**	**0**	**0.003**	**1**	**0**	**0**	**0**	**0**	**0.4 (2)**	**0.801**	$\Delta p, or$
H_{25}	**−0.015**	**0**	**0**	**0**	**0**	**1**	**0**	**0.000**	**0.2 (1)**	**0.669**	$s_r, b10$
H_{26}	0	0	0	−1	1	0	0	0	16.0 (3)	0.001	
H_{27}	0	0	0	−1	0	1	0	0	16.3 (3)	0.001	
H_{28}	**0**	**0**	**0**	**5.850**	**1**	**0**	**0**	**0**	**3.1 (2)**	**0.207**	$s_r, \Delta p, or$
H_{29}	**0**	**0**	**0**	**2.176**	**0**	**1**	**0**	**0**	**1.6 (2)**	**0.441**	$s_r, \Delta p, b10$
H_{30}	0	0	0	0	−1	1	0	0	12.2 (3)	0.007	
H_{31}	0	0	0	0	−1.471	1	0	0	11.5 (2)	0.003	
H_{32}	0	0	0	−2.111	1	1.111	0	0	16.1 (2)	0	
H_{33}	**0**	**0**	**0**	**3.485**	**−1**	**1**	**0**	**0**	**3.1 (2)**	**0.214**	$\Delta p, or$

is accepted. However, this is most likely due to inflation being stationary by itself. H_{25} shows that real money and nominal bond yields have a positive relation, which indicates an expected inflation effect. The 'Fisher parity'-hypotheses are rejected or exhibit the wrong sign. Additionally, for the combinations of inflation and interest rates (H_{33}) stationarity is accepted.

These preliminary results help to identify a valid long-run system. However, cointegration by itself is not indicative of the direction of causality between the variables. Instead, the test results have to be jointly evaluated with the α-matrix. This is the focus of the next section, where an identified long-run structure is presented. The analysis of the unrestricted Π and of the preliminary tests suggests that an over-identified long-run structure might consist of an output-stock market relation, a policy rule and a bond rate equation, but does not include a money demand relation. Additionally, inflation and capital flows might be stationary relations by themselves and, thus, represent two of the five cointegration vectors.

6.3.2.3 Identification of the Long-Run Cointegrating Relations

To identify the full cointegration structure the joint hypotheses H_6, H_{19} and H_{25} are tested together with inflation and capital flows as already stationary time series. The restrictions on the economically and empirically identified long-run structure are accepted with a p-value of 0.42 ($\chi^2(9) = 9.140$). Table 6.32 shows the cointegrating relations (β_1 to β_5) in the β'-matrix and the error-correction coefficients in the α-matrix. All β-coefficients are strongly significant and the rank conditions are accepted for the full cointegration space (see Table B.8 in Appendix B.2.5). Thus, the cointegration relations are linearly independent.

The graphs of the cointegrating relations are displayed in Appendix B.2.6 where the deterministic terms and short-term parameters are concentrated out.[53] It is notable that the first and third cointegration relation show relatively high persistence. In addition, information on parameter constancy based on forward and backward recursive tests, as shown in Appendix B.2.7, shows that parameter constancy for α_i and β_i ($i = 1, \ldots, 5$) is weak at the beginning of the sample. The parameter constancy tests show that the coefficients fluctuate over the sample period, especially for the backward recursive tests. A closer inspection demonstrates that while the absolute value of the coefficients fluctuates the signs do not change. This is important because it proves that the relationships between the variables do not reverse over time. Nevertheless, these findings are an indication to interpret the absolute value of the coefficients with caution.

Table B.9 in Appendix B.2.8 provides the structural representation of the cointegration space with weak exogeneity imposed on real money. This structure is

---

[53] This removes the seasonal fluctuations and outliers, which can be observed in the raw series. Hence, a clearer view of the stationarity of the long-run relations is presented (Brüggemann and Lütkepohl 2006, p. 692). See also Sect. 6.2.1.3.

Table 6.32 Euro area monthly data: the identified long-run structure (t-values in brackets)

β'

	m_r	s_r	y_r	Δp	or	$b10$	cf	*Trend*
Beta(1)	0.000 [NA]	**1.000** [NA]	**−16.21** [−15.017]	0.000 [NA]	0.000 [NA]	0.000 [NA]	0.000 [NA]	**0.019** [11.314]
Beta(2)	**−0.018** [−6.200]	0.000 [NA]	0.000 [NA]	0.000 [NA]	0.000 [NA]	**1.000** [NA]	0.000 [NA]	**0.000** [7.322]
Beta(3)	0.000 [NA]	**−0.003** [−9.367]	0.000 [NA]	0.000 [NA]	**1.000** [NA]	0.000 [NA]	0.000 [NA]	**0.000** [2.829]
Beta(4)	0.000 [NA]	0.000 [NA]	0.000 [NA]	**1.000** [NA]	0.000 [NA]	0.000 [NA]	0.000 [NA]	0.000 [NA]
Beta(5)	0.000 [NA]	0.000 [NA]	0.000 [NA]	0.000 [NA]	0.000 [NA]	0.000 [NA]	**1.000** [NA]	0.000 [NA]

α

	Alpha(1)	Alpha(2)	Alpha(3)	Alpha(4)	Alpha(5)
Δm_r	**−0.006** [−2.026]	0.482 [0.473]	−1.098 [−1.333]	−0.044 [−0.150]	0.108 [1.127]
Δs_r	**−0.066** [−2.110]	**−30.34** [−2.623]	**−27.01** [−2.888]	−4.930 [−1.492]	1.867 [1.723]
Δy_r	**0.012** [2.460]	2.066 [1.122]	−1.999 [−1.343]	0.277 [0.526]	0.183 [1.063]
$\Delta^2 p$	**−0.004** [−2.921]	−0.508 [−1.151]	−0.370 [−1.037]	**−1.000** [−7.933]	−0.015 [−0.368]
Δor	**−0.000** [−5.198]	**0.081** [2.459]	**−0.195** [−7.341]	**−0.021** [−2.228]	**−0.007** [−2.277]
$\Delta b10$	**−0.000** [−2.757]	**−0.168** [−5.096]	**−0.055** [−2.045]	0.017 [1.755]	0.004 [1.328]
Δcf	**0.007** [2.454]	**2.652** [2.674]	1.541 [1.922]	−0.341 [−1.203]	**−0.695** [−7.478]

accepted with a lower p-value of 0.226 ($\chi^2(14) = 17.597$), but the estimated results remain similar.

The first cointegration relation represents a relationship between trend-adjusted real income and the stock market:

$$s_{r,t} - 16.2(y_{r,t} - 0.001\ trend) \sim I(0), \tag{6.21}$$

where the stock market reacts positively to increases in real economic activity. This relationship works both ways because real output reacts positively to the stock market, describing wealth and balance sheet effects. It shows the self-reinforcing effects of optimism and confidence in real and financial markets and that the two variables are important to each other. This finding confirms the quarterly cointegration analysis of the euro area between 1980 and 2000 by Cassola and Morana (2002). They too, find a long-run relationship between the real stock market and real output (Cassola and Morana 2002, p. 20).

It is interesting that all other variables also have significant α-coefficients, further strengthening the importance of the above relation. However, the coefficients are extremely low, which suggests slow adjustment. While a relatively higher stock market (a positive residual of the above relation), on the one hand, pushes real money, inflation and the interest rates negatively, on the other hand, capital flows react positively to it. This shows that stock market advances improve the competitive position as an investment alternative. This leads to a substitution effect of money demand and interest-bearing investments. In addition, it also 'pulls' additional money into the euro area. All this reflects the self-reinforcing behavior of stock markets.

Obviously, the signs can be reversed to identify the adjustment behavior of the macro variables to innovations in real output. In line with theoretical aspects, real money, inflation and both interest rates react positively to real output advances which are relatively higher than stock market advances. The inflation rate's positive reaction can be interpreted in the framework of the short-run Phillips curve, where inflation increases with excess aggregate demand for goods (Juselius 2001, p. 344).

The second long-run relation describes a relationship between the level of real money and the bond rate:

$$b_t - 0.018m_{r,t} + 0.000\, trend \sim I(0), \tag{6.22}$$

where the bond rate reacts positively to real money. This can be interpreted as an expected inflation effect (see Sect. 3.2.1.2), where investors demand higher nominal bond returns as a result of increased money growth.[54] Whereas the bond rate is significantly correcting to this relation, real money is not. In addition, inspection of the α-coefficients shows that the overnight rate and capital flows adjust positively to deviations of this equilibrium and the stock market reacts negatively.

The reaction of the stock market is also evidence of the positive short-run adjustment of the stock market to advances in real money, which lasts until the equilibrium of real money and the bond rate is reestablished.

The third cointegrating relation shows a long-run equilibrium between the overnight rate and the stock market:

$$or - 0.003s_{r,t} - 0.000\, trend \sim I(0), \tag{6.23}$$

where the overnight rate reacts positively to stock market advances.[55] This indicates that the ECB follows the markets with its interest rate setting. This could also be a result of the stock market's reaction to real output, whereby, some information that the second pillar of the ECB monetary policy focuses on is incorporated. It is interesting to see that the stock market pushes this relationship but does not react to it. This indicates that monetary policy does not influence equity markets in the

[54] This is contrary to the hypothesis that abundant liquidity reduces the compensation for risk, which is often made responsible for low long-term interest rates (see literature overview in Taboga 2008, p. 2; Hördahl and Packer 2007, p. 6). This shows that the inflationary effect is higher.

[55] The low β-coefficient of the stock market variable can be rationalized by the extreme difference in the standard deviations of the two series. The residual standard error of the stock market is 360 times higher than that of the policy rate for monthly data. In general, the size of the coefficients has to be interpreted with caution. They usually can not be interpreted as elasticities, since a shock to one variable implies a shock to all variables in the long run. Thus, a ceteris paribus interpretation is generally invalid (Johansen 2009, pp. 8–9; Johansen 2005, pp. 97–100; Lütkepohl 1994, p. 393).

long run, but monetary policy nevertheless reacts to market movements and the two variables move up and down in tandem.

This is reasonable because interest rates rose along with the dot-com bull market, were drastically lowered in response to the bust in 2001, which also coincided with the terror attacks of September 11 and bottomed out in 2003, when markets started to rise again. Interest rates then followed with slow upward movements starting at the end of 2005. Recent history has shown that, in line with the deviations from this long-run equilibrium, this policy response was probably too late. It is clear, that this long-run steady state does not reflect a complete policy reaction function because other potentially important variables are missing. It nevertheless shows that policy makers were very reluctant to raise rates again in the middle of the decade. European central bankers were probably affected by the historically low rates set by their American counterparts.

As outlined above, the fourth and fifth β'-vectors show the stationary variables, inflation and capital flows, respectively (6.24) and (6.25):

$$\Delta p_t \sim I(0), \tag{6.24}$$

$$cf_t \sim I(0). \tag{6.25}$$

The α-coefficients show that inflation and capital flows error correct with strong significance and high coefficients. According to the α-coefficients, inflation reverts to the mean within one month and capital flows in less than two months.

In addition, positive deviations from the inflation rate lead to negative adjustment of the overnight rate. The third cointegration relation showed that deviations from the bond rate-real money equilibrium led to a positive adjustment of the overnight rate. As with the US analysis, this is a sign that expected inflation (as incorporated in the bond rate) plays a more prominent role than current inflation.

6.3.3 Short-Run Dynamics

As described in Sect. 6.2.3 this section applies a structural error-correction model and formulates stationary equations for each of the variables in the system. Hence, the analysis focuses on the dynamic short-run adjustment of each variable to the past and the other simultaneous variables in the system (Johansen 1995, p. 79). The starting point is estimating the multivariate dynamic equilibrium-correction model for the whole system. Identification of the p short-run equations requires at least $p-1$ just-identifying restrictions on each equation (Juselius 2006, p. 208). This is achieved by restricting current effects between the variables to zero. In addition, insignificant coefficients are removed from each single equation based on an LR test, which results in overidentified equations for each variable. The result is shown in Table 6.33. The dependent variables can be found in the top row as the column headings of each of the model equations. The row headings, on the other hand, indicate the conditioning variables.

Table 6.33 Euro area monthly data: short-run dynamics (t-values in brackets)

	Δm_r	Δs_r	Δy_r	$\Delta^2 p$	Δor	$\Delta b10$	Δcf
$\Delta m_{r,t}$	**1**	0	0	0	0	0	0
$\Delta s_{r,t}$	0	**1**	0	0	0	0	0
$\Delta y_{r,t}$	0	0	**1**	0	0	0	0
$\Delta^2 p_t$	0	0	0	**1**	0	0	0
Δor_t	0	0	0	0	**1**	0	0
$\Delta b10_t$	0	0	0	0	0	**1**	0
Δcf_t	0	0	0	0	0	0	**1**
$\Delta m_{r,t-1}$							
$\Delta s_{r,t-1}$	**0.017**					**0.001**	
	[2.21]					[2.16]	
$\Delta y_{r,t-1}$			**−0.306**		**−0.005**		
			[−3.80]		[−2.84]		
$\Delta^2 p_{t-1}$		**−3.698**					
		[−1.97]					
Δor_{t-1}	**−6.663**		**10.65**		**−0.212**		
	[−3.39]		[2.63]		[−2.79]		
$\Delta b10_{t-1}$	**−5.656**						**−14.26**
	[−2.36]						[−5.26]
Δcf_{t-1}			**−0.003**				
			[−2.27]				
$ecm1_{t-1}$	**−0.007**		**0.014**	**−0.002**	**−0.000**		
	[−3.86]		[4.83]	[−2.42]	[−5.05]		
$ecm2_{t-1}$					**0.082**	**−0.101**	
					[2.43]	[−3.54]	
$ecm3_{t-1}$	**−1.433**	**−19.15**			**−0.196**		
	[−2.29]	[−3.08]			[−7.32]		
$ecm4_{t-1}$				**−0.839**	**−0.019**	**0.021**	
				[−10.1]	[−2.67]	[3.02]	
$ecm5_{t-1}$					**−0.005**		**−7.874**
					[−2.21]		[−10.3]
$dum0004_{p,t}$							**−1.861**
							[−4.87]
$dum0102_{p,t}$	**0.021**				**−0.000**		**−1.107**
	[6.10]				[−1.97]		[−2.79]
$dum0201_{p,t}$				**0.004**	**0.000**		
				[2.90]	[3.73]		

The 74 zero restrictions of insignificant coefficients are accepted based on an LR test of over-identifying restrictions $\chi^2(74) = 79.998$ with a p-value of 0.30.
The analysis shows that real money reacts positively to lagged values of the stock market. This signifies that in the euro area wealth effects are stronger than

substitution effects in the short run. In addition, real money reacts negatively to both interest rates. The residuals of the first and third cointegration relation have a negative effect on real money.

The stock market only reacts to lagged values of inflation and the third long-run equilibrium (stock market-overnight rate relation). The negative effect of inflation is in keeping with theory (see Sect. 3.2.1.2). The reaction to the third ecm confirms the results of the long-run section. In addition, one would expect the stock market to react to the first cointegration relation as well, because the α-coefficient is significant. This means that the interpretation of the long-run relationship between the stock market and economic activity is closer to an aggregate demand for goods relation, where output grows with increased wealth instead of the other way around.

In the short term, real output is influenced by lagged values of itself, the overnight rate and capital flows. However, it is puzzling that the signs of the coefficients do not make sense economically. Additionally, real output equilibrium-corrects towards the first cointegration relation, as was already indicated in the long-run analysis.

Inflation does not react to any of the lagged variables of the system. However, it does exhibit error-correction behavior towards the fourth cointegration relation, which is the inflation relation and, hence, confirms the stationary behavior of the inflation rate in the euro area. Inflation is also negatively affected by the first ecm. This can be associated with an overheated economy, which leads to rising inflation.

As can already be seen in the analysis of the α-coefficients, the overnight rate is affected by all cointegration relations. In addition, lagged values of real output and the overnight rate itself have a negative effect on it.

The short-run analysis of the bond rate confirms the error-correcting behavior towards the second cointegration relation, which is the real money-bond rate relation, in line with the expected inflation effect on the bond rate. In addition, the bond rate is pushed by the residuals of actual inflation (the fourth cointegration relation) and the stock market.

Capital flows react negatively to the bond rate. An indication that bond investments are a prime target for international money. Again, this finding might be influenced by the financial turmoils in the beginning of the 21st century and the associated flight into safe assets. Especially after the dot-com bust, foreigners were eager to purchase bonds denominated in euro (ECB 2008b, p. 74; ECB 2005b, pp. 20–22; ECB 2005c, pp. 18–21). This can be ascribed to non-residents desire for low-risk euro denominated assets. In addition, capital flows show strong adjustment behavior to the fifth cointegration relation, which is the capital flows relation. This is another sign that capital flows are highly influenced by themselves and that deviations from the mean are quickly corrected.

Current effects are not modeled in the above equations. Instead they are left in the residuals. However, simultaneous effects have potential importance. Whereas correlation between the residuals is not problematic with respect to the long-run relations of the previous section, identification of the short-run structural equations requires uncorrelated residuals (Juselius 2006, p. 229). Table 6.34 shows the residual covariance matrix, in which large off-diagonal elements can be an indication of

Table 6.34 Euro area monthly data: correlation of structural residuals (standard deviations on diagonal)

	Δm_r	Δs_r	Δy_r	$\Delta^2 p$	Δor	$\Delta b10$	Δcf
Δm_r	*0.0036*						
Δs_r	0.12	*0.0431*					
Δy_r	−0.04	−0.14	*0.0067*				
$\Delta^2 p$	**−0.42**	0.09	−0.19	*0.0016*			
Δor	−0.02	0.08	−0.03	0.02	*0.0001*		
$\Delta b10$	0.11	0.19	−0.01	0.12	−0.07	*0.0001*	
Δcf	0.25	0.01	−0.01	−0.02	0.01	0.03	*0.3734*

significant current effects between the system variables. Especially the high value between real money and inflation must be critically recognized.[56]
One way to reduce residual correlation is to introduce current effects between the variables into the short-run structure. Adding current effects of real money to the inflation rate produces an insignificant regressor (t-value of 0.169) and does not reduce correlation between the two variables. The same is true for the current effects of inflation in the real money equation (insignificant coefficient with a t-value of 0.422). This does not neutralize the above results. However, the inability to perform a complete investigation of the short-run dynamics based on the available dataset must be acknowledged and more attention should be paid to the information included in the α-coefficients of the previous section.

6.3.4 *The Long-Run Impact of the Common Trends*

The C-matrix summarizes the long-run implications of the system. Circumstances where a shock to a monetary instrument has a significant long-run impact on market prices must prevail in order for central banks to have the ability to influence stock markets. Hence, when evaluating the effectiveness of monetary policy the long-run impact of shocks to money stock and the short-term interest rate (i.e., the overnight rate) on the stock market is of particular interest.[57]

The residual $\epsilon_{i,t}$ is interpreted as an estimate of the unanticipated shock to variable x_i. The estimated long-run impact of these shocks are reported in Table 6.35.[58] The C-matrix can be read column or row-wise. The columns show the long-run

[56] High residual correlation can result from the aggregation of the data over time, inadequately modeled expectations or omitted variables (Juselius 2006, pp. 239–240).

[57] An alternative is to use monetary instruments to control an intermediate target, such as the (real) long-term bond rate if the intermediate target has a long-run impact on stocks. However, for this to be manageable, cointegration between the policy instrument and the intermediate target is a necessity.

[58] For more information on the calculation and interpretation of the long-run impact matrix, see Sects. 5.1.2 and 6.2.4.

Table 6.35 Euro area monthly data: the long-run impact matrix (t-values in brackets)

The long-run impact matrix, C							
	$\hat{\epsilon}_{m_r}$	$\hat{\epsilon}_{s_r}$	$\hat{\epsilon}_{y_r}$	$\hat{\epsilon}_{\Delta p}$	$\hat{\epsilon}_{or}$	$\hat{\epsilon}_{b10}$	$\hat{\epsilon}_{cf}$
m_r	**0.844** [5.629]	0.024 [1.029]	0.095 [0.654]	−0.072 [−0.219]	−6.817 [−1.520]	0.892 [0.131]	0.295 [1.920]
s_r	2.166 [0.730]	**1.494** [3.258]	−3.586 [−1.246]	−12.30 [−1.897]	−65.01 [−0.732]	−25.71 [−1.914]	2.810 [0.923]
y_r	0.134 [0.730]	**0.092** [3.258]	−0.221 [−1.246]	−0.759 [−1.897]	−4.011 [−0.732]	−15.87 [−1.914]	0.173 [0.923]
Δp	0.000 [*NA*]	0.000 [*NA*]	0.000 [*NA*]	0.000 [*NA*]	0.000 [*NA*]	0.000 [*NA*]	0.000 [*NA*]
or	0.006 [0.730]	**0.004** [3.258]	−0.010 [−1.246]	−0.035 [−1.897]	−0.187 [−0.732]	−0.738 [−1.914]	0.008 [0.923]
$b10$	**0.015** [5.629]	0.000 [1.029]	0.002 [0.654]	−0.001 [−0.219]	−0.123 [−1.520]	0.016 [0.131]	0.005 [1.920]
cf	0.000 [*NA*]	0.000 [*NA*]	0.000 [*NA*]	0.000 [*NA*]	0.000 [*NA*]	0.000 [*NA*]	0.000 [*NA*]

impact of the cumulated shocks to a variable on all the variables in the system and the rows show which of the shocks have a long-run impact on the particular variable (Johansen 1995, pp. 49–50). Inflation and capital flows are immune to permanent shocks because they are stationary. Permanent shocks create non-stationarity. Thus, stationary variables are only affected by temporary shocks. Consequently, inflation and capital flows exhibit zero-rows in the long-run impact matrix.

Table 6.35 shows that only shocks to real money and to the stock market have significant long run effects on the included macro variables, which confirms the unit vector test in Sect. 6.3.2.2. Shocks to real money affect itself and the nominal long-term bond rate positively in the long run. The former confirms the procyclicality of the banking business, the latter investors' demand for higher nominal returns due to increased inflationary expectations. The analysis of shocks to real money also shows that the positive impact on the stock market is statistically insignificant.

The stock market has a positive effect on itself, which indicates that trend following and herding behavior, as well as rational speculation, amplify stock market dynamics. It also has a significant positive long-term influence on economic activity and on the overnight rate, which is in conformity with the above outlined cointegrating relations one and three.

Table B.10 in Appendix B.2.9 shows a further restricted version of the C-matrix. There, real money is restricted to be weakly exogenous. This has two consequences. First, it can not be subject to permanent shocks of other variables. Second, the cumulated shocks to real money define one common driving trend. This restriction changes the significance of the long-run impact of shocks on the bond rate. As such, shocks to the bond rate have a negative long-term impact on the stock market, real output, and the overnight rate.

To conclude, the choice of rank $r = 5$ was also the choice for five cointegrating relations and $p - r = 2$ common driving trends. The C-matrix suggests that the forces driving the system are mainly monetary and financial, represented as shocks to real money and the stock market.

Table 6.36 Euro area monthly data: results of main hypotheses

	Hypotheses/Questions	Result
H_1	Euro area stock market behavior shows strong persistence, i.e., shocks to the stock market have positive long-run effects on future developments	Yes
H_2	Long-run equilibria exist between stock prices and liquidity conditions	(Yes)
H_3	Liquidity conditions influence stock prices positively in the long run	No
H_4	Liquidity conditions influence stock prices positively in the short run	(Yes)
H_5	International capital flows have a positive long-run impact on the stock market behavior in the euro area	No
H_6	International capital flows have a positive short-run impact on the stock market behavior in the euro area	No
Q_1	Is the ECB able to influence stock prices in the long run?	No
Q_2	Is the ECB able to influence stock prices in the short run?	No

6.3.5 Conclusion

Table 6.36 shows that the results from the econometric analysis only confirm part of the main hypotheses. Innovations in the stock market have a permanent positive effect on future market developments. The long-run equilibria between liquidity conditions and the stock market is based on the third cointegration relation, which includes the overnight rate and the stock market. However, the stock market does not react to this relation. As such, the analysis shows that monetary policy reacted to stock market dynamics during the first 10 years of the ECB, confirming that the ECB takes asset price developments into account in its monetary policy strategy but does not target them directly (ECB 2005a, p. 59).

This is contrary to findings from Belke and Polleit (2006, pp. 346–348), who show that the one-month money market rate is the forcing variable but does not react to the stock market.[59] One explanation for the conflicting results is the application of a different timeframe (1974–2003) and that the main focus is on Germany. Consequently, the four ECB-years at the end of the sample only form a small share of the 30-year information set. The combined findings of the two analyses indicate that the ECB pays more attention to asset prices than the Bundesbank did, which could be a result of increased financial market turmoil or of the importance of the stock market for real developments. Real stock market levels long-run equilibrate with real output levels and both variables show error-correction behavior. This is

[59] Belke and Polleit (2006) test for cointegration between monetary policy, represented by the one-month money market rate, and stock market returns. Stock market returns are measured with three alternatives, namely 'stock price changes', 'dividend growth' and 'stock price changes minus dividend growth'. They focus on Germany and apply monthly data for the period 1974–2003. To avoid problems associated with time series being integrated of different order they apply the bounds testing approach proposed by Pesaran et al. (2001). Their empirical results show that the Bundesbank (and after 1999, the ECB) had a significant short and long-run impact on stock market returns. One limitation of the results is that the findings only hold for stock market returns when measured as dividend growth.

a confirmation of the ECB's strategy of paying attention to asset prices as leading indicators and also of their potential impact on consumer and investment spending as well as on the consumer price level (ECB 2005a, p. 59).

A stable long-run money demand relation could not be established. This confirms results of previous studies, in which stable money demand relations were identified for the years before the third stage of EMU but usually broke down after including the first years of the common currency.[60]

Researchers at the ECB provide an explanation for why real money and capital flows did not play a big role for stock markets (see, e.g., ECB 2005c, pp. 19–22; De Santis et al. 2008, pp. 11, 27–28). They argue that after the dot-com bust financial agents switched their investments from stocks to investments with less risk, such as money market funds.[61] However, this only changes the money stock if investments are made from abroad. An intra-euro area sale of stocks only changes the ownership structure but not the total amount of money. Nevertheless, the time frame for the empirical analysis is unfortunate because it starts with a long bear market after the dot-com bust and ends with more market turmoil due to the financial crisis. This makes it harder to establish a stable long-run relationship between developments in real money and the stock market.

The positive short-run effect of liquidity on the stock market is derived from the stock market adjustment behavior to the bond rate-real money relation. If this relationship is pushed out of equilibrium, then this deviation affects the stock market positively. Consequently, this link between liquidity conditions and the stock market is rather weak.

Additionally, the above analysis sheds light on a few other aspects of economic interest, mainly:

- Real money only has a significant α-coefficient in the stock market-goods demand relation. It is only included in the second cointegration relation but does not react to it. This also means that no stable money demand relation could be established. Instead, in the long run, money is pushed by shocks to itself. This is another indication for the procyclicality of credit supply. In addition, tests of weak exogeneity of real money are accepted. In the short run, real money is influenced positively by the stock market and negatively by both interest rates. Therefore, in the euro area the influence of the stock market on liquidity conditions (money and the short-term interest rate) is higher than the other way round, contrary to what was expected from the outset.
- Real output forms a long-run equilibria with the stock market where higher equity values increase real aggregate demand for goods, thereby, confirming the second part of transmission mechanism theory. This is also confirmed by the

[60] See Carstensen (2004, pp. 2–5) for an overview of euro area money demand literature.

[61] Greiber and Lemke (2005, pp. 17–19) establish a stable money demand relation by including a measure for macroeconomic uncertainty. The measure of uncertainty explains the increase in euro area money supply between 2001 and 2004.

long-run impact matrix. Shocks to the stock market push real output in the long run.

- Since the time series for inflation is integrated of order zero, it does not enter any of the other cointegration relations. In addition, it is not permanently affected by shocks to any of the other variables. The analysis also shows that, in the short run, inflation does not react to lagged values of the other variables but only to the first and fourth cointegration relation, which are the stock market-goods demand relation and the inflation rate relation itself. The positive reaction of the inflation rate to deviations from the aggregate demand for goods relation can be interpreted in the framework of the short-run Phillips curve, where inflation increases with excess aggregate demand for goods.
- As mentioned above, the short-term interest rate shows error-correction behavior to disequilibria between the stock market and itself. Shocks to the stock market also have a positive long-run impact on the overnight rate. This is logical because interest rates rose along with the dot-com bull market, were drastically lowered in response to the bust in 2001, which also coincided with the terror attacks of September 11, and bottomed out in 2003, when markets began rising again. Interest rates followed with a slow but persistent upward movement starting at the end of 2005. Recent history has shown that this policy response was probably too late, consistent with the deviations from this long-run equilibrium. This description is compatible with the finding that the ECB follows the Fed.[62] The imitation of the Fed's strong reaction after the burst of the dot-com bubble drove down interest rates to its lowest value in four decades. It is clear that the long-run steady state between the overnight rate and the stock market does not reflect a policy reaction function because other potentially important variables are missing. It nevertheless shows that policy makers were very hesitant to raise rates again in the middle of the decade. Euro area central bankers were probably affected by the historically low rates set by their American counterparts. In addition, the short rate adjusts in response to deviations from all cointegration relations. This confirms the ECB's approach of taking various economic indicators into account when setting its monetary policy, such as output developments, the inflation rate and also international developments, such as capital flows. However, it is peculiar that the policy rate reacts negatively to advances in inflation. This is a sign that euro area central bankers focus on future inflation instead of current inflation.
- The bond rate reacts positively to real money, indicating an expected inflation effect, where investors demand higher nominal bond returns as a result of increased money growth. In addition, analysis of the short run shows that the bond rate is pushed by the disequilibria of the inflation rate relation, which confirms the importance of expected and actual inflation for nominal yields.

[62] For an overview of literature exploring the leader-follower relationship between the Fed and the ECB see Belke and Cui (2009, pp. 4–7).

- Capital flows are found to be stationary and, thus, do not play a role in the other cointegration vectors. They are, however, negatively affected by the bond rate in the short run, which shows the importance of bond investments for international investors.

6.4 Japan: Quarterly Data

6.4.1 *Model Specification*

6.4.1.1 Data Overview, Deterministic Components and Lag Length

As outlined in Sect. 5.2.1, the data vector consists of the following variables:

$$x_t' = [m_r, s_r, y_r, \Delta p, or, b10, cf]_t\,, \tag{6.26}$$

where m_r is the log of real money (M3[63]), s_r is the log of real stock market levels (total market including dividends) and y_r is the log of real GDP. Real variables are transformed from nominal variables by applying the consumer price index, p, and, hence, Δp is the inflation rate. Short- and long-term interest rates are represented by the overnight interbank rate, or, and the yield on 10-year government bonds, $b10$, respectively. All interest rates have been converted to quarterly rates and divided by 100 to achieve comparability with the inflation rate. Capital flows, cf, are calculated in percent as a share of the total money stock M3.[64] They are derived from non-bank BoP transactions as described in Sect. 4.6.3.2 and Appendix A. All time series are obtained either from Datastream or the IMF BoP database and detailed information on specific sources of the data can be found in Appendix B.3.1. The data used for the analysis covers the last 25 years and consists of quarterly observations from 1983:3 to 2008:3. Figure 6.7 displays the time pattern of all variables in levels and first differences.

The graph for capital flows looks stationary in levels and differences. All other graphs only look stationary for the differenced series. Further characteristics of the

[63] M3 reflects cash currency in circulation plus deposits deposited at depository institutions. The former include banknotes and coins in circulation, the latter include deposit money (demand deposits, such as, among others, current and savings deposits) and quasi-money (such as, among others, time deposits, fixed savings and certificates of deposit) (Bank of Japan 2008, p. 1-1). The broader monetary aggregate 'L' includes too many investment alternatives, such as, among others, investment trusts and commercial paper issued by financial institutions. In addition, it is not as accurate as M3 as it relies more on estimations as a result of data limitations (Bank of Japan 2008, p. 2-1). Thus, it does not qualify as an alternative to M3. For level shifts and seasonal adjustment of the M3 time series see Bank of Japan (2008, pp. 2.19–2.20).

[64] The usage of a percentage value of a variable included in the system does not lead to any problems of statistical inference. It is important, though, that the model is well specified.

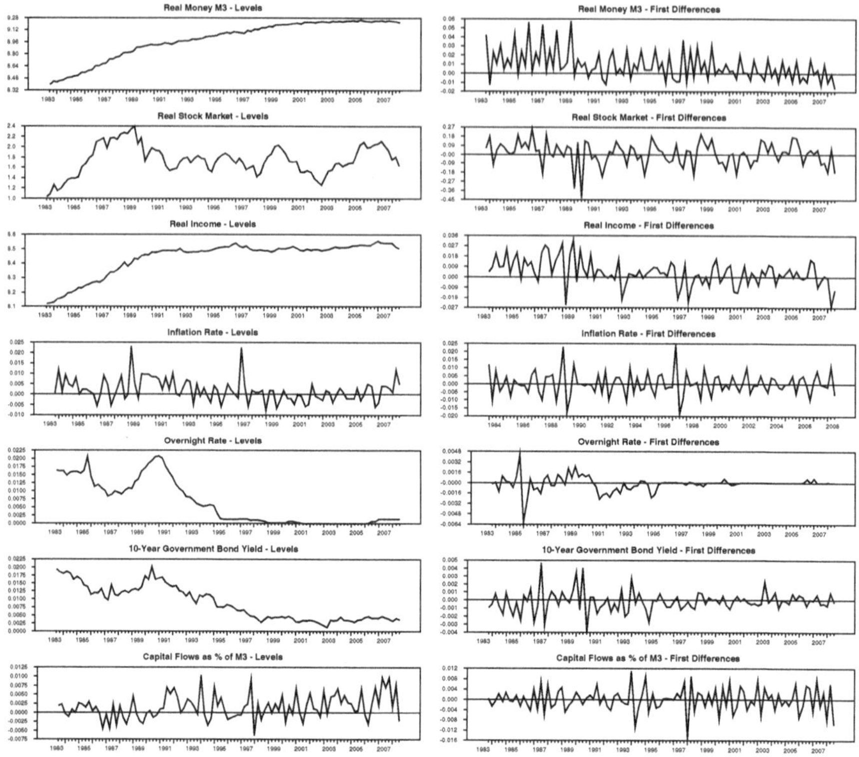

Fig. 6.7 Japan quarterly data in levels and first differences

data are that real money and real GDP seem to follow a trend. Thus, a deterministic (non-stochastic) trend should be allowed for in the model. However, the deterministic part of the trend changed after the real estate and stock market collapse at the beginning of 1990. This represents a mean shift in the differenced series. This structural break might require a shift dummy to model the change in expectations and risk perception inherent to the bust.

Deterministic Components

The above observations suggest the inclusion of the following deterministic components in the model (see also Sect. 6.2.1.1): an unrestricted constant, μ_0, a restricted linear trend, μ_1, and a restricted shift dummy, $\Phi_s D_{s,t}$. The CVAR model from (5.4) then becomes:

$$\Delta x_t = \alpha\beta' x_{t-1} + \sum_{i=1}^{k-1} \Gamma_i \Delta x_{t-1} + \Phi D_t + \mu_0 + \mu_1 + \Phi_s D_{s,t} + \epsilon_t, \qquad (6.27)$$

where $\mu_0 = \alpha\rho_0 + \gamma_0$, $\mu_1 = \alpha\rho_1 + \gamma_1$ and $\Phi_s = \alpha\delta_0 + \delta_1$, such that the parameters μ_0, μ_1 and Φ_s are decomposed in the direction of α and $\alpha_\perp$. Consequently, (6.27) becomes:

$$\Delta x_t = \alpha[\beta', \rho_0, \rho_1, \delta_0] \begin{bmatrix} x_{t-1} \\ 1 \\ t \\ D_{s,t} \end{bmatrix} + \sum_{i=1}^{k-1} \Gamma_i \Delta x_{t-1} + \Phi D_t + \gamma_0 + \gamma_1 + \delta_1 D_t^s + \epsilon_t. \tag{6.28}$$

The constant, μ_0, is unrestricted. The trend, μ_1, however, is restricted to the cointegration space. Hence, $\gamma_1 = 0$ and $(\gamma_0, \rho_0, \rho_1) \neq 0$.[65] With an unrestricted constant and a trend restricted to the cointegration space, linear trends ($\gamma_0 \neq 0$), but not quadratic trends ($\gamma_1 \neq 0$), are allowed for in the data. This specification ensures similarity in the rank test procedure because the trend might not cancel in the cointegration relations (Nielsen and Rahbek 2000, pp. 12–15). To ensure similarity in the presence of structural breaks a shift dummy must be included in the cointegration relations before determining the rank (Juselius 2006, p. 140). The shift dummy is restricted to the cointegration space: $\delta_0 \neq 0$ and $\delta_1 = 0$.

If $\rho_1 \neq 0$ and $\delta_0 \neq 0$ then the linear trend and the mean shift of the variables do not cancel in the cointegration relations, which will be formally tested in the model in Sect. 6.4.2.2, Table 6.45.

Dummy Variables

Misspecification tests show that normality is rejected and autocorrelation exists in the first two lags. [66] To ensure normality and reduce autocorrelation, dummies are included based on the economic calendar and the graphs of the standardized residuals, which have revealed some large outliers. Table 6.37 presents an overview. As already indicated above, the analysis of Japan requires one shift dummy, one permanent dummy and three transitory dummies. These intervention dummies are of the form $[0,\ldots,0,0,1,1,\ldots,1]$ for the shift dummy, denoted by $dumyyqq_s$; $[0,\ldots,0,1,0,\ldots,0]$ for the permanent blip dummy, denoted by $dumyyqq_p$; $[0,\ldots,0,1,-1,0,\ldots,0]$ for transitory blip dummies, denoted by $dumyyqq_t$ at time 19*yyqq* or 20*yyqq* (see also Sect. 6.2.1.1).

The stock market and real estate crash is modeled by a permanent shift in the intercepts of the long-run relations, combined with an impulse dummy around the transition from boom to bust. The impulse dummy in 1989 Q2 takes account of the fact that the shift in real income, inflation and the overnight rate already occurs

[65] These specifications correspond to case 4 in Juselius (2006, pp. 99–100) and model $H^*(r)$ in Johansen (1995, Equation (5.14), p. 81). In CATS it is processed via the use of det = cidrift.

[66] The test is not reported here at this stage. Instead, misspecification tests are reported for the specified model in Sect. 6.4.1.2.

Table 6.37 Japan quarterly data: intervention dummies

Dummy variable	Motivation	Impact on
$dum8504_t$	Repercussions of the Plaza Accord	Overnight rate
$dum8703_t$	Repercussions of the Louvre Accord	Bond rate
$dum8902_p$	Real estate and stock market bubble	Real income, inflation and overnight rate
$dum9001_s$ $(= D_s)$	Burst of real estate and stock market bubble	Real money, stock market and real income
$dum9702_t$	Increase in consumption tax	Inflation

Table 6.38 Japan quarterly data: information to determine lag length

Model	k	T	Regressive	Log-Likelihood	SC	H–Q	LM(1)	LM(k)
VAR(5)	5	99	46	4,059.060	−67.055	−72.081	0.156	0.259
VAR(4)	4	99	39	3,993.826	−68.012	−72.273	0.070	0.249
VAR(3)	3	99	32	3,936.923	−69.137	−72.633	0.016	0.419
VAR(2)	2	99	25	3,908.460	−70.836	**−73.567**	**0.249**	**0.776**
VAR(1)	1	99	18	3,825.680	**−71.438**	−73.405	0.000	0.000

in the second quarter of 1989, while the shift in real money and the stock market only starts in the first quarter of 1990.

Determination of the Lag Length

The two information criteria SC and H–Q are reported in Table 6.38 and are calculated for different values of lag length, k, where the smallest result suggests the ideal lag length. The last two columns in Table 6.38 report the LM test for autocorrelation of order 1 and k. Numbers in bold indicate the suggested lag length of the respective test.

Whereas the Schwartz criterion suggests one lag, the H–Q criterion proposes two lags. In addition, the LM test shows that there is left-over residual autocorrelation if only one lag is applied. Thus, a lag length of $k = 2$ is used for the analysis.[67]
The discussion in this section on lag length, deterministic components and dummy variables results in the following VAR(2) model (in error-correction form) for Japan:

$$\Delta x_t = \alpha \tilde{\beta}' \tilde{x}_{t-1} + \Gamma_1 \Delta x_{t-1} + \Phi D_t + \mu_0 + \epsilon_t, \tag{6.29}$$

where $x_t' = [m_r, s_r, y_r, \Delta p, or, b10, cf]_t$ and $\tilde{x}_t = \left[x_t', 1, trend, D_s\right]$ is a $((7 + 3) \times 1)$ data vector containing the p variables, a constant, a trend and the shift dummy. The cointegration vectors are represented by $\tilde{\beta} = \left[\beta', \rho_0, \rho_1, \delta_0\right]'$, which

[67] It is an empirical finding that two lags are mostly adequate to model the dynamics of the CVAR model (Johansen 1995, p. 4).

Table 6.39 Japan quarterly data: multivariate misspecification tests (p-values in brackets)

Test for no autocorrelation			
LM(1):	$\chi^2(49)$	=	55.294 [0.249]
LM(2):	$\chi^2(49)$	=	41.271 [0.776]
LM(3):	$\chi^2(49)$	=	52.882 [0.327]
LM(4):	$\chi^2(49)$	=	51.262 [0.385]
Test for normality	$\chi^2(14)$	=	21.292 [0.094]
Test for no Arch effects			
LM(1):	$\chi^2(784)$	=	841.998 [0.074]
LM(2):	$\chi^2(1568)$	=	1681.785 [**0.023**]
LM(3):	$\chi^2(2352)$	=	2455.448 [0.067]
LM(4):	$\chi^2(3136)$	=	2772.000 [1.000]

is a $((7 + 3) \times r)$ matrix with rank r. The analysis is based on 7×99 observations and conditions on the initial values (data points for 1983:3 to 1983:4). The unrestricted permanent and transitory dummy variables are contained in the vector $D_t = \left[dum8504_t,\ dum8703_t,\ dum8902_p,\ dum9702_t\right]$.

6.4.1.2 Misspecification Tests

Prior to determining the reduced rank of the model, the model must be well specified. Tables 6.39 and 6.40 report multivariate and univariate misspecification tests, respectively. The multivariate LM test shows no sign of autocorrelation in the first 4 lags (the null of the test is 'no autocorrelation').[68]

The normality tests are based on skewness and kurtosis.[69] The tests show that the null of the tests, normally distributed errors, is accepted in the multivariate case and for all individual time series except for the overnight rate. This is most likely due to its constant level for the last 15 years of the sample. This is acceptable because it is mainly a result of excess kurtosis and simulation studies have shown that kurtosis is less serious than skewness (Hendry and Juselius 2000, p. 7).

Additionally, tests for multivariate ARCH of order q (with $q = 1, \ldots, 4$) and univariate second order ARCH effects are reported.[70] There are signs for ARCH effects in the second lag, which results from inflation and the bond rate. However, Rahbek et al. (2002, p. 83) show that cointegration tests are robust against moderate residual ARCH effects.

[68] It is asymptotically distributed as χ^2 with p^2 degrees of freedom (Johansen 1995, p. 22).

[69] They are asymptotically χ^2-distributed, with $2p$ degrees of freedom in the multivariate and 2 degrees of freedom in the univariate case.

[70] The multivariate test statistic is approximately distributed as χ^2 with $\frac{q}{4}p^2(p + 1)^2$ degrees of freedom. The univariate test is approximately distributed as χ^2 with k degrees of freedom (Dennis 2006, pp. 179–180).

Table 6.40 Japan quarterly data: univariate misspecification tests (p-values in brackets)

	ARCH(2)	Normality	Skewness	Kurtosis
Δm_r	1.086 [0.581]	1.883 [0.390]	−0.314	3.148
Δs_r	3.861 [0.145]	1.008 [0.604]	−0.173	3.129
Δy_r	0.957 [0.620]	1.239 [0.538]	−0.234	3.109
$\Delta^2 p$	7.824 [**0.020**]	2.917 [0.233]	0.407	3.201
Δor	2.536 [0.281]	7.596 [**0.022**]	0.064	4.105
$\Delta b10$	13.21 [**0.001**]	1.926 [0.382]	0.149	3.364
Δcf	3.488 [0.175]	1.083 [0.582]	−0.061	3.213

6.4.1.3 Rank Determination

As outlined in Sect. 6.2.1.3 the following formal and informal test procedures are applied to determine the reduced rank of the system (Juselius 2006, p. 142):

- Trace test (formal LR test).
- Modulus of the roots of the companion matrix.
- Significance of the α-coefficients.
- Graphical inspection of the recursively calculated trace test statistics.
- Graphical inspection of the stationarity of the cointegration relations.

Trace Test

Table 6.41 furnishes an overview of the trace test results.[71] It reports the estimated eigenvalues, λ_i, the trace test, Q_r, the small sample Bartlett corrected trace test (Johansen 2002, pp. 1932–1940), Q_r^{Bart}, and the 95% quintile from the asymptotic distribution corrected for deterministic components, $C_r^{95\%}$. In addition, the table reports the p-value of the test statistic and the p-value of the Bartlett small sample corrections, p-value*, respectively. In this case, the Bartlett small sample corrections are irrelevant because the analysis is based on an effective sample of

[71] Equation (5.6) in Sect. 5.1.2 shows that, as a prerequisite for valid statistical inference, the variables can be integrated of first but not of higher order. Hence, it is important to ensure that no $I(2)$ variables are part of the data set. As outlined in Sect. 6.2.1.3 different criteria exist to analyze if $I(2)$-ness persists. Applying these criteria to the analysis of Japan shows that no $I(2)$-trends exist in the data. Because univariate unit root tests are used in most analyses, they are conducted as well, in spite of their many limitations in the multivariate setting. The ADF test and the PP test fail to reject the null hypothesis of the existence of a unit root at the 5% level for all variables in levels aside from the time series representing capital flows. The PP test is also rejected for inflation. In contrast, both tests reject the null hypothesis for the variables in first-differenced form of the series. Consequently, the variables are at most integrated of order one. The appropriate lags for the ADF

Table 6.41 Japan quarterly data: trace test of cointegration rank

$p-r$	r	λ_i	Q_r	Q_r^{Bart}	$C_r^{95\%}$	p-value	p-value*
7	0	0.630	312.396	281.609	183.259	0.000	0.000
6	1	0.533	213.961	190.097	146.379	0.000	0.000
5	2	0.408	138.570	115.765	113.306	0.000	0.034
4	3	0.346	86.616	72.839	84.103	0.032	**0.256**
3	4	0.195	44.627	38.779	58.797	**0.450**	0.725
2	5	0.141	23.208	20.586	37.166	0.616	0.770
1	6	0.079	8.161	2.732	18.825	0.715	0.997

99 observations. The trace test accepts the null of $p-r = 3$ unit roots and, therefore, $r = 4$.[72]

Roots of the Companion Matrix

The analysis of the modulus of the roots of the companion form matrix, as depicted in Table 6.42, shows that for $r = 4$ the modulus of the largest unrestricted root drops to 0.814, below the critical value of 0.85 for quarterly data. Hence, Table 6.42 also indicates rank $r = 4$.

Significance of Adjustment Coefficients α

The t-values of the α-coefficients indicate the significance of the equilibrium adjustment behavior of the relative variables. They are derived from the unrestricted

test are selected based on the Schwartz Criterion and the Akaike Information Criterion. The truncation point for the Newey–West adjustment, required for calculating the PP statistic, is determined by using the smallest integer greater than or equal to the sample size, T, to the power of $\frac{1}{4}$ (Greene 2003, p. 267). The test results are not reported here because of the questionable usefulness of univariate tests in a multivariate setting. Rao (2007, p. 1624) points out that these tests lack power and combinations of the many options of the tests almost always enable one to prove that the variables are I(1) in levels. Additionally, Muscatelli and Spinelli (2000, p. 724) refer to difficulties in using unit root tests as pre-tests if regime shifts are inherent to the model. For these and other reasons, Juselius (2006, p. 136) does not even discuss univariate unit root testing in her textbook on cointegration analysis. Instead, the stationarity of a variable is easily tested inside the multivariate model as a restriction on β (see Table 6.46 in Sect. 6.4.2.2). The advantage of the multivariate analysis is to define a well-specified model first and then test for stationarity. With univariate unit root tests, stationarity is tested before guaranteeing i.i.d. error terms, constant parameters and the absence of ARCH effects and before determining cointegration rank. The results of the ADF and PP tests are available on request.

[72] As a sensitivity analysis the trace test is performed with the intervention dummies excluded. The standard trace test borderline accepts $r = 3$ (p-value $= 0.058$). The additional rank of the trace test with dummies included results from the inclusion of the shift dummy, which allows for mean shifts in the cointegration relations. As mentioned above, this is the more correct specification.

Table 6.42 Japan quarterly data: modulus of the seven largest eigenvalue roots

$r = 7$	$r = 6$	$r = 5$	$r = 4$	$r = 3$	$r = 2$	$r = 1$	$r = 0$
1.000	1	1	1	1	1	1	1
0.879	**0.991**	1	1	1	1	1	1
0.879	0.876	**0.856**	1	1	1	1	1
0.875	0.876	0.856	**0.814**	1	1	1	1
0.645	0.597	0.561	0.814	**0.795**	1	1	1
0.645	0.597	0.561	0.513	0.504	**0.806**	1	1
0.422	0.417	0.415	0.443	0.504	0.554	**0.610**	1

Table 6.43 Japan quarterly data: t-values of the α-coefficients

	α						
	Alpha(1)	Alpha(2)	Alpha(3)	Alpha(4)	Alpha(5)	Alpha(6)	Alpha(7)
Δm_r	**(−2.688)**	**(7.965)**	(−0.510)	(−1.400)	(1.638)	(−1.081)	(−1.204)
Δs_r	(−1.877)	(−2.394)	(−0.072)	(−2.384)	**(3.684)**	(1.333)	(1.102)
Δy_r	(1.830)	**(4.608)**	**(−3.529)**	**(3.305)**	(2.044)	(−0.550)	(1.329)
$\Delta^2 p$	**(−4.185)**	**(−4.033)**	(−1.848)	(0.478)	(−1.789)	**(3.027)**	(−0.021)
Δor	**(6.156)**	(1.046)	(−0.184)	(0.357)	(1.098)	**(2.752)**	(−1.447)
$\Delta b10$	**(2.730)**	**(4.966)**	(1.892)	(−1.169)	(−2.300)	(2.223)	(1.066)
Δcf	(2.211)	(0.290)	**(−5.841)**	**(−4.134)**	(−0.647)	(−0.877)	(0.821)

estimates. As can be seen from Table 6.43, adjustment behavior to the first four equations is stronger and involves several variables. Nevertheless, the fifth and sixth relation also exhibit significant t-values, albeit with lower t-values.[73] As a result, the investigation of the adjustment coefficients' significance again points to a rank of $r = 4$.

The Recursive Graphs of the Trace Statistic

Figure 6.8 shows forward and backward recursively calculated graphs for the trace test statistic. The plots are normalized to the 5% significance level, represented by the horizontal line.

If $\lambda_i \neq 0$, the recursively calculated components of the trace statistic should grow linearly for $i = 1, \ldots, r$, but stay constant for $i = r + 1, \ldots, p$ (Juselius 2006, p. 142). Since four of the graphs show linear growth and are above or cross the 1-line (5% critical value), this also indicates a rank of $r = 4$. However, the graph of the fifth cointegration relation is borderline acceptable because it crosses the 1-line and is upward sloping, albeit only for the forward recursive test.

[73] The lower t-values are especially critical because the t-values of a given relation are no longer Student's t distributed if the relation is non-stationary. Instead, it is better to compare the t-values to the Dickey–Fuller distribution, where the critical values are larger. As a rule of thumb, the t-values should be close to 3.0 for the relation to still qualify as adjusting.

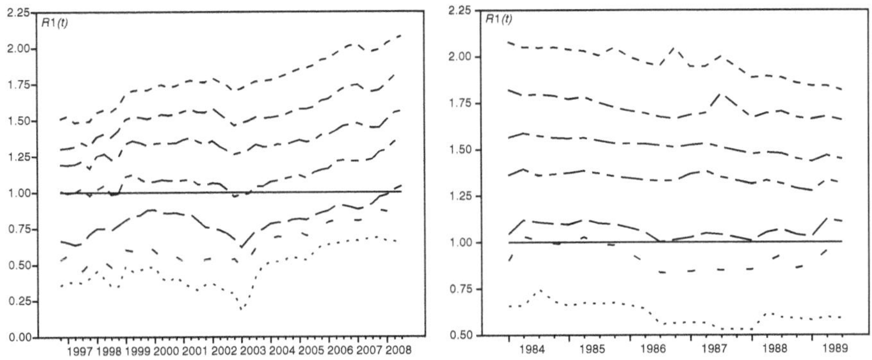

Fig. 6.8 Japan quarterly data: recursively calculated trace test statistics (forward, base sample 1984:01 to 1995:04, depicted left; backward, base sample 2008:03 to 1989:02, depicted right)

Graphical Analysis of the Cointegration Relations

Finally, Appendix B.3.2 depicts the graphs of the cointegrating relations of the unrestricted model. The graphs of the fifth, sixth and seventh relation show persistence and do not suggest mean-reversion behavior, whereas the first four graphs look fairly stationary. As a result, this indicator points to a rank of $r = 4$.

To conclude, the various information criteria used to determine the rank of the model mostly point to a rank of $r = 4$ and this is chosen for the subsequent analysis of the long-run equilibria. This also means that $p - r = 3$ common trends exist, which is also valid from an economic point of view since it is reasonable for a real, monetary and financial trend to exist. In addition, recursive tests show that the data describes a constant parameter regime. Figure 6.9 depicts the recursively calculated test of the log-likelihood. For both the forward and the backward recursive test the graph with short-run effects concentrated out, (R1(t)), stays under the line representing the 5% critical value. Thus, constancy of the overall model is accepted. Appendix B.3.3 provides further information on parameter constancy, such as the eigenvalues λ_i, the eigenvalue fluctuation test, the max test of β constancy and the test of β_t equals a known β. All confirm a constant parameter regime. As a result, the assumption of constant parameters, which is important for the valid identification of the long-run structure, is fulfilled.

6.4.2 *Identification of the Long-Run Structure*

6.4.2.1 Assessment of the Unrestricted Π-Matrix

To help facilitate the identification of an empirically acceptable long-run structure, the unrestricted Π is tentatively interpreted. However, the cointegration space can be rotated by taking proper linear combinations of the equations and, consequently, the final identified long-run structure does not have to reflect the initial suggestions from

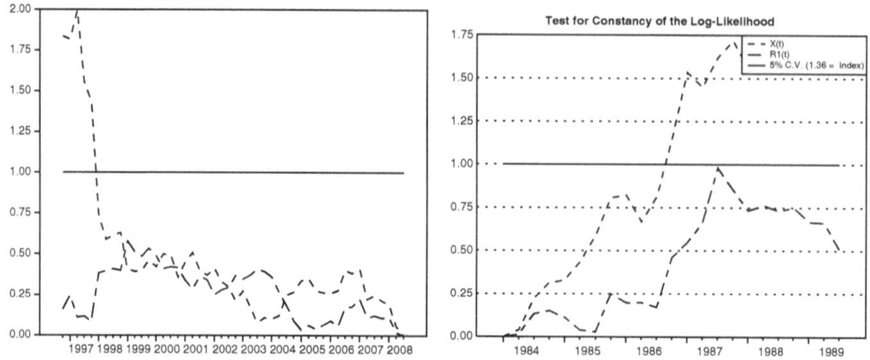

Fig. 6.9 Japan quarterly data: recursively calculated test of log-likelihood (forward, base sample 1984:01 to 1995:04, depicted left; backward, base sample 2008:03 to 1989:02, depicted right)

Table 6.44 Japan quarterly data: the unrestricted Π-matrix for a rank of 4 (t-values in brackets)

	Π								
	m_r	s_r	y_r	Δp	or	$b10$	cf	D_s9001	*Trend*
Δm_r	**−0.106** [−5.176]	0.004 [1.802]	**−0.159** [−4.895]	−0.364 [−1.399]	−0.211 [−1.401]	**−1.521** [−3.585]	−0.019 [−0.063]	**−0.004** [−8.027]	**0.004** [8.038]
Δs_r	−0.583 [−1.598]	**−0.120** [−3.142]	**1.978** [3.410]	−8.209 [−1.772]	**9.384** [3.506]	−9.760 [−1.292]	−6.976 [−1.290]	0.012 [1.420]	−0.010 [−1.174]
Δy_r	**0.058** [2.349]	**0.015** [5.850]	**−0.230** [−5.825]	0.208 [0.661]	**−0.992** [−5.454]	**1.697** [3.304]	−0.165 [−0.449]	**−0.002** [−2.797]	**0.001** [2.503]
$\Delta^2 p$	0.004 [0.359]	−0.002 [−1.598]	**0.076** [3.920]	**−0.744** [−4.822]	**0.294** [3.295]	0.426 [1.691]	−0.087 [−0.484]	**0.001** [3.269]	**−0.001** [−3.174]
Δor	**0.005** [2.712]	0.000 [1.916]	**−0.008** [−2.598]	**0.135** [5.327]	**−0.052** [−3.544]	0.048 [1.170]	−0.031 [−1.036]	0.000 [0.217]	−0.000 [−0.302]
$\Delta b10$	−0.006 [−1.864]	0.000 [1.151]	**−0.019** [−3.939]	**0.142** [3.778]	**−0.056** [−2.577]	**−0.168** [−2.744]	0.020 [0.454]	**−0.000** [−4.500]	**0.000** [4.454]
Δcf	−0.007 [−0.678]	−0.002 [−1.422]	0.019 [1.159]	−0.007 [−0.053]	0.122 [1.610]	0.095 [0.446]	**−1.118** [−7.304]	0.000 [0.395]	0.000 [0.071]

the unrestricted system. Also, the unrestricted Π-matrix may not be economically interpretable. Nevertheless, a rough indication of the long-run information in the data can be obtained. Basically, these estimates measure the combined effect of the cointegration relations in each of the equations (Johansen and Juselius 1992, p. 223).

The unrestricted Π-matrix for the chosen rank $r = 4$ is depicted in Table 6.44. The fact that the signs on the diagonal are negative and significant for all variables shows that all variables exhibit error-correction behavior. Real money is negatively related to real output and the bond rate. In addition, the shift dummy is highly significant for the money equation as already expected from the graphical inspection of the time series. The stock market is positively related to real output and the overnight rate.

The equation for real output shows an aggregate demand relation that is positively related to real money and the stock market and shows a positive deterministic trend. Real output is also positively related to the bond rate but negatively influenced by the overnight rate.

Inflation reacts positively to the overnight rate and deviations of real output. This is an early indication of the Bank of Japan's (BoJ) inability to fight deflation. The overnight rate reacts positively to real money and inflation but reacts negatively to real output. The bond rate equation is negatively related to real output and the overnight rate and positively to inflation (expected inflation effect). Finally, the last equation shows that capital flows only show error-correction behavior to deviations of their own mean. It turns out that capital flows are stationary by themselves. As a result, this equation already describes a cointegrating relation with only one variable.

Table B.12 in Appendix B.3.4 shows the α- and β'-matrices of the partitioned unrestricted Π-matrix. The α-coefficients can indicate which variables are strongly adjusting to long-run equilibria and which variables are more on the pushing side. The estimated α-matrix shows that all variables but the overnight rate show significant adjustment behavior in more than one relation.

The following section outlines preliminary tests for purposes of assessment structure and providing additional information.

6.4.2.2 Preliminary Hypotheses Testing

This section is divided into preliminary tests for β' and α. Automated tests on β' include the potential to exclude variables from the long-run relations and stationarity of individual variables. The α-matrix is formally analyzed for weak exogeneity and unit vectors. Afterwards, single cointegration tests are conducted.[74] This is to test for potential long-run equilibria as outlined in the section on long-run economic relations (5.2). This helps to facilitate the final identification of the long-run structure and provides additional insight on information contained in the data set.

Table 6.45 demonstrates that exclusion of any of the variables is strongly rejected. It also shows that the inclusion of the shift dummy is essential.

Table 6.46 reports the tests for long-run stationarity. Tests are carried out without a restricted trend, with the restricted trend and with the restricted trend as well as the shift dummy included in the cointegrating relations. Stationarity for capital flows is strongly accepted for all three tests and, thus, capital flows may represent a cointegrating vector of their own.

Tables 6.47 and 6.48 test restrictions on α. The test of weak exogeneity is equivalent to testing a zero row in the α-matrix. It denotes a non-error-correcting variable that can be considered weakly exogenous for the long-run parameters β'. If the test is accepted, this also means that the sum of the cumulated empirical shocks to the variable in question defines one common driving trend. Table 6.47 shows that weak exogeneity is borderline accepted for the stock market.

The test of a unit vector in α tests for the opposite, namely whether a variable is exclusively adjusting. If the unit vector test is accepted, the properties of the relevant variable are that its shocks have no permanent effect on any of the other variables

---

[74] All test statistics on α and β are asymptotically distributed as χ^2 because the asymptotic distribution is mixed Gaussian (Johansen 1995, pp. 177–178). As a result, the usual statistical inference can be applied (Johansen and Juselius 1994, p. 16).

Table 6.45 Japan quarterly data: test of variable exclusion (p-values in brackets)

Test of exclusion											
r	DGF	5% C.V.	m_r	s_r	y_r	Δp	or	$b10$	cf	D_s9001	*Trend*
4	4	9.488	27.277 [0.000]	11.609 [0.021]	31.693 [0.000]	69.408 [0.000]	12.470 [0.014]	17.744 [0.001]	29.293 [0.000]	23.928 [0.000]	20.004 [0.000]

Table 6.46 Japan quarterly data: test of variable stationarity (p-values in brackets)

Test of stationarity									
r	DGF	5% C.V.	m_r	s_r	y_r	Δp	or	$b10$	cf
4	5	11.070	31.719 [0.000]	36.259 [0.000]	40.641 [0.000]	31.256 [0.000]	29.710 [0.000]	26.616 [0.000]	**3.547** [0.616]
Restricted trend included in the cointegrating relations									
4	4	9.488	28.265 [0.000]	23.806 [0.000]	28.470 [0.000]	28.454 [0.000]	29.121 [0.000]	28.530 [0.000]	**2.837** [0.585]
Restricted trend and shift-dummy included in the cointegrating relations									
4	3	7.815	27.509 [0.000]	19.052 [0.000]	17.791 [0.000]	18.858 [0.000]	27.692 [0.000]	23.961 [0.000]	**2.676** [0.444]

Table 6.47 Japan quarterly data: test of weak exogeneity (p-values in brackets)

Test of weak exogeneity									
r	DGF	5% C.V.	m_r	s_r	y_r	Δp	or	$b10$	cf
4	4	9.488	42.237 [0.000]	**8.800** [0.066]	26.932 [0.000]	23.960 [0.000]	27.089 [0.000]	23.241 [0.000]	28.010 [0.000]

Table 6.48 Japan quarterly data: test for a unit vector in the α-matrix (p-values in brackets)

Test of unit vector in alpha									
r	DGF	5% C.V.	m_r	s_r	y_r	Δp	or	$b10$	cf
4	3.000	7.815	13.666 [0.003]	18.421 [0.000]	**7.066** [0.070]	14.824 [0.002]	29.832 [0.000]	21.499 [0.000]	**1.713** [0.634]

in the system and it can be regarded as endogenous. The transitory shocks do not cumulate into trends, instead they die out over time. Consequently, together, the two tests of α can identify the pulling and pushing forces of the system. Table 6.48 shows that the test is borderline accepted for real output and strongly accepted for capital flows.

In addition to the above tests on single variables, the focus of the remaining preliminary tests is on single cointegration relations. The idea is to analyze if stable relationships between the economic variables can be identified by linear relations. Testing follows the theoretical connections outlined in Chap. 3 and Sect. 5.2, summarized in Table 5.1. The hypotheses are of the form:

$$\beta = (H\phi, \psi_1, \psi_2, \psi_3), \qquad (6.30)$$

where H is the design matrix, ϕ contains the restricted parameters and ψ_i is a vector of parameters which are freely estimated. It is important to note that each hypothesis in Table 6.49 tests restrictions on a single vector but leaves the other cointegration vectors unrestricted (Johansen and Juselius 1992, pp. 233–236).

Table 6.49 is an overview of the single cointegration test results. Its structure corresponds to Table 5.2. However, since the rank is set to $r = 4$, a minimum of 4 restrictions has to be set to formally test for cointegration.[75] Therefore, only those theoretical relations of Table 5.2 can be formally tested, which restrict at least four of the parameters (all but H_{11} do). In addition, since capital flows are found to be inherently stationary, the variable can not be part of another cointegration relation or adjust to a non-stationary variable (Juselius 2001, p. 343). The test results are still shown for purposes of comparison consistency and in order to keep the final long-run structure open. However, for relations including capital flows, one must keep in mind that stationarity might be a result of the already stationary capital flows instead of the combination of variables.
Hypotheses H_1 to H_8 test for cointegration between stocks and the other variables. Even though stationarity is accepted for hypotheses H_3, H_7 and H_8, the stock market variable does not exhibit significant adjustment behavior to any of the stationary relations. Cointegration by itself does not speak to the direction of causality between the variables. Instead, the test results have to be jointly evaluated with the α-matrix. The last column shows that real money, inflation and the long-term interest rate react to the third relation, with very high coefficients on the long-term real interest rate. In addition, the relations including capital flows are stationary, again with high coefficients on the capital flows variable. As mentioned above, this is most likely a result of the inherent stationarity of capital flows.

H_9 to H_{16} test monetary relations. Only the money demand relation incorporating real output and inflation (H_{12}) is accepted. However, error-correcting behavior of real money is borderline rejected.

'Policy rules' (H_{17} to H_{19}) are all rejected. Hypotheses H_{20} to H_{23} focus on potential stationary aggregate demand for goods relations. H_{21} shows that output reacts positively to deviations in the real bond rate. Hence, H_{21} indicates an IS-type relation in the long-run structure, albeit with relatively high coefficients of the real interest rate.

Under the headline 'Inflation and interest rates' cointegration between inflation and the nominal interest rates ('Fisher parity') as well as between the interest rates themselves ('expectations hypothesis') is tested. The 'Fisher parity'-hypothesis is accepted for the real long-term interest rate in the strong form (H_{27}, i.e., with proportionality imposed) and the weak form (H_{29}, i.e., free parameters). Additionally,

---

[75] The reason for this is the $\chi^2(v)$-distribution of the single cointegration test with v being the number of degrees of freedom. The degrees of freedom are derived from the decrease in the number of free parameters. They are calculated as $v = no.of restr. - rank + 1$. As a result, the number of restrictions has to be a minimum of four to obtain one degree of freedom and, thus, have testable results. Put in a different way, one can always impose $r - 1$ restrictions without changing the value of the likelihood function. Then the system is just identified. However, only over-identified systems can be formally tested (Juselius 2006, p. 215). Hence, more than $r - 1$ restrictions must be imposed.

Table 6.49 Japan quarterly data: testing the stationarity of single relations

	m_r	s_r	y_r	Δp	or	$b10$	cf	$D_s 9001$	*Trend*	$\chi^2(v)$	p-value	$sign.\alpha$
						Demand for stocks						
H_1	2.323	1	0	0	0	0	0	0.089	−0.105	15.8 (2)	0.000	
H_2	0	1	0	−42.35	42.35	0	0	0.065	−0.064	17.0 (2)	0.000	
H_3	**0**	**1**	**0**	**−670.6**	**0**	**670.6**	**0**	**−0.059**	**0.082**	**1.5 (2)**	**0.466**	$m_r, \Delta p, b10$
H_4	0	1	0	0	−9.283	0	0	0.042	−0.053	20.3 (2)	0.000	
H_5	0	1	0	0	0	−24.88	0	0.038	−0.052	21.1 (2)	0.000	
H_6	0	1	−15.22	0	0	0	0	−0.164	0.166	10.0 (2)	0.007	
H_7	**0**	**1**	**0**	**0**	**0**	**0**	**−635.9**	**0.032**	**−0.023**	**2.3 (2)**	**0.318**	cf
H_8	**16.28**	**1**	**0**	**0**	**0**	**0**	**896.7**	**0.293**	**−0.401**	**0.3 (1)**	**0.593**	cf
						Money demand						
H_9	1	0	−1	0	0	0	0	−0.018	0.008	26.1 (3)	0.000	
H_{10}	1	0	0	0	−20.53	20.53	0	−0.054	0.027	26.3 (2)	0.000	
H_{11}	1	0	1.011	0	0.454	17.98	0	0.029	−0.031		no test	
H_{12}	**1**	**0**	**0.575**	**20.93**	**0**	**0**	**0**	**0.027**	**−0.029**	**1.0 (1)**	**0.330**	$s_r, \Delta p$
H_{13}	1	0.430	0	0	0	0	0	0.038	−0.045	15.8 (2)	0.000	
H_{14}	1	0.329	0	0	−0.437	0.437	0	0.025	−0.033	18.3 (1)	0.000	
H_{15}	1	0.294	−1	0	0	0	0	0.015	−0.021	11.6 (2)	0.003	
H_{16}	1	0.259	−1	0	−2.101	2.101	0	0.010	−0.017	12.0 (1)	0.001	
						Policy rules						
H_{17}	0	0	0	−2.687	1	0	0	0	0	11.7 (3)	0.008	
H_{18}	0	0	0.483	0	1	0	0	0.008	−0.007	12.4 (2)	0.002	
H_{19}	0	−0.108	0	0	1	0	0	−0.005	0.006	20.3 (2)	0.000	

(continued)

Table 6.49 (Continued)

	m_r	s_r	y_r	Δp	or	$b10$	cf	D_s9001	*Trend*	$\chi^2(v)$	p-value	$sign.\alpha$
						Demand for goods						
H_{20}	0	0	1	−4.070	4.070	0	0	0.014	−0.010	9.5 (2)	0.009	
H_{21}	**0**	**0**	**1**	**−45.44**	**0**	**45.44**	**0**	**0.006**	**−0.005**	**1.5 (2)**	**0.477**	$m_r, \Delta p, b10$
H_{22}	−0.021	0	1	0	0	0	0	0.016	−0.015	17.8 (2)	0.000	
H_{23}	−0.241	−0.093	1	0	0	0	0	0.006	−0.005	6.5 (1)	0.011	
						Inflation and interest rates						
H_{24}	0.031	0	−0.031	1	0	0	0	0	0	16.5 (3)	0.001	
H_{25}	−0.002	0	0	0	0	1	0	0.003	−0.002	26.9 (2)	0.000	
H_{26}	0	0	0	−1	1	0	0	0	0	25.8 (4)	0.000	
H_{27}	**0**	**0**	**0**	**−1**	**0**	**1**	**0**	**0**	**0**	**6.3 (4)**	**0.171**	$m_r, \Delta p, b10$
H_{28}	0	0	0	1	−0.372	0	0	0	0	11.7 (3)	0.008	
H_{29}	**0**	**0**	**0**	**1**	**0**	**−0.857**	**0**	**0**	**0**	**5.8 (3)**	**0.122**	$\Delta p, b10$
H_{30}	0	0	0	0	−1	1	0	−0.002	0	27.0 (4)	0.000	
H_{31}	0	0	0	0	−0.022	1	0	0.001	0	27.5 (3)	0.000	
H_{32}	**0**	**0**	**0**	**57.05**	**1**	**−58.05**	**0**	**−0.003**	**0**	**6.3 (3)**	0.099	$y_r, \Delta p, b10$
H_{33}	0	0	0	2.635	−1	1	0	0.001	0	18.4 (3)	0.000	

the combination of inflation and interest rates (H_{32}), is stationary as well. However, this is most likely due to the inherent stationarity of the real long-term interest rate.

6.4.2.3 Identification of the Long-Run Cointegrating Relations

The identification procedure is based on the outlined economic theory and the preliminary testing of the econometric model in the previous section. An empirically and economically uniquely identified long-run structure can be obtained by imposing different linear restrictions on the cointegrating relations.

The restrictions on the identified long-run structure are accepted with a p-value of 0.20 ($\chi^2(11) = 14.652$). Appendix B.3.5 shows that the rank conditions are accepted for the full cointegration space. This means that the four cointegration relations are linearly independent and, as such, can not be replaced by each other. The graphs of the cointegrating relations are displayed in Appendix B.3.6 with the deterministic terms and short-term parameters concentrated out.[76] They all describe stationary behavior.

Graphical overviews of forward and backward recursive tests of parameter constancy in Appendix B.3.7 show that parameter constancy for α_i and β_i ($i = 1, \ldots, 4$) is for the most part given. However, parameters of the first two cointegration relations become distorted during the Asian financial crisis between 1997 and 1998. Since both relations incorporate the stock market variable, this might be a result of the turmoil in financial markets worldwide. The third and fourth cointegration relations exhibit constant parameters over the whole sample period.

The structural representation of the cointegration space is depicted in Table 6.50 with the estimated eigenvectors β and the weights α.
The first cointegrating relation describes the long-run relationship between real money, the stock market and inflation:

$$m_{r,t} + 0.033 s_{r,t} + 20.1 \Delta p_t + 0.018 D_s - 0.020 trend \sim I(0), \qquad (6.31)$$

where real money is negatively related to the stock market and inflation. Hence, for Japan, the substitution effect is stronger than the wealth effect. It is notable, though, that the β-coefficient of the stock market is only borderline significant. The negative effect of the stock market might be a result of the long period of poorly performing stocks after 1990. Investors sold stocks and invested in safe assets, such as money.[77] Inflation was low or negative, so that wealth could be stored better in bank accounts than with equity investments. The negative effect of inflation is in accordance with theory since inflation increases the opportunity costs of holding money. However, in the case of Japan it could also be a result of the prevailing deflationary tendencies.

[76] This removes the seasonal fluctuations and outliers, which can be observed in the raw series and, thus, provides a clearer picture (Brüggemann and Lütkepohl 2006, p. 692). See also Sect. 6.2.1.3.

[77] The negative relationship between money and the stock market confirms findings of Humpe and Macmillan (2009, p. 115), who analyze monthly data from 1965 to 2005.

Table 6.50 Japan quarterly data: the identified long-run structure (t-values in brackets)

β'	m_r	s_r	y_r	Δp	or	$b10$	cf	D_s9001	$Trend$
Beta(1)	**1.000** [NA]	**0.033** [1.813]	0.000 [NA]	**20.10** [16.67]	0.000 [NA]	0.000 [NA]	0.000 [NA]	**0.018** [12.78]	**−0.020** [−14.20]
Beta(2)	0.000 [NA]	**−0.060** [−5.001]	**1.000** [NA]	0.000 [NA]	**3.019** [4.896]	0.000 [NA]	0.000 [NA]	**0.011** [11.33]	**−0.010** [−10.34]
Beta(3)	0.000 [NA]	0.000 [NA]	0.000 [NA]	**−1.000** [NA]	0.000 [NA]	**1.000** [NA]	0.000 [NA]	**0.000** [3.310]	0.000 [NA]
Beta(4)	0.000 [NA]	0.000 [NA]	0.000 [NA]	0.000 [NA]	0.000 [NA]	0.000 [NA]	**1.000** [NA]	0.000 [NA]	0.000 [NA]

α	Alpha(1)	Alpha(2)	Alpha(3)	Alpha(4)
Δm_r	**−0.089** [−4.760]	**−0.120** [−3.727]	**−1.442** [−4.024]	0.005 [0.018]
Δs_r	**−0.716** [−2.139]	**2.021** [3.521]	−5.723 [−0.893]	−6.973 [−1.359]
Δy_r	**0.070** [3.027]	**−0.230** [−5.799]	**1.176** [2.654]	−0.142 [−0.399]
$\Delta^2 p$	−0.006 [−0.565]	**0.046** [2.381]	**0.569** [2.633]	−0.040 [−0.230]
Δor	**0.006** [3.270]	−0.005 [−1.480]	0.000 [0.009]	−0.032 [−1.094]
$\Delta b10$	−0.000 [−0.162]	**−0.014** [−2.877]	**−0.144** [−2.713]	0.044 [1.040]
Δcf	0.011 [1.113]	0.024 [1.447]	0.146 [0.788]	**−1.030** [−6.915]

Deflation leads people to increase their money demand because it is more attractive to save and purchase goods at a later point in time.

The α-coefficients show that real money and the stock market are significantly adjusting to this relation. Inflation, on the other hand, does not react to this relation. Thus, real money and the stock market do not have an influence on inflation, but inflation affects both variables. Additionally, deviations from this long-run equilibrium push real output and the overnight rate.

The second β'-vector describes an aggregate demand for goods relation:

$$y_{r,t} - 0.060 s_{r,t} + 3.019 or_t + 0.011 D_s - 0.010 trend \sim I(0), \qquad (6.32)$$

where demand for goods is driven by wealth and balance sheet effects as represented by stock market movements. In addition, real output is negatively affected by the short-term interest rate. A closer look at the α-coefficients reveals that real output and the stock market significantly error correct to this long-run relationship. As such, it can also be interpreted as the stock market reacting positively to real output and the overnight rate.[78] In addition, deviations from this equilibrium have negative

[78] The positive relationship between economic activity and the stock market confirms findings of Humpe and Macmillan (2009, p. 115). The positive long-run relationship between the stock market and the overnight rate confirms the findings of Mukherjee and Naka (1995, pp. 231–232), who find the same relation in their CVAR analysis of the Japanese market.

effects on real money and the bond rate but exhibit positive effects on the inflation rate. This confirms the finding of the previous cointegration relation that the transaction effect on money demand is dominated by other factors. Moreover, it shows that inflation is driven by real developments instead of money growth. The positive reaction of the inflation rate can be interpreted in the framework of the short-run Phillips curve, where inflation increases with excess aggregate demand for goods (Juselius 2001, p. 344).

The third long-run relation confirms the Fisher hypothesis and describes a stable long-term real interest rate:

$$b10_t - \Delta p_t + 0.000 D_s \sim I(0). \tag{6.33}$$

Analysis of the short-run adjustment shows that real money reacts negatively to movements in the long-term real interest rate, which can be associated with the higher opportunity costs of holding money. Real output reacts positively, which, at first glance, seems economically implausible. However, if positive deviations from the long-run equilibrium are associated with higher expected future inflation, then the positive reaction of real output might stem from the different interpretation of inflationary effects in Japan. While inflation is perceived as negative for business in other countries, in Japan deflation was the bigger fear. Deflation led people to postpone purchases. As a result, higher expected inflation might increase consumption and benefit economic activity.

The last cointegrating relation consists of the capital flows variable, which is stationary on its own:

$$cf_t \sim I(0), \tag{6.34}$$

The α-coefficient shows that capital flows error correct with high significance. The other variables do not adjust to movements in capital flows.

6.4.3 Short-Run Dynamics

While the previous analysis focuses on stable long-run economic relations, this section applies a structural error-correction model and formulates stationary equations for each of the variables in the system (see Sect. 6.2.3). Hence, the analysis focuses on the dynamic short-run adjustment of each variable to the past and the other simultaneous variables in the system (Johansen 1995, p. 79). The starting point is estimating the multivariate dynamic equilibrium-correction model for the whole system. Identification of the p short-run equations requires at least $p-1$ just-identifying restrictions on each equation (Juselius 2006, p. 208). This is achieved by restricting current effects between the variables to zero. In addition, insignificant coefficients are removed from each single equation based on an LR test, which results in overidentified equations for each variable. The 68 zero restrictions of insignificant coefficients are accepted with a p-value of 0.44 ($\chi^2(68) = 69.16$). Table 6.51 provides an overview. The dependent variables can be found in the top

Table 6.51 Japan quarterly data: short-run dynamics (t-values in brackets)

	Δm_r	Δs_r	Δy_r	$\Delta^2 p$	Δor	$\Delta b10$	Δcf
$\Delta m_{r,t}$	**1**	0	0	0	0	0	0
$\Delta s_{r,t}$	0	**1**	0	0	0	0	0
$\Delta y_{r,t}$	0	0	**1**	0	0	0	0
$\Delta^2 p_t$	0	0	0	**1**	0	0	0
Δor_t	0	0	0	0	**1**	0	0
$\Delta b10_t$	0	0	0	0	0	**1**	0
Δcf_t	0	0	0	0	0	0	**1**
$\Delta m_{r,t-1}$	**−0.499**		**−0.328**	**0.130**			
	[−4.81]		[−2.69]	[2.34]			
$\Delta s_{r,t-1}$						**0.004**	
						[4.82]	
$\Delta y_{r,t-1}$					**0.018**	**0.041**	
					[2.60]	[3.85]	
$\Delta^2 p_{t-1}$	**−0.274**	**5.597**	**−0.552**		**−0.065**	**−0.078**	
	[−2.04]	[2.52]	[−3.62]		[−4.71]	[−3.84]	
Δor_{t-1}					**0.168**		**−0.617**
					[2.95]		[−2.06]
$\Delta b10_{t-1}$	**1.149**			**−0.571**	**0.197**		
	[2.09]			[−2.15]	[4.21]		
Δcf_{t-1}	**−0.270**					**−0.062**	
	[−2.07]					[−2.97]	
$ecm1_{t-1}$	**−0.074**	**−0.385**	**0.058**		**0.005**		**0.010**
	[−4.59]	[−3.10]	[3.09]		[5.12]		[2.98]
$ecm2_{t-1}$	**−0.145**		**−0.231**	**0.045**	**−0.005**		
	[−6.90]		[−9.51]	[4.81]	[−2.83]		
$ecm3_{t-1}$	**−1.196**		**0.752**	**0.710**		**−0.136**	
	[−3.64]		[1.98]	[6.68]		[−4.45]	
$ecm4_{t-1}$					**−0.048**		**−0.938**
					[−2.45]		[−9.09]
$dum8504_{t,t}$					**0.005**		
					[13.8]		
$dum8703_{t,t}$						**0.004**	
						[5.63]	
$dum8902_{p,t}$	**−0.016**		**−0.033**	**0.020**	**0.003**		
	[−2.44]		[−4.49]	[5.72]	[4.33]		
$dum9001_{p,t}$		**−0.408**	**−0.015**	**0.007**		**0.003**	
		[−3.77]	[−1.99]	[2.23]		[2.91]	
$dum9702_{t,t}$				**0.007**			
				[3.26]			

row as the column headings of each of the model equations. The row headings, on the other hand, indicate the conditioning variables.

The analysis of the short-run dynamics shows that real money reacts negatively to lagged values of itself, the inflation rate and capital flows but positively to the long-term interest rate. Real money error corrects to the first cointegration relation, which is the money demand relation. In addition, the disequilibrium errors of the second and third cointegration relation negatively affect real money.

The stock market only reacts to the inflation rate and error corrects towards the first ecm. This confirms that, in Japan, inflationary tendencies are perceived as good for the economy and the stock market.

Real output is negatively related to lagged values of real money and inflation and shows error-correcting behavior to the second cointegration relation, which is the goods demand relation. The first and the third ecm push real output in the short run. This confirms the information from the short-run adjustment coefficients α of the long-run structure.

Inflation reacts positively to real money and negatively to the bond rate. Moreover, deviations of the second and third cointegration relation push the inflation rate. However, information impulses from the lagged values and from the ecms is contradictory. In the short run, the bond rate has a negative and a positive effect on inflation. The significance of the ecm-coefficient ($t - value = 6.50$) is much higher than the one from the lagged value of the bond rate ($t - value = 2.18$), which may indicate its higher relevancy.

The overnight rate is positively influenced by real output, the bond rate and itself. Inflation has a negative effect. Additionally, deviations from the first cointegration relation push the overnight rate and the disequilibrium errors of the second and fourth cointegration relation have a negative effect on the overnight rate.

The bond rate is pushed by the stock market and real output and reacts negatively to inflation and capital flows. The positive effect of real output is in line with the simple valuation model that is often used to assess whether bonds are fairly priced (Becker 2007, p. 9). It assumes that the nominal yield of a risk-free bond should equal the yield of the underlying economy as a whole. That means that, over the long run, government bond yields should be the same as nominal GDP growth rates. In addition, the short-run analysis shows the adjustment behavior of the bond rate towards the long-term real interest rate ($ecm3$).

Capital flows react negatively to the overnight rate. This establishes that, in the short run, low interest rates drive capital outflows in the form of carry trades. In addition, capital flows show strong adjustment behavior towards the fourth cointegration relation, which is the capital flows relation.

One downside of the above equations is that current effects are not modeled. Instead they are left in the residuals. However, simultaneous effects have potential importance. Whereas correlation between the residuals is a non-issue for the long-run relations of the previous section, identification of the short-run structural equations requires uncorrelated residuals (Juselius 2006, p. 229). Table 6.52 shows the residual covariance matrix, in which large off-diagonal elements can be an

Table 6.52 Japan quarterly data: correlation of structural residuals (standard deviations on diagonal)

	Δm_r	Δs_r	Δy_r	$\Delta^2 p$	Δor	$\Delta b10$	Δcf
Δm_r	*0.006*						
Δs_r	−0.11	*0.108*					
Δy_r	0.15	0.11	*0.007*				
$\Delta^2 p$	**−0.54**	0.14	−0.29	*0.004*			
Δor	0.02	0.13	−0.08	0.29	*0.001*		
$\Delta b10$	−0.13	−0.14	0.01	0.29	0.22	*0.001*	
Δcf	0.01	0.14	0.16	−0.01	−0.25	0.05	*0.003*

Table 6.53 Japan quarterly data: correlation of structural residuals after allowing for current effects (standard deviations on diagonal)

	Δm_r	Δs_r	Δy_r	$\Delta^2 p$	Δor	$\Delta b10$	Δcf
Δm_r	*0.005*						
Δs_r	−0.06	*0.108*					
Δy_r	0.06	0.11	*0.007*				
$\Delta^2 p$	**−0.20**	0.13	−0.29	*0.004*			
Δor	0.15	0.13	−0.08	0.29	*0.001*		
$\Delta b10$	−0.01	−0.14	0.01	0.28	0.22	*0.001*	
Δcf	0.01	0.14	0.16	−0.01	−0.25	0.05	*0.003*

indication of significant current effects between the system variables. Correlation between real money and inflation must be critically recognized.[79]
One way to reduce residual correlation is to introduce current effects between the variables into the short-run structure. Adding current effects of the inflation rate to the real money equation helps to reduce the correlation between the two variables from −0.54 to −0.20 (see Table 6.53).

Table 6.54 shows the slightly changed short-run structure after allowing for current effects. The only difference is that for the real money equation, the coefficients of the bond rate and of the third ecm become insignificant. The other results remain similar.

6.4.4 *The Long-Run Impact of the Common Trends*

The C-matrix provides the key to understanding the long-run implications of the model. Central banks can only influence stock markets where a shock to a monetary instrument has a significant long-run impact on the stock market. Hence, when evaluating the effectiveness of monetary policy the long-run impact of shocks to the

[79] High residual correlation can result from the aggregation of the data over time, inadequately modeled expectations or omitted variables (Juselius 2006, pp. 239–240).

Table 6.54 Japan quarterly data: short-run dynamics allowing for current effects (t-values in brackets)

	Δm_r	Δs_r	Δy_r	$\Delta^2 p$	Δor	$\Delta b10$	Δcf
$\Delta m_{r,t}$	**1**	0	0	0	0	0	0
$\Delta s_{r,t}$	0	**1**	0	0	0	0	0
$\Delta y_{r,t}$	0	0	**1**	0	0	0	0
$\Delta^2 p_t$	−0.634	0	0	**1**	0	0	0
Δor_t	0	0	0	0	**1**	0	0
$\Delta b10_t$	0	0	0	0	0	**1**	0
Δcf_t	0	0	0	0	0	0	**1**
$\Delta m_{r,t-1}$	**−0.400**		**−0.324**	**0.126**			
	[−3.65]		[−2.65]	[2.26]			
$\Delta s_{r,t-1}$						**0.004**	
						[4.76]	
$\Delta y_{r,t-1}$					**0.018**	**0.041**	
					[2.58]	[3.83]	
$\Delta^2 p_{t-1}$	**−0.284**	**5.580**	**−0.550**		**−0.065**	**−0.078**	
	[−2.13]	[2.52]	[−3.25]		[−4.73]	[−3.86]	
Δor_{t-1}					**0.167**		**−0.618**
					[2.94]		[−2.06]
$\Delta b10_{t-1}$	0.837			**−0.578**	**0.197**		
	[1.57]			[−2.18]	[4.21]		
Δcf_{t-1}	**−0.289**					**−0.063**	
	[−2.21]					[−2.97]	
$ecm1_{t-1}$	**−0.074**	**−0.384**	**0.059**		**0.005**		**0.010**
	[−4.63]	[−3.09]	[3.10]		[5.12]		[2.98]
$ecm2_{t-1}$	**−0.115**		**−0.231**	**0.044**	**−0.005**		
	[−4.15]		[−9.50]	[4.77]	[−2.83]		
$ecm3_{t-1}$	−0.720		**0.755**	**0.694**		**−0.136**	
	[−1.65]		[1.99]	[6.50]		[−4.46]	
$ecm4_{t-1}$					**−0.048**		**−0.938**
					[−2.46]		[−9.09]
$dum8504_{t,t}$					**0.005**		
					[13.8]		
$dum8703_{t,t}$						**0.004**	
						[5.65]	
$dum8902_{p,t}$	−0.003		**−0.033**	**0.021**	**0.003**		
	[−0.33]		[−4.49]	[5.76]	[4.33]		
$dum9001_{p,t}$		**−0.401**	**−0.016**	**0.008**		**0.003**	
		[−3.69]	[−2.05]	[2.21]		[2.95]	
$dum9702_{t,t}$				**0.008**			
				[3.47]			

Table 6.55 Japan quarterly data: the long-run impact matrix (t-values in brackets)

The long-run impact matrix, C							
	$\hat{\epsilon}_{m_r}$	$\hat{\epsilon}_{s_r}$	$\hat{\epsilon}_{y_r}$	$\hat{\epsilon}_{\Delta p}$	$\hat{\epsilon}_{or}$	$\hat{\epsilon}_{b10}$	$\hat{\epsilon}_{cf}$
m_r	0.264 [1.270]	**−0.048** [−1.964]	−0.304 [−1.369]	−1.406 [−1.798]	−0.493 [−0.260]	**−8.693** [−2.986]	0.063 [0.110]
s_r	−1.461 [−0.900]	**0.722** [3.733]	**5.057** [2.915]	−2.554 [−0.418]	12.93 [0.872]	11.65 [0.513]	−5.392 [−1.209]
y_r	**−0.215** [−2.124]	**0.033** [2.775]	**0.299** [2.764]	**−0.785** [−2.066]	**−3.181** [−3.447]	0.005 [0.004]	−0.140 [−0.505]
Δp	−0.011 [−1.134]	0.001 [1.072]	0.007 [0.684]	**0.074** [2.074]	0.004 [0.041]	**0.414** [3.110]	0.006 [0.215]
or	0.042 [1.781]	0.003 [1.151]	0.001 [0.053]	**0.209** [2.354]	**1.310** [6.062]	0.229 [0.692]	−0.060 [−0.929]
$b10$	−0.011 [−1.134]	0.001 [1.072]	0.007 [0.684]	**0.074** [2.074]	0.004 [0.041]	**0.414** [3.110]	0.006 [0.215]
cf	0.000 [NA]	0.000 [NA]	0.000 [NA]	0.000 [NA]	0.000 [NA]	0.000 [NA]	0.000 [NA]

short-term interest rate and to the money supply on the stock market is of particular interest.[80]

The residual $\epsilon_{i,t}$ is interpreted as an estimate of the unanticipated shock to variable x_i. The estimated long-run impact of these cumulated shocks is reported in Table 6.55 and is calculated from the estimates of the restricted VAR model as

$$C = \tilde{\beta}_{\perp}\alpha_{\perp}^{'}, \qquad (6.35)$$

where $\tilde{\beta}_{\perp} = \beta_{\perp}(\alpha_{\perp}^{'}\beta_{\perp})^{-1}$ and $\alpha_{\perp}, \beta_{\perp}$ are the $(p \times p - r)$ orthogonal compliments of α and β (Johansen 1995, pp. 49–50). Since C has reduced rank, only $p - r = 3$ linear combinations of the $p = 7$ innovations, ϵ_t, have permanent effects.

The C-matrix can be read column or row-wise. The columns show the long-run impact of a shock to a variable on each of the variables in the system and the rows show which of the shocks have a long-run impact on the particular variable.
The C-matrix in Table 6.55 shows that, in the long run, shocks to both the stock market and the bond rate have negative effects on real money. Since both assets serve as substitutes for money, the substitution effect is more dominant than the wealth effect in the long run.

Cumulated shocks to stock prices and real income influence stock market developments in the long run. The former is a sign of herding, trend-following behavior and rational speculation of economic agents. The latter indicates the importance of real developments for the stock market. The C-matrix also shows that for the period under investigation, the BoJ did not have the ability to influence stock market developments in the long run.

[80] An alternative could be to use monetary instruments to control an intermediate target, such as the (real) long-term bond rate if the intermediate target has a long-run impact on stocks. However, for this to be manageable, cointegration between the policy instrument and the intermediate target is a necessity.

That aside, the C-matrix shows that shocks to both real output and the stock market have positive long-run effects on the level of economic activity. At the same time, shocks to real money, inflation and the overnight rate translate into weaker economic growth in the long run. This confirms the finding of the long-run relations.

Shocks to the bond rate translate into higher inflation and vice versa. Also at interest is the non-existent long-term impact of the overnight rate on inflation, which indicates that the BoJ was unable to permanently influence inflation over the last 25 years. In addition to the importance of global forces on the inflation rate, this confirms the 'liquidity trap', which restricted Japanese monetary policy after the burst of the stock market and real estate bubbles.

6.4.5 Conclusion

The analysis of Japan has produced results which differ from those of the US and euro area analyses. Japan's economy is also characterized by different circumstances as a result of the real estate and stock market bubble and burst at the end of the 1980s. The 1990s are often described as the lost decade for Japan, with no real growth in aggregate output. In addition, Japan is the only country with a high share of deflationary time periods over the timeframe under consideration. The severe differences in economic developments before and after 1990 required the inclusion of a shift dummy to account for the changing risk perception and reduced optimism of economic agents. This enabled a constant parameter regime.

Table 6.56 shows that the results of the main hypotheses are rejected. The long-run structure of the cointegration space shows that stock markets dynamically adjust to excess liquidity. However, the money demand relation is different from classical money demand relations, which usually include aggregate demand for goods. In the case of Japan, the strongest influence on money demand comes from price developments. Money demand increases with reduced inflation or deflation in the long and in the short run. This characterizes Japan's problems over the past 18 years. Because economic agents expected deflationary developments they increased their money holdings and postponed purchases of real goods. One alternative to money holdings is to buy stocks. The stock market is the second factor influencing money demand. It shows a substitution effect. The more the stock market rose the more people invested in stocks again, thereby, reducing money demand. This is also confirmed by the analysis of the long-run impact matrix, where shocks to the stock market and to the bond rate have a negative long-run impact on money holdings because alternative investments become more attractive. Surprisingly, aggregate real output does not play a role for money demand. This could result from the rather flat output developments since the end of the boom/bust cycle.

Table 6.56 also shows that confidence and optimism are important factors for the development of stock prices. The table shows that the self-reinforcing and trend-following behavior of stock markets can be found not only in countries with mostly

Table 6.56 Japan quarterly data: results of main hypotheses

	Hypotheses/Questions	Result
H_1	Stock market behavior in Japan shows strong persistence, i.e., shocks to the stock market have positive long-run effects on future developments	Yes
H_2	Long-run equilibria exist between stock prices and liquidity conditions	(Yes)
H_3	Liquidity conditions influence stock prices positively in the long run	No
H_4	Liquidity conditions influence stock prices positively in the short run	No
H_5	International capital flows have a positive long-run impact on the stock market behavior in Japan	No
H_6	International capital flows have a positive short-run impact on the stock market behavior in Japan	No
Q_1	Is the BoJ able to influence stock prices in the long run?	No
Q_2	Is the BoJ able to influence stock prices in the short run?	No

rising (US) but also in countries with mostly falling (Japan) stock markets. In addition, stock market developments are driven by changes in economic activity.

The analysis of Japan also confirms the stock market's importance for aggregate output, the second part of transmission mechanism theory. The stock market enters positively into the second cointegration relation, which is the demand for goods relation. In addition, shocks to the stock market have a positive long-run impact on real output.

In addition, the above analysis sheds light on a few other aspects of economic interest, mainly:

- The Fisher parity holds for the long-term real interest rate. Both inflation and the bond rate react towards this long-run equilibrium.
- The inflation rate reacts positively to deviations from the aggregate demand for goods relation, which can be interpreted in the framework of the short-run Phillips curve, where inflation increases with excess aggregate demand for goods.
- The short-term interest rate is pushed by the equilibrium errors of the money demand relation but does not show error correction behavior to any of the other cointegration relations. In the short run, it is pushed by lagged values of real output, the bond rate and itself. In addition, it reacts negatively to the inflation rate.
- Capital flows are found to be stationary and, thus, do not play a role in the other cointegration vectors. Furthermore, shocks to capital flows do not have any long-term impacts on any of the other variables. In the short run, capital flows are negatively affected by the short-term interest rate, which tentatively indicates the importance of the carry trade for capital flows into and out of Japan. It would appear that international capital flows are more driven by exports and imports and less by financial flows. This is contrary to what one would expect from the outset, especially with the large volume of carry trades in mind. Nevertheless, Japan is an industrial and export as well as import-dependent country.

6.5 United Kingdom: Quarterly Data

6.5.1 Model Specification

6.5.1.1 Data Overview, Deterministic Components and Lag Length

As in the other country analyses, the data vector consists of the following seven variables:

$$x_t' = [m_r, s_r, y_r, \Delta p, or, b10, cf]_t\,, \qquad (6.36)$$

where m_r is the log of real money (M4[81]), s_r is the log of real stock market levels (total market including dividends) and y_r is the log of real GDP. Real variables are transformed from nominal variables by applying the consumer price index, p. Hence, Δp is the inflation rate. Short and long-term interest rates are represented by the overnight interbank rate, or, and the yield on 10-year government bonds, $b10$, respectively. All interest rates have been converted to quarterly rates and divided by 100 to achieve comparability with the inflation rate. Capital flows, cf, are calculated in percent as a share of the total money stock M4. Capital flows are derived from non-bank BoP transactions as described in Sect. 4.6.3.2 and Appendix A. All time series are obtained either from Datastream or the IMF BoP database. Detailed information on the specific sources of the data are reported in Appendix B.4.1. The data used for the analysis covers the last 25 years and consists of quarterly observations from 1983:1 to 2008:3.[82] Figure 6.10 displays the time pattern of all variables in levels and first differences.

All graphs look stationary for the differenced series. The series in levels, however, show a lot of persistence. In addition, real money, the stock market and real GDP seem to follow a trend. Thus, an unrestricted constant and a restricted trend are included in the model.[83]

Dummy Variables

Misspecification tests show that normality is rejected and ARCH effects exist in the second and third lag.[84] To ensure normality and reduce ARCH effects, dummies

---

[81] The time series for nominal money (M4) was corrected for an additive outlier in the third quarter of 1997 before entering the analysis. The additive outlier is based on the September 1997 opt-in to the monetary control arrangements exercised by banks in the Channel Islands and the Isle of Man, which was related to their reclassification as non-resident (Bank of England (2003, p. 6)).

[82] The motivation for starting the sample period in 1983 is to ensure a constant parameter regime. Therefore, the volatile and high-inflation period of the 1970s and the beginning of the 1980s is excluded. Moreover, 1983 also coincides with a general increase in international capital flows due to the abolition of previous control measures in many western economies and with the beginning of more efficient electronic transmission technologies.

[83] For a discussion of deterministic components in the model, see Sect. 6.2.1.1.

[84] Test results are not reported here at this stage. Instead, misspecification tests are reported for the specified model in Sect. 6.5.1.2.

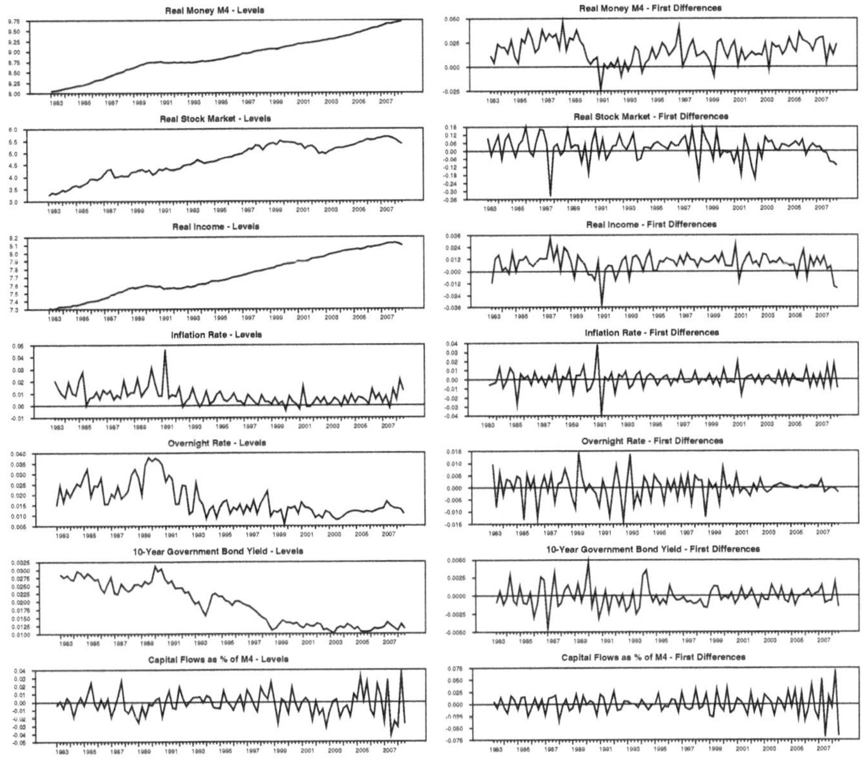

Fig. 6.10 UK quarterly data in levels and first differences

Table 6.57 UK quarterly data: intervention dummies

Dummy variable	Motivation	Impact on
$dum8704_p$	Black Friday stock market crash in October	Stock market
$dum9001_p$	German re-unification[a]	Bond rate
$dum9102_p$	Recession[b]	Real money, real output and inflation

[a] Homer and Sylla (2005, p. 669).
[b] The UK entered into recession because the bond rate was kept too high. Monetary policy focus was on the exchange rate instead of economic activity, thereby, increasing the severity of the recession. It also reduced real money holdings (higher opportunity costs) and dampened inflation.

are included based on the economic calendar and the graphs of the standardized residuals, which have revealed some large outliers. Table 6.57 provides an overview. Modeling data for the UK requires three permanent dummies.[85] Analysis of the residuals pointed to the inclusion of additional dummies, e.g., for the overnight

[85] For an overview of the different kinds of dummies see Sect. 6.2.1.1.

Table 6.58 UK quarterly data: information to determine lag length

Model	k	T	Regressive	Log-Likelihood	SC	H–Q	LM(1)	LM(k)
VAR(5)	5	101	43	3,709.828	−59.708	−64.346	0.003	0.316
VAR(4)	4	101	36	3,648.484	−60.732	−64.616	0.081	0.571
VAR(3)	3	101	29	3,611.999	−62.249	−65.377	0.416	0.513
VAR(2)	2	101	22	3,569.528	−63.647	−66.020	**0.053**	**0.070**
VAR(1)	1	101	15	3,535.901	**−65.220**	**−66.838**	0.011	0.011

rate. However, this increased autocorrelation and was stricken, because the model is specified well enough in their absence.

Determination of the Lag Length

The two information criteria SC and H–Q are reported in Table 6.58 and are calculated for different values of lag length, k, where the smallest result suggests the ideal lag length. The last two columns in Table 6.58 report the LM test for autocorrelation of order 1 and k. Numbers in bold indicate the suggested lag length of the respective test.

Both criteria (SC, H–Q) suggest one lag. However, the LM test shows that there is left-over residual autocorrelation if only one lag is applied. Thus, a lag length of $k = 2$ is used for the analysis.

The discussion in this section on lag length, deterministic components and dummy variables results in the following VAR(2) model (in error-correction form) for UK quarterly data:

$$\Delta x_t = \alpha \tilde{\beta}' \tilde{x}_{t-1} + \Gamma_1 \Delta x_{t-1} + \Phi D_t + \mu_0 + \epsilon_t, \tag{6.37}$$

where $x_t' = [m_r, s_r, y_r, \Delta p, or, b10, cf]_t$ and $\tilde{x}_t = \left[x_t', 1, trend\right]$ is a $((7+2) \times 1)$ data vector containing the p variables, a constant and a trend. The cointegration vectors are represented by $\tilde{\beta} = \left[\beta', \rho_0, \rho_1\right]'$, which is a $((7+2) \times r)$ matrix with rank r. The analysis is based on 7×101 observations and conditions on the initial values (data points for 1983:1 to 1983:2). The dummy variables are contained in the vector $D_t = \left[dum8704_p,\ dum9001_p,\ dum9102_p\right]$.

6.5.1.2 Misspecification Tests

The model must be well specified to be able to determine the reduced rank of the model. Tables 6.59 and 6.60 report multivariate and univariate misspecification tests, respectively. The multivariate LM test shows that the null of the test (‘no autocorrelation’) is only borderline accepted for the first two lags.[86]

[86] It is asymptotically distributed as χ^2 with p^2 degrees of freedom (Johansen 1995, p. 22).

Table 6.59 UK quarterly data: multivariate misspecification tests (p-values in brackets)

Test for no autocorrelation			
LM(1):	$\chi^2(49)$	=	65.950 [0.053]
LM(2):	$\chi^2(49)$	=	64.289 [0.070]
LM(3):	$\chi^2(49)$	=	61.513 [0.108]
LM(4):	$\chi^2(49)$	=	52.745 [0.331]
Test for normality	$\chi^2(14)$	=	22.082 [0.077]
Test for no Arch effects			
LM(1):	$\chi^2(784)$	=	858.685 [**0.032**]
LM(2):	$\chi^2(1568)$	=	1651.301 [0.070]
LM(3):	$\chi^2(2352)$	=	2507.490 [**0.013**]
LM(4):	$\chi^2(3136)$	=	2828.000 [1.000]

Table 6.60 UK quarterly data: univariate misspecification tests (p-values in brackets)

	ARCH(2)	Normality	Skewness	Kurtosis
Δm_r	1.387 [0.500]	0.154 [0.926]	0.046	2.919
Δs_r	1.658 [0.437]	1.254 [0.534]	−0.250	3.055
Δy_r	1.907 [0.385]	0.282 [0.868]	0.024	2.992
$\Delta^2 p$	8.959 [**0.011**]	5.637 [0.060]	0.468	3.924
Δor	5.689 [0.058]	3.617 [0.164]	−0.017	3.635
$\Delta b10$	4.772 [0.092]	8.125 [**0.017**]	−0.301	4.225
Δcf	22.271 [**0.000**]	1.660 [0.436]	−0.024	3.333

The normality tests are based on skewness and kurtosis.[87] The tests show that the null of the tests, normally distributed errors, is accepted in the multivariate case and for all individual time series aside from the bond rate. This is adequate because it is a result of excess kurtosis and simulation studies have shown that kurtosis is not as substantial as skewness (Hendry and Juselius 2000, p. 7).
Additionally, tests for multivariate ARCH of order q (with $q = 1, \ldots, 4$) and univariate second order ARCH effects are reported.[88] There are signs for ARCH effects in the first and third lag of the system and individually for inflation and capital flows. However, Rahbek et al. (2002, p. 83) show that cointegration tests are robust against moderate residual ARCH effects.

[87] They are asymptotically χ^2-distributed, with $2p$ degrees of freedom in the multivariate and 2 degrees of freedom in the univariate case.

[88] The multivariate test statistic is approximately distributed as χ^2 with $\frac{q}{4}p^2(p+1)^2$ degrees of freedom. The univariate test is approximately distributed as χ^2 with k degrees of freedom (Dennis 2006, pp. 179–180).

6.5.1.3 Rank Determination

As outlined in Sect. 6.2.1.3 the following formal and informal test procedures are applied to determine the reduced rank of the system (Juselius 2006, p. 142):

- Trace test (formal LR test).
- Modulus of the roots of the companion matrix.
- Significance of the α-coefficients.
- Graphical inspection of the recursively calculated trace test statistics.
- Graphical inspection of the stationarity of the cointegration relations.

Trace Test

Table 6.61 provides an overview of the trace test results.[89] It reports the estimated eigenvalues, λ_i, the trace test, Q_r, the small sample Bartlett corrected trace test (Johansen 2002, pp. 1932–1940), Q_r^{Bart}, and the 95% quintile from the asymptotic distribution corrected for deterministic components, $C_r^{95\%}$. In addition, the table reports the p-value of the test statistic and the p-value of the Bartlett small sample corrections, p-value*, respectively. The trace test and the Bartlett corrected trace test accept the null of $p - r = 4$ unit roots and, therefore, $r = 3$.[90]

[89] Equation (5.6) in Sect. 5.1.2 shows that, as a prerequisite for valid statistical inference, the variables can be integrated of first but not of higher order. Hence, it is important to ensure that no $I(2)$ variables are part of the data set. As outlined in Sect. 6.2.1.3 different criteria exist to analyze if $I(2)$-ness persists. Applying these criteria to UK data shows that no $I(2)$-trends exist in the data. Because univariate unit root tests are used in most analyses, they are conducted as well, in spite of their many limitations in the multivariate setting. The ADF test and the PP test fail to reject the null hypothesis of the existence of a unit root at the 5% level for all variables in levels aside from the time series representing capital flows. The PP test is also rejected for inflation. In contrast, both tests reject the null hypothesis for the variables in first-differenced form of the series. Consequently, the variables are at most integrated of order one. The appropriate lags for the ADF test are selected based on the Schwartz Criterion and the Akaike Information Criterion. The truncation point for the Newey–West adjustment, required for calculating the PP statistic, is determined by using the smallest integer greater than or equal to the sample size, T, to the power of $\frac{1}{4}$ (Greene 2003, p. 267). The test results are not reported here because of the questionable usefulness of univariate tests in a multivariate setting. Rao (2007, p. 1624) points out that these tests lack power and combinations of the many options of the tests almost always enable one to prove that the variables are I(1) in levels. Additionally, Muscatelli and Spinelli (2000, p. 724) refer to difficulties in using unit root tests as pre-tests if regime shifts are inherent to the model. For these and other reasons, Juselius (2006, p. 136) does not even discuss univariate unit root testing in her textbook on cointegration analysis. Instead, the stationarity of a variable is easily tested inside the multivariate model as a restriction on β (see Table 6.66 in Sect. 6.5.2.2). The advantage of the multivariate analysis is to define a well-specified model first and then test for stationarity. With univariate unit root tests, stationarity is tested before guaranteeing i.i.d. error terms, constant parameters and the absence of ARCH effects and before determining cointegration rank. The results of the ADF and PP tests are available on request.

[90] As a sensitivity analysis the trace test is performed with the intervention dummies excluded. The results are confirmed as both test statistics suggest a rank of three.

Table 6.61 UK quarterly data: trace test of cointegration rank

$p-r$	r	λ_i	Q_r	Q_r^{Bart}	$C_r^{95\%}$	p-value	p-value*
7	0	0.535	246.913	220.648	150.348	0.000	0.000
6	1	0.473	169.491	152.534	117.451	0.000	0.000
5	2	0.356	104.721	95.140	88.554	0.002	0.015
4	3	0.255	60.244	54.431	63.659	**0.096**	**0.242**
3	4	0.112	30.453	27.676	42.770	0.482	0.645
2	5	0.101	18.407	14.217	25.731	0.324	0.645
1	6	0.073	7.693	7.518	12.448	0.286	0.303

Table 6.62 UK quarterly data: modulus of the seven largest eigenvalue roots

$r=7$	$r=6$	$r=5$	$r=4$	$r=3$	$r=2$	$r=1$	$r=0$
0.994	1	1	1	1	1	1	1
0.994	**0.985**	1	1	1	1	1	1
0.951	0.985	**0.913**	1	1	1	1	1
0.552	0.568	0.741	**0.658**	1	1	1	1
0.552	0.568	0.498	0.658	**0.612**	1	1	1
0.500	0.497	0.498	0.496	0.612	**0.561**	1	1
0.500	0.497	0.475	0.496	0.491	0.480	**0.558**	1

Roots of the Companion Matrix

The analysis of the modulus of the roots of the companion form matrix, as depicted in Table 6.62, shows that for $r = 4$ the modulus of the largest unrestricted root drops to 0.658, and, thus, well below the critical value of 0.85 for quarterly data. Therefore, Table 6.62 indicates rank $r = 4$.

Significance of Adjustment Coefficients α

The t-values of the α-coefficients provide an indication for the significance of the equilibrium adjustment behavior of the relative variables. They are derived from the unrestricted estimates. As can be seen from Table 6.63, adjustment behavior to the first three relations is stronger and involves several variables. Nevertheless, the fourth relation also exhibits significant albeit lower t-values.[91] As a result, the investigation of the adjustment coefficients' significance points to a rank of $r = 3$ but also allows for a rank of $r = 4$.

[91] The lower t-values are especially critical because the t-values of a given relation are no longer Student's t distributed if the relation is non-stationary. Instead, it is better to compare the t-values to the Dickey–Fuller distribution, where the critical values are larger. As a rule of thumb, the t-values should be close to 3.0 for the relation to still qualify as adjusting.

Table 6.63 UK quarterly data: t-values of the α-coefficients

	α						
	Alpha(1)	Alpha(2)	Alpha(3)	Alpha(4)	Alpha(5)	Alpha(6)	Alpha(7)
Δm_r	(−1.755)	(2.337)	(1.236)	(−1.011)	(2.453)	(−0.894)	(−1.588)
Δs_r	(1.829)	(0.325)	(−0.253)	(0.312)	(−1.006)	(0.840)	**(−2.567)**
Δy_r	(−1.392)	(−0.393)	**(4.054)**	(2.402)	(−0.499)	(−2.107)	(−0.933)
$\Delta^2 p$	**(5.288)**	**(−5.789)**	(1.066)	(−1.406)	(0.504)	(1.297)	(1.075)
Δor	(1.506)	**(4.416)**	**(4.997)**	**(−2.711)**	(−0.882)	(0.440)	(0.480)
$\Delta b10$	(−1.412)	(−0.388)	(2.213)	**(3.068)**	(1.269)	(1.985)	(1.086)
Δcf	**(−6.834)**	**(−4.426)**	(2.057)	(−2.180)	(−0.413)	(1.073)	(−0.662)

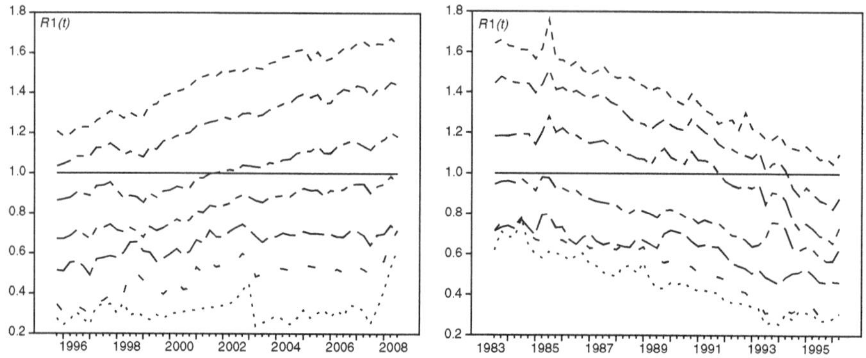

Fig. 6.11 UK quarterly data: recursively calculated trace test statistics (forward, base sample 1983:03 to 1995:04, depicted left; backward, base sample 2008:03 to 1996:02, depicted right)

The Recursive Graphs of the Trace Statistic

Figure 6.11 shows forward and backward recursively calculated graphs for the trace test statistic. The plots are normalized to the 5% significance level, represented by the horizontal line. If $\lambda_i \neq 0$, the recursively calculated components of the trace statistic should grow linearly for $i = 1, \ldots, r$, but stay constant for $i = r+1, \ldots, p$ (Juselius 2006, p. 142). Four of the graphs show linear growth but only three are above or cross the 1-line (5% critical value). Hence, the graphical inspection of the trace statistic confirms a rank of $r = 3$.

Graphical Analysis of the Cointegration Relations

The graphs of the cointegrating relations of the unrestricted model are depicted in Appendix B.4.2. Whereas the first three graphs clearly look stationary, the last three relations show clear persistent behavior. The fourth relation could be interpreted as either stationary or non-stationary. As a result, this indicator points to a rank of either $r = 3$ or $r = 4$.

To conclude, the various information criteria used to determine the rank of the model mostly point to a rank of $r = 3$ and this is chosen for the subsequent analysis

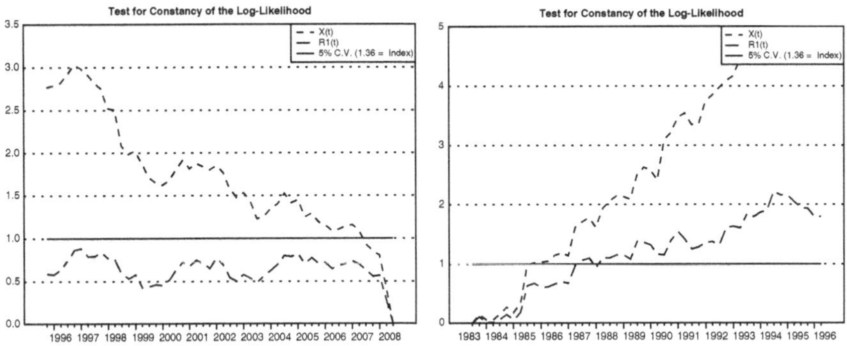

Fig. 6.12 UK quarterly data: recursively calculated test of log-likelihood (forward, base sample 1983:03 to 1995:04, depicted left; backward, base sample 2008:03 to 1996:02, depicted right)

of the long-run equilibria.[92] This also means that $p-r = 4$ common trends exist. In addition, recursive tests show that the data describes a constant parameter regime. Figure 6.12 depicts the recursively calculated test of the log-likelihood. Whereas the forward test is clearly accepted,[93] the backward calculated test statistic takes a long time to drop under the line. This is probably due to the exclusion of some intervention dummies because of the connected autocorrelation. However, as additional tests on parameter constancy show, constancy of the overall model is accepted (see the tests in Appendix B.4.3 on eigenvalues λ_i, eigenvalue fluctuations, the max test of β constancy and the test of β_t equals a known β, Figs. B.46–B.49, respectively). As a result, the assumption of constant parameters, which is important for valid identification of the long-run structure, is fulfilled.

6.5.2 *Identification of the Long-Run Structure*

6.5.2.1 Assessment of the Unrestricted Π-Matrix

To help facilitate the identification of an empirically acceptable long-run structure, the unrestricted Π is tentatively interpreted. However, the cointegration space can be rotated by taking proper linear combinations of the equations. Consequently, the final identified long-run structure does not have to reflect the initial suggestions from the unrestricted system. Also, the unrestricted Π-matrix may not be economically interpretable. Nevertheless, a rough indication of the long-run information in the data can be obtained. Basically, these estimates measure the combined effect of the cointegration relations in each of the equations (Johansen and Juselius 1992, p. 223).

---

[92] Since the rank test procedures would also allow for a rank of $r = 4$, the identified cointegration relations are tested for this choice of rank as well. This sensitivity analysis confirms the derived results.

[93] The graph with short-run effects concentrated out, (R1(t)), stays under the line representing the 5% critical value.

The unrestricted Π-matrix for the chosen rank $r = 3$ is depicted in Table 6.64. Analysis of the diagonal shows that the variables do not exhibit as much error-correcting behavior as the same variables in the other country analyses. Money, the stock market, output and the bond rate either have positive signs or are insignificant or both. Inflation, the short rate and capital flows, on the other hand, have significant and negative coefficients on the diagonal. Thus, a first indication of the analysis of the unrestricted Π is that the three cointegrating relations reflect an inflation rate, an overnight rate and a capital flows relation.

Since the relations for the stock market and the bond rate have no significant coefficients, they are potentially weakly exogenous to the system. This might be a result of the importance of the world financial hub in London, reflecting international rather than national developments.
In addition, Table 6.64 establishes that inflation reacts positively to real money and the overnight rate and negatively to the stock market. The overnight rate reacts positively to real money, the stock market and real output. Finally, the last equation shows that capital flows demonstrate error-correction behavior towards all other variables aside from the inflation rate.

Table B.15 in Appendix B.4.4 shows the α- and β'-matrices of the partitioned unrestricted Π-matrix. The α-coefficients can indicate which variables strongly adjust to long-run equilibria and which variables are more on the pushing side. The estimated α-matrix suggests that inflation, the overnight rate and capital flows show significant adjustment behavior to at least two relations. The stock market does not react to any of the relations, another sign for its weak exogeneity.

6.5.2.2 Preliminary Hypotheses Testing

This section is divided into preliminary tests for β' and α. Automated tests on β' include the possibility to exclude variables from the long-run relations and stationarity of individual variables. The α-matrix is formally analyzed for weak exogeneity

Table 6.64 UK quarterly data: the unrestricted Π-matrix for a rank of 3 (t-values in brackets)

	Π							
	m_r	s_r	y_r	Δp	or	$b10$	cf	*Trend*
Δm_r	0.002 [0.262]	**0.006** [2.873]	0.024 [0.947]	**0.880** [2.588]	**−0.633** [−2.014]	−0.304 [−1.559]	−0.043 [−0.446]	−0.000 [−1.228]
Δs_r	0.076 [1.330]	−0.019 [−1.152]	0.196 [0.995]	−2.493 [−0.940]	−0.887 [−0.361]	2.740 [1.797]	1.192 [1.583]	−0.002 [−0.767]
Δy_r	0.005 [0.812]	**0.005** [2.832]	0.031 [1.566]	0.034 [0.129]	**−0.556** [−2.291]	−0.271 [−1.794]	**−0.191** [−2.566]	**−0.001** [−2.069]
$\Delta^2 p$	**0.006** [2.080]	**−0.005** [−5.667]	0.008 [0.737]	**−1.079** [−7.720]	**0.262** [2.023]	**0.353** [4.390]	0.016 [0.393]	−0.000 [−0.279]
Δor	**0.015** [5.294]	**0.003** [3.806]	**0.059** [6.087]	0.190 [1.445]	**−0.796** [−6.560]	0.098 [1.303]	0.064 [1.732]	**−0.001** [−6.319]
$\Delta b10$	−0.000 [−0.089]	0.001 [1.838]	0.001 [0.412]	0.016 [0.365]	−0.040 [−1.003]	−0.039 [−1.574]	−0.024 [−1.917]	−0.000 [−0.752]
Δcf	**−0.060** [−5.752]	**0.010** [3.398]	**−0.167** [−4.624]	0.565 [1.159]	**1.192** [2.644]	**−2.022** [−7.220]	**−1.116** [−8.073]	**0.002** [3.642]

Table 6.65 UK quarterly data: test of variable exclusion (p-values in brackets)

Test of exclusion										
r	DGF	5% C.V.	m_r	s_r	y_r	Δp	or	$b10$	cf	*Trend*
3	3	7.815	**5.657** [0.130]	8.193 [0.042]	12.379 [0.006]	40.330 [0.000]	23.277 [0.000]	**5.384** [0.146]	38.187 [0.000]	24.128 [0.000]

Table 6.66 UK quarterly data: test of variable stationarity (p-values in brackets)

Test of stationarity									
r	DGF	5% C.V.	m_r	s_r	y_r	Δp	or	$b10$	cf
3	5	11.070	35.358 [0.000]	36.216 [0.000]	35.468 [0.000]	28.507 [0.000]	32.764 [0.000]	36.510 [0.000]	14.925 [0.011]
Restricted trend included in the cointegrating relations									
3	4	9.488	33.592 [0.000]	35.702 [0.000]	32.496 [0.000]	**9.352** [0.053]	17.532 [0.002]	13.225 [0.010]	14.784 [0.005]

Table 6.67 UK quarterly data: test of weak exogeneity (p-values in brackets)

Test of weak exogeneity									
r	DGF	5% C.V.	m_r	s_r	y_r	Δp	or	$b10$	cf
3	3	7.815	**7.445** [0.059]	**2.943** [0.401]	8.807 [0.032]	34.132 [0.000]	17.176 [0.001]	**3.751** [0.290]	33.402 [0.000]

and unit vectors. Afterwards, single cointegration tests are conducted. This is to test for potential long-run equilibria as outlined in the section on long-run economic relations (5.2).[94] It will help facilitate the final identification of the long-run structure and provide additional insight on information contained in the data set.

Table 6.65 provides LR tests for the exclusion of any variable from the cointegration relations. It shows that exclusion of real money and the bond rate are accepted with a p-value of 0.13 and 0.15, respectively.

Table 6.66 reports the tests for long-run stationarity. It shows that stationarity is strongly rejected for all variables. However, trend-stationarity is borderline accepted for the inflation rate. Hence, inflation might but does not have to be, one cointegration vector on its own. The final long-run structure will show that inflation can not be made stationary on its own but in combination with the other variables.

Table 6.67 tests for weak exogeneity, which is equivalent to testing a zero row in the α-matrix. This means that a variable is not error correcting but can be considered weakly exogenous for the long-run parameters β. If the test is accepted, this also means that the sum of the cumulated empirical shocks to the variable in question define one common driving trend. Table 6.67 shows that the test is borderline accepted for real money (p-value 0.059) and very significantly accepted for the stock market (p-value 0.401) and the bond rate (p-value 0.290).

[94] All test statistics on α and β are asymptotically distributed as χ^2 because the asymptotic distribution is mixed Gaussian (Johansen 1995, pp. 177–178). As a result, the usual statistical inference can be applied (Johansen and Juselius 1994, p. 16).

Table 6.68 UK quarterly data: test for a unit vector in the α-matrix (p-values in brackets)

Test of unit vector in alpha									
r	DGF	5% C.V.	m_r	s_r	y_r	Δp	or	$b10$	cf
3	4.000	9.488	30.935 [0.000]	34.363 [0.000]	15.601 [0.004]	**5.815** [0.213]	**8.337** [0.080]	22.532 [0.000]	10.607 [0.031]

The test of a unit vector in α tests if a variable is exclusively adjusting. Acceptance of the unit vector test demonstrates that shocks to the relevant variable only have transitory effects on the other variables in the system and it can be regarded as endogenous. Thus, the two tests of α can identify the pulling and pushing forces of the system. Table 6.68 shows that shocks to the inflation rate and the overnight rate only have transitory effects. This is a weak indication that the Bank of England (BoE) did not have a long-run impact on the inflation rate or on the performance of the stock market by exerting influence on the overnight rate. However, the p-value is fairly low.

In addition to the above tests on single variables, the focus of the remaining preliminary tests is on single cointegration relations. The idea is to analyze if stable relationships between the economic variables can be identified by linear relations. Testing follows the theoretical connections outlined in Chap. 3 and Sect. 5.2, summarized in Table 5.1. The hypotheses are of the form:

$$\beta = (H\phi, \psi_1, \psi_2), \tag{6.38}$$

where H is the design matrix, ϕ contains the restricted parameters and ψ_i is a vector of parameters which are freely estimated. It is important to note that each hypothesis in Table 6.69 tests restrictions on a single vector but leaves the other cointegration vectors unrestricted (Johansen and Juselius 1992, pp. 233–236).

Table 6.69 provides an overview of the single cointegration test results. It follows the structure of Table 5.2 exactly. Accepted hypotheses are indicated in bold. The table shows that only a few hypotheses are accepted; hence, limited cointegration exists between the variables. This was already indicated in the analysis of the unrestricted Π. In addition, examination of the last column, which points out the variables that react to deviations of the long-run equilibria, allows the conclusion that mostly inflation, the overnight rate and capital flows show error-correcting behavior. This is consistent with the other preliminary tests.

Hypotheses H_1 to H_8 test for cointegration between stocks and the other variables. Only H_8 is accepted, which represents a relation between the stock market, real money and capital flows. However, the stock market variable does not exhibit significant adjustment behavior towards this relation. Cointegration by itself is not meaningful with respect to the direction of causality between the variables. Instead, the test results have to be jointly evaluated with the α-matrix. The last column shows that H_8 can be interpreted as a capital flows relation, where capital flows increase with rising stock prices and decrease with abundant liquidity available in the economy.

Table 6.69 UK quarterly data: testing the stationarity of single relations

	m_r	s_r	y_r	Δp	or	$b10$	cf	*Trend*	$\chi^2(v)$	p-value	*sign.* α
					Demand for stocks						
H_1	−2.982	1	0	0	0	0	0	0.020	28.0 (3)	0.000	
H_2	0	1	0	112.2	−112.2	0	0	−0.031	10.8 (3)	0.013	
H_3	0	1	0	454.3	0	−454.3	0	−0.066	9.6 (3)	0.022	
H_4	0	1	0	0	−122.8	0	0	−0.047	14.7 (3)	0.002	
H_5	0	1	0	0	0	−1,418	0	−0.329	13.1 (3)	0.004	
H_6	0	1	−9.626	0	0	0	0	0.051	30.7 (3)	0.000	
H_7	0	1	0	0	0	0	−87.37	−0.020	12.6 (3)	0.005	
H_8	**−3.684**	**1**	**0**	**0**	**0**	**0**	**−54.57**	**0.032**	**2.0 (2)**	**0.367**	cf
					Money demand						
H_9	1	0	−1	0	0	0	0	−0.005	33.8 (4)	0.000	
H_{10}	1	0	0	0	−32.77	32.77	0	−0.014	16.0 (3)	0.001	
H_{11}	**1**	**0**	**2.003**	**0**	**−33.31**	**−9.095**	**0**	**−0.039**	**1.6 (1)**	**0.211**	$\Delta p, or, b10$
H_{12}	**1**	**0**	**5.722**	**−164.0**	**0**	**0**	**0**	**−0.079**	**3.8 (2)**	**0.149**	$m_r, \Delta p, or$
H_{13}	1	−0.335	0	0	0	0	0	−0.007	28.0 (3)	0.000	
H_{14}	1	0.140	0	0	−38.83	38.83	0	−0.017	15.0 (2)	0.001	
H_{15}	1	−0.265	−1	0	0	0	0	0	27.2 (3)	0.000	
H_{16}	1	1.417	−1	0	−189.6	189.6	0	−0.035	17.9 (2)	0.000	
					Policy rules						
H_{17}	0	0	0	−1.836	1	0	0	0	12.2 (4)	0.016	
H_{18}	**0**	**0**	**−0.100**	**0**	**1**	**0**	**0**	**0.001**	**7.3 (3)**	**0.062**	m_r, or
H_{19}	0	−0.008	0	0	1	0	0	0	14.7 (3)	0.002	

(continued)

Table 6.69 (Continued)

	m_r	s_r	y_r	Δp	or	$b10$	cf	*Trend*	$\chi^2(v)$	p-value	*sign.* α
					Demand for goods						
H_{20}	0	0	1	17.31	−17.31	0	0	−0.010	12.2 (3)	0.007	
H_{21}	**0**	**0**	**1**	**−31.55**	**0**	**31.55**	**0**	**−0.005**	**6.1 (3)**	**0.106**	$m_r, \Delta p, cf$
H_{22}	0.199	0	1	0	0	0	0	−0.005	32.1 (3)	0.000	
H_{23}	−0.953	0.251	1	0	0	0	0	0	27.2 (2)	0.000	
					Inflation and interest rates						
H_{24}	0.017	0	−0.017	1	0	0	0	0	13.2 (4)	0.011	
H_{25}	−0.007	0	0	0	0	1	0	0	12.1 (3)	0.007	
H_{26}	0	0	0	−1	1	0	0	0	28.5 (5)	0.000	
H_{27}	0	0	0	−1	0	1	0	0	29.8 (5)	0.000	
H_{28}	0	0	0	−1.836	1	0	0	0	12.2 (4)	0.016	
H_{29}	**0**	**0**	**0**	**−1.86**	**0**	**1**	**0**	**0**	**8.6 (4)**	**0.073**	$m_r, \Delta p, cf$
H_{30}	0	0	0	0	−1	1	0	0	21.4 (5)	0.001	
H_{31}	0	0	0	0	−1.071	1	0	0	21.1 (4)	0.000	
H_{32}	0	0	0	0.080	1	−1.080	0	0	21.4 (4)	0.000	
H_{33}	0	0	0	−0.367	−1	1	0	0	20.1 (4)	0.000	

H_9 to H_{16} test monetary relations. Only the relation incorporating real output and inflation (H_{12}) could be interpreted as a money demand relation because real money shows error-correcting behavior.

'Policy rules' (H_{17} to H_{19}) show that deviations from real output drive the overnight rate (H_{18}). This indicates that the BoE pays special attention to real developments when conducting monetary policy. However, it is only borderline accepted and probably requires the inclusion of other variables to fully define a policy rule relation.

Hypotheses H_{20} to H_{23} focus on potential stationary aggregate demand for goods relations, but output does not react to the IS-type relation (H_{21}), the only one for which stationarity is accepted.

Under the headline 'Inflation and interest rates' cointegration between inflation and the nominal interest rates ('Fisher parity') as well as between the interest rates themselves ('expectations hypothesis') is tested. Only the 'Fisher parity'-hypothesis is borderline accepted in its weak form for the real long-term interest rate (H_{29}, i.e., with free parameters).

6.5.2.3 Identification of the Long-Run Cointegrating Relations

The identification procedure is based on the outlined economic theory and the preliminary testing of the econometric model in the previous section. An empirically and economically uniquely identified long-run structure can be obtained by imposing different linear restrictions on the cointegrating relations.

The restrictions on the identified long-run structure are accepted with a p-value of 0.33 ($\chi^2(5) = 5.742$). The structure is formally and empirically identified because all β-coefficients are strongly significant (Juselius and MacDonald 2004, p. 18). In addition, Appendix B.4.5 shows that the rank conditions are accepted for the full cointegration space. This signifies that the three cointegration relations are linearly independent and, as such, can not be replaced by each other.

The graphs of the cointegrating relations are displayed in Appendix B.4.6 with the deterministic terms and short-term parameters concentrated out.[95] They all describe stationary behavior. Graphical overviews of forward and backward recursive tests of parameter constancy in Appendix B.4.7 show that parameter constancy for α_i and β_i ($i = 1, \ldots, 3$) is broadly accepted. Parameter values seem to fluctuate during the dot-com bubble and burst but the sign of the coefficients remain the same. The structural representation of the cointegration space is depicted in Table 6.70 with the estimated eigenvectors β and the weights α.

The first cointegrating relation describes a monetary policy rule including the stock market and output:

[95] This removes the seasonal fluctuations and outliers, which can be observed in the raw series and, thus, provides a clearer picture (Brüggemann and Lütkepohl 2006, p. 692). See also Sect. 6.2.1.3.

Table 6.70 UK quarterly data: the identified long-run structure (t-values in brackets)

	β'							
	m_r	s_r	y_r	Δp	or	$b10$	cf	*Trend*
Beta(1)	0.000 [NA]	**−0.007** [−3.509]	**−0.104** [−6.071]	0.000 [NA]	**1.000** [NA]	0.000 [NA]	0.000 [NA]	**0.001** [7.661]
Beta(2)	**0.083** [4.898]	**−0.021** [−3.736]	0.000 [NA]	0.000 [NA]	0.000 [NA]	0.000 [NA]	**1.000** [NA]	**−0.001** [−2.933]
Beta(3)	0.000 [NA]	0.000 [NA]	**−0.068** [−4.353]	**1.000** [NA]	**0.292** [3.349]	**−0.454** [−2.844]	0.000 [NA]	**0.001** [4.635]

	α		
	Alpha(1)	Alpha(2)	Alpha(3)
Δm_r	**−0.889** [−2.783]	−0.066 [−0.681]	**0.832** [2.447]
Δs_r	0.103 [0.041]	1.215 [1.604]	−2.423 [−0.909]
Δy_r	**−0.642** [−2.612]	−0.144 [−1.943]	0.042 [0.159]
$\Delta^2 p$	**0.616** [4.665]	0.013 [0.325]	**−1.083** [−7.712]
Δor	**−0.670** [−5.162]	0.057 [1.448]	0.181 [1.313]
$\Delta b10$	−0.056 [−1.337]	−0.011 [−0.905]	0.026 [0.588]
Δcf	**0.938** [2.071]	**−1.154** [−8.441]	0.489 [1.016]

$$or_t - 0.007 s_{r,t} - 0.104(y_{r,t} - 0.01\ trend) \sim I(0), \tag{6.39}$$

where the overnight rate reacts positively to real stock market levels and trend-adjusted real output. Analysis of the α-coefficients reveals that the overnight rate shows strong error-correcting behavior towards this relation. The size of the α-coefficient indicates that equilibrium is restored in less than two quarters. Moreover, the α-coefficients show that equilibrium errors of the long-run relation have a negative effect on real money and positive effects on inflation and capital flows. Real output seems to be primarily responsible for pushing this relation out of equilibrium.

The second β'-vector represents a relationship between capital flows, real money and the stock market:

$$cf_t + 0.083 m_{r,t} - 0.021 s_{r,t} - 0.001\ trend \sim I(0), \tag{6.40}$$

where capital flows react positively to stock market advances and negatively to the level of real money available. Since the stock market's reaction to this long-run equilibrium is insignificant (t-value $= 1.6$), it is not statistically significantly driven by capital flows and real money developments even though the signs of the coefficients are correct. Instead, for the UK, it is the other way round, capital inflows are attracted by higher stock prices. Additionally, the negative relation with domestic money stock indicates that capital inflows decrease or capital outflows increase if domestic liquidity rises. This could be a result of limited investment alternatives and less incentive to borrow internationally since abundant liquidity is available at home. The size of the α-coefficient indicates fast equilibrium correction. It takes capital flows approximately one quarter to restore equilibrium.

The third long-run relation describes a relationship between inflation, real output and the interest rates:

$$\Delta p_t - 0.068 y_{r,t} + 0.292 or_t - 0.454 b10_t + 0.001 \, trend \sim I(0), \qquad (6.41)$$

where inflation reacts positively to real output and the bond rate and negatively to the overnight rate. The positive reaction to the bond rate shows that higher bond yields lead to a cost-push effect of higher financing costs (Juselius and MacDonald 2004, p. 23). This relation already indicates the strong ability of the BoE to affect macro variables, especially inflation. This is confirmed by the analysis of the unrestricted C-matrix, where whether the cumulated shocks to a variable have any long-run impact on the other variables is tested (see Sect. 6.5.4). Analysis of the α-coefficients shows that real money is pushed by this relation.

Table B.17 in Appendix B.4.8 shows the identified long-run structure with weak exogeneity imposed on stock markets and the bond rate. It turns out that the coefficients and the significance of the results remain similar. This long-run structure is accepted with a p-value of 0.39 ($\chi^2(11) = 11.614$), which is even higher than the original one. The exogeneity of the stock market and the bond rate indicates the importance of London as a global financial hub. As a result, domestic developments are less important for financial markets in the UK.

6.5.3 Short-Run Dynamics

Whereas the previous analysis focuses on stable long-run economic relations, this section applies a structural error-correction model and formulates stationary equations for each of the variables in the system (see Sect. 6.2.3). The 70 zero restrictions of insignificant coefficients are strongly accepted based on an LR test of over-identifying restrictions with a p-value of 0.94 ($\chi^2(70) = 52.23$). Table 6.71 provides an overview. The dependent variables can be found in the top row as the column headings of each of the model equations. The row headings, on the other hand, indicate the conditioning variables.

The analysis of the short-run dynamics shows that real money reacts positively to lagged values of itself. Moreover, the residuals of the first cointegration relation affect real money negatively and the third ecm affects real money positively.

The stock market is strongly exogenous because it only reacts to the 1987 stock market crash dummy. Real output, too, does not react to lagged values of the other variables. It does, however, react to the first and second ecm. Hence, it reacts to deviations of monetary policy and capital flows equilibria.

Inflation reacts positively to lagged values of itself. Deviations of the first cointegration relation push the inflation rate. In addition, it error corrects to the third ecm, which is the inflation rate relation and, thus, confirms the above findings.

Table 6.71 UK quarterly data: short-run dynamics (t-values in brackets)

	Δm_r	Δs_r	Δy_r	$\Delta^2 p$	Δor	$\Delta b10$	Δcf
$\Delta m_{r,t}$	**1**	0	0	0	0	0	0
$\Delta s_{r,t}$	0	**1**	0	0	0	0	0
$\Delta y_{r,t}$	0	0	**1**	0	0	0	0
$\Delta^2 p_t$	0	0	0	**1**	0	0	0
Δor_t	0	0	0	0	**1**	0	0
$\Delta b10_t$	0	0	0	0	0	**1**	0
Δcf_t	0	0	0	0	0	0	**1**
$\Delta m_{r,t-1}$	**0.513**						
	[6.14]						
$\Delta s_{r,t-1}$							
$\Delta y_{r,t-1}$							
$\Delta^2 p_{t-1}$				**0.174**		**−0.049**	
				[2.46]		[−2.77]	
Δor_{t-1}							**−0.851**
							[−2.84]
$\Delta b10_{t-1}$							
Δcf_{t-1}							
$ecm1_{t-1}$	**−0.908**		**−0.399**	**0.506**	**−0.658**	**−0.074**	**1.448**
	[−4.09]		[−2.62]	[4.95]	[−6.79]	[−3.08]	[4.62]
$ecm2_{t-1}$			**−0.112**				**−1.151**
			[−2.38]				[−12.3]
$ecm3_{t-1}$	**0.946**			**−1.184**	**0.202**		
	[4.36]			[−11.3]	[2.28]		
$dum8704_{p,t}$		**−0.426**					**0.045**
		[−5.83]					[3.22]
$dum9001_{p,t}$						**0.005**	
						[4.29]	
$dum9102_{p,t}$	**−0.026**			**0.025**			
	[−2.69]			[6.55]			

The behavior of the overnight rate is opposite that of the inflation rate in the short run. It error corrects to the first cointegration relation and is pushed by the third one. This also indicates a relationship between inflation and the short-term interest rate, where monetary policy reacts to increasing inflation. The subsequent increase in the policy rate brings the inflation rate back down to desired levels.

The bond rate reacts negatively to inflation and the first ecm. And, finally, capital flows show strong adjustment behavior to the second cointegration relation, which

Table 6.72 UK quarterly data: correlation of structural residuals (standard deviations on diagonal)

	Δm_r	Δs_r	Δy_r	$\Delta^2 p$	Δor	$\Delta b10$	Δcf
Δm_r	*0.009*						
Δs_r	0.19	*0.077*					
Δy_r	0.25	0.12	*0.008*				
$\Delta^2 p$	**−0.36**	−0.26	**−0.45**	*0.004*			
Δor	−0.05	−0.06	−0.07	0.16	*0.004*		
$\Delta b10$	−0.15	**−0.32**	−0.05	0.32	−0.07	*0.001*	
Δcf	0.04	0.14	−0.01	0.13	0.12	0.06	*0.014*

is the capital flows relation. Capital flows also react negatively to lagged values of the overnight rate and are pushed by deviations from the first cointegration relation.

According to Table 6.71 most of the autoregressive coefficients are insignificant and, thus, restricted to 0. The bulk of explanatory power in the short run is based on the inclusion of the ecms. The equilibrium-correcting coefficients are mostly highly significant, indicating a potential loss of information if the VAR model had only been estimated in first differences.

One downside of the above equations is that current effects are not modeled. Instead they are left in the residuals. However, simultaneous effects are potentially important. Whereas correlation between the residuals is a non-issue for the long-run relations of the previous section, identification of the short-run structural equations requires uncorrelated residuals (Juselius 2006, p. 229). Table 6.72 shows the residual covariance matrix, in which large off-diagonal elements can be an indication of significant current effects between the system variables. Correlation between real output and inflation, real money and inflation as well as the stock market and the bond rate must be critically recognized.[96]

One way to reduce residual correlation is to introduce current effects between the variables into the short-run structure. Adding current effects of real output to the inflation equation and the bond rate to the stock market equation helps to reduce correlation between the variables (see Table 6.73).[97] However, the coefficients of the current effects turn out to be insignificant. The results of the short-run analysis remain the same if current effects are modeled. Table 6.74 shows the almost identical short-run structure after allowing for current effects.

[96] High residual correlation can result from the aggregation of the data over time, inadequately modeled expectations or omitted variables (Juselius 2006, pp. 239–240).

[97] Other combinations of current effects were tested but did not reduce correlation between the variables. These included current effects of inflation in the real money and the real output inflation, real money in the inflation rate equation and the current effects of the stock market in the bond rate equation.

Table 6.73 UK quarterly data: correlation of structural residuals after allowing for current effects (standard deviations on diagonal)

	Δm_r	Δs_r	Δy_r	$\Delta^2 p$	Δor	$\Delta b10$	Δcf
Δm_r	*0.009*						
Δs_r	0.17	*0.074*					
Δy_r	0.25	0.13	*0.008*				
$\Delta^2 p$	**−0.34**	−0.20	**−0.27**	*0.004*			
Δor	−0.05	−0.07	−0.06	0.15	*0.004*		
$\Delta b10$	−0.15	**−0.14**	−0.05	0.33	−0.08	*0.001*	
Δcf	0.04	0.17	−0.01	0.14	0.12	0.06	*0.014*

6.5.4 The Long-Run Impact of the Common Trends

The C-matrix provides the key to understanding the long-run implications of the model. A condition precedent to the ability of central banks to influence stock markets is that a shock to a monetary instrument has a significant long-run impact on the stock market. Hence, when evaluating the effectiveness of monetary policy, the long-run impact of shocks to the short-term interest rate and to the money supply on the stock market is of particular interest.

The residual $\epsilon_{i,t}$ is interpreted as an estimate of the unanticipated shock to variable x_i. The estimated long-run impact of the cumulated shocks is reported in Table 6.75 and is calculated from the estimates of the restricted VAR model as

$$C = \tilde{\beta}_{\perp}\alpha'_{\perp}, \tag{6.42}$$

where $\tilde{\beta}_{\perp} = \beta_{\perp}(\alpha'_{\perp}\beta_{\perp})^{-1}$ and $\alpha_{\perp}$, $\beta_{\perp}$ are the $(p \times p - r)$ orthogonal compliments of α and β (Johansen 1995, pp. 49–50). Since C has reduced rank, $p - r = 4$ linear combinations of the $p = 7$ innovations, ϵ_t, have permanent effects.

The C-matrix can be read column or row-wise. The columns show the long-run impact of a shock to a variable on each of the variables in the system and the rows show which of the shocks have a long-run impact on the particular variable.

The C-matrix in Table 6.75 shows that, in the long run, shocks to real money affect real money positively and capital flows negatively. The former is an indication of the procyclicality of credit creation, the latter shows that positive liquidity in the home country reduces the need to borrow from abroad and reduces the attractiveness of home country investments to foreign investors.

Cumulated shocks to the stock market influence stock market developments positively in the long run. This confirms the results of the other country analyses and indicates the importance of herding and trend-following behavior as well as rational speculation of economic agents for stock market developments. In addition, shocks to the stock market have a positive effect on both interest rates and capital flows. This is in line with the findings of the cointegration relations. The C-matrix also shows that, for the period under investigation, the BoE was incapable of influencing stock market developments in the long run, because no other variable had a

Table 6.74 UK quarterly data: short-run dynamics allowing for current effects (t-values in brackets)

	Δm_r	Δs_r	Δy_r	$\Delta^2 p$	Δor	$\Delta b10$	Δcf
$\Delta m_{r,t}$	**1**	0	0	0	0	0	0
$\Delta s_{r,t}$	0	**1**	0	0	0	0	0
$\Delta y_{r,t}$	0	0	**1**	−0.11	0	0	0
$\Delta^2 p_t$	0	0	0	**1**	0	0	0
Δor_t	0	0	0	0	**1**	0	0
$\Delta b10_t$	0	−10.96	0	0	0	**1**	0
Δcf_t	0	0	0	0	0	0	**1**
$\Delta m_{r,t-1}$	**0.510** [6.10]						
$\Delta s_{r,t-1}$							
$\Delta y_{r,t-1}$							
$\Delta^2 p_{t-1}$				**0.174** [2.45]		**−0.050** [−2.69]	
Δor_{t-1}							**−0.851** [−2.84]
$\Delta b10_{t-1}$							
Δcf_{t-1}							
$ecm1_{t-1}$	**−0.904** [−4.06]		**−0.383** [−2.51]	**0.459** [3.64]	**−0.660** [−6.80]	**−0.075** [−2.97]	**1.466** [4.69]
$ecm2_{t-1}$			**−0.123** [−2.40]				**−1.144** [−12.1]
$ecm3_{t-1}$	**0.954** [4.39]			**−1.196** [−11.4]	**0.199** [2.25]		
$dum8704_{p,t}$		**−0.421** [−5.78]					**0.045** [3.23]
$dum9001_{p,t}$						**0.006** [4.52]	
$dum9102_{p,t}$	**−0.025** [−2.68]		**−0.031** [−3.99]	**0.021** [2.96]			

permanent effect on stock market developments. Since it is found to be strongly exogenous, this confirms previous findings.

Aside from that, the C-matrix shows that shocks to real output have positive long-run effects on the level of economic activity, the inflation rate and the short-term interest rate.

Shocks to inflation, on the other hand, do not have any permanent effects, which was already indicated by the unit vector test in Sect. 6.5.2.2. In addition, shocks to the overnight rate translate into lower values for real money, real output, inflation

Table 6.75 UK quarterly data: the long-run impact matrix (t-values in brackets)

The long-run impact matrix, C							
	$\hat{\epsilon}_{m_r}$	$\hat{\epsilon}_{s_r}$	$\hat{\epsilon}_{y_r}$	$\hat{\epsilon}_{\Delta p}$	$\hat{\epsilon}_{or}$	$\hat{\epsilon}_{b10}$	$\hat{\epsilon}_{cf}$
m_r	**1.687** [4.084]	0.046 [1.602]	0.356 [1.097]	0.763 [1.025]	**−2.065** [−2.205]	−0.677 [−0.478]	−0.178 [−1.032]
s_r	−0.642 [−0.366]	**0.994** [8.120]	0.437 [0.316]	−2.265 [−0.717]	0.083 [0.021]	−1.767 [−0.294]	1.024 [1.395]
y_r	−0.240 [−0.901]	0.031 [1.645]	**1.143** [5.458]	−0.544 [−1.133]	**−1.501** [−2.486]	−0.201 [−0.221]	−0.175 [−1.571]
Δp	−0.009 [−0.440]	0.001 [0.785]	**0.057** [3.741]	−0.025 [−0.699]	**−0.124** [−2.805]	**0.426** [6.376]	−0.016 [−1.978]
or	−0.029 [−0.876]	**0.010** [4.272]	**0.122** [4.625]	−0.072 [−1.194]	**−0.155** [−2.048]	−0.033 [−0.288]	−0.011 [−0.799]
$b10$	−0.002 [−0.066]	**0.004** [2.052]	0.034 [1.474]	−0.019 [−0.364]	**−0.149** [−2.239]	**0.946** [9.416]	−0.017 [−1.352]
cf	**−0.153** [−3.671]	**0.017** [5.721]	−0.021 [−0.627]	−0.110 [−1.463]	0.173 [1.829]	0.020 [0.138]	**0.036** [2.057]

and the bond rate. Shocks to the bond rate increase inflation in the long run (cost-push effect of higher financing costs). Lastly, shocks to capital flows are only borderline significant.

As previously stated, the stock market and the bond rate can also be restricted to be weakly exogenous. This restriction is accepted with a p-value of 0.39 ($\chi^2(11) = 11.61$). This only changes the long-run impact matrix as in so far as the bond rate is not subject to permanent shocks of the other variables and shocks to capital flows become completely insignificant (see Table B.18 in Appendix B.4.9). The implications remain the same.

6.5.5 Conclusion

As stated in the introduction, confidence and optimism are important factors for the development of stock prices. In addition, one objective of this contribution is to test whether or not abundant liquidity enforces the upward spiral of stock prices. Whereas the self-reinforcing and trend-following behavior of stock markets could be found in the data, the latter hypothesis does not hold for the UK for the timeframe under consideration. The analysis of the variables in levels and in first differences shows that the stock market behaves strongly exogenous and is not influenced by any of the other variables, neither in the long run nor in the short run. Two explanations are possible but are not tested herein. First, as is the case in the US analysis, one could argue that excess liquidity was not invested in stocks but in housing, culminating in a massive housing boom. The analyses of Belke et al. (2008, pp. 416–420) and Giese and Tuxen (2007, pp. 22–24) support this point on a global basis. Second, London, as a world financial hub, attracts huge capital investments and also invests heavily abroad. As a result, stock market conditions in the UK might, to a large extent, be driven by international conditions. The second argument, however,

Table 6.76 UK quarterly data: results of main hypotheses

	Hypotheses/Questions	Result
H_1	UK stock market behavior shows strong persistence, i.e., shocks to the stock market have positive long-run effects on future developments	Yes
H_2	Long-run equilibria exist between stock prices and liquidity conditions	(Yes)
H_3	Liquidity conditions influence stock prices positively in the long run	No
H_4	Liquidity conditions influence stock prices positively in the short run	No
H_5	International capital flows have a positive long-run impact on the stock market behavior in the UK	No
H_6	International capital flows have a positive short-run impact on the stock market behavior in the UK	No
Q_1	Is the BoE able to influence stock prices in the long run?	No
Q_2	Is the BoE able to influence stock prices in the short run?	No

seems weaker than the first because capital flows do not influence stock market developments either.

Table 6.76 confirms that the results of the econometric analysis do not support the main hypotheses. Instead, the strong exogeneity of real stock market levels rules out any influence of monetary factors on stock markets. However, the long-run cointegration relations show that the short-term interest rate and capital flows react positively to stock market developments. The first is an indication of the BoE's progressive view on including asset prices in monetary policy setting. The second is a confirmation of the 'pull' effect because capital inflows increase when stock markets rise.

In addition, the above analysis sheds light on a few other aspects of economic interest, mainly:

- Supply of real money is very procyclical since it reacts positively to lagged values of itself in the short run and innovations in real money have a permanent long-run effect on the money stock.
- Real aggregate demand for goods does not react much to developments of the system variables. However, the test for weak exogeneity of real output is rejected with a p-value of 0.011 ($\chi^2(8) = 19.87$). The main reason for this is the long-run impact of shocks to the overnight rate. They have a negative effect on economic activity.
- The analysis shows that inflation is positively influenced by real output and the bond rate (overheated economy and long-term financing cost-push effect) and negatively by the short-term interest rate. This shows that the BoE is able to influence price developments. The long-run impact matrix confirms this since shocks to the overnight rate have a negative long-run impact on inflation.
- The short-term interest rate builds a long-run equilibrium with real output and the stock market. The C-matrix confirms the importance of these two variables for policy setting in the UK. Analysis of the short run shows that the policy rate also reacts to deviations from the inflation rate relation. It does not come as a surprise that the BoE informally takes stock market developments into account

since central bank officials were alert to the importance of asset prices early on (see, for example, King (2006, p. 7)).
- The test for weak exogeneity of the bond rate is accepted. Another sign that financial market developments (stock market and fixed income) are determined by international developments instead of domestic conditions.
- Capital flows are non-stationary in the UK analysis and enter the long-run structure. The second cointegration relation describes the relationship between capital flows, real money and the stock market. However, the important role of international capital flows for UK financial markets can not be proven econometrically. Capital flows do not have any impact on stock or bond markets, neither in the long nor in the short run. Instead, the opposite is true, capital flows are attracted by positive stock market developments.

6.6 Australia: Quarterly Data

6.6.1 *Model Specification*

6.6.1.1 Data Overview, Deterministic Components and Lag Length

As in the other country analyses, the data vector (6.43) lists the seven variables:

$$x_t^{\prime} = [m_r, s_r, y_r, \Delta p, or, b10, cf]_t \,, \tag{6.43}$$

where m_r is the log of real broad money,[98] s_r is the log of real stock market levels (total market including dividends) and y_r is the log of real GDP. Real variables are transformed from nominal variables by applying the consumer price index, p. Hence, Δp is the inflation rate. Short and long-term interest rates are represented by the overnight interbank rate, or, and the yield on 10-year government bonds, $b10$, respectively. All interest rates have been converted to quarterly rates and divided by 100 to achieve comparability with the inflation rate. Capital flows, cf, are calculated in percent as a share of the total money stock (broad money). Capital flows are derived from non-bank BoP transactions as described in Sect. 4.6.3.2 and Appendix A. All time series are obtained either from Datastream or the IMF BoP database. Detailed information on the specific sources of the data can be found in Appendix B.5.1. The data used for the analysis covers the last 25 years and consists of quarterly observations from 1983:1 to 2008:3.

Figure 6.13 displays the time pattern of all variables in levels and first differences. All graphs look stationary for the differenced series. The series in levels, however,

[98] In addition to the elements included in the monetary aggregate M3, broad money also covers borrowing from the private sector by Non-Bank Financial Institutions, less the latter's holdings of currency and bank deposits.

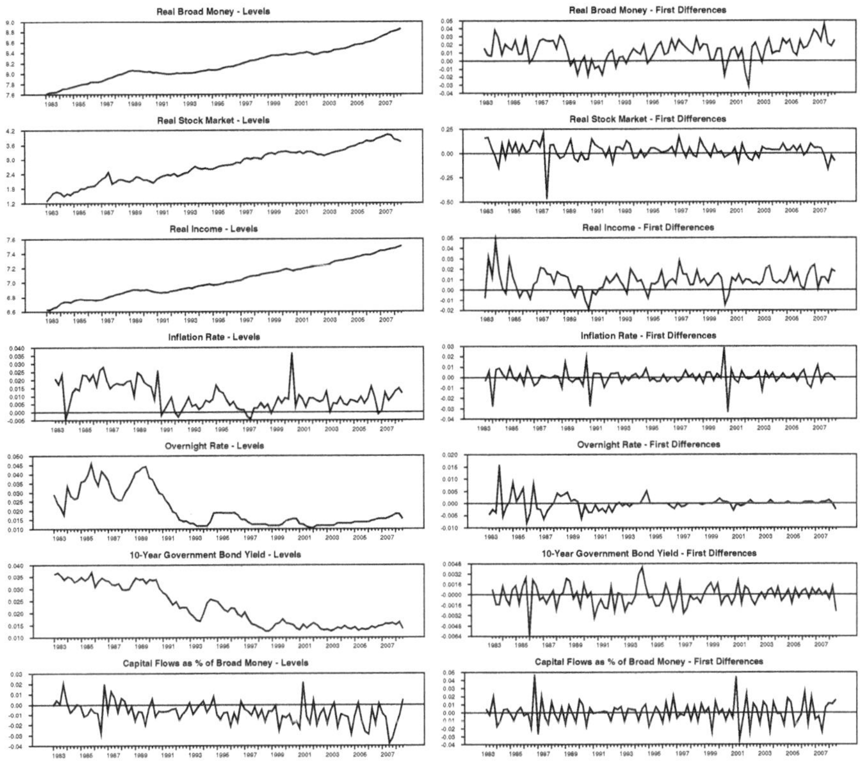

Fig. 6.13 Australia quarterly data in levels and first differences

show a lot of persistence. In addition, real money, the stock market and real GDP seem to follow a trend. Thus, an unrestricted constant and a restricted trend are included in the model.[99]

Dummy Variables

Misspecification tests show that normality is rejected and ARCH effects exist in the first, second and third lag.[100] To ensure normality and reduce ARCH effects, dummies are included based on the economic calendar and the graphs of the standardized residuals, which have revealed some large outliers. Table 6.77 provides an overview. Modeling data for Australia requires five permanent dummies.[101]

[99] For a discussion of deterministic components in the model, see Sect. 6.2.1.1.

[100] The test is not reported here at this stage. Instead, misspecification tests are reported for the specified model in Sect. 6.6.1.2.

[101] For an overview of the different kinds of dummies see Sect. 6.2.1.1.

Table 6.77 Australia quarterly data: intervention dummies

Dummy variable	Motivation	Impact on
$dum8401_p$	High and strongly fluctuating inflation rate	Overnight rate
$dum8601_p$	World bond market fluctuations	Bond rate
$dum8704_p$	Black Friday stock market crash in October	Stock market
$dum0003_p$	Permanent increase of general sales tax	Inflation, real money and real output
$dum0202_p$	Exchange rate devaluation and asset substitution[a]	Real money

[a] The unwinding of long positions in Australian Dollars led to a depreciation of the Australian currency, which affected money holdings. In addition, real money has been affected by banks' substitution between certificates of deposit and bank bills as well as offshore borrowing by financial institutions because the latter are not included in the monetary aggregate (Reserve Bank of Australia Bulletin 2002, p. 47).

Table 6.78 Australia quarterly data: information to determine lag length

Model	k	T	Regressive	Log-Likelihood	SC	H–Q	LM(1)	LM(k)
VAR(5)	5	101	45	3,795.492	−60.765	−65.619	0.413	0.465
VAR(4)	4	101	38	3,732.699	−61.760	−65.859	0.314	0.007
VAR(3)	3	101	31	3,689.942	−63.152	−66.497	0.234	0.176
VAR(2)	2	101	24	3,646.554	−64.532	−67.121	0.811	0.084
VAR(1)	1	101	17	3,590.284	**−65.657**	**−67.491**	**0.118**	**0.118**

Determination of the Lag Length

The two information criteria SC and H–Q are reported in Table 6.78 and are calculated for different values of lag length, k, where the smallest result suggests the ideal lag length. The last two columns in Table 6.78 report the LM test for autocorrelation of order 1 and k. Numbers in bold indicate the suggested lag length of the respective test.

All three criteria point to one lag. However, to perform the analysis of short-run dynamics a minimum of two lags has to be included. Hence, a lag length of $k = 2$ is used for the analysis.[102]

The discussion in this section on lag length, deterministic components and dummy variables results in the following VAR(2) model (in error-correction form) for Australia quarterly data:

$$\Delta x_t = \alpha \tilde{\beta}' \tilde{x}_{t-1} + \Gamma_1 \Delta x_{t-1} + \Phi D_t + \mu_0 + \epsilon_t, \tag{6.44}$$

where $x_t' = [m_r, s_r, y_r, \Delta p, or, b10, cf]_t$ and $\tilde{x}_t = \left[x_t', 1, trend\right]$ is a $((7+2) \times 1)$ data vector containing the p variables, a constant and a trend. The cointegration

[102] Empirically, two lags are mostly adequate to model the dynamics of the CVAR model (Johansen 1995, p. 4).

Table 6.79 Australia quarterly data: multivariate misspecification tests (p-values in brackets)

Test for no autocorrelation			
LM(1):	$\chi^2(49)$	=	40.191 [0.811]
LM(2):	$\chi^2(49)$	=	63.203 [0.084]
LM(3):	$\chi^2(49)$	=	53.737 [0.298]
LM(4):	$\chi^2(49)$	=	51.233 [0.386]
Test for normality	$\chi^2(14)$	=	18.461 [0.187]
Test for no Arch effects			
LM(1):	$\chi^2(784)$	=	864.338 [**0.024**]
LM(2):	$\chi^2(1568)$	=	1675.571 [**0.029**]
LM(3):	$\chi^2(2352)$	=	2481.565 [**0.031**]
LM(4):	$\chi^2(3136)$	=	2828.000 [1.000]

vectors are represented by $\tilde{\beta} = \left[\beta', \rho_0, \rho_1\right]'$, which is a $((7+2) \times r)$ matrix with rank r. The analysis is based on 7×101 observations and conditions on the initial values (data points for 1983:1 to 1983:2) and the dummy variables are contained in the vector $D_t = \left[dum8401_p,\ dum8601_p,\ dum8704_p,\ dum0003_p,\ dum0202_p\right]$.

6.6.1.2 Misspecification Tests

The model must be well specified to be able to determine the reduced rank of the model. Tables 6.79 and 6.80 report multivariate and univariate misspecification tests, respectively. The multivariate LM test shows that the null of the test ('no autocorrelation') is accepted for the first four lags.[103]

The normality tests are based on skewness and kurtosis.[104] The tests show that the null of the tests, normally distributed errors, is accepted in the multivariate case and for all individual time series aside from the overnight rate. This is acceptable because it is mainly a result of excess kurtosis and simulation studies have shown that kurtosis is less serious than skewness (Hendry and Juselius 2000, p. 7).

Additionally, tests for multivariate ARCH of order q (with $q = 1, \ldots, 4$) and univariate second order ARCH effects are reported.[105] There are signs for ARCH effects in the first three lags of the system and individually for the bond rate. However, Rahbek et al. (2002, p. 83) show that cointegration tests are robust against

---

[103] It is asymptotically distributed as χ^2 with p^2 degrees of freedom (Johansen 1995, p. 22).

[104] They are asymptotically χ^2-distributed, with $2p$ degrees of freedom in the multivariate and 2 degrees of freedom in the univariate case.

[105] The multivariate test statistic is approximately distributed as χ^2 with $\frac{q}{4}p^2(p+1)^2$ degrees of freedom. The univariate test is approximately distributed as χ^2 with k degrees of freedom (Dennis 2006, pp. 179–180).

Table 6.80 Australia quarterly data: univariate misspecification tests (p-values in brackets)

	ARCH(2)	Normality	Skewness	Kurtosis
Δm_r	3.996 [0.136]	0.714 [0.700]	−0.082	3.113
Δs_r	3.679 [0.159]	0.177 [0.915]	−0.037	2.633
Δy_r	2.950 [0.229]	4.316 [0.116]	0.320	3.734
$\Delta^2 p$	4.198 [0.123]	3.024 [0.221]	−0.249	3.532
Δor	0.930 [0.628]	8.256 [**0.016**]	0.280	4.230
$\Delta b10$	8.589 [**0.014**]	1.990 [0.370]	0.321	2.898
Δcf	2.757 [0.252]	1.854 [0.396]	0.199	3.326

moderate residual ARCH effects. Since most test statistics are accepted, the model seems to describe the data well.

6.6.1.3 Rank Determination

As outlined in Sect. 6.2.1.3 the following formal and informal test procedures are applied to determine the reduced rank of the system (Juselius 2006, p. 142):

- Trace test (formal LR test).
- Modulus of the roots of the companion matrix.
- Significance of the α-coefficients.
- Graphical inspection of the recursively calculated trace test statistics.
- Graphical inspection of the stationarity of the cointegration relations.

Trace Test

Table 6.81 provides an overview of the trace test results. [106] It reports the estimated eigenvalues, λ_i, the trace test, Q_r, the small sample Bartlett corrected trace test (Johansen 2002, pp. 1932–1940), Q_r^{Bart}, and the 95% quintile from the asymptotic distribution corrected for deterministic components, $C_r^{95\%}$. In addition, the table reports the p-value of the test statistic and the p-value of the Bartlett small sample corrections, p-value*, respectively. In this case, the Bartlett small sample

[106] Equation (5.6) in Sect. 5.1.2 shows that, as a prerequisite for valid statistical inference, the variables can be integrated of first but not of higher order. Hence, it is important to ensure that no $I(2)$ variables are part of the data set. As outlined in Sect. 6.2.1.3 different criteria exist to analyze if $I(2)$-ness persists. Applying these criteria to the analysis of Australia shows that no $I(2)$-trends exist in the data. Because univariate unit root tests are used in most analyses, they are conducted as well, in spite of their many limitations in the multivariate setting. The ADF test and the PP test fail to reject the null hypothesis of the existence of a unit root at the 5% level for all variables in levels aside from the time series representing capital flows.The PP test is also rejected for inflation.

Table 6.81 Australia quarterly data: trace test of cointegration rank

$p-r$	r	λ_i	Q_r	Q_r^{Bart}	$C_r^{95\%}$	p-value	p-value*
7	0	0.504	206.222	184.780	150.348	0.000	0.000
6	1	0.341	135.444	122.104	117.451	0.002	0.024
5	2	0.325	93.268	84.235	88.554	0.021	**0.101**
4	3	0.223	53.545	45.067	63.659	**0.273**	0.646
3	4	0.170	28.035	23.281	42.770	0.624	0.863
2	5	0.071	9.184	7.839	25.731	0.948	0.979
1	6	0.017	1.744	1.612	12.448	0.970	0.976

corrections are probably irrelevant since the analysis is based on an effective sample of 101 observations.

The trace test accepts the null of $p - r = 4$ unit roots and, therefore, $r = 3$.[107]

Roots of the Companion Matrix

The analysis of the modulus of the roots of the companion form matrix, as depicted in Table 6.82, shows that for $r = 4$ the modulus of the largest unrestricted root drops to 0.843, and for $r = 3$ it drops to 0.837. As a result, it is difficult to discriminate between rank 3 or 4 based on the information of the roots from the companion matrix.

Significance of Adjustment Coefficients α

The t-values of the α-coefficients give an indication of the significance of the equilibrium adjustment behavior of the relative variables. They are derived from the

In contrast, both tests reject the null hypothesis for the variables in first-differenced form of the series. Consequently, the variables are at most integrated of order one. The appropriate lags for the ADF test are selected based on the Schwartz Criterion and the Akaike Information Criterion. The truncation point for the Newey–West adjustment, required for calculating the PP statistic, is determined by using the smallest integer greater than or equal to the sample size, T, to the power of $\frac{1}{4}$ (Greene 2003, p. 267). The test results are not reported here because of the questionable usefulness of univariate tests in a multivariate setting. Rao (2007, p. 1624) points out that these tests lack power and combinations of the many options of the tests almost always enable one to prove that the variables are I(1) in levels. Additionally, Muscatelli and Spinelli (2000, p. 724) refer to difficulties in using unit root tests as pre-tests if regime shifts are inherent to the model. For these and other reasons, Juselius (2006, p. 136) does not even discuss univariate unit root testing in her textbook on cointegration analysis. Instead, the stationarity of a variable is easily tested inside the multivariate model as a restriction on β (see Table 6.86 in Sect. 6.6.2.2). The advantage of the multivariate analysis is to define a well-specified model first and then test for stationarity. With univariate unit root tests, stationarity is tested before guaranteeing i.i.d. error terms, constant parameters and the absence of ARCH effects and before determining cointegration rank. The results of the ADF and PP tests are available on request.

[107] As a sensitivity analysis the trace test is performed with the intervention dummies excluded. The results are confirmed as both test statistics suggest a rank of three.

Table 6.82 Australia quarterly data: modulus of the seven largest eigenvalue roots

$r = 7$	$r = 6$	$r = 5$	$r = 4$	$r = 3$	$r = 2$	$r = 1$	$r = 0$
0.952	1	1	1	1	1	1	1
0.952	**0.923**	1	1	1	1	1	1
0.922	0.923	**0.915**	1	1	1	1	1
0.922	0.868	0.915	**0.843**	1	1	1	1
0.841	0.835	0.861	0.843	**0.837**	1	1	1
0.517	0.543	0.541	0.541	0.534	**0.576**	1	1
0.517	0.543	0.541	0.541	0.534	0.576	**0.455**	1

Table 6.83 Australia quarterly data: t-values of the α-coefficients

	α						
	Alpha(1)	Alpha(2)	Alpha(3)	Alpha(4)	Alpha(5)	Alpha(6)	Alpha(7)
Δm_r	(−0.613)	**(−2.856)**	**(4.587)**	(−0.719)	(2.097)	(0.397)	(0.527)
Δs_r	(−0.556)	(2.318)	(−0.046)	(0.904)	(−0.875)	(1.568)	(0.948)
Δy_r	(0.246)	(2.254)	(1.176)	(−0.549)	(2.453)	(−0.932)	(0.900)
$\Delta^2 p$	(0.975)	**(−3.995)**	**(−5.245)**	(1.363)	(−0.494)	(−0.208)	(0.263)
Δor	(2.118)	(−0.438)	(0.777)	**(3.935)**	(2.176)	(1.035)	(−0.263)
$\Delta b10$	(−0.915)	(−0.802)	**(2.597)**	**(4.050)**	(−0.787)	(−1.369)	(−0.074)
Δcf	**(8.437)**	(−0.195)	(0.871)	(−0.639)	(−1.509)	(−0.672)	(0.434)

unrestricted estimates. As can be seen from Table 6.83, adjustment behavior to the first three relations is stronger and involves several variables. Nevertheless, the fourth relation also exhibits significant t-values. However, a closer look at the α and β-coefficients of the overnight rate in the fourth relation reveals that they share the same sign and, hence, do not indicate adjustment behavior. Consequently, the investigation of the adjustment coefficients' significance points to a rank of $r = 3$ but also allows for a rank of $r = 4$.

The Recursive Graphs of the Trace Statistic

Figure 6.14 shows forward and backward recursively calculated graphs for the trace test statistic. The plots are normalized to the 5% significance level, represented by the horizontal line.

If $\lambda_i \neq 0$, the recursively calculated components of the trace statistic should grow linearly for $i = 1, \ldots, r$, but stay constant for $i = r + 1, \ldots, p$ (Juselius 2006, p. 142). Three of the graphs show linear growth and are above or cross the 1-line (5% critical value). As such, the graphical inspection of the trace statistic confirms a rank of $r = 3$.

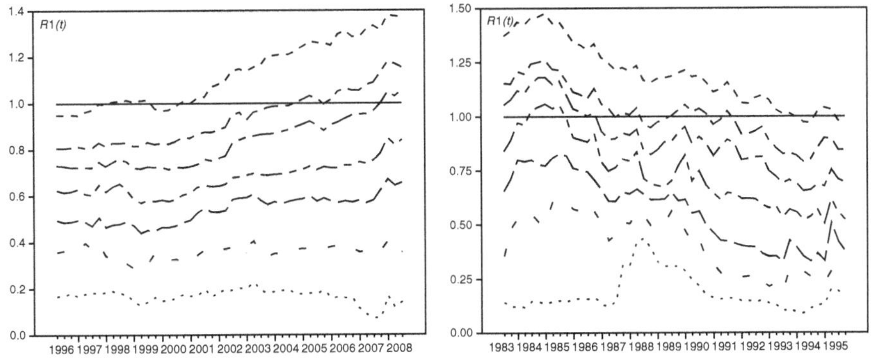

Fig. 6.14 Australia quarterly data: recursively calculated trace test statistics (forward, base sample 1983:03 to 1996:02, depicted left; backward, base sample 2008:03 to 1995:04, depicted right)

Graphical Analysis of the Cointegration Relations

The graphs of the cointegrating relations of the unrestricted model can be found in Appendix B.5.2. Whereas the first three graphs look clearly stationary, the last two relations show clear persistent behavior. The fourth and fifth relation could be interpreted as either stationary or non-stationary. As a result, this indicator points to a rank between $r = 3$ and $r = 5$.

To conclude, the various information criteria used to determine the rank of the model mostly point to a rank of $r = 3$ and this was chosen for the subsequent analysis of the long-run equilibria.[108] That also means that $p - r = 4$ common trends exist. In addition, recursive tests show that the data describes a constant parameter regime. Figure 6.15 depicts the recursively calculated test of the log-likelihood. Whereas the forward test is clearly accepted,[109] the backward calculated test statistic takes a long time to drop under the line. However, since additional tests confirm parameter constancy, constancy of the overall model is accepted (see the tests in Appendix B.5.3 on eigenvalues λ_i, eigenvalue fluctuations, the max test of β constancy and the test of β_t equals a known β, Figs. B.58–B.61, respectively). As a result, the assumption of constant parameters, which is important for valid identification of the long-run structure, is fulfilled.

[108] Since the above test results would have also allowed for a rank of $r = 4$ the identified long-run structure and other results were also validated for this choice of rank. This sensitivity analysis confirms the results for $r = 3$.

[109] The graph with short-run effects concentrated out, (R1(t)), stays under the line representing the 5% critical value.

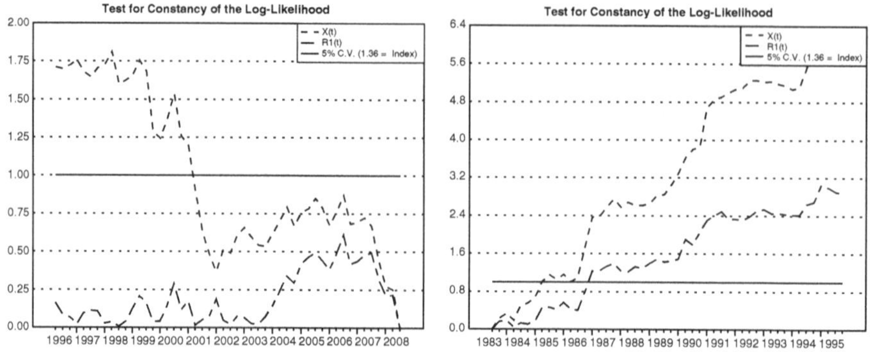

Fig. 6.15 Australia quarterly data: recursively calculated test of log-likelihood (forward, base sample 1983:03 to 1996:02, depicted left; backward, base sample 2008:03 to 1995:04, depicted right)

6.6.2 Identification of the Long-Run Structure

6.6.2.1 Assessment of the Unrestricted Π-Matrix

To help facilitate the identification of an empirically acceptable long-run structure, the unrestricted Π-matrix is tentatively interpreted.[110] These estimates measure the combined effect of the cointegration relations in each of the equations (Johansen and Juselius 1992, p. 223).

The unrestricted Π-matrix for the chosen rank of $r = 3$ is depicted in Table 6.84. Signs and t-values of the coefficients on the diagonal indicate which variables show error-correction behavior and might be part of the cointegration relations. Real money, inflation and capital flows all have significant and negative coefficients. Thus, a first indication of the analysis of the unrestricted Π is that the three cointegrating relations reflect a money demand, an inflation and a capital flows relation.

A closer look shows that real money reacts positively to the stock market, real output and the overnight rate, representing a classical money demand relation where higher wealth, increased transaction volume and lower opportunity costs increase money demand.

The stock market's adjustment behavior is insignificant (t-value $= -1.765$), but indicates a positive relationship with real money and a negative one with real output.

[110] However, the cointegration space can be rotated by taking proper linear combinations of the equations. Consequently, the final identified long-run structure does not have to reflect the initial suggestions from the unrestricted system. Also, the unrestricted Π-matrix may not be economically interpretable. Nevertheless, a rough indication of the long-run information in the data can be obtained.

Table 6.84 Australia quarterly data: the unrestricted Π-matrix for a rank of 3 (t-values in brackets)

	Π							
	m_r	s_r	y_r	Δp	or	$b10$	cf	*Trend*
Δm_r	**−0.107** [−4.484]	**0.032** [4.513]	**0.185** [3.919]	0.211 [1.050]	**0.285** [2.252]	−0.229 [−1.118]	−0.025 [−0.157]	**−0.001** [−3.834]
Δs_r	0.300 [1.766]	−0.089 [−1.765]	**−0.703** [−2.099]	2.017 [1.410]	0.178 [0.197]	−2.508 [−1.718]	1.110 [0.990]	**0.004** [2.210]
Δy_r	0.030 [1.416]	−0.009 [−1.400]	−0.076 [−1.805]	**0.416** [2.329]	−0.021 [−0.183]	−0.401 [−2.202]	0.022 [0.160]	0.000 [1.795]
$\Delta^2 p$	−0.009 [−0.786]	0.003 [0.739]	**0.054** [2.271]	**−0.617** [−6.105]	−0.121 [−1.907]	**0.664** [6.439]	−0.121 [−1.532]	**−0.000** [−2.491]
Δor	−0.000 [−0.049]	0.000 [0.067]	0.003 [0.302]	0.028 [0.630]	−0.044 [−1.560]	0.016 [0.356]	**−0.071** [−1.991]	−0.000 [−0.612]
$\Delta b10$	−0.007 [−1.920]	**0.002** [1.933]	0.010 [1.447]	0.028 [0.963]	0.030 [1.594]	−0.038 [−1.269]	0.013 [0.578]	−0.000 [−1.310]
Δcf	**0.047** [2.028]	**−0.013** [−1.968]	−0.033 [−0.729]	**0.440** [2.255]	**−0.932** [−7.579]	0.376 [1.888]	**−1.254** [−8.197]	−0.000 [−0.600]

Inflation is positively related to advances in real output and the bond rate. It appears that the two interest rates do not react to the other variables. This is a first indication of the Reserve Bank of Australia's (RBoA) ability to externally determine short-term interest rates. Finally, the last equation shows that capital flows show error-correction behavior towards all other variables aside from real output and the bond rate.

Table B.20 in Appendix B.5.4 shows the α- and β'-matrices of the partitioned unrestricted Π-matrix. The α-coefficients indicate which variables strongly adjust to long-run equilibria and which variables are more on the pushing side. The estimated α-matrix confirms that the three cointegration relations might be a money demand, an inflation rate and a capital flows relation.

The following section outlines preliminary tests for informative and assessment structure purposes.

6.6.2.2 Preliminary Hypotheses Testing

This section is divided into preliminary tests for β' and α. Automated tests on β' include the possibility to exclude variables from the long-run relations and the stationarity of individual relations. The α-matrix is formally analyzed for weak exogeneity and unit vectors. Afterwards, single cointegration tests are conducted. This is to test for potential long-run equilibria as outlined in the section on long-run economic relations (5.2).[111] This will help facilitate the final identification of the long-run structure and provides additional insight on information contained in the data set.

[111] All test statistics on α and β are asymptotically distributed as χ^2 because the asymptotic distribution is mixed Gaussian (Johansen 1995, pp. 177–178). As a result, the usual statistical inference can be applied (Johansen and Juselius 1994, p. 16).

Table 6.85 Australia quarterly data: test of variable exclusion (p-values in brackets)

Test of exclusion										
r	DGF	5% C.V.	m_r	s_r	y_r	Δp	or	$b10$	cf	*Trend*
3	3	7.815	16.980 [0.001]	14.849 [0.002]	11.199 [0.011]	16.954 [0.001]	9.640 [0.022]	3.665 [0.300]	44.034 [0.000]	**7.481** [0.058]

Table 6.86 Australia quarterly data: test of variable stationarity (p-values in brackets)

Test of stationarity									
r	DGF	5% C.V.	m_r	s_r	y_r	Δp	or	$b10$	cf
3	5	11.070	27.655 [0.000]	25.848 [0.000]	29.140 [0.000]	29.425 [0.000]	31.994 [0.000]	33.255 [0.000]	17.440 [0.004]
Restricted trend included in the cointegrating relations									
3	4	9.488	27.244 [0.000]	19.828 [0.001]	24.495 [0.000]	13.099 [0.011]	24.923 [0.000]	23.888 [0.000]	**6.972** [0.137]

Table 6.87 Australia quarterly data: test of weak exogeneity (p-values in brackets)

Test of weak exogeneity									
r	DGF	5% C.V.	m_r	s_r	y_r	Δp	or	$b10$	cf
3	3	7.815	13.764 [0.003]	**4.514** [0.211]	**4.421** [0.219]	14.419 [0.002]	**3.064** [0.382]	**3.285** [0.350]	41.398 [0.000]

Table 6.85 provides LR tests for the exclusion of any variables from the cointegration relations. It shows that exclusion of the trend is borderline accepted with a p-value of 0.058. However, the final long-run structure shows that trends are needed in the cointegration relations.
Table 6.86 reports the tests for long-run stationarity. It shows that stationarity is strongly rejected for all variables. However, trend-stationarity is accepted for capital flows. Hence, capital flows could be one cointegration vector on its own.
Table 6.87 tests for weak exogeneity, which is equivalent to testing a zero row in the α-matrix. This means that a variable is not error correcting but can be considered weakly exogenous for the long-run parameters β. If the test is accepted, this also means that the sum of the cumulated empirical shocks to the variable in question defines one common driving trend. Table 6.87 shows that the test is accepted for the stock market, real output, the overnight rate and the bond rate and, thus, confirms the analysis of the unrestricted Π-matrix.
The test of a unit vector in α tests if a variable is exclusively adjusting. If the unit vector test is accepted, the properties of the relevant variable are that its shocks only have transitory effects on the other variables in the system and it can be regarded as endogenous. Thus, the two tests of α can identify the pulling and pushing forces of the system. Table 6.88 shows that shocks to real money, the inflation rate and capital flows only have transitory effects. It confirms the mirror image of the unit vector test compared to the test on weak exogeneity. In conclusion, the stock market, real output and the interest rates seem to represent the pushing forces of the system and real money, inflation and capital flows seem to characterize the pulling forces.

Table 6.88 Australia quarterly data: test for a unit vector in the α-matrix (p-values in brackets)

Test of unit vector in alpha										
r	DGF	5% C.V.	m_r	s_r	y_r	Δp	or	$b10$	cf
3	4.000	9.488	**5.349** [0.253]	30.000 [0.000]	22.640 [0.000]	**7.276** [0.122]	22.289 [0.000]	18.908 [0.001]	**5.243** [0.263]

In addition to the above tests on single variables, the focus of the remaining preliminary tests is on single cointegration relations. The idea is to analyze if stable relationships between the economic variables can be identified by linear relations. Testing follows the theoretical connections outlined in Chap. 3 and Sect. 5.2, summarized in Table 5.1. The hypotheses are of the form:

$$\beta = (H\phi, \psi_1, \psi_2), \tag{6.45}$$

where H is the design matrix, ϕ contains the restricted parameters and ψ_i is a vector of parameters which are freely estimated. It is important to note that each hypothesis in Table 6.89 tests restrictions on a single vector but leaves the other cointegration vectors unrestricted (Johansen and Juselius 1992, pp. 233–236).

Table 6.89 provides an overview of the single cointegration test results. It mirrors the structure of Table 5.2. Accepted hypotheses are indicated in bold. The table shows that only a few hypotheses are accepted; hence, limited cointegration exists between the variables. This was already indicated by the analysis of the unrestricted Π.[112]

Hypotheses H_1 to H_8 test for cointegration between stocks and the other variables. Only H_3 and H_7 are accepted. However, the coefficients of the real long-term interest rate (in H_3) and of capital flows (in H_7) are very high. In addition, the stock market variable does not exhibit significant adjustment behavior to either relation.

H_9 to H_{16} test monetary relations. Only the relation incorporating real output and inflation (H_{12}) could be interpreted as a money demand relation but real money does not show error-correcting behavior.

'Policy rules' (H_{17} to H_{19}) show that the overnight rate does not react to the other variables. This is an indication that the RBoA determines the overnight rate exogenously.

Hypotheses H_{20} to H_{23} focus on potential stationary aggregate demand for goods relations. H_{21} shows that output reacts to the long-term real interest rate. This represents an IS-type relation. Stationarity is also accepted for H_{23}. However,

[112] In addition, since capital flows are found to be inherently stationary and, thus, integrated of order 0, the variable can not be part of another cointegration relation or adjust to a non-stationary variable (Juselius 2001, p. 343). The test results are still shown for purposes of comparison because every country analysis shows the same preliminary tests and in order to keep the final long-run structure open. However, for relations including capital flows, one must keep in mind that the stationarity might be a result of the already stationary capital flows instead of the combination of variables.

Table 6.89 Australia quarterly data: testing the stationarity of single relations

	m_r	s_r	y_r	Δp	or	$b10$	cf	*Trend*	$\chi^2(v)$	p-value	*sign.* α
					Demand for stocks						
H_1	0.216	1	0	0	0	0	0	−0.021	19.7 (3)	0.000	
H_2	0	1	0	77.40	−77.40	0	0	−0.027	13.3 (3)	0.004	
H_3	**0**	**−0.002**	**0**	**−1**	**0**	**1**	**0**	**0**	**1.0 (3)**	**0.806**	$y_r, \Delta p$
H_4	0	1	0	0	15.24	0	0	−0.016	15.9 (3)	0.001	
H_5	0	1	0	0	0	33.18	0	−0.011	13.9 (3)	0.003	
H_6	0	1	2.919	0	0	0	0	−0.041	16.1 (3)	0.001	
H_7	**0**	**1**	**0**	**0**	**0**	**0**	**−1,608**	**−0.231**	**6.6 (3)**	**0.086**	cf
H_8	−4.73	1	0	0	0	0	−583.7	−0.054	6.2 (2)	0.045	
					Money demand						
H_9	1	0	−1	0	0	0	0	0.001	27.9 (4)	0.000	
H_{10}	1	0	0	0	−24.73	24.73	0	−0.009	18.0 (3)	0.000	
H_{11}	1	0	−2.962	0	−5.770	21.14	0	0.017	11.9 (1)	0.001	
H_{12}	**1**	**0**	**−6.845**	**46.92**	**0**	**0**	**0**	**0.049**	**3.1 (2)**	**0.217**	$y_r, \Delta p$
H_{13}	1	4.632	0	0	0	0	0	−0.097	19.7 (3)	0.000	
H_{14}	1	−0.409	0	0	−22.06	22.06	0	−0.001	13.6 (2)	0.001	
H_{15}	1	−0.871	−1	0	0	0	0	0.015	18.9 (3)	0.000	
H_{16}	1	−0.285	−1	0	−9.828	9.828	0	0.004	6.8 (2)	0.033	

(continued)

Table 6.89 (Continued)

	m_r	s_r	y_r	Δp	or	$b10$	cf	*Trend*	$\chi^2(v)$	p-value	*sign.* α
					Policy rules						
H_{17}	**0**	**0**	**0**	**−1.763**	**1**	**0**	**0**	**0**	**5.3 (4)**	**0.256**	$y_r, \Delta p, cf$
H_{18}	0	0	−0.167	0	1	0	0	0.002	18.9 (3)	0.000	
H_{19}	0	0.066	0	0	1	0	0	−0.001	15.9 (3)	0.001	
					Demand for goods						
H_{20}	0	0	1	11.86	−11.86	0	0	−0.010	9.8 (3)	0.020	
H_{21}	**0**	**0**	**1**	**−36.50**	**0**	**36.50**	**0**	**−0.003**	**0.2 (3)**	**0.978**	$y_r, \Delta p$
H_{22}	−0.350	0	1	0	0	0	0	−0.004	18.4 (3)	0.000	
H_{23}	**−0.442**	**0.133**	**1**	**0**	**0**	**0**	**0**	**−0.006**	**1.1 (2)**	**0.567**	m_r, s_r
					Inflation and interest rates						
H_{24}	0.067	0	−0.067	1	0	0	0	0	18.0 (4)	0.001	
H_{25}	−0.010	0	0	0	0	1	0	0	22.9 (3)	0.000	
H_{26}	0	0	0	−1	1	0	0	0	16.1 (5)	0.006	
H_{27}	**0**	**0**	**0**	**−1**	**0**	**1**	**0**	**0**	**8.9 (5)**	**0.111**	$y_r, \Delta p$
H_{28}	**0**	**0**	**0**	**−1.763**	**1**	**0**	**0**	**0**	**5.3 (4)**	**0.256**	$y_r, \Delta p, cf$
H_{29}	**0**	**0**	**0**	**−1.509**	**0**	**1**	**0**	**0**	**3.5 (4)**	**0.471**	$y_r, \Delta p$
H_{30}	0	0	0	0	−1	1	0	0	23.2 (5)	0.000	
H_{31}	0	0	0	0	−0.917	1	0	0	22.9 (4)	0.000	
H_{32}	**0**	**0**	**0**	**17.85**	**1**	**−18.85**	**0**	**0**	**8.9 (4)**	**0.063**	Δp
H_{33}	0	0	0	−0.582	−1	1	0	0	20.8 (4)	0.000	

instead of real output real money reacts to this relation. This relation resembles the money demand relation that was already indicated in the unrestricted Π-matrix.

Under the headline 'Inflation and interest rates' cointegration between inflation and the nominal interest rates ('Fisher parity') as well as between the interest rates themselves ('expectations hypothesis') is tested. The 'Fisher parity'-hypothesis is accepted for the real long-term interest rate (H_{27}). However, identification of the long-run structure shows that it is not accepted as part of the final long-run structure. Instead it has to be amended by real output, which is equal to hypothesis H_{21}.

6.6.2.3 Identification of the Long-Run Cointegrating Relations

The identification procedure is based on the outlined economic theory and the preliminary testing of the econometric model in the previous section. By imposing different linear restrictions on the cointegrating relations an empirically and economically uniquely identified long-run structure can be obtained.

To identify the full cointegration structure the joint hypotheses H_{21} and H_{23} are tested together with capital flows as an already stationary time series. The restrictions on the identified long-run structure are accepted with a p-value of 0.29 ($\chi^2(9) = 10.847$). The structure is formally and empirically identified because all β-coefficients are strongly significant (Juselius and MacDonald 2004, p. 18). In addition, Appendix B.5.5 shows that the rank conditions are accepted for the full cointegration space. This means that the three cointegration relations are linearly independent and, as such, can not be replaced by each other.

The graphs of the cointegrating relations are displayed in Appendix B.5.6 with the deterministic terms and short-term parameters concentrated out.[113] They all describe stationary behavior. Graphical overviews of forward and backward recursive tests of parameter constancy in Appendix B.5.7 show that parameter constancy for α_i and β_i $(i = 1, \ldots, 3)$ is broadly accepted. Parameter coefficients of the second cointegration relation fluctuate strongly at the beginning of the 1990s and at the end of the sample. However, the signs of the coefficients remain constant. The structural representation of the cointegration space is depicted in Table 6.90 with the estimated eigenvectors β and the weights α.
The first cointegrating vector describes a money demand relation augmented with the stock market:

$$m_{r,t} - 0.312 s_{r,t} - 2.299 y_{r,t} + 0.014 trend \sim I(0), \tag{6.46}$$

where money demand reacts positively to higher GDP levels and to stock market advances. The positive reaction to output growth represents transaction based

[113] This removes the seasonal fluctuations and outliers, which can be observed in the raw series and, thus, provides a clearer picture (Brüggemann and Lütkepohl 2006, p. 692). See also Sect. 6.2.1.3.

Table 6.90 Australia quarterly data: the identified long-run structure (t-values in brackets)

	m_r	s_r	y_r	Δp	or	$b10$	cf	Trend
Beta(1)	**1.000** [NA]	**−0.312** [−5.860]	**−2.299** [−11.945]	0.000 [NA]	0.000 [NA]	0.000 [NA]	0.000 [NA]	**0.014** [7.723]
Beta(2)	0.000 [NA]	0.000 [NA]	**1.000** [NA]	**−37.850** [−7.522]	0.000 [NA]	**37.850** [7.522]	0.000 [NA]	**−0.003** [−2.471]
Beta(3)	0.000 [NA]	0.000 [NA]	0.000 [NA]	0.000 [NA]	0.000 [NA]	0.000 [NA]	**1.000** [NA]	**0.000** [6.030]

α	Alpha(1)	Alpha(2)	Alpha(3)
Δm_r	**−0.101** [−4.701]	−0.007 [−1.298]	0.069 [0.446]
Δs_r	**0.299** [1.960]	−0.056 [−1.479]	1.006 [0.902]
Δy_r	0.020 [1.036]	**−0.011** [−2.351]	0.126 [0.901]
$\Delta^2 p$	−0.011 [−1.034]	**0.017** [6.271]	−0.117 [−1.476]
Δor	−0.004 [−0.833]	−0.001 [−0.594]	−0.034 [−0.954]
$\Delta b10$	−0.006 [−1.933]	−0.001 [−1.258]	0.005 [0.230]
Δcf	**0.043** [2.026]	−0.007 [−1.319]	**−1.249** [−8.177]

increases in money demand. The positive reaction to stock market developments shows that the wealth effect is stronger than the substitution effect.

The α-coefficients show that not only real money but also the stock market adjust significantly to this relation. Although the stock market's reaction is only borderline significant, this indicates that the stock market reacts positively to real money and excess liquidity in the system. This shows that monetary developments have played a bigger role in the Australian stock market than in the other countries. One explanation of this could be the dominant commodity sector in the Australian market. Belke et al. (2009, pp. 21–23) show that global excess liquidity leads to commodity price increases. In which case, a larger share of commodity-related companies listed on the stock market might be responsible for the relationship between money and stocks.[114] The t-values of the adjustment coefficients show that real money adjusts more significantly but the coefficients show that the speed of adjustment is higher for the stock market. It takes the stock market approximately three quarters to restore equilibrium while it takes real money ten quarters.

Further investigation of the α-coefficients shows that capital flows react positively to deviations of this relation. The reaction of capital flows shows that, for the case of Australia, the 'pull' channel as suggested by Baks and Kramer (1999, p. 6) prevails. The 'pull' channel basically states the following: if domestic money stock

[114] Approximately 200 of the 500 companies listed in the All Ordinaries Share Price Index do business in commodity-related areas (Standard & Poor's 2009).

increases lead to higher domestic asset prices and foreign investors are attracted by these asset price increases, then capital will flow in from abroad (a 'pull' of capital from abroad). These inflows can further drive domestic asset price inflation.

The second β'-vector represents a relationship between output, inflation and the bond rate:

$$y_{r,t} + 37.9(b10_t - \Delta p_t) - 0.003trend \sim I(0), \tag{6.47}$$

where real output reacts negatively to the long-term real interest rate. This represents a classical IS-type relationship. The high coefficients for inflation and the bond rate could indicate that this relation should be interpreted as an inflation rate relation.[115] The high significance of the inflation α-coefficient also suggests this. Ergo, inflation is positively affected by advances in real output and increases in the bond rate. This is consistent with the theory that higher utilization (due to output growth) results in price increases. In addition, higher bond yields lead to a cost-push effect due to higher financing costs and can be associated with higher expected inflation (Juselius and MacDonald 2004, p. 23).

The last cointegrating relation consists of the capital flows variable, which is stationary if a small trend is included:

$$cf_t + 0.00014trend \sim I(0). \tag{6.48}$$

The α-coefficient shows that capital flows strongly and significantly error correct in less than one quarter. In addition, the trend shows that outflows grow faster than inflows, albeit very slowly.

Weak exogeneity was tested for the bond rate and the stock market both separately and together. These long-run structures were still accepted but reduced the p-value to 0.12, 0.19 and 0.09, respectively. The main results remain similar.

To find out if the cumulated shocks to a variable have any long-run impact on other variables Sect. 6.6.4 analyzes the unrestricted C-matrix. There the focus is also on the controllability of stock markets.

6.6.3 *Short-Run Dynamics*

While the previous analysis focuses on stable long-run economic relations, this section applies a structural error-correction model and formulates stationary equations for each of the variables in the system (see Sect. 6.2.3). The 81 zero restrictions of insignificant coefficients were accepted based on an LR test of over-identifying

[115] However, the size of the coefficients has to be interpreted with caution. They usually can not be interpreted as elasticities, since a shock to one variable implies a shock to all variables in the long run. Thus, a ceteris paribus interpretation is generally invalid (Johansen 2009, pp. 8–9; Johansen 2005, pp. 97–100; Lütkepohl 1994, p. 393). In addition, The low β-coefficient of the real output variable can be rationalized by the difference of the standard deviations of the two series. The residual standard error of real output is 7 times higher than that of the bond rate.

Table 6.91 Australia quarterly data: short-run dynamics (t-values in brackets)

	Δm_r	Δs_r	Δy_r	$\Delta^2 p$	Δor	$\Delta b10$	Δcf
$\Delta m_{r,t}$	**1**	0	0	0	0	0	0
$\Delta s_{r,t}$	0	**1**	0	0	0	0	0
$\Delta y_{r,t}$	0	0	**1**	0	0	0	0
$\Delta^2 p_t$	0	0	0	**1**	0	0	0
Δor_t	0	0	0	0	**1**	0	0
$\Delta b10_t$	0	0	0	0	0	**1**	0
Δcf_t	0	0	0	0	0	0	**1**
$\Delta m_{r,t-1}$				**0.100**			
				[2.80]			
$\Delta s_{r,t-1}$							
$\Delta y_{r,t-1}$	**0.304**		**0.304**				**0.217**
	[3.03]		[3.66]				[2.04]
$\Delta^2 p_{t-1}$					**0.087**		
					[3.43]		
Δor_{t-1}		**−5.353**					
		[−2.36]					
$\Delta b10_{t-1}$	**−1.447**				**0.522**		
	[−2.68]				[3.91]		
Δcf_{t-1}							
$ecm1_{t-1}$	**−0.108**					**−0.006**	**0.035**
	[−6.63]					[−2.76]	[1.94]
$ecm2_{t-1}$				**0.019**			
				[9.38]			
$ecm3_{t-1}$							**−1.082**
							[−10.8]
$dum8401_{p,t}$	**0.020**		**0.037**	**−0.022**	**0.016**		
	[2.07]		[4.45]	[−4.38]	[7.58]		
$dum8601_{p,t}$					**−0.010**	**−0.007**	
					[−4.81]	[−4.70]	
$dum8704_{p,t}$		**−0.520**					
		[−7.55]					
$dum0003_{p,t}$	**−0.038**		**−0.022**	**0.030**			
	[−3.96]		[−2.67]	[6.24]			
$dum0202_{p,t}$	**−0.047**						
	[−5.83]						

restrictions with a p-value of 0.63 ($\chi^2(81) = 76.28$). Table 6.91 provides the results. The dependent variables can be found in the top row as the column headings of each of the model equations. The row headings, on the other hand, indicate the conditioning variables.

The analysis of the short-run dynamics shows that real money reacts positively to lagged values of real output (increased transaction volume) and negatively to lagged values of the bond rate (opportunity costs of holding money). In addition, real money shows error-correction behavior to the first cointegration relation, which is the money demand relation.

The stock market shows a strong negative reaction to lagged values of the overnight rate. This demonstrates the RBoA's ability to influence stock prices in the short run. The analysis of the short-run dynamics also shows that the stock market does not react to any of the cointegration relations. This also confirms the interpretation of the first cointegration relation as a money demand relation instead of a stock market relation.

Real output only reacts to lagged values of itself. Inflation reacts positively to lagged values of real money and is pushed by the second cointegration relation. This supports the notion that the second cointegration relation is an inflation rate relation rather than an IS-type aggregate demand relation. In which case, inflation reacts positively to advances in real output and the bond rate in the long run.

Table 6.91 also shows that the overnight rate reacts positively to inflation and the bond rate in the short run. This suggests that inflation (actual and expected) is important for Australian monetary policy decisions.

The bond rate only reacts to the money demand relation and only with a small coefficient. This indicates that part of the excess liquidity is channeled into bond investments. Capital flows increase in response to lagged values of real output and react strongly to the third β-vector, which is the stationary capital flows vector. Additionally, they are pushed by the residuals of the money demand relation, which confirms the aforementioned 'pull' channel effect.

The downside of the above equations is that current effects are not modeled. Instead they are left in the residuals. However, simultaneous effects may have potential importance. Whereas correlation between the residuals is not problematic in the long-run analyses of the previous and the following section, identification of the short-run structural equations requires uncorrelated residuals (Juselius 2006, p. 229). Table 6.92 shows the residual covariance matrix, in which large off-diagonal elements indicate significant current effects between the system variables. Correlation between real money and real output, real money and inflation, as well as between the two interest rates must be critically recognized.[116]

One way to reduce residual correlation is to introduce current effects between the variables into the short-run structure. Adding current effects of the bond rate to the short rate equation helps to reduce correlation between the variables (see Table 6.93). However, although other combinations of current effects were tested, correlation between the variables was not reduced. These tests included current effects of inflation and real output in the real money inflation and vice versa. Unfortunately, the coefficients of the current effects proved insignificant and did

[116] High residual correlation can result from the aggregation of the data over time, inadequately modeled expectations or omitted variables (Juselius 2006, pp. 239–240).

Table 6.92 Australia quarterly data: correlation of structural residuals (standard deviations on diagonal)

	Δm_r	Δs_r	Δy_r	$\Delta^2 p$	Δor	$\Delta b10$	Δcf
Δm_r	*0.010*						
Δs_r	0.10	*0.070*					
Δy_r	**0.48**	0.22	*0.009*				
$\Delta^2 p$	**−0.27**	−0.03	−0.20	*0.005*			
Δor	0.19	0.05	−0.03	0.12	*0.002*		
$\Delta b10$	0.00	−0.11	−0.01	0.06	**0.36**	*0.001*	
Δcf	0.01	0.09	0.20	0.08	−0.17	0.03	*0.009*

Table 6.93 Australia quarterly data: correlation of structural residuals after allowing for current effects (standard deviations on diagonal)

	Δm_r	Δs_r	Δy_r	$\Delta^2 p$	Δor	$\Delta b10$	Δcf
Δm_r	*0.010*						
Δs_r	0.11	*0.070*					
Δy_r	**0.48**	0.22	*0.009*				
$\Delta^2 p$	**−0.28**	−0.03	−0.20	*0.005*			
Δor	0.20	0.13	−0.02	0.08	*0.002*		
$\Delta b10$	0.00	−0.10	−0.01	0.05	−0.23	*0.001*	
Δcf	0.01	0.09	0.20	0.08	−0.19	0.03	*0.009*

not reduce residual correlation between the variables. The results of the short-run analysis remain almost identical if current effects between the two interest rates are modeled. Table 6.94 shows the short-run structure after allowing for current effects. The structure is accepted based on an LR test of over-identifying restrictions with a p-value of 0.69 ($\chi^2(80) = 72.93$).

6.6.4 The Long-Run Impact of the Common Trends

The C-matrix is integral to understanding the long-run implications of the model. In order for a central bank to influence the stock market it is essential that shocks to a monetary instrument have a significant long-run impact on the stock market. Hence, when evaluating the effectiveness of monetary policy, the long-run impact of shocks to the short-term interest rate and to the money supply on the stock market is of particular interest.

The residual $\epsilon_{i,t}$ is interpreted as an estimate of the unanticipated shock to variable x_i. The estimated long-run impact of the cumulated shocks is reported in Table 6.95 and is calculated from the estimates of the restricted VAR model as

$$C = \tilde{\beta}_{\perp}\alpha_{\perp}', \tag{6.49}$$

Table 6.94 Australia quarterly data: short-run dynamics allowing for current effects (t-values in brackets)

	Δm_r	Δs_r	Δy_r	$\Delta^2 p$	Δor	$\Delta b10$	Δcf
$\Delta m_{r,t}$	**1**	0	0	0	0	0	0
$\Delta s_{r,t}$	0	**1**	0	0	0	0	0
$\Delta y_{r,t}$	0	0	**1**	0	0	0	0
$\Delta^2 p_t$	0	0	0	**1**	0	0	0
Δor_t	0	0	0	0	**1**	0	0
$\Delta b10_t$	0	0	0	0	0.9	**1**	0
Δcf_t	0	0	0	0	0	0	**1**
$\Delta m_{r,t-1}$				**0.104**			
				[2.93]			
$\Delta s_{r,t-1}$							
$\Delta y_{r,t-1}$	**0.303**		**0.302**				**0.216**
	[3.02]		[3.64]				[2.03]
$\Delta^2 p_{t-1}$					**0.085**		
					[3.41]		
Δor_{t-1}		**−5.355**					
		[−2.36]					
$\Delta b10_{t-1}$	**−1.489**				**0.484**		
	[−2.76]				[3.63]		
Δcf_{t-1}							
$ecm1_{t-1}$	**−0.115**					**−0.008**	**0.040**
	[−6.86]					[−3.22]	[2.19]
$ecm2_{t-1}$				**0.018**			
				[9.32]			
$ecm3_{t-1}$							**−1.082**
							[−10.8]
$dum8401_{p,t}$	**0.020**		**0.037**	**−0.022**	**0.016**		
	[2.05]		[4.45]	[−4.38]	[7.61]		
$dum8601_{p,t}$					**−0.005**	**−0.007**	
					[−1.21]	[−4.74]	
$dum8704_{p,t}$		**−0.516**					
		[−7.51]					
$dum0003_{p,t}$	**−0.038**		**−0.022**	**0.030**			
	[−3.97]		[−2.68]	[6.24]			
$dum0202_{p,t}$	**−0.047**						
	[−5.83]						

where $\tilde{\beta}_\perp = \beta_\perp(\alpha'_\perp\beta_\perp)^{-1}$ and $\alpha_\perp, \beta_\perp$ are the $(p \times p-r)$ orthogonal compliments of α and β (Johansen 1995, pp. 49–50). As C has reduced rank, only $p - r = 4$ linear combinations of the $p = 7$ innovations, ϵ_t, have permanent effects.

The C-matrix can be read column or row-wise. The columns show the long-run impact of a shock to a variable on each of the variables in the system and the rows show which of the shocks have a long-run impact on the particular variable.

Table 6.95 Australia quarterly data: the long-run impact matrix (t-values in brackets)

The long-run impact matrix, C							
	$\hat{\epsilon}_{m_r}$	$\hat{\epsilon}_{s_r}$	$\hat{\epsilon}_{y_r}$	$\hat{\epsilon}_{\Delta p}$	$\hat{\epsilon}_{or}$	$\hat{\epsilon}_{b10}$	$\hat{\epsilon}_{cf}$
m_r	**1.003** [2.612]	0.156 [1.611]	**2.325** [2.486]	2.310 [1.716]	−1.658 [−1.110]	−2.903 [−1.303]	0.231 [0.581]
s_r	**1.449** [2.745]	**0.531** [3.987]	**−3.584** [−2.788]	−0.357 [−0.193]	−2.487 [−1.210]	−5.741 [−1.874]	0.225 [0.411]
y_r	0.240 [1.379]	−0.004 [−0.093]	**1.497** [3.535]	1.053 [1.727]	−0.384 [−0.568]	−0.485 [−0.480]	0.070 [0.389]
Δp	0.019 [0.642]	0.014 [1.833]	**0.189** [2.564]	**0.226** [2.129]	−0.201 [−1.703]	**0.828** [4.715]	0.019 [0.609]
or	0.042 [0.854]	**0.026** [2.043]	**0.251** [2.077]	0.313 [1.801]	**0.844** [4.376]	0.199 [0.691]	−0.003 [−0.065]
$b10$	0.013 [0.488]	**0.014** [2.084]	**0.150** [2.288]	**0.198** [2.107]	−0.190 [−1.824]	**0.841** [5.402]	0.017 [0.621]
cf	0.000 [NA]	0.000 [NA]	0.000 [NA]	0.000 [NA]	0.000 [NA]	0.000 [NA]	0.000 [NA]

The C-matrix in Table 6.95 establishes that, in the long run, shocks to real money affect real money and the stock market positively. The former is an indication of the procyclicality of credit creation, the latter confirms the leading hypothesis of this contribution that liquidity conditions have a positive effect on stock markets.

Cumulated shocks to the stock market positively influence stock market developments in the long run. This confirms the results of the other country analyses and indicates the importance of herding and trend-following behavior as well as rational speculation of economic agents for stock market developments. In addition, shocks to the stock market have a positive effect on both interest rates.

Aside from that, the C-matrix shows that shocks to real output have positive long-run effects on real money, inflation, both interest rates and the level of economic activity itself. In addition, the shocks have negative effects on the stock market, which is a surprising and unusual finding.

Shocks to inflation influence the bond rate and vice versa. Another sign of the strong stationarity of the long-term real interest rate.

The C-matrix also shows that shocks to real output, the stock market and inflation (borderline insignificant) influence the overnight rate. This is a sign that the RBoA already takes all three factors into account when conducting its monetary policy. Analysis of the shocks to the overnight rate reveals that the signs of the coefficients are negative for all three variables (stock market, output, inflation). However, the coefficients turn out to be statistically insignificant (for inflation only borderline insignificant). It is, thus, questionable if the policies of the RBoA have the desired long-run effects.

6.6.5 Conclusion

The findings for Australia confirm that positive shocks to the stock market have a positive impact on future developments of the Australian stock market. One explanation for this, as stated in the introduction, is the importance of investors' confidence and optimism. In addition, one objective of this contribution is to test whether or not abundant liquidity enforces the upward spiral of stock prices. This is also confirmed by the long-run cointegration relations and the long-run impact matrix. The first cointegration relation shows that the Australian stock market reacts to excess liquidity in the system. Additionally, the long-run impact matrix confirms that shocks to real money translate into higher stock prices in the long run. One explanation for the strong connection between money and stock prices in the case of Australia is the importance of the commodity sector. Belke et al. (2009, pp. 21–23) as well as Browne and Cronin (2007, p. 22) show that global liquidity has a positive impact on commodity prices. Since Australia has a large share of commodity related companies (such as mining) listed on the stock market the positive liquidity effect on commodity prices also increased revenues of mining companies and might have led to higher stock market levels.[117]

Table 6.96 shows the answers to the main hypotheses based on the results of the econometric analysis. Aside from the non-existent importance of capital flows the hypotheses are mainly confirmed. The analysis also shows that the RBoA has the ability to influence the stock market in the short run. For the long run, the negative impact turns out to be statistically insignificant.

In addition, the above analysis elucidates a few other aspects of economic interest, primarily:

- A stable money demand relation could be identified where real output and stock market levels are the main driving factors. Real output seems to be especially important for money demand. First, it is part of the cointegration relation. Second, shocks to real output have a positive long-run effect on money developments. And, third, real money reacts to lagged values of real output in the short run. Additionally, the bond rate has a negative effect on money holdings

Table 6.96 Australia quarterly data: results of main hypotheses

	Hypotheses/Questions	Result
H_1	The behavior of the stock market in Australia shows strong persistence, i.e., shocks to the stock market have positive long-run effects on future developments	Yes
H_2	Long-run equilibria exist between stock prices and liquidity conditions	Yes
H_3	Liquidity conditions influence stock prices positively in the long run	Yes
H_4	Liquidity conditions influence stock prices positively in the short run	Yes
H_5	International capital flows have a positive long-run impact on the stock market behavior in Australia	No
H_6	International capital flows have a positive short-run impact on the stock market behavior in Australia	No
Q_1	Is the RBoA able to influence stock prices in the long run?	No
Q_2	Is the RBoA able to influence stock prices in the short run?	Yes

[117] Approximately 200 of the 500 companies listed in the All Ordinaries Share Price Index do business in commodity-related areas (Standard & Poor's 2009).

in the short run. This indicates short-run portfolio reallocations due to higher opportunity costs.

- Real aggregate demand for goods has a negative relationship with the long-term real interest rate, as expected from theoretical considerations. However, it is only borderline significant. Also, the analysis of the short run and of the long-run impact matrix shows that economic activity is only influenced by itself.
- The analysis shows that a positive long-run relationship exists between inflation and the bond rate, as well as economic activity. This indicates the importance of the long-run interest rate for financing costs and the resulting cost-push effect of higher interest rates on inflation. An alternative interpretation is to regard higher nominal long-term interest rates as increased expected inflation and investors' demand for compensation for it. For Australia, monetary developments only affect inflation in the short run. More precisely, inflation reacts to higher lagged values of money growth.
- The short-term interest rate is not part of and does not react to any of the long-run cointegration relations. The long-run impact matrix of shocks to the variables, however, demonstrates that the policy rate is positively influenced by shocks to the stock market, real output and also inflation (borderline insignificant). In the short term, the policy rate reacts to inflation and the bond rate (as a proxy for expected inflation). These findings illustrate the RBoA's consideration of asset prices as well as economic activity and inflation when setting interest rates.
- The bond rate moves parallel to the inflation rate, which results in a stationary long-term real interest rate.
- Capital flows are found to be trend-stationary and, thus, do not play a role in the other cointegration vectors. Shocks to capital flows also do not have any long-run impact on any of the other variables, neither in the long nor in the short run. Consequently, capital flows seem to be unimportant for domestic developments in Australia. Capital inflows are attracted by excess liquidity in connection with higher asset prices as well as economic activity.

6.7 South Korea: Quarterly Data

6.7.1 Model Specification

6.7.1.1 Data Overview, Deterministic Components and Lag Length

The data vector for the country analysis of South Korea consists of the following variables:

$$x_t' = [m_r, s_r, y_r, \Delta p, or, b10, cf]_t \,, \tag{6.50}$$

where m_r is the log of real money (M2), s_r is the log of real stock market levels (total market including dividends) and y_r is the log of real GDP. Nominal variables are transformed to real variables by applying the consumer price index, p, and, hence, Δp is the inflation rate. Short and long-term interest rates are represented by the money market rate, or, and the 10-year government bond yield, $b10$. All interest rates have been converted to quarterly rates and divided by 100 to achieve comparability with the inflation rate. Capital flows, cf, are calculated in percent as a share of the total money stock (M2). Capital flows are derived from non-bank BoP transactions as described in Sect. 4.6.3.2 and Appendix A. All time series are obtained either from Datastream or the IMF BoP database and detailed information on specific sources of the data can be found in Appendix B.6.1. The data used for the analysis covers the last 25 years and consists of quarterly observations from 1983:1 to 2008:3.

Figure 6.16 displays the time pattern of all variables in levels and first differences. The graph for inflation looks stationary in levels and differences. All other graphs only look stationary for the differenced series. Further characteristics of the data are that real money, real stock prices and real GDP seem to follow a trend. Thus, a deterministic (non-stochastic) trend should be allowed for in the model. However, it seems that the deterministic part of the trend changed after the Asian financial crisis in 1997/1998. This represents a mean shift in the differenced series. This structural

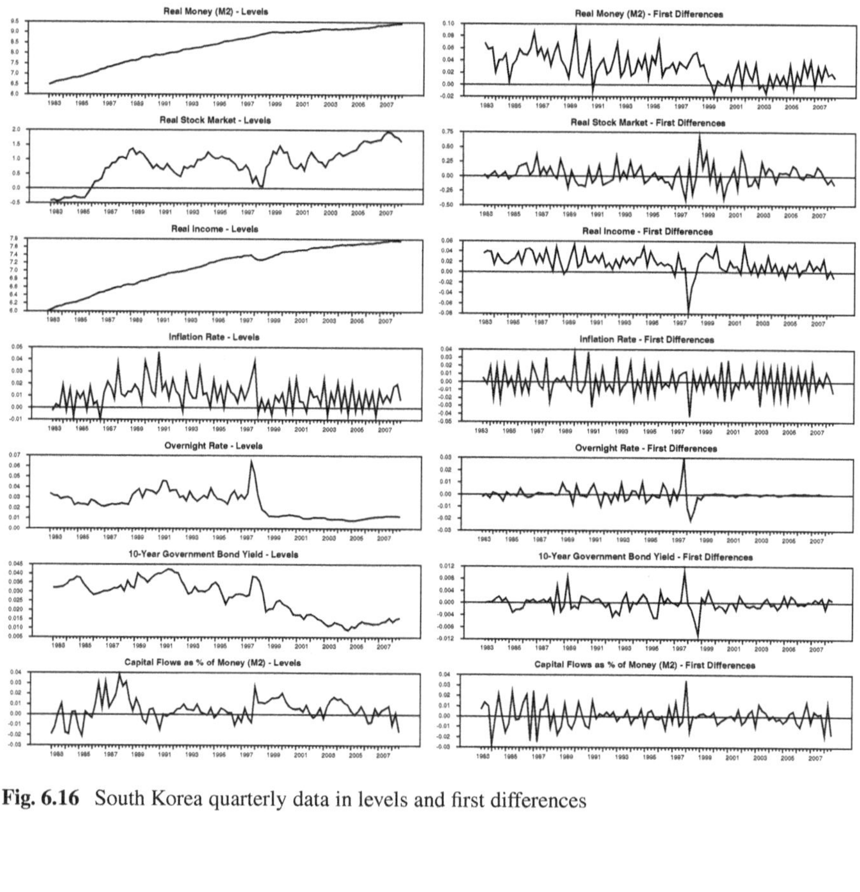

Fig. 6.16 South Korea quarterly data in levels and first differences

break might require a shift dummy to model the change in expectations and risk perception inherent with the bust.

Deterministic Components

The above observations suggest including the following deterministic components in the model (see also Sect. 6.2.1.1): an unrestricted constant, μ_0, a restricted linear trend, μ_1, and a restricted shift dummy, $\Phi_s D_{s,t}$. The CVAR model from (5.4) then becomes

$$\Delta x_t = \alpha\beta' x_{t-1} + \sum_{i=1}^{k-1} \Gamma_i \Delta x_{t-1} + \Phi D_t + \mu_0 + \mu_1 + \Phi_s \, , D_{s,t} + \epsilon_t \quad (6.51)$$

where $\mu_0 = \alpha\rho_0 + \gamma_0$, $\mu_1 = \alpha\rho_1 + \gamma_1$ and $\Phi_s = \alpha\delta_0 + \delta_1$, such that the parameters μ_0, μ_1 and Φ_s are decomposed in the direction of α and $\alpha_\perp$. Consequently, (6.51) becomes

$$\Delta x_t = \alpha[\beta', \rho_0, \rho_1, \delta_0] \begin{bmatrix} x_{t-1} \\ 1 \\ t \\ D_{s,t} \end{bmatrix} + \sum_{i=1}^{k-1} \Gamma_i \Delta x_{t-1} + \Phi D_t + \gamma_0 + \gamma_1 + \delta_1 D_t^s + \epsilon_t. \quad (6.52)$$

The constant, μ_0, is unrestricted. The trend, μ_1, however, is restricted to the cointegration space. Hence, $\gamma_1 = 0$ and $(\gamma_0, \rho_0, \rho_1) \neq 0$.[118] With an unrestricted constant and a trend restricted to the cointegration space, linear trends ($\gamma_0 \neq 0$), but not quadratic trends ($\gamma_1 \neq 0$), are allowed for in the data. This specification ensures similarity in the rank test procedure because the trend might not cancel in the cointegration relations (Nielsen and Rahbek 2000, pp. 12–15). To ensure similarity in the presence of structural breaks the shift dummy needs to be included in the cointegration relations before determining the rank (Juselius 2006, p. 140). The shift dummy is restricted to the cointegration space: $\delta_0 \neq 0$ and $\delta_1 = 0$.

If $\rho_1 \neq 0$ and $\delta_0 \neq 0$ then the linear trend and the mean shift of the variables do not cancel in the cointegration relations, which will be formally tested in the model in Sect. 6.7.2.2, Table 6.105.

[118] These specifications correspond to case 4 in Juselius (2006, pp. 99–100) and model $H^*(r)$ in Johansen (1995, Equation (5.14), p. 81). In CATS it is processed via the use of det = cidrift.

Table 6.97 South Korea quarterly data: intervention dummies

Dummy variable	Motivation	Impact on
$dum9404_t$	Market expectations of tightened monetary policy due to rapid economic growth[a]	Overnight rate
$dum9704_s (= D_s)$	Asian financial crisis	Overnight rate, bond rate, stock market and inflation
$dum9704_p$[b]	Asian financial crisis	Overnight rate, bond rate, stock market and inflation
$dum0201_p$	Banks' increased extension of consumer loans	Real money and real output

[a] The Bank of Korea (1995, p. 15)

[b] The shift dummy ($dum9704_s$) is restricted to lie in the cointegration space. As a result, its difference ($\Delta dum9704_s = dum9704_p$) should be included as an unrestricted permanent blip dummy in the VAR equations (Juselius 2006, p. 109).

Dummy Variables

The misspecification test shows that normality is rejected and autocorrelation exists in the first lag.[119] To ensure normality and reduce autocorrelation, dummies are included based on the economic calendar and the graphs of the standardized residuals, which have revealed some large outliers. These intervention dummies are used to account for significant political or institutional events and reforms. These interventions frequently show up as extraordinarily large shocks in the VAR analysis and, thereby, violate the normality assumption. Table 6.97 gives an overview. The analysis of South Korea quarterly data requires one transitory, two permanent and one shift dummy.

Determination of the Lag Length

To guarantee valid statistical inference it is crucial to test for the satisfaction of the assumptions underlying the model. This includes the determination of the lag length as well as tests to exclude serial correlation, conditional heteroscedasticity and deviations from Gaussian white noise, which is the focus of the next section.

The two information criteria SC and H–Q are reported in Table 6.98. The last two columns in Table 6.98 report the LM test for autocorrelation of order 1 and k. Numbers in bold indicate the suggested lag length of the respective test.
Both criteria (SC, H–Q) suggest one lag. However, the LM test shows that there is left-over residual autocorrelation if only one lag is applied. In addition, to perform the analysis of short-run dynamics a minimum of two lags has to be included. Thus, a lag length of $k = 2$ is used for the analysis.

[119] The test is not reported here at this stage. Instead, misspecification tests are reported for the specified model in Sect. 6.7.1.2.

Table 6.98 South Korea quarterly data: information to determine lag length

Model	k	T	Regressive	Log-Likelihood	SC	H–Q	LM(1)	LM(k)
VAR(5)	5	101	45	3,578.688	−56.471	−61.326	0.222	0.176
VAR(4)	4	101	38	3,509.565	−57.342	−61.441	0.030	0.253
VAR(3)	3	101	31	3,468.507	−58.768	−62.112	0.094	0.002
VAR(2)	2	101	24	3,430.966	−60.263	−62.852	**0.068**	**0.874**
VAR(1)	1	101	17	3,377.388	**−61.441**	**−63.275**	0.002	0.002

The discussion in this section on lag length, deterministic components and dummy variables results in the following VAR(2) model (in error-correction form) for South Korea:

$$\Delta x_t = \alpha \tilde{\beta}' \tilde{x}_{t-1} + \Gamma_1 \Delta x_{t-1} + \Phi D_t + \mu_0 + \epsilon_t, \tag{6.53}$$

where $x_t' = [m_r, s_r, y_r, \Delta p, or, b10, cf]_t$ and $\tilde{x}_t = \left[x_t', 1, trend, D_s\right]$ is a $((7+3) \times 1)$ data vector containing the p variables, a constant, a trend and the shift dummy. The cointegration vectors are represented by $\tilde{\beta} = \left[\beta', \rho_0, \rho_1, \delta_0\right]'$, which is a $((7+3) \times r)$ matrix with rank r. The analysis is based on 7×101 observations and conditions on the initial values (data points for 1983:1 to 1983:2). The unrestricted permanent and transitory dummy variables are contained in the vector $D_t = \left[dum9404_t, \ dum9704_p, \ dum0201_p\right]$.

6.7.1.2 Misspecification Tests

Before one may determine the reduced rank of the model, the model must be well specified. Tables 6.99 and 6.100 report multivariate and univariate misspecification tests, respectively. The multivariate LM test shows no sign of autocorrelation in the first 4 lags (the null of the test is 'no autocorrelation').[120]
The normality tests are based on skewness and kurtosis.[121] The null of the tests is normally distributed errors. Tables 6.99 and 6.100 show that normality is accepted for the multivariate case and for the univariate case for all variables but capital flows. This is acceptable because it is mainly a result of excess kurtosis and simulation studies have shown that kurtosis is less serious than skewness (Hendry and Juselius 2000, p. 7).
Additionally, tests for multivariate ARCH of order q (with $q = 1, \ldots, 4$) and univariate second order ARCH effects are reported.[122] There are signs of ARCH effects

[120] It is asymptotically distributed as χ^2 with p^2 degrees of freedom (Johansen 1995, p. 22).

[121] They are asymptotically χ^2-distributed, with $2p$ degrees of freedom in the multivariate and 2 degrees of freedom in the univariate case.

[122] The multivariate test statistic is approximately distributed as χ^2 with $\frac{q}{4}p^2(p+1)^2$ degrees of freedom. The univariate test is approximately distributed as χ^2 with k degrees of freedom (Dennis 2006, pp. 179–180).

Table 6.99 South Korea quarterly data: multivariate misspecification tests (p-values in brackets)

Test for no autocorrelation			
LM(1):	$\chi^2(49)$	=	64.489 [0.068]
LM(2):	$\chi^2(49)$	=	37.953 [0.874]
LM(3):	$\chi^2(49)$	=	64.420 [0.069]
LM(4):	$\chi^2(49)$	=	40.785 [0.792]
Test for normality	$\chi^2(14)$	=	12.905 [0.534]
Test for no Arch effects			
LM(1):	$\chi^2(784)$	=	880.786 [**0.010**]
LM(2):	$\chi^2(1568)$	=	1715.778 [**0.045**]
LM(3):	$\chi^2(2352)$	=	2535.085 [**0.040**]
LM(4):	$\chi^2(3136)$	=	2828.000 [1.000]

Table 6.100 South Korea quarterly data: univariate misspecification tests (p-values in brackets)

	ARCH(2)	Normality	Skewness	Kurtosis
Δm_r	1.905 [0.386]	0.818 [0.664]	0.130	2.554
Δs_r	4.287 [0.117]	0.210 [0.900]	0.058	2.641
Δy_r	8.254 [**0.016**]	2.111 [0.348]	−0.225	3.366
$\Delta^2 p$	0.770 [0.680]	0.331 [0.847]	0.029	3.010
Δor	9.111 [**0.011**]	0.686 [0.710]	0.164	3.016
$\Delta b10$	3.692 [0.158]	0.925 [0.630]	0.211	3.009
Δcf	1.584 [0.453]	9.735 [**0.008**]	0.278	4.385

in the first three lags of the system and individually for real income and the overnight rate. However, Rahbek et al. (2002, p. 83) show that cointegration tests are robust against moderate residual ARCH effects.

6.7.1.3 Rank Determination

As outlined in Sect. 6.2.1.3 the following formal and informal test procedures are applied to determine the reduced rank of the system (Juselius 2006, p. 142):

- Trace test (formal LR test).
- Modulus of the roots of the companion matrix.
- Significance of the α-coefficients.
- Graphical inspection of the recursively calculated trace test statistics.
- Graphical inspection of the stationarity of the cointegration relations.

Table 6.101 South Korea quarterly data: trace test of cointegration rank

$p-r$	r	λ_i	Q_r	Q_r^{Bart}	$C_r^{95\%}$	p-value	p-value*
7	0	0.617	321.328	289.857	183.085	0.000	0.000
6	1	0.508	224.287	204.632	146.033	0.000	0.000
5	2	0.440	152.574	138.378	112.653	0.000	0.000
4	3	0.353	94.083	86.367	83.095	0.006	0.028
3	4	0.246	50.129	45.799	57.492	**0.185**	**0.337**
2	5	0.147	21.650	19.190	35.774	0.604	0.751
1	6	0.054	5.608	4.992	17.751	0.827	0.876

Trace Test

Table 6.101 gives an overview of the trace test results.[123] It reports the estimated eigenvalues, λ_i, the trace test, Q_r, the small sample Bartlett corrected trace test (Johansen 2002, pp. 1932–1940), Q_r^{Bart}, and the 95% quintile from the asymptotic distribution corrected for deterministic components, $C_r^{95\%}$. In addition, the table reports the p-value of the test statistic and the p-value of the Bartlett small sample corrections, p-value*, respectively.
The trace test and the Bartlett small sample trace test accept the null of $p - r = 3$ unit roots and, therefore, $r = 4$. These test results are a first indication for rank $r = 4$. However, it is important to include the other information criteria mentioned above.

[123] Equation (5.6) in Sect. 5.1.2 shows that, as a prerequisite for valid statistical inference, the variables can be integrated of first but not of higher order. Hence, it is important to ensure that no $I(2)$ variables are part of the data set. As outlined in Sect. 6.2.1.3 different criteria exist to analyze if $I(2)$-ness persists. Applying these criteria to the analysis of South Korea shows that no $I(2)$-trends exist in the data. Because univariate unit root tests are used in most analyses, they are conducted as well, in spite of their many limitations in the multivariate setting. The ADF test and the PP test fail to reject the null hypothesis of the existence of a unit root at the 5% level for all variables in levels aside from the time series representing capital flows. The PP test is also rejected for inflation. In contrast, both tests reject the null hypothesis for the variables in first-differenced form of the series. Consequently, the variables are at most integrated of order one. The appropriate lags for the ADF test are selected based on the Schwartz Criterion and the Akaike Information Criterion. The truncation point for the Newey–West adjustment, required for calculating the PP statistic, is determined by using the smallest integer greater than or equal to the sample size, T, to the power of $\frac{1}{4}$ (Greene 2003, p. 267). The test results are not reported here because of the questionable usefulness of univariate tests in a multivariate setting. Rao (2007, p. 1624) points out that these tests lack power and combinations of the many options of the tests almost always enable one to prove that the variables are I(1) in levels. Additionally, Muscatelli and Spinelli (2000, p. 724) refer to difficulties in using unit root tests as pre-tests if regime shifts are inherent to the model. For these and other reasons, Juselius (2006, p. 136) does not even discuss univariate unit root testing in her textbook on cointegration analysis. Instead, the stationarity of a variable is easily tested inside the multivariate model as a restriction on β (see Table 6.106 in Sect. 6.7.2.2). The advantage of the multivariate analysis is to define a well-specified model first and then test for stationarity. With univariate unit root tests, stationarity is tested before guaranteeing i.i.d. error terms, constant parameters and the absence of ARCH effects and before determining cointegration rank. The results of the ADF and PP tests are available on request.

Table 6.102 South Korea quarterly data: modulus of the seven largest eigenvalue roots

$r = 7$	$r = 6$	$r = 5$	$r = 4$	$r = 3$	$r = 2$	$r = 1$	$r = 0$
0.885	1	1	1	1	1	1	1
0.885	**0.863**	1	1	1	1	1	1
0.879	0.835	**0.789**	1	1	1	1	1
0.624	0.613	0.623	**0.687**	1	1	1	1
0.624	0.613	0.623	0.687	**0.652**	1	1	1
0.492	0.494	0.623	0.670	0.652	**0.583**	1	1
0.492	0.494	0.500	0.343	0.433	0.583	**0.579**	1

Roots of the Companion Matrix

The analysis of the modulus of the roots of the companion form matrix, as depicted in Table 6.102, shows that for $r = 4$ the modulus of the largest unrestricted root drops to 0.687 and, as such, far away from a unit root. Thus, Table 6.102 also indicates rank $r = 4$ but also accepts $r = 5$ since the largest unrestricted root already drops to 0.789.

Significance of Adjustment Coefficients α

The t-values of the α-coefficients give an indication of the significance of the equilibrium adjustment behavior of the relative variables. They are derived from the unrestricted estimates and can be used to identify the cointegration rank. As can be seen from Table 6.103, adjustment behavior to the first five equations is stronger and involves several variables, whereas for the sixth relation only one variable and none for the seventh equation show significant t-values and the t-value is lower.[124] Therefore, the investigation of the adjustment coefficients' significance points to a rank of $r = 5$.

The Recursive Graphs of the Trace Statistic

Figure 6.17 shows the forward and backward recursively calculated graphs for the trace statistic. The plots are normalized to the 5% significance level, represented by the horizontal line.

If $\lambda_i \neq 0$, the recursively calculated components of the trace statistic should grow linearly for $i = 1, \ldots, r$, but stay constant for $i = r + 1, \ldots, p$ (Juselius 2006, p. 142). While five of the graphs cross or are above the 1-line only four are upward

[124] This is especially so since the t-values of a given relation are no longer Student's t distributed if the relation is non-stationary. Instead, it is better to compare the t-values to the Dickey–Fuller distribution, where the critical values are larger. As a rule of thumb, the t-values should be close to 3.0 for the relation to still qualify as adjusting.

Table 6.103 South Korea quarterly data: t-values of the α-coefficients

	α						
	Alpha(1)	Alpha(2)	Alpha(3)	Alpha(4)	Alpha(5)	Alpha(6)	Alpha(7)
Δm_r	**(−6.130)**	**(−2.465)**	(−1.969)	(−1.862)	(2.046)	(−2.008)	(−1.177)
Δs_r	(1.161)	(1.523)	**(−5.378)**	(0.822)	**(−3.240)**	(0.119)	(−1.253)
Δy_r	**(3.275)**	**(−3.729)**	(−1.433)	(0.315)	(−1.280)	**(−3.417)**	(0.548)
$\Delta^2 p$	**(7.094)**	**(5.283)**	(2.353)	**(−4.368)**	(0.129)	(−0.091)	(−0.196)
Δor	**(8.417)**	(−1.343)	(−0.648)	(2.224)	(2.450)	(1.113)	(−1.072)
$\Delta b10$	**(3.815)**	**(−6.686)**	(−0.365)	**(−2.833)**	(−0.852)	(2.121)	(0.560)
Δcf	(−0.557)	(−1.479)	**(3.452)**	(−0.237)	**(−3.888)**	(−0.720)	(−1.393)

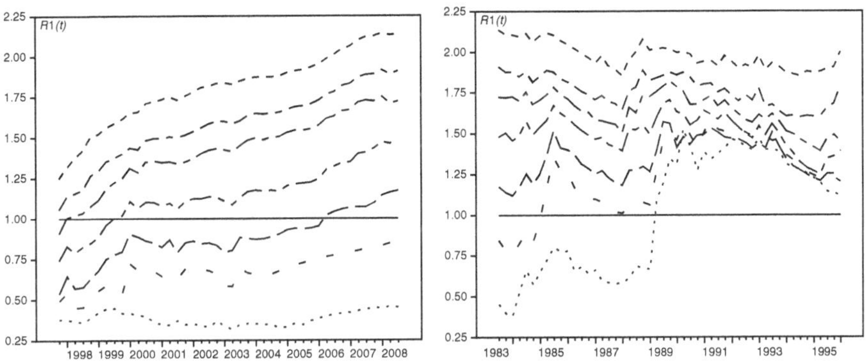

Fig. 6.17 South Korea quarterly data: recursively calculated trace test statistics (forward, base sample 1983:03 to 1997:04, depicted left; backward, base sample 2008:03 to 1996:01, depicted right)

trending for the backward recursive test. Hence, this indicates a rank of $r = 4$. However, the graph of the fifth cointegration relation is borderline acceptable because it shows linear growth for the forward recursive test. Based on this criteria, a rank of $r = 5$ would be borderline acceptable as well.

Graphical Analysis of the Cointegration Relations

Finally, Appendix B.6.2 depicts the graphs of the cointegrating relations of the unrestricted model. The graphs of the sixth and seventh relation show persistent behavior and do not suggest mean-reversion behavior, whereas the first four graphs look clearly stationary. The fifth graph is a borderline case. However, it shows persistence and does not cross the 0-line as frequently as the graphs of the first four relations. As a result, this indicator points to a rank of $r = 4$.

In sum, the various information criteria used to determine the rank of the model all point to or allow for a rank of $r = 4$ and this is chosen for the subsequent analysis of the long-run equilibria. That also means that $p - r = 3$ common trends exist, which is also valid from an economic point of view since it is reasonable for a real,

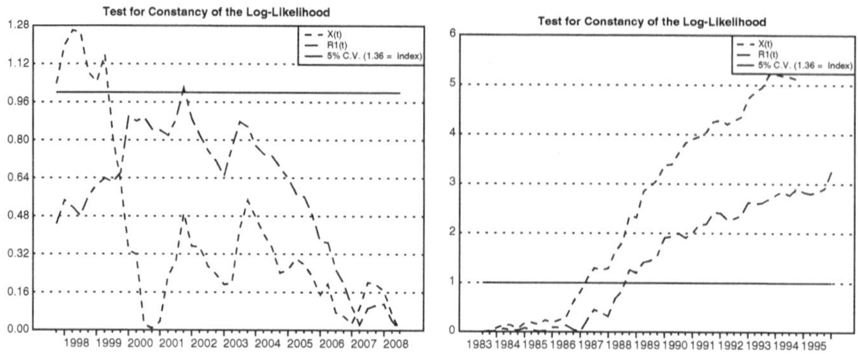

Fig. 6.18 South Korea quarterly data: recursively calculated test of log-likelihood (forward, base sample 1983:03 to 1997:04, depicted left; backward, base sample 2008:03 to 1996:01, depicted right)

monetary and financial trend to exist. In addition, recursive tests show that the data describes a constant parameter regime. Figure 6.18 depicts the recursively calculated log-likelihood. The forward recursive test shows that the graph with short-run effects concentrated out, (R1(t)), stays under the line. The line represents the 5% critical value. The backward test, however, takes a long time to drop under the line. To further investigate this, Appendix B.6.3 provides additional information on parameter constancy, such as the eigenvalues λ_i, the eigenvalue fluctuation test, the max test of β constancy and the test of β_t equals a known β. They all confirm a constant parameter regime. As a result, the assumption of constant parameters, which is important for valid identification of the long-run structure, is fulfilled and constancy of the overall model is accepted.

6.7.2 *Identification of the Long-Run Structure*

6.7.2.1 Assessment of the Unrestricted Π-Matrix

The unrestricted Π-matrix for the chosen rank $r = 4$ is depicted in Table 6.104. The fact that the signs of the coefficients on the diagonal are negative and statistically significant for all variables shows that they exhibit error-correction behavior.
The first row shows that money is positively related to inflation and capital flows and negatively to the interest rate spread. The stock market equation already indicates the importance of monetary developments for the South Korean stock market. It is positively related to money stock and capital flows and negatively to the short term interest rate. The negative relation with real output is surprising and differs from the findings of the other country analyses.

The equation for real output shows an aggregate demand relation that is positively related to real money and negatively to the long-term interest rate. The latter

Table 6.104 South Korea quarterly data: the unrestricted Π-matrix for a rank of 4 (t-values in brackets)

	Π								
	m_r	s_r	y_r	Δp	or	$b10$	cf	D_s9704	*Trend*
Δm_r	**−0.092**	0.001	−0.076	**0.784**	**1.677**	**−1.166**	**0.753**	**−0.003**	**0.005**
	[−4.110]	[0.122]	[−1.890]	[2.158]	[3.935]	[−2.340]	[3.652]	[−4.668]	[5.088]
Δs_r	**0.753**	**−0.245**	**−1.592**	1.986	**−8.522**	7.664	**8.581**	0.004	0.015
	[3.308]	[−4.587]	[−3.913]	[0.540]	[−1.976]	[1.520]	[4.111]	[0.607]	[1.565]
Δy_r	**0.053**	0.007	**−0.109**	0.289	0.005	**−1.316**	−0.128	−0.000	0.000
	[2.794]	[1.571]	[−3.217]	[0.942]	[0.014]	[−3.125]	[−0.737]	[−0.209]	[0.165]
$\Delta^2 p$	**0.061**	0.000	**0.072**	**−1.358**	0.019	0.319	**−0.179**	**0.002**	**−0.004**
	[6.454]	[0.170]	[4.239]	[−8.882]	[0.108]	[1.521]	[−2.062]	[10.050]	[−9.667]
Δor	**0.029**	0.001	**−0.018**	−0.041	**−0.317**	−0.077	**−0.127**	**0.000**	**−0.001**
	[6.683]	[0.631]	[−2.309]	[−0.569]	[−3.785]	[−0.792]	[−3.144]	[3.646]	[−3.696]
$\Delta b10$	**0.009**	**0.003**	**−0.018**	−0.025	**0.196**	**−0.453**	−0.040	0.000	−0.000
	[3.108]	[5.149]	[−3.533]	[−0.544]	[3.707]	[−7.328]	[−1.579]	[0.042]	[−0.719]
Δcf	**−0.030**	**0.011**	**0.058**	0.005	0.317	−0.405	**−0.385**	−0.000	−0.001
	[−2.029]	[3.118]	[2.182]	[0.019]	[1.120]	[−1.224]	[−2.815]	[−0.650]	[−0.807]

confirms findings from the other country analyses that long-term rates are more important than short-term rates for investment decisions.

Inflation is driven by developments of real money and real output and is negatively related to international capital flows. The overnight rate is positively related to real money and negatively to output and capital flows. At first sight, this seems unusual because one would expect policy makers to increase interest rates with increasing output. It seems as if output behaves peculiarly in the South Korean analysis.

The bond rate reacts positively to real money (expected inflation effect), the overnight rate (term structure of interest rates) and the stock market. In addition, it is negatively related to real output. The last variable, capital flows, is positively driven by stock market and economic activity developments and negatively related to increases in money. The positive relations show that foreign money is attracted by booming stock markets and industrial developments. The negative relation with money may be a result of abundant money already in place and, thus, less incentive to borrow from abroad.

Table B.23 in Appendix B.6.4 shows the α- and β'-matrices of the partitioned unrestricted Π-matrix. The α-coefficients can indicate which variables are strongly adjusting to long-run equilibria and which variables are more on the pushing side. The estimated α-matrix shows that all variables significantly adjust towards at least one cointegration relation.

The following section outlines preliminary tests for purposes of assessment structure and providing additional information.

6.7.2.2 Preliminary Hypotheses Testing

This section is divided into preliminary tests for β' and α. Automated tests on β' include the potential to exclude variables from the long-run relations and stationarity of individual variables. The α-matrix is formally analyzed for weak exogeneity and

Table 6.105 South Korea quarterly data: test of variable exclusion (p-values in brackets)

Test of exclusion											
r	DGF	5% C.V.	m_r	s_r	y_r	Δp	or	$b10$	cf	D_s9704	*Trend*
4	4	9.488	24.291 [0.000]	24.404 [0.000]	25.941 [0.000]	30.668 [0.000]	23.148 [0.000]	28.459 [0.000]	32.640 [0.000]	18.674 [0.001]	21.855 [0.000]

Table 6.106 South Korea quarterly data: test of variable stationarity (p-values in brackets)

Test of stationarity									
r	DGF	5% C.V.	m_r	s_r	y_r	Δp	or	$b10$	cf
4	5	11.070	35.255 [0.000]	29.160 [0.000]	33.727 [0.000]	22.484 [0.000]	32.145 [0.000]	44.459 [0.000]	33.897 [0.000]
Restricted trend included in the cointegrating relation(s)									
4	4	9.488	33.238 [0.000]	28.037 [0.000]	33.584 [0.000]	22.267 [0.000]	22.799 [0.000]	31.852 [0.000]	28.439 [0.000]
Restricted trend and shift-dummy included in the cointegrating relations									
4	3	7.815	29.819 [0.000]	23.864 [0.000]	22.597 [0.000]	22.170 [0.000]	22.656 [0.000]	30.484 [0.000]	17.851 [0.000]

unit vectors. Afterwards, single cointegration tests are conducted. This is to test for potential long-run equilibria as outlined in the section on long-run economic relations (5.2).[125] This will help facilitate the final identification of the long-run structure and provides additional insight on information contained in the data set.

Table 6.105 provides LR tests for the exclusion of any variable from the cointegration relations. If the test is accepted, a zero restriction can be imposed on the coefficient of the variable in all cointegration relations. The test is rejected for all variables. This also confirms the inclusion of the shift dummy to account for changing expectations and risk perceptions after the Asian financial crisis.

Table 6.106 reports the tests for long-run stationarity. None of the variables are accepted as stationary even after allowing for a trend and the shift dummy.

Tables 6.107 and 6.108 test restrictions on α. The test of weak exogeneity is equivalent to testing a zero row in the α-matrix. This means that a variable is not error correcting but can be considered weakly exogenous for the long-run parameters β'. If the test is accepted, this also means that the sum of the cumulated empirical shocks to the variable in question defines one common driving trend. Table 6.107 shows that weak exogeneity is accepted for capital flows, albeit with a low p-value. This is nevertheless an interesting finding when compared to the country analyses of the developed countries. There, capital flows are either stationary or shocks to capital flows have only transitory shocks. This shows that for South Korea, capital flows are mostly determined outside of the country. This also alludes to the danger of sudden capital reversals.

[125] All test statistics on α and β are asymptotically distributed as χ^2 because the asymptotic distribution is mixed Gaussian (Johansen 1995, pp. 177–178). As a result, the usual statistical inference can be applied (Johansen and Juselius 1994, p. 16).

Table 6.107 South Korea quarterly data: test of weak exogeneity (p-values in brackets)

Test of weak exogeneity									
r	DGF	5% C.V.	m_r	s_r	y_r	Δp	or	$b10$	cf
4	4	9.488	31.207 [0.000]	16.728 [0.002]	17.620 [0.001]	42.786 [0.000]	42.665 [0.000]	36.924 [0.000]	**7.854** [0.097]

Table 6.108 South Korea quarterly data: test for a unit vector in the α-matrix (p-values in brackets)

Test of unit vector in alpha									
r	DGF	5% C.V.	m_r	s_r	y_r	Δp	or	$b10$	cf
4	3.000	7.815	16.855 [0.001]	8.895 [0.031]	28.394 [0.000]	**1.574** [0.665]	17.453 [0.001]	8.077 [0.044]	18.994 [0.000]

The test of a unit vector in α tests for the opposite, namely if a variable is exclusively adjusting. If the unit vector test is accepted, the properties of the relevant variable are that its shocks have no permanent effect on any of the other variables in the system and it can be regarded as endogenous. The transitory shocks do not cumulate into trends, instead, they die out over time. Consequently, together the two tests of α can identify the pulling and pushing forces of the system. Table 6.108 shows that shocks to inflation only have transitory effects.

In addition to the above tests on single variables, the focus of the remaining preliminary tests is on single cointegration relations. The idea is to analyze if stable relationships between the economic variables can be identified by linear relations. Testing follows the theoretical connections outlined in Chap. 3 and Sect. 5.2, summarized in Table 5.1. The hypotheses are of the form:

$$\beta = (H\phi, \psi_1, \psi_2, \psi_3), \tag{6.54}$$

where H is the design matrix, ϕ contains the restricted parameters and ψ_i is a vector of parameters which are freely estimated. It is important to note that each hypothesis in Table 6.109 tests restrictions on a single vector but leaves the other cointegration vectors unrestricted (Johansen and Juselius 1992, pp. 233–236). Table 6.109 provides an overview of the single cointegration test results. It is structured the same as Table 5.2.[126]

[126] Since the rank is set to $r = 4$, a minimum of 4 restrictions has to be set to formally test for cointegration. The reason for this is the $\chi^2(v)$-distribution of the single cointegration test with v being the number of degrees of freedom. The degrees of freedom are derived from the decrease in the number of free parameters. They are calculated as $v = no.of restr. - rank + 1$. As a result, the number of restrictions has to be a minimum of four to obtain one degree of freedom and, thus, have testable results. Put in a different way, one can always impose $r - 1$ restrictions without changing the value of the likelihood function. Then the system is just identified. However, only over-identified systems can be formally tested (Juselius 2006, p. 215). Hence, more than $r - 1$ restrictions must be imposed. Therefore, only those theoretical relations of Table 5.2, which restrict at least four of the parameters (all but H_{11} do) can be formally tested.

Table 6.109 South Korea quarterly data: testing the stationarity of single relations

	m_r	s_r	y_r	Δp	or	$b10$	cf	D_s9001	*Trend*	$\chi^2(v)$	p-value	*sign.* α
						Demand for stocks						
H_1	−3.346	1	0	0	0	0	0	−0.074	0.103	15.8 (2)	0.000	
H_2	0	1	0	−249.9	249.9	0	0	0.047	−0.047	9.2 (2)	0.010	
H_3	0	0.000	0	−1	0	1	0	0.000	0.000	14.7 (2)	0.001	
H_4	0	1	0	0	−74.63	0	0	0.004	−0.015	15.3 (2)	0.000	
H_5	0	1	0	0	0	−57.36	0	0.013	−0.032	16.6 (2)	0.000	
H_6	0	1	−1.552	0	0	0	0	0.013	0.009	22.4 (2)	0.000	
H_7	0	1	0	0	0	0	−66.5	−0.044	−0.019	19.0 (2)	0.000	
H_8	−1.787	1	0	0	0	0	−37.61	−0.067	0.046	18.3 (1)	0.000	
						Money demand						
H_9	1	0	−1	0	0	0	0	0.034	−0.012	33.1 (3)	0.000	
H_{10}	1	0	0	0	531.6	−531.6	0	0.068	−0.165	9.1 (2)	0.011	
H_{11}	1	0	−1.374	0	−4.501	−9.267	0	0.008	−0.007		no test	
H_{12}	**1**	**0**	**0.069**	**−15.85**	**0**	**0**	**0**	**0.028**	**−0.039**	**0.27 (1)**	**0.604**	$m_r, \Delta p$
H_{13}	1	−0.299	0	0	0	0	0	0.022	−0.031	15.8 (2)	0.000	
H_{14}	**1**	**−0.295**	**0**	**0**	**−31.26**	**31.26**	**0**	**0.022**	**−0.024**	**2.1 (1)**	**0.143**	$m_r, s_r, b10$
H_{15}	1	−0.278	−1	0	0	0	0	0.009	−0.008	15.8 (2)	0.000	
H_{16}	**1**	**−0.292**	**−1**	**0**	**−42.09**	**42.09**	**0**	**0.008**	**0.002**	**2.2 (1)**	**0.136**	$m_r, b10$

(continued)

Table 6.109 (Continued)

	m_r	s_r	y_r	Δp	or	$b10$	cf	D_s9001	*Trend*	$\chi^2(v)$	p-value	*sign.* α
						Policy rules						
H_{17}	0	0	0	−1.115	1	0	0	0.000	0	10.9 (3)	0.012	
H_{18}	0	0	−0.106	0	1	0	0	−0.001	0.002	21.0 (2)	0.000	
H_{19}	0	−0.013	0	0	1	0	0	0	0	15.3 (2)	0.000	
						Demand for goods						
H_{20}	**0**	**0**	**1**	**−9.771**	**9.771**	**0**	**0**	**0.014**	**−0.02**	**1.2 (2)**	**0.553**	$\Delta p, or$
H_{21}	**0**	**0**	**1**	**−10.93**	**0**	**10.93**	**0**	**0.014**	**−0.021**	**2.4 (2)**	**0.298**	$m_r, y_r, \Delta p, b10$
H_{22}	−0.028	0	1	0	0	0	0	0.014	−0.021	22.5 (2)	0.000	
H_{23}	−2.612	0.719	1	0	0	0	0	−0.046	0.059	15.2 (1)	0.000	
						Inflation and interest rates						
H_{24}	−0.003	0	0.003	1	0	0	0	0	0	22.0 (3)	0.000	
H_{25}	−0.06	0	0	0	0	1	0	−0.002	0.002	23.8 (2)	0.000	
H_{26}	0	0	0	−1	1	0	0	0.000	0	11.1 (4)	0.026	
H_{27}	0	0	0	−1	0	1	0	0.000	0	17.3 (4)	0.002	
H_{28}	0	0	0	−1.115	1	0	0	0.000	0	10.9 (3)	0.012	
H_{29}	0	0	0	−1.562	0	1	0	0	0	16.0 (3)	0.001	
H_{30}	0	0	0	0	−1	1	0	0	0	26.5 (4)	0.000	
H_{31}	0	0	0	0	−2.242	1	0	0	0	23.4 (3)	0.000	
H_{32}	0	0	0	−1.156	1	0.156	0	0	0	10.9 (3)	0.012	
H_{33}	0	0	0	1.951	−1	1	0	0	0	21.0 (3)	0.000	

Hypotheses H_1 to H_8 test for cointegration between stocks and the other variables. None of the outlined relations is accepted. Hence, a stock market relation does not exist in the form stated by hypotheses H_1 to H_8.

H_9 to H_{16} test monetary relations. The test for a stationary liquidity relation (H_7) is rejected. If amended with the stock market and the yield spread (H_{16}) the liquidity relation becomes stationary. In addition, real money shows significant adjustment behavior towards this relation. Thus, H_{16} represents a classical money demand relation where demand increases with expanding economic activity (transaction effect), with rising stock prices (wealth effect) and decreases with a higher yield spread (opportunity cost of holding money). In addition, hypotheses H_{12} and H_{14} are also accepted, showing a positive reaction of money to higher inflation.

'Policy rules' (H_{17} to H_{19}) are harder to test for since the monetary policy target is unknown. Hence, deviations from the target inflation rate, the target output level or the target stock market level are uncertain and cannot be measured directly. One possibility is to test for monetary policy reactions to changes in the inflation rate (independent of a target level) and to deviations of real output and real stock market levels from their trend. As can be seen in Table 6.109 all three tests are rejected.

Hypotheses H_{20} to H_{23} focus on potential stationary aggregate demand for goods relations. H_{20} and H_{21} show that output reacts negatively to deviations in the real short-term rate and the real long-term rate. This indicates an IS-type relation in the long-run structure.

Under the headline 'Inflation and interest rates' cointegration between inflation and the nominal interest rates ('Fisher parity') as well as between the interest rates themselves ('expectations hypothesis') is tested. None of these hypotheses are accepted.

In sum, the preliminary tests suggest that an over-identified long-run structure should include a money demand and an aggregate demand for goods relation. In addition, the analysis of the unrestricted Π-matrix showed a relationship of the stock market with money, capital flows and output and a positive relation between real money and inflation.

6.7.2.3 Identification of the Long-Run Cointegrating Relations

The restrictions on the identified long-run structure are accepted with a p-value of 0.62 ($\chi^2(7) = 5.314$). This shows that the imposed restrictions describe the data well. The structure is formally and empirically identified because all β-coefficients are strongly significant (Juselius and MacDonald 2004, p. 18). Appendix B.6.5 shows that the rank conditions are accepted for the full cointegration space. This means that the four cointegration relations are linearly independent and, as such, can not be replaced by each other.

Table 6.110 South Korea quarterly data: the identified long-run structure (t-values in brackets)

β'									
	m_r	s_r	y_r	Δp	or	$b10$	cf	D_s9704	*Trend*
Beta(1)	**−3.068** [−5.377]	**1.000** [*NA*]	**8.607** [7.123]	0.000 [*NA*]	0.000 [*NA*]	0.000 [*NA*]	**−47.87** [−11.58]	0.000 [*NA*]	**−0.103** [−9.754]
Beta(2)	**1.000** [*NA*]	**−0.278** [−8.989]	**−1.000** [*NA*]	0.000 [*NA*]	**−35.66** [−10.98]	**35.66** [10.98]	0.000 [*NA*]	**0.009** [4.660]	0.000 [*NA*]
Beta(3)	**−0.068** [−11.15]	0.000 [*NA*]	0.000 [*NA*]	**1.000** [*NA*]	0.000 [*NA*]	0.000 [*NA*]	0.000 [*NA*]	**−0.002** [−10.46]	**0.003** [10.72]
Beta(4)	0.000 [*NA*]	0.000 [*NA*]	**1.000** [*NA*]	**−10.59** [−13.64]	0.000 [*NA*]	**10.59** [13.64]	0.000 [*NA*]	**0.013** [17.25]	**−0.021** [−47.06]

α				
	Alpha(1)	Alpha(2)	Alpha(3)	Alpha(4)
Δm_r	**−0.016** [−3.736]	**−0.046** [−3.678]	**1.263** [3.359]	0.053 [1.502]
Δs_r	**−0.169** [−3.940]	**0.262** [2.127]	0.657 [0.178]	−0.299 [−0.859]
Δy_r	0.003 [0.857]	0.003 [0.302]	**−1.067** [−3.380]	**−0.128** [−4.309]
$\Delta^2 p$	0.003 [1.749]	0.001 [0.274]	**−0.896** [−5.681]	**0.039** [2.654]
Δor	**0.003** [3.353]	**0.008** [3.207]	**−0.452** [−6.116]	**−0.036** [−5.192]
$\Delta b10$	0.001 [1.558]	**−0.006** [−4.314]	**−0.313** [−6.941]	**−0.027** [−6.353]
Δcf	**0.008** [2.698]	−0.006 [−0.737]	−0.078 [−0.314]	−0.024 [−1.027]

The graphs of the cointegrating relations are displayed in Appendix B.6.6, with the deterministic terms and short-term parameters concentrated out.[127] In addition, graphical overviews of forward and backward recursive tests of parameter constancy in Appendix B.6.7 show that parameter constancy for α_i and β_i ($i = 1, \ldots, 4$) is mainly given. However, the backward recursive tests show unexplained strong fluctuations in the first years of the 1990s. Parameter constancy is stronger for the second part of the sample. The structural representation of the cointegration space is depicted in Table 6.110 with the estimated eigenvectors β and the weights α. The first β'-vector describes a relationship between the stock market, internal and external liquidity and real output:

$$s_{r,t} - 3.068m_{r,t} + 8.607y_{r,t} - 47.87cf_t - 0.103trend \sim I(0), \tag{6.55}$$

where stock prices increase with real money and capital inflows but decrease with increased economic activity.[128] The last part seems unusual since economic

[127] This removes the seasonal fluctuations and outliers, which can be observed in the raw series and, thus, provides a clearer picture (Brüggemann and Lütkepohl 2006, p. 692). See also Sect. 6.7.1.3.

[128] The high β-coefficient of the capital flows variable can be rationalized by the extreme difference of the standard deviations of the two series. The residual standard error of the stock market is 16 times higher than that of capital flows. In general, the size of the coefficients has to be interpreted with caution. They usually can not be interpreted as elasticities, since a shock to one variable

performance is expected to be positive for stock market developments. However, as the preliminary tests on single relations showed, the above relation is not stationary if output is excluded (see H_8). Nevertheless, this relation shows the importance of liquidity conditions for the stock market. Contrary to the previous country analyses, which focused on developed economies, international capital flows play a key role for South Korea. This reflects the lack of depth in financial markets in developing countries; thus, international developments and investments matter more.[129] The α-coefficient of the stock market suggests that the adjustment process is rather slow and it might take up to six quarters to restore equilibrium.

The α-coefficients also show that, in addition to the stock market variable, capital flows are significantly adjusting to this relation. Hence, one could also interpret this relation as a capital flows relation where capital flows are attracted by rising stock prices and increased economic activity but decrease when abundant liquidity is already available inside the country. The equilibrium errors of this relation also push the overnight rate positively. Real money pushes this long-run steady state out of equilibrium.

The second long-run relation describes a money demand relation:

$$m_{r,t} - y_{r,t} - 0.278 s_{r,t} + 35.66(b10_t - or_t) + 0.009 D_s \sim I(0), \qquad (6.56)$$

where money demand increases with expanding economic activity (y_r) and wealth (s_r) and decreases with higher opportunity costs of holding money ($b10 - or$). Real money, the stock market and both interest rates react significantly to this relation. This shows, that in addition to real money and capital flows, excess liquidity also has a positive impact on the stock market.

The third cointegrating relation describes a relationship between real money and inflation:

$$\Delta p_t - 0.068 m_{r,t} - 0.002 D_s + 0.003\ trend \sim I(0). \qquad (6.57)$$

Both, inflation and money react to this relation, albeit inflation with higher significance. Thus, money and inflation feed into each other. In addition, both interest rates and output dynamically adjust in response to deviations from this equilibrium.

The last long-run equilibrium exists between real output and the long-term real interest rate:

$$y_{r,t} + 10.59(b10_t - \Delta p_t) + 0.013 D_s - 0.021\ trend \sim I(0), \qquad (6.58)$$

where aggregate demand for goods increases with lower long-term real interest rates. Hence, this relationship represents a classical IS-type relation. The α-coefficients show that output, inflation and both interest rates react to this relation.

implies a shock to all variables in the long run. Thus, a ceteris paribus interpretation is generally invalid (Johansen 2009, pp. 8–9; Johansen 2005, pp. 97–100; Lütkepohl 1994, p. 393).

[129] Noland (2005, p. 2) points out that the liberalization process of capital controls exacerbated the influence of international capital flows because it created incentives for short-term bank borrowing.

The positive reaction of the inflation rate can be interpreted in the framework of the short-run Phillips curve, where inflation increases with excess aggregate demand for goods (Juselius 2001, p. 344). Together with the third cointegration relation this shows that the overnight rate reacts to real output and inflation.

6.7.3 *Short-Run Dynamics*

While the previous section focused on stable long-run economic relations, this section applies a structural error-correction model and formulates stationary equations for each of the variables in the system. Hence, the analysis focuses on the dynamic short-run adjustment of each variable to the past and the other simultaneous variables in the system (Johansen 1995, p. 79). First, the long-run equilibria (the cointegration relations) are uniquely identified in the reduced form error-correction model and are fixed according to the prior analysis (with no restrictions on the short-run parameters). As a result, the variables in differences and the residuals of the equilibrium errors (the regressors in the short-run analysis) are stationary and the usual regression analysis can be applied.

The starting point is estimating the multivariate dynamic equilibrium-correction model for the whole system. Identification of the p short-run equations requires at least $p-1$ just-identifying restrictions on each equation (Juselius 2006, p. 208). This is achieved by restricting current effects between the variables to zero. In addition, insignificant coefficients are removed from each single equation based on an LR test, which results in overidentified equations for each variable. The result is the parsimonious model shown in Table 6.111. The dependent variables can be found in the top row as the column headings of each of the model equations. The row headings, on the other hand, indicate the conditioning variables.

The 55 zero restrictions of insignificant coefficients are accepted based on an LR test of over-identifying restrictions $\chi^2(55) = 57.558$ with a p-value of 0.38. The analysis of the short-run dynamics shows that real money reacts positively to lagged values of real output. Real money reacts negatively to lagged values of the short-term interest rate and capital flows. This is surprising since higher short-term interest rates usually increase money demand. In the short run, real money is pushed by deviations from the first cointegration relation and shows equilibrium-correction behavior towards the second and third cointegration relation.

The stock market reacts positively to lagged values of real money and reacts towards the equilibrium of the first cointegration relation, which is the stock market relation. This shows that stock prices are affected by liquidity conditions in the long run and in the short run.

In addition, Table 6.111 shows that real output is positively affected by lagged values of itself and the stock market and reacts negatively to the short-term interest rate. Additionally, real output is pushed by deviations of the first cointegration relation, which is the stock market relation. This is another sign for the importance of the stock market for economic developments. The third ecm (inflation-real money

Table 6.111 South Korea quarterly data: short-run dynamics (t-values in brackets)

	Δm_r	Δs_r	Δy_r	$\Delta^2 p$	Δor	$\Delta b10$	Δcf
$\Delta m_{r,t}$	**1**	0	0	0	0	0	0
$\Delta s_{r,t}$	0	**1**	0	0	0	0	0
$\Delta y_{r,t}$	0	0	**1**	0	0	0	0
$\Delta^2 p_t$	0	0	0	**1**	0	0	0
Δor_t	0	0	0	0	**1**	0	0
$\Delta b10_t$	0	0	0	0	0	**1**	0
Δcf_t	0	0	0	0	0	0	**1**
$\Delta m_{r,t-1}$		**3.013**				**−0.033**	
		[4.04]				[−3.25]	
$\Delta s_{r,t-1}$			**0.031**				
			[3.79]				
$\Delta y_{r,t-1}$	**0.210**		**0.199**				
	[2.13]		[2.25]				
$\Delta^2 p_{t-1}$					**0.147**		**−0.285**
					[3.27]		[−2.20]
Δor_{t-1}	**−1.427**		**−1.057**	**0.340**			
	[−4.73]		[−3.97]	[2.93]			
$\Delta b10_{t-1}$							
Δcf_{t-1}	**−0.333**				**0.099**		**−0.259**
	[−2.06]				[2.97]		[−2.91]
$ecm1_{t-1}$	**−0.010**	**−0.040**	**0.012**		**0.005**	**0.001**	**0.003**
	[−3.48]	[−2.91]	[5.30]		[7.76]	[2.32]	[3.17]
$ecm2_{t-1}$	**−0.063**				**0.007**	**−0.001**	
	[−7.30]				[4.43]	[−6.50]	
$ecm3_{t-1}$	**0.420**		**−0.810**	**−0.608**	**−0.372**	**−0.283**	
	[1.95]		[−3.14]	[−8.37]	[−6.09]	[−7.99]	
$ecm4_{t-1}$			**−0.081**	**0.050**	**−0.023**	**−0.021**	**−0.048**
			[−3.22]	[7.34]	[−3.61]	[−6.24]	[−2.91]
$dum9404_{t,t}$					**0.008**		
					[4.32]		
$dum9704_{p,t}$		**−0.432**		**0.025**	**0.033**	**0.012**	
		[−2.94]		[4.31]	[11.3]	[6.31]	
$dum0201_{p,t}$	**0.049**	**0.331**	**0.044**				
	[3.55]	[2.33]	[3.26]				

relation) has a negative effect on output. Last, the short-run analysis confirms the error-correction behavior towards the long-run real interest rate, which represents the fourth cointegration relation.

Inflation reacts positively to the short rate. In addition, inflation shows error-correction behavior towards the third and fourth cointegration relation. This is a first indication of adverse effects of the policy rate on inflation dynamics. It is further confirmed by the long-run impact of the policy rate (see Sect. 6.7.4).

The short-term interest rate increases with lagged values of inflation and capital flows. In addition, both interest rates react to all cointegration relations. The overnight rate error corrects to the money demand relation and is pushed by the first ecm. Residuals of the third and fourth cointegration relation have a negative effect on the policy rate.

The bond rate, too, is mostly influenced by the ecms. It error corrects to the money demand and aggregate demand for goods relation and is pushed by the first ecm. Residuals of the third cointegration relation have a negative effect on the bond rate.

Capital flows react negatively to inflation and itself. In addition, it confirms the error-correction behavior towards the first cointegration relation of the long-run analysis. Residuals of the fourth cointegration relation (aggregate demand for goods) have a negative effect on capital flows.

Table 6.111 shows that many of the autoregressive coefficients are insignificant and, thus, restricted to zero. The bulk of explanatory power in the short run is based on the inclusion of the ecms. The equilibrium-correcting coefficients are mostly highly significant, indicating the potential loss of information if the VAR model had only been estimated in first differences.

One downside of the above equations is that current effects are not modeled. Instead they are left in the residuals. However, simultaneous effects are potentially important. Whereas correlation between the residuals is not problematic for the long-run relations of the previous section, identification of the short-run structural equations requires uncorrelated residuals (Juselius 2006, p. 229). Table 6.112 shows the residual covariance matrix, in which large off-diagonal elements can be an indication of significant current effects between the system variables. The values between real money and inflation, real money and the bond rate, between the stock market and capital flows and between the overnight rate and capital flows are a bit too high.[130]

One way to reduce residual correlation is to introduce current effects between the variables into the short-run structure. Adding the current effects of real money to the inflation rate and the bond rate equation and current effects of capital flows to the stock market equation helps to reduce the correlation between the variables, even though they are insignificant (see Table 6.113). The positive, albeit borderline insignificant, current effects of capital flows on stock market developments confirms the importance of capital flows for the stock market analysis of South Korea. Unfortunately, the correlation between the overnight rate and capital flows could not be reduced further. Table 6.114 shows the slightly changed short-run structure after allowing for current effects. The implications remain the same.

[130] High residual correlation can be a result of aggregation of the data over time, inadequately modeled expectations or result from omitted variables (Juselius 2006, pp. 239–240).

Table 6.112 South Korea quarterly data: correlation of structural residuals (standard deviations on diagonal)

	Δm_r	Δs_r	Δy_r	$\Delta^2 p$	Δor	$\Delta b10$	Δcf
Δm_r	*0.014*						
Δs_r	0.04	*0.154*					
Δy_r	0.21	0.15	*0.013*				
$\Delta^2 p$	**−0.27**	−0.04	−0.18	*0.006*			
Δor	−0.08	0.19	−0.02	0.07	*0.003*		
$\Delta b10$	**−0.31**	−0.08	0.02	−0.01	0.18	*0.002*	
Δcf	0.03	**0.33**	0.03	0.13	**−0.28**	−0.06	*0.010*

Table 6.113 South Korea quarterly data: correlation of structural residuals after allowing for current effects (standard deviations on diagonal)

	Δm_r	Δs_r	Δy_r	$\Delta^2 p$	Δor	$\Delta b10$	Δcf
Δm_r	*0.014*						
Δs_r	0.03	*0.146*					
Δy_r	0.21	0.16	*0.013*				
$\Delta^2 p$	**−0.22**	−0.08	−0.17	*0.006*			
Δor	−0.08	0.29	−0.02	0.07	*0.003*		
$\Delta b10$	**−0.15**	−0.07	0.06	−0.08	0.18	*0.002*	
Δcf	0.04	**0.04**	0.04	0.13	**−0.28**	−0.07	*0.010*

6.7.4 The Long-Run Impact of the Common Trends

The C-matrix provides the key to understanding the long-run implications of the model. The Bank of Korea (BoK) can only influence the stock market if a shock to a monetary instrument has a significant impact on the stock market. Hence, when evaluating the effectiveness of monetary policy the long-run impact of shocks to the short-term interest rate and to the money supply on the stock market is of particular interest.

The residual $\epsilon_{i,t}$ is interpreted as an estimate of the unanticipated shock to variable x_i. The estimated long-run impact of these cumulated shocks is reported in Table 6.115 and is calculated from the estimates of the restricted VAR model as

$$C = \tilde{\beta}_{\perp}\alpha_{\perp}^{'}, \tag{6.59}$$

where $\tilde{\beta}_{\perp} = \beta_{\perp}(\alpha_{\perp}^{'}\beta_{\perp})^{-1}$ and $\alpha_{\perp}, \beta_{\perp}$ are the $(p \times p - r)$ orthogonal compliments of α and β (Johansen 1995, pp. 49–50). Since C has reduced rank, only $p - r = 3$ linear combinations of the $p = 7$ innovations, ϵ_t, have permanent effects.

The C-matrix can be read column or row-wise. The columns show the long-run impact of a shock to a variable on each of the variables in the system and the rows show which of the shocks have a long-run impact on the particular variable.
The C-matrix in Table 6.115 confirms the findings of the previous sections. Shocks to real money have a permanent long-term effect on real money (procyclicality of

Table 6.114 South Korea quarterly data: short-run dynamics allowing for current effects (t-values in brackets)

	Δm_r	Δs_r	Δy_r	$\Delta^2 p$	Δor	$\Delta b10$	Δcf
$\Delta m_{r,t}$	**1**	0	0	−0.02	0	−0.02	0
$\Delta s_{r,t}$	0	**1**	0	0	0	0	0
$\Delta y_{r,t}$	0	0	**1**	0	0	0	0
$\Delta^2 p_t$	0	0	0	**1**	0	0	0
Δor_t	0	0	0	0	**1**	0	0
$\Delta b10_t$	0	0	0	0	0	**1**	0
Δcf_t	0	4.4	0	0	0	0	**1**
$\Delta m_{r,t-1}$		**3.193**				**−0.030**	
		[4.21]				[−2.84]	
$\Delta s_{r,t-1}$			**0.030**				
			[3.76]				
$\Delta y_{r,t-1}$	**0.232**		**0.194**				
	[2.21]		[2.19]				
$\Delta^2 p_{t-1}$					**0.135**		**−0.252**
					[3.04]		[−1.83]
Δor_{t-1}	**−1.530**		**−1.065**	**0.333**			
	[−4.87]		[−3.98]	[2.83]			
$\Delta b10_{t-1}$							
Δcf_{t-1}	**−0.359**				**0.096**		**−0.306**
	[−2.10]				[2.86]		[−3.24]
$ecm1_{t-1}$	**−0.011**	**−0.049**	**0.012**		**0.005**	**0.001**	**0.003**
	[−3.56]	[−3.25]	[5.34]		[7.83]	[1.94]	[2.99]
$ecm2_{t-1}$	**−0.064**				**0.007**	**−0.007**	
	[−7.19]				[4.41]	[−5.79]	
$ecm3_{t-1}$	**0.447**		**−0.830**	**−0.581**	**−0.371**	**−0.275**	
	[1.94]		[−3.19]	[−6.05]	[−6.04]	[−7.66]	
$ecm4_{t-1}$			**−0.084**	**0.051**	**−0.024**	**−0.020**	**−0.048**
			[−3.29]	[6.63]	[−3.82]	[−6.07]	[−2.73]
$dum9404_{t,t}$					**0.008**		
					[4.27]		
$dum9704_{p,t}$		**−0.452**		**0.025**	**0.033**	**0.011**	
		[−3.04]		[4.28]	[11.2]	[6.21]	
$dum0201_{p,t}$	**0.051**	**0.359**	**0.043**				
	[3.44]	[2.51]	[3.21]				

money supply), the stock market (liquidity conditions hypothesis), inflation (quantity theory of money), the overnight rate and the bond rate (increased inflation expectations). The impact on the overnight rate, however, is contrary to the expected 'liquidity effect' (see Sect. 4.3).

Table 6.115 South Korea quarterly data: the long-run impact matrix (t-values in brackets)

	The long-run impact matrix, C						
	$\hat{\epsilon}_{m_r}$	$\hat{\epsilon}_{s_r}$	$\hat{\epsilon}_{y_r}$	$\hat{\epsilon}_{\Delta p}$	$\hat{\epsilon}_{or}$	$\hat{\epsilon}_{b10}$	$\hat{\epsilon}_{cf}$
m_r	**1.027** [4.976]	0.004 [0.251]	0.264 [1.209]	0.651 [1.416]	**3.361** [3.109]	−3.714 [−1.823]	**1.013** [2.237]
s_r	**3.582** [2.133]	**0.464** [3.681]	−2.742 [−1.543]	4.014 [1.072]	11.20 [1.272]	−6.265 [−0.378]	**13.63** [3.697]
y_r	0.165 [1.260]	0.005 [0.481]	**0.787** [5.686]	0.433 [1.485]	−0.902 [−1.315]	−2.067 [−1.600]	0.505 [1.758]
Δp	**0.070** [4.976]	0.000 [0.251]	0.018 [1.209]	0.045 [1.416]	**0.230** [3.109]	−0.254 [−1.823]	**0.069** [2.237]
or	**0.051** [3.012]	**−0.004** [−3.011]	**−0.050** [−2.774]	−0.022 [−0.571]	**0.347** [3.922]	−0.056 [−0.337]	−0.070 [−1.897]
$b10$	**0.055** [4.393]	−0.000 [−0.193]	**−0.056** [−4.276]	0.004 [0.131]	**0.315** [4.832]	−0.059 [−0.479]	0.022 [0.791]
cf	0.039 [0.949]	**0.010** [3.366]	0.067 [1.563]	0.120 [1.321]	−0.144 [−0.673]	−0.265 [−0.658]	**0.311** [3.473]

Shocks to the stock market have a positive effect on future market developments and capital flows and negative impact on the overnight rate, which is quite surprising.

Table 6.115 also shows the positive long-run impact of real output on itself and the negative impact on both interest rates, in line with the findings of the preliminary tests. Tests of a unit vector in alpha already pointed to only temporary effects of inflation (see Sect. 6.7.2.2). This is confirmed here since the effects of shocks to inflation are all insignificant. Shocks to the overnight rate affect real money, inflation and both interest rates positively. Lastly, shocks to capital flows affect real money, the stock market, inflation and itself positively. These findings confirm the importance of liquidity conditions for the stock market in Seoul.

6.7.5 Conclusion

The introduction stated that confidence and optimism are important factors for the development of stock prices. In addition, one objective of this contribution is to test whether or not abundant liquidity amplifies the upward and downward spirals of stock prices. Both hypotheses can be fully accepted for South Korea.

Table 6.116 shows the answers to the main hypotheses from the results of the econometric analysis. South Korea has made substantial economic progress over the last 25 years. It completed the transition from a developing country to a developed economy. This might be the main reason for the importance of international capital flows for stock market movements. Unlike financial markets in developed countries, the financial market in South Korea has less depth. This is especially true for the first part of the sample. As a result, international developments, as well as investments from abroad, play a more prominent role than for developed economies.

While the question of monetary conditions' importance can be clearly answered, the ability of the BoK to influence asset prices can not. A closer inspection of

Table 6.116 South Korea quarterly data: results of main hypotheses

	Hypotheses/Questions	Result
H_1	Korean stock market behavior shows strong persistence, i.e., shocks to the stock market have positive long-run effects on future developments	Yes
H_2	Long-run equilibria exist between stock prices and liquidity conditions	Yes
H_3	Liquidity conditions influence stock prices positively in the long run	Yes
H_4	Liquidity conditions influence stock prices positively in the short run	Yes
H_5	International capital flows have a positive long-run impact on the stock market behavior in South Korea	Yes
H_6	International capital flows have a positive short-run impact on the stock market behavior in South Korea	Yes
Q_1	Is the BoK is able to influence stock prices in the long run?	No
Q_2	Is the BoK able to influence stock prices in the short run?	No

the second cointegration relation reveals that the stock market reacts negatively to advances in the overnight rate. However, since the whole relation should be interpreted as a money demand relation, the strength of the relationship between the short-term interest rate and the stock market is questionable. In addition, preliminary tests of stationary relations show that cointegration does not exist between the overnight rate and the stock market without including additional variables. There is also no direct link between the overnight rate and the stock market in the short run. However, lagged values of the overnight rate have a negative effect on money holdings, which in turn also decreases stock prices in the short run. To conclude, the ability of the BoK to influence stock prices is very limited.

The above analysis also sheds light on a few other aspects of economic interest, mainly:

- A stable money demand relation could be identified where real output and stock market levels increase money demand whereas the interest rate spread has a negative relationship with real money. Real output also affects money holdings in the short run. While both, the overnight rate and capital flows have a negative short-run effect on money holdings, shocks to either variable have a positive permanent long-term effect on the money stock. This suggests that money stock developments are supply-driven in the short run and demand-driven in the long run. The positive effect of the stock market on money demand shows that, for South Korea, the wealth effect is stronger than the substitution effect.
- Real aggregate demand for goods has a negative relationship with the long-term real interest rate, as expected from theoretical considerations. The analysis of the short run and of the long-run impact matrix shows that economic activity is mainly influenced by itself. In addition, the stock market has positive effects and the overnight rate negative effects on economic activity in the short run.
- The analysis shows that inflation is influenced by monetary developments. Inflation reacts positively to the amount of money and the cumulated shocks to real money have a positive long-run impact on inflation. In addition, the inflation rate reacts positively to deviations from the aggregate demand for goods relation, which can be interpreted in the framework of the short-run Phillips curve,

where inflation increases with excess aggregate demand for goods. Consequently, inflation is a monetary phenomenon in the long run and is influenced by real developments in the short run. The analysis also shows that the short-term interest rate and capital flows affect inflation positively. While the positive impact of capital flows can be explained with spillover effects of global inflation, the effect of the short-term interest rate is surprising and probably unwanted.

- The short-term interest rate reacts to all cointegration relations and shocks to all variables but inflation and the bond rate have an impact on the overnight rate. This indicates that the BoK focuses more on economic activity and the stock market than on inflation. In other words, Korean central bankers pay more attention to an overheating economy than to actual inflation. However, the BoK cites inflation as their prime monetary policy objective, followed by financial stability. The analysis shows, that the setting of the favored policy instrument, the short-term interest rate, has a positive effect on current inflation. Monetary policy had the opposite effect of what it was designed to do. One explanation might be derived from the difference between current and future inflation. However, since shocks to the overnight rate also have a positive long-run impact on real money and the bond rate, it is most likely, that future inflation is also positively affected by the overnight rate.
- The bond rate moves parallel to the inflation rate and reacts to lagged values of real money in the short run. It seems that inflationary expectations drive long-term interest rates in South Korea.
- As mentioned above, capital flows play a positive role for stock market developments and are also attracted by stock market advances. This confirms the major role of 'hot money' in leading to the build up of the asset price bubble in Asia in the 1990s and the subsequent burst once the direction of financial flows was reversed.

6.8 Thailand: Quarterly Data

6.8.1 Model Specification

6.8.1.1 Data Overview, Deterministic Components and Lag Length

Unlike the previous country analyses the data vector for Thailand does not include the long-term interest rate because until 1996 there were no outstanding government bonds (Inoguchi 2007, p. 392). As can be seen from the chart in Fig. 6.19, the yield on long-term government bonds, as provided by the main economic indicators from the OECD, was fixed for extended periods. This is a result of data unavailability. In addition, before the Asian financial crisis, the Thailand bond market was heavily regulated and had a very low trading volume due to the inefficient infrastructure of tax and information disclosure procedures.[131] As a result, the long-term interest rate is inoperative for the purposes of the econometric analysis. Consequently, the data vector for Thailand consists of only the following variables:

$$x_t^{'} = [m_r, s_r, y_r, \Delta p, or, cf]_t \tag{6.60}$$

where m_r is the log of real money (M3), s_r is the log of real stock market levels (total market including dividends) and y_r is the log of real GDP.[132] Real variables are transformed from nominal variables by applying the consumer price index, p, and, hence, Δp is the inflation rate. Short term interest rates are represented by the overnight interbank rate, or. Interest rates have been converted to quarterly rates and divided by 100 to achieve comparability with the inflation rate. Capital flows, cf, are calculated in percent as a share of the total money stock M3. They are derived from non-bank BoP transactions as described in Sect. 4.6.3.2 and Appendix A. All time series are obtained either from Datastream or the IMF BoP database and detailed information on specific sources of the data can be found in Appendix B.7.1. The data used for the analysis covers the last 22 years and consists of quarterly observations from 1987:1 to 2008:3.[133]
Figure 6.19 displays the time pattern of all variables in levels and first differences. All graphs look stationary for the differenced series and non-stationary for the time series in levels. Further characteristics of the data are that real money and real GDP seem to follow a trend. Thus, a deterministic (non-stochastic) trend should be allowed for in the model. However, the deterministic part of the trend changed after the Asian financial crisis and the stock market collapse in 1997. This represents a mean shift in the differenced series. This structural break might require a shift dummy to model the change in expectations and risk perception intrinsic to the bust.

Deterministic Components

The above observations suggest including the following deterministic components in the model (see also Sect. 6.2.1.1): an unrestricted constant, μ_0, a restricted linear trend, μ_1, and a restricted shift dummy, $\Phi_s D_{s,t}$. The CVAR model from (5.4) then becomes

$$\Delta x_t = \alpha\beta^{'} x_{t-1} + \sum_{i=1}^{k-1} \Gamma_i \Delta x_{t-1} + \Phi D_t + \mu_0 + \mu_1 + \Phi_s D_{s,t} + \epsilon_t, \tag{6.61}$$

---

[131] For a detailed presentation of the developments of the Thai bond market see Ganjarerndee (2001, pp. 642–684).

[132] The time series for nominal GDP is based on two time series because information on quarterly GDP data is only published from 1993 onwards. To cover a longer time frame, growth rates of the manufacturing production index are applied for earlier years.

[133] As mentioned above, quarterly GDP figures could not be obtained or calculated for earlier years. Therefore, compared to the other quarterly country analyses the time frame is shorter.

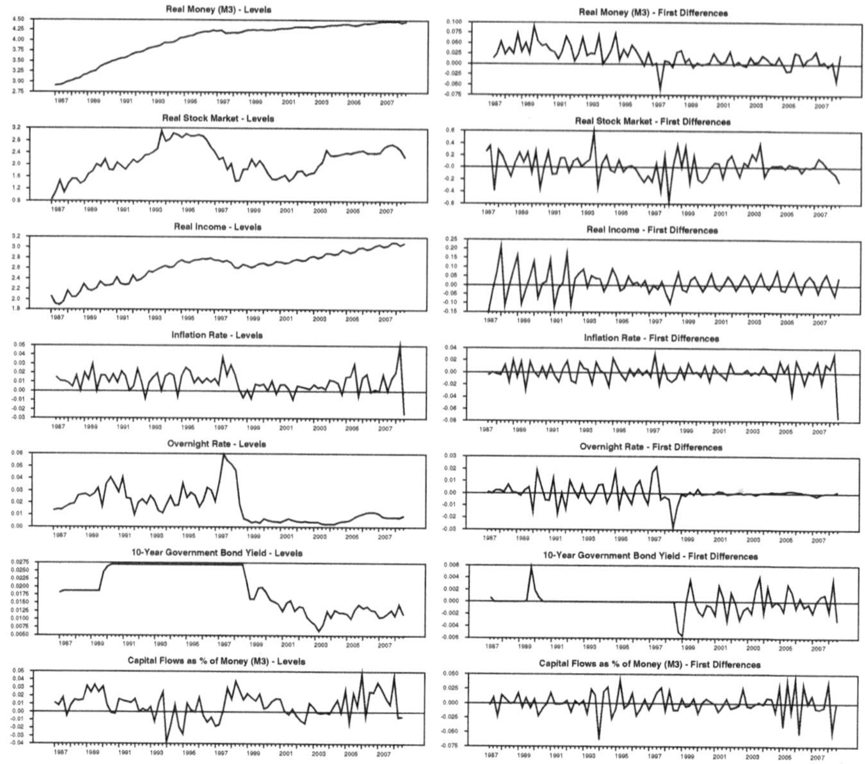

Fig. 6.19 Thailand quarterly data in levels and first differences

where $\mu_0 = \alpha\rho_0 + \gamma_0$, $\mu_1 = \alpha\rho_1 + \gamma_1$ and $\Phi_s = \alpha\delta_0 + \delta_1$, such that the parameters μ_0, μ_1 and Φ_s are decomposed in the direction of α and $\alpha_\perp$. Consequently, (6.61) becomes

$$\Delta x_t = \alpha[\beta^{'}, \rho_0, \rho_1, \delta_0]\begin{bmatrix} x_{t-1} \\ 1 \\ t \\ D_{s,t} \end{bmatrix} + \sum_{i=1}^{k-1} \Gamma_i \Delta x_{t-1} + \Phi D_t + \gamma_0 + \gamma_1 + \delta_1 D_t^s + \epsilon_t. \tag{6.62}$$

The constant, μ_0, is unrestricted. The trend, μ_1, however, is restricted to the cointegration space. Hence, $\gamma_1 = 0$ and $(\gamma_0, \rho_0, \rho_1) \neq 0$.[134] With an unrestricted constant and a trend restricted to the cointegration space, linear trends ($\gamma_0 \neq 0$), but not quadratic trends ($\gamma_1 \neq 0$), are allowed for in the data. This specification ensures similarity in the rank test procedure because the trend might not cancel in

[134] These specifications correspond to case 4 in Juselius (2006, pp. 99–100) and model $H^*(r)$ in Johansen (1995, Equation (5.14), p. 81). In CATS it is processed via the use of det = cidrift.

Table 6.117 Thailand quarterly data: intervention dummies

Dummy variable	Motivation	Impact on
$dum8901_p$	Strong economic expansion	Real income
$dum9703_s(D_s)$	Asian financial crisis	Real money, overnight rate, inflation
$dum9703_p$[136]	Asian financial crisis	Real money, overnight rate
$dum0802_t$	Food and energy price bonanza	Inflation

the cointegration relations (Nielsen and Rahbek 2000, pp. 12–15). To ensure similarity in the presence of structural breaks, the shift dummy needs to be included in the cointegration relations before determining the rank (Juselius 2006, p. 140). The shift dummy is restricted to the cointegration space: $\delta_0 \neq 0$ and $\delta_1 = 0$.

If $\rho_1 \neq 0$ and $\delta_0 \neq 0$ then the linear trend and the mean shift of the variables do not cancel in the cointegration relations, which will be formally tested in the model in Sect. 6.8.2.2, Table 6.125.

Dummy Variables

Misspecification tests show that normality is rejected and ARCH effects exist in the first three lags.[135] To ensure normality and reduce ARCH effects, dummies are included based on the economic calendar and the graphs of the standardized residuals, which have revealed some large outliers. Table 6.117 provides an overview.

The analysis of Thailand quarterly data requires one shift dummy, two permanent dummies and one transitory dummy.

Determination of the Lag Length

Since earlier data points for GDP are unavailable the usual test statistics can only be calculated for one or two lags. The two information criteria SC and H–Q are reported in Table 6.118. The last two columns in Table 6.118 report the LM test for autocorrelation of order 1 and k. Numbers in bold indicate the suggested lag length of the respective test. Although all test statistics suggest one lag, two lags are incorporated in the analysis since short-run dynamics are also modeled. This would not be possible if only one lag were included since the model is specified in levels and differences.

The discussion in this section on lag length, deterministic components and dummy variables results in the following VAR(2) model (in error-correction form) for Thailand:

---

[135] The test is not reported here at this stage. Instead, misspecification tests are reported for the specified model in Sect. 6.8.1.2.

Table 6.118 Thailand quarterly data: information to determine lag length

Model	k	T	Regressive	Log-Likelihood	SC	H–Q	LM(1)	LM(k)
VAR(2)	2	85	22	2,152.611	−43.751	−46.018	0.334	0.120
VAR(1)	1	85	16	2,121.179	**−44.893**	**−46.542**	**0.271**	**0.271**

Table 6.119 Thailand quarterly data: multivariate misspecification tests (p-values in brackets)

Test for no autocorrelation			
LM(1):	$\chi^2(36)$	=	39.064 [0.334]
LM(2):	$\chi^2(36)$	=	46.154 [0.120]
LM(3):	$\chi^2(36)$	=	41.058 [0.258]
LM(4):	$\chi^2(36)$	=	48.437 [0.081]
Test for normality	$\chi^2(12)$	=	20.483 [0.058]
Test for no Arch effects			
LM(1):	$\chi^2(441)$	=	471.295 [0.154]
LM(2):	$\chi^2(882)$	=	929.807 [0.128]
LM(3):	$\chi^2(1323)$	=	1410.766 [**0.046**]
LM(4):	$\chi^2(1764)$	=	1785.000 [0.358]

$$\Delta x_t = \alpha \tilde{\beta}' \tilde{x}_{t-1} + \Gamma_1 \Delta x_{t-1} + \Phi D_t + \mu_0 + \epsilon_t, \qquad (6.63)$$

where $x_t' = [m_r, s_r, y_r, \Delta p, or, cf]_t$ and $\tilde{x}_t = \left[x_t', 1, trend, D_s\right]$ is a $((6+3) \times 1)$ data vector containing the p variables, a constant, a trend and the shift dummy. The cointegration vectors are represented by $\tilde{\beta} = \left[\beta', \rho_0, \rho_1, \delta_0\right]'$, which is a $((6+3) \times r)$ matrix with rank r. The analysis is based on 6×85 observations and conditions on the initial values (data points for 1987:1 to 1987:2). The unrestricted permanent and transitory dummy variables are contained in the vector $D_t = \left[dum8901_p, dum9703_p, dum0802_t\right]$.

6.8.1.2 Misspecification Tests

To determine the reduced rank of the model, the model must be well specified. Tables 6.119 and 6.120 report multivariate and univariate misspecification tests, respectively. The multivariate LM test shows no sign of autocorrelation in the first 4 lags (the null of the test is 'no autocorrelation').[137]
The normality tests are based on skewness and kurtosis.[138] The tests show that the null of the tests, normally distributed errors, is borderline accepted in the multivariate case and accepted for all individual time series aside from the inflation rate. This

[137] It is asymptotically distributed as χ^2 with p^2 degrees of freedom (Johansen 1995, p. 22).

[138] They are asymptotically χ^2-distributed, with $2p$ degrees of freedom in the multivariate and 2 degrees of freedom in the univariate case.

Table 6.120 Thailand quarterly data: univariate misspecification tests (p-values in brackets)

	ARCH(2)	Normality	Skewness	Kurtosis
Δm_r	1.928 [0.381]	0.019 [0.990]	0.026	2.709
Δs_r	0.397 [0.820]	3.323 [0.190]	0.323	2.483
Δy_r	3.316 [0.191]	5.019 [0.081]	−0.116	3.852
$\Delta^2 p$	2.157 [0.340]	6.380 [**0.041**]	0.000	4.012
Δor	4.504 [0.105]	2.870 [0.238]	0.137	3.543
Δcf	5.075 [0.079]	0.533 [0.766]	−0.159	2.954

is acceptable because it is a result of excess kurtosis and simulation studies have shown that kurtosis is not as serious as skewness (Hendry and Juselius 2000, p. 7). Additionally, tests for multivariate ARCH of order q (with $q = 1, \dots, 4$) and univariate second order ARCH effects are reported.[139] There are signs for ARCH effects in the third lag. However, Rahbek et al. (2002, p. 83) show that cointegration tests are robust against moderate residual ARCH effects. Since the main test statistics are accepted, the model describes the data well.

6.8.1.3 Rank Determination

As outlined in Sect. 6.2.1.3 the following formal and informal test procedures are applied to determine the reduced rank of the system (Juselius 2006, p. 142):

- Trace test (formal LR test).
- Modulus of the roots of the companion matrix.
- Significance of the α-coefficients.
- Graphical inspection of the recursively calculated trace test statistics.
- Graphical inspection of the stationarity of the cointegration relations.

Trace Test

Table 6.121 contains an overview of the trace test results.[140] It reports the estimated eigenvalues, λ_i, the trace test, Q_r, the small sample Bartlett corrected trace test (Johansen 2002, pp. 1932–1940), Q_r^{Bart}, and the 95% quintile from the asymptotic distribution corrected for deterministic components, $C_r^{95\%}$. In addition, the table

[139] The multivariate test statistic is approximately distributed as χ^2 with $\frac{q}{4}p^2(p+1)^2$ degrees of freedom. The univariate test is approximately distributed as χ^2 with k degrees of freedom (Dennis 2006, pp. 179–180).

[140] Equation (5.6) in Sect. 5.1.2 shows that, as a prerequisite for valid statistical inference, the variables can be integrated of first but not of higher order. Hence, it is important to ensure that no $I(2)$ variables are part of the data set. As outlined in Sect. 6.2.1.3 different criteria exist to analyze if $I(2)$-ness persists. Applying these criteria to the analysis of Thailand shows that no $I(2)$-trends exist in the data. Because univariate unit root tests are used in most analyses, they are conducted as well, in spite of their many limitations in the multivariate setting.The ADF test and the PP test fail

Table 6.121 Thailand quarterly data: trace test of cointegration rank

$p-r$	r	λ_i	Q_r	Q_r^{Bart}	$C_r^{95\%}$	p-value	p-value*
6	0	0.639	222.806	203.038	148.371	0.000	0.000
5	1	0.445	136.187	124.623	113.219	0.001	0.007
4	2	0.367	86.129	79.462	82.263	0.024	**0.080**
3	3	0.255	47.248	42.399	55.747	**0.217**	0.404
2	4	0.133	22.240	19.826	33.810	0.419	0.562
1	5	0.112	10.131	5.410	16.721	0.255	0.639

reports the p-value of the test statistic and the p-value of the Bartlett small sample corrections, p-value*, respectively.

The trace test accepts the null of $p - r = 3$ unit roots and, therefore, $r = 3$. The Bartlett corrected test accepts $r = 2$. These test results are a first indication for a rank of $r = 3$ or $r = 2$.

Roots of the Companion Matrix

The analysis of the modulus of the roots of the companion form matrix, as depicted in Table 6.122, shows that for $r = 4$ the modulus of the largest unrestricted root drops to 0.71 and, thus, below the critical value of 0.85 for quarterly data. As such, Table 6.122 establishes rank $r = 4$.

---

to reject the null hypothesis of the existence of a unit root at the 5% level for all variables in levels aside from the time series representing capital flows. The PP test is also rejected for inflation. In contrast, both tests reject the null hypothesis for the variables in the first-differenced form of the series. Consequently, the variables are at most integrated of order one. The appropriate lags for the ADF test are selected based on the Schwartz Criterion and the Akaike Information Criterion. The truncation point for the Newey–West adjustment, required for calculating the PP statistic, is determined by using the smallest integer greater than or equal to the sample size, T, to the power of $\frac{1}{4}$ (Greene 2003, p. 267). The test results are not reported here because of the questionable usefulness of univariate tests in a multivariate setting. Rao (2007, p. 1624) points out that these tests lack power and combinations of the many options of the tests almost always enable one to prove that the variables are I(1) in levels. Additionally, Muscatelli and Spinelli (2000, p. 724) refer to difficulties in using unit root tests as pre-tests if regime shifts are inherent to the model. For these and other reasons, Juselius (2006, p. 136) does not even discuss univariate unit root testing in her textbook on cointegration analysis. Instead, the stationarity of a variable is easily tested inside the multivariate model as a restriction on β (see Table 6.126 in Sect. 6.8.2.2). The advantage of the multivariate analysis is to define a well-specified model first and then test for stationarity. With univariate unit root tests, stationarity is tested before guaranteeing i.i.d. error terms, constant parameters and the absence of ARCH effects and before determining cointegration rank. The results of the ADF and PP tests are available on request.

Table 6.122 Thailand quarterly data: modulus of the six largest eigenvalue roots

$r = 6$	$r = 5$	$r = 4$	$r = 3$	$r = 2$	$r = 1$	$r = 0$
0.980	1	1	1	1	1	1
0.822	**0.981**	1	1	1	1	1
0.822	0.726	**0.710**	1	1	1	1
0.459	0.549	0.618	**0.703**	1	1	1
0.433	0.427	0.446	0.453	**0.424**	1	1
0.433	0.427	0.446	0.453	0.420	**0.509**	1

Table 6.123 Thailand quarterly data: t-values of the α-coefficients

			α			
	Alpha(1)	Alpha(2)	Alpha(3)	Alpha(4)	Alpha(5)	Alpha(6)
Δm_r	(−1.533)	(−1.888)	(0.650)	(0.535)	**(−3.407)**	(0.486)
Δs_r	**(4.266)**	(−1.177)	(−1.112)	(−1.541)	(−1.314)	**(2.581)**
Δy_r	**(−4.281)**	**(4.029)**	**(−4.373)**	(−1.392)	(−0.640)	(1.288)
$\Delta^2 p$	**(7.320)**	**(4.881)**	(0.685)	(1.769)	(1.356)	(−0.623)
Δor	(2.459)	(−1.026)	**(−3.577)**	(−1.384)	(0.630)	**(−2.516)**
Δcf	(2.113)	**(2.790)**	**(3.698)**	**(−2.960)**	(−1.854)	(0.377)

Significance of Adjustment Coefficients α

The t-values of the α-coefficients provide an indication of the significance of the equilibrium adjustment behavior of the relative variables. They are derived from the unrestricted estimates. As can be seen from Table 6.123, adjustment behavior to the first three equations is stronger and involves several variables. Nevertheless, the other relations also exhibit significant albeit lower t-values.[141] As a result, the investigation of the adjustment coefficients' significance points to a rank of $r = 3$.

The Recursive Graphs of the Trace Statistic

Figure 6.20 shows forward and backward recursively calculated graphs for the trace test statistic. The plots are normalized to the 5% significance level, represented by the horizontal line.

If $\lambda_i \neq 0$, the recursively calculated components of the trace statistic should grow linearly for $i = 1, \ldots, r$, but stay constant for $i = r + 1, \ldots, p$ (Juselius 2006, p. 142). As four of the graphs show linear growth and are above or cross the 1-line (5% critical value), this indicates a rank of $r = 4$.

[141] The lower t-values are especially critical because the t-values of a given relation are no longer Student's t distributed if the relation is non-stationary. Instead, it is better to compare the t-values to the Dickey–Fuller distribution, where the critical values are larger. As a rule of thumb, the t-values should be close to 3.0 for the relation to still qualify as adjusting.

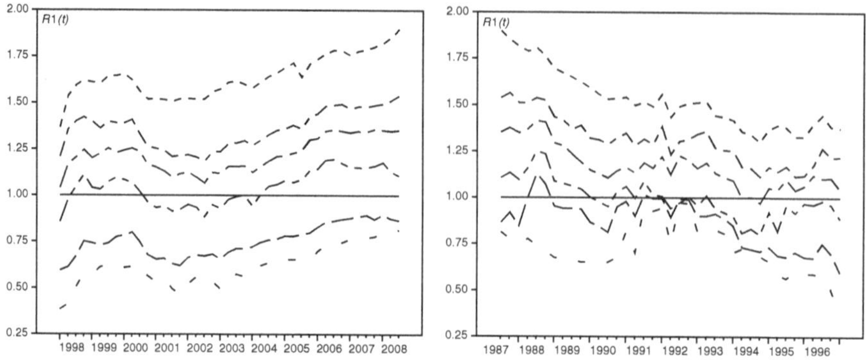

Fig. 6.20 Thailand quarterly data: recursively calculated trace test statistics (forward, base sample 1987:03 to 1998:01, depicted left; backward, base sample 2008:03 to 1997:01, depicted right)

Graphical Analysis of the Cointegration Relations

Finally, Appendix B.7.2 depicts the graphs of the cointegrating relations of the unrestricted model. The graphs of the fifth and sixth relation show persistent behavior and do not strongly suggest mean-reversion behavior, whereas the first three graphs look fairly stationary. The fourth graph looks borderline stationary, but also exhibits some persistence. As a result, this indicator points to a rank of either $r = 3$ or $r = 4$.

To conclude, the various information criteria used to determine the rank of the model mostly point to a rank of either $r = 3$ or $r = 4$. The formal trace test and especially the t-values of the α-coefficients strongly point to $r = 3$ and this is chosen for the subsequent analysis of the long-run equilibria.[142] That also means that $p - r = 3$ common trends exist, which is also valid from an economic point of view since it is reasonable for a real, monetary and financial trend to exist.

In addition, recursive tests show that the data describes a constant parameter regime. Figure 6.21 depicts the recursively calculated test of the log-likelihood. For the forward recursive test, the graph with short-run effects concentrated out, (R1(t)), stays under the line representing the 5% critical value. It takes some time, however, for the backward recursive test to drop under the line. Therefore, Appendix B.7.3 provides further information on parameter constancy, such as the eigenvalues λ_i, the eigenvalue fluctuation test, the max test of β constancy and the test of β_t equals a known β. All confirm a constant parameter regime. As a result, the assumption of constant parameters, which is important for valid identification of the long-run structure, is fulfilled.

[142] As the above test results would have also allowed for a rank of $r = 4$, the identified long-run structure and other results were also validated for this choice of rank. This sensitivity analysis confirms the results for $r = 3$.

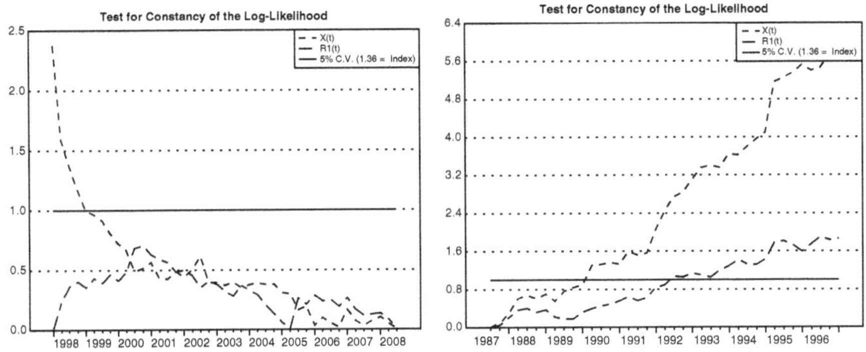

Fig. 6.21 Thailand quarterly data: recursively calculated test of log-likelihood (forward, base sample 1987:03 to 1998:01, depicted left; backward, base sample 2008:03 to 1997:01, depicted right)

6.8.2 *Identification of the Long-Run Structure*

6.8.2.1 Assessment of the Unrestricted Π-Matrix

To help facilitate the identification of an empirically acceptable long-run structure, the unrestricted Π is tentatively interpreted. However, the cointegration space can be rotated by taking proper linear combinations of the equations. Consequently, the final identified long-run structure does not have to reflect the initial suggestions from the unrestricted system. Also, the unrestricted Π-matrix may not be economically interpretable. Nevertheless, a rough indication of the long-run information in the data can be obtained. Basically, these estimates measure the combined effect of the cointegration relations in each of the equations (Johansen and Juselius 1992, p. 223).

The unrestricted Π-matrix for the chosen rank $r = 3$ is depicted in Table 6.124. The fact that the signs on the diagonal are negative and significant for all variables but real money shows that these variables exhibit error-correction behavior. Real money is only borderline significantly related to the inflation rate. This is a first sign that real money might be weakly exogenous. In addition, the shift dummy is highly significant for most equations as already expected from the graphical inspection of the time series.

The stock market equation represents a demand for stocks relation, where demand increases with real money and real output and decreases with advances in the overnight rate. Real output is positively related to the stock market and negatively related to real money. Inflation reacts positively to deviations of real output and negatively to capital flows. The overnight rate reacts positively to real money. Finally, the last equation reveals that capital flows react negatively to real money and inflation but react positively to advances in the overnight rate.

Table B.26 in Appendix B.7.4 shows the α- and β'-matrices of the partitioned unrestricted Π-matrix. The α-coefficients can indicate which variables are strongly adjusting to long-run equilibria and which variables are more on the pushing side.

Table 6.124 Thailand quarterly data: the unrestricted Π-matrix for a rank of 3 (*t*-values in brackets)

	m_r	s_r	y_r	Δp	or	cf	D_s9703	*Trend*
Δm_r	0.000 [0.033]	−0.008 [−1.247]	0.002 [0.033]	**0.602** [2.180]	−0.075 [−0.321]	0.154 [1.599]	−0.001 [−0.727]	0.001 [0.378]
Δs_r	**0.382** [3.428]	**−0.166** [−2.153]	**2.458** [3.575]	−5.811 [−1.826]	**−7.960** [−2.977]	0.699 [0.630]	**0.036** [4.211]	**−0.063** [−4.034]
Δy_r	**−0.051** [−2.382]	**0.090** [6.049]	**−0.859** [−6.486]	0.326 [0.531]	0.970 [1.884]	−0.193 [−0.903]	**−0.008** [−5.011]	**0.017** [5.627]
$\Delta^2 p$	0.002 [0.374]	0.005 [1.660]	**0.080** [2.955]	**−1.042** [−8.342]	0.099 [0.942]	**−0.256** [−5.876]	**0.002** [4.800]	**−0.002** [−3.880]
Δor	**0.015** [3.759]	−0.002 [−0.884]	0.041 [1.680]	−0.057 [−0.495]	**−0.348** [−3.624]	0.073 [1.822]	**0.001** [2.780]	**−0.001** [−2.479]
Δcf	**−0.024** [−2.533]	0.005 [0.846]	0.044 [0.769]	**−0.971** [−3.636]	**0.697** [3.106]	**−0.385** [−4.138]	0.000 [0.623]	−0.001 [−0.488]

Table 6.125 Thailand quarterly data: test of variable exclusion (*p*-values in brackets)

r	DGF	5% C.V.	m_r	s_r	y_r	Δp	or	cf	D_s9001	*Trend*
3	3	7.815	**2.163** [0.539]	22.696 [0.000]	47.088 [0.000]	32.460 [0.000]	25.659 [0.000]	9.059 [0.029]	20.606 [0.000]	32.787 [0.000]

The estimated α-matrix demonstrates that all variables except real money show strong and significant adjustment behavior in more than one relation. Real money does not react to any of the cointegration relations, which is another sign of its potential weak exogeneity.

6.8.2.2 Preliminary Hypotheses Testing

This section is divided into preliminary tests for β' and α. Automated tests on β' include the possibility to exclude variables from the long-run relations and stationarity of individual variables. The α-matrix is formally analyzed for weak exogeneity and unit vectors. Afterwards, single cointegration tests are conducted. This is to test for potential long-run equilibria as outlined in the section on long-run economic relations (5.2).[143] Table 6.125 shows that exclusion of real money is strongly accepted. It also shows that the inclusion of the shift dummy is essential.

Table 6.126 reports the tests for long-run stationarity. Tests are carried out without a restricted trend, with a restricted trend included and with a restricted trend and the shift dummy included in the cointegrating relations. Stationarity for the overnight rate is strongly accepted for all three tests and, thus, the overnight rate represents a cointegrating vector of its own.

[143] All test statistics on α and β are asymptotically distributed as χ^2 because the asymptotic distribution is mixed Gaussian (Johansen 1995, pp. 177–178). As a result, the usual statistical inference can be applied (Johansen and Juselius 1994, p. 16).

Table 6.126 Thailand quarterly data: test of variable stationarity (p-values in brackets)

Test of stationarity								
r	DGF	5% C.V.	m_r	s_r	y_r	Δp	or	cf
3	5	11.070	26.594 [0.000]	29.080 [0.000]	28.722 [0.000]	20.852 [0.001]	**3.189** [0.671]	18.942 [0.002]
Restricted trend included in the cointegrating relations								
3	4	9.488	26.603 [0.000]	28.990 [0.000]	21.195 [0.000]	16.986 [0.002]	**3.187** [0.527]	17.913 [0.001]
Restricted trend and shift-dummy included in the cointegrating relations								
3	3	7.815	26.594 [0.000]	26.673 [0.000]	12.476 [0.006]	12.315 [0.006]	**2.475** [0.480]	14.029 [0.003]

Table 6.127 Thailand quarterly data: test of weak exogeneity (p-values in brackets)

Test of weak exogeneity								
r	DGF	5% C.V.	m_r	s_r	y_r	Δp	or	cf
3	3	7.815	**4.490** [0.213]	14.687 [0.002]	23.888 [0.000]	38.036 [0.000]	11.947 [0.008]	11.303 [0.010]

Table 6.128 Thailand quarterly data: test for a unit vector in the α-matrix (p-values in brackets)

Test of unit vector in alpha								
r	DGF	5% C.V.	m_r	s_r	y_r	Δp	or	cf
3	3.000	7.815	22.236 [0.000]	16.910 [0.001]	**1.794** [0.616]	12.229 [0.007]	16.097 [0.001]	10.490 [0.015]

Tables 6.127 and 6.128 test restrictions on α. The test of weak exogeneity is equivalent to testing a zero row in the α-matrix. A finding of acceptance means that a variable is not error correcting but can be considered weakly exogenous for the long-run parameters β'. If the test is accepted, this also means that the sum of the cumulated empirical shocks to the variable in question defines one common driving trend. Table 6.127 shows that weak exogeneity is accepted for real money.
The test of a unit vector in α tests for the opposite, namely if a variable is exclusively adjusting. If the unit vector test is accepted, the properties of the relevant variable are that its shocks have no permanent effect on any of the other variables in the system and it can be regarded as endogenous. The transitory shocks do not cumulate into trends, instead they die out over time. Consequently, together, the two tests of α can identify the pulling and pushing forces of the system. Table 6.128 shows that the test is accepted for real output.
In addition to the above tests on single variables, the focus of the remaining preliminary tests is on single cointegration relations. The idea is to analyze if stable relationships between the economic variables can be identified by linear relations. Testing follows the theoretical connections outlined in Chap. 3 and Sect. 5.2, summarized in Table 5.1. The hypotheses are of the form:

$$\beta = (H\phi, \psi_1, \psi_2), \tag{6.64}$$

where H is the design matrix, ϕ contains the restricted parameters and ψ_i is a vector of parameters which are freely estimated. It is important to note that each hypothesis in Table 6.129 tests restrictions on a single vector but leaves the other cointegration vectors unrestricted (Johansen and Juselius 1992, pp. 233–236).

Table 6.129 gives an overview of the single cointegration test results. Its structure mirrors Table 5.2. However, since the long-term interest rate is not part of the data vector many potentially stationary relations can not be tested. Table 6.129 shows blanks for the hypotheses that include the bond rate. The numbering is unchanged to allow for comparisons between countries. In addition, since the short-term interest rate is found to be inherently stationary and, thus, integrated of order 0, the variable can not be part of another cointegration relation or adjust to a non-stationary variable (Juselius 2001, p. 343).[144] As a result, insight from the preliminary testing for Thailand is limited.

Hypotheses H_1 to H_8 test for cointegration between stocks and the other variables. Even though stationarity is accepted for hypotheses H_2, H_4 and H_6, the stock market variable only exhibits significant adjustment behavior to H_6.[145] The last column shows that the short-term interest rate reacts to the second and fourth relation, which is most likely a result of the inherent stationarity of the overnight rate.

H_9 to H_{16} test monetary relations. Only the money demand relation, incorporating the overnight rate, (H_{11}), is accepted. This is in line with the previous findings that real money is either long-run excludable or at least weakly exogenous.

'Policy rules' (H_{17} to H_{19}) are all accepted. Again, this is due to the stationarity of the overnight rate itself.

Hypotheses H_{20} to H_{23} focus on potential stationary goods demand relations. H_{23} shows that output reacts positively to advances in the stock market and negatively to real money.

Under the headline 'Inflation and interest rates' cointegration between inflation and the nominal interest rates ('Fisher parity') as well as between the interest rates themselves ('expectations hypothesis') is tested. The 'Fisher parity'-hypothesis is accepted for the real short-term interest rate in the strong form (H_{26}, i.e., with proportionality imposed) and the weak form (H_{28}, i.e., with free parameters).

As mentioned above, due to the stationary overnight rate and the non-existent long-term rate, the teachings of these preliminary tests are limited. H_6 does show, however, a valid cointegration relation between real output and the stock market where both variables react to each other. Together with the stationary overnight rate, these could represent two cointegration vectors. Thus, one additional cointegration relation needs to be found. To do so, it is helpful to consult the unrestricted Π-matrix (Table 6.124) and the partitioned unrestricted Π-matrices (Table B.26 in

---

[144] The test results are still shown for purposes of comparison because every country analysis shows the same preliminary tests and in order to keep the final long-run structure open. However, for relations including the overnight rate, one must keep in mind that the stationarity might be a result of the already stationary overnight rate time series instead of the combination of variables.

[145] Cointegration by itself is not indicative of the direction of causality between the variables. Instead, the test results have to be jointly evaluated with the α-matrix.

Table 6.129 Thailand quarterly data: testing the stationarity of single relations

	m_r	s_r	y_r	Δp	or	cf	D_s9001	*Trend*	$\chi^2(v)$	p-value	$sign.\alpha$
					Demand for stocks						
H_1	−4.095	1	0	0	0	0	−0.197	0.205	26.9 (2)	0.000	
H_2	**0**	**1**	**0**	**−256.1**	**256.1**	**0**	**0.054**	**−0.037**	**3.4 (2)**	**0.183**	$\Delta p, or$
H_3											
H_4	**0**	**1**	**0**	**0**	**−118.2**	**0**	**0.059**	**−0.074**	**1.0 (2)**	**0.596**	or, cf
H_5											
H_6	**0**	**1**	**−8.681**	**0**	**0**	**0**	**−0.064**	**0.146**	**0.0 (2)**	**0.992**	$s_r, y_r, \Delta p$
H_7	0	1	0	0	0	−156.2	0.166	−0.125	13.5 (2)	0.001	
H_8	−2.203	1	0	0	0	−134.5	0.083	−0.036	13.4 (1)	0.000	
					Money demand						
H_9	1	0	−1	0	0	0	0.019	−0.013	14.5 (3)	0.002	
H_{10}											
H_{11}	**1**	**0**	**1.379**	**0**	**−25.22**	**0**	**0.050**	**−0.071**	**0.8 (1)**	**0.367**	or, cf
H_{12}	1	0	47.47	−381.5	0	0	0.664	−1.154	6.5 (1)	0.011	
H_{13}	1	−0.244	0	0	0	0	0.048	−0.050	26.9 (2)	0.000	
H_{14}											
H_{15}	1	0.039	−1	0	0	0	0.020	−0.015	13.9 (2)	0.001	
H_{16}											

(continued)

Table 6.129 (Continued)

	m_r	s_r	y_r	Δp	or	cf	D_s9001	*Trend*	$\chi^2(v)$	p-value	$sign.\alpha$
					Policy rules						
H_{17}	**0**	**0**	**0**	**−0.380**	**1**	**0**	**0.000**	**0**	**2.4 (3)**	**0.501**	$s_r, \Delta p, or$
H_{18}	**0**	**0**	**−0.065**	**0**	**1**	**0**	**−0.001**	**0.002**	**1.6 (2)**	**0.451**	s_r, or
H_{19}	**0**	**−0.008**	**0**	**0**	**1**	**0**	**0**	**0.001**	**1.0 (2)**	**0.596**	or
					Demand for goods						
H_{20}	**0**	**0**	**1**	**−16.44**	**16.44**	**0**	**0.012**	**−0.020**	**2.6 (2)**	**0.267**	$\Delta p, or$
H_{21}											
H_{22}	−0.364	0	1	0	0	0	0	−0.010	10.9 (2)	0.004	
H_{23}	**0.017**	**−0.116**	**1**	**0**	**0**	**0**	**0.008**	**−0.017**	**0.0 (1)**	**0.923**	s_r, y_r
					Inflation and interest rates						
H_{24}	0.006	0	−0.006	1	0	0	0	0	12.8 (3)	0.005	
H_{25}											
H_{26}	**0**	**0**	**0**	**−1**	**1**	**0**	**0.000**	**0**	**3.8 (4)**	**0.429**	$\Delta p, or$
H_{27}											
H_{28}	**0**	**0**	**0**	**−0.380**	**1**	**0**	**0.000**	**0**	**2.4 (3)**	**0.501**	$s_r, \Delta p, or$
H_{29}											
H_{30}											
H_{31}											
H_{32}											
H_{33}											

Appendix B.7.4), which show that the inflation rate and capital flows adjust to all three cointegration relations and to several variables.

6.8.2.3 Identification of the Long-Run Cointegrating Relations

The identification procedure is based on the outlined economic theory and the preliminary testing of the econometric model in the previous section. Thus, by imposing different linear restrictions on the cointegrating relations an empirically and economically uniquely identified long-run structure can be obtained.

The restrictions on the identified long-run structure are accepted with a p-value of 0.52 ($\chi^2(8) = 7.124$). The structure is formally and empirically identified because all β-coefficients are strongly significant (Juselius and MacDonald 2004, p. 18). In addition, Appendix B.7.5 shows that the rank conditions are accepted for the full cointegration space. This means that the three cointegration relations are linearly independent and, as such, can not be replaced by each other.

The graphs of the cointegrating relations are displayed in Appendix B.7.6 with the deterministic terms and short-term parameters concentrated out.[146] They all describe stationary behavior. Graphical overviews of forward and backward recursive tests of parameter constancy in Appendix B.7.7 show that parameter constancy for α_i and β_i ($i = 1, \ldots, 3$) is given.

The structural representation of the cointegration space is depicted in Table 6.130 with the estimated eigenvectors β and the weights α.

The first cointegrating relation describes the relationship between real output and the stock market:

$$y_{r,t} - 0.091 s_{r,t} + 0.009 D_s - 0.019 trend \sim I(0), \qquad (6.65)$$

where real output is positively related to the stock market and vice versa. The α-coefficients show that real output and the stock market significantly adjust to this relation. The significance of the adjustment is higher for real output. The coefficients suggest that it takes real output between one and two quarters to restore equilibrium and the stock market less than one quarter to do so. This fast adjustment process confirms the importance of the two variables to each other. In addition, deviations from this long-run equilibrium have a positive effect on inflation and the overnight rate. The positive reaction of the inflation rate can be interpreted in the framework of the short-run Phillips curve, where inflation increases with excess aggregate demand for goods (Juselius 2001, p. 344).

The second β'-vector describes a relationship between inflation, the stock market and capital flows:

[146] This removes the seasonal fluctuations and outliers, which can be observed in the raw series and, thus, provides a clearer picture (Brüggemann and Lütkepohl 2006, p. 692). See also Sect. 6.2.1.3.

Table 6.130 Thailand quarterly data: the identified long-run structure (t-values in brackets)

β'	m_r	s_r	y_r	Δp	or	cf	D_s9001	$Trend$
Beta(1)	0.000 [NA]	**−0.091** [−7.826]	**1.000** [NA]	0.000 [NA]	0.000 [NA]	0.000 [NA]	**0.009** [14.78]	**−0.019** [−26.79]
Beta(2)	0.000 [NA]	**−0.012** [−4.368]	0.000 [NA]	**1.000** [NA]	0.000 [NA]	**0.205** [3.709]	**−0.001** [−5.540]	**0.001** [4.581]
Beta(3)	0.000 [NA]	0.000 [NA]	0.000 [NA]	0.000 [NA]	**1.000** [NA]	0.000 [NA]	0.000 [NA]	0.000 [NA]

α	Alpha(1)	Alpha(2)	Alpha(3)
Δm_r	0.003 [0.044]	**0.602** [2.028]	−0.017 [−0.071]
Δs_r	**2.505** [3.583]	−4.162 [−1.214]	**−8.382** [−3.086]
Δy_r	**−0.829** [−6.095]	0.275 [0.412]	0.809 [1.531]
$\Delta^2 p$	**0.070** [2.576]	**−1.114** [−8.350]	0.154 [1.460]
Δor	**0.053** [2.126]	0.020 [0.165]	**−0.379** [−3.918]
Δcf	0.079 [1.293]	**−0.948** [−3.179]	0.442 [1.871]

$$\Delta p_t - 0.012 s_{r,t} + 0.205 cf_t - 0.001 D_s + 0.001 trend \sim I(0), \tag{6.66}$$

where inflation reacts positively to stock market advances and negatively to capital flows. The first relationship shows that asset price inflation translates into consumer price inflation. This information is meaningful for purposes of monetary policy implementation. The second part is surprising because the expectation is that capital flows increase domestic inflation. However, analysis of the α-coefficients shows that both variables, inflation and capital flows, error correct to this relation. Hence, this relation can also be interpreted as a capital flows relation where capital flows are attracted by stock market advances and react negatively to higher inflation. This behavior is consistent with theory. Both coefficients show an adjustment speed of roughly one quarter to restore equilibrium. Since the significance of the α-coefficient of inflation is higher, this relation is normalized on the β-coefficient of inflation. The stock market does not react to this relation.

The last cointegrating relation consists of the overnight rate variable, which is stationary on its own:

$$or_t \sim I(0). \tag{6.67}$$

The α-coefficient confirms that the overnight rate shows significant adjustment behavior. In addition, the stock market has a strong negative reaction to advances in the overnight rate. This indicates the Bank of Thailand's (BoT) ability to influence the stock market.

To find out if the cumulated shocks to a variable have any long-run impact on other variables Sect. 6.8.4 analyzes the unrestricted C-matrix. There, the focus is also on the controllability of the stock market.

Table 6.131 Thailand quarterly data: short-run dynamics (t-values in brackets)

	Δm_r	Δs_r	Δy_r	$\Delta^2 p$	Δor	Δcf
$\Delta m_{r,t}$	**1**	0	0	0	0	0
$\Delta s_{r,t}$	0	**1**	0	0	0	0
$\Delta y_{r,t}$	0	0	**1**	0	0	0
$\Delta^2 p_t$	0	0	0	**1**	0	0
Δor_t	0	0	0	0	**1**	0
Δcf_t	0	0	0	0	0	**1**
$\Delta m_{r,t-1}$	**0.221**		**1.015**			**−0.439**
	[2.93]		[3.76]			[−4.33]
$\Delta s_{r,t-1}$		**−0.277**	**−0.055**			
		[−3.13]	[−2.68]			
$\Delta y_{r,t-1}$						
$\Delta^2 p_{t-1}$			**1.515**	**−0.166**		
			[3.35]	[2.19]		
Δor_{t-1}		**−5.693**				
		[−2.42]				
Δcf_{t-1}						**−0.484**
						[−5.79]
$ecm1_{t-1}$	**0.100**	**0.864**	**−0.249**	**−0.045**	**0.037**	
	[5.23]	[3.56]	[−4.60]	[−3.45]	[4.49]	
$ecm2_{t-1}$			**−1.175**	**−0.627**		**−0.581**
			[−2.38]	[−6.90]		[−3.11]
$ecm3_{t-1}$		**−6.811**		**0.214**	**−0.357**	**0.404**
		[−3.62]		[2.87]	[−5.89]	[3.21]
$dum8901_{p,t}$			**0.118**			
			[3.44]			
$dum9703_{p,t}$	**−0.083**			**0.026**	**0.030**	
	[−5.79]			[3.86]	[5.52]	
$dum0802_{t,t}$	**−0.035**			**0.039**		
	[−3.57]			[7.75]		

6.8.3 *Short-Run Dynamics*

While the previous analysis focuses on stable long-run economic relations, this section applies a structural error-correction model and formulates stationary equations for each of the variables in the system (see Sect. 6.2.3). The 45 zero restrictions of insignificant coefficients are accepted based on an LR test of over-identifying restrictions $\chi^2(45) = 35.023$ with a p-value of 0.86. Table 6.131 provides an overview. The dependent variables can be found in the top row as the column headings of each of the model equations. The row headings, on the other hand, indicate the conditioning variables.

The analysis of the short-run dynamics shows that real money reacts positively to lagged values of itself and is pushed by deviations from the first cointegration relation.

The stock market is negatively affected by lagged values of itself and by the overnight rate. In addition, it reacts to the first cointegration relation, which is the real output-stock market relation, and to the third cointegration relation, which is the overnight rate. This shows the strong negative reaction of the stock market to movements in the overnight rate.

Real output is positively driven by lagged values of real money and inflation and shows error-correcting behavior to the first ecm. In addition, real output reacts negatively to lagged values of the stock market and to the second ecm, which is contradictory to the long-run behavior of stocks and output, as demonstrated in the first cointegration relation. This might be a result of high residual correlation between the variables in the system. In addition, the significance is lower than the short-run adjustment to the first cointegration relation.

Inflation reacts negatively to itself and shows error-correcting behavior to the second cointegration relation, which is the inflation rate relation. Furthermore, the first ecm has a negative effect on inflation and the third ecm a positive effect.

The overnight rate is not influenced by any of the lagged variables but it reacts to the third cointegration relation, which is the overnight rate relation. Moreover, it is pushed by deviations from the first cointegration relation, which indicates that the BoT reacts to higher economic activity.

Capital flows react negatively to real money and itself and positively to deviations in the overnight rate (ecm3). In addition, it shows adjustment behavior to the second cointegration relation, which is the capital flows relation.

Table 6.131 shows that many of the autoregressive coefficients are insignificant and, thus, restricted to 0. The bulk of explanatory power in the short run is based on the inclusion of the ecms. The equilibrium-correcting coefficients are mostly highly significant, indicating the potential loss of information if the VAR model had only been estimated in first differences.

One downside of the above equations is that current effects are not modeled. Instead they are left in the residuals. However, simultaneous effects have potential importance. Whereas correlation between the residuals is not problematic in the long-run relations of the previous section, identification of the short-run structural equations requires uncorrelated residuals (Juselius 2006, p. 229). Table 6.132 shows the residual covariance matrix, in which large off-diagonal elements can be an indication of significant current effects between the system variables. Correlation between real money and inflation, between the stock market and the overnight rate and the stock market and capital flows and between real output and inflation must be critically recognized.

One way to reduce residual correlation is to introduce current effects between the variables into the short-run structure. Adding current effects of the inflation rate to the real money and real output equation as well as current effects of the stock market to the overnight rate and capital flows equations helps to reduce correlation (see Table 6.133). Nevertheless, overall correlation remains high. This might be

Table 6.132 Thailand quarterly data: correlation of structural residuals (standard deviations on diagonal)

	Δm_r	Δs_r	Δy_r	$\Delta^2 p$	Δor	Δcf
Δm_r	*0.015*					
Δs_r	0.34	*0.174*				
Δy_r	0.21	0.13	*0.037*			
$\Delta^2 p$	**−0.58**	−0.07	**−0.46**	*0.008*		
Δor	−0.34	**−0.44**	−0.07	0.10	*0.006*	
Δcf	0.26	**0.40**	−0.04	0.09	−0.29	*0.015*

Table 6.133 Thailand quarterly data: correlation of structural residuals after allowing for current effects (standard deviations on diagonal)

	Δm_r	Δs_r	Δy_r	$\Delta^2 p$	Δor	Δcf
Δm_r	*0.013*					
Δs_r	0.36	*0.176*				
Δy_r	0.10	0.15	*0.036*			
$\Delta^2 p$	**−0.40**	−0.07	**−0.39**	*0.008*		
Δor	−0.32	**−0.26**	−0.05	0.10	*0.006*	
Δcf	0.23	**0.10**	−0.06	0.10	−0.16	*0.014*

the reason for some peculiar findings of the short-run dynamics. As a result, these findings must be interpreted with caution.

Table 6.134 shows the slightly changed short-run structure after allowing for current effects. The main results remain the same.

6.8.4 The Long-Run Impact of the Common Trends

The C-matrix is vital to understanding the long-run implications of the model. Central banks ability to influence the stock market is conditioned upon a shock to a monetary instrument having a significant long-run impact on the stock market. Hence, when evaluating the effectiveness of monetary policy the long-run impact of shocks to the short-term interest rate and to the money supply on the stock market is of particular interest.

The residual $\epsilon_{i,t}$ is interpreted as an estimate of the unanticipated shock to variable x_i. The estimated long-run impact of these cumulated shocks is reported in Table 6.135 and is calculated from the estimates of the restricted VAR model as

$$C = \tilde{\beta}_{\perp}\alpha'_{\perp}, \tag{6.68}$$

where $\tilde{\beta}_{\perp} = \beta_{\perp}(\alpha'_{\perp}\beta_{\perp})^{-1}$ and $\alpha_{\perp}, \beta_{\perp}$ are the $(p \times p - r)$ orthogonal compliments of α and β (Johansen 1995, pp. 49–50). Because C has reduced rank, only $p-r = 3$ linear combinations of the $p = 6$ innovations, ϵ_t, have permanent effects.

Table 6.134 Thailand quarterly data: short-run dynamics allowing for current effects (t-values in brackets)

	Δm_r	Δs_r	Δy_r	$\Delta^2 p$	Δor	Δcf
$\Delta m_{r,t}$	**1**	0	0	0	0	0
$\Delta s_{r,t}$	0	**1**	0	0	−0.01	0.03
$\Delta y_{r,t}$	0	0	**1**	0	0	0
$\Delta^2 p_t$	**−0.43**	0	−0.46	**1**	0	0
Δor_t	0	0	0	0	**1**	0
Δcf_t	0	0	0	0	0	**1**
$\Delta m_{r,t-1}$	**0.300**		**0.980**			**−0.465**
	[3.48]		[3.62]			[−4.36]
$\Delta s_{r,t-1}$		**−0.333**	**−0.058**			
		[−3.38]	[−2.82]			
$\Delta y_{r,t-1}$						
$\Delta^2 p_{t-1}$			**1.371**	**−0.194**		
			[2.78]	[−2.22]		
Δor_{t-1}		**−6.856**				
		[−2.64]				
Δcf_{t-1}						**−0.468**
						[−5.58]
$ecm1_{t-1}$	**0.096**	**0.928**	**−0.254**	**−0.049**	**0.041**	
	[5.40]	[3.64]	[−4.71]	[−3.28]	[4.12]	
$ecm2_{t-1}$			**−1.421**	**−0.675**		**−0.543**
			[−2.45]	[−6.22]		[−2.92]
$ecm3_{t-1}$		**−7.117**		**0.225**	**−0.396**	**0.476**
		[−3.69]		[2.51]	[−5.24]	[3.72]
$dum8901_{p,t}$			**0.117**			
			[3.39]			
$dum9703_{p,t}$	**−0.069**			**0.027**	**0.030**	
	[−4.73]			[3.56]	[5.50]	
$dum0802_{t,t}$	**−0.017**			**0.040**		
	[−1.33]			[7.18]		

The C-matrix can be read column or row-wise. The columns show the long-run impact of a shock to a variable on each of the variables in the system and the rows show which of the shocks have a long-run impact on the particular variable.
The C-matrix in Table 6.135 shows that, in the long run, shocks to both real money and the inflation rate have positive effects on real money. The effect of the inflation rate is only borderline significant and real money can be restricted to be weakly exogenous. The test of weak exogeneity of real money is accepted with a p-value of 0.34 ($\chi^2(11) = 12.338$). The C-matrix with weak exogeneity imposed is presented in Table B.29 in Appendix B.7.9.

Table 6.135 Thailand quarterly data: the long-run impact matrix (t-values in brackets)

The long-run impact matrix, C						
	$\hat{\epsilon}_{m_r}$	$\hat{\epsilon}_{s_r}$	$\hat{\epsilon}_{y_r}$	$\hat{\epsilon}_{\Delta p}$	$\hat{\epsilon}_{or}$	$\hat{\epsilon}_{cf}$
m_r	**1.648** [5.163]	−0.009 [−0.618]	0.119 [1.293]	**0.869** [2.001]	0.863 [1.246]	0.117 [1.106]
s_r	5.053 [1.587]	**0.627** [4.461]	1.248 [1.364]	0.359 [0.083]	−11.08 [−1.603]	0.164 [0.156]
y_r	0.460 [1.587]	**0.057** [4.461]	0.114 [1.364]	0.033 [0.083]	−1.009 [−1.603]	0.015 [0.156]
Δp	**0.117** [2.933]	**0.006** [3.680]	0.007 [0.641]	**0.130** [2.401]	**−0.207** [−2.394]	**−0.109** [−8.265]
or	0.000 [NA]	0.000 [NA]	0.000 [NA]	0.000 [NA]	0.000 [NA]	0.000 [NA]
cf	**−0.286** [−2.293]	0.004 [0.666]	0.034 [0.959]	**−0.615** [−3.621]	0.388 [1.430]	**0.543** [13.10]

Only cumulated shocks to the stock market influence stock market developments in the long run. This is a sign of herding, trend-following behavior and rational speculation of economic agents. The signs for real money (positive) and the overnight rate (negative) are correct but they are borderline insignificant. This changes when real money is restricted to be weakly exogenous. Then, the negative impact of shocks to the overnight rate becomes significant.

Aside from that, the C-matrix shows that shocks to the stock market have positive long-run effects on the level of economic activity. This confirms the findings of the long-run relations.

In addition, shocks to real money and the stock market translate into higher inflation. Shocks to capital flows and the overnight rate, on the other hand, reduce inflation in the long run. Hence, the BoT has is able to fight inflation in the long run.

Capital flows are negatively affected by cumulated shocks to real money and to inflation and positively by shocks to itself. The latter shows the persistence of capital flows to and from Thailand. These circumstances worsened the Asian financial crisis.

6.8.5 Conclusion

Table 6.136 shows that the results of the main hypotheses are mixed. The hypothesis that confidence and optimism are important factors for the development of stock prices is confirmed. In addition, one objective of this contribution is to test whether or not abundant liquidity enforces the upward spiral of stock prices. This hypothesis does not hold for Thailand for the timeframe under consideration. Instead, real stock market levels long-run equilibrate with real output levels, where both variables show error-correction behavior. Also, capital flows do not affect the Thai stock market, neither in the long run nor in the short run. Instead it is the other way round. This finding holds throughout most country analyses. Capital flows are attracted by rising levels of stock prices. In addition, abundant domestic liquidity has a negative effect on capital flows because investment opportunities become more scarce.

Table 6.136 Thailand quarterly data: results of main hypotheses

	Hypotheses/Questions	Result
H_1	Thailand's stock market behavior shows strong persistence, i.e., shocks to the stock market have positive long-run effects on future developments	Yes
H_2	Long-run equilibria exist between stock prices and liquidity conditions	No
H_3	Liquidity conditions influence stock prices positively in the long run	No
H_4	Liquidity conditions influence stock prices positively in the short run	No
H_5	International capital flows have a positive long-run impact on the stock market behavior in Thailand	No
H_6	International capital flows have a positive short-run impact on the stock market behavior in Thailand	No
Q_1	Is the BoT able to influence stock prices in the long run?	Yes
Q_2	Is the BoT able to influence stock prices in the short run?	Yes

In addition to financial stability, the above analysis provides another argument for why monetary policy should react to stock market levels; shocks to the stock market translate into higher inflation. The ability of the central bank to influence stock market developments is given, very strongly so in the short run, but also in the long run. Shocks to the policy rate have a negative impact on the stock market in the long run, albeit the effect is only borderline statistically significant.

The analysis of Thailand also confirms the stock market's importance for aggregate output, the second part of transmission mechanism theory. The stock market enters positively into the first cointegration relation, which is the aggregate demand for goods relation. In addition, shocks to the stock market have a positive long-run impact on real output.

The above analysis also sheds light on a few other aspects of economic interest, mainly:

- Real money is weakly exogenous to the system. In the short run, real money only reacts to lagged values of itself and is pushed by the residuals of the real output-stock market relation.
- The analysis shows that inflation is influenced by monetary developments and the stock market. The cumulated shocks to real money have a positive long-run impact on inflation. In addition, the inflation rate reacts positively to deviations from the aggregate demand relation, which can be interpreted in the framework of the short-run Phillips curve, where inflation increases with excess aggregate demand for goods. Consequently, inflation is a monetary phenomenon in the long run and is influenced by real developments in the short run. The analysis also shows that the short-term interest rate affects inflation negatively. Hence, the BoT has the ability to fight inflation by setting the short-term policy rate.
- The short-term interest rate shows stationary behavior over the period under investigation. This indicates that the BoT often reversed course in monetary policy setting. This is contrary to the behavior of the established central banks of the large industrialized countries, such as the Fed or the BoE. There, the behavior of

central bankers is very persistent. This means that once rates are lowered instead of further increased they will be lowered for some time and vice versa.

- As mentioned above, capital flows are attracted by stock market advances. In addition, they react negatively to increased domestic inflation.

6.9 Brazil: Quarterly Data

6.9.1 Model Specification

6.9.1.1 Data Overview, Deterministic Components and Lag Length

As with the country analysis for Thailand the data vector for Brazil does not include the long-term interest rate. A continuous bond market did not exist for most of the time period under investigation and is, therefore, not useful for the analysis. As a result, the data vector for Brazil consists of only the following variables:

$$x_t' = [m_r, s_r, y_r, \Delta p, or, cf]_t \,, \tag{6.69}$$

where m_r is the log of real money (M2), s_r is the log of real stock market levels (total market including dividends) and y_r is the log of real GDP. Real variables are transformed from nominal variables by applying the consumer price index, p, and, hence, Δp is the inflation rate. Short term interest rates are represented by the overnight interbank rate, or. Interest rates have been converted to quarterly rates and divided by 100 to achieve comparability with the inflation rate. Capital flows, cf, are calculated in percent as a share of the total money stock M2. They are derived from non-bank BoP transactions as described in Sect. 4.6.3.2 and Appendix A. All time series are obtained either from Datastream or the IMF BoP database and detailed information on specific sources of the data can be found in Appendix B.8.1. The data used for the analysis only covers the last 14 years and consists of quarterly observations from 1995:1 to 2008:3.[147]

Figure 6.22 displays the time pattern of all variables in levels and first differences. All graphs look stationary for the differenced series. The series in levels, however, show a lot of persistence. In addition, real money, the stock market and real GDP seem to follow a trend. Thus, an unrestricted constant and a restricted trend are included in the model.[148]

[147] The time frame had to be shortened compared to the other quarterly country analyses due to periods of hyperinflation during the 1980s and at the beginning of the 1990s. As a result, no reasonable time series for money and inflation are available before the mid 1990s and a constant parameter regime could not have been achieved.

[148] For a discussion of deterministic components in the model, see Sect. 6.2.1.1.

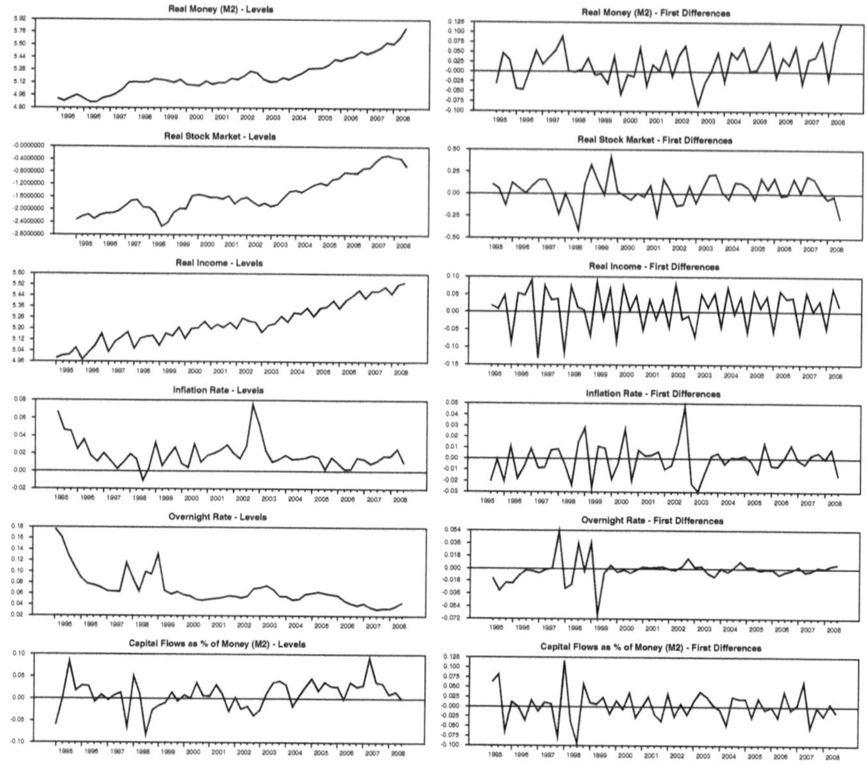

Fig. 6.22 Brazil quarterly data in levels and first differences

Dummy Variables

Misspecification tests show that normality is rejected, autocorrelation exists in the fourth lag and ARCH effects exist in the second lag.[149] To ensure normality and reduce autocorrelation and ARCH effects, dummies are included based on the economic calendar and the graphs of the standardized residuals, which have revealed some large outliers. Table 6.137 provides an overview. Modeling data for Brazil requires two permanent and three transitory dummies.[150]

Determination of the Lag Length

Since earlier data points for real money and inflation are unavailable the usual test statistics can only be calculated for one or two lags. The two information criteria SC

[149] The test is not reported here at this stage. Instead, misspecification tests are reported for the specified model in Sect. 6.9.1.2.

[150] For an overview of the different kinds of dummies see Sect. 6.2.1.1.

Table 6.137 Brazil quarterly data: intervention dummies

Dummy variable	Motivation	Impact on
$dum9704_p$	Increased risk perception due to the Asian financial crisis	Overnight rate & capital flows
$dum9802_t$	Increased volatility due to the Asian financial crisis	Overnight rate
$dum9901_t$	Increased volatility due to the Asian financial crisis	Overnight rate
$dum0204_p$	Rising fuel and food prices	Inflation
$dum0702_t$	Strong capital inflows due to commodity-related portfolio investment	Capital flows

Table 6.138 Brazil quarterly data: information to determine lag length

Model	k	T	Regressive	Log-Likelihood	SC	H–Q	LM(1)	LM(k)
VAR(2)	2	53	22	1,361.471	−41.488	−44.508	0.122	0.855
VAR(1)	1	53	16	1,330.740	**−43.025**	**−45.222**	**0.175**	**0.175**

and H–Q are reported in Table 6.138. The last two columns in Table 6.138 report the LM test for autocorrelation of order 1 and k. Numbers in bold indicate the suggested lag length of the respective test. Although all test statistics suggest one lag, two lags are incorporated in the analysis since short-run dynamics are also modeled. This would not be possible if only one lag were included because the model is specified in levels and differences.

The discussion in this section on lag length, deterministic components and dummy variables results in the following VAR(2) model (in error-correction form) for Brazil quarterly data:

$$\Delta x_t = \alpha\tilde{\beta}'\tilde{x}_{t-1} + \Gamma_1\Delta x_{t-1} + \Phi D_t + \mu_0 + \epsilon_t, \tag{6.70}$$

where $x_t' = [m_r, s_r, y_r, \Delta p, or, cf]_t$ and $\tilde{x}_t = \left[x_t', 1, trend\right]$ is a $((6+2) \times 1)$ data vector containing the p variables, a constant and a trend. The cointegration vectors are represented by $\tilde{\beta} = \left[\beta', \rho_0, \rho_1\right]'$, which is a $((6+2) \times r)$ matrix with rank r. The analysis is based on 6×55 observations and conditions on the initial values (data points for 1995:1 to 1995:2). The dummy variables are contained in the vector $D_t = \left[dum9704_p,\ dum9802_t,\ dum9901_t,\ dum0204_p,\ dum0702_t\right]$.

6.9.1.2 Misspecification Tests

The model must be well specified to determine the reduced rank of the model. Tables 6.139 and 6.140 report multivariate and univariate misspecification tests,

Table 6.139 Brazil quarterly data: multivariate misspecification tests (p-values in brackets)

Test for no autocorrelation			
LM(1):	$\chi^2(36)$	=	46.015 [0.122]
LM(2):	$\chi^2(36)$	=	27.190 [0.855]
LM(3):	$\chi^2(36)$	=	22.638 [0.960]
LM(4):	$\chi^2(36)$	=	47.660 [0.093]
Test for normality	$\chi^2(12)$	=	16.879 [0.154]
Test for no Arch effects			
LM(1):	$\chi^2(441)$	=	484.359 [0.075]
LM(2):	$\chi^2(882)$	=	946.465 [0.065]
LM(3):	$\chi^2(1323)$	=	1113.000 [1.000]
LM(4):	$\chi^2(1764)$	=	1113.000 [1.000]

Table 6.140 Brazil quarterly data: univariate misspecification tests (p-values in brackets)

	ARCH(2)	Normality	Skewness	Kurtosis
Δm_r	0.232 [0.890]	0.891 [0.641]	−0.212	2.446
Δs_r	1.396 [0.498]	2.365 [0.307]	0.002	3.458
Δy_r	0.292 [0.864]	8.431 [**0.015**]	0.812	4.977
$\Delta^2 p$	0.780 [0.677]	4.570 [0.102]	0.692	3.739
Δor	0.277 [0.871]	1.344 [0.511]	−0.080	2.179
Δcf	2.650 [0.266]	0.913 [0.634]	−0.227	3.043

respectively. The multivariate LM test shows that the null of the test ('no autocorrelation') is accepted for the first four lags.[151]

The normality tests are based on skewness and kurtosis.[152] The tests show that the null of the tests, normally distributed errors, is accepted in the multivariate case and for all individual time series except real output.

Additionally, tests for multivariate ARCH of order q (with $q = 1, \dots, 4$) and univariate second order ARCH effects are reported.[153] There are no signs of ARCH effects in the system or individually. Since most test statistics are accepted, the model appears to describe the data well.

[151] It is asymptotically distributed as χ^2 with p^2 degrees of freedom (Johansen 1995, p. 22).

[152] They are asymptotically χ^2-distributed, with $2p$ degrees of freedom in the multivariate and 2 degrees of freedom in the univariate case.

[153] The multivariate test statistic is approximately distributed as χ^2 with $\frac{q}{4}p^2(p+1)^2$ degrees of freedom. The univariate test is approximately distributed as χ^2 with k degrees of freedom (Dennis 2006, pp. 179–180).

6.9.1.3 Rank Determination

As outlined in Sect. 6.2.1.3 the following formal and informal test procedures are applied to determine the reduced rank of the system (Juselius 2006, p. 142):

- Trace test (formal LR test).
- Modulus of the roots of the companion matrix.
- Significance of the α-coefficients.
- Graphical inspection of the recursively calculated trace test statistics.
- Graphical inspection of the stationarity of the cointegration relations.

Trace Test

Table 6.141 provides an overview of the trace test results.[154] It reports the estimated eigenvalues, λ_i, the trace test, Q_r, the small sample Bartlett corrected trace test (Johansen 2002, pp. 1932–1940), Q_r^{Bart}, and the 95% quintile from the asymptotic distribution corrected for deterministic components, $C_r^{95\%}$. In addition, the table reports the p-value of the test statistic and the p-value of the Bartlett small sample corrections, p-value*, respectively. In this case, the Bartlett small sample corrections are probably more relevant because the analysis is only based on an effective sample of 55 observations.

[154] Equation (5.6) in Sect. 5.1.2 shows that, as a prerequisite for valid statistical inference, the variables can be integrated of first but not of higher order. Hence, it is important to ensure that no $I(2)$ variables are part of the data set. As outlined in Sect. 6.2.1.3 different criteria exist to analyze if $I(2)$-ness persists. Applying these criteria to the analysis of Brazil shows that no $I(2)$-trends exist in the data. Because univariate unit root tests are used in most analyses, they are conducted as well, in spite of their many limitations in the multivariate setting. The ADF test and the PP test fail to reject the null hypothesis of the existence of a unit root at the 5% level for all variables in levels aside from the time series representing the overnight rate and capital flows. The PP test is also rejected for inflation. In contrast, both tests reject the null hypothesis for the variables in first-differenced form of the series. Consequently, the variables are at most integrated of order one. The appropriate lags for the ADF test are selected based on the Schwartz Criterion and the Akaike Information Criterion. The truncation point for the Newey–West adjustment, required for calculating the PP statistic, is determined by using the smallest integer greater than or equal to the sample size, T, to the power of $\frac{1}{4}$ (Greene 2003, p. 267). The test results are not reported here because of the questionable usefulness of univariate tests in a multivariate setting. Rao (2007, p. 1624) points out that these tests lack power and combinations of the many options of the tests almost always enable one to prove that the variables are I(1) in levels. Additionally, Muscatelli and Spinelli (2000, p. 724) refer to difficulties in using unit root tests as pre-tests if regime shifts are inherent to the model. For these and other reasons, Juselius (2006, p. 136) does not even discuss univariate unit root testing in her textbook on cointegration analysis. Instead, the stationarity of a variable is easily tested inside the multivariate model as a restriction on β (see Table 6.146 in Sect. 6.9.2.2). The advantage of the multivariate analysis is to define a well-specified model first and then test for stationarity. With univariate unit root tests, stationarity is tested before guaranteeing i.i.d. error terms, constant parameters and the absence of ARCH effects and before determining cointegration rank. The results of the ADF and PP tests are available on request.

Table 6.141 Brazil quarterly data: trace test of cointegration rank

$p-r$	r	λ_i	Q_r	Q_r^{Bart}	$C_r^{95\%}$	p-value	p-value*
6	0	0.838	221.096	174.633	117.451	0.000	0.000
5	1	0.634	124.711	98.008	88.554	0.000	0.008
4	2	0.512	71.462	54.263	63.659	0.009	**0.248**
3	3	0.372	33.442	25.059	42.770	**0.320**	0.786
2	4	0.102	8.774	7.160	25.731	0.960	0.988
1	5	0.057	3.097	2.990	12.448	0.855	0.867

Table 6.142 Brazil quarterly data: modulus of the seven largest eigenvalue roots

$r=6$	$r=5$	$r=4$	$r=3$	$r=2$	$r=1$	$r=0$
0.902	1	1	1	1	1	1
0.900	**0.880**	1	1	1	1	1
0.900	0.880	**0.761**	1	1	1	1
0.528	0.527	0.535	**0.833**	1	1	1
0.528	0.527	0.535	0.448	**0.803**	1	1
0.504	0.503	0.530	0.448	0.456	**0.715**	1

The trace test accepts the null of $p-r=3$ unit roots and, therefore, $r=3$ and the Bartlett corrected trace test accepts the null of $p-r=4$ unit roots and, therefore, $r=2$.

Roots of the Companion Matrix

The analysis of the modulus of the roots of the companion form matrix, as depicted in Table 6.142, shows that for $r=4$ the modulus of the largest unrestricted root drops to 0.761 and, thus, well below the critical value of 0.85 for quarterly data. Hence, Table 6.142 accepts a rank of $r=4$.

Significance of Adjustment Coefficients α

The t-values of the α-coefficients provide an indication of the significance of the equilibrium adjustment behavior of the relative variables. They are derived from the unrestricted estimates. As can be seen from Table 6.143, adjustment behavior to the first three relations is stronger and involves several variables. Nevertheless, the fourth relation also exhibits significant t-values, albeit with lower t-values. As a result, the investigation of the adjustment coefficients' significance points to a rank of $r=3$ but also allows for a rank of $r=4$.

Table 6.143 Brazil quarterly data: t-values of the α-coefficients

	α					
	Alpha(1)	Alpha(2)	Alpha(3)	Alpha(4)	Alpha(5)	Alpha(6)
Δm_r	(−0.952)	(−1.960)	(−0.992)	(0.676)	(−2.287)	(0.399)
Δs_r	(−0.746)	(−0.876)	**(3.778)**	(−0.764)	(−0.385)	(1.483)
Δy_r	(1.879)	(2.339)	**(−4.081)**	**(−3.279)**	(−0.586)	(0.853)
$\Delta^2 p$	(1.047)	(−1.725)	**(4.272)**	**(−3.280)**	(−0.151)	(−0.960)
Δor	**(13.89)**	**(−3.470)**	**(−2.889)**	(0.632)	(−0.058)	(0.037)
Δcf	**(−7.603)**	**(−6.520)**	(0.832)	(−1.279)	(0.980)	(0.566)

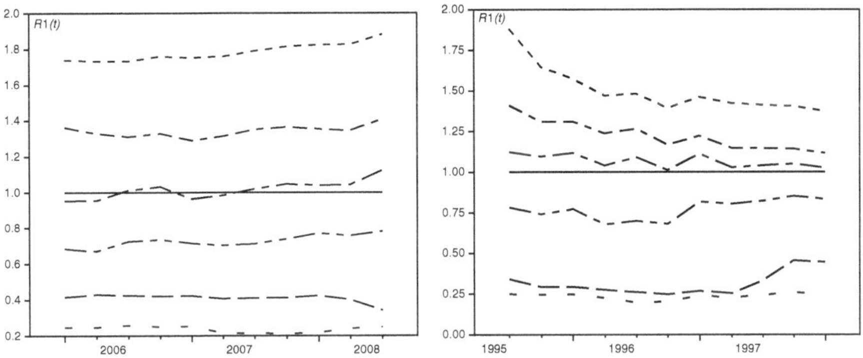

Fig. 6.23 Brazil quarterly data: recursively calculated trace test statistics (forward, base sample 1995:03 to 2006:01, depicted left; backward, base sample 2008:03 to 1998:01, depicted right)

The Recursive Graphs of the Trace Statistic

Figure 6.23 shows forward and backward recursively calculated graphs for the trace test statistic. The plots are normalized to the 5% significance level, represented by the horizontal line.

If $\lambda_i \neq 0$, the recursively calculated components of the trace statistic should grow linearly for $i = 1, \ldots, r$, but stay constant for $i = r + 1, \ldots, p$ (Juselius 2006, p. 142). Three of the graphs show linear growth and are above or cross the 1-line (5% critical value). Hence, the graphical inspection of the trace statistic confirms a rank of $r = 3$.[155]

[155] One should recognize, however, that due to the shorter investigation period, recursive tests do not provide as much information as in the other country analyses. The main reason for this is that a big timeframe in the middle of the analysis is not covered because it is needed to calculate the recursive series. Therefore, recursive tests for Brazil must be interpreted with caution.

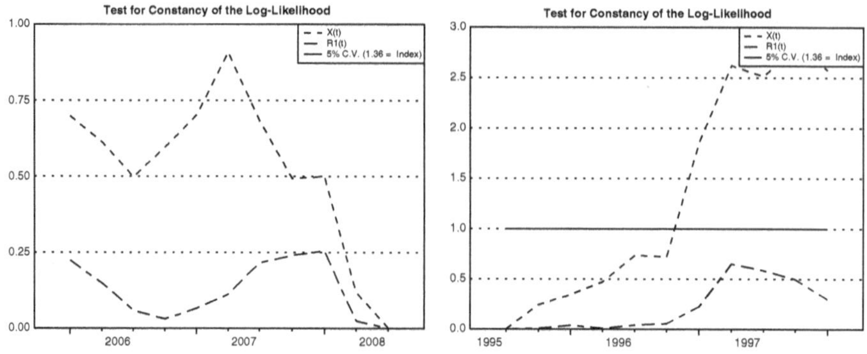

Fig. 6.24 Brazil quarterly data: recursively calculated test of log-likelihood (forward, base sample 1995:03 to 2006:01, depicted left; backward, base sample 2008:03 to 1998:01, depicted right)

Graphical Analysis of the Cointegration Relations

The graphs of the cointegrating relations of the unrestricted model are depicted in Appendix B.8.2. Whereas the first four graphs look stationary, the last two relations show persistent behavior. Hence, this indicator points to a rank of $r = 4$.

To conclude, the various information criteria used to determine the rank of the model mostly point to a rank of $r = 3$ or $r = 4$. However, as the Bartlett corrected trace test only suggests a rank of $r = 2$, a rank of four appears to be invalid. Thus, rank three is chosen for the subsequent analysis of the long-run equilibria.[156] That also means that $p - r = 3$ common trends exist, which is valid from an economic point of view since it is reasonable for a real, monetary and financial trend to exist.

In addition, recursive tests show that the data describes a constant parameter regime. Figure 6.24 depicts the recursively calculated test of the log-likelihood. Both tests are clearly accepted.[157] Additional tests on parameter constancy confirm that constancy of the overall model is accepted (see the tests in Appendix B.8.3 on eigenvalues λ_i, eigenvalue fluctuations, the max test of β constancy and the test of β_t equals a known β, Figs. B.96–B.99, respectively). As a result, the assumption of constant parameters, which is important for valid identification of the long-run structure, is fulfilled.

---

[156] To ensure reliable results the identified long-run structure is also tested for $r = 4$. These sensitivity tests confirm the results obtained for rank three.

[157] In the graph with short-run effects concentrated out, (R1(t)), stays under the line representing the 5% critical value.

Table 6.144 Brazil quarterly data: the unrestricted Π-matrix for a rank of 3 (*t*-values in brackets)

	m_r	s_r	y_r	Δp	or	cf	*Trend*
Δm_r	−0.054 [−1.422]	0.025 [1.594]	0.047 [0.277]	0.112 [0.974]	0.126 [0.750]	**−0.360** [−2.248]	−0.000 [−0.170]
Δs_r	**−0.584** [−2.632]	**−0.256** [−2.813]	**3.643** [3.666]	**−2.456** [−3.644]	**2.172** [2.207]	0.650 [0.694]	**−0.014** [−3.712]
Δy_r	**0.136** [4.045]	**0.030** [2.170]	**−0.669** [−4.462]	**0.368** [3.618]	**−0.489** [−3.293]	0.090 [0.639]	**0.003** [4.448]
$\Delta^2 p$	**−0.045** [−2.552]	**−0.025** [−3.497]	**0.309** [3.929]	**−0.209** [−3.911]	0.068 [0.866]	0.045 [0.603]	**−0.001** [−3.973]
Δor	**0.034** [4.535]	**−0.007** [−2.195]	**−0.094** [−2.806]	**0.051** [2.238]	**−0.438** [−13.16]	−0.020 [−0.640]	**0.000** [2.847]
Δcf	**−0.262** [−8.518]	**0.045** [3.566]	**0.690** [5.021]	−0.047 [−0.500]	**1.094** [8.035]	**−0.910** [−7.027]	**−0.003** [−4.702]

6.9.2 Identification of the Long-Run Structure

6.9.2.1 Assessment of the Unrestricted Π-Matrix

To help facilitate the identification of an empirically acceptable long-run structure, the unrestricted Π is tentatively interpreted. However, the cointegration space can be rotated by taking proper linear combinations of the equations. Consequently, the final identified long-run structure does not have to reflect the initial suggestions from the unrestricted system. Also, the unrestricted Π-matrix may not be economically interpretable. Nevertheless, a rough indication of the long-run information in the data can be obtained. Basically, these estimates measure the combined effect of the cointegration relations in each of the equations (Johansen and Juselius 1992, p. 223).

The unrestricted Π-matrix for the chosen rank $r = 3$ is depicted in Table 6.144. At first glance, according to the unrestricted Π-matrix most variables adjust to each other. Upon closer inspection, the diagonal shows that all coefficients have a negative sign and, thus, show error-correcting behavior. However, the coefficient for real money is insignificant. This signifies that real money might be weakly exogenous. In addition, Table 6.144 shows that the stock market is positively related to real output and the overnight rate and negatively related to real money and inflation.

The equation for real output represents an aggregate demand relation where real output is driven by advances in real money and the stock market and reacts negatively to higher short-term interest rates.

The information on the inflation rate is unanticipated because inflation reacts negatively to real money and the stock market. The overnight rate reacts positively to real money and inflation and negatively to the stock market and real output. Finally, the last equation shows that capital flows show error-correction behavior towards all other variables aside from the inflation rate. As seen in most other country analyses, higher stock market levels, economic activity and interest rates increase capital inflows while abundant domestic liquidity has a negative effect on capital inflows.

Table B.31 in Appendix B.8.4 shows the α- and β'-matrices of the partitioned unrestricted Π-matrix. The α-coefficients can indicate which variables strongly

Table 6.145 Brazil quarterly data: test of variable exclusion (p-values in brackets)

Test of exclusion										
r	DGF	5% C.V.	m_r	s_r	y_r	Δp	or	cf	$Trend$
3	3	7.815	32.831 [0.000]	16.154 [0.001]	13.752 [0.003]	**2.764** [0.429]	60.338 [0.000]	26.496 [0.000]	9.260 [0.026]

Table 6.146 Brazil quarterly data: test of variable stationarity (p-values in brackets)

Test of stationarity								
r	DGF	5% C.V.	m_r	s_r	y_r	Δp	or	cf
3	4	9.488	36.861 [0.000]	33.348 [0.000]	35.828 [0.000]	**9.383** [0.052]	20.687 [0.000]	32.259 [0.000]
Restricted trend included in the cointegrating relations								
3	3	7.815	34.214 [0.000]	35.768 [0.000]	31.818 [0.000]	9.382 [0.025]	18.081 [0.000]	24.749 [0.000]

adjust to long-run equilibria and which variables are more on the pushing side. The estimated α-matrix shows that all variables except real money show significant adjustment behavior to at least one cointegration relation.

The following section outlines preliminary tests for purposes of assessment structure and providing additional information.

6.9.2.2 Preliminary Hypotheses Testing

This section is divided into preliminary tests for β' and α. Automated tests on β' include the potential to exclude variables from the long-run relations and stationarity of individual variables. The α-matrix is formally analyzed for weak exogeneity and unit vectors. Afterwards, single cointegration tests are conducted. This is to test for potential long-run equilibria as outlined in the section on long-run economic relations (5.2).[158] This will help ease the final identification of the long-run structure and provides additional insight on information contained in the data set.

Table 6.145 provides LR tests for the exclusion of any variable from the cointegration relations. It shows that exclusion of the inflation rate is accepted with a p-value of 0.43. The final long-run structure confirms this finding since inflation is not part of any of the cointegration relations.

Table 6.146 reports the tests for long-run stationarity. It shows that stationarity is borderline accepted for the inflation rate.

Table 6.147 tests for weak exogeneity, which is equivalent to testing a zero row in the α-matrix. It means that a variable is not error correcting but can be considered weakly exogenous for the long-run parameters β. If the test is accepted, this also means that the sum of the cumulated empirical shocks to the variable in question

[158] All test statistics on α and β are asymptotically distributed as χ^2 because the asymptotic distribution is mixed Gaussian (Johansen 1995, pp. 177–178). As a result, the usual statistical inference can be applied (Johansen and Juselius 1994, p. 16).

Table 6.147 Brazil quarterly data: test of weak exogeneity (p-values in brackets)

Test of weak exogeneity								
r	DGF	5% C.V.	m_r	s_r	y_r	Δp	or	cf
3	3	7.815	**4.541** [0.209]	10.850 [0.013]	9.983 [0.019]	8.122 [0.044]	61.006 [0.000]	41.620 [0.000]

Table 6.148 Brazil quarterly data: test for a unit vector in the α-matrix (p-values in brackets)

Test of unit vector in alpha								
r	DGF	5% C.V.	m_r	s_r	y_r	Δp	or	cf
3	3.000	7.815	30.917 [0.000]	19.405 [0.000]	11.015 [0.012]	17.298 [0.001]	**2.835** [0.418]	**6.047** [0.109]

define one common driving trend. Table 6.147 shows that the test is accepted for real money (p-value 0.21), which confirms previous findings.

The test of a unit vector in α tests whether a variable is exclusively adjusting. If the unit vector test is accepted, the properties of the relevant variable are that its shocks only have transitory effects on the other variables in the system and it can be regarded as endogenous. Thus, the two tests of α can identify the pulling and pushing forces of the system. Table 6.148 shows that shocks to the overnight rate and to capital flows only have transitory effects. This indicates that monetary policy in Brazil did not have a long-run impact on the inflation rate or on the performance of the stock market by influencing the overnight rate.

In addition to the above tests on single variables, the focus of the remaining preliminary tests is on single cointegration relations. The idea is to analyze if stable relationships between the economic variables can be identified by linear relations. Testing follows the theoretical connections outlined in Chap. 3 and Sect. 5.2, summarized in Table 5.1. The hypotheses are of the form:

$$\beta = (H\phi, \psi_1, \psi_2), \tag{6.71}$$

where H is the design matrix, ϕ contains the restricted parameters and ψ_i is a vector of parameters which are freely estimated. It is important to note that each hypothesis in Table 6.149 tests restrictions on a single vector but leaves the other cointegration vectors unrestricted (Johansen and Juselius 1992, pp. 233–236).

Table 6.149 gives an overview of the single cointegration test results. It is structured the same as Table 5.2. However, since the long-term interest rate is not part of the data vector many potentially stationary relations can not be tested. Table 6.129 shows blanks for the hypotheses that include the bond rate. The numbering is unchanged to make comparisons between countries easier. Accepted hypotheses are indicated in bold.

Hypotheses H_1 to H_8 test for cointegration between stocks and the other variables. H_4 and H_8 are accepted, but the stock market only reacts to the latter relation. This represents a relation between the stock market, real money and capital flows. Hence, the stock market reacts positively to domestic and international liquidity conditions. H_9 to H_{16} test monetary relations. None of them are accepted.

Table 6.149 Brazil quarterly data: testing the stationarity of single relations

	m_r	s_r	y_r	Δp	or	cf	*Trend*	$\chi^2(v)$	p-value	$sign.\alpha$
					Demand for stocks					
H_1	−2.181	1	0	0	0	0	0.007	30.5 (2)	0.000	
H_2	0	1	0	−56.38	56.38	0	−0.007	10.9 (2)	0.004	
H_3										
H_4	**0**	**1**	**0**	**0**	**34.20**	**0**	**−0.016**	**5.7 (2)**	**0.058**	y_r, or
H_5										
H_6	0	1	−9.685	0	0	0	0.049	14.4 (2)	0.001	
H_7	0	1	0	0	0	−19.59	−0.012	14.0 (2)	0.001	
H_8	**−1.873**	**1**	**0**	**0**	**0**	**−15.38**	**0.006**	**1.0 (1)**	**0.329**	s_r, cf
					Money demand					
H_9	1	0	−1	0	0	0	−0.011	33.9 (3)	0.000	
H_{10}										
H_{11}										
H_{12}	1	0	−0.405	34.38	0	0	−0.010	8.3 (1)	0.004	
H_{13}	1	−0.458	0	0	0	0	−0.003	30.5 (2)	0.000	
H_{14}										
H_{15}	0	−0.256	−1	0	0	0	−0.001	31.9 (2)	0.000	
H_{16}										

(continued)

Table 6.149 (Continued)

	m_r	s_r	y_r	Δp	or	cf	*Trend*	$\chi^2(v)$	p-value	$sign.\alpha$
					Policy rules					
H_{17}	0	0	0	−12.41	1	0	0	9.2 (3)	0.026	
H_{18}	0	0	0.192	0	1	0	−0.001	13.4 (2)	0.001	
H_{19}	**0**	**0.029**	**0**	**0**	**1**	**0**	**0**	**5.7 (2)**	**0.058**	y_r, or
					Demand for goods					
H_{20}	0	0	1	−7	7.042	0	−0.010	11.6 (2)	0.003	
H_{21}										
H_{22}	−0.235	0	1	0	0	0	−0.005	27.5 (2)	0.000	
H_{23}	**−0.135**	**−0.077**	**1**	**0**	**0**	**0**	**−0.004**	**2.3 (1)**	**0.131**	s_r, y_r, or
					Inflation and interest rates					
H_{24}	0.017	0	−0.017	1	0	0	0	8.9 (3)	0.031	
H_{25}										
H_{26}	0	0	0	−1	1	0	0	15.4 (4)	0.004	
H_{27}										
H_{28}	0	0	0	−12.41	1	0	0	9.2 (3)	0.026	
H_{29}										
H_{30}										
H_{31}										
H_{32}										
H_{33}										

'Policy rules' (H_{17} to H_{19}) show that the overnight rate reacts negatively to deviations from stock market levels (H_{19}). However, this is nonsensical and it is only borderline accepted. This relation probably requires the inclusion of other variables to fully define a policy rule relation.

Hypotheses H_{20} to H_{23} focus on potential stationary aggregate demand for goods relations. Real output reacts positively to real money and the stock market (H_{23}), a finding in line with most other country analyses.

Under the headline 'Inflation and interest rates' cointegration between inflation and the nominal interest rates ('Fisher parity') as well as between the interest rates themselves ('expectations hypothesis') is tested. None of them are accepted. This is primarily a result of inflation being long-run excludable.

6.9.2.3 Identification of the Long-Run Cointegrating Relations

The identification procedure is based on the outlined economic theory and the preliminary testing of the econometric model in the previous section. By imposing different linear restrictions on the cointegrating relations an empirically and economically uniquely identified long-run structure can be obtained.

The restrictions on the identified long-run structure are accepted with a p-value of 0.70 ($\chi^2(6) = 3.833$). The structure is formally and empirically identified because all β-coefficients are strongly significant (Juselius and MacDonald 2004, p. 18). In addition, Appendix B.8.5 shows that the rank conditions are accepted for the full cointegration space. This means that the three cointegration relations are linearly independent and, as such, can not be replaced by each other.

The graphs of the cointegrating relations are displayed in Appendix B.8.6 with the deterministic terms and short-term parameters concentrated out.[159] They all describe stationary behavior. Graphical overviews of forward and backward recursive tests of parameter constancy in Appendix B.8.7 show that parameter constancy for α_i and β_i $(i = 1, \ldots, 3)$ is clearly accepted.

The structural representation of the cointegration space is depicted in Table 6.150 with the estimated eigenvectors β and the weights α.

The first cointegrating relation describes the relationship between liquidity conditions and the stock market:

$$s_{r,t} - 1.488 m_{r,t} - 14.601 cf_t \sim I(0), \tag{6.72}$$

where the stock market reacts positively to both domestic and external liquidity conditions. Hence, for Brazil, domestic money holdings and especially capital flows from abroad influence stock market developments.[160] The stock market

[159] This removes the seasonal fluctuations and outliers, which can be observed in the raw series and, thus, provides a clearer picture (Brüggemann and Lütkepohl 2006, p. 692). See also Sect. 6.2.1.3.

[160] The high β-coefficient of the capital flows variable can be rationalized by the extreme difference in the standard deviations of the two series. The residual standard error of the stock market is eight

Table 6.150 Brazil quarterly data: the identified long-run structure (t-values in brackets)

	β'						
	m_r	s_r	y_r	Δp	or	cf	*Trend*
Beta(1)	**−1.488** [−15.94]	**1.000** [*NA*]	0.000 [*NA*]	0.000 [*NA*]	0.000 [*NA*]	**−14.60** [−12.23]	0.000 [*NA*]
Beta(2)	0.000 [*NA*]	0.000 [*NA*]	0.000 [*NA*]	0.000 [*NA*]	**1.000** [*NA*]	**0.534** [8.590]	0.000 [*NA*]
Beta(3)	**−0.255** [−10.40]	0.000 [*NA*]	**1.000** [*NA*]	0.000 [*NA*]	**2.154** [21.48]	0.000 [*NA*]	**−0.004** [−11.37]

	α		
	Alpha(1)	Alpha(2)	Alpha(3)
Δm_r	0.023 [1.108]	−0.016 [−0.041]	0.078 [0.385]
Δs_r	**−0.301** [−2.435]	**−6.622** [−2.744]	**3.773** [3.071]
Δy_r	**0.060** [3.626]	**1.571** [4.823]	**−0.932** [−5.621]
$\Delta^2 p$	−0.019 [−1.816]	**−0.506** [−2.514]	**0.235** [2.288]
Δor	−0.007 [−1.631]	**−0.219** [−2.731]	**−0.094** [−2.310]
Δcf	**0.051** [3.067]	−0.338 [−1.037]	**0.639** [3.852]

error corrects towards this long-run steady state. The adjustment process takes approximately three quarters to restore equilibrium.

The α-coefficients also show that capital flows significantly adjust to this relation as well. This means that this relation could also be interpreted as a capital flows relation. Viewing the cointegration relation from that angle, the same pattern that exists in most other country analyses can be detected. More specifically, capital flows are attracted by good stock market performance but react negatively to abundant domestic liquidity. Thus, capital inflows decrease or capital outflows increase if domestic liquidity rises. This is potentially a result of limited investment alternatives and less incentive to borrow internationally when abundant liquidity is available at home. In addition, analysis of the α-coefficients reveals that real output reacts positively to deviations of the above equilibrium.

The second β'-vector represents a relationship between the overnight rate and capital flows:

$$or_t + 0.534cf_t \sim I(0), \tag{6.73}$$

where the overnight rate reacts negatively to capital inflows, that is, short-term interest rates decrease as liquidity enters Brazil. This makes sense from a supply and demand point of view. It is surprising, though, that capital flows play such a strong

times higher than that of capital flows. In general, the size of the coefficients has to be interpreted with caution. They usually can not be interpreted as elasticities, since a shock to one variable implies a shock to all variables in the long run. Thus, a ceteris paribus interpretation is generally invalid (Johansen 2009, pp. 8–9; Johansen 2005, pp. 97–100; Lütkepohl 1994, p. 393).

role for the overnight rate. Analysis of the α-coefficients shows that the equilibrium errors affect the stock market and inflation negatively and real output positively.

The third long-run relation describes an aggregate demand for goods relation:

$$y_{r,t} - 0.255m_{r,t} + 2.154or_t - 0.004trend \sim I(0), \quad (6.74)$$

where real output grows with rising money stock, decreases with higher short-term interest rates and follows a positive deterministic trend. Real output exhibits fast error-correction speed, taking roughly one quarter to restore the long-run steady state. Analysis of the α-coefficients also shows that deviations from the aggregate demand for goods equilibrium push the stock market, inflation and capital flows. The positive reaction of the inflation rate can be interpreted in the framework of the short-run Phillips curve, where inflation increases with excess aggregate demand for goods (Juselius 2001, p. 344). The many significant α-coefficients confirm the analysis of the unrestricted Π, which established that most variables react to each other.

The restriction of real money to be weakly exogenous is accepted with a p-value of 0.56 ($\chi^2(9) = 7.775$) for the final identified long-run structure. However, this restriction does not change the above described results since real money already does not react to any of the cointegration relations.

6.9.3 Short-Run Dynamics

While the previous analysis focuses on stable long-run economic relations, this section applies a structural error-correction model and formulates stationary equations for each of the variables in the system (see Sect. 6.2.3).The 53 zero restrictions of insignificant coefficients are strongly accepted based on an LR test of over-identifying restrictions with a p-value of 0.65 ($\chi^2(53) = 48.383$). Table 6.151 provides an overview. The dependent variables can be found in the top row as the column headings of each of the model equations. The row headings, on the other hand, indicate the conditioning variables.

The analysis of the short-run dynamics shows that real money reacts positively to lagged values of itself, the inflation rate and capital flows. Additionally, real money is negatively affected by the second ecm, which represents the relationship between the overnight rate and capital flows. It shows error-correction behavior towards the third cointegration relation, which indicates that real output and the overnight rate affect real money positively. This is compatible with standard money demand theory (see Sect. 3.3). The stock market only reacts to the dummy variable that represents the Asian financial crisis.

Real output does not react to lagged values of any of the variables but shows error-correcting behavior to the third cointegration relation, which is the aggregate demand relation. In addition, it is pushed by the first and second ecm.

Table 6.151 Brazil quarterly data: short-run dynamics (t-values in brackets)

	Δm_r	Δs_r	Δy_r	$\Delta^2 p$	Δor	Δcf
$\Delta m_{r,t}$	**1**	0	0	0	0	0
$\Delta s_{r,t}$	0	**1**	0	0	0	0
$\Delta y_{r,t}$	0	0	**1**	0	0	0
$\Delta^2 p_t$	0	0	0	**1**	0	0
Δor_t	0	0	0	0	**1**	0
Δcf_t	0	0	0	0	0	**1**
$\Delta m_{r,t-1}$	**0.405**			**0.175**	**0.066**	**−0.206**
	[3.42]			[3.52]	[2.87]	[−2.78]
$\Delta s_{r,t-1}$					**−0.012**	
					[−2.65]	
$\Delta y_{r,t-1}$					**0.084**	**−0.388**
					[2.99]	[−4.34]
$\Delta^2 p_{t-1}$	**0.429**			**−0.206**	**0.107**	**−0.553**
	[1.95]			[−2.01]	[2.03]	[−3.41]
Δor_{t-1}						
Δcf_{t-1}	**0.310**					
	[2.99]					
$ecm1_{t-1}$			**0.045**			**0.062**
			[3.34]			[10.9]
$ecm2_{t-1}$	**−0.882**		**1.118**			
	[−4.36]		[4.34]			
$ecm3_{t-1}$	**0.351**		**−0.688**		**−0.180**	**0.427**
	[2.93]		[−5.43]		[−11.0]	[8.43]
$dum9704_{p,t}$		**−0.328**			**0.052**	**−0.065**
		[−2.26]			[10.8]	[−3.78]
$dum9802_{t,t}$					**−0.026**	**0.028**
					[−7.22]	[2.55]
$dum9901_{t,t}$				**0.028**	**0.049**	
				[3.67]	[13.7]	
$dum0204_{p,t}$	**−0.109**		**−0.051**	**0.039**		
	[−4.29]		[−2.81]	[3.40]		
$dum0702_{t,t}$						**0.040**
						[3.79]

The inflation rate reacts positively to lagged values of real money and negatively to itself. The latter is a sign of its borderline stationarity. The inflation rate does not react to any of the cointegration residuals, a confirmation that it is long-run excludable (see Sect. 6.9.2.2).

The overnight rate reacts positively to real money, real output and the inflation rate and negatively to the stock market. While it is heavily influenced by capital

Table 6.152 Brazil quarterly data: correlation of structural residuals (standard deviations on diagonal)

	Δm_r	Δs_r	Δy_r	$\Delta^2 p$	Δor	Δcf
Δm_r	*0.025*					
Δs_r	0.02	*0.146*				
Δy_r	**0.28**	0.09	*0.018*			
$\Delta^2 p$	**−0.32**	0.26	−0.17	*0.011*		
Δor	−0.16	−0.05	0.04	−0.07	*0.005*	
Δcf	−0.25	**0.49**	−0.08	0.23	−0.12	*0.017*

flows in the long run, they do not play a role in short-run developments. In addition, it shows error correction towards the third cointegration relation.

Capital flows are negatively affected by lagged values of real money, real output and the inflation rate and, thus, the opposite of the overnight rate. This might be a reason for the negative long-run relationship between the two variables. In addition, it shows error-correction behavior towards the first cointegration relation and is pushed by the residuals of the last one.

One downside of the above equations is that current effects are not modeled. Instead they are left in the residuals. However, simultaneous effects have potential importance. Whereas correlation between the residuals is a non-issue for the long-run relations of the previous section, identification of the short-run structural equations requires uncorrelated residuals (Juselius 2006, p. 229). Table 6.152 shows the residual covariance matrix, in which large off-diagonal elements can be an indication of significant current effects between the system variables. Correlation between real money and real output, between real money and inflation and especially between the stock market and capital flows must be critically recognized. One way to reduce residual correlation is to introduce current effects between the variables into the short-run structure. Adding current effects of real money to the output equation and capital flows to the stock market equation helps to reduce correlation between the variables (see Table 6.153).[161] The results of the short-run analysis remain similar if current effects are modeled. The current effects of capital flows in the stock market equation show the importance of international capital flows for stock market developments in Brazil. Table 6.154 shows the minimally changed short-run structure after allowing for current effects.

6.9.4 The Long-Run Impact of the Common Trends

The C-matrix is crucial to understanding the long-run implications of the model. A condition precedent to a central bank's ability to influence the stock market is

[161] Other combinations of current effects were tested but did not reduce correlation between the variables. These included the current effects of inflation in the real money equation and vice versa.

Table 6.153 Brazil quarterly data: correlation of structural residuals after allowing for current effects (standard deviations on diagonal)

	Δm_r	Δs_r	Δy_r	$\Delta^2 p$	Δor	Δcf
Δm_r	*0.025*					
Δs_r	0.07	*0.136*				
Δy_r	**0.02**	0.14	*0.017*			
$\Delta^2 p$	**−0.32**	0.22	−0.08	*0.011*		
Δor	−0.16	−0.03	0.07	−0.07	*0.005*	
Δcf	−0.24	**0.38**	0.00	0.21	−0.12	*0.017*

that a shock to a monetary instrument has a significant long-run impact on the stock market. Hence, when evaluating the effectiveness of monetary policy, the long-run impact of shocks to the short-term interest rate and to the money supply on the stock market is of particular concern.

The residual $\epsilon_{i,t}$ is interpreted as an estimate of the unanticipated shock to variable x_i. The estimated long-run impact of the cumulated shocks is reported in Table 6.155 and is calculated from the estimates of the restricted VAR model as

$$C = \tilde{\beta}_{\perp}\alpha_{\perp}^{'}, \tag{6.75}$$

where $\tilde{\beta}_{\perp} = \beta_{\perp}(\alpha_{\perp}^{'}\beta_{\perp})^{-1}$ and $\alpha_{\perp}, \beta_{\perp}$ are the $(p \times p - r)$ orthogonal compliments of α and β (Johansen 1995, pp. 49 50). As C has reduced rank, only $p - r = 3$ linear combinations of the $p = 6$ innovations, ϵ_t, have permanent effects.

The C-matrix can be read column or row-wise. The columns show the long-run impact of a shock to a variable on each of the variables in the system and the rows show which of the shocks have a long-run impact on the particular variable. A first look at the C-matrix in Table 6.155 shows that, compared to the other country analyses, most shocks are transitory. Capital flows and the overnight rate only have transitory shocks; that is, they do not affect any of the variables in the long run. Inflation and output only affect themselves. Hence, it is mostly real money and the stock market that exert permanent shocks on the other variables.

In the long run, shocks to real money affect the overnight rate positively. Consequently, the 'liquidity effect' (see Sect. 4.3) does not hold in the long run. In addition, real money has the above described negative effect on capital flows. This shows that positive liquidity in the home country reduces the need to borrow from abroad and reduces the attractiveness of home country investments to foreign investors. However, both effects are only borderline significant.

Cumulated shocks to the stock market positively influence stock market developments in the long run. This confirms the results of the other country analyses and indicates the importance of herding, trend-following behavior and rational speculation of economic agents for stock market developments. In addition, shocks to the stock market have a positive effect on economic activity – more evidence that the second part of the transmission mechanism holds.

Table 6.154 Brazil quarterly data: short-run dynamics allowing for current effects (t-values in brackets)

	Δm_r	Δs_r	Δy_r	$\Delta^2 p$	Δor	Δcf
$\Delta m_{r,t}$	**1**	0	0.19	0	0	0
$\Delta s_{r,t}$	0	**1**	0	0	0	0
$\Delta y_{r,t}$	0	0	**1**	0	0	0
$\Delta^2 p_t$	0	0	0	**1**	0	0
Δor_t	0	0	0	0	**1**	0
Δcf_t	0	0.9	0	0	0	**1**
$\Delta m_{r,t-1}$	**0.435**			**0.164**	**0.068**	**−0.239**
	[3.54]			[3.23]	[2.94]	[−3.04]
$\Delta s_{r,t-1}$					**−0.012**	
					[−2.62]	
$\Delta y_{r,t-1}$					**0.084**	**−0.413**
					[3.01]	[−4.37]
$\Delta^2 p_{t-1}$	**0.493**			**−0.228**	**0.108**	**−0.610**
	[2.05]			[−2.18]	[2.06]	[−3.55]
Δor_{t-1}						
Δcf_{t-1}	**0.320**					
	[3.04]					
$ecm1_{t-1}$			**0.049**			**0.065**
			[3.70]			[10.6]
$ecm2_{t-1}$	**−0.909**		**1.296**			
	[−4.46]		[4.64]			
$ecm3_{t-1}$	**0.365**		**−0.764**		**−0.181**	**0.454**
	[3.02]		[−5.67]		[−11.1]	[8.37]
$dum9704_{p,t}$		**−0.262**			**0.052**	**−0.064**
		[−1.86]			[10.8]	[−3.76]
$dum9802_{t,t}$					**−0.026**	**0.030**
					[−7.21]	[2.60]
$dum9901_{t,t}$				**0.027**	**0.049**	
				[3.61]	[13.7]	
$dum0204_{p,t}$	**−0.111**		**−0.037**	**0.040**		
	[−4.36]		[−1.83]	[3.41]		
$dum0702_{t,t}$						**0.041**
						[3.71]

6.9.5 Conclusion

Table 6.156 shows the answers to the main hypotheses from the results of the econometric analysis. The introduction hypothesized that confidence and optimism are important factors for the development of stock prices. In addition, one objective of this contribution is to test whether or not abundant liquidity amplifies the upward

Table 6.155 Brazil quarterly data: the long-run impact matrix (t-values in brackets)

The long-run impact matrix, C						
	$\hat{\epsilon}_{m_r}$	$\hat{\epsilon}_{s_r}$	$\hat{\epsilon}_{y_r}$	$\hat{\epsilon}_{\Delta p}$	$\hat{\epsilon}_{or}$	$\hat{\epsilon}_{cf}$
m_r	4.023 [1.871]	0.097 [0.743]	0.759 [0.815]	2.879 [1.455]	−2.344 [−0.861]	−1.363 [−1.195]
s_r	−9.351 [−1.895]	**0.730** [2.436]	2.171 [1.016]	−7.855 [−1.730]	6.431 [1.029]	3.841 [1.467]
y_r	−0.181 [−0.705]	**0.071** [4.553]	**0.276** [2.484]	−0.221 [−0.937]	0.183 [0.563]	0.114 [0.839]
Δp	0.395 [1.243]	−0.007 [−0.340]	0.242 [1.759]	**1.138** [3.892]	−0.498 [−1.239]	−0.148 [−0.880]
or	**0.561** [2.008]	−0.021 [−1.263]	−0.038 [−0.315]	0.444 [1.728]	−0.363 [−1.026]	−0.215 [−1.449]
cf	**−1.050** [−2.008]	0.040 [1.263]	0.071 [0.315]	−0.831 [−1.728]	0.679 [1.026]	0.402 [1.449]

Table 6.156 Brazil quarterly data: results of main hypotheses

	Hypotheses/Questions	Result
H_1	Stock market behavior in Brazil shows strong persistence, i.e., shocks to the stock market have positive long-run effects on future developments	Yes
H_2	Long-run equilibria exist between stock prices and liquidity conditions	Yes
H_3	Liquidity conditions influence stock prices positively in the long run	Yes
H_4	Liquidity conditions influence stock prices positively in the short run	No
H_5	International capital flows have a positive long-run impact on the stock market behavior in Brazil	Yes
H_6	International capital flows have a positive short-run impact on the stock market behavior in Brazil	Yes
Q_1	Is the Banco Central do Brasil able to influence stock prices in the long run?	No
Q_2	Is the Banco Central do Brasil able to influence stock prices in the short run?	No

and downward spirals of stock prices. Both hypotheses can be accepted for Brazil. Brazil has a history of hyperinflation and devaluations of its currency. Nevertheless, investors from abroad continue to demand Brazilian bonds and invest heavily in the Brazilian stock market. This might be the main reason for the importance of international capital flows for stock market movements. Unlike financial markets in developed countries, the financial market in Brazil has less depth. As a result, international developments, as well as investments from abroad, play a more prominent role than for developed economies. In addition, these results confirm the findings for Australia and South Korea. Real money is more important in countries where the stock market contains a high share of commodity-related companies (Australia) and for Emerging Markets (South Korea). Brazil combines both characteristics.

The results also show that the central bank of Brazil was unable to influence stock market developments in the short and in the long run.

In addition, the above analysis elucidates a few other aspects of economic interest, mainly:

- Real money is exogenous in the long run but is reacts positively to lagged values of inflation, capital flows and itself in the short run.

- Real aggregate demand for goods is driven by advances in real money supply and reacts negatively to higher short-term interest rates. In addition, shocks to the stock market have a positive long-run effect on economic activity, which proves that the link between stocks and output, which resembles the second part of the transmission mechanism, holds.
- The analysis shows that inflation is long-run excludable from the system. In the short run it reacts positively to increases in real money and to deviations from the aggregate demand relation. The latter finding can be interpreted in the framework of the short-run Phillips curve, where inflation increases with excess aggregate demand for goods.
- The short-term interest rate builds a long-run equilibrium with capital flows. An economic reason is that liquidity inflows reduce the price for short-term borrowing. A closer look at the short-run dynamics offers an alternative explanation. It shows that the reactions to lagged values of the variables and to the ecm of capital flows and the short term interest rate are opposite. Consequently, the negative long-run relation could also result from simultaneous reactions to similar shocks but in opposite directions.
- Capital flows are attracted by positive stock market performance and react negatively to abundant domestic liquidity.

Chapter 7
Summary of Empirical Analysis and Policy Implications

7.1 Empirical Findings of Main Hypotheses: Cross-Country Comparisons

This section provides an aggregated overview of the results of the main hypotheses. Below is a brief overview. This is followed by a detailed discussion of the findings and an analysis of how these findings relate to other studies. Table 7.1 shows the empirical results of the hypotheses with respect to the main objectives of this contribution across the eight regions of the analysis. At first glance, one can derive seven main conclusions:

1. Stock market performance shows long-run persistence in all countries. It is long-run persistent because shocks to the stock market exhibit a significant positive long-run impact on future stock market developments. This suggests that investors' behavior patterns, such as herding and rational speculation, play a prominent role in stock market ups and downs.
2. Long-run equilibria between liquidity conditions and the stock market exist across most countries, often with real output as part of the cointegration relation. This indicates that the variables are subject to a common driving trend and are tied together. This confirms the procyclical interplay of stock market levels, real money and real output as hypothesized in the introduction and theoretically outlined in Sect. 3.2.3.2. However, it is notable that the stock market does not directly react to liquidity conditions in half of the countries. Instead, liquidity conditions and, especially, economic activity are often affected by stock market developments.
3. A positive long-run effect of real money on the stock market is only found in Australia, South Korea and Brazil. Positive short-run effects are present in the euro area analysis, in Australia and in South Korea.
4. Capital flows play an important role for stock market developments in Emerging Markets (South Korea and Brazil) but are irrelevant for the established and deep financial markets of industrialized countries.
5. According to the empirical analysis, the ability of central banks to influence stock markets appears to be very limited. Only the BoT is able to exercise a direct long

M. Wiedmann, *Money, Stock Prices and Central Banks*, Contributions to Economics,
DOI 10.1007/978-3-7908-2647-0_7, © Springer-Verlag Berlin Heidelberg 2011

Table 7.1 Findings from the empirical analysis – main hypotheses

	Hypothesis/question	US	Euro area	Japan	UK	Australia	South Korea	Thailand	Brazil
H_1	Market agents' behavior leads to strong persistence in stock market developments	**Yes**	**Yes**	**Yes**	**Yes**	**Yes**	**Yes**	**Yes**	**Yes**
H_2	Long-run equilibria exist between stock prices and liquidity conditions	**(Yes)**	**(Yes)**	**(Yes)**	**(Yes)**	**Yes**	**Yes**	No	**Yes**
H_3	Liquidity conditions influence stock prices positively in the long run	No	No	No	No	**Yes**	**Yes**	No	**Yes**
H_4	Liquidity conditions influence stock prices positively in the short run	No	**Yes**	No	No	**Yes**	**Yes**	No	No
H_5	International capital flows have a positive long-run impact on stock market behavior	No	No	No	No	No	**Yes**	No	**Yes**
H_6	International capital flows have a positive short-run impact on stock market behavior	No	No	No	No	No	**Yes**	No	**Yes**
Q_1	Are central banks able to influence stock prices in the long run?	No	No	No	No	No	No	**Yes**	No
Q_2	Are central banks able to influence stock prices in the short run?	No	No	No	No	**Yes**	No	**Yes**	No
	Stock market strongly exogenous	**Yes**	No	No	**Yes**	No	No	No	No

and short-run effect on stock markets. In addition, the RBoA is able to affect stock markets in the short run.

6. The stock market is strongly exogenous in the US and in the UK. This means that none of the included domestic macro variables has a significant effect on stock market performance, neither in the long nor in the short run. This raises the question of whether global forces are important for stock market developments in these countries.[1]
7. In general, the interplay between the domestic economic variables, which are included in the analyses, differs between the economies. While a few common relations can be established, most countries are subject to individual trends and behavior. This suggests that domestic developments should still play the major role in monetary policy analysis, notwithstanding the importance of global developments and international spillover effects.

A more sophisticated picture of the above findings can be obtained by investigating the respective hypotheses in more detail. Table 7.2 provides an extensive overview of the effects of the included macro variables on the stock market in the long and short run. It is constructed to cover all aspects of the empirical analysis, including long-run effects and equilibria (columns a to e) as well as short-run dynamics (columns f to j).

Columns a and b show which cumulated shocks to the variables have a significant positive or negative long-run impact on stock markets, respectively. Columns c to e provide information derived from the long-run cointegration relations, which can be interpreted as economic equilibria between the variables. Columns c and d show to which of the variables the stock market is related in the long run and dynamically adjusts in the short run. This is based on the cointegration relations depicted in column f. Column e, on the other hand, shows cointegration relations, in which the stock market variable is present but the stock market does not react to disequilibria.[2]

Short-run dynamics are divided into adjustment to the equilibrium errors of the cointegration relations and significant effects of lagged variables. More precisely, on the one hand, column f documents the cointegration relations, to which the stock market shows error-correction behavior. Columns g and h, on the other hand, demonstrate to which disequilibrium errors the stock market reacts without being part of the cointegration relation. Finally, columns i and j describe positive and negative significant effects of lagged values of the variables in first differences. These are derived by applying the full information maximum likelihood estimator

[1] For example, Bagliano and Morana (2009, p. 441) find strong evidence of international comovement among real stock returns. However, preliminary cointegration analysis between the included stock market indices and global forces did not suggest that a common trend exists, which drives stock markets across countries.

[2] To enhance readability of the table the coefficients to the parameters of the cointegration relations are left out. The idea here is to gain understanding of significant relationships between the variables. A more detailed view of the cointegration relations is presented in the respective country analyses.

Table 7.2 Impact of macro variables on stock market developments

	Long run					Short run				
	Common trends		Cointegration			Adjustment to cointegration relations			Effects of lagged variables	
	Positive impact of cumulated shocks to variable	Negative impact of cumulated shocks to variable	Positively related to	Negatively related to	Part of but not reacting to it	Equilibrium correcting to deviations from CI relation	Pushed positively by deviations from CI relation	Pushed negatively by deviations from CI relation	Positive significant effect	Negative significant effect
	a	*b*	*c*	*d*	*e*	*f*	*g*	*h*	*i*	*j*
USA	Real stocks				$y_r - m_r - s_r - trend$					
Euro area	Real stocks		Real output		$or - s_r$	$s_r - (y_r - trend)$		$b10 - m_r$		Inflation
Japan	Real stocks		Real output	Real money		$m_r + s_r + \Delta p$			Inflation	
	Real output		Short rate	Inflation		$y_r - s_r + or$				
UK	Real stocks				$or - s_r - y_r$ $cf + m_r - s_r$					
Australia	Real money	Real output	Real money	Real output		$m_r - s_r - y_r + trend$				Short rate
	Real stocks		Excess liquidity							
South Korea	Real money		Real money	Real output		$s_r - m_r + y_r - cf - trend$	$m_r - s_r - y_r + (b10 - or)$		Real money	
	Real stocks Capital flows		Capital flows							
Thailand	Real stocks	Short rate	Real output		$\Delta p - s_r + cf$	$y_r - sr - trend$		or	Real stocks	Short rate
Brazil	Real stocks		Real money			$s_r - m_r - cf$	$y_r - m_r + or - trend$	$or + cf$	Capital flows	
			Capital flows							

in simultaneous equation modeling. Dissecting the findings in Table 7.1 with the help of Table 7.2 adds insight to the above described main conclusions.

Stock Market Persistence

One objective of this contribution, as hypothezised in the introduction, is to test whether or not confidence and optimism of market participants are important factors for the development of stock prices. The empirical findings show that past stock market movements are more important for stock market developments in the long run than in the short run. While the persistent long-run effect is statistically valid in every country in the empirical analyses, significant short-run effects can only be identified in the analysis of Thailand. This suggests that confidence and optimism of market participants are very persistent and translate into self-reinforcing and trend-following behavior (see Sect. 3.2.3.2).[3] It also confirms that rational speculation can be reasonable even if markets diverge from fundamental values (Trichet 2005, p. 2). It is still lucrative to bet on rising prices, if stocks can be sold at a higher level before the market corrects. Thus, unaccountably high levels on the stock market can result from rational speculation and people's perception that they can leave the market before it changes course. This is in line with findings from Brunnermeier and Nagel (2004) on hedge fund behavior during the dot-com boom. The same logic and self-reinforcing effects apply in a downturn as a result of overconfidence turning into debilitating uncertainty. This empirical finding of long-run stock market movements coincides with the erratic short-run behavior of stock markets. This means that bearish developments in a bull market and bullish developments in a bear market are acceptable characteristics of the long-term persistence of stock markets. In addition, this empirical finding adds to the evidence of the stock market's susceptibility to bubbles and crises and the often observed phenomenon that upturns and downturns last longer than widely expected.[4] It is important to acknowledge that the finding that past shocks to the stock market have a long-run significant effect only serves as an indication of the significance of behavioral aspects for stock market developments. However, since variables that represent the level of confidence or optimism or the extent of rational speculation do not enter the analysis, this is not directly tested herein. Better measurements of rational speculation, herding and the level of confidence and optimism of investors are necessary to extend this analysis and gain further insight into their respective short and long-run importance for the stock market.[5]

---

[3] For a theoretical model that describes the persistence of stock market bubbles, see Abreu and Brunnermeier (2003, pp. 178–197).

[4] For example, Alan Greenspan's warning of 'irrational exuberance' in 1996 came four years before the end of the dot-com bubble, with the Dow trading at 6.500 points and perhaps too early to be taken seriously by market participants (Ito 2003, p. 549).

[5] The main focus in this contribution is on the interplay between money and stock prices and the role of central banks. Therefore, behavioral aspects of stock markets are only tested in so far as their role is inherently assumed in the long-run persistence of stock markets.

Long-Run Equilibria Between Liquidity Conditions and the Stock Market

Liquidity and real output developments appear to play a role for stock markets. The long-run equilibria between the stock market, liquidity and/or real output (depicted in columns *e* and *f* in Table 7.2) show that these variables are often subject to a common driving trend. One explanation for this could be the oft cited 'animal spirits', which might represent a common driving trend that affects all three variables (Mishkin 2001, p. 16; Keynes 1936, pp. 161–162). The three aspects of the economy have inherent procyclicality in common. This means that current developments amplify the existing trend. Sprinkel (1964, p. vii) describes this by saying that "[i]t is the basic thesis of this exposition that economic and stock price changes have a common 'cause', changes in money, which directly influence the demand for assets such as common stock as well as the demand for goods and services". This contribution, however, maintains that the direction of causality is not so clear. It does show, though, that the variables are tied together. However, the combination of variables that react to reestablish the long-run equilibrium differs across countries. This finding on the long-run relations is in line with previous cointegration analyses.[6] The results in Table 7.2 show that the stock market does not react to these long-run equilibria in the four most developed economies. This shows that while the hypothesis of existent long-run equilibria can be accepted, it is, nevertheless, an unsatisfying finding and contrary to the stock market behavior that was expected from the outset. This is confirmed by the findings of the next hypotheses.

Effects of Liquidity Conditions on Stock Market Developments

Another objective of this contribution is to test whether or not abundant liquidity amplifies the upward and downward spirals of stock prices, which is represented by hypotheses H_3 and H_4 in Table 7.1. A closer look at Table 7.2 reveals that real money does not affect stock prices in the four most developed financial markets, namely, the US, the euro area, Japan and the UK. This is contrary to the widespread belief that "developments in monetary aggregates and credit play an important role in the development of asset price boom episodes" (Trichet 2005, p. 5).[7] Real money developments do, however, play a role for Australia, and for two of the three developing countries included in the analysis, South Korea and Brazil.[8] As such, the results on the liquidity hypotheses are mixed. This coincides with the analysis of

[6] See, for example, Ratanapakorn and Sharma (2007), Kwon and Shin (1999) and Mukherjee and Naka (1995). However, since the cointegration space is not restricted in these analyses, their confirmation has to be interpreted with caution.

[7] One has to keep in mind, though, that the empirical findings herein are based on boom and non-boom conditions. The focus is on the total sample and the general relationship between money and stock prices instead of being restricted to boom and bust phases.

[8] South Korea is regarded as a developing country even though it is by now considered developed. However, since the analysis focuses on the last 25 years, it is fair to say that over that time period it was in transition from a developing to a developed country.

previous research on the subject, where no clear answer is provided. Instead, results differ between the analyses and across time (see Chap. 2). Economists still argue over whether or not a relationship exists, and if it does exist, how important it is and in which direction causality runs.[9]

Different country-specific reasons might help to explain why liquidity conditions affect the stock market in developed countries less than in developing economies. First, over the period under investigation, abundant liquidity might not have been predominantly channeled to the stock market but into real estate.[10] The real estate bubbles in the US, the UK and parts of Europe at the beginning of the 1990s and the first years of the new millennium exemplify this. This is further indicated by the analyses of Belke et al. (2008, pp. 416–420) and Giese and Tuxen (2007, pp. 22–24), who identify the positive impact of global liquidity on global real estate prices, but not on global stock markets. Even though their analyses are based on global liquidity, strong movements in housing prices might be the prime reason for the missing direct link between money and stocks in the US, the UK and the euro area.[11]

Rising house prices, however, would also serve as an argument for the Australian market, for which the positive effect of real money on stocks could be proven. This difference leads to a second argument. Liquidity conditions facilitated a major bull market in global commodities.[12] This, in turn, had a positive impact on the Australian stock market, which has a high share of commodity-related stocks.[13] Hence, this could explain the stronger role of real money for stock prices in Australia in comparison to the above mentioned developed countries.

Third, economic circumstances can explain the results of the Japanese analysis. The extended period of economic stagnation and difficulties in the banking sector after the burst of the stock market and real estate bubbles distort the relationship between money and stock prices. The BoJ's policy of 'quantitative easing' has not led to goods or asset price inflation because the BoJ was unable to alter the economic agents' expectations.[14] Deflationary expectations led people to save more and invest less in goods or stock markets. The positive short-term influence of inflation on the stock market is indicative of this (see column i in Table 7.2). While in other countries inflation is negative for the stock market, this is not true for Japan. The reason for this can be found in the different perception of inflation. After the bust

[9] Positive findings are stronger for analyses that exclusively focus on boom-bust episodes, such as Adalid and Detken (2007) and Bruggeman (2007). However, even in boom-bust analyses, it is difficult to prove the importance of real money developments for the stock market econometrically, see, for example, Pepper and Oliver (2006) and Congdon (2005).

[10] Since housing prices are not included in the analysis, this is not tested herein.

[11] Greiber and Setzer (2007, pp. 15–17) support this finding in their US analysis.

[12] This, again, is not tested herein since commodity price indices are not part of the system. For analyses, which identify the positive impact of global liquidity on global commodity prices, see, for example, Belke et al. (2009, pp. 21–23) and Browne and Cronin (2007, pp. 19–22, 30–31).

[13] Approximately 200 of the 500 companies listed in the All Ordinaries Share Price Index conduct business in commodity related areas (Standard & Poor's 2009).

[14] In addition, a portion of the created liquidity has been invested abroad (carry trades).

of the stock market and real estate bubbles, Japan's main concern was deflation rather than inflation. Hence, inflation was perceived as an indication of improving economic conditions and, consequently, helped to spur stock market advances.

Fourth, financial markets in the first four countries of the empirical analysis are so deep that additional money only plays a subordinate role for stock market developments as a whole. Consequently, liquidity conditions have a bigger impact on emerging countries' less developed financial markets. This is in line with the finding that capital flows are important for stock markets in developing economies, but do not play a role for the deep financial markets of developed countries. In addition, Gudmundsson (2008, p. 7) points out that the transmission mechanism alters with changes in domestic financial markets. When financial markets develop and mature, the effectiveness of policy instruments changes. In Gudmundsson's view the interest rate channel is weaker if bond markets are underdeveloped and short-term credit intermediation is dominated by banks. In this case, which is the case for the developing economies, changes in the money supply have a greater impact on the economy and potentially on the stock market.

While the above reasons appear to be plausible explanations of the missing direct effect of money on stock markets, the empirical findings herein are weaker than expected. The above reasoning is not tested herein and, hence, should not be confused with the results of the empirical analysis. The overarching hypothesis of this contribution it that liquidity conditions play a role for stock market developments. With the exception of Australia, this is not confirmed for developed economies. It has been proven, though, for emerging market countries.

Capital Flows and the Stock Market

A third objective is to understand how global liquidity conditions, in the form of capital flows, affect the stock market (hypotheses H_5 and H_6 in Table 7.1). The focus is on net capital flows because they represent the share of global liquidity that actually flows into a given country. A closer inspection of the importance of capital flows shows the following. The time series for capital flows is found to be stationary in half of the countries, namely the US, the euro area, Japan and Australia. This has the direct consequence that capital flows and the stock market can not form a long-run relation because cointegration can not exist between stationary and non-stationary variables. Nevertheless, cumulated shocks to capital flows could have a permanent effect on the stock market. In addition, the stock market could react to lagged values of capital flows in the short run. This is not the case for any of the developed countries. This is in line with previous findings, as stated by Warnock and Warnock (2006, p. 1): "evidence of any meaningful impact of capital flows on large economies is scarce."[15]

[15] This was one reason not to focus on the traditional measure of capital flows, which is the current account of the BoP, but to determine, which parts of capital flows affect monetary aggregates

Capital flows do play an important role in the long and short run for South Korea and Brazil. This confirms that external financing is more important for emerging economies than for established markets. Unlike financial markets in developed countries, the financial markets in South Korea and Brazil have less depth but are still very open. As a result, international developments as well as investments from abroad play a more prominent role. As such, it is reasonable for central banks in emerging economies to closely monitor international capital flows.

Ability of Central Banks to Influence Stock Markets

The final aim of this contribution is to test whether or not central banks are able to influence stock prices. The empirical findings show that the ability to influence the stock market is limited.[16] Table 7.1 documents that only in Australia and in Thailand are stock markets negatively influenced by the central bank policy rate. One could argue that the money market rate does not completely reflect central banks' actions. Instead the target rate should be used. However, both interest rates move closely together. In addition, the market-determined overnight rate has one main advantage. Monetary policy is closely followed and anticipated by economic agents. Consequently, central bank communication can affect markets without altering the short-term target rate. Often, changes in the market interest rate happen before the policy action. As a result, the important monetary impulse for the markets takes effect before the announcement. Consequently, the subsequent 'actual monetary policy shock' has no effect (Meltzer 1995, p. 50).

It is often argued that the 'surprise' element of monetary policy might be the part of monetary policy that is relevant for financial markets (Kuttner 2001, pp. 533–535). The surprise could be a result of central bank communication or of unexpected interest rate changes. This reasoning is confirmed by findings of Bernanke and Kuttner (2005, p. 1253). They conclude that for the US only monetary policy surprises can explain part of stock market variability. The econometric method applied herein only includes monetary policy expectations in so far as they can be explained by the other macro variables in the system. The unexpected part is left in the residuals of the overnight rate. Consequently, the residual $\epsilon_{i,t}$ is interpreted as an estimate of the unanticipated shock to variable x_i. The estimated long-run impact of these cumulated shocks is analyzed in the long-run impact matrix and is calculated from the estimates of the restricted VAR model. This shows that if the 'surprise' element of monetary policy were important for stock markets it would show up in the

(see Sect. 4.6.3). Unfortunately, this has not delivered much additional insight for the behavior of developed economies' stock markets.

[16] This finding confirms previous analyses of the effectiveness of changes in the policy rate. For an overview of the policy rate and house prices, see Kohn (2008, p. 5) and the mentioned articles. One should note, though, that most articles focus on the fed funds rate and the US market. This contribution, however, confirms this result for other markets as well.

analysis herein.[17] Nevertheless, no variable that represents expectations of market participants enters the analysis. Therefore, the critical value of the interest rate that leads market agents to alter their expectations of future developments is unclear. Consequently, whether certain threshold values of the policy rate that trigger stock market reversals exist can not be analyzed.

The disappointing finding concerning central banks' inability to influence stock markets should be kept in mind in the current policy debate over the question of how to deal with asset prices in monetary policy. To improve the reasoning in this discussion, it is crucial to, on the one hand, understand central banks' abilities to affect other macro variables and, on the other hand, to analyze, which variables affect monetary policy decisions. This is one focus of the next section. On the basis of this improved understanding of central banks' actions and their consequences, policy recommendations have been set forth in Sect. 7.2.2.

7.2 Policy Implications

7.2.1 Monetary Policy: Current State

Before outlining potential policy reorientation strategies in Sect. 7.2.2, here, the current state of monetary policy, according to the results of the empirical analysis, is described. Table 7.3 provides an overview of the empirical findings on hypotheses related to monetary policy.[18] The first section of the table focuses on hypotheses derived from monetary transmission mechanism theory. It shows that for four countries (Japan, UK, South Korea, and Brazil) the respective central banks are able to influence economic activity via the short-term interest rate. This means that the interest rate channel holds. In addition, Table 7.3 documents that real money has a positive significant effect on the level of economic activity in the US and in Thailand.[19] This is a strong indication for the US to revisit the importance of monetary aggregates, especially M3. Moreover, it provides an opportunity for these countries to try to influence the money supply to increase monetary policy effectiveness with respect to the business cycle.

However, for the US, real money is found to be weakly exogenous (see Table C.1 in Appendix C, which is constructed analog to Table 7.2). This does not mean that the Fed can not influence monetary developments, but it indicates that the fed

---

[17] In addition, since all variables are treated as endogenous from the outset, the analysis is not subject to an endogeneity bias (Ehrmann and Fratzscher 2004, p. 722). This is advantageous because interest rate changes are not considered purely exogenous.

[18] Confirmation of hypotheses in brackets, (yes), demonstrates that the effect is only significant in the short run.

[19] One explanation of the strong role of money in the US economy can be derived from the importance of the financial sector for US GDP. Up to the current financial crisis, abundant liquidity enabled banking sector revenues and profits to propel in comparison to other sectors.

Table 7.3 Findings from empirical analysis: Additional hypotheses

Hypothesis/question	US	Euro area	Japan	UK	Australia	South Korea	Thailand	Brazil
Monetary transmission mechanism								
– Direct link between interest rates and economic activity	No	No	**Yes**	**Yes**	No	**(Yes)**	No	**Yes**
– Direct link between real money and economic activity	**Yes**	No	No	No	No	No	**(Yes)**	No
– Link between monetary policy and equity prices	No	No	No	No	**Yes**	No	**Yes**	No
– Link between stock prices and economic activity	**Yes**	**Yes**	**Yes**	No	No	**(Yes)**	**Yes**	**Yes**
Procyclicality of money	**Yes**	**Yes**	No	**Yes**	**Yes**	**Yes**	**Yes**	No
Effects of stock market developments on money demand								
– Wealth effects	No	**(Yes)**	No	No	**Yes**	**Yes**	No	No
– Substitution effects	**(Yes)**	No	**Yes**	No	No	No	No	No
Positive impact of excess aggregate demand for goods on inflation in the short run	**Yes**	**Yes**	**Yes**	No	**Yes**	**Yes**	**Yes**	No

funds rate might not be the ideal tool. Alternatives could include changes in minimum reserve requirements and treasury bond transactions by the Fed. In doing so, the Fed has the potential to affect the money supply; however, these alternatives are not included in the empirical analysis. Table C.1 also shows that real money itself is the dominant factor for monetary developments in the short and in the long run across all countries except Japan. This confirms the inherent procyclicality of credit supply, which is best dealt with via regulatory measures and changes in minimum reserve requirements (Kohn 2008, p. 6). The impact of the stock market on money developments is ambiguous and is individual to the respective country (see Table 7.3).

Many theories of the monetary transmission mechanism, such as the asset price channel, the balance sheet channel and the liquidity effects view, are based on the initial relationship between interest rates and asset prices (Mishkin 1995, pp. 5–9). As shown in the last section and restated in Table 7.3, this link only holds for two countries. However, the second part of these transmission mechanism theories, namely the link between stock prices and economic activity, can be confirmed for six of the eight regions. This means that central banks, which focus on constant inflation rates along with economic growth, should pay attention to developments on the stock market. This is an important finding because some economists argue that the integration and globalization of financial markets along with financial deregulation and innovation complicates the relationship between financial markets and the real economy (Ferguson 2005, p. 1; Friedman 1993, pp. 186–189). The empirical findings in this contribution validate the relationship between stock prices and economic activity.[20]

Analog to the structure of Table 7.2, Table C.2 in Appendix C shows how economic activity is affected by the macro variables included in the system. As can be seen, on the one hand, real output is positively affected by past shocks to itself, by the stock market and by real money. On the other hand, the overnight rate, the bond rate and inflation have a negative impact on real output. In addition to the confirmation of the second part of the transmission mechanism theories, the extensive overview in Table C.2 allows for two main conclusions. First, it confirms the important procyclical interplay of liquidity conditions, the stock market and economic activity. Second, while some central banks are already able to influence economic activity, they could improve their effectiveness in the area of business cycle smoothing by paying more attention to stock market and money developments.

Most central banks focus primarily on the inflation rate and then on economic growth. Table C.3 in Appendix C shows the effects of the macro variables on inflation. Columns *f* to *h* show that inflation dynamically adjusts to excess aggregate demand for goods in the short run in all countries but the UK and Brazil (see also Table C.3). This conforms to the short-run Phillips curve explanation. Column *a*

[20] See also Reinhart and Rogoff (2009, pp. 4–10) and Helbling and Terrones (2003, pp. 69–70) for consequences of stock market and real estate busts for the real economy. See Mauro (2000, p. 3) for an overview of studies that document the positive relation between the stock market and economic activity.

shows that, in the long run, it is mostly shocks to real money and to the bond rate that exert a positive effect on inflation. While the former is as expected, the latter can be rationalized via higher financing costs that translate into higher prices. In addition, the positive effect of the bond rate may also indicate the importance of global factors for price developments. With capital being abundant and increasingly mobile, the long-term interest rate is subject to global forces and, in turn, affects the inflation rate. Table C.3 also shows that the short-term interest rate only has a significant negative effect on inflation in the UK and in Thailand. Taken together, the findings of the empirical analysis demonstrate the importance of monetary, financial and real developments for central bank policy making.

The empirical findings show that most central banks are more successful in influencing economic activity as compared to inflation or the stock market. One could argue that over the last 25 years price developments have constantly been under pressure from global competition, sinking long-term yields and global labor supply shocks (Bini Smaghi 2007, p. 3). In addition, the independence of central banks improved, which helped to stabilize inflation expectations on a low level. As a result, central bankers did not have to use their policy instruments as much to keep inflation under control. Instead, circumstances permitted them to pay more attention to the business cycle. If the business cycle was the 'real' objective, they were rather successful because, up until the financial crisis, output growth was more stable than ever before. However, by following this goal, they might have helped to exacerbate asset price ups and downs with delayed consequences for the real economy. Additionally, by facilitating low inflation rates and reduced output volatility they might have increased the vulnerability of financial markets to crises because risk-perception decreased and leverage rose, encouraging investors to place ever larger bets.

To improve the understanding of the likeliness of this scenario, one must gain further insight into the respective importance of economic variables for monetary policy and into the drivers of monetary policy decisions. Table C.4 in Appendix C shows how the overnight rate is affected by the macro variables. Looking at positive long-run effects (columns a and c), one can see that the stock market and/or real output affect the policy rate in all developed economies (US, euro area, UK, Australia) aside from Japan. Japan's policy rate is affected by inflation in the long run. A different picture arises for the developing countries. The main factors for the policy rate in South Korea and Brazil are real money in the long run and inflation in the short run. This fits perfectly with the above outlined scenario. Since inflation is higher and central bank credibility is lower in emerging economies the main objective of the central bank is to fight inflation. To do so, central bankers monitor monetary developments and react to higher real money because of a potential expected inflation effect and higher future inflation. In the short run they initiate direct measures as a consequence of higher actual inflation.

The main conclusions drawn from this discussion are that monetary policy objectives can be widened in conjunction with the state of development of the economy as a whole and with institutional conditions, such as central bank independence and credibility. Central bankers in industrialized economies already concentrate more on developments in real output and the stock market than inflation. This is according to the empirical analysis of which variables affect the overnight rate and is also suspected by academics (Knight 2006, p. 2). In addition, the empirical findings establish that changes in the overnight rate are most effective in influencing real economic activity. The effects on inflation are very limited. This leads to the assumption that central banks can keep inflation in check by affecting expectations via communication but not through the setting of the policy rate.[21] This could be a result of the following circumstances:

- Well-anchored inflation expectations due to excellent central bank reputation and increasing central bank independence.[22]
- Inflation-depressing global forces, such as enhanced global competition, decreasing and low long-term interest rates and ample global labor supply.

In addition to allowing for a focus on price developments, these circumstances endow central bankers with more flexibility to exert influence on economic conditions. Policy recommendations are discussed in the next section.

7.2.2 Monetary Policy and Asset Prices: Recommendations

7.2.2.1 Monetary Policy Reorientation: A Case for a Shift Towards Increased Importance of Asset Prices

Historically, monetary policy strategy was refocused after important misalignments of macro variables. For example, high inflation periods in the 1970s led to increased importance of monetary aggregates. Unstable money demand functions in the 1980s and 1990s led many central banks to ignore monetary aggregates. Instead, they focused on 'official' or 'unofficial' inflation targeting and applied a short-term interest rate as the preferred monetary policy instrument. This historical pattern of central bank behavior is a strong argument in favor of refocusing monetary policy strategy, especially in the wake of the global financial crisis.

This strategy reorientation could include a shift of central banks' focus towards asset prices along with consumer prices. A direct targeting of asset prices is, so far, unprecedented. However, recent history has confirmed that financial and real estate markets are prone to bubbles, which results in reduced efficiency of capital markets and financial intermediation and potentially devastating consequences for the real economy after the burst of the bubble. The current crisis supports proponents of a

[21] See article in the Wall Street Journal (WSJ) on Cleveland Fed Inflation Model that predicts low inflation rates 30 years into the future (WSJ 2009, p. 1). This is one example of anchoring inflation expectations without changing the policy rate.

[22] See also Blanchard and Riggi (2009, pp. 18–19) for an analysis on changes in the macroeconomic effects of oil prices. They find that the lower importance of oil prices for economic activity is mainly due to vanishing wage indexation and credible monetary policy.

'leaning against the wind'-policy; tightening monetary policy more than required from inflationary expectations could help to reduce the costs of an asset price bust, which might include increased inflation variability and reduced real growth (Adalid and Detken 2007, p. 7).[23] Nevertheless, the discussion on whether or not central banks should use monetary policy to fight financial imbalances is still ongoing.[24] Bernanke and Gertler (1999, p. 19), who are among the opponents of a 'leaning against the wind'-strategy,[25] point out that asset price fluctuations should only be of concern to central bankers if two conditions are satisfied. The first is the subjection of asset price volatility to non-fundamental factors. The second prerequisite is that asset price developments, which are unrelated to fundamental conditions, have a significant impact on other parts of the economy, mainly real output. Where these conditions are met, asset price volatility can result in economic instability and, hence, should be a cause for concern and influence monetary policy decisions.

The empirical findings in this contribution show that the two conditions are met and, consequently, that superior monetary policy is heedful of asset prices. First, the analysis shows that the stock market is strongly persistent (see Table 7.1 in Sect. 7.1). This means that shocks to the stock market have a positive significant long-run effect on the stock market. This suggests that confidence and optimism of market participants are very persistent and translate into self-reinforcing and trend-following behavior.[26] It also indicates that the stock market is prone to bubbles. Second, the empirical analysis shows the importance of stock market movements for developments in real economic activity. Table 7.3 in Sect. 7.2.1 summarizes that a significant positive link between stock prices and economic activity exists in all analyzed countries except the UK and Australia. Hence, pronounced stock market downturns can lead to severe economic contraction.

There are two noteworthy limitations. On the one hand, stock market persistence can only serve as an indication of the importance of non-fundamental movements due to 'animal spirits', herding or (ir-)rational speculation. It does not prove the existence of these behavioral aspects since they are not directly measured and not part of the empirical analysis. More research on potential measurement alternatives, their behavior over time and their influence on the stock market is necessary. On the

[23] 'Leaning against the wind' does not include direct targeting of asset prices but the central bank's willingness to tighten monetary policy at the margin. The effect of this tightening should slow down asset price growth, which is regarded as excessive and, thereby, decrease the chances of future financial instability and depressed growth (Assenmacher-Wesche and Gerlach 2008, p. 1). See also ECB (2005a, pp. 56–59) for a discussion on the bandwidth of potential monetary policy responses to asset price bubbles.

[24] For extensive discussions on the question of whether or not central banks should pay attention to asset prices, the reader is referred to, for example, Cecchetti et al. (2000), Bernanke and Gertler (1999), Smets (1997) and Goodhart (1995), who share different views on this question. In addition, Detken and Smets (2004, pp. 23–30) present a very objective literature overview of theoretical aspects of the ideal policy response to asset price booms and busts.

[25] See also Bernanke (2002).

[26] As theoretically outlined in Sect. 3.2.3.2, market psychology and irrational as well as rational behavior on the part of investors can lead to non-fundamental movements of stock markets.

other hand, Bernanke and Gertler's second prerequisite only focuses on the effect of non-fundamental movements in asset prices on the real economy. The analysis herein, however, establishes the relationship between movements in stock prices and real economic activity, independent of whether or not the price movement is based on fundamentals. It is difficult to imagine, though, that anyone could ever establish a clear division between fundamental and non-fundamental movements (ECB 2005a, p. 48). As such, the second limitation appears to be less important than the first.

Independent of the above mentioned shortcomings, if one assumes that central bankers' objectives, beyond inflation, are stable real output growth and financial stability, then the two empirical findings taken together are a strong case for the inclusion of asset prices in monetary policy making. In conclusion, a forward-looking central bank, which wants to achieve the three above mentioned goals of monetary policy, should take asset prices more prominently into account.

Of course, opponents of an asset price factor in monetary policy might point out that central banks have the option of dealing with asset price busts without targeting misalignments during upturns. This is comparable to the 'Greenspan-Put', which refers to Alan Greenspan's response to asset price bubbles during his reign as Fed Chairman. He believed that deviations from fundamental levels could not be identified a priori. Hence, bubbles can only be recognized as such after the bust. This led him to the conclusion that they are best dealt with after bursting by strongly loosening monetary policy to reduce the intensity of the subsequent recession.[27] At first glance this strategy seems favorable all around. Investors are happy that the central bank does not interfere with rising stock prices because they enjoy the wealth effects. Rising stock prices also support economic growth,[28] which, in turn, reduces unemployment. Unfortunately, the difficulty inherent with this strategy is a result of the lopsided dealing with asset price movements. Since the liquidity that is pumped into the system is not taken out of the system once economic circumstances improve, the additional liquidity is the basis for the next bubble. Although this is not part of the empirical analysis, stylized facts of the last 20 years indicate this. The 1987 stock market crash was followed by a housing boom-bust cycle in the beginning of the 1990s. The dot-com boom had a short setback in 1998 due to the collapse of the LTCM hedge fund before peaking in 2001. The biggest crisis of the last 20 years

---

[27] Greenspan (2002, p. 3) points to two problems which make 'pricking' bubbles particularly difficult. First, one must distinguish between a bubble and a fundamentally justified increase in prices. Second is the bluntness of monetary policy instruments. He considers interest rates to be too inaccurate to conquer bubbles without endangering the economy. On the one hand, if the rise in rates is too small, monetary policy may have no effect, or contrary effects. For example, economic agents may think the central bank has full control and, thus, be encouraged in their investing behavior. On the other hand, if the increase is too large, the economy may not face a bubble, but may dive directly into a recession instead. Therefore, in his opinion, it is wiser to wait until bubbles burst and to fight the aftereffects with monetary easing. This attitude was also elucidated in his mid 1999 congressional testimony, in which he stated that the policymakers duty is "to mitigate the fallout when it occurs and, hopefully, ease the transition to the next expansion" (Greenspan 1999, p. 7).

[28] See Sect. 5.2.2 for theoretical reasons, which are confirmed by the findings from the empirical analysis.

is the global financial crisis that started in 2007. The one thing that all events have in common is the tremendous support by the Fed following the onset of crises, be it in the form of extremely loose monetary policy or in organizing safety packages for LTCM. The message is the same: "don't worry investor, enjoy market upturns because we will take care of it if things get ugly." Central bank support of crippled stock markets leads to increases in moral hazard and encourages risk-taking among investors and banks (The Economist 2007, p. 6; Issing 2004, p. 2). Thereby, central banks sow the seeds of the next boom-bust episode.

In addition, the lop-sided dealing with asset bubbles in the past has required ever stronger monetary policy responses. To fight the dot-com bust, the Fed reduced interest rates to historically low levels last seen in the 1960s. The response to the current global financial crisis led to a policy rate approaching zero, unprecedented in Fed history. All this serves as an indication that the lopsided treatment of asset price ups and downs increases financial instability. This, however, does not mean that the strong response to crises is bad in itself. It does demonstrate, though, that earlier actions, during the boom phase, could lead to more favorable outcomes.

If central banks addressed asset prices, one of the biggest challenges would be to legitimize their actions to the public. Central bankers would have to justify monetary tightening in a phase of booming asset prices as well as low and stable consumer goods inflation. Through their actions they would slow down economic growth and erode prosperity (Borio and Lowe 2003, p. 261). Booms are popular. Therefore, at the time of central bank involvement, public understanding would be limited and communication would prove difficult (Caruana 2003, p. 540). This argument points to the difficulties in acting against asset price misalignments. However, it does not state that the idea of tackling them is intrinsically bad.

Instead, the difficulties trace back to the reputation of central bank employees and their own utility functions. The positive reputation that they have built up by providing low and stable inflation and successfully anchoring inflation expectations, might suffer through drastic responses to rising asset prices. Therefore, the central bank would have to explain the reasoning behind its actions to the public. However, explaining asset price bubbles and their consequences to the general public might prove difficult. Rather than giving such an explanation late in the bubble, it should be stated early on that the purpose of monetary policy is to help ensure economic and financial stability (Mussa 2003, p. 50). Of course, the border between contributing to macroeconomic stability and being the only one responsible for it is narrow. It is important not to push central banks into that position. On the other hand, "central banks will simply have to face up to the fact that their fundamental task is not to maximize their popularity" (Mussa 2003, p. 50). In addition, the aftermath of the global financial crisis can be used to create greater central bank transparency of their objectives and potential actions. Central bankers around the globe have the unique opportunity to increase awareness of the general public that central banks also focus on financial stability, which might include actions against asset price exaggerations. The understanding of the general public might have never been better than in the wake of the global financial crisis.

Speeches of leading central bankers and economists at international organizations confirm the heightened interest in asset price movements. Nevertheless, they remain cautious about how and whether to deal with asset price volatility.[29]

However, the focus in this contribution, is not only to lead the debate on whether or not asset prices should be included in monetary policy making, but also to bring this discussion to the next level – understanding whether or not central banks actually have the ability to fight asset price exaggerations (Kohn 2008, pp. 4–6). Put in a different way: do policy-controlled instruments have stable effects on asset prices? The next section outlines options that central banks have to deal with asset price booms.

7.2.2.2 Options Central Banks have to Influence Asset Prices

The previous section made the case that ideal monetary policy takes asset prices into account and, if need be, tries to influence them. The empirical analysis across the eight countries finds that only the Australian and Thai central banks are able to affect stock prices via changes in the short-term interest rate.[30] If changes in the central bank policy rate do not have a clear effect, the follow-up question is then: what other options do central bankers have to influence the stock market? The findings from the empirical analysis, taken together with findings of other authors, suggest that central banks in developed and developing economies should focus on mainly two things: first, the extent of money and credit growth and, second, credible asset price-related communication strategies. In addition, central bankers in emerging economies should also try to influence the extent of capital flows.

Money and Credit

The empirical analysis shows that stock markets in Australia, South Korea and Brazil are directly affected by the developments of real money (see Table 7.1 in Sect. 7.1). In addition, cointegration between real money, real output and the stock market demonstrates that stable long-run relations exist across most countries. This means that they are pushed by one common trend and are 'bound'. This might be a result of the inherent procyclicality of the three variables and the 'animal spirits', which drive all three variables. However, the stock market does not react to this

---

[29] See, for example, Kohn (2008), Stark (2007), Knight (2006), Trichet (2005), Ferguson (2005) and Issing (2004). In addition, Mishkin (2009, p. 1) acknowledges in a recent Financial Times article that credit boom bubbles should be targeted by central banks. All other asset price bubbles, however, should not. His reasoning is based on the devastating consequences of a credit boom bust compared to the milder repercussions of asset boom busts.

[30] In addition, it is widely assumed that increases in the policy rate must be so high as to have a significant effect on asset prices that this might lead to unproportionally high costs for the real economy (ECB 2005a, p. 57; Issing 2004, p. 2).

cointegration relation in the four most industrialized countries, namely, the US, the euro area, Japan and the UK. One potential explanation for the non-existent direct effect of money on stocks is that excess liquidity has not been invested in stocks but in housing, leading to a real estate boom at the beginning of the 1990s and culminating in the global housing boom in the first years of the new millennium. However, since house prices are not included in the empirical analysis, this is not tested herein. Nevertheless, the analysis by Greiber and Setzer (2007, pp. 15–17), which focuses on the US as well as analyses focusing on global conditions by Belke et al. (2008, pp. 416–420) and Giese and Tuxen (2007, pp. 22–24), support this point.

If it is assumed that money and credit developments play a central role in the formation of asset price exaggerations,[31] then central banks have two main options to reduce asset price misalignments: first, altering minimum reserve requirements and, second, changing regulations. Increasing minimum reserve requirements is comparable to a tax on financial intermediation, which can reduce credit growth without altering the short-term interest rate (see also Sect. 4.4.1). This helps to reduce leverage in the system, thereby, increasing financial stability.[32] In most countries, regulations can not be directly changed by central bank officials. However, they can lead the discussion and try to exert pressure on regulatory offices to adapt regulations to increase financial stability. The empirical analysis shows that one main driver of financial instability is the inherent procyclicality, which is apparent with developments in money supply. The reason behind this is that banks tend to decrease their risk weighting in an upturn and, thus, increase their borrowing. The reverse is true for downturns. One solution is to introduce capital requirements that act as buffers over the business cycle (Moreno 2003, p. 525; IMF 2000, p. 106). Increasing capital requirements during economic upturns and decreasing them during downturns flattens credit lending.[33] Regulation has the potential to be a more effective tool than the policy rate (Kohn 2008, p. 6; Trichet 2005, p. 8).

The two measures differ in how quickly they take effect. While implementing regulatory change requires time-consuming efforts, the consequences of altering minimum reserve requirements are immediate. This shows that the two instruments need to be used together, minimum reserve requirements for the short-term perspective and financial regulation to ensure long-term soundness of the system.

---

[31] Issing (2004, p. 2) points out that most asset price booms have been accompanied "by strong money and/or credit growth". In addition, Reinhart and Rogoff (2008, pp. 24–33) find that costly banking crises are usually preceded by large capital inflows, credit booms and asset price booms.

[32] In addition, high leverage levels can be associated with costlier boom-bust phases (Trichet 2005, p. 4). Consequently, lower leverage levels may help to lower the costs of a potential post-boom recession.

[33] Schwartz (2002, p. 11) presents flexible capital requirements as a policy alternative for the BoJ in the 1980s. In her opinion, capital requirements that change with the ratio of a loan category to total loan portfolio could have led to healthier bank balance sheets and a sounder financial system. If ratios rise too high, banks would have to liquidate assets to keep the ratio in line with the capital requirements. As a result, the portfolios of Japanese banks would not have been as biased and as vulnerable to the subsequent downturn.

One drawback is that higher regulation might lead to an increase in less regulated non-bank financial institutions (Kent and Lowe 1997, p. 21). Consequently, counter-cyclical regulation must be imposed on all parts of the financial system.[34]

Communication and Credibility

The empirical analysis indicates that stock markets are prone to bubbles and that behavioral aspects, such as rational speculation and herding, play a key role (see Sect. 7.1). This is confirmed by a study by Brunnermeier and Nagel (2004), who analyze hedge fund behavior during the dot-com bubble. Their findings show that it is profitable to ride a bubble even if investors are aware of the non-fundamental increases. Consequently, even if a bubble is recognized, it does not mean that rational investors will instantly try to prick it. Instead, these investors ride the bubble or wait at the sidelines until a majority is formed that is ready to bring stock prices back to fundamental values. Brunnermeier and Nagel's argument is based on the observation that rational investors can not coordinate to bet against the bubble. If they did, they could make big profits. However, since coordination is not feasible, it is too risky for the individual investor to bet against (non-)fundamental increases in prices.

Rising asset prices may reflect two things. They may either be justified by fundamentals or they may represent a market exaggeration. The task for any economic agent is to find out which of the two cases describes a better assessment of the current situation. From this reasoning it can be concluded that better information for the general public hampers the formation and sustainability of bubbles (Kroszner 2003, p. 8). Transparency increases would help to reduce the information asymmetry and insecurity of economic circumstances.[35] Investors who assume that other market participants have superior information tend to follow their lead and intensify market movements through their behavior. Greater transparency would help to reduce herding behavior (Trichet 2003, p. 20). It has to be noted, though, that central bank communication with respect to asset price misalignments can be very difficult. The level of sophistication of central banks' audiences differs and the mentioning

[34] Other regulatory measures could be helpful to stabilize financial markets but are beyond the scope of this contribution. Münchau (2009, p. 1) suggests focusing on potential causes of bubbles, such as the size of the financial sector, the too-big-to-fail issue and bankers' extreme tendency to load on risk.

[35] In addition, transparency also has the potential to reduce stock price volatility. This is based on the assumption that monetary policy is not predictable and transparent enough for investors to form consistent long-run expectations. Consequently, stock prices fluctuate more than necessary. Stock price volatility could be reduced if the central bank reduced uncertainty of subsequent policy rate changes because the 'option value of waiting' of portfolio and investment decisions would be reduced (Belke and Polleit 2006, p. 336).

of the word ‘bubble’ could lead to unpredictable outcomes (Filardo 2004, p. 17). As such, any communication has to be worded cautiously. This, however, is true for all aspects of central bank communication, independent of the focus, be it inflation, the economy, wages or asset prices.

Even if central banks do not have superior information in comparison to market participants, they can send credible signals to the market via communication. This might lead market participants to reassess their views on current price developments. Analog to the theoretical model developed in Abreu and Brunnermeier (2003, pp. 178–197), the drastically simplified line of actions and effects could look as follows:

1. Some rational market participants realize that stock prices are deviating from fundamental values. Whereas the ‘efficient market hypothesis’ claims that rational investors, who identify price misalignments, would sell the asset short in order to make a profit, it is assumed here, that investors know that they alone can not initiate a ‘rational’ correction. Instead, it is profitable to ride the bubble and observe potential exit signs closely. The main reason for the persistence of stock market developments is that investors can not coordinate their actions. As such, they wait for signals that suggest that a critical number of investors has recognized the bubble and are prepared to sell.
2. A central bank reaction in the form of communication (or backed by actions in the policy rate or minimum reserve requirements) can influence the balance between market participants that are on the buy side and on the sell side. It is important that the central bank sends a credible signal that shows that it is willing to react to market misalignments if need be. Consequently, investors’ expectations can be altered and they are able to realize the limited upside potential and potential downward threats of their investments.
3. If the shift to the sell side is big enough, the market will correct back to fundamental levels and the central bank achieves the desired outcome without having to raise interest rates to undesired levels, which would adversely affect output growth.

It is important, here, to stress the credibility of central bank communication. As mentioned above, the public does not perceive fighting asset price booms as a good thing. If central bankers fought asset price booms their personal reputation would suffer. The problem is that this would lead market participants to expect that central bankers will not follow through on their warnings. Hence, to effectively strengthen the rational sellers in a developing non-fundamental boom phase the central bank would have to take action beyond communication, for example, in the form of changes in interest rates or minimum reserve requirements. If their communication is perceived as credible, central banks increase transparency and alter expectations of market participants regarding future stock market movements without adverse effects on economic activity related to interest rate increases.

Capital Flows

The empirical analysis shows that capital flows do not play a role for the deep financial markets of developed economies. However, the picture is different for emerging economies. There, capital flows are one major factor that influences stock market developments in the short and in the long run (see Table 7.1 in Sect. 7.1). Previous financial crisis in Latin America, Asia and Eastern Europe have shown the susceptibility of financial stability to sudden capital flow reversals. The question remains, which options do central banks have to avoid financial instability stemming from excessive capital inflows or outflows. Hesitancy over containing capital flows stems from the fact that capital flows come with many benefits for borrowers and lenders, such as improved resource allocation, the ability to smooth consumption over time and increased opportunities to manage and diversify risks. While consensus exists that strict capital controls are unfavorable, weaker measures that have the potential to disrupt capital flows are still open for discussion (Mishkin 1999, p. 722).

In October 2009, in order to slow the appreciation of the Brazil real, Brazil imposed a 2% tax on capital inflows invested in equities and fixed income (Wheatley 2009, p. 1). The idea is to target volatile portfolio flows but leave foreign direct investment in the productive economy tax free. As a result, Brazil is to be able to reap the benefits of capital flows and to reduce speculative short-term portfolio capital flows, which have often been subject to rapid reversals in the past (Singh and Weisse 1998, p. 618).

Weaker forms of capital flow manipulation include changes in the reserve requirements on foreign currency liabilities compared to liabilities in national currency. Bolder measures include negative interest rates on domestic currency deposits by foreigners. This measure was taken by the Swiss central bank in 1972 and again from 1977 to 1979 to reduce massive capital inflows, which led to a strong appreciation of the Swiss franc (Pollock 2009, p. 1–2).

While it is clear that more research is necessary to determine the advantages and disadvantages of temporary measures of capital controls, it is also clear that central bankers in emerging economies can not afford to ignore capital flows. The findings of the empirical analysis show that capital flows are a major determinant of stock prices and, as such, need to be taken into account in monetary policy.

Chapter 8
Concluding Remarks

This contribution applies the CVAR model to analyze the long-run behavior and short-run dynamics of stock markets across five developed and three emerging economies. The governing thought is that liquidity conditions play an important role for stock market developments. Liquidity conditions enter the analysis from three angles: in the form of a broad monetary aggregate, the interbank overnight rate and net capital flows, which represent the share of global liquidity that arrives in the respective country. A second objective is to understand whether central banks are able to influence the stock market.

The empirical findings demonstrate that the widely assumed impact of real money developments on stock prices in developed economies is very limited. Aside from Australia, no significant effects can be identified. A potential reason for the non-existent effect on stock prices could be that the abundant liquidity is being directed into real estate and commodities. However, since these assets are not part of the empirical analysis, more research on liquidity is necessary to fully understand the consequences of rapid money growth.

The empirical analysis establishes, however, that real money, real output and the stock market form a stationary cointegration relation in most countries. This demonstrates that these variables are driven by a common trend. The forces behind this common trend must be analyzed further. The starting hypothesis should be that the common trend is based on 'animal spirits' of market agents, which increase the inherent procyclicality of all three variables. This is further indicated by the self-reinforcing effects of stock price developments, which are present in the data across all countries because shocks to the stock market have a significant long-run impact on future stock prices. These self-reinforcing effects could be the result of behavioral effects, such as, among others, over-confidence, rational speculation or herding. However, since these variables do not enter the empirical analysis, the empirical findings serve only as an indication and additional research is required to further prove the importance of investors' rational and irrational behavior for stock market developments.

The findings of the empirical analysis differ for developing countries. Here, liquidity conditions play a significant role for stock market behavior. Both real money and capital flows have a significant positive short and long-run impact on stock

M. Wiedmann, *Money, Stock Prices and Central Banks*, Contributions to Economics, DOI 10.1007/978-3-7908-2647-0_8, © Springer-Verlag Berlin Heidelberg 2011

prices in South Korea and Brazil. In addition, the short-term interest rate influences the stock market negatively in Thailand.

The ability of central banks to affect stock prices through changes in the policy rate is very limited. While this is in line with previous findings, it raises two follow-up questions, which have not yet been answered: first, if the policy rate has no significant effect on equity valuations, what does this mean for our current understanding of transmission mechanism theories that incorporate equity prices.[1] Second, which monetary policy instruments have a superior ability to affect stock prices in a desired way? It is especially crucial to understand this because the findings of the empirical analysis show that stock price developments have a significant effect on the real economy. Consequently, this contribution argues that central bankers should pay more attention to asset price developments and consider alternative instruments to influence stock prices, such as changes in the minimum reserve requirement or active communication. While the difficulty of communicating asset price-based policy changes to the public has been recognized, the timing, right in the aftermath of the global financial crisis, could not be better. The chances for investors and the general public to understand might never be higher than now.

The empirical findings demonstrate the need for future research across several dimensions. These research topics can best be described along the three main objectives of this contribution: first, to improve the understanding of stock market behavior, second, to analyze the consequences of abundant liquidity in developed economies, since it is not the main driving force of stock markets and, third, options and effects of monetary policy.

According to the findings herein, future research on stock markets should focus on:

- The importance of behavioral aspects, such as variables that measure ‘animal spirits’, ‘optimism’, ‘confidence’, ‘trust’ or the level of speculation. Obviously, one challenge here is to identify measures that capture these soft aspects of the economy. Aside from survey-based data series that capture business and consumer sentiment, one could imagine including risk measurements such as the ‘itraxx crossover’ index to capture market sentiment.[2] Additionally, data on internet searches might be used to improve measures of investors’ behavior (The Economist 2009a, p. 1). This also has the advantage that data becomes available earlier than other macro data and, hence, is more consistent with data on stock prices.
- The finding that the stock market is strongly exogenous in the analysis of the US and the UK indicate that national measures might not be enough to explain stock market developments. Instead, in today’s globalized world, it could be that global

[1] Many theories of the monetary transmission mechanism, such as the asset price channel, the balance sheet channel and the liquidity effects view, are based on the initial relationship between interest rates and asset prices (Mishkin 1995, pp. 5–9).

[2] For an example of a constructed measure of ‘uncertainty’, see Greiber and Lemke (2005, pp. 5–6, 10–13).

factors are important for national stock market developments. This is related to the question of whether or not stock market developments across countries are interrelated. If that was the case, then global common trends could be responsible for stock market developments. Further research in this direction might also shed light on the question of spillover effects between economies, which is important to develop coordination policies.

Second, future research on liquidity conditions should include:

- Similar cointegration analyses on a country level but including real estate prices, commodity prices and/or aggregated asset price time series in order to extend the analysis herein. This would enable a better understanding of the recipients of liquidity and the consequences for stability and inflation. In addition, the analysis could be used to determine whether other asset prices are as important for the real economy as stock prices.
- In addition, since capital flows turned out not to play a role for the financial markets of developed economies, an alternative would be to incorporate global liquidity measures in the analysis to analyze how global conditions affect domestic macro variables.
- The analysis herein has also shown that it proved difficult to establish valid long-run money demand relations, which help to determine the level of excess liquidity in the system. An approach for further research could be to focus on higher frequency data and shorter time periods. This would ensure sufficient data points and, at the same time, would allow for structural breaks in money demand.

Last, future research on central bank policy should build on the following arguments:

- Since stock market developments are important for economic activity but monetary policy, in the form changes in the policy rate, has a very limited effect on stock prices, the effects of alternative central bank instruments need to be analyzed. Namely, consequences of altering the level of minimum reserve requirements and active, asset price-related information need to be better understood. The main focus of the research should be laid on the question of how central banks' actions affect asset prices as compared to economic activity. This enables central bankers to better weigh potential costs and benefits of early action against asset price misalignments.
- Since asset prices are assumed to be interest-rate sensitive, they are an important component of some transmission mechanism theories. If this transmission channel is disrupted, as is indicated by the empirical findings, the "reliability and the effectiveness of policy are degraded. In the worst case, policy's room for maneuver may be narrowed or even severely compromised, and risks of a policy blunder are heightened" (Ferguson 2005, p. 2). The findings show that the postulated connections in transmission mechanism theories between policy rate changes and the stock market are non-existent or weak. While the second part of the theory, to wit, the connection between equity prices and the economy, holds, too little is known about the first part. This demonstrates the need for further analyses of transmission mechanism theories that incorporate asset prices.

- Since the variability of the empirical results across countries is rather high, this indicates the need for central banks to focus on their respective regional developments. Consequently, more research is needed on a country basis, especially outside the US and the euro area. This is not to say that central banks should not pay attention to global developments. On the contrary, they should try to determine, which global factors influence national variables, which, in turn, also affect the price level, economic growth and financial stability.

At the moment, it looks like central bankers around the world are not able to pursue two important goals at the same time, namely to control goods price inflation and asset price volatility. However, since both are prerequisites for financial stability and stable output growth, it is time to concentrate research on the question of how both objectives can be achieved.

Appendix A
Details on the Calculation of the Capital Flows Time Series

The time series representing capital flows are based on the methodology of the 'monetary presentation of the balance of payments' as described in Sect. 4.6.3.2.[1] The underlying data series used to calculate the 'capital flows' time series are derived from the 'Analytic Presentation' and the 'Standard Presentation' of the 'Country Tables View' section of the IMF BoP Statistics. Table A.1 provides an overview of how the time series are calculated, albeit small differences can be found for the individual countries as a result of data reporting. The table shows detailed calculation steps and sources of subseries for the example of Japan with data from Q1 to Q3 of 2008.[2] As outlined in Sect. 4.6.3.2, the basic idea is to split transactions into bank and non-bank transactions. In the BoP data the non-bank resident sector is comprised of the positions 'general government' and 'other sectors', which includes other financial intermediaries, non-financial companies and households (IMF 1993, pp. 37–50).[3]

The sign conventions reflect inflows (+) and outflows (−). Inflows result from an increase in liabilities and a decrease in assets. Outflows, on the other hand, result from an increase in assets or a decrease in liabilities. This means that a positive value of transactions of non-financial agents is equal to a decrease in foreign assets of the non-bank resident sector which equals an increase in external assets of the banking sector and with it an increase in domestic money supply. The final time series is obtained by converting the USD value into national currency, applying the average exchange rate of the period (IMF 1993, pp. 33–34).[4]

[1] Further details and applications are presented in the ECB Occasional Paper No. 96 (Be Duc et al. 2008).

[2] Japan, which is the third country in the empirical analysis, is chosen because of limited data availability for the US analysis and calculations by the ECB for the euro area analysis, which are the first two countries in the empirical analysis.

[3] Unfortunately, the capital flows time series are affected by data limitations: current and capital account transactions, direct investment as well as errors and omissions can not be split into bank and non-bank transactions. The assumption is that the external transactions of the banking sector have a neutral impact on these positions. Consequently, they are allocated to the non-bank sector (see Table A.1).

[4] Since the 5th edition of the BoP Manual is not clear about which conversion rates to apply, the use of average rates was double-checked with the Statistics Division of the IMF.

M. Wiedmann, *Money, Stock Prices and Central Banks*, Contributions to Economics, DOI 10.1007/978-3-7908-2647-0

Table A.1 Calculation example for capital flows time series: Japan

BoP position		Units	Scale	Database	BOP series code	Descriptor	Q1 2008	Q2 2008	Q3 2008
Current and capital account balance		USD	Billions	Anal. pres.	1584981..9...	TOTAL, GROUPS A PLUS B	61.0	36.0	37.9
Direct investment									
By resident units abroad		USD	Billions	Anal. pres.	1584505..9...	DIRECT INVESTMENT ABROAD: NET	−29.3	−17.9	−21.0
By non-resident units in the reporting economy		USD	Billions	Anal. pres.	1584555Z.9...	DI IN REPORTING ECON EXCL GRP E	10.2	6.3	1.7
Portfolio investment									
Assets	Non-banks	USD	Billions	Stand. pres.	1584612..9...	PI GEN GOVT EQTY SECURITIES AS: NET	0.0	0.0	0.0
		USD	Billions	Stand. pres.	1584614..9...	PI OTH SECT EQTY SECURITIES AS: NET	−12.4	−4.9	−2.9
		USD	Billions	Stand. pres.	1584622..9...	PI GEN GOVT BONDS & NOTES AS: NET	0.7	−0.6	−0.2
		USD	Billions	Stand. pres.	1584624..9...	PI OTH SECT BONDS & NOTES AS: NET	−64.5	−23.1	−17.7
		USD	Billions	Stand. pres.	1584632..9...	PI GEN GOVT MONEY MAR INSTRU AS: NET	0.0	0.0	0.0
		USD	Billions	Stand. pres.	1584634..9...	PI OTH SECT MONEY MAR INSTRU AS: NET	−0.9	−1.2	0.7
		USD	Billions	*calculation*		PI Assets (non-banks)	−77.2	−29.8	−20.0
Liabilities	Non-banks	USD	Billions	Stand. pres.	1584664..9...	PI OTH SECT EQTY SECURITIES LB: NET	−59.5	47.1	−41.4
		USD	Billions	Stand. pres.	1584672..9...	PI GEN GOVT BONDS & NOTES LB: NET	−6.7	−5.0	34.0
		USD	Billions	Stand. pres.	1584674..9...	PI OTH SECT BONDS & NOTES LB: NET	−1.1	−2.9	−2.3
		USD	Billions	Stand. pres.	1584682..9...	PI GEN GOVT MONEY MAR INSTRU LB: NET	17.4	45.8	−4.1
		USD	Billions	Stand. pres.	1584684..9...	PI OTH SECTMONEY MAR INSTRUU LB: NET	0.1	0.4	−0.1
		USD	Billions	*calculation*		PI Liabilities (non-banks)	−49.8	85.5	−13.8

(continued)

Table A.1 (Continued)

BoP position		Units	Scale	Database	BOP series code	Descriptor	Q1 2008	Q2 2008	Q3 2008
Other investment									
Assets	Non-banks	USD	Billions	Anal. pres.	1584704..9...	OTHER INVEST ASSETS GEN GOVT	−0.2	1.5	−4.5
		USD	Billions	Anal. pres.	1584728..9...	OTHER INVEST ASSETS OTH SECT	−43.4	81.6	−35.2
		USD	Billions	*calculation*		OI Assets (non-banks)	−43.7	83.1	−39.7
Liabilities	Non-banks	USD	Billions	Anal. pres.	1584753ZB9...	OI LIAB EXCLUDING GRP E GEN GOVT	4.0	−2.0	36.0
		USD	Billions	Anal. pres.	1584753ZD9...	OI LIAB EXCLUDING GRP E OTH SECT	120.0	−94.4	−5.0
		USD	Billions	*calculation*		OI Liabilities (non-banks)	124.0	−96.4	31.0
Financial derivatives									
		USD	Billions	Stand. pres.	1584912..9...	FINAN DERIV GEN GOVT: NET	0.0	0.0	0.0
		USD	Billions	Stand. pres.	1584914..9...	FINAN DERIV OTHER SECTORS: NET	6.1	−3.5	3.0
		USD	Billions	*calculation*		Fin. Deriv. (non-banks)	6.2	−3.6	3.0
Errors and Omissions		USD	Billions	Anal. pres.	1584998..9...	NET ERRORS AND OMISSIONS	13.5	12.5	−1.3
Total		USD	Billions	*calculation*		Total	14.9	75.7	−22.3
			Units	Anal. pres.	1580101..4...	NC/US$ PERIOD AVG	105.2	104.5	107.6
Total in local currency		JPY	Billions	*calculation*		Total in Yen	1,563.2	7,913.3	−2,400.9

Appendix B
Additional Information of Empirical Analysis

B.1 United States of America: Quarterly Data

B.1.1 Data Sources (Table B.1)

Table B.1 US quarterly data: data sources

m	Variable	Nominal money, not seasonally adjusted (NSA)
	Datastream name	US MONEY M3 CURN
	Datastream Mnemonic	USQ59MC.A
	Data source	IMF IFS
s	Variable	Nominal stock market level, NSA
	Datastream name	US-DS Market - TOT RETURN IND
	Datastream Mnemonic	TOTMKUS(RI)
	Data source	Datastream
y	Variable	Nominal gross domestic product, seasonally adjusted (SA)
	Datastream name	US GDP (AR) CURA
	Datastream Mnemonic	USOEX001B
	Data source	Main Economic Indicators, Copyright OECD
p	Variable	Consumer price index, NSA
	Datastream name	US CPI NADJ
	Datastream Mnemonic	USQ64...F
	Data source	IMF IFS
ff	Variable	Short-term interest rate, NSA
	Datastream name	US FEDERAL FUNDS (EFFECTIVE) - MIDDLE RATE
	Datastream Mnemonic	FRFEDFD
	Data source	Federal Reserve Bank of New York
*b*10	Variable	Long-term interest rate, NSA
	Datastream name	US TREASURY CONSTANT MATURITIES 10 YR - MIDDLE RATE

(continued)

Table B.1 (Continued)

	Datastream Mnemonic	FRTCM10
	Data source	Federal Reserve
cf	Variable	
		Capital flows (changes in net foreign assets of the banking system), NSA
	Time series name	US FOREIGN ASSETS, NET (BANKING SURVEY) CURN
	Data source	IMF IFS

B.1.2 Graphs of the Cointegrating Relations of the Unrestricted Model (Fig. B.1)

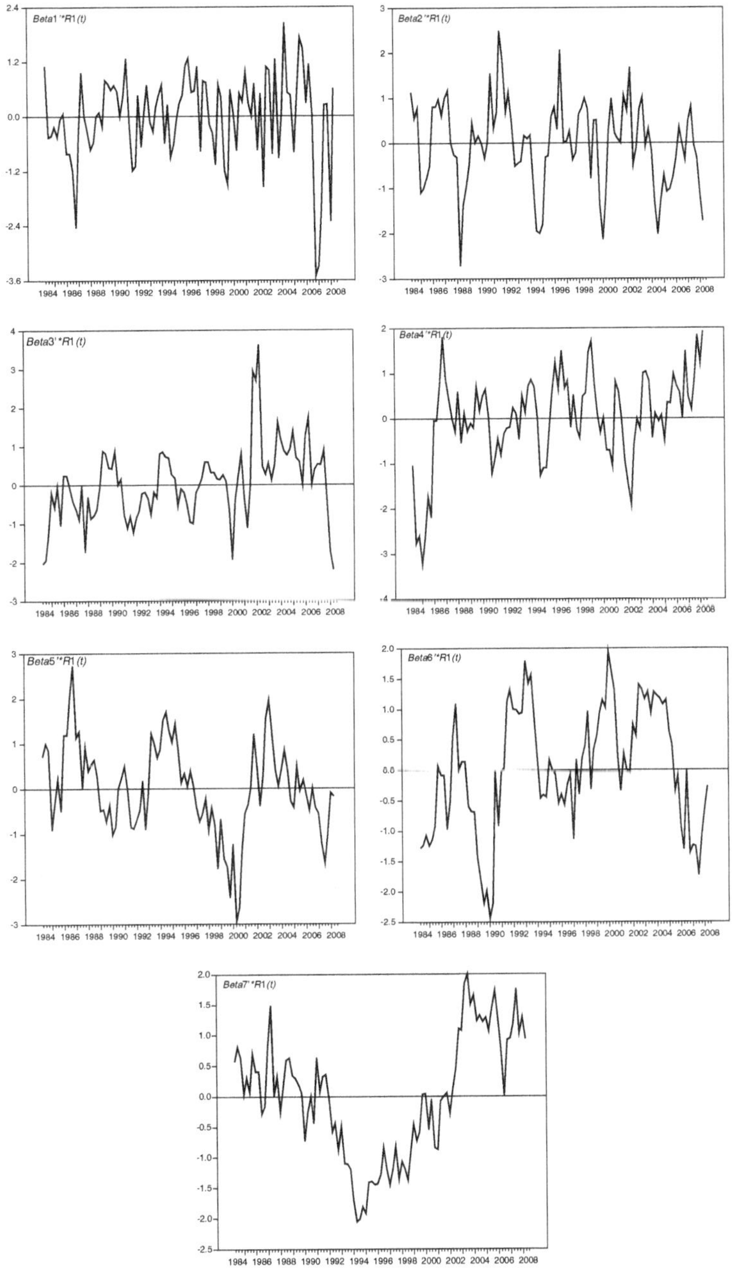

Fig. B.1 US quarterly data: the cointegration relations ($\beta_1, \ldots, \beta_7$) of the unrestricted model

B.1.3 Forward and Backward Recursive Tests for Parameter Constancy of the Unidentified System with Rank $r = 4$ Imposed (Figs. B.2, B.3, B.4, and B.5)

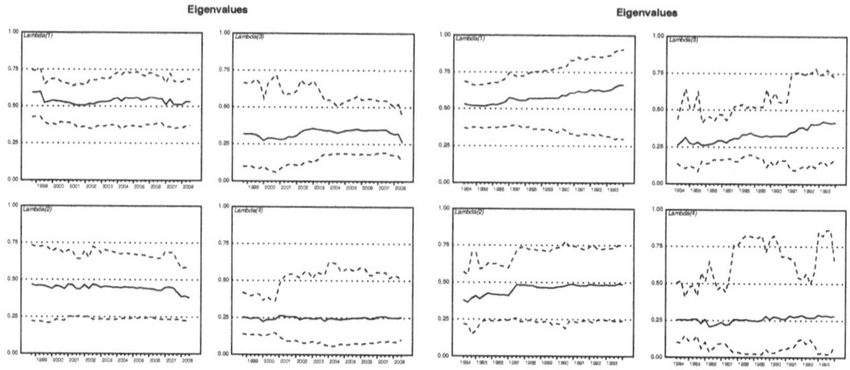

Fig. B.2 US quarterly data: recursively calculated eigenvalues λ_i (forward, base sample 1984:02 to 1998:04, depicted left; backward, base sample 2008:03 to 1994:01, depicted right)

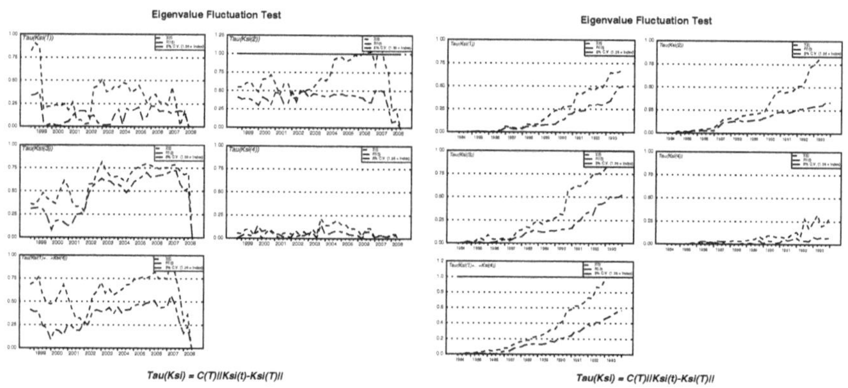

Fig. B.3 US quarterly data: recursively calculated eigenvalue fluctuation test (forward, base sample 1984:02 to 1998:04, depicted left; backward, base sample 2008:03 to 1994:01, depicted right)

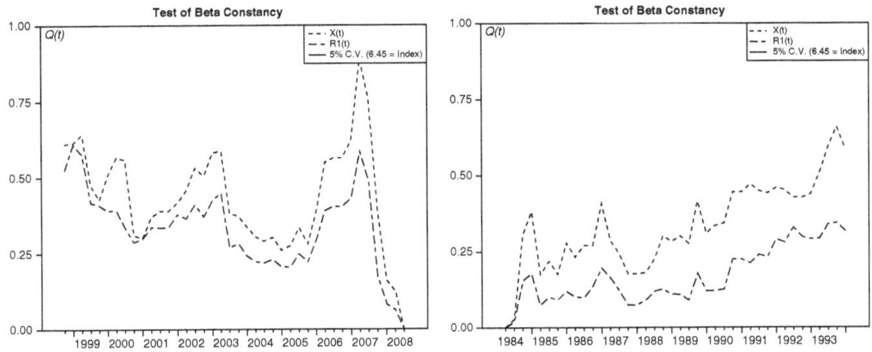

Fig. B.4 US quarterly data: recursively calculated test of β constancy (forward, base sample 1984:02 to 1998:04, depicted left; backward, base sample 2008:03 to 1994:01, depicted right)

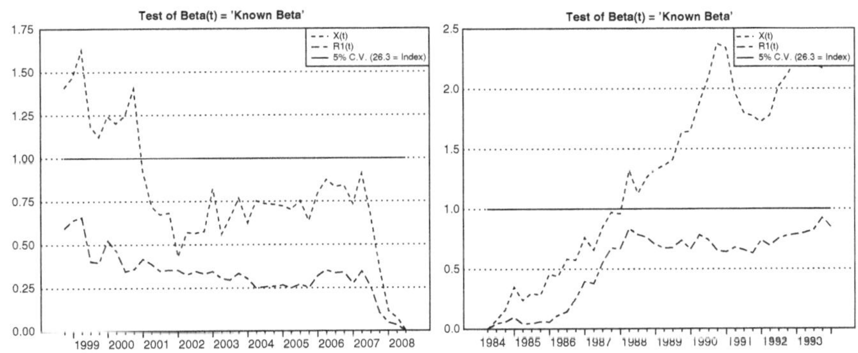

Fig. B.5 US quarterly data: recursively calculated test of β_t equals a known β (forward, base sample 1984:02 to 1998:04, depicted left; backward, base sample 2008:03 to 1994:01, depicted right)

B.1.4 The Partitioned Unrestricted Π-Matrices (Table B.2)

Table B.2 US quarterly data: the partitioned unrestricted Π-matrices based on 4 cointegrating vectors (t-values in brackets)

β'								
	m_r	s_r	y_r	Δp	ff	$b10$	cf	*Trend*
Beta(1)	−0.001	0.002	−0.052	1.000	0.159	−0.443	−0.357	0.000
Beta(2)	0.040	0.008	−0.272	−0.462	1.000	−0.939	−0.272	0.001
Beta(3)	0.020	0.005	−0.178	0.774	−0.513	0.131	1.000	0.001
Beta(4)	0.003	0.004	−0.000	−0.139	−0.274	1.000	−0.182	−0.000

α				
	Alpha(1)	Alpha(2)	Alpha(3)	Alpha(4)
Δm_r	0.131 [0.265]	**0.615** [1.936]	−0.013 [−0.065]	0.842 [1.766]
Δs_r	−2.616 [−0.658]	1.308 [0.513]	2.398 [1.482]	1.781 [0.465]
Δy_r	**0.600** [2.106]	**0.465** [2.542]	0.154 [1.331]	0.195 [0.711]
$\Delta^2 p$	**−1.116** [−6.511]	−0.102 [−0.925]	**−0.179** [−2.566]	**−0.455** [−2.751]
Δff	0.142 [1.742]	**−0.335** [−6.415]	−0.023 [−0.684]	−0.065 [−0.832]
$\Delta b10$	**0.260** [4.289]	−0.025 [−0.643]	−0.025 [−1.011]	**−0.300** [−5.137]
Δcf	**0.770** [3.178]	0.063 [0.404]	**−0.452** [−4.588]	**0.591** [2.532]

B.1.5 Rank Conditions of the Identified Long-Run Structure

Checking formal identification of the restrictions imposed by:

H_1'							
0	0	1	0	0	0	0	0
1	0	0	0	0	0	0	0
0	1	0	0	0	0	0	0
0	0	0	0	0	0	0	1

H_2'							
0	0	0	1	0	0	0	0
1	0	−1	0	0	0	0	0
0	0	0	0	0	0	0	1

H_3'							
0	0	0	1	−1	0	0	0
0	0	0	0	−1	1	0	0

H_4'							
0	0	0	0	0	0	1	0

The set of restrictions imposed by $H_1, \ldots H_4$ are formally identifying if for all i and $k = 1, \ldots, r-1$ and any set of indices $1 \le i_1 < \cdots < i_k \le r$ not containing i it holds that

$$R\left(i.i_1, \ldots, i_k\right) = rank\left(R_i'\left[H_{i_1} \cdots H_{i_k}\right]\right) \ge k$$

where $R_i = H_{1\perp}$ for all i. The conditions are summarized in Table B.3:

Table B.3 US quarterly data: rank conditions of the identified long-run structure

Rank Conditions					
$R(i.j)$		$R(i.jk)$		$R(i.jkl)$	
(1.2):	1	(1.23):	3	(1.234):	4
(1.3):	2	(1.24):	2		
(1.4):	1	(1.34):	3		
(2.1):	2	(2.13):	4	(2.134):	5
(2.3):	2	(2.14):	3		
(2.4):	1	(2.34):	3		
(3.1):	4	(3.12):	5	(3.124):	6
(3.2):	3	(3.14):	5		
(3.4):	1	(3.24):	4		
(4.1):	4	(4.12):	5	(4.123):	7
(4.2):	3	(4.13):	6		
(4.3):	2	(4.23):	5		

B.1.6 Graphs of the Cointegrating Relations of the Identified Long-Run Structure (Fig. B.6)

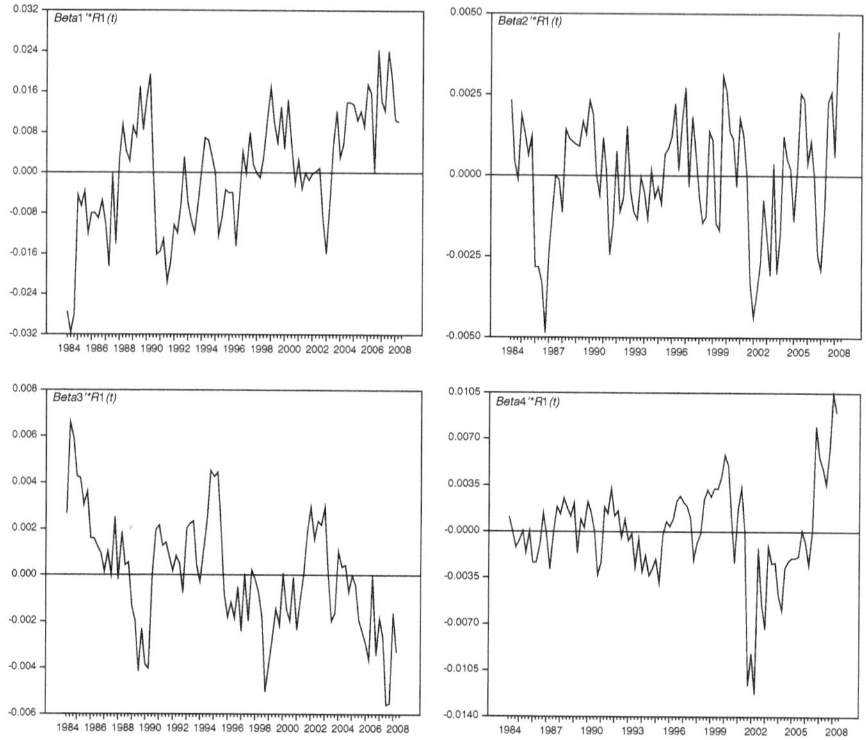

Fig. B.6 US quarterly data: the cointegration relations ($\beta_1, \ldots, \beta_4$) of the restricted model

B.1.7 *Tests for Parameter Constancy of the Identified Long-Run Structure (Fig. B.7, B.8, B.9, B.10, B.11, B.12, B.13, and B.14)*

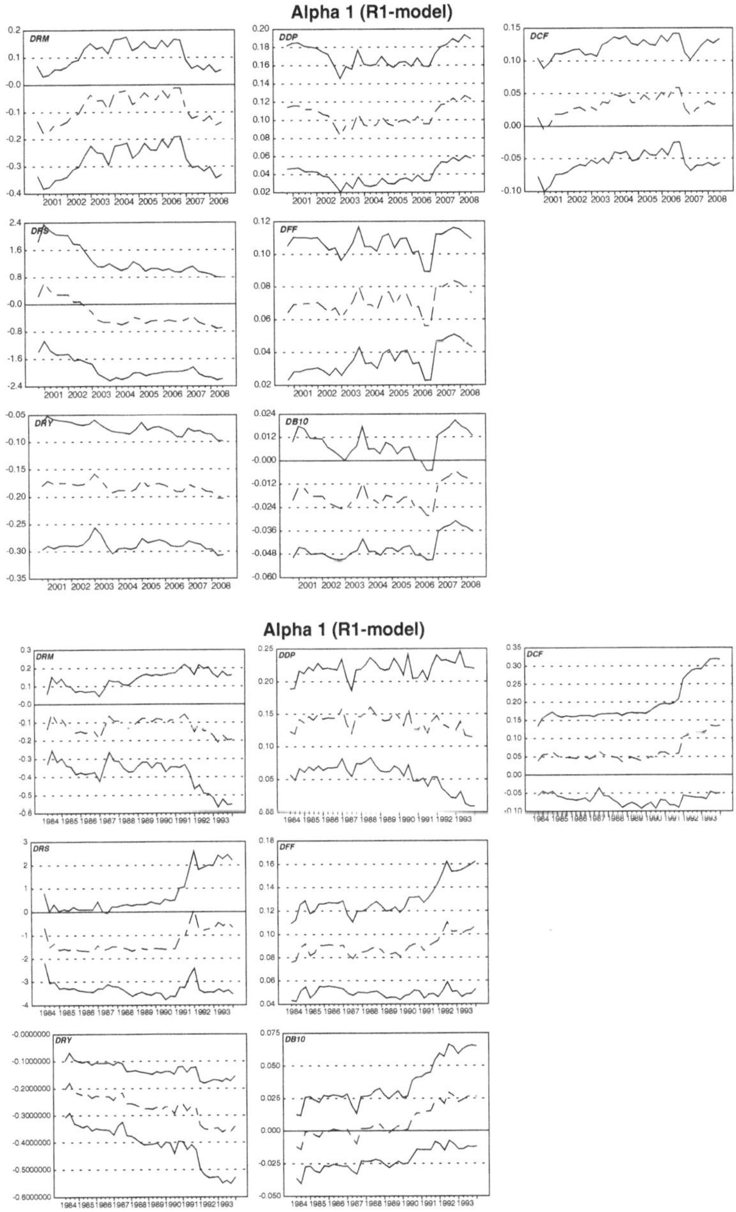

Fig. B.7 US quarterly data: recursively calculated αs of the first cointegration relation (forward, base sample 1984:02 to 1998:04, depicted above; backward, base sample 2008:03 to 1994:01, depicted below)

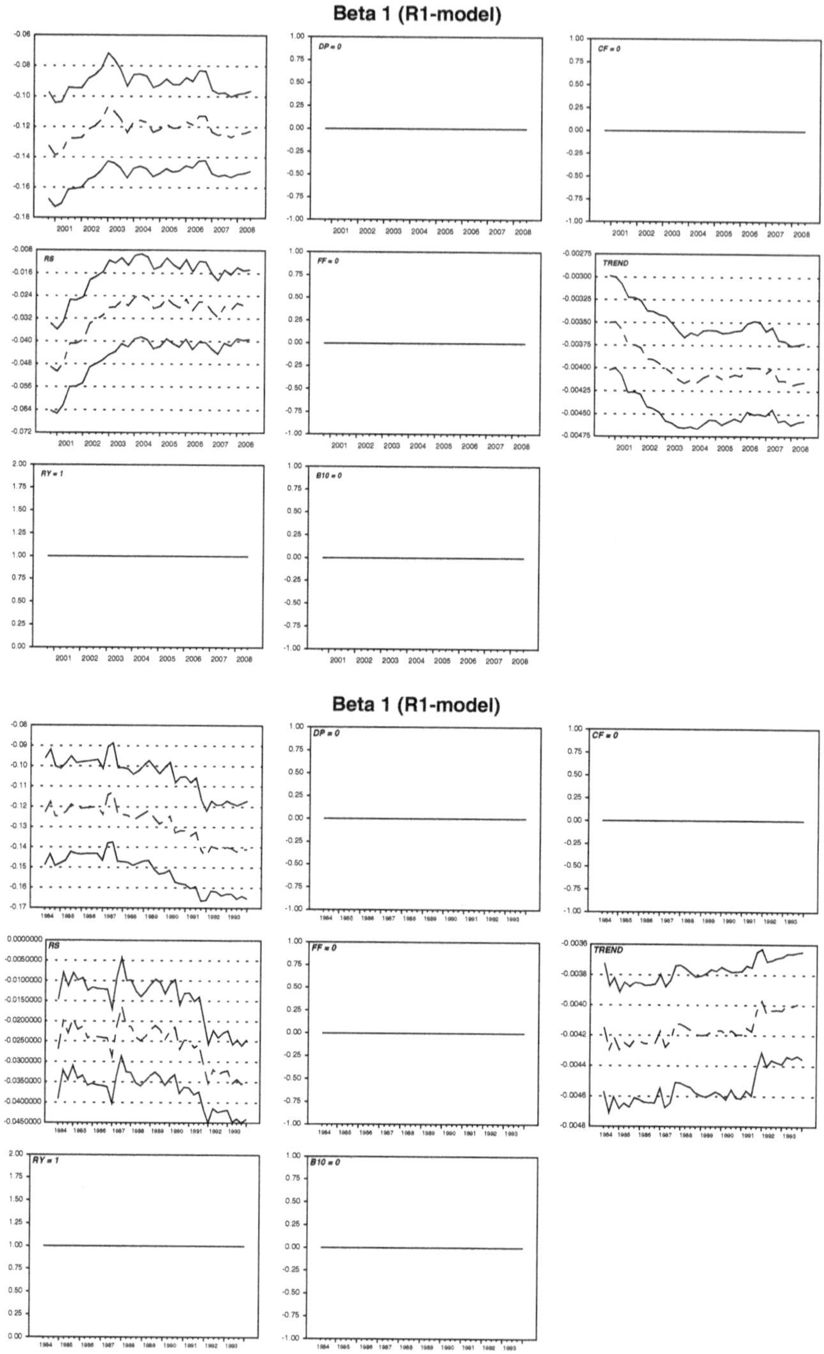

Fig. B.8 US quarterly data: recursively calculated βs of the first cointegration relation (forward, base sample 1984:02 to 1998:04, depicted above; backward, base sample 2008:03 to 1994:01, depicted below)

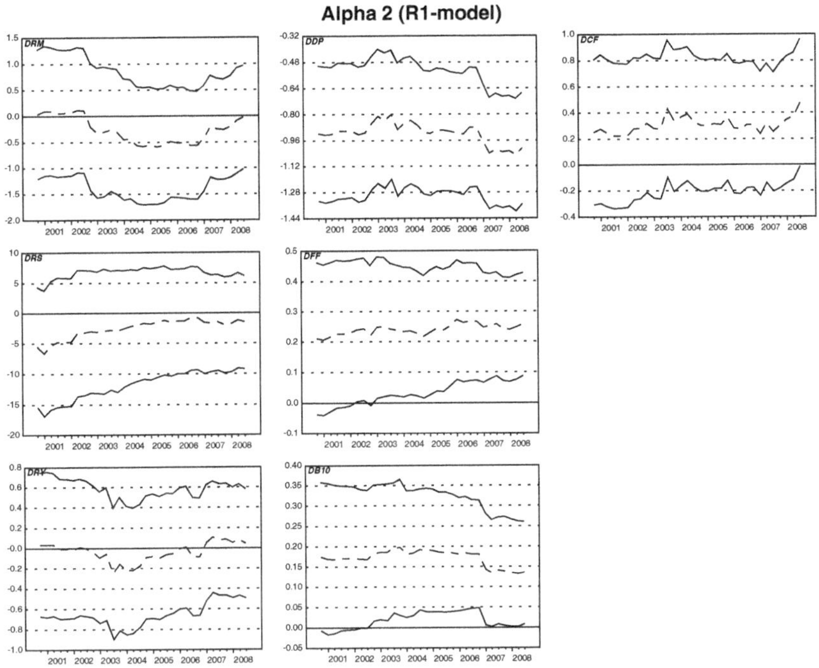

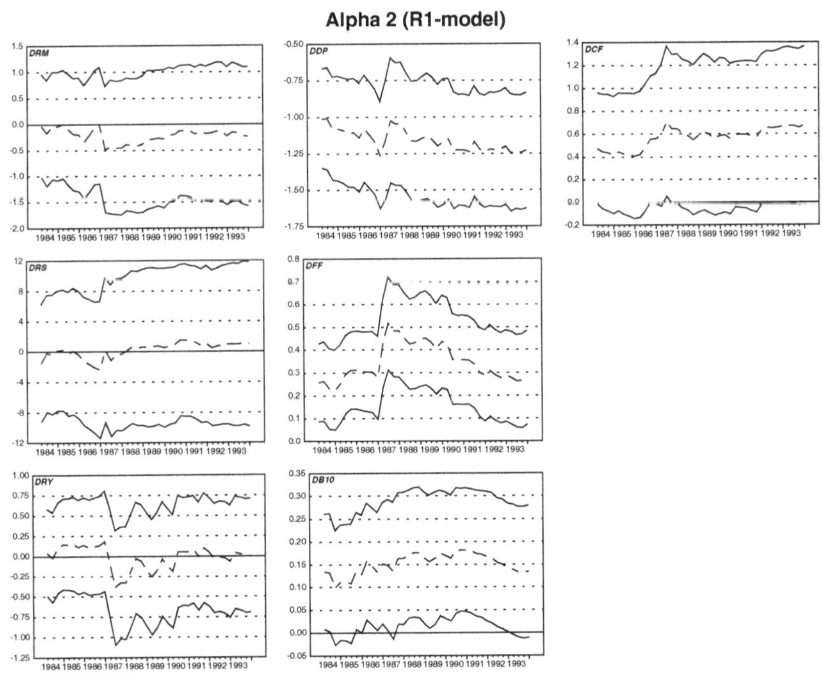

Fig. B.9 US quarterly data: recursively calculated αs of the second cointegration relation (forward, base sample 1984:02 to 1998:04, depicted above; backward, base sample 2008:03 to 1994:01, depicted below)

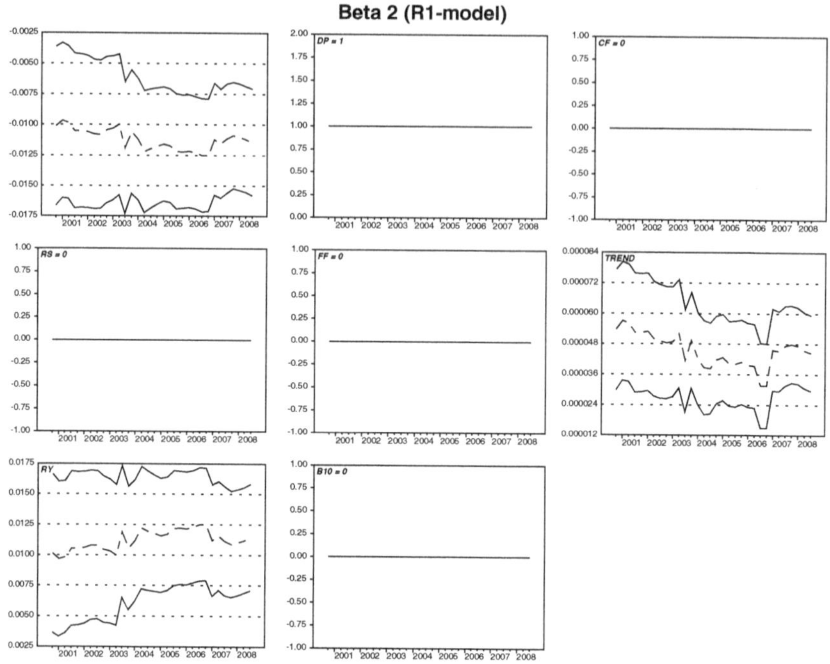

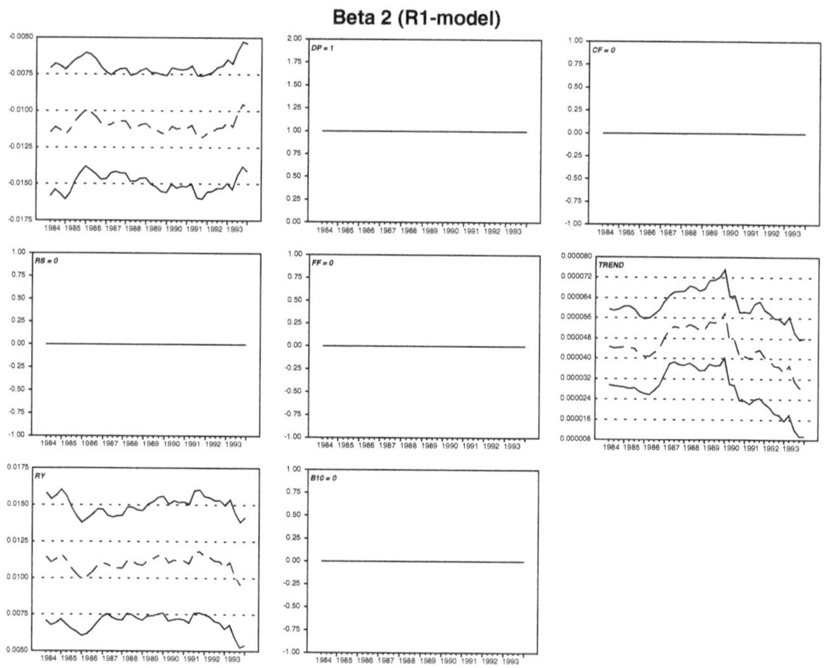

Fig. B.10 US quarterly data: recursively calculated βs of the second cointegration relation (forward, base sample 1984:02 to 1998:04, depicted above; backward, base sample 2008:03 to 1994:01, depicted below)

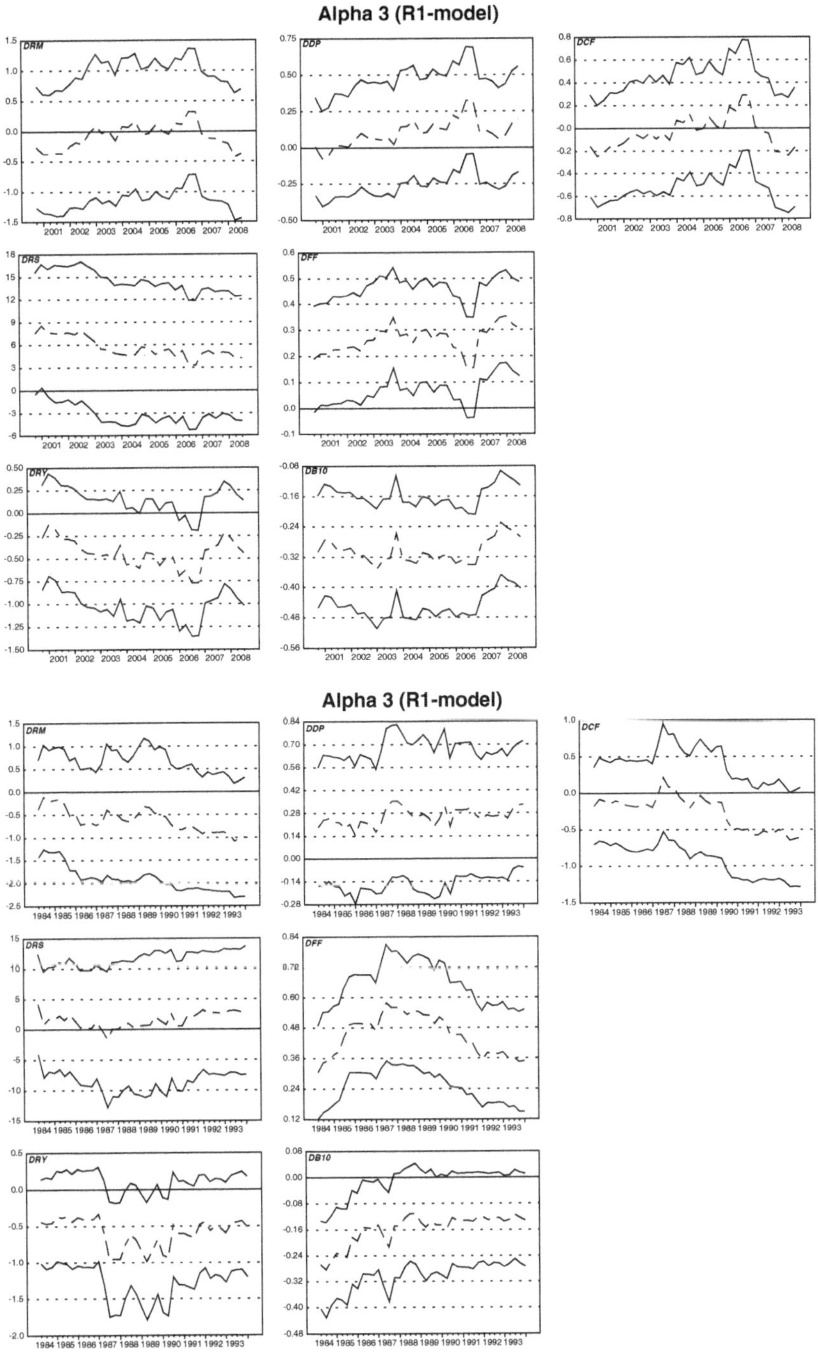

Fig. B.11 US quarterly data: recursively calculated αs of the third cointegration relation (forward, base sample 1984:02 to 1998:04, depicted above; backward, base sample 2008:03 to 1994:01, depicted below)

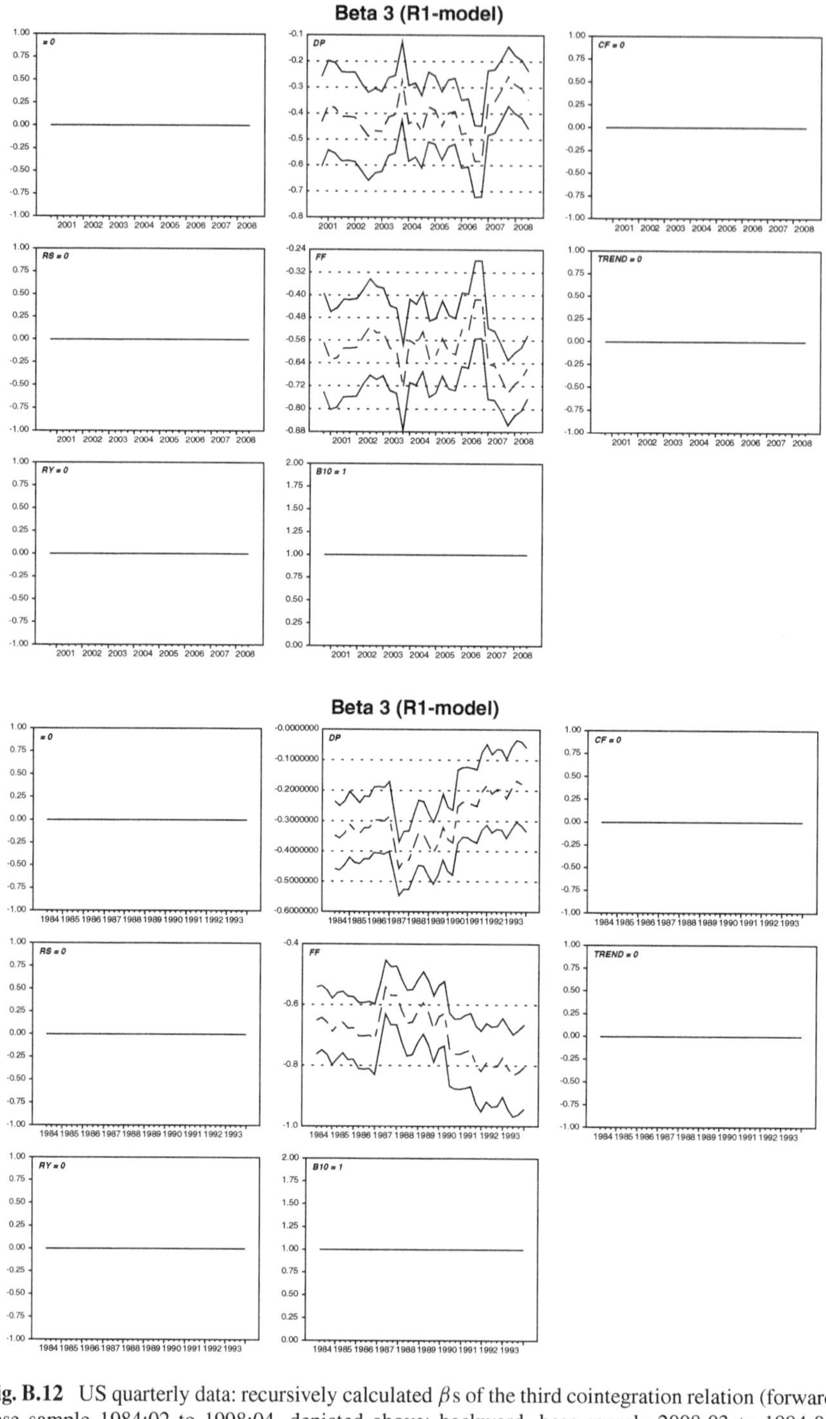

Fig. B.12 US quarterly data: recursively calculated βs of the third cointegration relation (forward, base sample 1984:02 to 1998:04, depicted above; backward, base sample 2008:03 to 1994:01, depicted below)

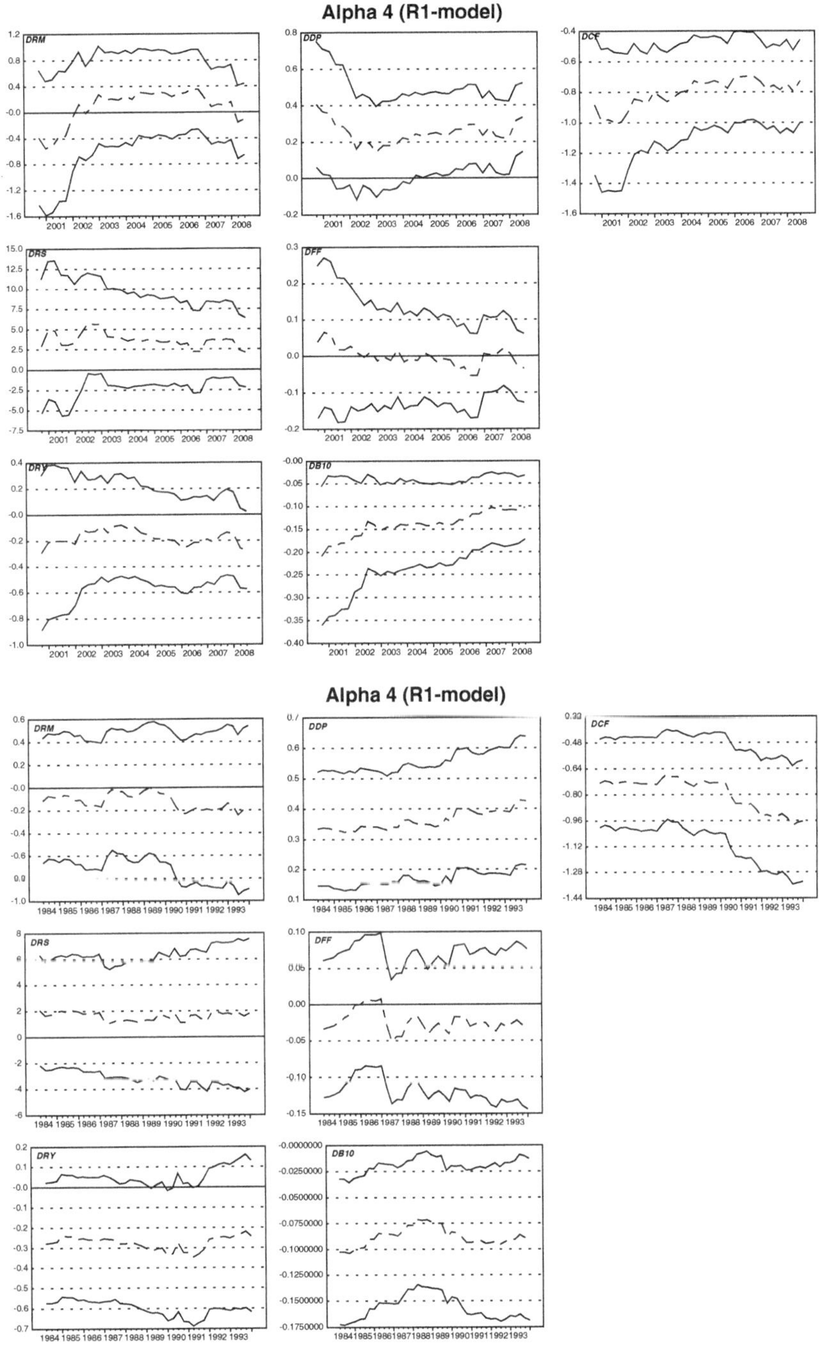

Fig. B.13 US quarterly data: recursively calculated αs of the fourth cointegration relation (forward, base sample 1984:02 to 1998:04, depicted above; backward, base sample 2008:03 to 1994:01, depicted below)

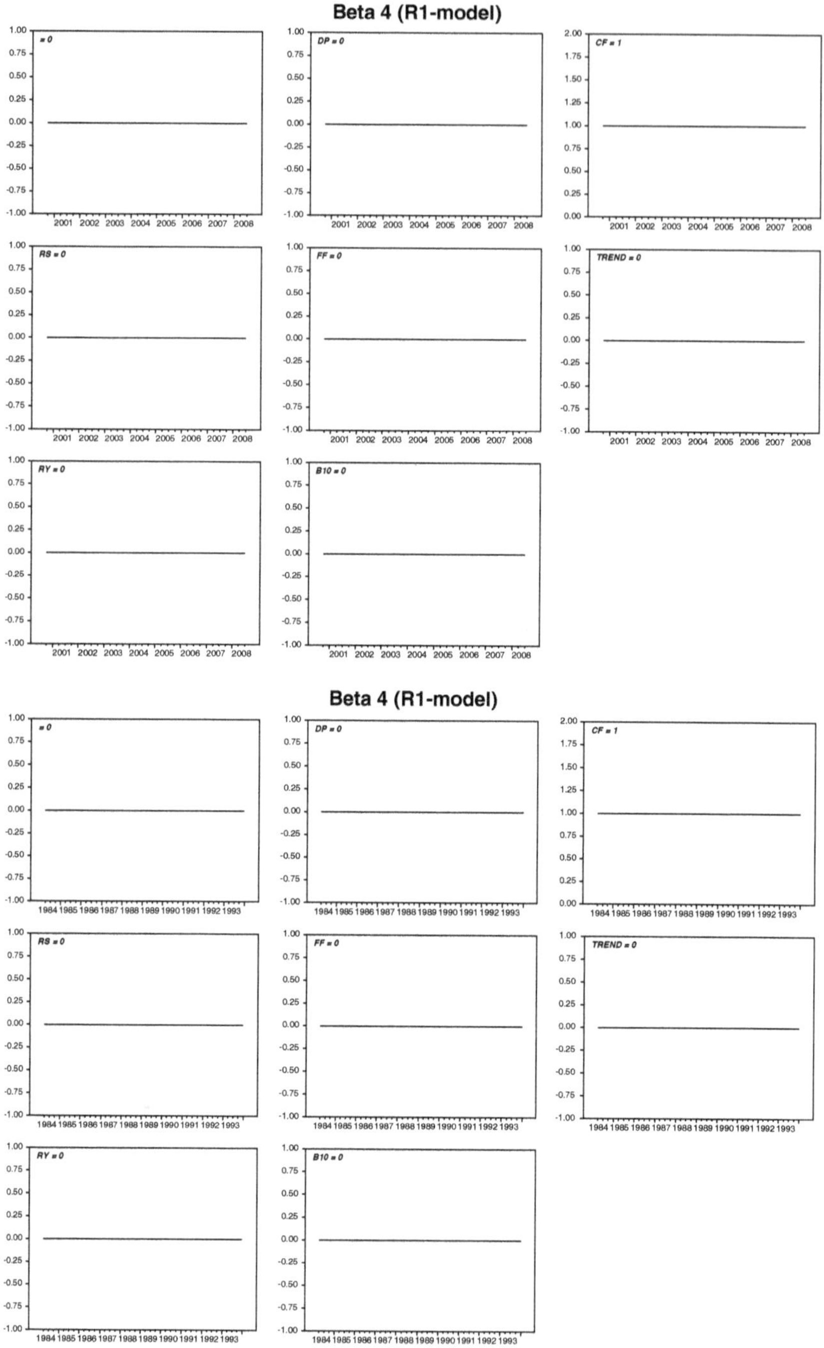

Fig. B.14 US quarterly data: recursively calculated βs of the fourth cointegration relation (forward, base sample 1984:02 to 1998:04, depicted above; backward, base sample 2008:03 to 1994:01, depicted below)

B.1.8 The Identified Long-Run Structure with Weak Exogeneity Imposed (Table B.4)

Table B.4 US quarterly data: the identified long-run structure with weak exogeneity imposed on real money and the stock market (t-values in brackets)

β'								
	m_r	s_r	y_r	Δp	*ff*	$b10$	cf	*Trend*
Beta(1)	**−0.127** [−9.415]	**−0.026** [−4.115]	**1.000** [*NA*]	0.000 [*NA*]	0.000 [*NA*]	0.000 [*NA*]	0.000 [*NA*]	**−0.004** [−19.16]
Beta(2)	**−0.012** [−5.235]	0.000 [*NA*]	**0.012** [5.235]	**1.000** [*NA*]	0.000 [*NA*]	0.000 [*NA*]	0.000 [*NA*]	**0.000** [5.816]
Beta(3)	0.000 [*NA*]	0.000 [*NA*]	0.000 [*NA*]	**−0.318** [−5.387]	**−0.682** [−11.56]	**1.000** [*NA*]	0.000 [*NA*]	0.000 [*NA*]
Beta(4)	0.000 [*NA*]	0.000 [*NA*]	0.000 [*NA*]	0.000 [*NA*]	0.000 [*NA*]	0.000 [*NA*]	**1.000** [*NA*]	0.000 [*NA*]

α				
	Alpha(1)	Alpha(2)	Alpha(3)	Alpha(4)
Δm_r	0.000 [0.000]	0.000 [0.000]	0.000 [0.000]	0.000 [0.000]
Δs_r	0.000 [0.000]	0.000 [0.000]	0.000 [0.000]	0.000 [0.000]
Δy_r	**−0.174** [−3.100]	0.093 [0.328]	−0.402 [−1.332]	−0.282 [−1.773]
$\Delta^2 p$	**0.095** [2.660]	**−1.032** [−5.762]	0.141 [0.734]	**0.323** [3.212]
Δff	**0.079** [4.597]	**0.252** [2.922]	**0.314** [3.408]	−0.030 [−0.623]
$\Delta b10$	−0.016 [−1.201]	**0.137** [2.103]	**−0.270** [−3.865]	**−0.108** [−2.940]
Δcf	0.066 [1.319]	0.467 [1.868]	−0.101 [−0.379]	**−0.706** [−5.029]

B.1.9 The Long-Run Impact of the Common Trends with Weak Exogeneity Imposed (Table B.5)

Table B.5 US quarterly data: the long-run impact matrix with weak exogeneity imposed on real money and the stock market (t-values in brackets)

The Long-Run Impact Matrix, C							
	$\hat{\epsilon}_{m_r}$	$\hat{\epsilon}_{s_r}$	$\hat{\epsilon}_{y_r}$	$\hat{\epsilon}_{\Delta p}$	$\hat{\epsilon}_{ff}$	$\hat{\epsilon}_{b10}$	$\hat{\epsilon}_{cf}$
m_r	**2.489** [3.741]	−0.028 [−0.355]	1.896 [1.005]	1.155 [0.764]	4.036 [1.192]	2.790 [0.859]	−0.827 [−0.716]
s_r	−1.186 [−0.390]	**1.463** [4.029]	2.866 [0.333]	1.745 [0.253]	6.100 [0.395]	4.217 [0.284]	−1.249 [−0.237]
y_r	**0.286** [2.388]	**0.034** [2.393]	0.315 [0.928]	0.192 [0.706]	0.671 [1.101]	0.464 [0.794]	−0.137 [−0.662]
Δp	**0.026** [3.798]	−0.001 [−0.901]	0.018 [0.961]	0.011 [0.730]	0.039 [1.140]	0.027 [0.822]	−0.008 [−0.685]
ff	−0.042 [−0.533]	0.013 [1.389]	0.365 [1.615]	0.222 [1.228]	0.777 [1.917]	0.537 [1.381]	−0.159 [−1.152]
$b10$	−0.021 [−0.380]	0.009 [1.344]	0.255 [1.641]	0.155 [1.248]	0.543 [1.948]	0.375 [1.404]	−0.111 [−1.170]
cf	0.000 [NA]	0.000 [NA]	0.000 [NA]	0.000 [NA]	0.000 [NA]	0.000 [NA]	0.000 [NA]

B.2 Euro Area: Monthly Data

B.2.1 Data Sources (Table B.6)

Table B.6 Euro area monthly data: data sources

m	Variable	Nominal money
	Datastream name	MONEY SUPPLY: M3 (EP)
	Datastream Mnemonic	EMECBM3.A
	Data source	EUROPEAN CENTRAL BANK
s	Variable	Nominal stock market level[315]
	Datastream name	EMU-DS Market – TOT RETURN IND
	Datastream Mnemonic	TOTMKEM(RI)
	Data source	Datastream
y_r	Variable	Industrial production (real)
	Datastream name	EM INDUSTRIAL PRODUCTION SADJ
	Datastream Mnemonic	EMI66..CE
	Data source	IMF IFS
p	Variable	Consumer price index
	Datastream name	EM CPI - ALL ITEMS (HARMONISED, NSA) NADJ
	Datastream Mnemonic	EMCPHARMF
	Data source	EUROSTAT
or	Variable	Short-term interest rate
	Datastream name	EURO OVERNIGHTINDEX AVERAGE(EONIA)-OFFERED RATE
	Datastream Mnemonic	EUEONIA(IO)
	Data source	FBE and ACI
$b10$	Variable	Long-term interest rate
	Datastream name	EM LONG TERM GOVT.BOND YIELDS – MAASTRICHT DEFINITION (AVG.) NADJ
	Datastream Mnemonic	EMESEFIGR
	Data source	Datastream
cf	Variable	Capital flows (monetary presentation of the BoP)
	Datastream name	EM BOP: TRANSACTIONS IN EXTERNAL COUNTERPART OF M3 CURN
	Datastream Mnemonic	EMEB12BMA
	Data source	EUROPEAN CENTRAL BANK

[315] Time series only available in USD. Thus, the data series is converted into EUR using the EUR/USD exchange rate.

B.2.2 Graphs of the Cointegrating Relations of the Unrestricted Model (Fig. B.15)

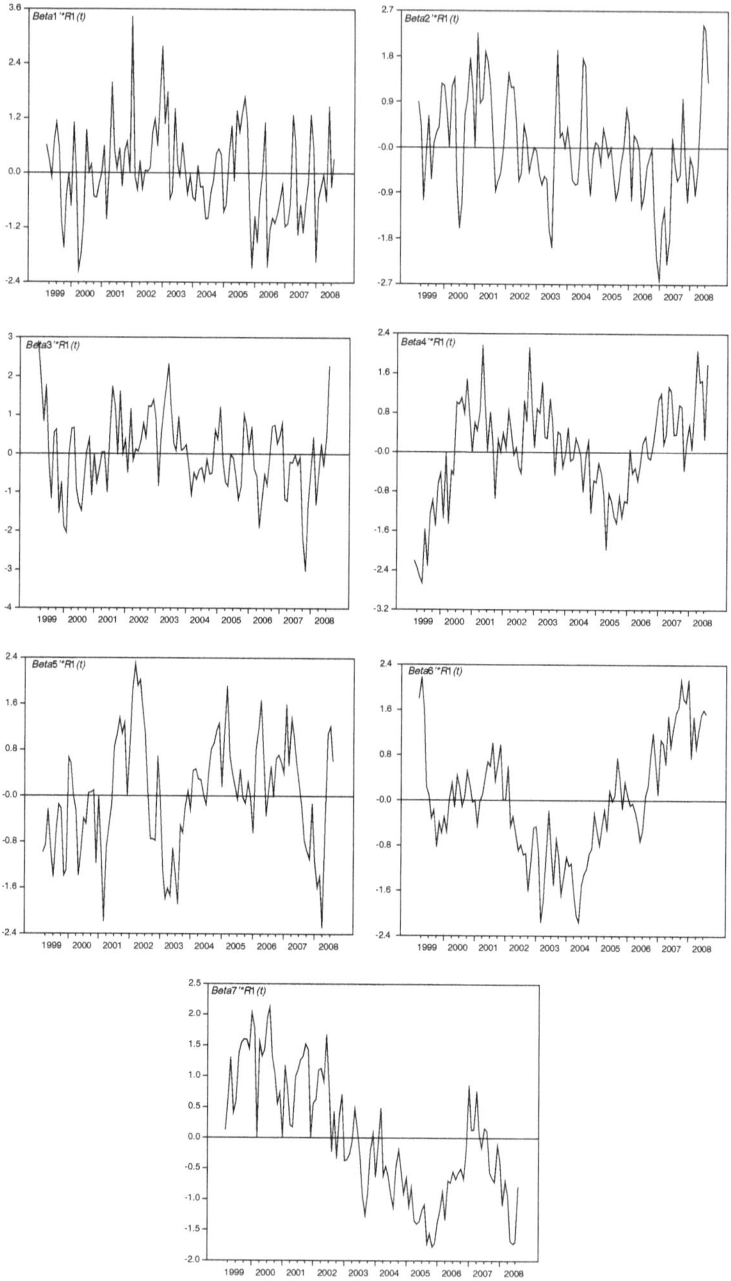

Fig. B.15 Euro area monthly data: the cointegration relations $(\beta_1, \ldots, \beta_7)$ of the unrestricted model

B.2.3 Forward and Backward Recursive Tests for Parameter Constancy of the Unidentified System with Rank $r = 5$ Imposed (Figs. B.16, B.17, B.18, and B.19)

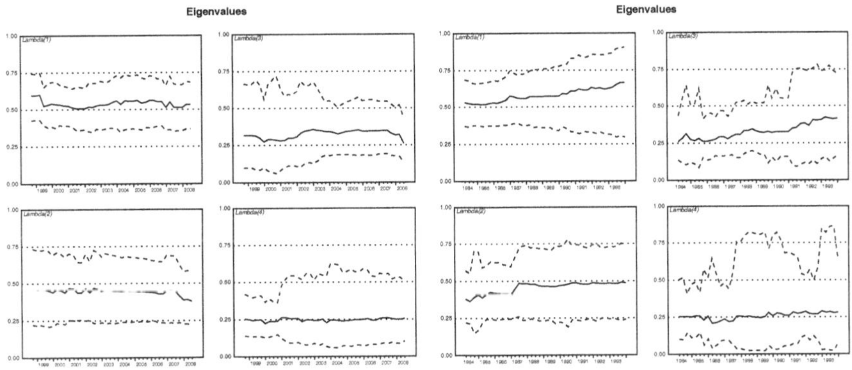

Fig. B.16 Euro area monthly data: recursively calculated eigenvalues λ_i (forward, base sample 1999:03 to 2003:12, depicted left; backward, base sample 2008:09 to 2003:12, depicted right)

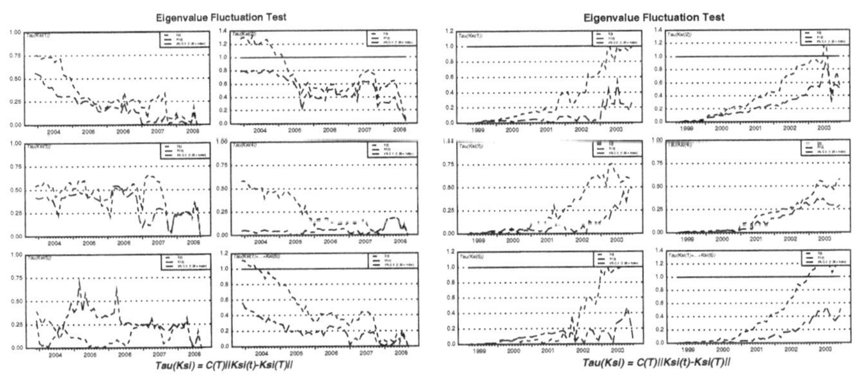

Fig. B.17 Euro area monthly data: recursively calculated eigenvalue fluctuation test (forward, base sample 1999:03 to 2003:12, depicted left; backward, base sample 2008:09 to 2003:12, depicted right)

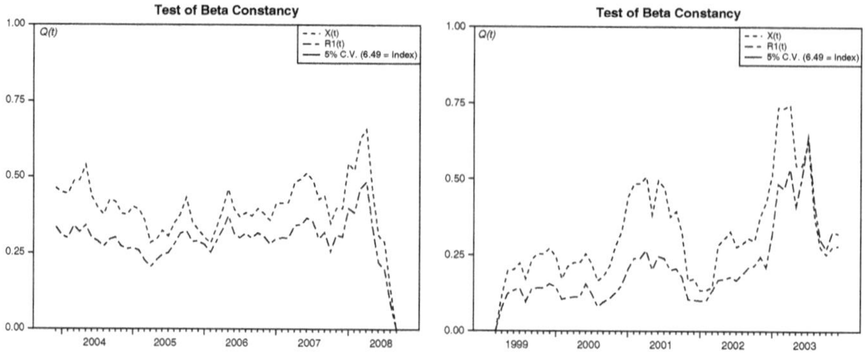

Fig. B.18 Euro area monthly data: recursively calculated test of β constancy (forward, base sample 1999:03 to 2003:12, depicted left; backward, base sample 2008:09 to 2003:12, depicted right)

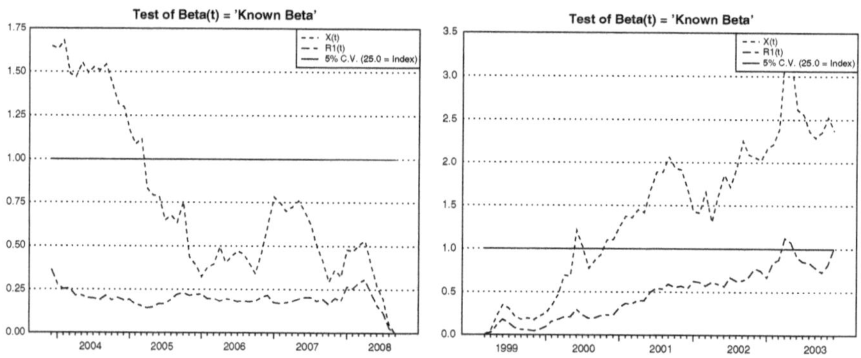

Fig. B.19 Euro area monthly data: recursively calculated test of β_t equals a known β (forward, base sample 1999:03 to 2003:12, depicted left; backward, base sample 2008:09 to 2003:12, depicted right) test of β_t equals a known β

B.2.4 The Partitioned Unrestricted Π-Matrices (Table B.7)

Table B.7 Euro area monthly data: the partitioned unrestricted Π-matrices based on 5 cointegrating vectors (t-values in brackets)

β'								
	m_r	s_r	y_r	Δp	or	$b10$	cf	*Trend*
Beta(1)	0.003	0.000	−0.044	0.407	1.000	−0.508	0.022	0.000
Beta(2)	−0.021	−0.000	−0.030	0.047	0.485	1.000	−0.184	0.000
Beta(3)	0.002	−0.001	−0.031	−0.360	1.000	−0.374	−0.008	0.000
Beta(4)	−0.015	−0.005	0.032	−0.069	1.000	0.666	0.036	0.000
Beta(5)	−0.017	0.003	−0.055	−0.052	0.489	1.000	0.029	0.000

α					
	Alpha(1)	Alpha(2)	Alpha(3)	Alpha(4)	Alpha(5)
Δm_r	−0.760 [−1.500]	−0.730 [−1.458]	−0.575 [−1.010]	0.601 [1.755]	0.819 [1.115]
Δs_r	−10.08 [−1.757]	**−13.06** [−2.305]	4.273 [0.663]	**−9.753** [−2.517]	**−16.35** [−1.965]
Δy_r	0.319 [0.356]	−0.950 [−1.074]	−0.185 [−0.184]	**−2.420** [−4.002]	**4.860** [3.741]
$\Delta^2 p$	**−1.362** [−6.179]	−0.135 [−0.619]	**1.278** [5.161]	−0.016 [−0.105]	−0.557 [−1.741]
Δor	**−0.134** [−8.326]	0.019 [1.208]	**−0.096** [−5.334]	−0.007 [−0.600]	−0.009 [−0.365]
$\Delta b10$	0.022 [1.305]	**−0.046** [−2.806]	−0.008 [−0.414]	−0.021 [−1.834]	**−0.074** [−3.058]
Δcf	−0.746 [−1.504]	**3.515** [7.174]	0.817 [1.465]	−0.425 [−1.269]	−0.319 [−0.443]

B.2.5 Rank Conditions of the Identified Long-Run Structure

Checking formal identification of the restrictions imposed by:

H_1'							
0	1	0	0	0	0	0	0
0	0	1	0	0	0	0	0
0	0	0	0	0	0	0	1

H_2'							
0	0	0	0	0	1	0	0
1	0	0	0	0	0	0	0
0	0	0	0	0	0	0	1

H_3'							
0	0	0	0	1	0	0	0
0	1	0	0	0	0	0	0
0	0	0	0	0	0	0	1

H_4'							
0	0	0	1	0	0	0	0

H_5'							
0	0	0	0	0	0	1	0

The set of restrictions imposed by $H_1, \ldots H_5$ are formally identifying if for all i and $k = 1, \ldots, r-1$ and any set of indices $1 \leq i_1 < \cdots < i_k \leq r$ not containing i it holds that

$$R\left(i.i_1, \ldots, i_k\right) = rank\left(R_i'\left[H_{i_1} \cdots H_{i_k}\right]\right) \geq k$$

where $R_i = H_{1\perp}$ for all i. The conditions are summarized in Table B.8:

Table B.8 Euro area monthly data: rank conditions of the identified long-run structure

Rank Conditions							
$R(i.j)$		$R(i.jk)$		$R(i.jkl)$		$R(i.jklm)$	
(1.2):	2	(1.23):	3	(1.234):	4	(1.2345):	5
(1.3):	1	(1.24):	3	(1.235):	4		
(1.4):	1	(1.25):	3	(1.245):	4		
(1.5):	1	(1.34):	2	(1.345):	3		
		(1.35):	2				
		(1.45):	2				
(2.1):	2	(2.13):	3	(2.134):	4	(2.1345):	5
(2.3):	2	(2.14):	3	(2.135):	4		
(2.4):	1	(2.15):	3	(2.145):	4		
(2.5):	1	(2.34):	3	(2.345):	4		
		(2.35):	3				
		(2.45):	2				
(3.1):	1	(3.12):	3	(3.124):	4	(3.1245):	5
(3.2):	2	(3.14):	2	(3.125):	4		
(3.4):	1	(3.15):	2	(3.145):	3		
(3.5):	1	(3.24):	3	(3.245):	4		
		(3.25):	3				
		(3.45):	2				
(4.1):	3	(4.12):	5	(4.123):	6	(4.1235):	7
(4.2):	3	(4.13):	4	(4.125):	6		
(4.3):	3	(4.15):	4	(4.135):	5		
(4.5):	1	(4.23):	5	(4.235):	6		
		(4.25):	4				
		(4.35):	4				
(5.1):	3	(5.12):	5	(5.123):	6	(5.1234):	7
(5.2):	3	(5.13):	4	(5.124):	6		
(5.3):	3	(5.14):	4	(5.134):	5		
(5.4):	1	(5.23):	5	(5.234):	6		
		(5.24):	4				
		(5.34):	4				

B.2.6 Graphs of the Cointegrating Relations of the Identified Long-Run Structure (Fig. B.20)

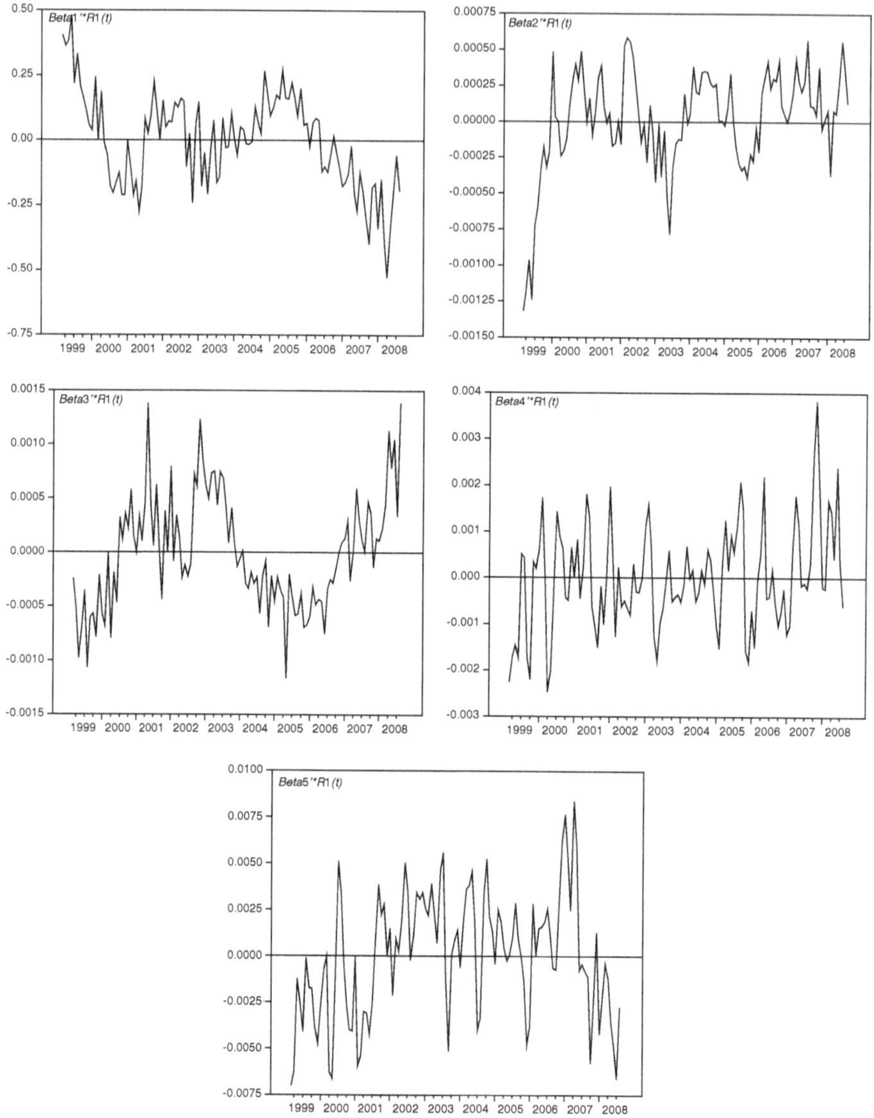

Fig. B.20 Euro area monthly data: the cointegration relations ($\beta_1, \ldots, \beta_5$) of the restricted model

B.2.7 Tests for Parameter Constancy of the Identified Long-Run Structure (Figs. B.21, B.22, B.23, B.24, B.25, B.26, B.27, B.28, B.29, and B.30)

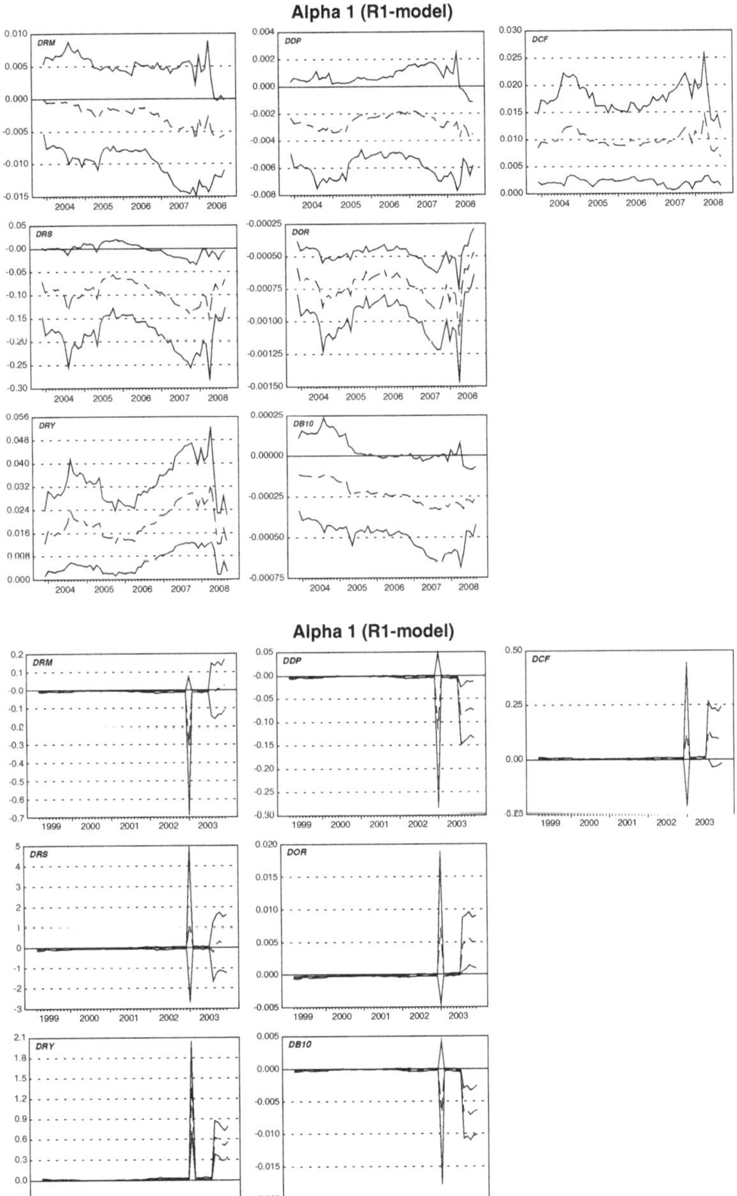

Fig. B.21 Euro area monthly data: recursively calculated αs of the first cointegration relation (forward, base sample 1999:03 to 2003:12, depicted above; backward, base sample 2008:09 to 2003:12, depicted below)

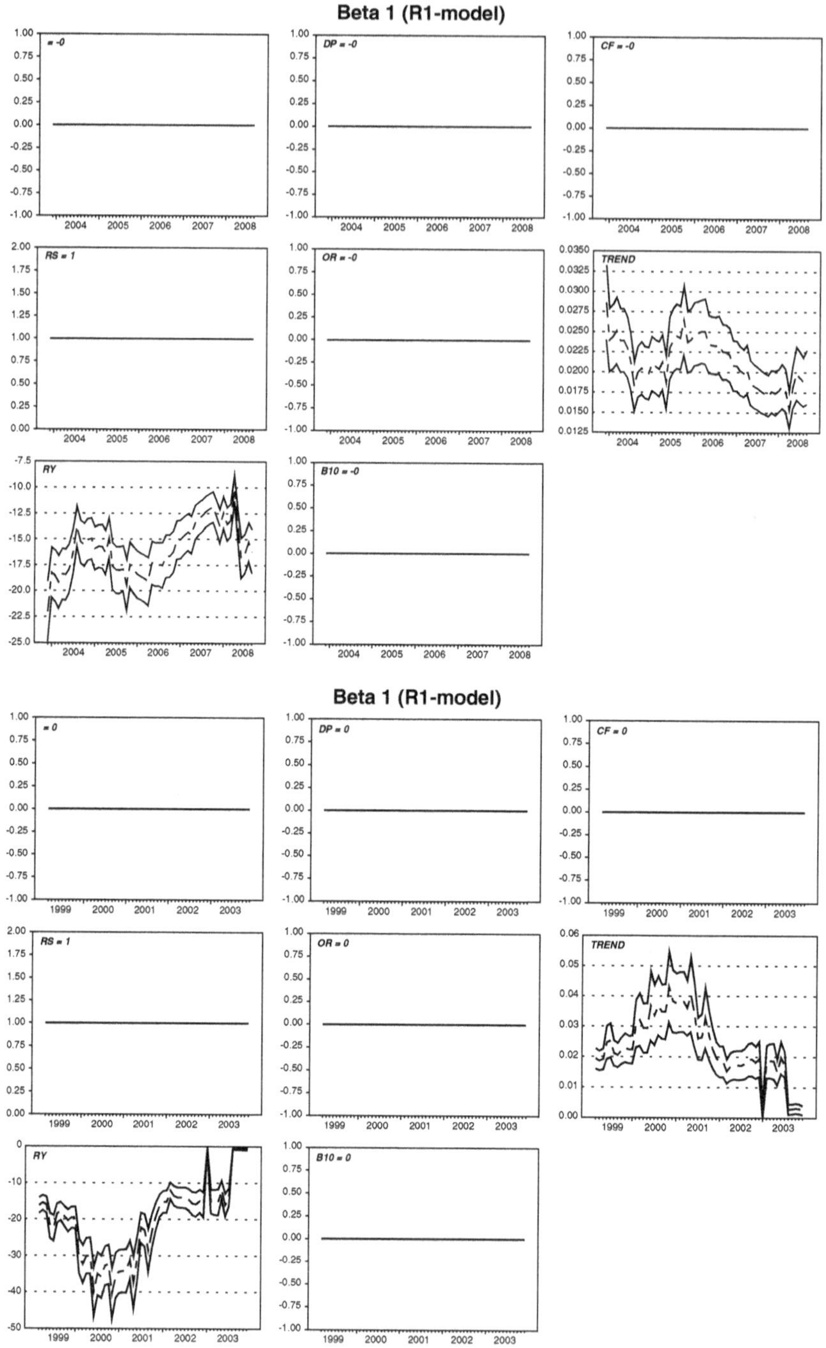

Fig. B.22 Euro area monthly data: recursively calculated βs of the first cointegration relation (forward, base sample 1999:03 to 2003:12, depicted above; backward, base sample 2008:09 to 2003:12, depicted below)

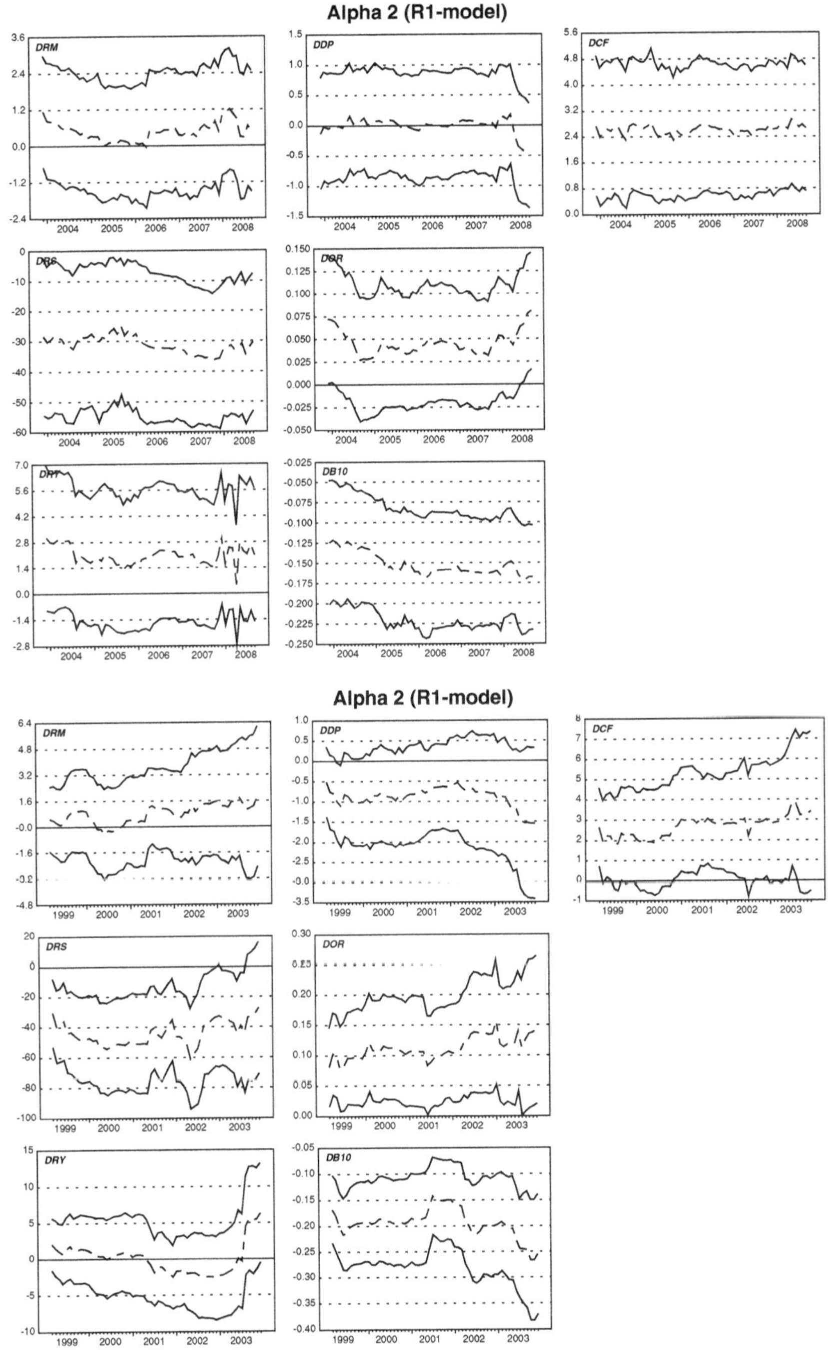

Fig. B.23 Euro area monthly data: recursively calculated αs of the second cointegration relation (forward, base sample 1999:03 to 2003:12, depicted above; backward, base sample 2008:09 to 2003:12, depicted below)

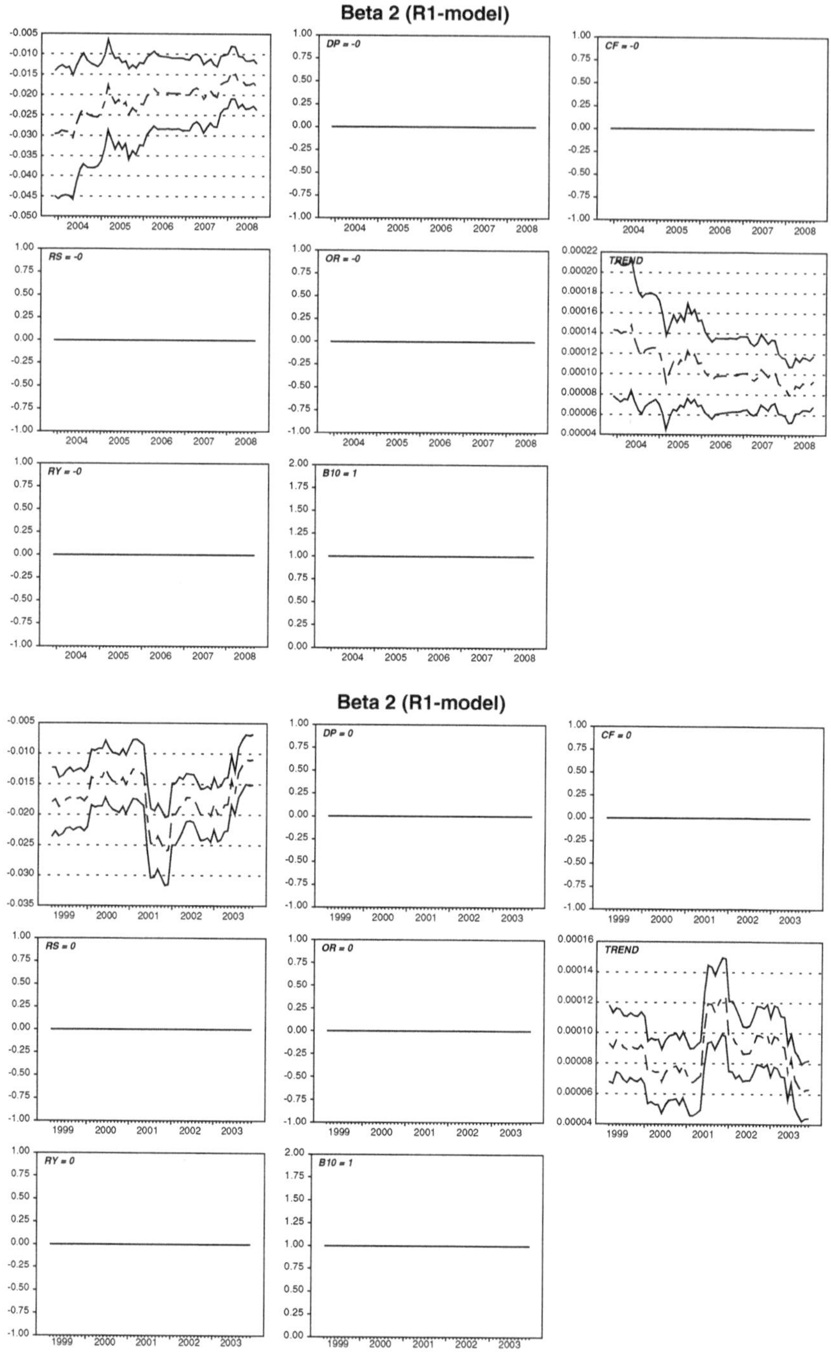

Fig. B.24 Euro area monthly data: recursively calculated βs of the second cointegration relation (forward, base sample 1999:03 to 2003:12, depicted above; backward, base sample 2008:09 to 2003:12, depicted below)

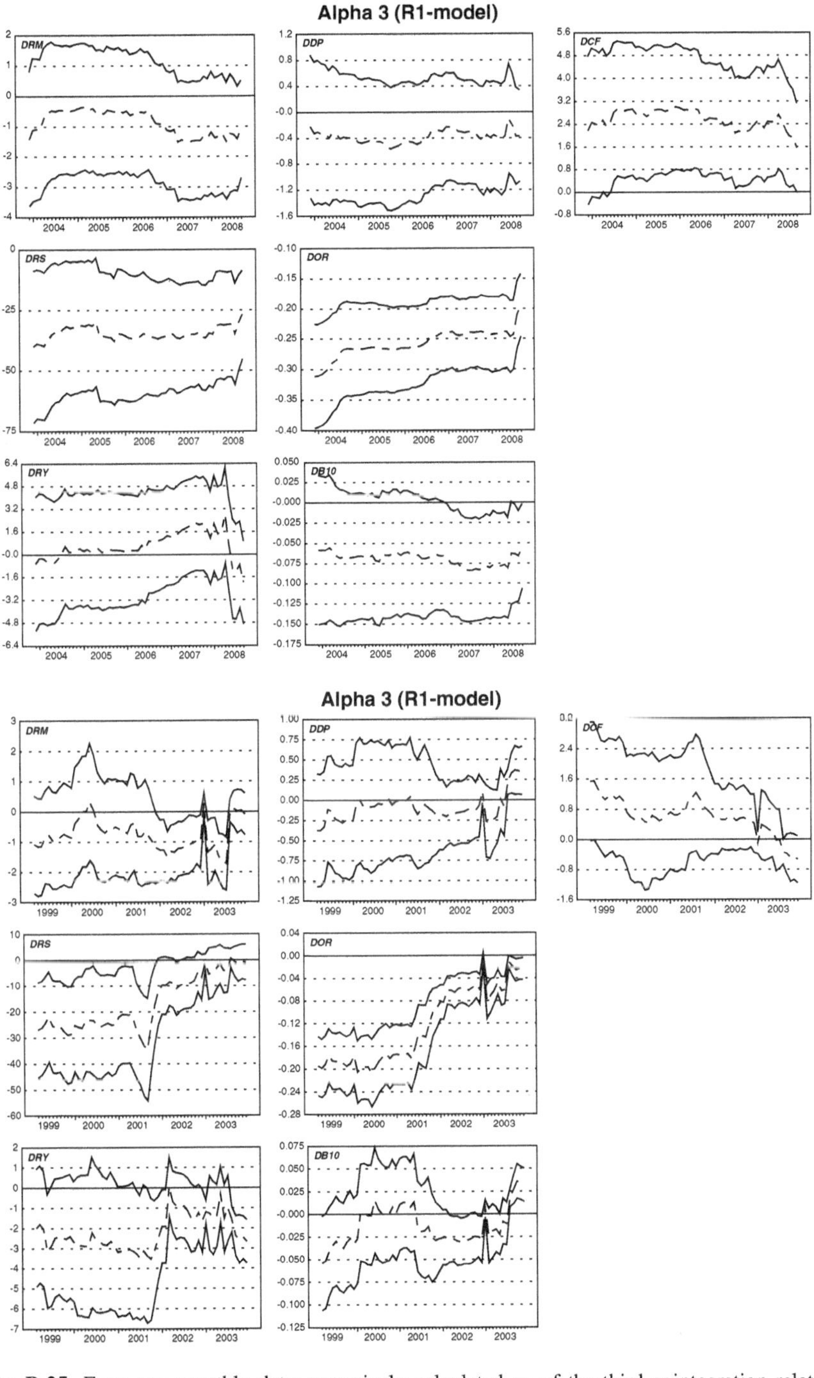

Fig. B.25 Euro area monthly data: recursively calculated αs of the third cointegration relation (forward, base sample 1999:03 to 2003:12, depicted above; backward, base sample 2008:09 to 2003:12, depicted below)

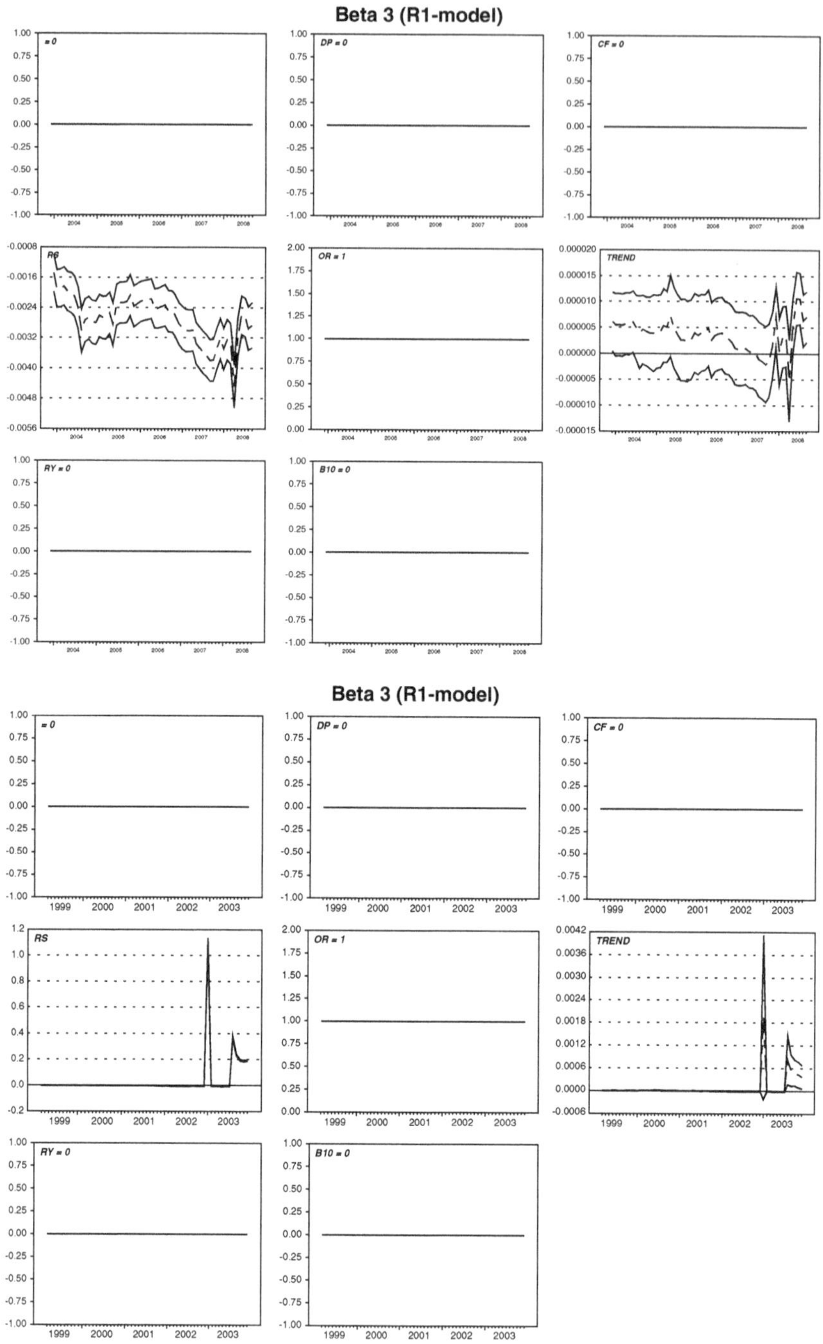

Fig. B.26 Euro area monthly data: recursively calculated βs of the third cointegration relation (forward, base sample 1999:03 to 2003:12, depicted above; backward, base sample 2008:09 to 2003:12, depicted below)

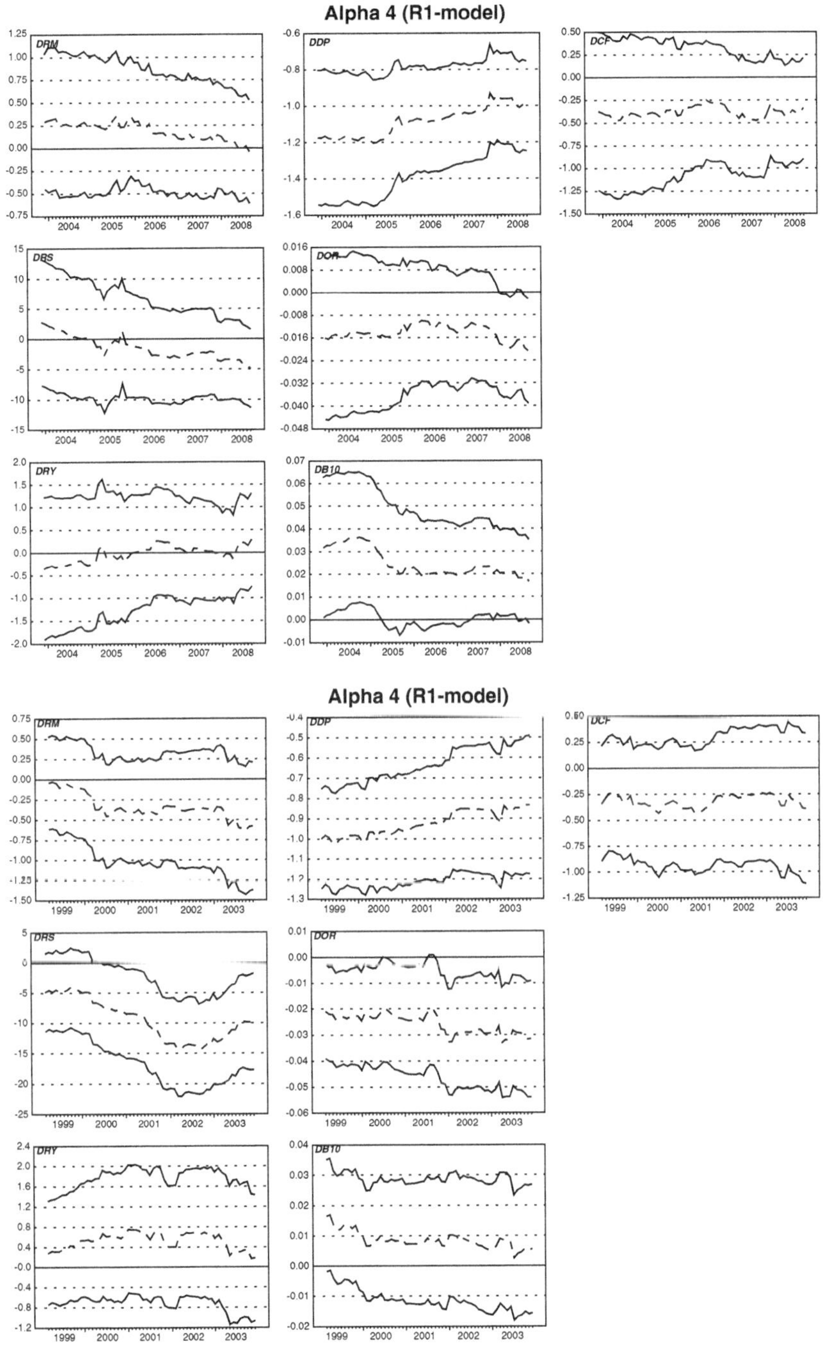

Fig. B.27 Euro area monthly data: recursively calculated αs of the fourth cointegration relation (forward, base sample 1999:03 to 2003:12, depicted above; backward, base sample 2008:09 to 2003:12, depicted below)

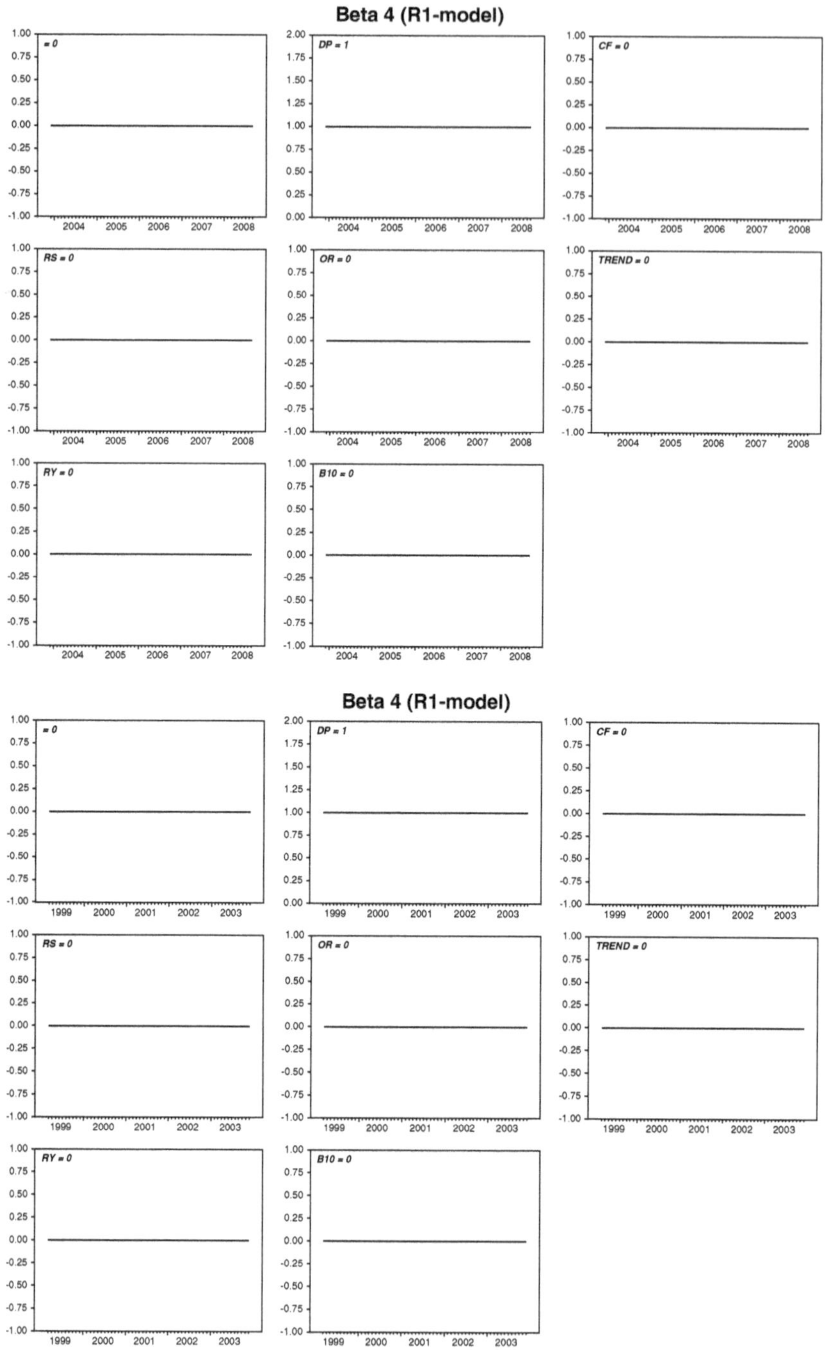

Fig. B.28 Euro area monthly data: recursively calculated βs of the fourth cointegration relation (forward, base sample 1999:03 to 2003:12, depicted above; backward, base sample 2008:09 to 2003:12, depicted below)

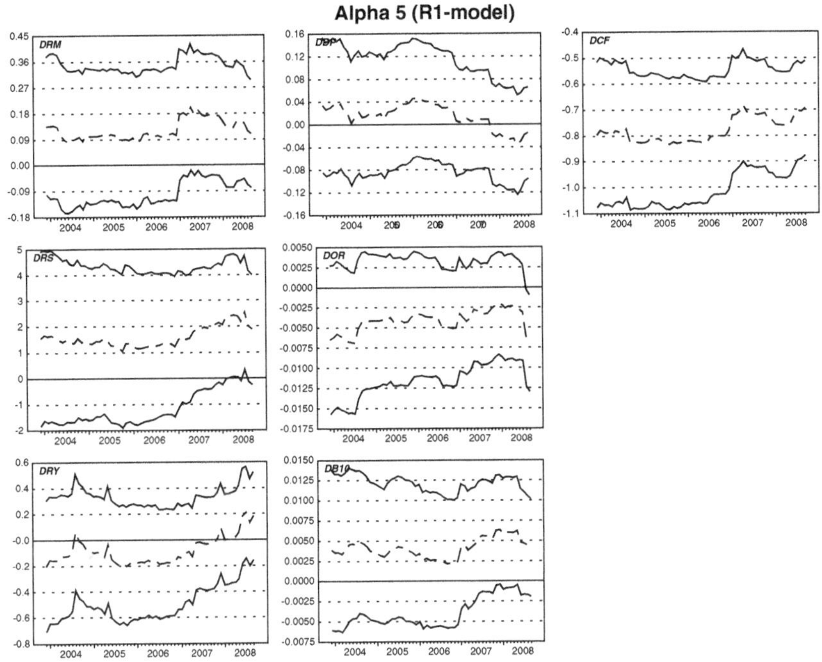

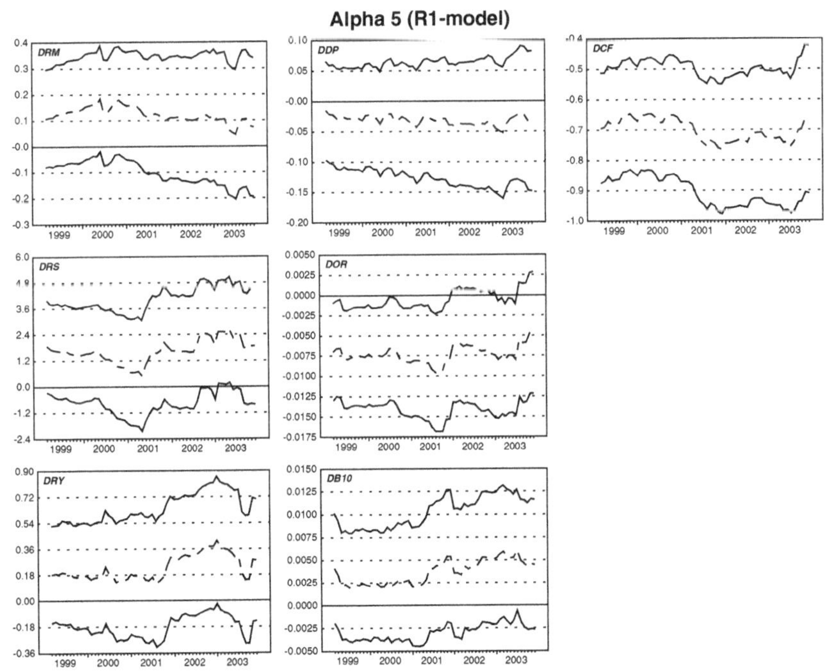

Fig. B.29 Euro area monthly data: recursively calculated αs of the fifth cointegration relation (forward, base sample 1999:03 to 2003:12, depicted above; backward, base sample 2008:09 to 2003:12, depicted below)

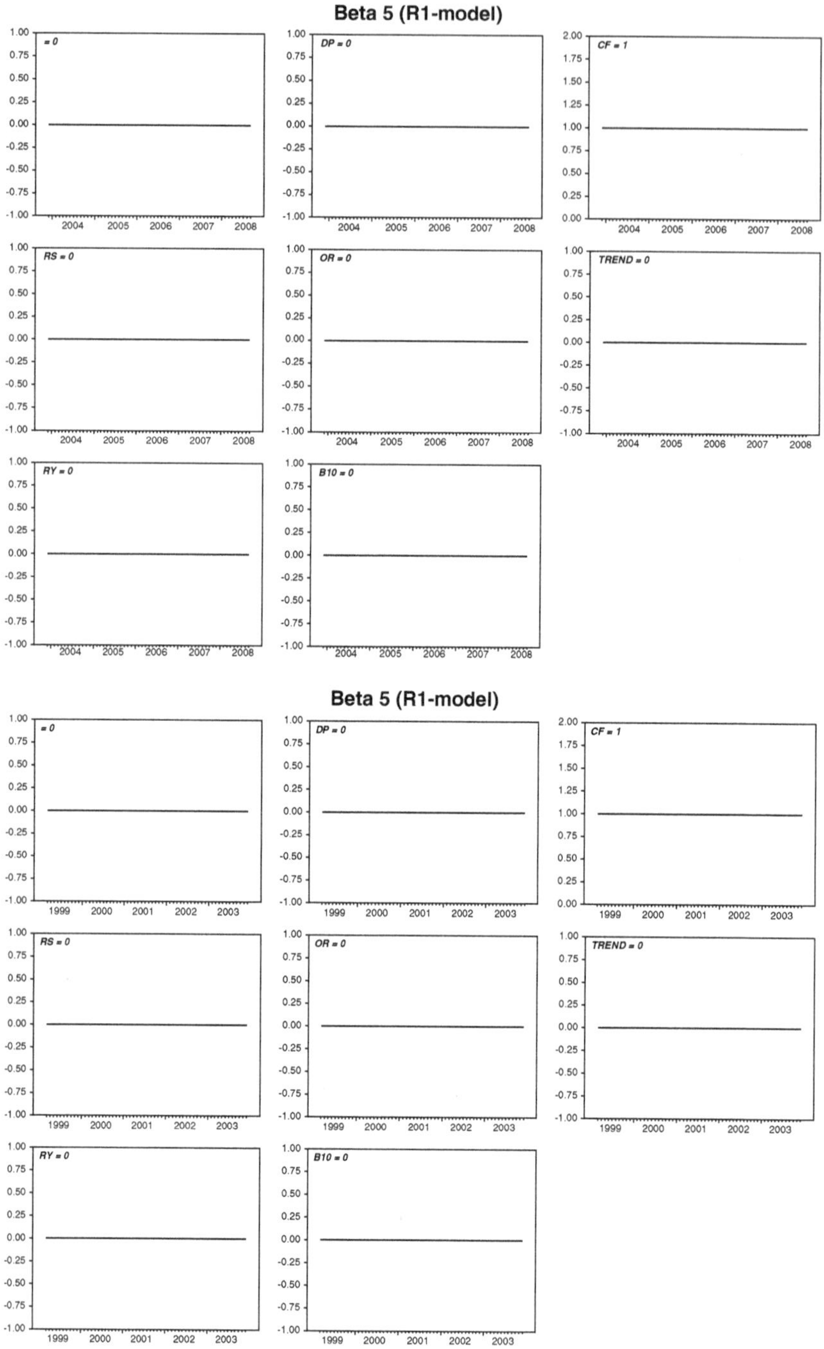

Fig. B.30 Euro area monthly data: recursively calculated βs of the fifth cointegration relation (forward, base sample 1999:03 to 2003:12, depicted above; backward, base sample 2008:09 to 2003:12, depicted below)

B.2.8 The Identified Long-Run Structure with Weak Exogeneity Imposed (Table B.9)

Table B.9 Euro area monthly data: the identified long-run structure with weak exogeneity imposed on real money (t-values in brackets)

	β'							
	m_r	s_r	y_r	Δp	or	$b10$	cf	*Trend*
Beta(1)	0.000 [NA]	**1.000** [NA]	**−15.09** [−15.38]	0.000 [NA]	0.000 [NA]	0.000 [NA]	0.000 [NA]	**0.019** [12.02]
Beta(2)	**−0.018** [−6.217]	0.000 [NA]	0.000 [NA]	0.000 [NA]	0.000 [NA]	**1.000** [NA]	0.000 [NA]	**0.000** [7.260]
Beta(3)	0.000 [NA]	**−0.003** [−9.852]	0.000 [NA]	0.000 [NA]	**1.000** [NA]	0.000 [NA]	0.000 [NA]	**0.000** [2.355]
Beta(4)	0.000 [NA]	0.000 [NA]	0.000 [NA]	**1.000** [NA]	0.000 [NA]	0.000 [NA]	0.000 [NA]	0.000 [NA]
Beta(5)	0.000 [NA]	0.000 [NA]	0.000 [NA]	0.000 [NA]	0.000 [NA]	0.000 [NA]	**1.000** [NA]	0.000 [NA]

	α				
	Alpha(1)	Alpha(2)	Alpha(3)	Alpha(4)	Alpha(5)
Δm_r	0.000 [0.000]	0.000 [0.000]	0.000 [0.000]	0.000 [0.000]	0.000 [0.000]
Δs_r	**−0.066** [−1.848]	**−31.86** [−2.787]	**−25.88** [−2.727]	−4.994 [−1.528]	1.704 [1.580]
Δy_r	**0.016** [2.731]	2.103 [1.159]	−1.583 [−1.052]	0.245 [0.472]	0.186 [1.089]
$\Delta^2 p$	**−0.005** [−3.702]	−0.393 [−0.902]	−0.656 [−1.811]	**−0.987** [−7.911]	0.005 [0.112]
Δor	**−0.001** [−5.256]	**0.081** [2.473]	**−0.202** [−7.448]	**−0.020** [−2.164]	**−0.007** [−2.182]
$\Delta b10$	**−0.000** [−2.288]	**−0.167** [−5.125]	**−0.051** [−1.897]	0.017 [1.807]	0.003 [1.123]
Δcf	**0.009** [2.930]	**2.470** [2.563]	**1.912** [2.390]	−0.343 [−1.244]	**−0.718** [−7.896]

B.2.9 The Long-Run Impact of the Common Trends with Weak Exogeneity Imposed (Table B.10)

Table B.10 Euro area monthly data: the long-run impact matrix with weak exogeneity imposed on real money (t-values in brackets)

The Long-Run Impact Matrix, C							
	$\hat{\epsilon}_{m_r}$	$\hat{\epsilon}_{s_r}$	$\hat{\epsilon}_{y_r}$	$\hat{\epsilon}_{\Delta p}$	$\hat{\epsilon}_{or}$	$\hat{\epsilon}_{b10}$	$\hat{\epsilon}_{cf}$
m_r	**0.982** [6.077]	−0.004 [−0.175]	0.010 [0.075]	0.034 [0.108]	0.067 [0.018]	0.751 [0.113]	−0.003 [−0.021]
s_r	3.167 [0.997]	**1.331** [3.179]	−3.736 [−1.362]	−12.11 [−1.956]	−23.84 [−0.318]	**−26.79** [−2.043]	1.042 [0.373]
y_r	0.210 [0.997]	**0.088** [3.179]	−0.248 [−1.362]	−0.803 [−1.956]	−1.580 [−0.318]	**−17.75** [−2.043]	0.069 [0.373]
Δp	−0.000 [NA]	−0.000 [NA]	0.000 [NA]	0.000 [NA]	0.000 [0.318]	0.000 [NA]	−0.000 [NA]
or	0.009 [0.997]	**0.004** [3.179]	−0.011 [−1.362]	−0.036 [−1.956]	−0.071 [−0.318]	**−0.802** [−2.043]	0.003 [0.373]
$b10$	**0.018** [6.077]	−0.000 [−0.175]	0.000 [0.075]	0.001 [0.108]	0.001 [0.018]	0.014 [0.113]	−0.000 [−0.021]
cf	0.000 [NA]	0.000 [NA]	0.000 [NA]	0.000 [NA]	0.000 [NA]	0.000 [NA]	0.000 [NA]

B.3 Japan: Quarterly Data

B.3.1 Data Sources (Table B.11)

Table B.11 Japan quarterly data: data sources

m	Variable	Nominal money M3, NSA
	Datastream name	JP MONEY SUPPLY: M3 (METHO-BREAK, APR. 2003) (EP) CURN
	Datastream Mnemonic	JPM3CDF.A
	Data source	Bank of Japan
s	Variable	Nominal stock market level, NSA
	Datastream name	JAPAN-DS Market - TOT RETURN IND
	Datastream Mnemonic	TOTMKJP(RI)
	Data source	Datastream
y	Variable	Nominal gross domestic product, SA
	Datastream name	JP GDP (AR) CURA
	Datastream Mnemonic	JPGDP...B
	Data source	Cabinet Office, Japan
p	Variable	Consumer price index, NSA
	Datastream name	JP CPI: NATIONAL MEASURE NADJ
	Datastream Mnemonic	JPCPIGNAF
	Data source	Statistics Bureau of MIC
or	Variable	Short-term interest rate, NSA
	Datastream name	JP OVERNIGHT UNCOLLATERISED CALL MONEY RATE (AVG.)
	Datastream Mnemonic	JPCALMTH
	Data source	Bank of Japan
*b*10	Variable	Long-term interest rate, NSA
	Datastream name	JP INTEREST-BEARING GOVERNMENT BONDS - 10-YEAR (EP)
	Datastream Mnemonic	JPGBOND.
	Data source	Main Economic Indicators, Copyright OECD
cf	Variable	Capital flows, NSA
	Time series name	External Counterpart of Money
	Data source	Constructed by author (see Appendix A), original data series from IMF BoP database

B.3.2 Graphs of the Cointegrating Relations of the Unrestricted Model (Fig. B.31)

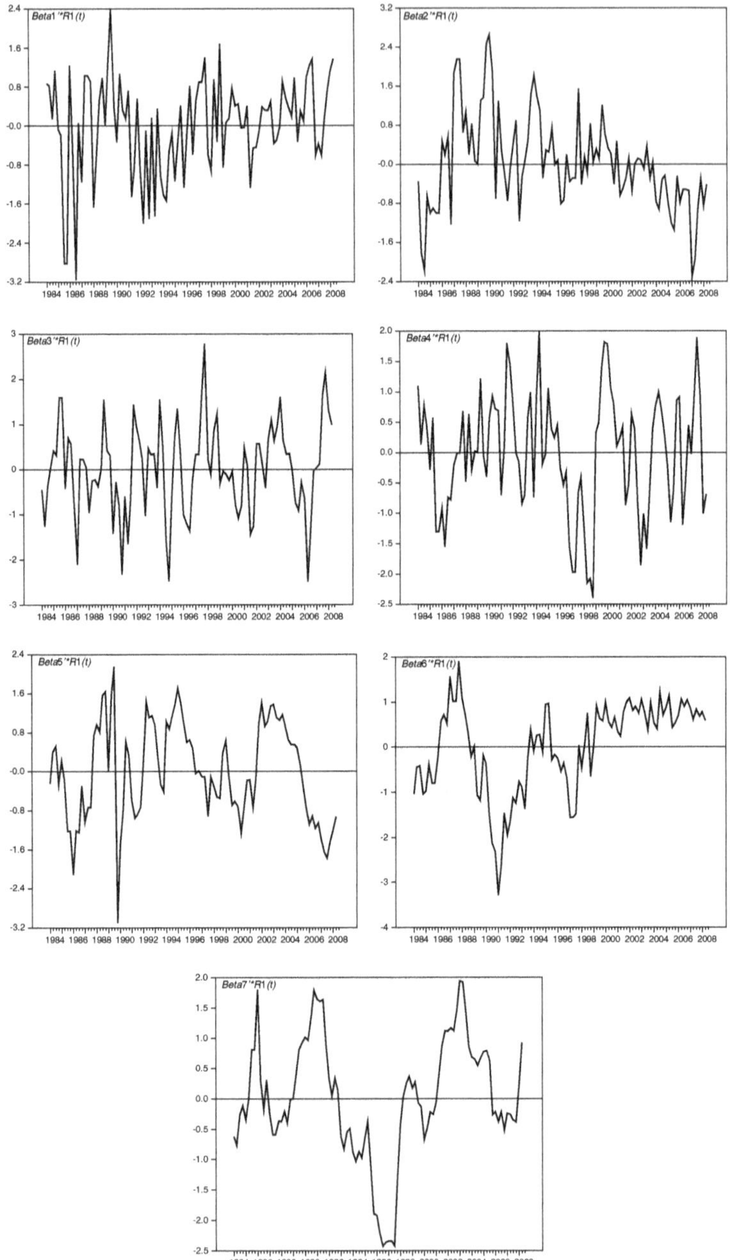

Fig. B.31 Japan quarterly data: the cointegration relations ($\beta_1, \ldots, \beta_7$) of the unrestricted model

B.3.3 Forward and Backward Recursive Tests for Parameter Constancy of the Unidentified System with Rank $r = 4$ Imposed (Figs. B.32, B.33, B.34, and B.35)

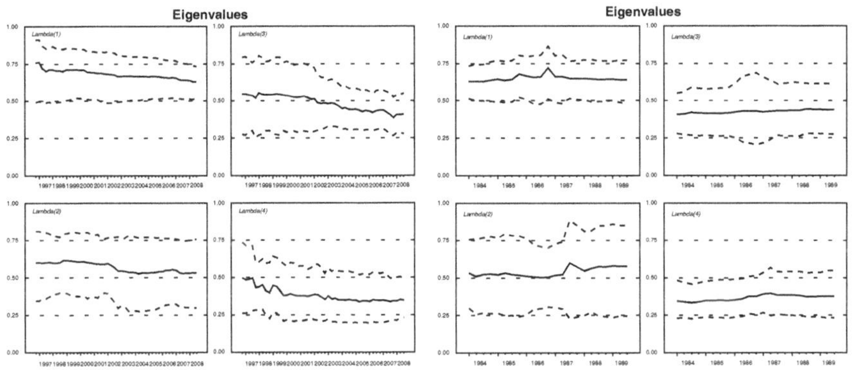

Fig. B.32 Japan quarterly data: recursively calculated eigenvalues λ_i (forward, base sample 1984:01 to 1995:04, depicted left; backward, base sample 2008:03 to 1989:02, depicted right)

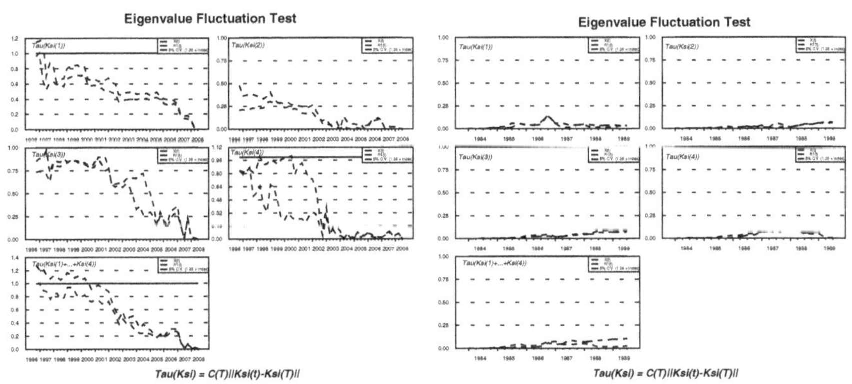

Fig. B.33 Japan quarterly data: recursively calculated eigenvalue fluctuation test (forward, base sample 1984:01 to 1995:04, depicted left; backward, base sample 2008:03 to 1989:02, depicted right)

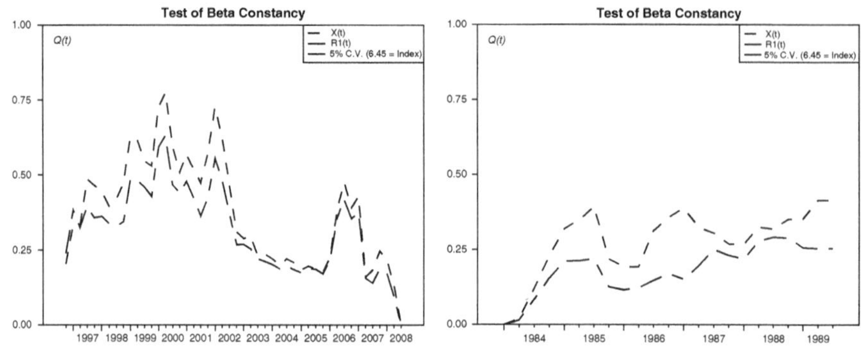

Fig. B.34 Japan quarterly data: recursively calculated test of β constancy (forward, base sample 1984:01 to 1995:04, depicted left; backward, base sample 2008:03 to 1989:02, depicted right)

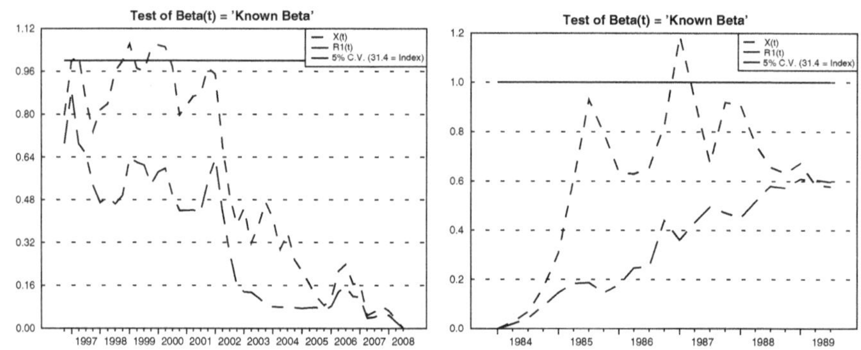

Fig. B.35 Japan quarterly data: recursively calculated test of β_t equals a known β (forward, base sample 1984:01 to 1995:04, depicted left; backward, base sample 2008:03 to 1989:02, depicted right)

B.3.4 The Partitioned Unrestricted Π-Matrices (Table B.12)

Table B.12 Japan quarterly data: the partitioned unrestricted Π-matrices based on 4 cointegrating vectors (t-values in brackets)

β'									
	m_r	s_r	y_r	Δp	or	$b10$	cf	D_s9001	*Trend*
Beta(1)	0.042	0.002	−0.038	1.000	−0.309	0.345	−0.267	0.000	−0.000
Beta(2)	0.063	−0.007	0.208	−0.285	0.555	1.000	−0.196	0.003	−0.003
Beta(3)	0.022	0.002	−0.002	−0.445	−0.024	1.000	−0.949	0.000	−0.000
Beta(4)	0.048	0.006	−0.052	−0.049	−0.347	1.000	0.610	0.000	−0.000

α				
	Alpha(1)	Alpha(2)	Alpha(3)	Alpha(4)
Δm_r	**−0.616** [−2.619]	**−0.989** [−7.760]	0.116 [0.496]	−0.436 [−1.364]
Δs_r	−7.270 [−1.737]	**5.029** [2.216]	0.279 [0.067]	**−12.56** [−2.206]
Δy_r	0.505 [1.774]	**−0.689** [−4.469]	**0.972** [3.423]	**1.240** [3.205]
$\Delta^2 p$	**−0.550** [−3.946]	**0.287** [3.802]	0.242 [1.742]	0.086 [0.451]
Δor	**0.133** [5.844]	−0.012 [−0.993]	0.004 [0.174]	0.011 [0.339]
$\Delta b10$	**0.088** [2.586]	**−0.087** [−4.703]	−0.061 [−1.792]	−0.051 [−1.107]
Δcf	**0.259** [2.191]	−0.018 [−0.287]	**0.684** [5.787]	**−0.660** [−4.096]

B.3.5 Rank Conditions of the Identified Long-Run Structure

Checking formal identification of the restrictions imposed by:

H_1'								
1	0	0	0	0	0	0	0	0
0	1	0	0	0	0	0	0	0
0	0	0	1	0	0	0	0	0
0	0	0	0	0	0	0	1	0
0	0	0	0	0	0	0	0	1

H_2'								
0	1	0	0	0	0	0	0	0
0	0	1	0	0	0	0	0	0
0	0	0	0	1	0	0	0	0
0	0	0	0	0	0	0	1	0
0	0	0	0	0	0	0	0	1

H_3'								
0	0	0	−1	0	1	0	0	0
0	0	0	0	0	0	0	1	0

H_4'								
0	0	0	0	0	0	1	0	0

The set of restrictions imposed by $H_1, \ldots H_r$ are formally identifying if for all i and $k = 1, \ldots, r-1$ and any set of indices $1 \leq i_1 < \cdots < i_k \leq r$ not containing i it holds that

$$R\left(i.i_1, \ldots, i_k\right) = rank\left(R_i'\left[H_{i_1} \cdots H_{i_k}\right]\right) \geq k$$

where $R_i = H_{1\perp}$ for all i. The conditions are summarized in Table B.13:

Table B.13 Japan quarterly data: rank conditions of the identified long-run structure

Rank Conditions					
$R(i.j)$		$R(i.jk)$		$R(i.jkl)$	
(1.2):	2	(1.23):	3	(1.234):	4
(1.3):	1	(1.24):	3		
(1.4):	1	(1.34):	2		
(2.1):	2	(2.13):	3	(2.134):	4
(2.3):	1	(2.14):	3		
(2.4):	1	(2.34):	2		
(3.1):	4	(3.12):	6	(3.124):	7
(3.2):	4	(3.14):	5		
(3.4):	1	(3.24):	5		
(4.1):	5	(4.12):	7	(4.123):	8
(4.2):	5	(4.13):	6		
(4.3):	2	(4.23):	6		

B.3.6 Graphs of the Cointegrating Relations of the Identified Long-Run Structure (Fig. B.36)

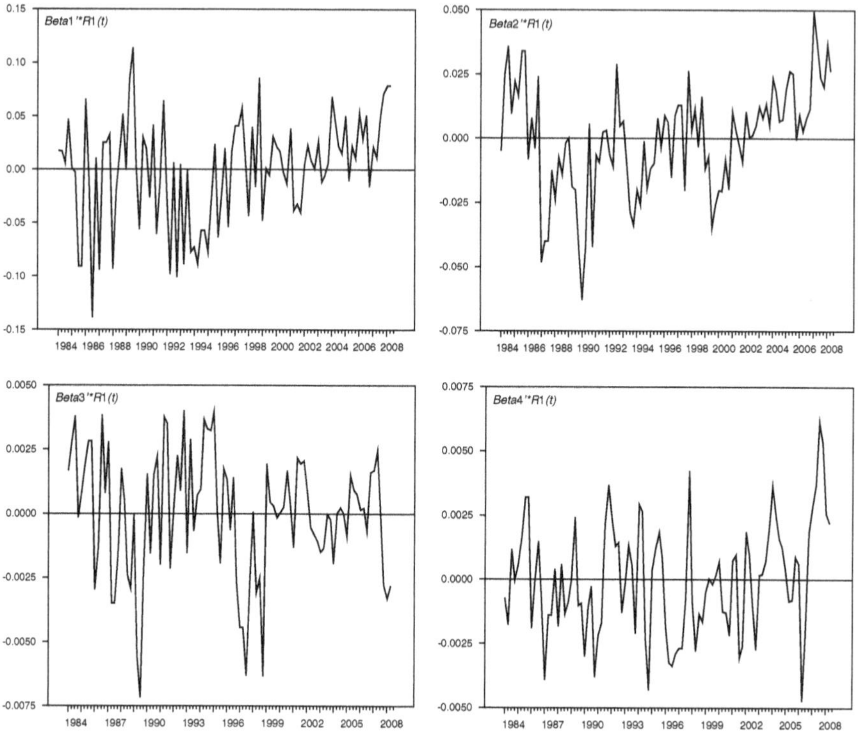

Fig. B.36 Japan quarterly data: the cointegration relations ($\beta_1, \ldots, \beta_4$) of the restricted model

B.3.7 Tests for Parameter Constancy of the Identified Long-Run Structure (Figs. B.37, B.38, B.39, B.40, B.41, B.42, B.43, and B.44)

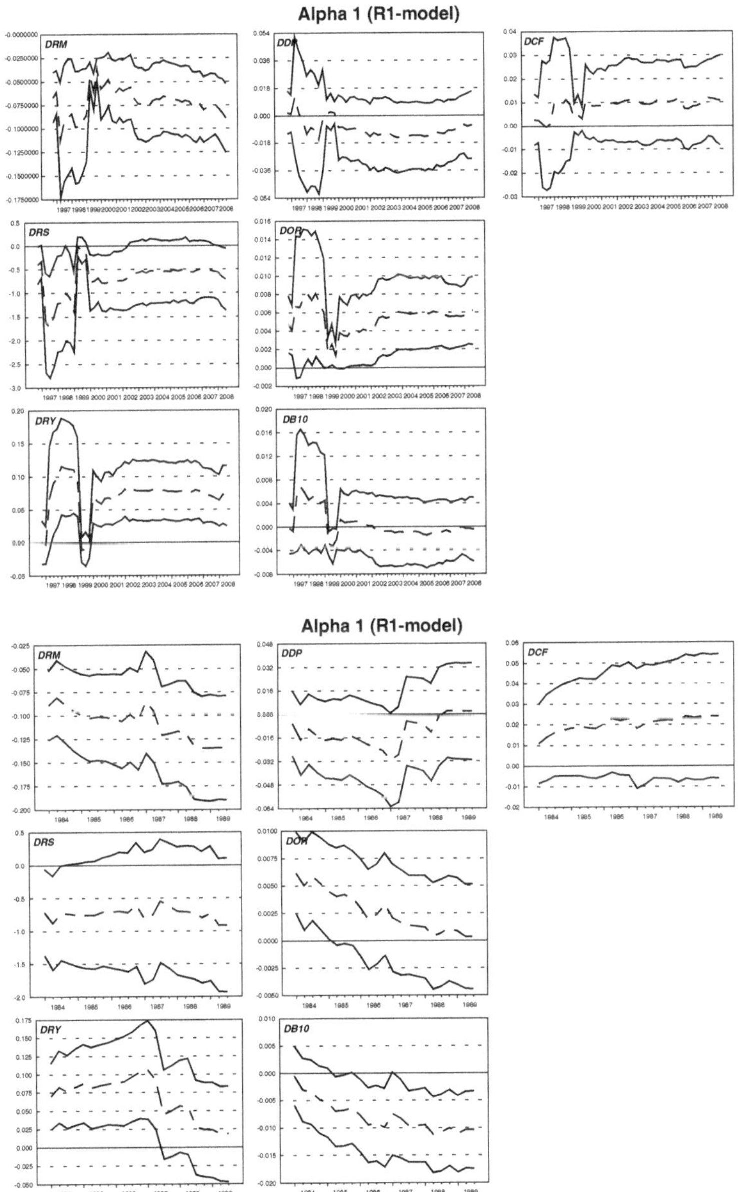

Fig. B.37 Japan quarterly data: recursively calculated αs of the first cointegration relation (forward, base sample 1984:01 to 1995:04, depicted above; backward, base sample 2008:03 to 1989:02, depicted below)

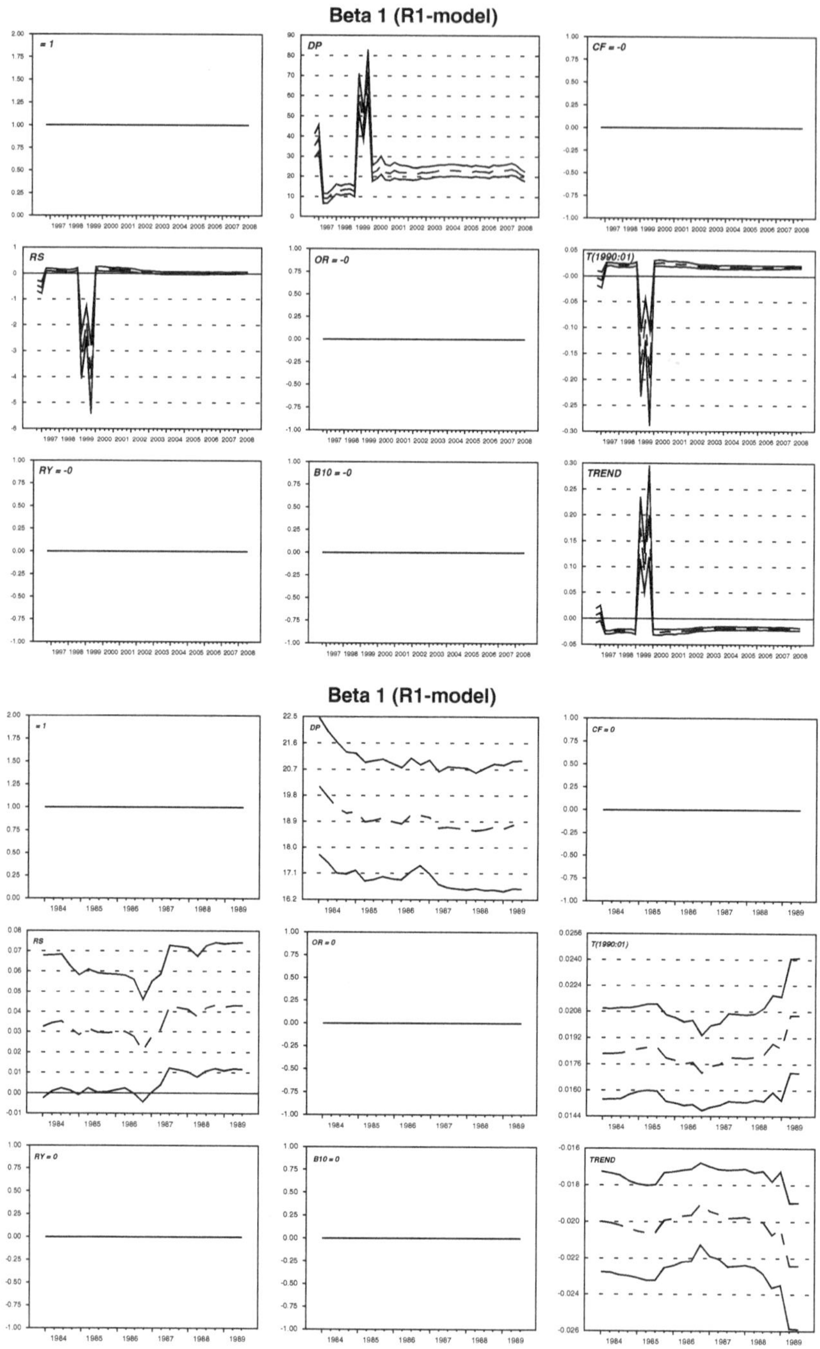

Fig. B.38 Japan quarterly data: recursively calculated βs of the first cointegration relation (forward, base sample 1984:01 to 1995:04, depicted above; backward, base sample 2008:03 to 1989:02, depicted below)

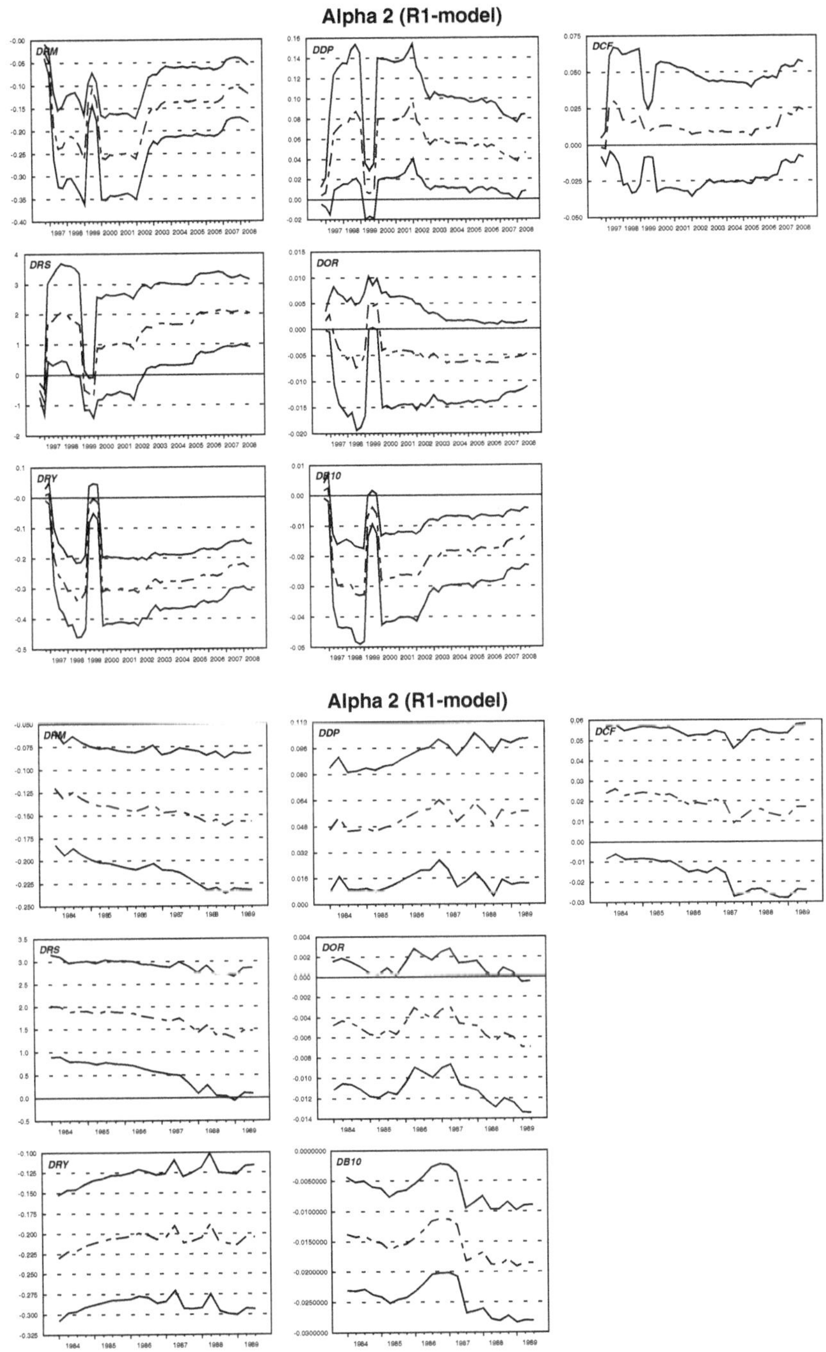

Fig. B.39 Japan quarterly data: recursively calculated αs of the second cointegration relation (forward, base sample 1984:01 to 1995:04, depicted above; backward, base sample 2008:03 to 1989:02, depicted below)

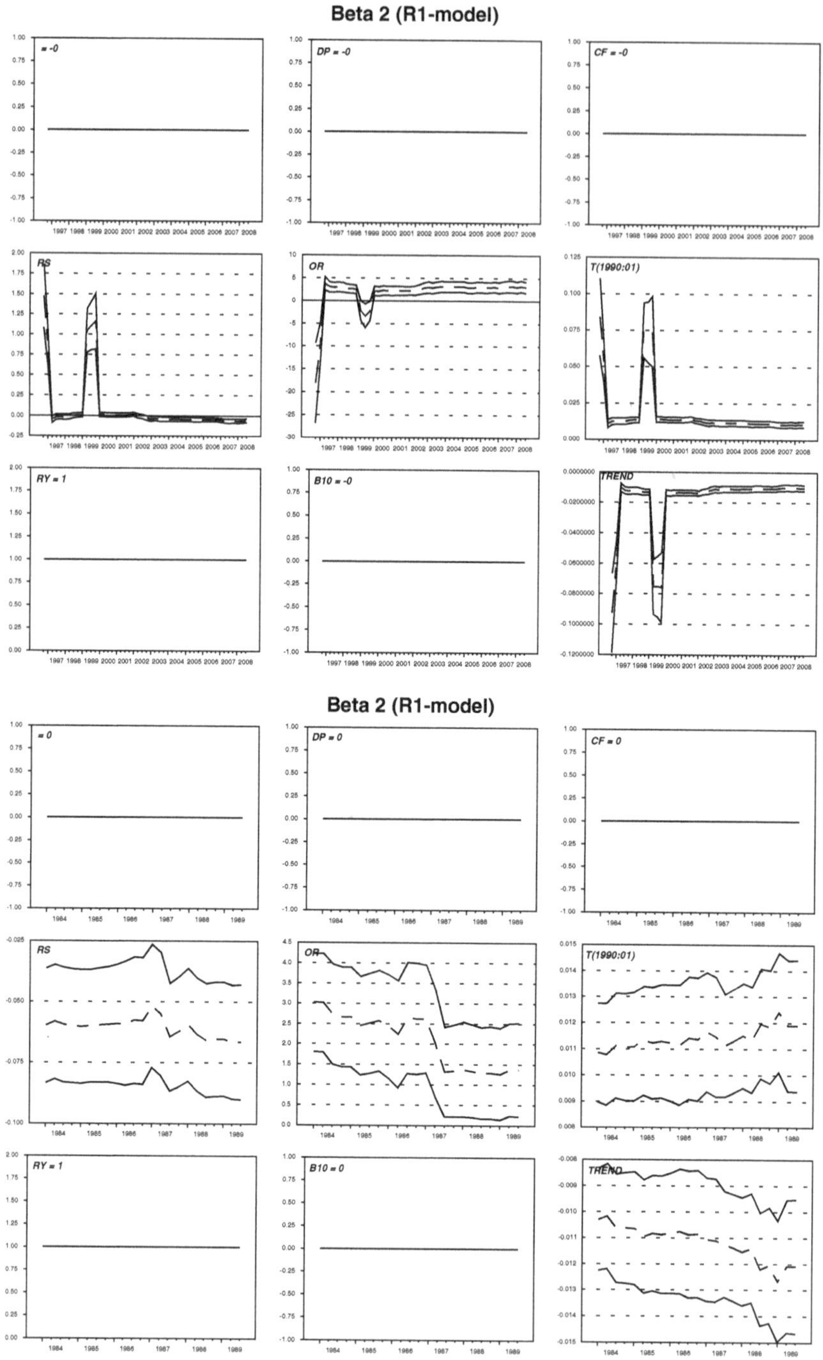

Fig. B.40 Japan quarterly data: recursively calculated βs of the second cointegration relation (forward, base sample 1984:01 to 1995:04, depicted above; backward, base sample 2008:03 to 1989:02, depicted below)

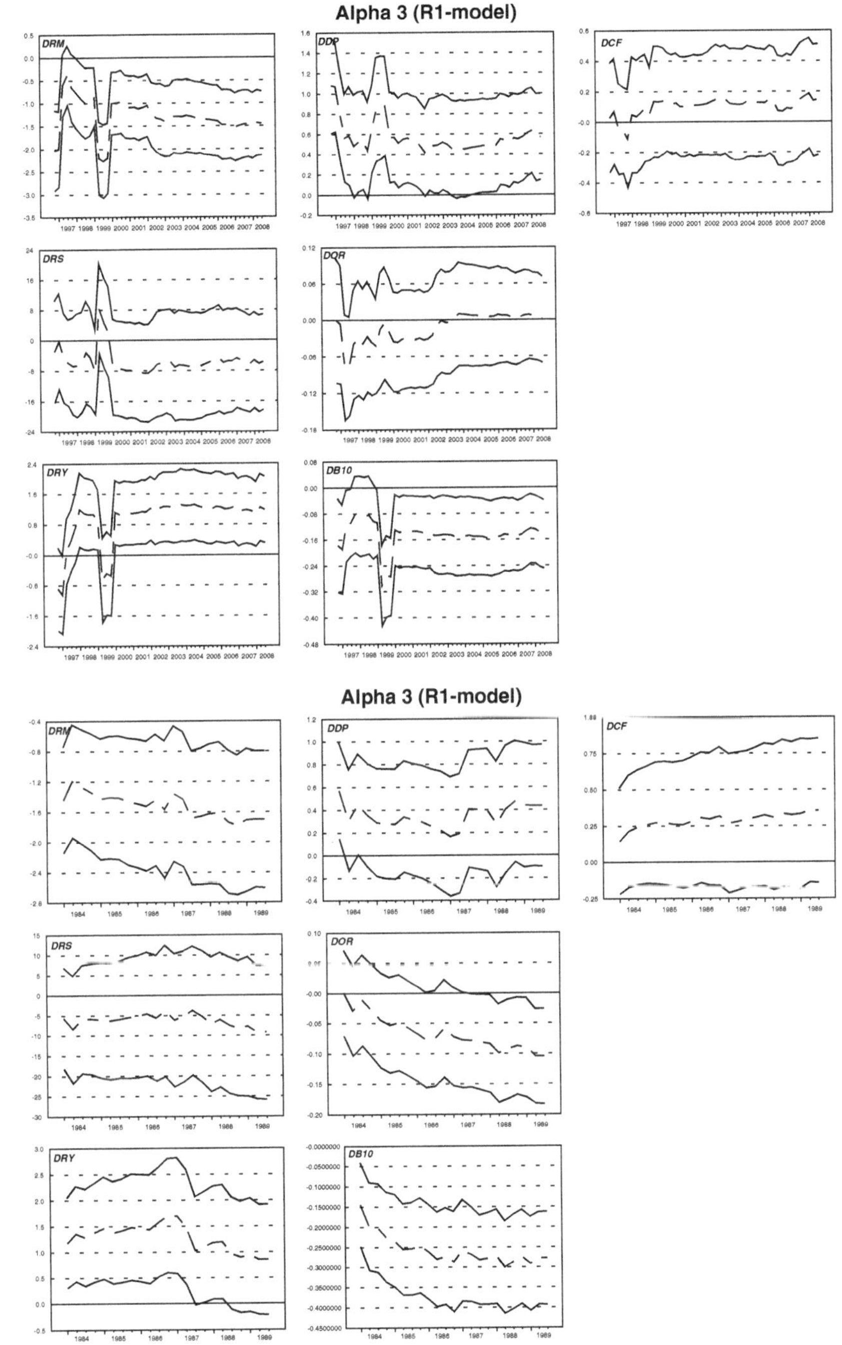

Fig. B.41 Japan quarterly data: recursively calculated αs of the third cointegration relation (forward, base sample 1984:01 to 1995:04, depicted above; backward, base sample 2008:03 to 1989:02, depicted below)

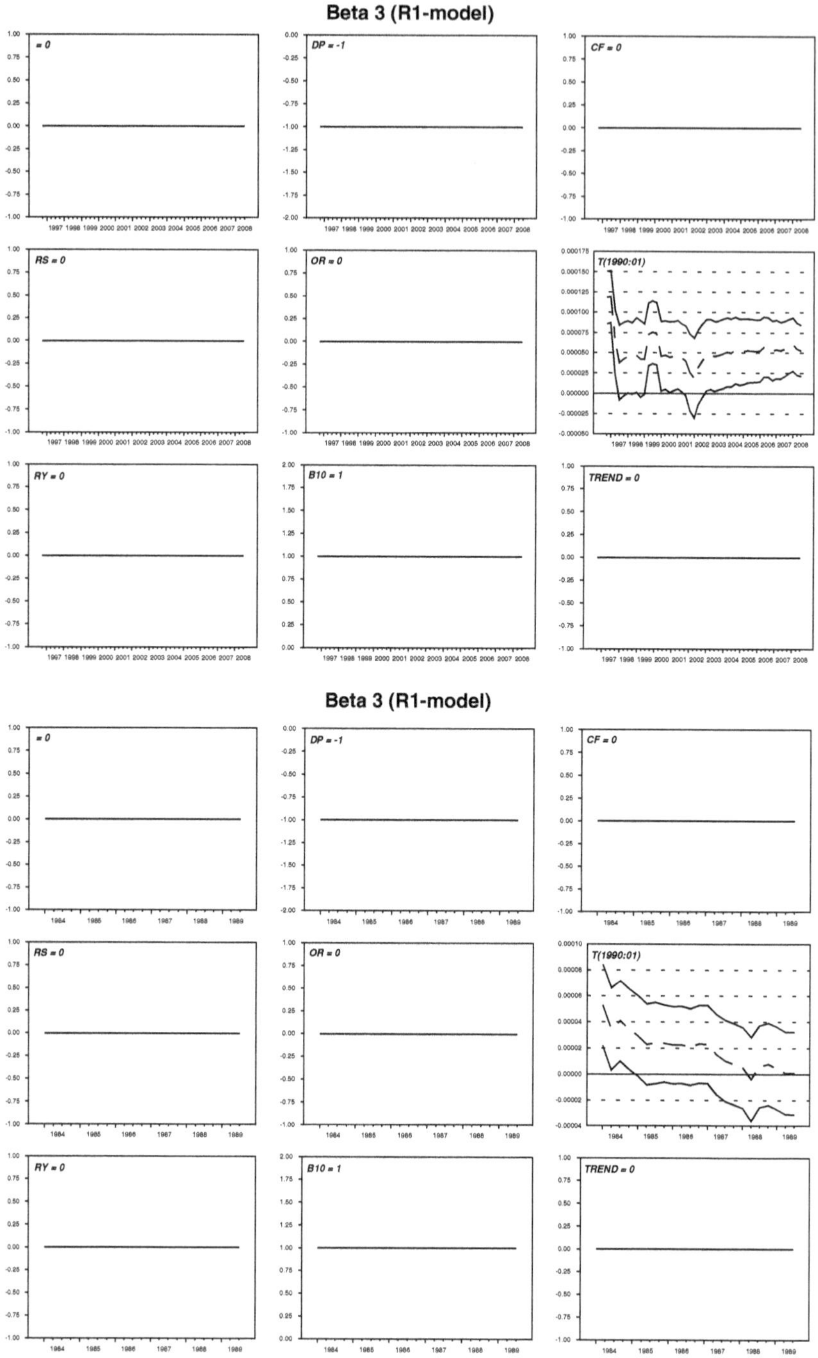

Fig. B.42 Japan quarterly data: recursively calculated βs of the third cointegration relation (forward, base sample 1984:01 to 1995:04, depicted above; backward, base sample 2008:03 to 1989:02, depicted below)

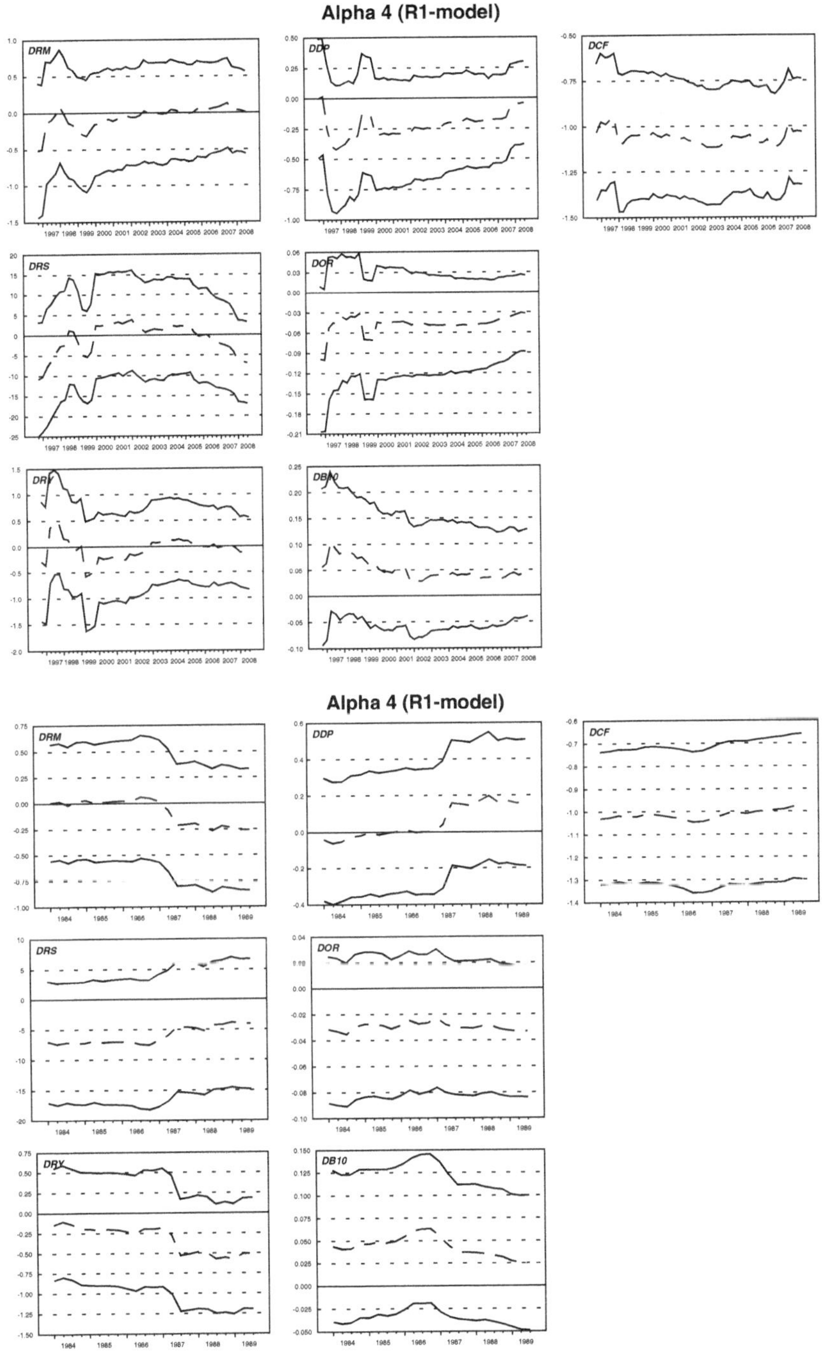

Fig. B.43 Japan quarterly data: recursively calculated αs of the fourth cointegration relation (forward, base sample 1984:01 to 1995:04, depicted above; backward, base sample 2008:03 to 1989:02, depicted below)

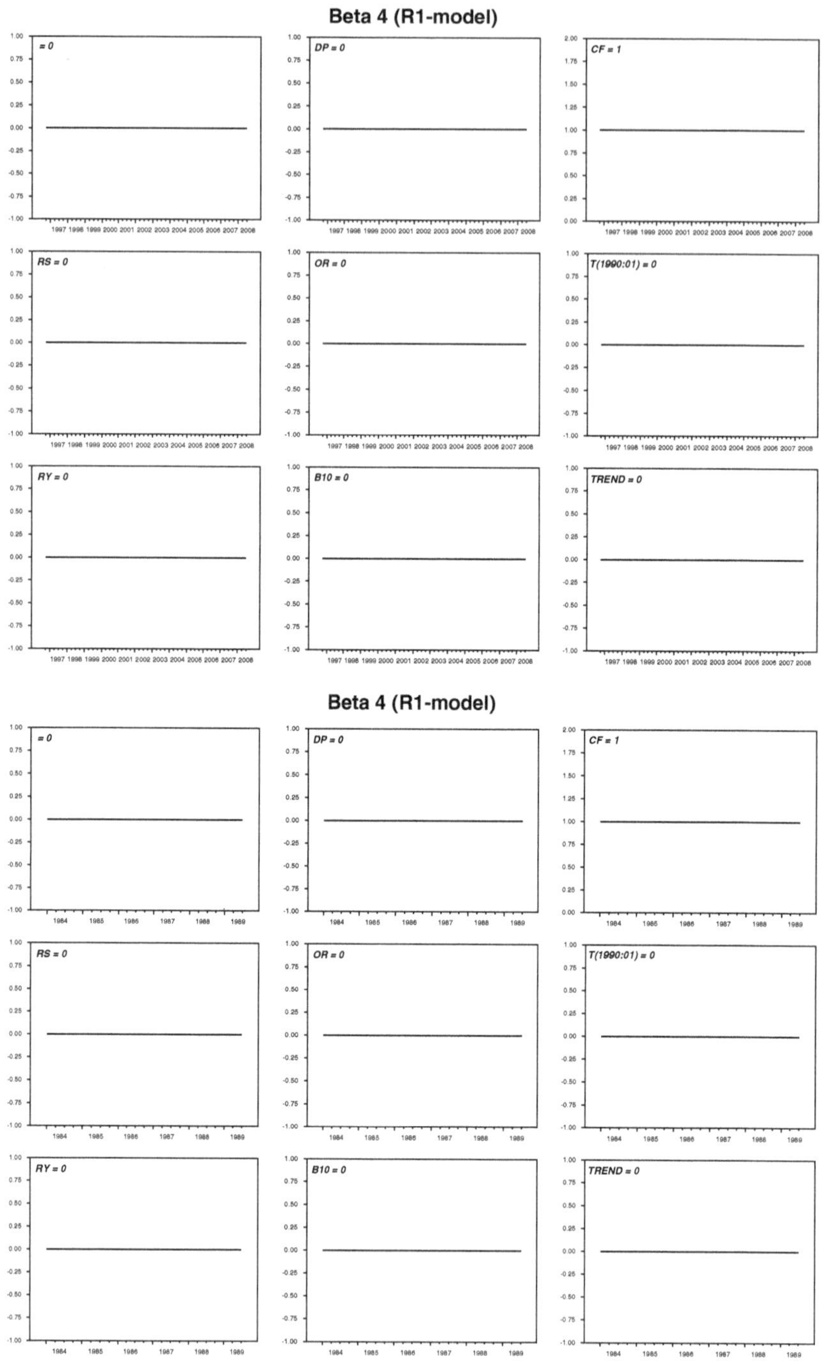

Fig. B.44 Japan quarterly data: recursively calculated βs of the fourth cointegration relation (forward, base sample 1984:01 to 1995:04, depicted above; backward, base sample 2008:03 to 1989:02, depicted below)

B.4 United Kingdom: Quarterly Data

B.4.1 Data Sources (Table B.14)

Table B.14 UK quarterly data: data sources

m	Variable	Nominal money M4, NSA
	Datastream name	UK MONEY SUPPLY M4(END QUARTER LEVEL) CURN
	Datastream Mnemonic	UKM4Q...A
	Data source	Bank of England
s	Variable	Nominal stock market level, NSA
	Datastream name	UK-DS Market -TOT RETURN IND
	Datastream Mnemonic	TOTMKUK(RI)
	Data source	Datastream
y	Variable	Nominal gross domestic product, SA
	Datastream name	UK GROSSDOMESTIC PRODUCT (MARKET PRICES) CURA
	Datastream Mnemonic	UKYBHA..B
	Data source	Office for National Statistics
p	Variable	Consumer price index, NSA
	Datastream name	UK CPI NADJ
	Datastream Mnemonic	UKOCP009F
	Data source	Main Economic Indicators, Copyright OECD
or	Variable	Short-term interest rate, NSA
	Datastream name	UK INTERBANK OVERNIGHT- MIDDLE RATE
	Datastream Mnemonic	LDNIBON
	Data source	Tradition
*b*10	Variable	Long-term interest rate, NSA
	Datastream name	UK GROSS REDEMPTION YIELD ON 10 YEAR GILT EDGED STOCKS(AVE)
	Datastream Mnemonic	UKMEDYLD
	Data source	Bank of England
cf	Variable	Capital flows, NSA
	Time series name	External Counterpart of Money
	Data source	Constructed by author (see Appendix A), original data series from IMF BoP database

B.4.2 Graphs of the Cointegrating Relations of the Unrestricted Model (Fig. B.45)

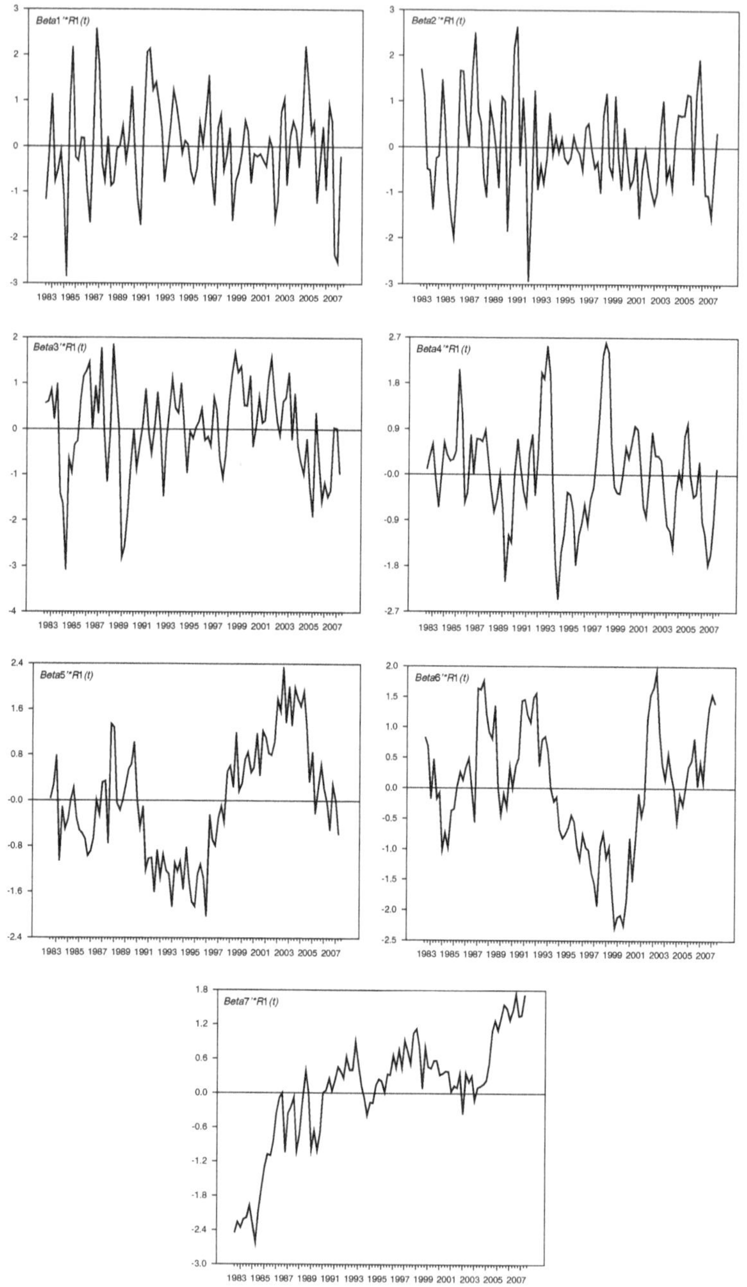

Fig. B.45 UK quarterly data: the cointegration relations ($\beta_1, \ldots, \beta_7$) of the unrestricted model

B.4.3 Forward and Backward Recursive Tests for Parameter Constancy of the Unidentified System with Rank $r = 3$ Imposed (Figs. B.46, B.47, B.48, and B.49)

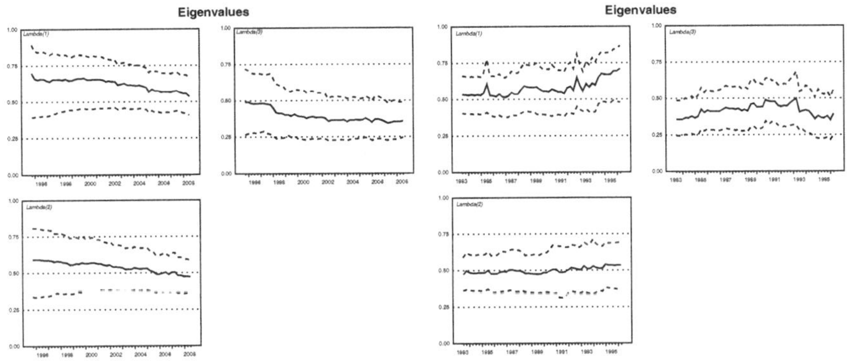

Fig. B.46 UK quarterly data: recursively calculated eigenvalues λ_i (forward, base sample 1983:03 to 1995:04, depicted left; backward, base sample 2008:03 to 1996:02, depicted right)

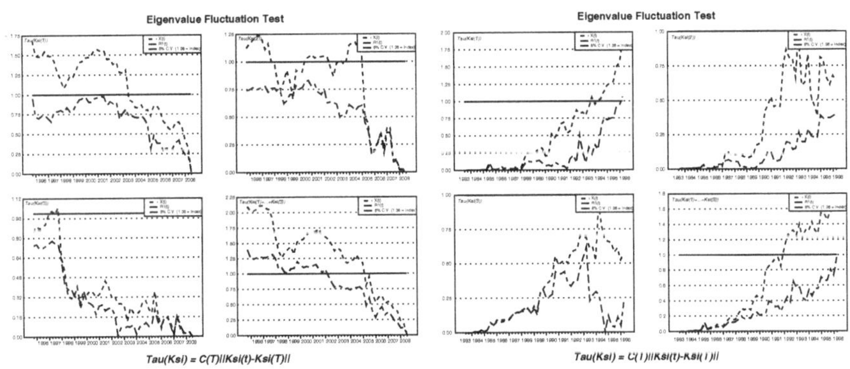

Fig. B.47 UK quarterly data: recursively calculated eigenvalue fluctuation test (forward, base sample 1983:03 to 1995:04, depicted left; backward, base sample 2008:03 to 1996:02, depicted right)

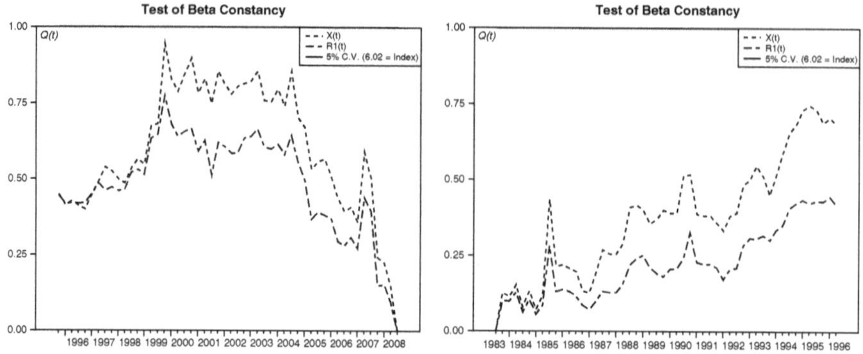

Fig. B.48 UK quarterly data: recursively calculated test of β constancy (forward, base sample 1983:03 to 1995:04, depicted left; backward, base sample 2008:03 to 1996:02, depicted right)

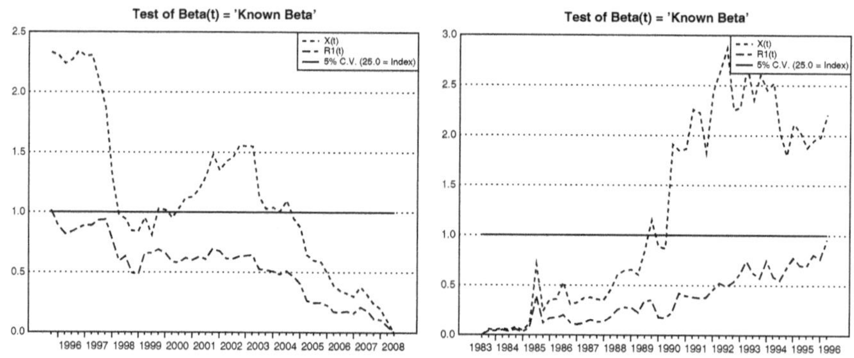

Fig. B.49 UK quarterly data: recursively calculated test of β_t equals a known β (forward, base sample 1983:03 to 1995:04, depicted left; backward, base sample 2008:03 to 1996:02, depicted right)

B.4.4 The Partitioned Unrestricted Π*-Matrices (Table B.15)*

Table B.15 UK quarterly data: the partitioned unrestricted Π-matrices based on 4 cointegrating vectors (t-values in brackets)

	β'							
	m_r	s_r	y_r	Δp	or	$b10$	cf	*Trend*
Beta(1)	−0.024	0.006	−0.062	1.000	0.255	−0.834	−0.314	0.001
Beta(2)	0.012	0.004	0.052	1.000	−0.852	0.082	0.218	−0.001
Beta(3)	−0.016	−0.005	−0.072	0.195	1.000	0.101	0.150	0.001

	α		
	Alpha(1)	Alpha(2)	Alpha(3)
Δm_r	0.387 [1.672]	**0.545** [2.225]	−0.268 [−1.177]
Δs_r	−3.176 [−1.757]	0.598 [0.313]	0.433 [0.243]
Δy_r	0.236 [1.320]	−0.070 [−0.373]	**−0.677** [−3.844]
$\Delta^2 p$	**−0.491** [−5.160]	**−0.569** [−5.649]	−0.097 [−1.040]
Δor	−0.129 [−1.446]	**0.401** [4.241]	**−0.422** [−4.798]
$\Delta b10$	0.039 [1.311]	−0.011 [−0.360]	**−0.060** [−2.054]
Δcf	**2.198** [6.624]	**−1.506** [−4.290]	**−0.651** [1.993]

B.4.5 Rank Conditions of the Identified Long-Run Structure

Checking formal identification of the restrictions imposed by:

H_1'							
0	0	0	0	1	0	0	0
0	0	0	0	0	0	0	1
0	1	0	0	0	0	0	0
0	0	1	0	0	0	0	0

H_2'							
0	0	0	0	0	0	1	0
1	0	0	0	0	0	0	0
0	1	0	0	0	0	0	0
0	0	0	0	0	0	0	1

H_3'							
0	0	0	1	0	0	0	0
0	0	1	0	0	0	0	0
0	0	0	0	0	1	0	0
0	0	0	0	0	0	0	1
0	0	0	0	1	0	0	0

The set of restrictions imposed by $H_1, \ldots H_3$ are formally identifying if for all i and $k = 1, \ldots, r-1$ and any set of indices $1 \leq i_1 < \cdots < i_k \leq r$ not containing i it holds that

$$R\,(i.i_1, \ldots, i_k) = rank\left(R_i'\left[H_{i_1} \cdots H_{i_k}\right]\right) \geq k$$

where $R_i = H_{1\perp}$ for all i. The conditions are summarized in Table B.16:

Table B.16 UK quarterly data: rank conditions of the identified long-run structure

Rank Conditions			
$R(i.j)$		$R(i.jk)$	
(1.2):	2	(1.23):	4
(1.3):	2		
(2.1):	2	(2.13):	4
(2.3):	4		
(3.1):	1	(3.12):	3
(3.2):	3		

B.4.6 Graphs of the Cointegrating Relations of the Identified Long-Run Structure (Fig. B.50)

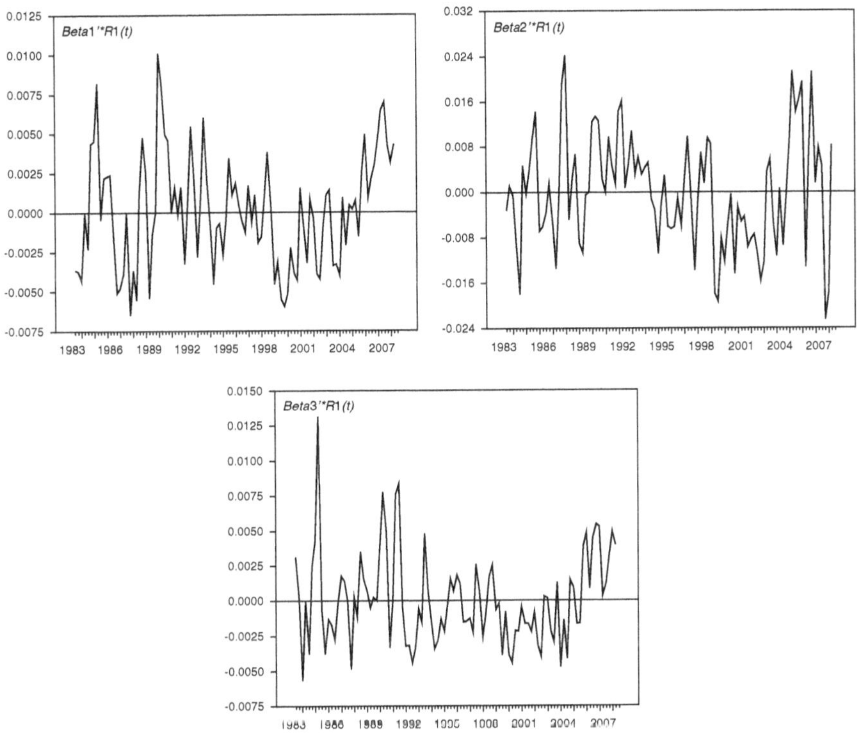

Fig. B.50 UK quarterly data: the cointegration relations ($\beta_1, \ldots, \beta_3$) of the restricted model

B.4.7 Tests for Parameter Constancy of the Identified Long-Run Structure (Figs. B.51, B.52, B.53, B.54, B.55, and B.56)

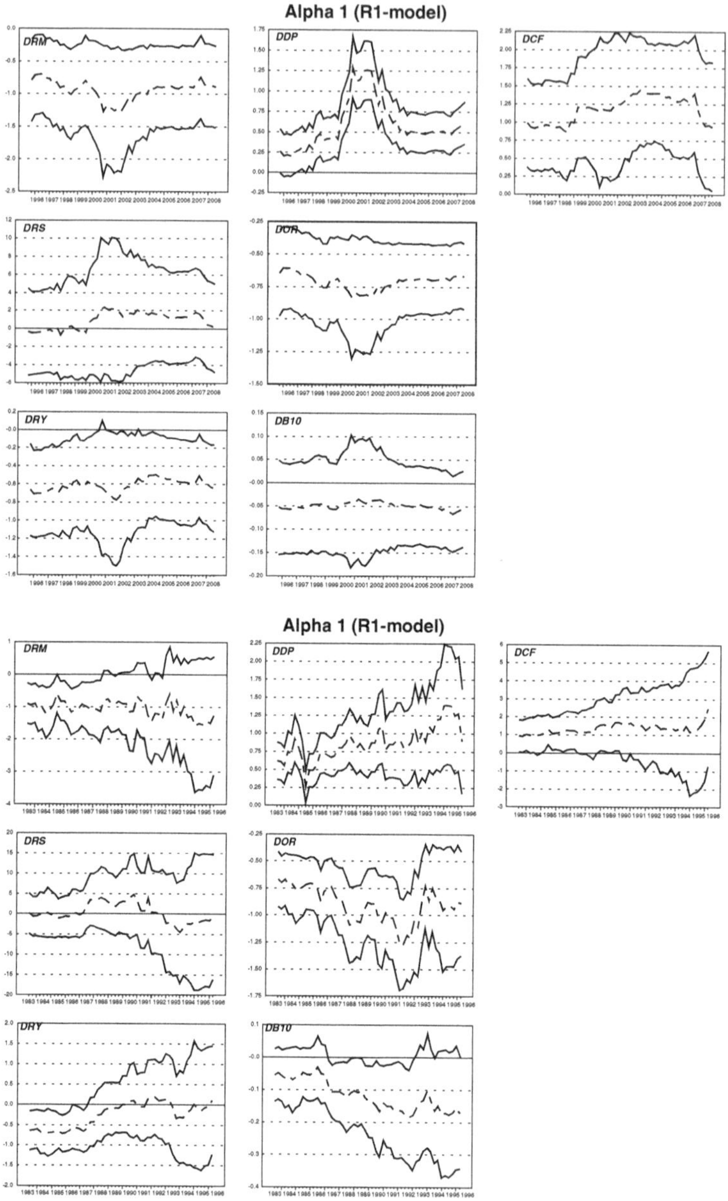

Fig. B.51 UK quarterly data: recursively calculated αs of the first cointegration relation (forward, base sample 1983:03 to 1995:04, depicted above; backward, base sample 2008:03 to 1996:02, depicted below)

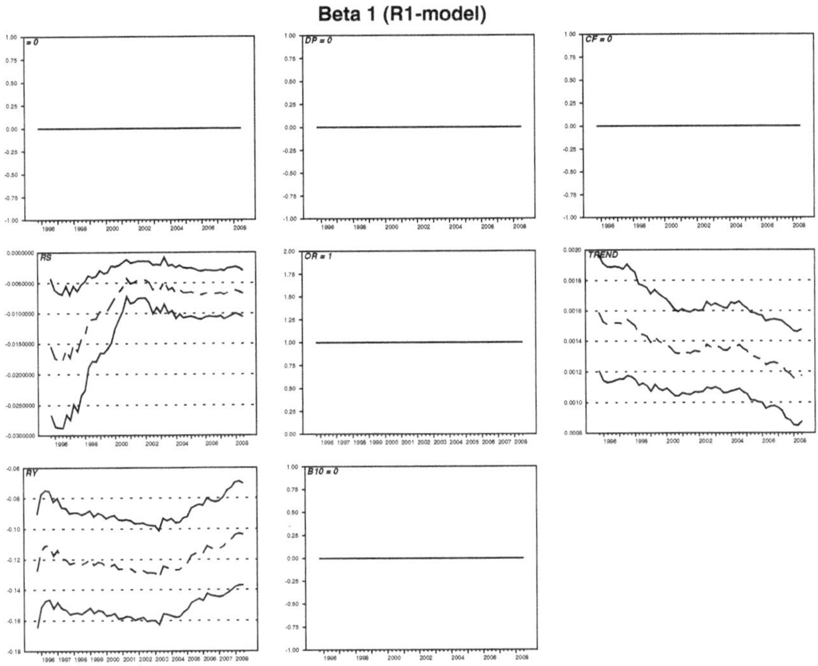

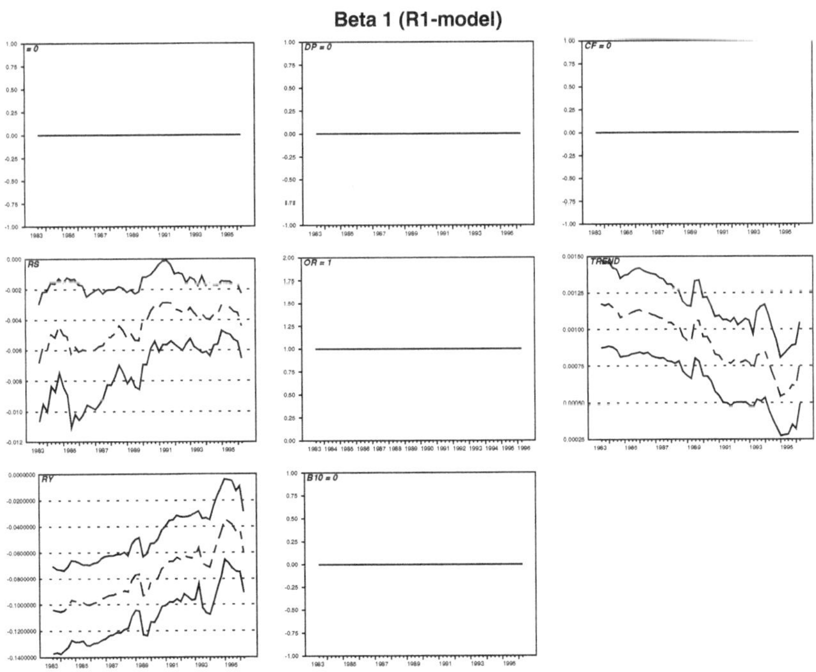

Fig. B.52 UK quarterly data: recursively calculated βs of the first cointegration relation (forward, base sample 1983:03 to 1995:04, depicted above; backward, base sample 2008:03 to 1996:02, depicted below)

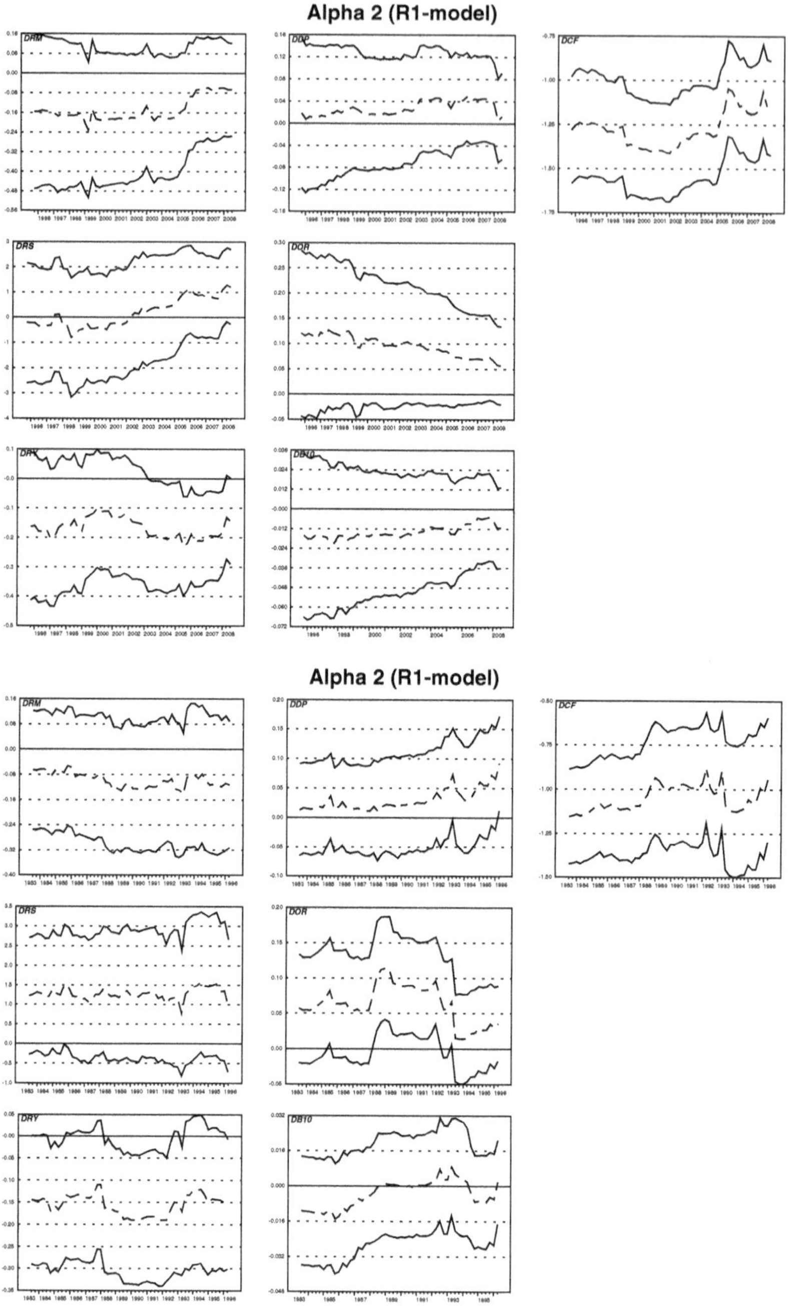

Fig. B.53 UK quarterly data: recursively calculated αs of the second cointegration relation (forward, base sample 1983:03 to 1995:04, depicted above; backward, base sample 2008:03 to 1996:02, depicted below)

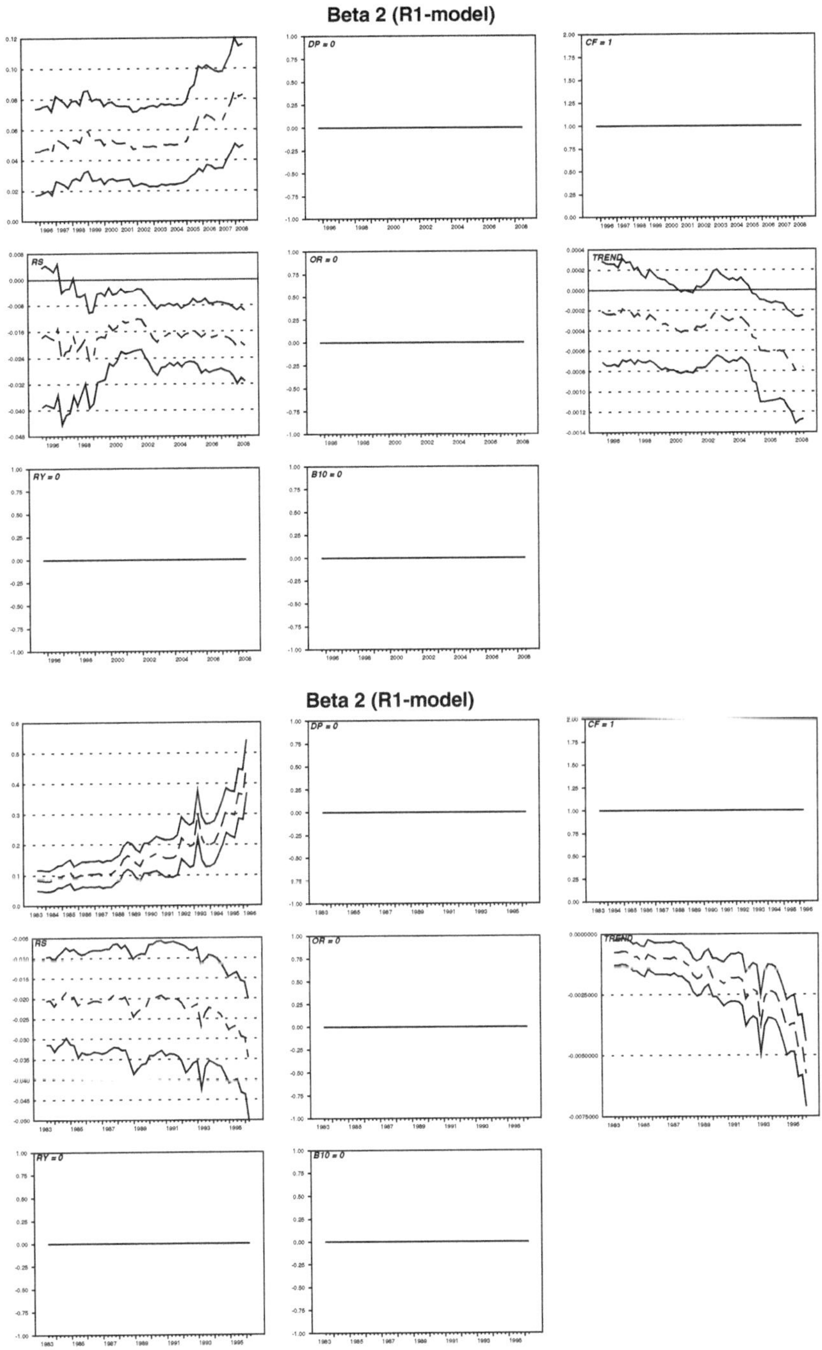

Fig. B.54 UK quarterly data: recursively calculated βs of the second cointegration relation (forward, base sample 1983:03 to 1995:04, depicted above; backward, base sample 2008:03 to 1996:02, depicted below)

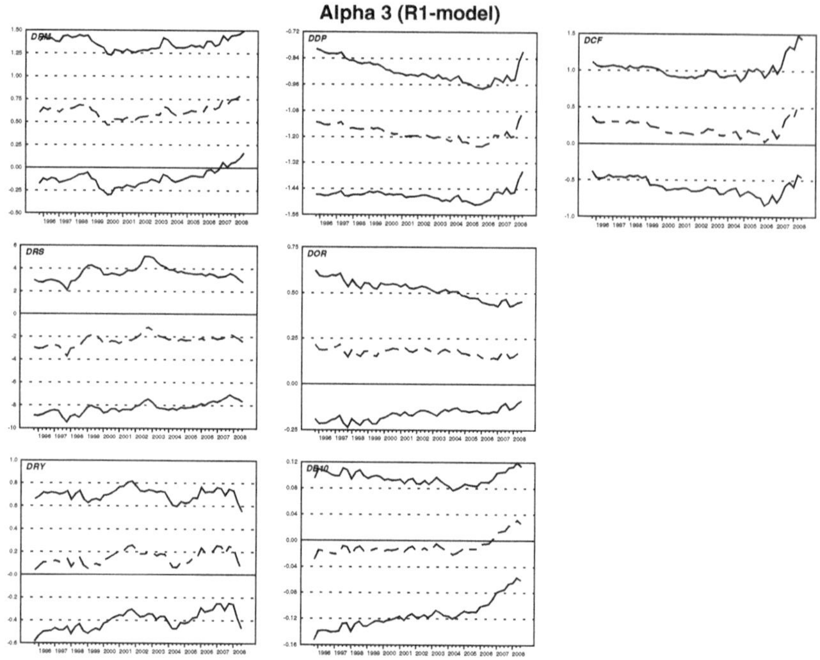

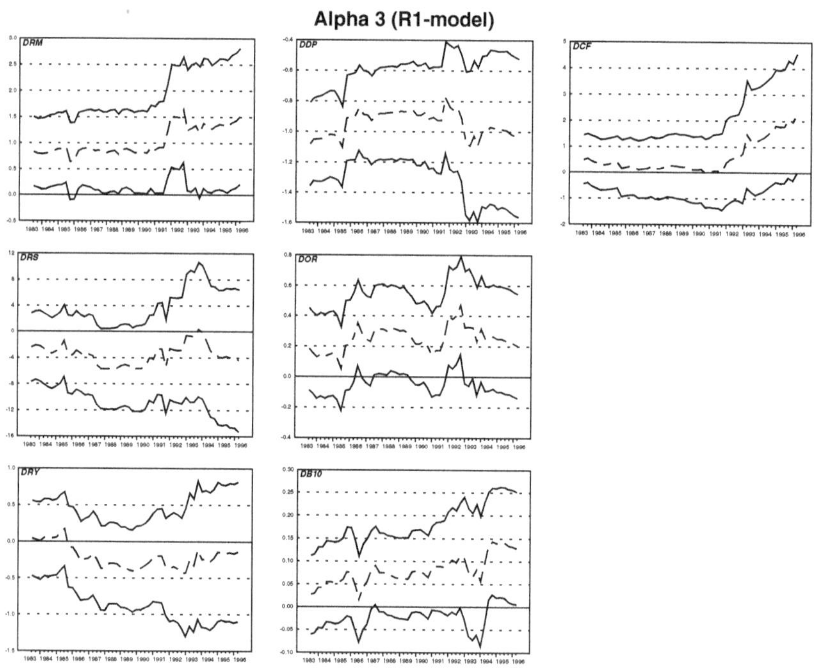

Fig. B.55 UK quarterly data: recursively calculated αs of the third cointegration relation (forward, base sample 1983:03 to 1995:04, depicted above; backward, base sample 2008:03 to 1996:02, depicted below)

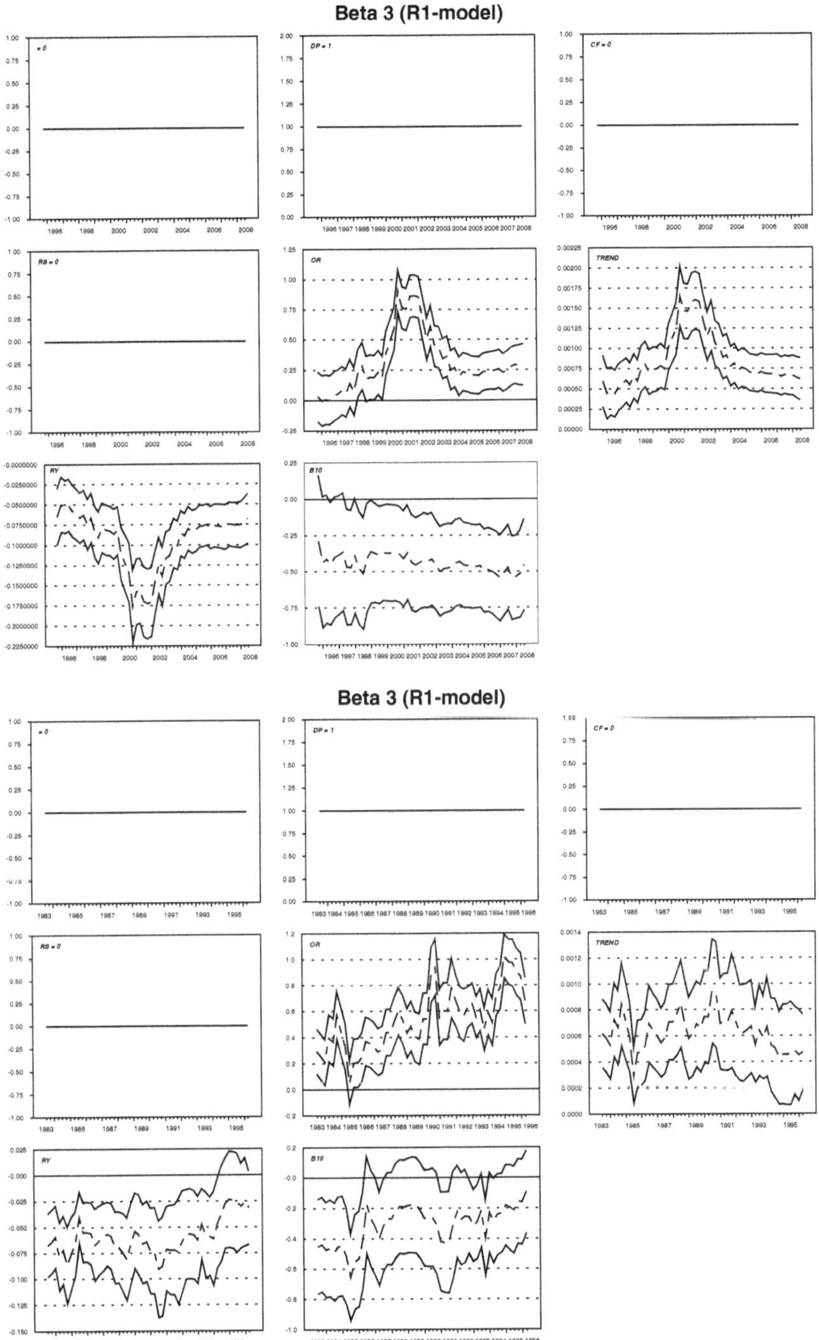

Fig. B.56 UK quarterly data: recursively calculated βs of the third cointegration relation (forward, base sample 1983:03 to 1995:04, depicted above; backward, base sample 2008:03 to 1996:02, depicted below)

B.4.8 *The Identified Long-Run Structure with Weak Exogeneity Imposed (Table B.17)*

Table B.17 UK quarterly data: the identified long-run structure with weak exogeneity imposed on the stock market and the bond rate (t-values in brackets)

	β'							
	m_r	s_r	y_r	Δp	or	$b10$	cf	*Trend*
Beta(1)	0.000 [*NA*]	**−0.007** [−3.609]	**−0.100** [−5.733]	0.000 [*NA*]	**1.000** [*NA*]	0.000 [*NA*]	0.000 [*NA*]	**0.001** [7.369]
Beta(2)	**0.087** [5.023]	**−0.021** [−3.740]	0.000 [*NA*]	0.000 [*NA*]	0.000 [*NA*]	0.000 [*NA*]	**1.000** [*NA*]	**−0.001** [−2.952]
Beta(3)	0.000 [*NA*]	0.000 [*NA*]	**−0.061** [−3.974]	**1.000** [*NA*]	**0.231** [2.642]	**−0.416** [−2.596]	0.000 [*NA*]	**0.001** [4.249]

	α		
	Alpha(1)	Alpha(2)	Alpha(3)
Δm_r	**−0.867** [−2.829]	−0.102 [−1.070]	**0.907** [2.694]
Δs_r	0.000 [0.000]	0.000 [0.000]	0.000 [0.000]
Δy_r	**−0.653** [−2.773]	**−0.167** [−2.274]	0.073 [0.281]
$\Delta^2 p$	**0.601** [4.801]	0.035 [0.897]	**−1.119** [−8.146]
Δor	**−0.683** [−5.477]	0.060 [1.539]	0.193 [1.409]
$\Delta b10$	0.000 [0.000]	0.000 [0.000]	0.000 [0.000]
Δcf	**1.093** [2.525]	**−1.183** [−8.761]	0.553 [1.163]

B.4.9 *The Long-Run Impact of the Common Trends with Weak Exogeneity Imposed (Table B.18)*

Table B.18 UK quarterly data: the long-run impact matrix with weak exogeneity imposed on the stock market and the bond rate (t-values in brackets)

	The Long-Run Impact Matrix, C						
	$\hat{\epsilon}_{m_r}$	$\hat{\epsilon}_{s_r}$	$\hat{\epsilon}_{y_r}$	$\hat{\epsilon}_{\Delta p}$	$\hat{\epsilon}_{or}$	$\hat{\epsilon}_{b10}$	$\hat{\epsilon}_{cf}$
m_r	**1.668** [3.857]	0.056 [1.746]	0.393 [1.173]	0.857 [1.098]	**−2.198** [−2.258]	−0.619 [−0.411]	−0.285 [−1.527]
s_r	−0.612 [−0.329]	**1.080** [7.896]	0.987 [0.685]	−0.687 [−0.205]	−1.025 [−0.245]	−1.194 [−0.184]	−0.159 [−0.197]
y_r	−0.271 [−0.945]	0.036 [1.727]	**1.155** [5.191]	−0.541 [−1.043]	**−1.616** [−2.501]	−0.210 [−0.209]	−0.237 [−1.913]
Δp	−0.001 [−0.032]	0.001 [0.783]	**0.053** [4.096]	−0.018 [−0.589]	**−0.086** [−2.270]	**0.403** [6.866]	−0.012 [−1.701]
or	−0.032 [−0.863]	**0.012** [4.335]	**0.123** [4.317]	−0.059 [−0.892]	**−0.170** [−2.048]	−0.030 [−0.233]	−0.025 [−1.570]
$b10$	0.021 [0.744]	0.004 [1.745]	0.029 [1.336]	0.003 [0.055]	−0.066 [−1.055]	**0.983** [10.20]	−0.009 [−0.758]
cf	**−0.158** [−3.638]	**0.018** [5.709]	−0.013 [−0.389]	−0.089 [−1.137]	0.169 [1.730]	0.028 [0.187]	0.021 [1.141]

B.5 Australia: Quarterly Data

B.5.1 Data Sources (Table B.19)

Table B.19 Australia quarterly data: data sources

m	Variable	Nominal broad money, SA[a]
	Datastream name	MONEY SUPPLY - BROAD MONEY (SEE AUM6...OB)
	Datastream Mnemonic	AUM6....B
	Data source	Reserve Bank of Australia
s	Variable	Nominal stock market level, NSA
	Datastream name	AUSTRALIA-DS Market
	Datastream Mnemonic	TOTMKAU(RI)
	Data source	Datastream
y	Variable	Nominal gross domestic product, SA
	Datastream name	GDP
	Datastream Mnemonic	AUGDP...B
	Data source	Australian Bureau of Statistics
p	Variable	Consumer price index, NSA
	Datastream name	CPI
	Datastream Mnemonic	AUCONPRCF
	Data source	Australian Bureau of Statistics
or	Variable	Short-term interest rate, NSA[a]
	Datastream name	MONEY MARKET RATE (FEDERAL FUNDS)
	Datastream Mnemonic	AUI60B..
	Data source	IMF IFS
*b*10	Variable	Long-term interest rate, NSA[b]
	Datastream name	AUSTRALIA BOND YIELD 10 YEAR
	Datastream Mnemonic	ABND10Y
	Data source	Reserve Bank of Australia
cf	Variable	Capital flows, NSA
	Time series name	External Counterpart of Money
	Data source	Constructed by author (see Appendix A), original data series from IMF BoP database

[a]Since quarterly data for this time series is constructed as the average value of the quarter, the values of the last month in the quarter of monthly data are applied instead.
[b]beginning of quarter, eins hochgeschoben, wie aufschreiben ...

B.5.2 Graphs of the Cointegrating Relations of the Unrestricted Model (Fig. B.57)

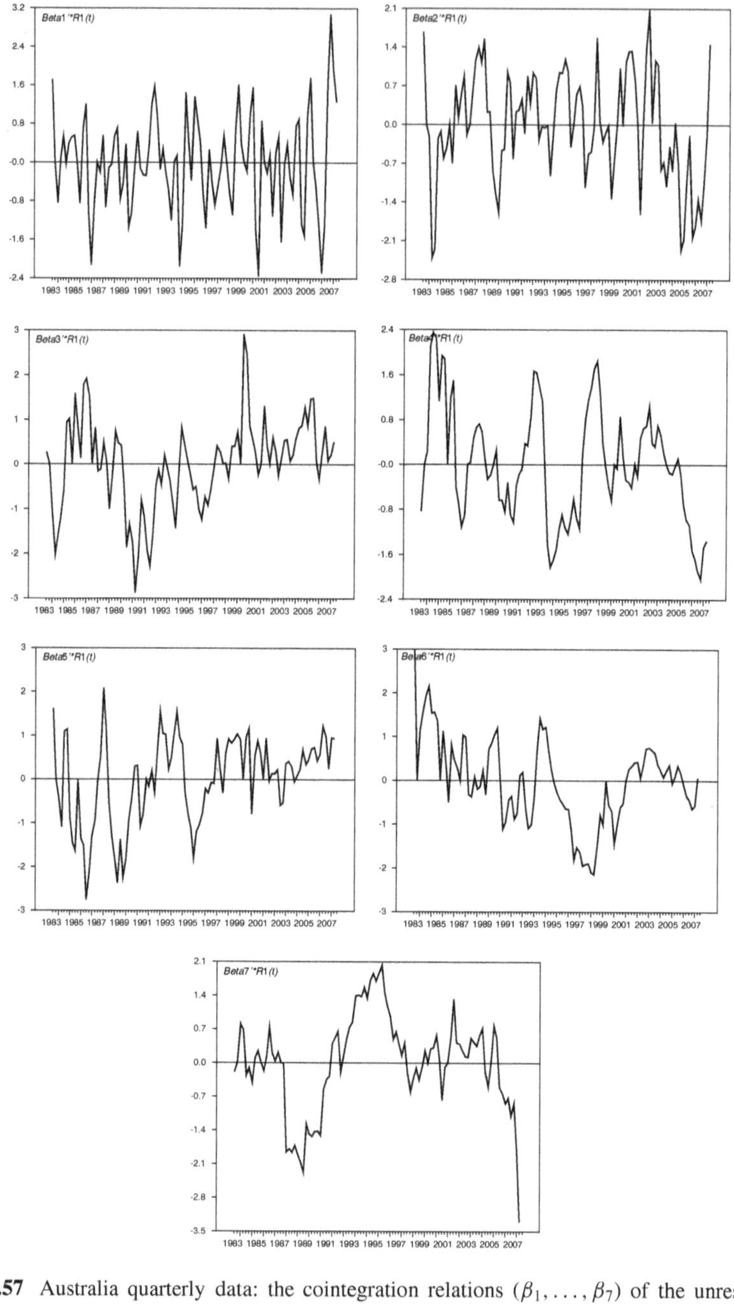

Fig. B.57 Australia quarterly data: the cointegration relations ($\beta_1, \ldots, \beta_7$) of the unrestricted model

B.5.3 Forward and Backward Recursive Tests for Parameter Constancy of the Unidentified System with Rank $r = 3$ Imposed (Figs. B.58, B.59, B.60, and B.61)

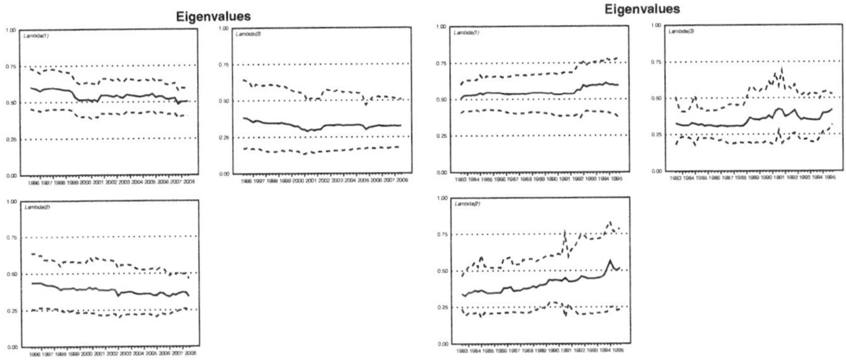

Fig. B.58 Australia quarterly data: recursively calculated eigenvalues λ_i (forward, base sample 1983:03 to 1996:02, depicted left; backward, base sample 2008:03 to 1995:04, depicted right)

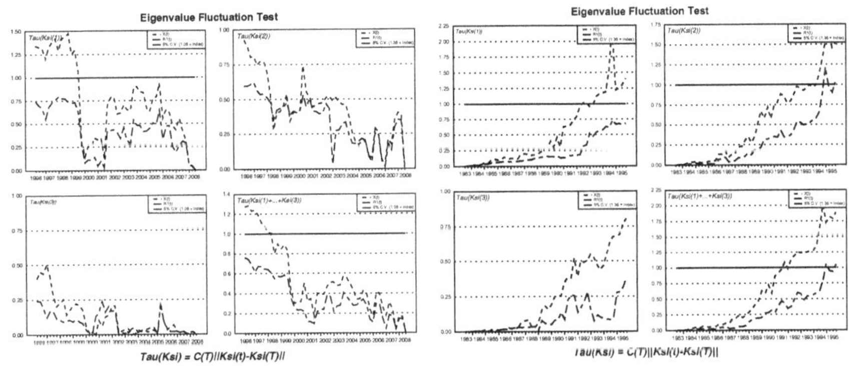

Fig. B.59 Australia quarterly data: recursively calculated eigenvalue fluctuation test (forward, base sample 1983:03 to 1996:02, depicted left; backward, base sample 2008:03 to 1995:04, depicted right)

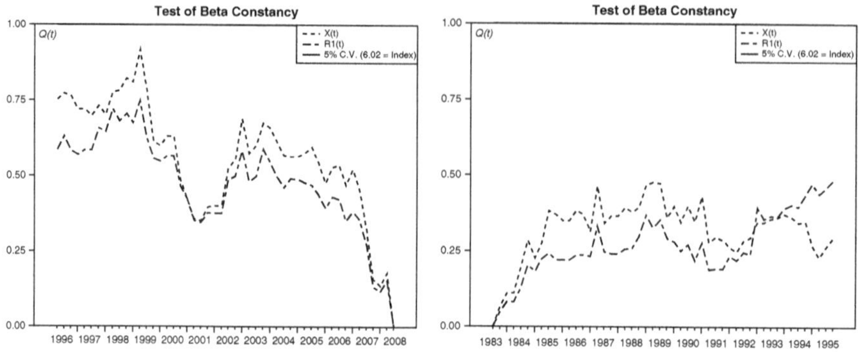

Fig. B.60 Australia quarterly data: recursively calculated test of β constancy (forward, base sample 1983:03 to 1996:02, depicted left; backward, base sample 2008:03 to 1995:04, depicted right)

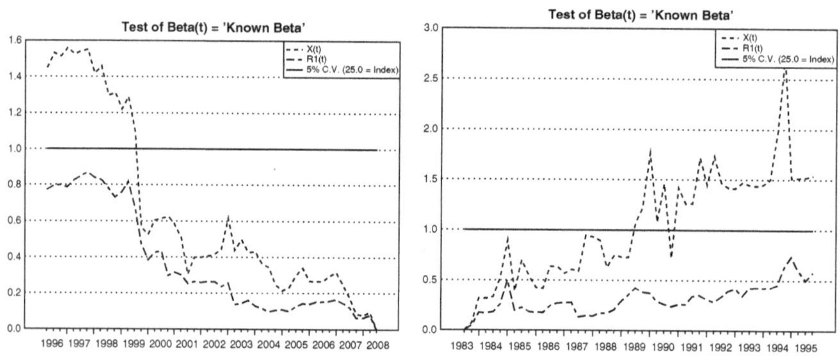

Fig. B.61 Australia quarterly data: recursively calculated test of β_t equals a known β (forward, base sample 1983:03 to 1996:02, depicted left; backward, base sample 2008:03 to 1995:04, depicted right)

B.5.4 The Partitioned Unrestricted Π-Matrices (Table B.20)

Table B.20 Australia quarterly data: the partitioned unrestricted Π-matrices based on 4 cointegrating vectors (t-values in brackets)

	β'							
	m_r	s_r	y_r	Δp	or	$b10$	cf	*Trend*
Beta(1)	−0.048	0.014	0.042	−0.282	0.777	−0.370	1.000	0.000
Beta(2)	−0.139	0.041	0.311	−0.957	0.118	1.000	−0.220	−0.002
Beta(3)	−0.075	0.023	0.089	1.000	0.267	−0.961	−0.046	−0.000

	α		
	Alpha(1)	Alpha(2)	Alpha(3)
Δm_r	0.092 [0.597]	**0.403** [2.784]	**0.622** [4.470]
Δs_r	0.596 [0.543]	**−2.330** [−2.264]	−0.044 [−0.045]
Δy_r	−0.032 [−0.237]	**−0.279** [−2.170]	0.140 [1.132]
$\Delta^2 p$	−0.075 [−0.964]	**0.287** [3.952]	**−0.363** [−5.188]
Δor	−0.067 [−1.924]	0.013 [0.398]	0.022 [0.706]
$\Delta b10$	0.019 [0.840]	0.016 [0.736]	**0.049** [2.384]
Δcf	**−1.243** [−8.301]	0.027 [0.191]	0.116 [0.857]

B.5.5 Rank Conditions of the Identified Long-Run Structure

Checking formal identification of the restrictions imposed by:

H_1'							
1	0	0	0	0	0	0	0
0	1	0	0	0	0	0	0
0	0	1	0	0	0	0	0
0	0	0	0	0	0	0	1

H_2'							
0	0	1	0	0	0	0	0
0	0	0	−1	0	1	0	0
0	0	0	0	0	0	0	1

H_3'							
0	0	0	0	0	0	1	0
0	0	0	0	0	0	0	1

The set of restrictions imposed by $H_1, \ldots H_3$ are formally identifying if for all i and $k = 1, \ldots, r-1$ and any set of indices $1 \leq i_1 < \cdots < i_k \leq r$ not containing i it holds that

$$R\left(i.i_1, \ldots, i_k\right) = rank\left(R_i'\left[H_{i_1} \cdots H_{i_k}\right]\right) \geq k$$

where $R_i = H_{1\perp}$ for all i. The conditions are summarized in Table B.21:

Table B.21 Australia quarterly data: rank conditions of the identified long-run structure

Rank Conditions			
$R(i.j)$		$R(i.jk)$	
(1.2):	1	(1.23):	2
(1.3):	1		
(2.1):	2	(2.13):	3
(2.3):	1		
(3.1):	3	(3.12):	4
(3.2):	2		

B.5.6 Graphs of the Cointegrating Relations of the Identified Long-Run Structure (Fig. B.62)

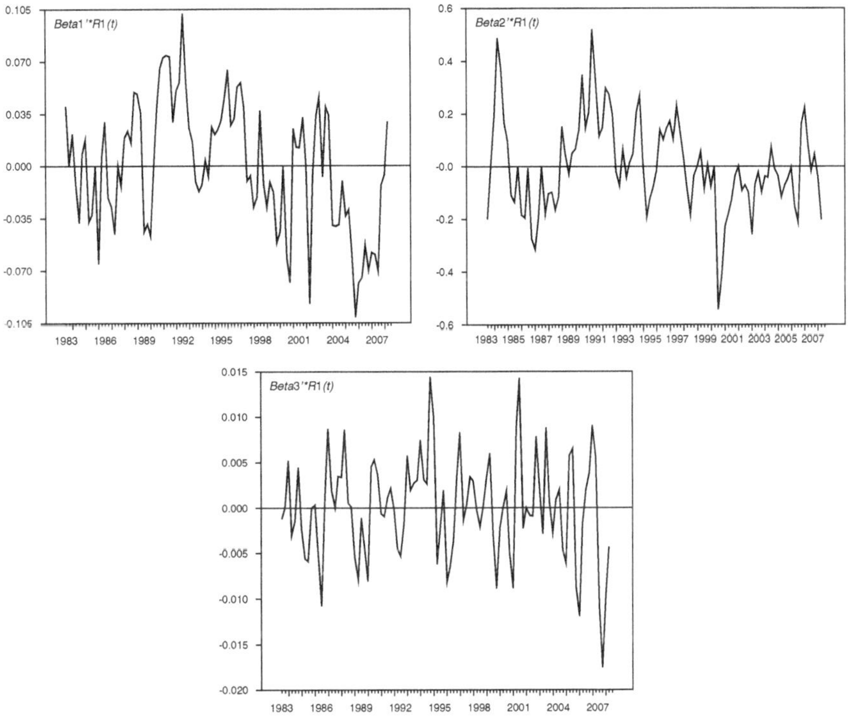

Fig. B.62 Australia quarterly data: the cointegration relations ($\beta_1, \ldots, \beta_3$) of the restricted model

B.5.7 Tests for Parameter Constancy of the Identified Long-Run Structure (Figs. B.63, B.64, B.65, B.66, B.67, and B.68)

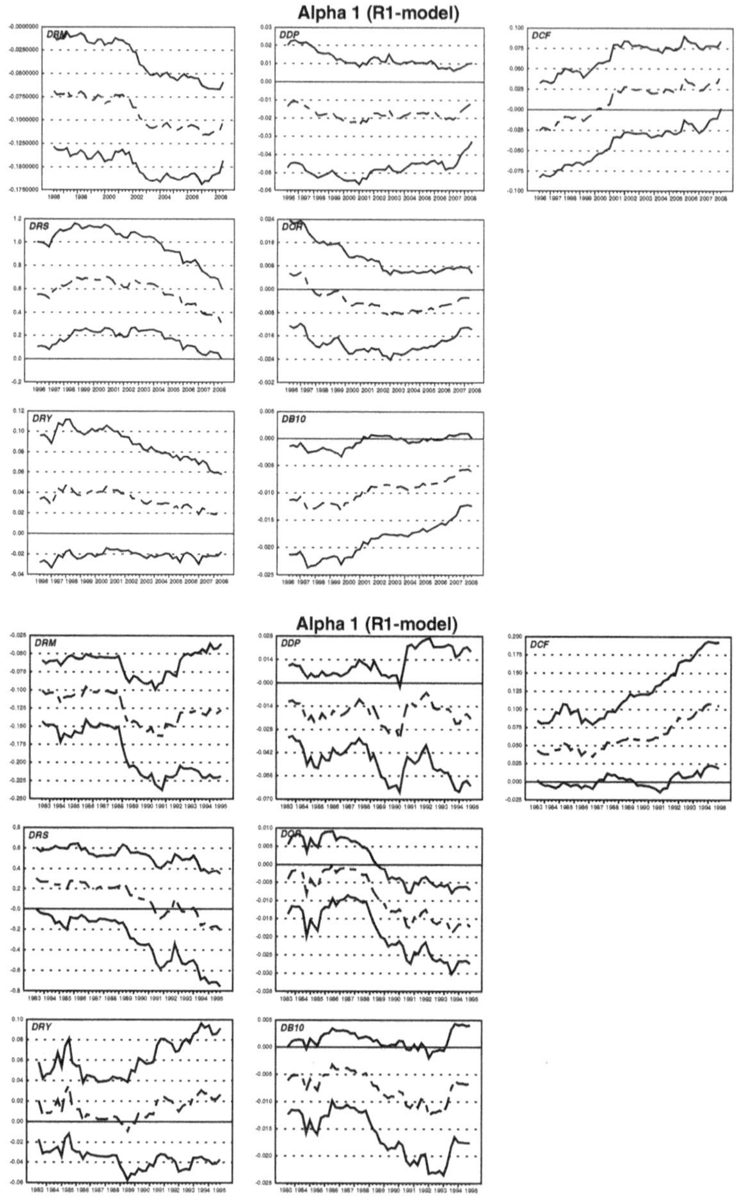

Fig. B.63 Australia quarterly data: recursively calculated αs of the first cointegration relation (forward, base sample 1983:03 to 1996:02, depicted above; backward, base sample 2008:03 to 1995:04, depicted below)

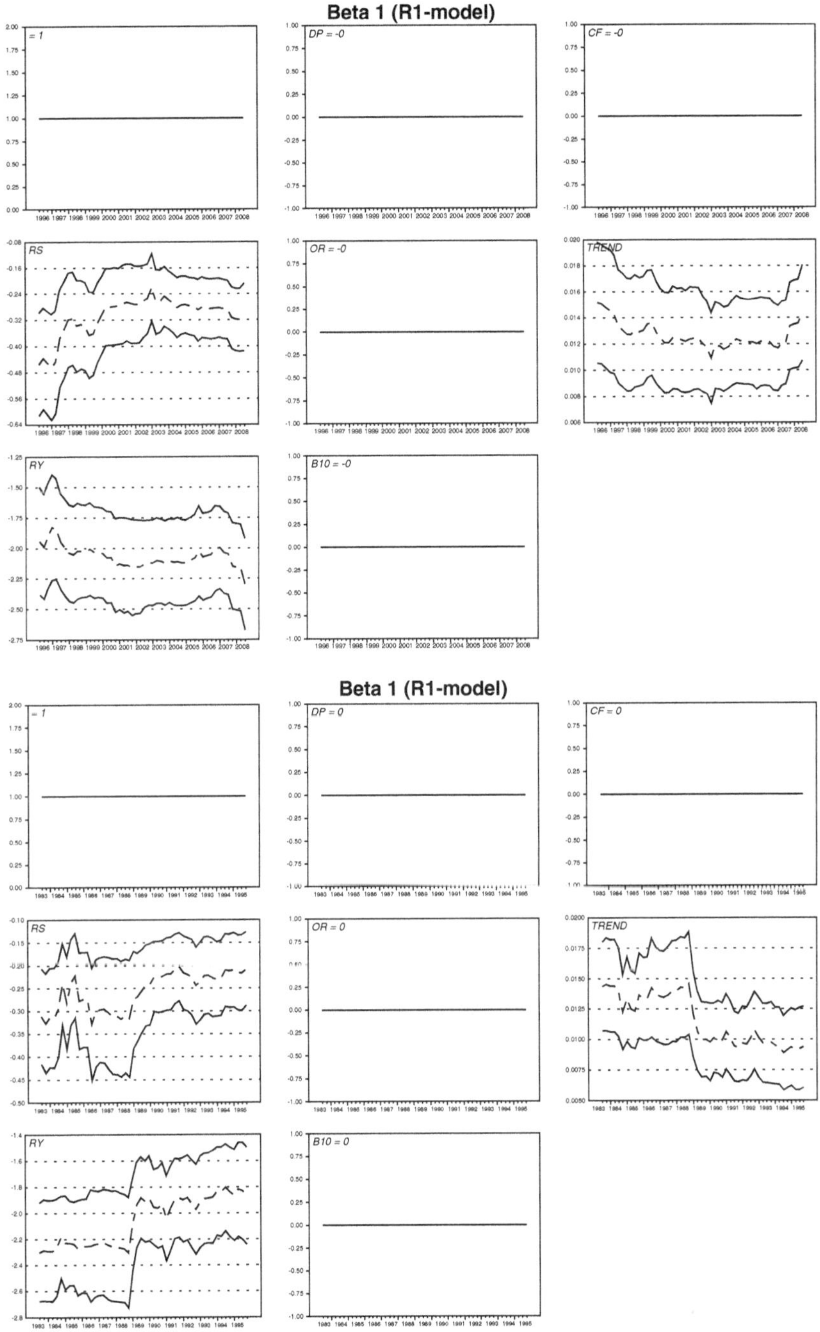

Fig. B.64 Australia quarterly data: recursively calculated βs of the first cointegration relation (forward, base sample 1983:03 to 1996:02, depicted above; backward, base sample 2008:03 to 1995:04, depicted below)

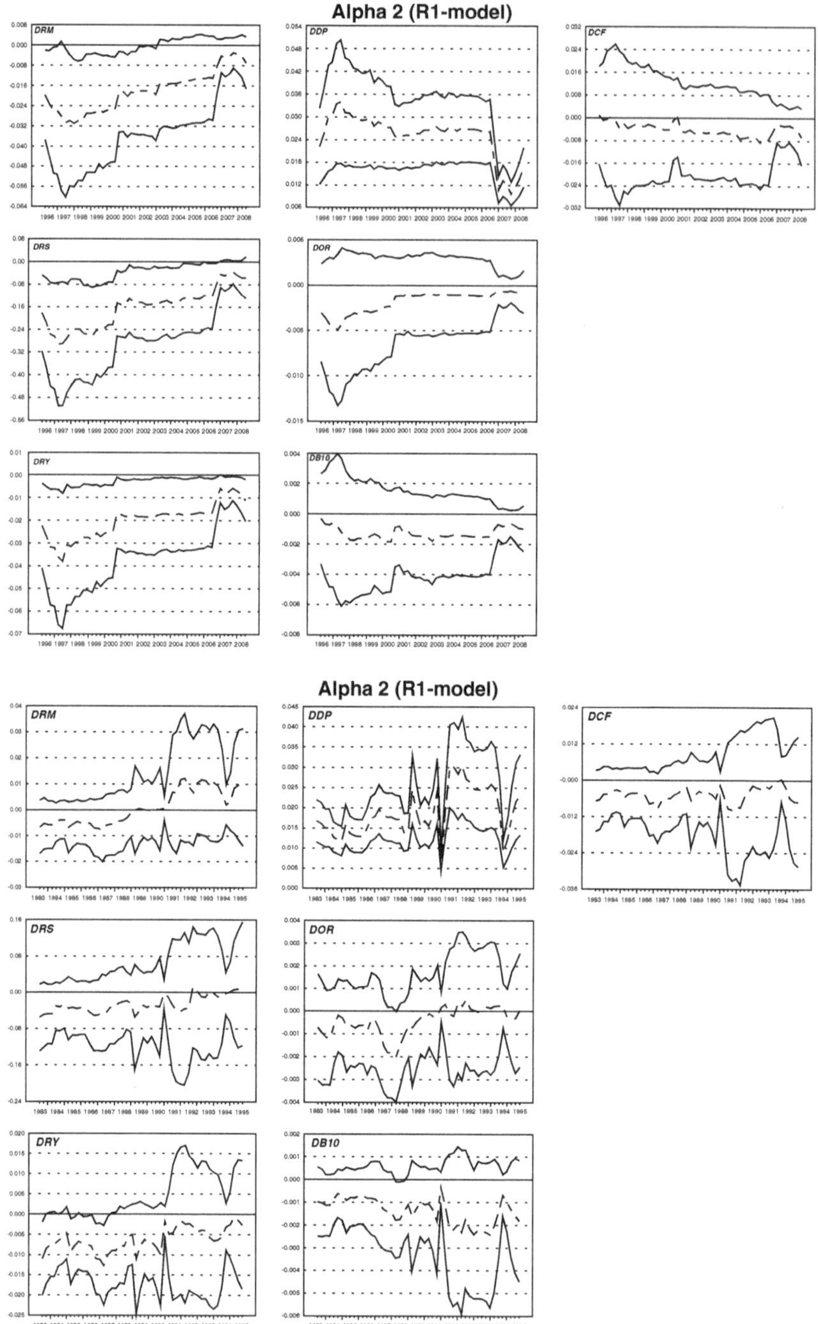

Fig. B.65 Australia quarterly data: recursively calculated αs of the second cointegration relation (forward, base sample 1983:03 to 1996:02, depicted above; backward, base sample 2008:03 to 1995:04, depicted below)

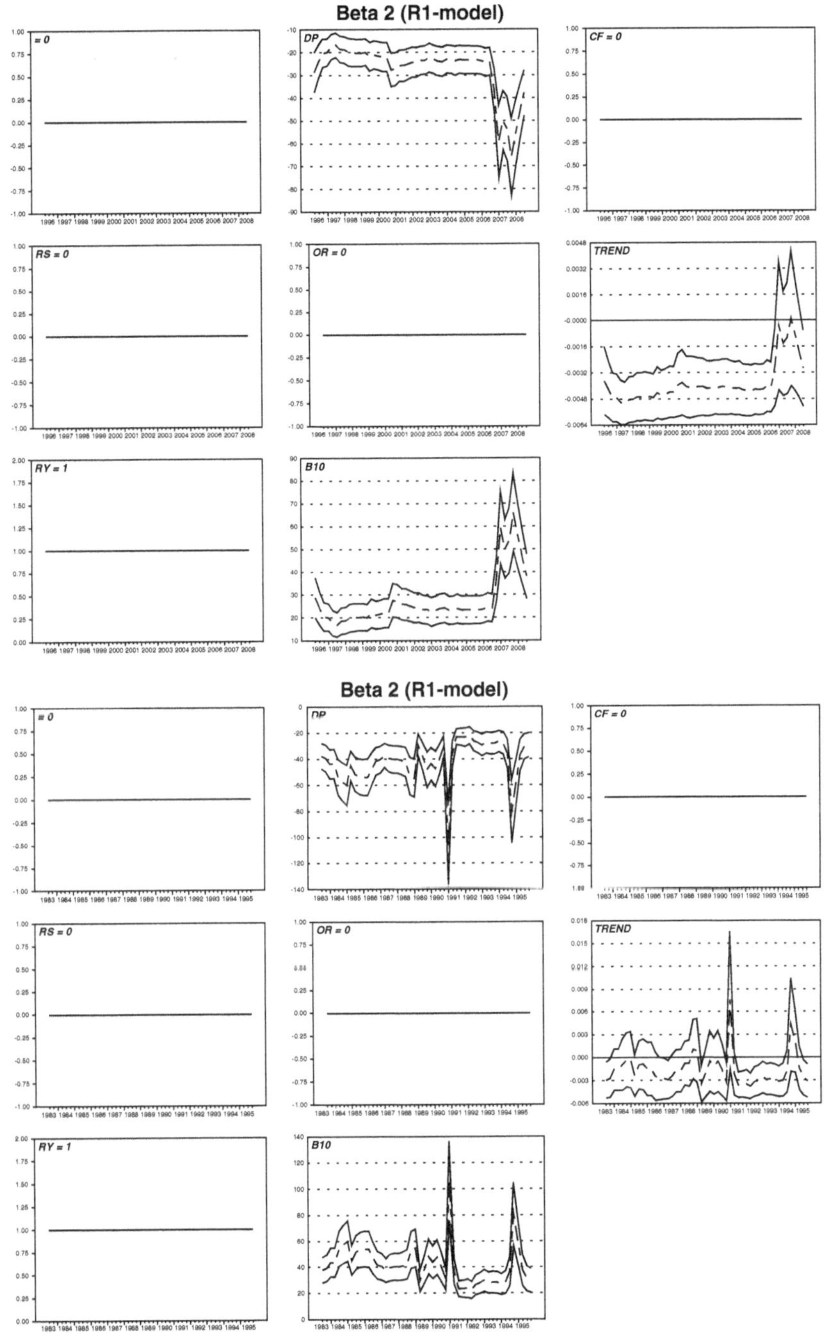

Fig. B.66 Australia quarterly data: recursively calculated βs of the second cointegration relation (forward, base sample 1983:03 to 1996:02, depicted above; backward, base sample 2008:03 to 1995:04, depicted below)

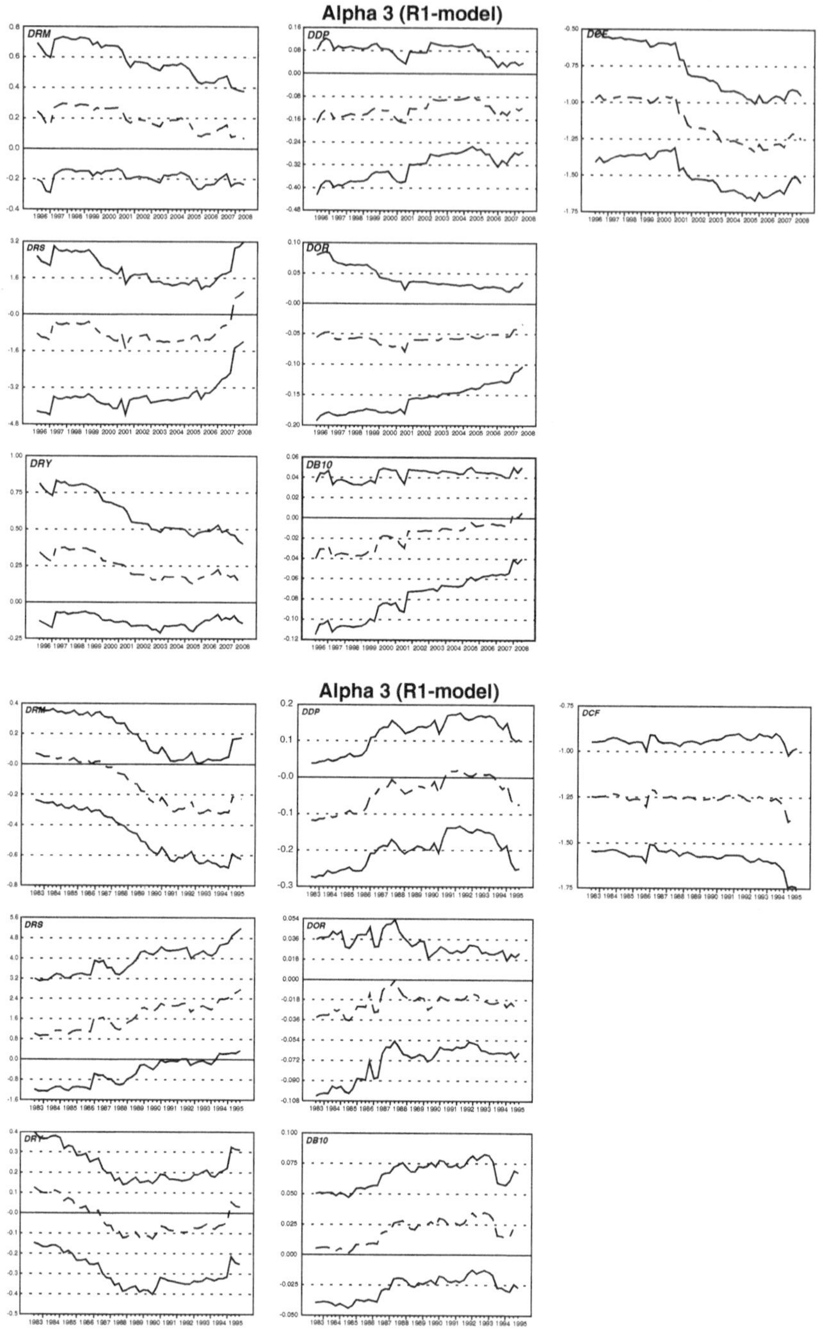

Fig. B.67 Australia quarterly data: recursively calculated αs of the third cointegration relation (forward, base sample 1983:03 to 1996:02, depicted above; backward, base sample 2008:03 to 1995:04, depicted below)

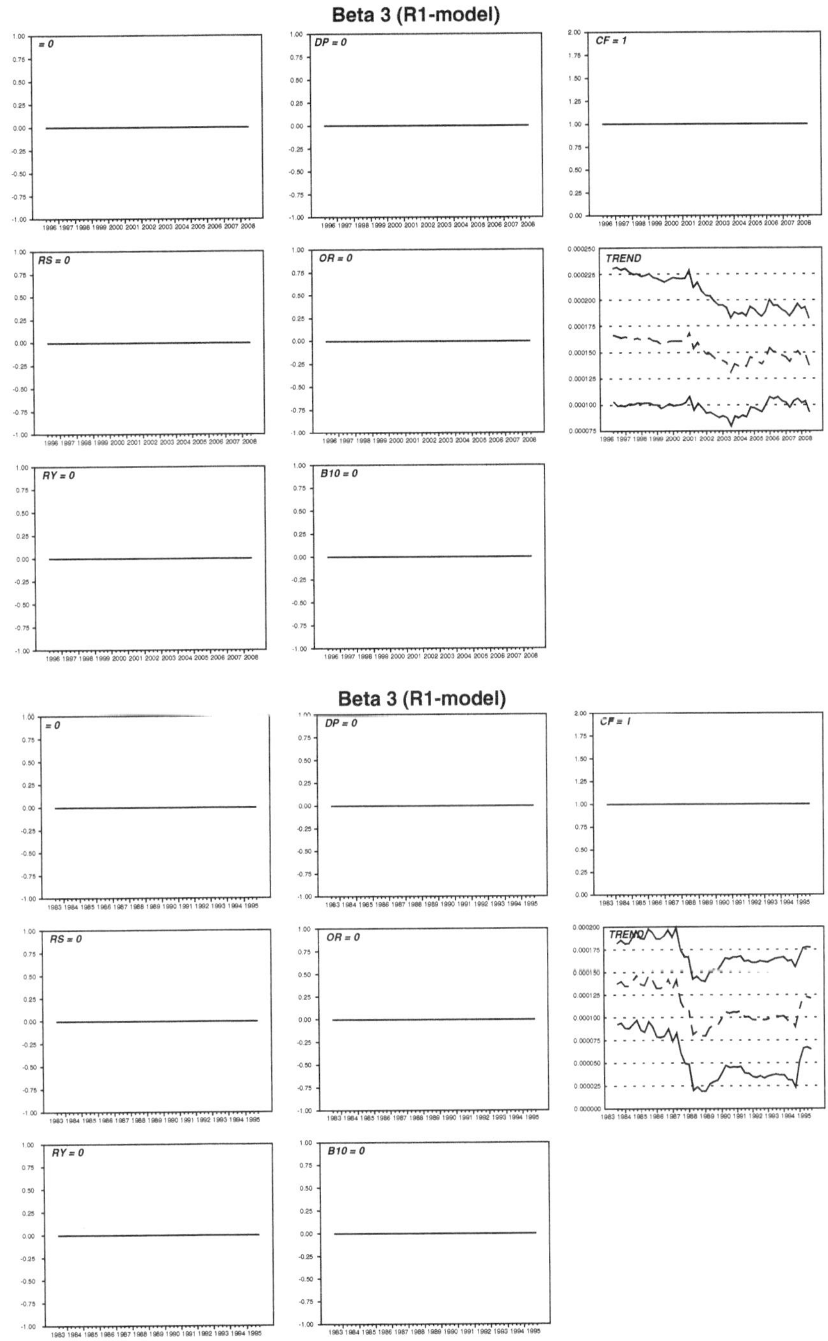

Fig. B.68 Australia quarterly data: recursively calculated βs of the third cointegration relation (forward, base sample 1983:03 to 1996:02, depicted above; backward, base sample 2008:03 to 1995:04, depicted below)

B.6 South Korea: Quarterly Data

B.6.1 Data Sources (Table B.22)

Table B.22 South Korea quarterly data: data sources

m	Variable	Nominal money, NSA
	Datastream name	MONEY SUPPLY - M2 (EP)
	Datastream Mnemonic	KOM2....A
	Data source	The Bank of Korea
s	Variable	Nominal stock market level, NSA
	Datastream name	KOREA-DS Marke
	Datastream Mnemonic	TOTMKKO(RI)
	Data source	Datastream
y	Variable	Nominal gross domestic product, SA
	Datastream name	GDP
	Datastream Mnemonic	KOGDP...B
	Data source	The Bank of Korea
p	Variable	Consumer price index, NSA
	Datastream name	CPI
	Datastream Mnemonic	KOCONPRCF[a]
	Data source	National Statistical Office
or	Variable	Short-term interest rate, NSA
	Datastream name	MONEY MARKET RATE (FEDERAL FUNDS)
	Datastream Mnemonic	KOI60B..[a]
	Data source	IMF IFS
*b*10	Variable	Long-term interest rate, NSA
	Datastream name	GOVT BOND YIELD - LONGTERM
	Datastream Mnemonic	KOI61...[a]
	Data source	IMF IFS
cf	Variable	Capital flows, NSA
	Time series name	External Counterpart of Money
	Data source	Constructed by author (see Appendix A), original data series from IMF BoP database

[a] Since quarterly data for this time series is constructed as the average value of the quarter, the values of the last month in the quarter of monthly data are applied instead.

B.6.2 Graphs of the Cointegrating Relations of the Unrestricted Model (Fig. B.69)

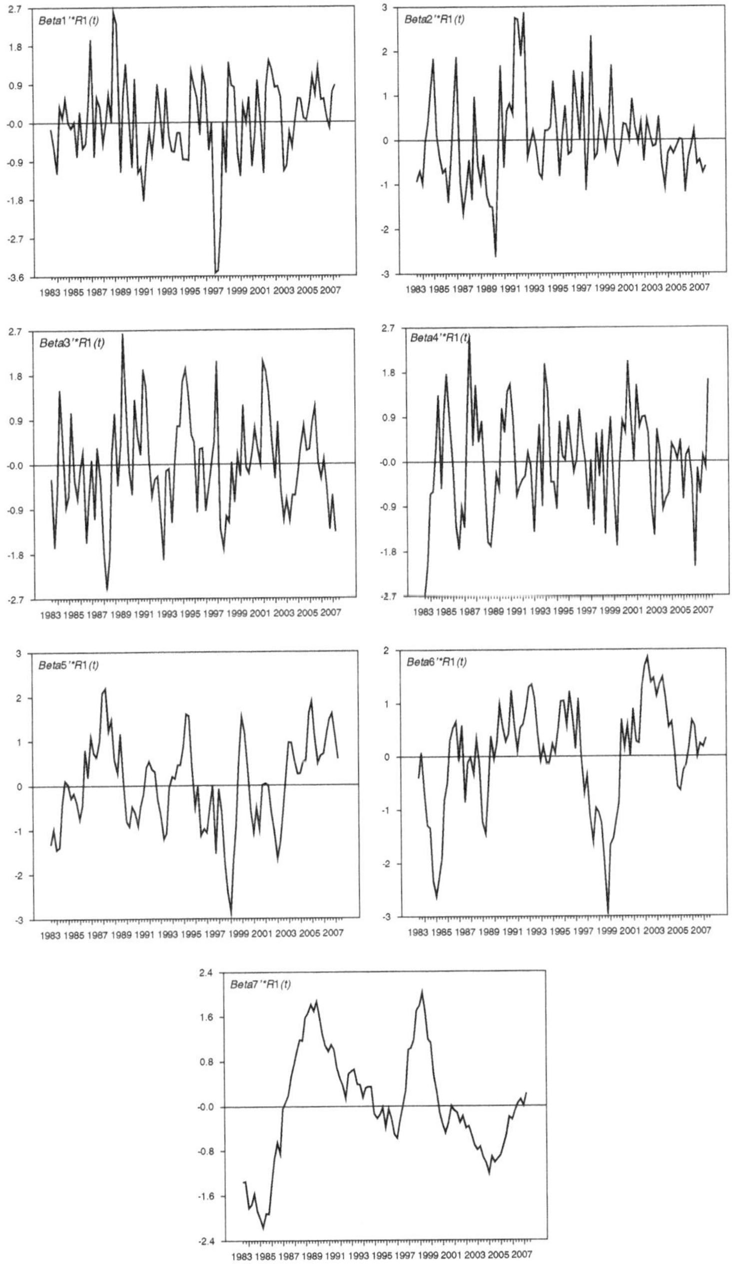

Fig. B.69 South Korea quarterly data: the cointegration relations ($\beta_1, \ldots, \beta_7$) of the unrestricted model

B.6.3 Forward and Backward Recursive Tests for Parameter Constancy of the Unidentified System with Rank r = 4 Imposed (Figs. B.70, B.71, B.72, and B.73)

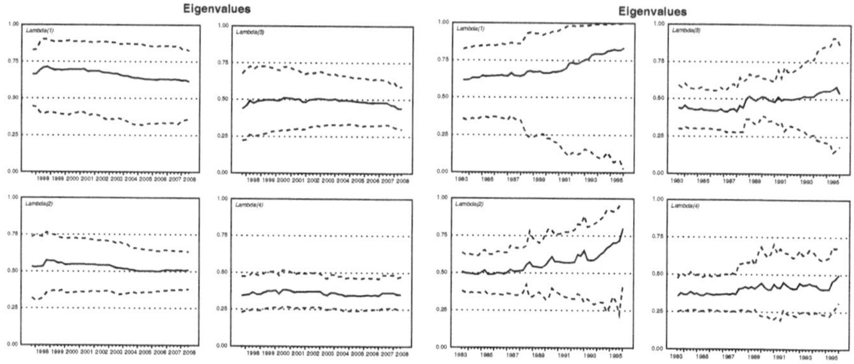

Fig. B.70 South Korea quarterly data: recursively calculated eigenvalues λ_i (forward, base sample 1983:03 to 1997:04, depicted left; backward, base sample 2008:03 to 1996:01, depicted right)

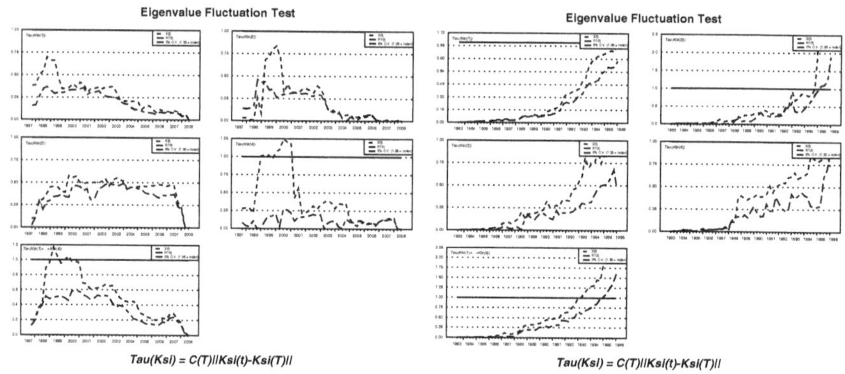

Fig. B.71 South Korea quarterly data: recursively calculated eigenvalue fluctuation test (forward, base sample 1983:03 to 1997:04, depicted left; backward, base sample 2008:03 to 1996:01, depicted right)

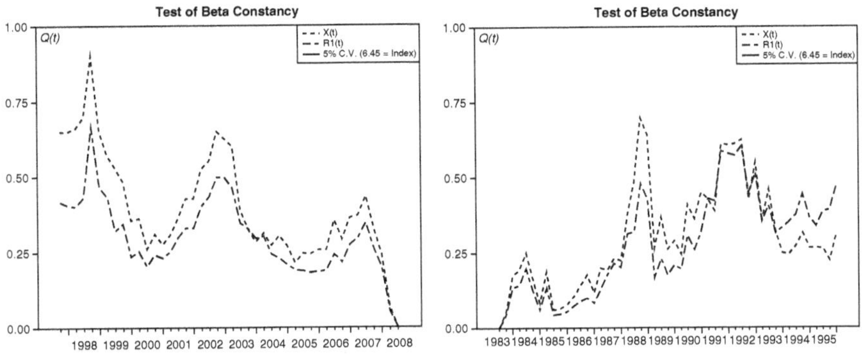

Fig. B.72 South Korea quarterly data: recursively calculated test of constant β (forward, base sample 1983:03 to 1997:04, depicted left; backward, base sample 2008:03 to 1996:01, depicted right)

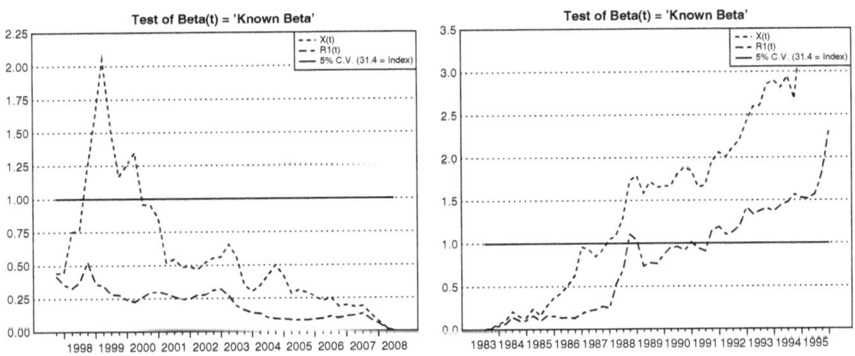

Fig. B.73 South Korea quarterly data: recursively calculated test of β_t equals a known β (forward, base sample 1983:03 to 1997:04, depicted left; backward, base sample 2008:03 to 1996:01, depicted right)

B.6.4 The Partitioned Unrestricted Π-Matrices (Table B.23)

Table B.23 South Korea quarterly data: the partitioned unrestricted Π-matrices based on 4 cointegrating vectors (t-values in brackets)

β'

	m_r	s_r	y_r	Δp	or	$b10$	cf	D_s9704	*Trend*
Beta(1)	−0.145	−0.004	0.034	1.000	0.917	0.372	0.533	−0.003	0.005
Beta(2)	0.006	−0.008	0.045	−0.386	−0.366	1.000	0.106	0.001	−0.001
Beta(3)	0.058	−0.021	−0.194	0.390	−0.213	0.002	1.000	−0.000	0.003
Beta(4)	0.011	0.004	0.012	−0.765	1.000	−0.687	0.160	0.001	−0.001

α

	Alpha(1)	Alpha(2)	Alpha(3)	Alpha(4)
Δm_r	**0.779** [5.858]	**−0.997** [−2.355]	0.336 [1.882]	0.669 [1.779]
Δs_r	−1.477 [−1.097]	6.167 [1.439]	**9.188** [5.083]	−2.954 [−0.777]
Δy_r	**−0.346** [−3.075]	**−1.252** [−3.500]	0.203 [1.346]	−0.094 [−0.296]
$\Delta^2 p$	**−0.397** [−7.092]	**0.941** [5.281]	**−0.177** [−2.352]	**0.691** [4.367]
Δor	**−0.211** [−8.088]	−0.107 [−1.291]	0.022 [0.623]	**−0.158** [−2.137]
$\Delta b10$	**−0.061** [−3.715]	**−0.342** [−6.509]	0.008 [0.356]	**0.129** [2.758]
Δcf	0.045 [0.514]	−0.384 [−1.365]	**−0.378** [−3.186]	0.054 [0.218]

B.6.5 Rank Conditions of the Identified Long-Run Structure

Checking formal identification of the restrictions imposed by:

H_1'								
0	1	0	0	0	0	0	0	0
1	0	0	0	0	0	0	0	0
0	0	0	0	0	0	1	0	0
0	0	1	0	0	0	0	0	0
0	0	0	0	0	0	0	0	1

H_2'								
1	0	−1	0	0	0	0	0	0
0	1	0	0	0	0	0	0	0
0	0	0	0	−1	1	0	0	0
0	0	0	0	0	0	0	1	0

H_3'								
1	0	0	0	0	0	0	0	0
0	0	0	1	0	0	0	0	0
0	0	0	0	0	0	0	1	0
0	0	0	0	0	0	0	0	1

H_4'								
0	0	1	0	0	0	0	0	0
0	0	0	−1	0	1	0	0	0
0	0	0	0	0	0	0	1	0
0	0	0	0	0	0	0	0	1

The set of restrictions imposed by $H_1, \ldots H_4$ are formally identifying if for all i and $k = 1, \ldots, r-1$ and any set of indices $1 \leq i_1 < \cdots < i_k \leq r$ not containing i it holds that

$$R\left(i.i_1, \ldots, i_k\right) = rank\left(R_i' \left[H_{i_1} \cdots H_{i_k}\right]\right) \geq k$$

where $R_i = H_{1\perp}$ for all i. The conditions are summarized in Table B.24:

Table B.24 South Korea quarterly data: rank conditions of the identified long-run structure

Rank Conditions					
$R(i.j)$		$R(i.jk)$		$R(i.jkl)$	
(1.2):	2	(1.23):	3	(1.234):	4
(1.3):	2	(1.24):	3		
(1.4):	2	(1.34):	3		
(2.1):	3	(2.13):	4	(2.134):	5
(2.3):	3	(2.14):	4		
(2.4):	3	(2.34):	4		
(3.1):	3	(3.12):	4	(3.124):	5
(3.2):	3	(3.14):	4		
(3.4):	2	(3.24):	4		
(4.1):	3	(4.12):	4	(4.123):	5
(4.2):	3	(4.13):	4		
(4.3):	2	(4.23):	4		

B.6.6 *Graphs of the Cointegrating Relations of the Identified Long-Run Structure (Fig. B.74)*

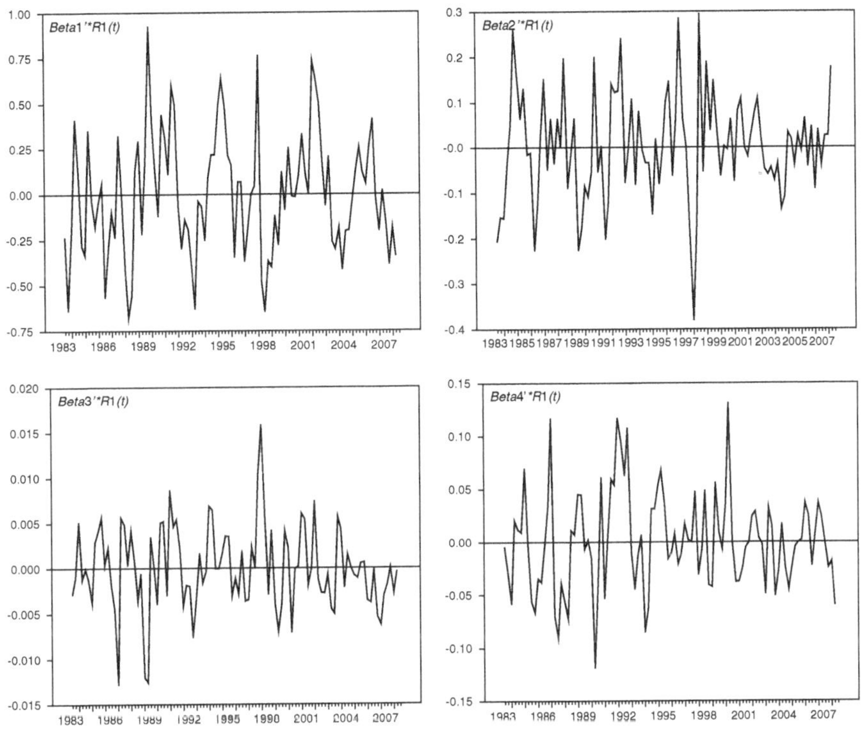

Fig. B.74 South Korea quarterly data: the cointegration relations ($\beta_1, \ldots, \beta_4$) of the restricted model

B.6.7 Tests for Parameter Constancy of the Identified Long-Run Structure (Figs. B.75, B.76, B.77, B.78, B.79, B.80, B.81, and B.82)

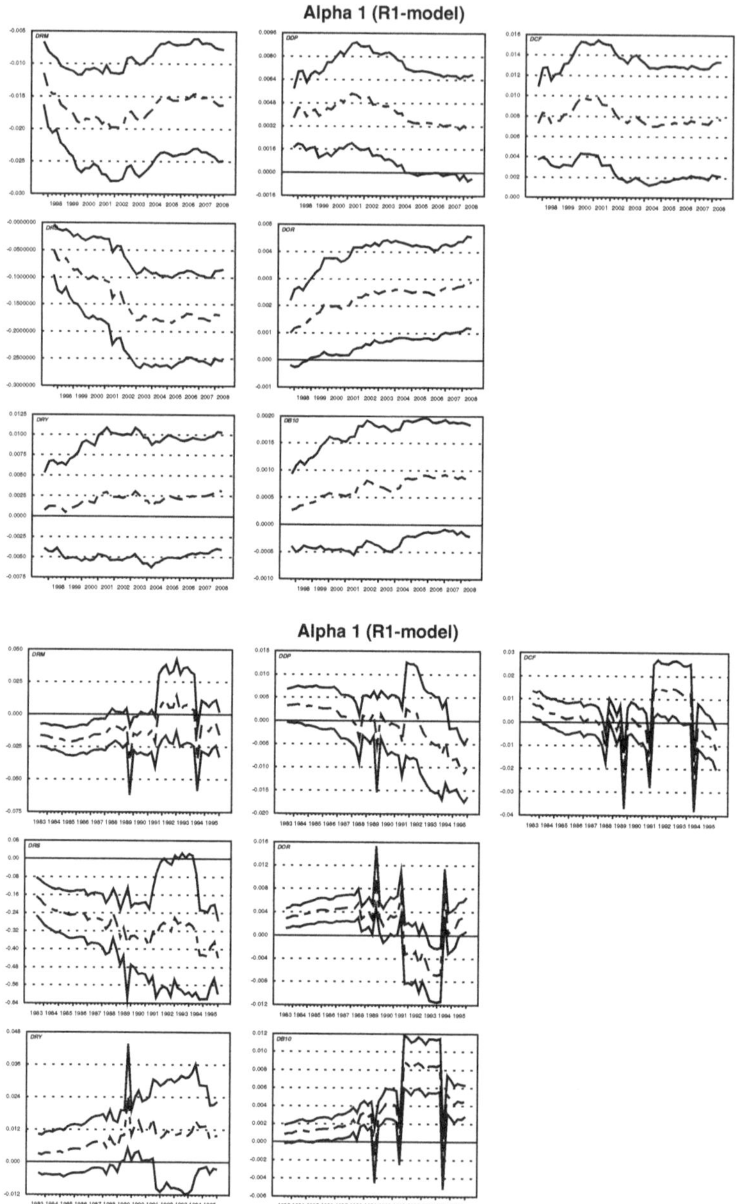

Fig. B.75 South Korea quarterly data: recursively calculated αs of the first cointegration relation (forward, base sample 1983:03 to 1997:04, depicted above; backward, base sample 2008:03 to 1996:01, depicted below)

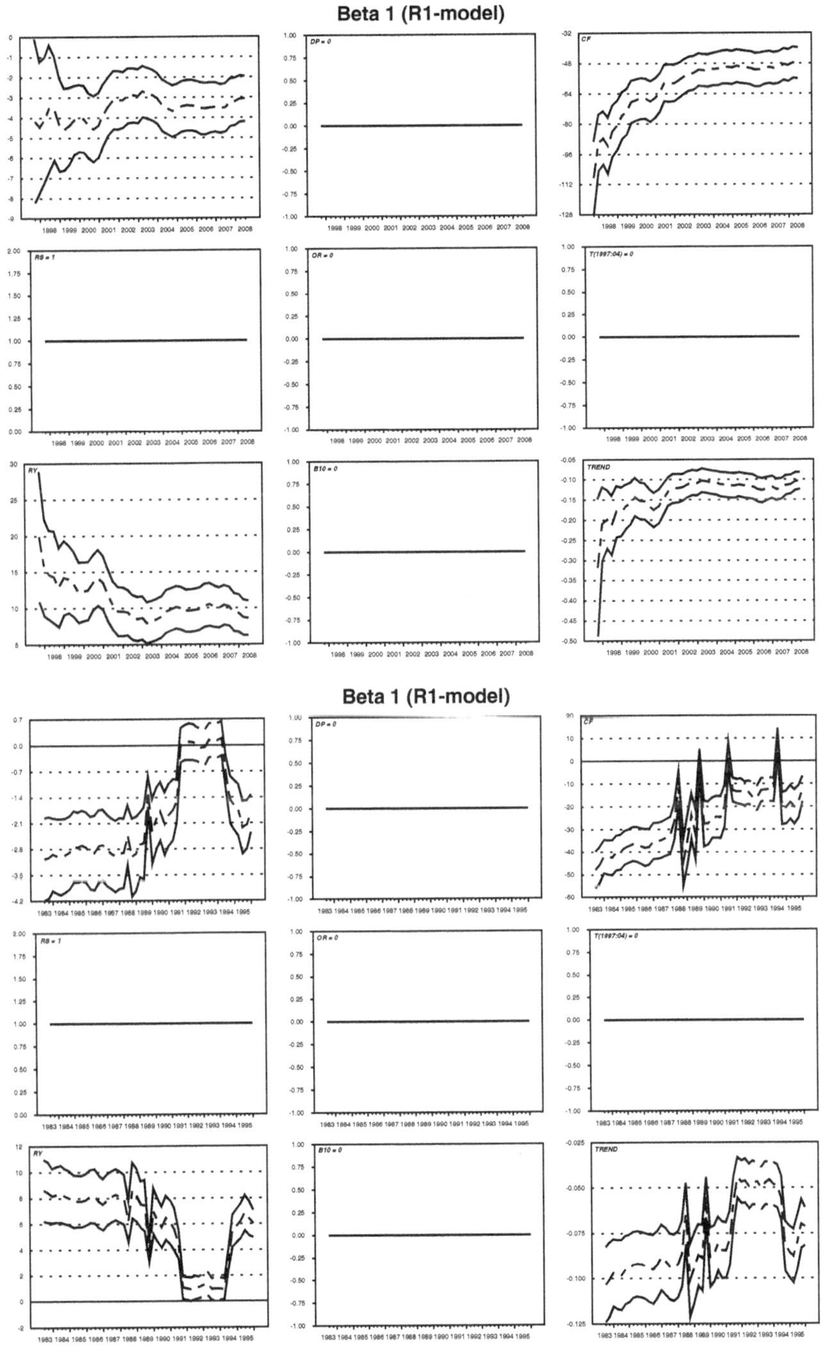

Fig. B.76 South Korea quarterly data: recursively calculated βs of the first cointegration relation (forward, base sample 1983:03 to 1997:04, depicted above; backward, base sample 2008:03 to 1996:01, depicted below)

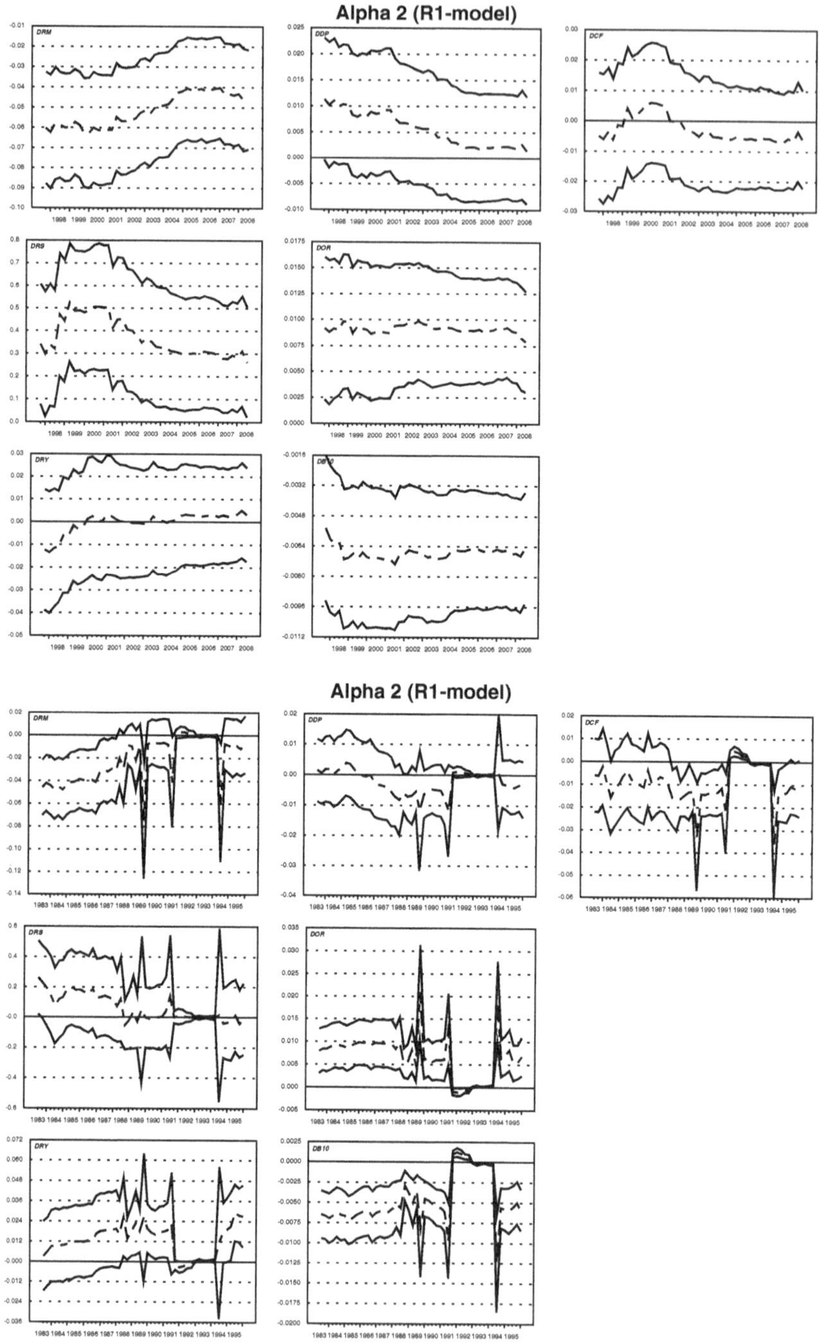

Fig. B.77 South Korea quarterly data: recursively calculated αs of the second cointegration relation (forward, base sample 1983:03 to 1997:04, depicted above; backward, base sample 2008:03 to 1996:01, depicted below)

Beta 2 (R1-model)

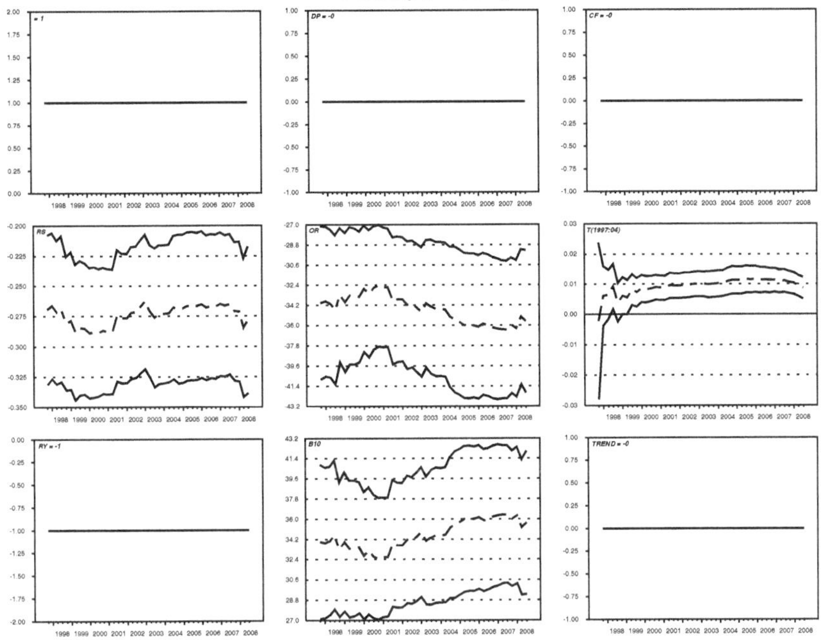

Beta 2 (R1-model)

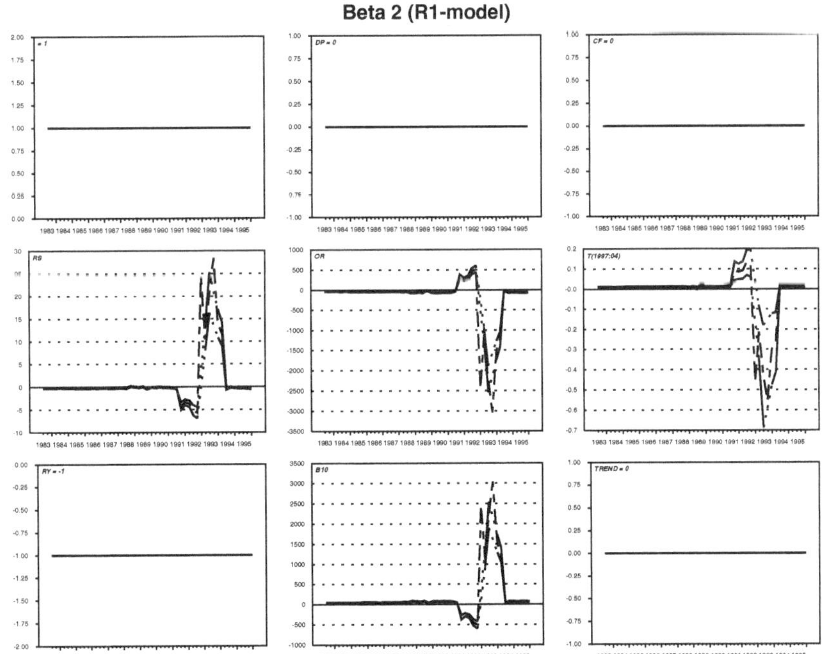

Fig. B.78 South Korea quarterly data: recursively calculated βs of the second cointegration relation (forward, base sample 1983:03 to 1997:04, depicted above; backward, base sample 2008:03 to 1996:01, depicted below)

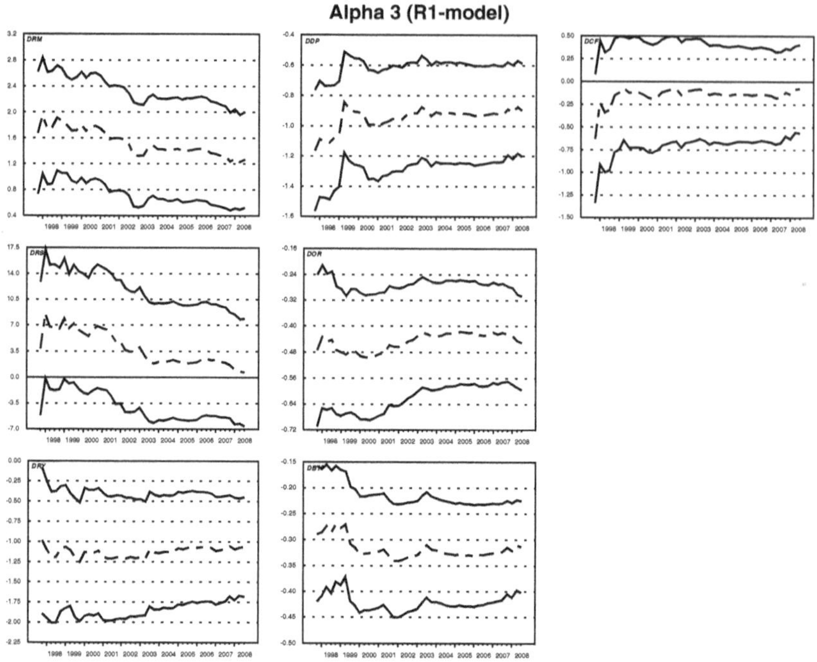

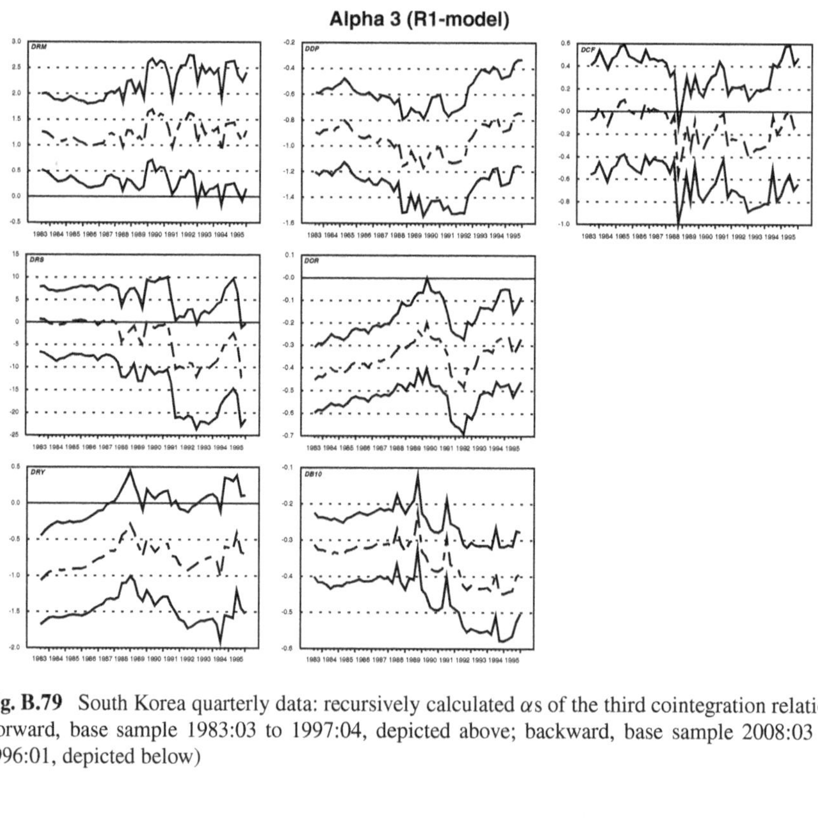

Fig. B.79 South Korea quarterly data: recursively calculated αs of the third cointegration relation (forward, base sample 1983:03 to 1997:04, depicted above; backward, base sample 2008:03 to 1996:01, depicted below)

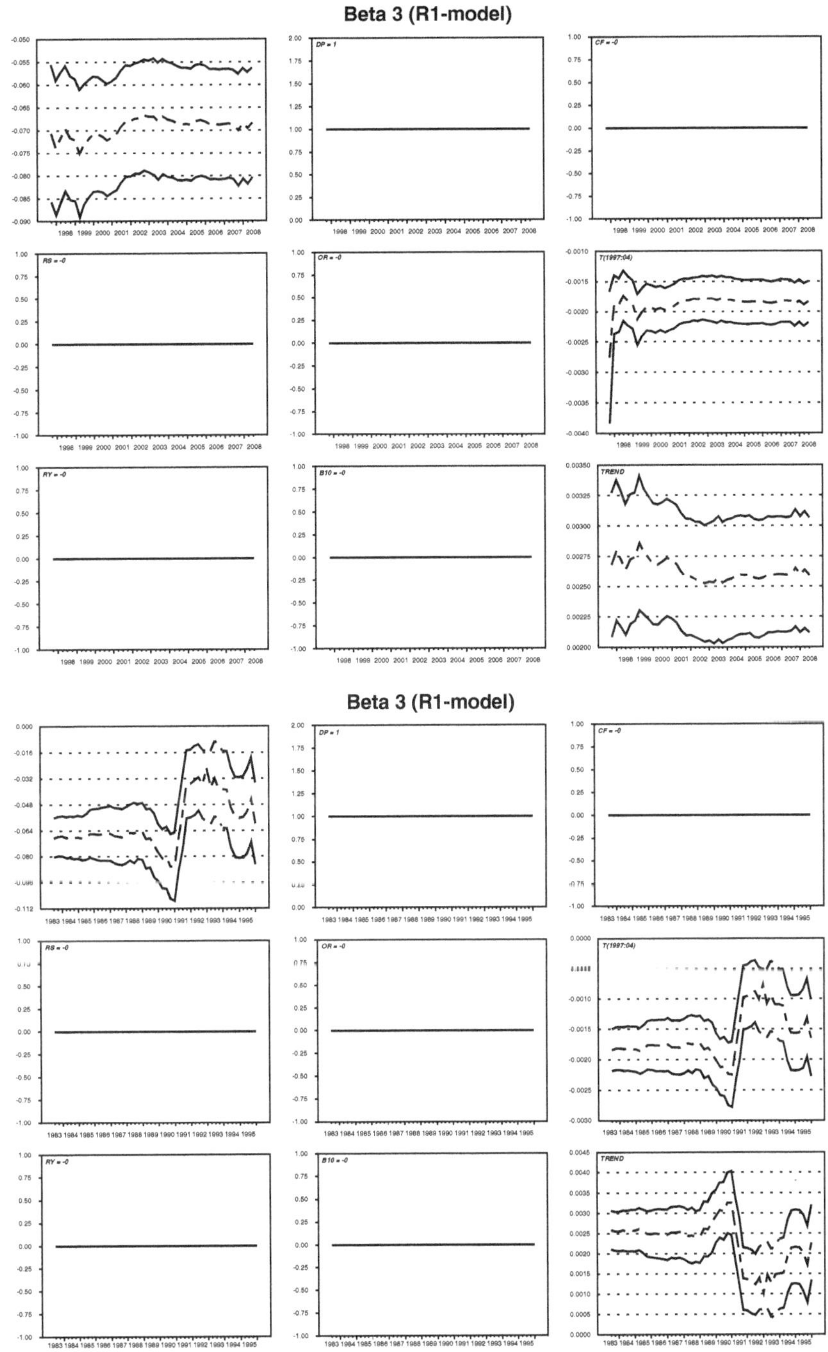

Fig. B.80 South Korea quarterly data: recursively calculated βs of the third cointegration relation (forward, base sample 1983:03 to 1997:04, depicted above; backward, base sample 2008:03 to 1996:01, depicted below)

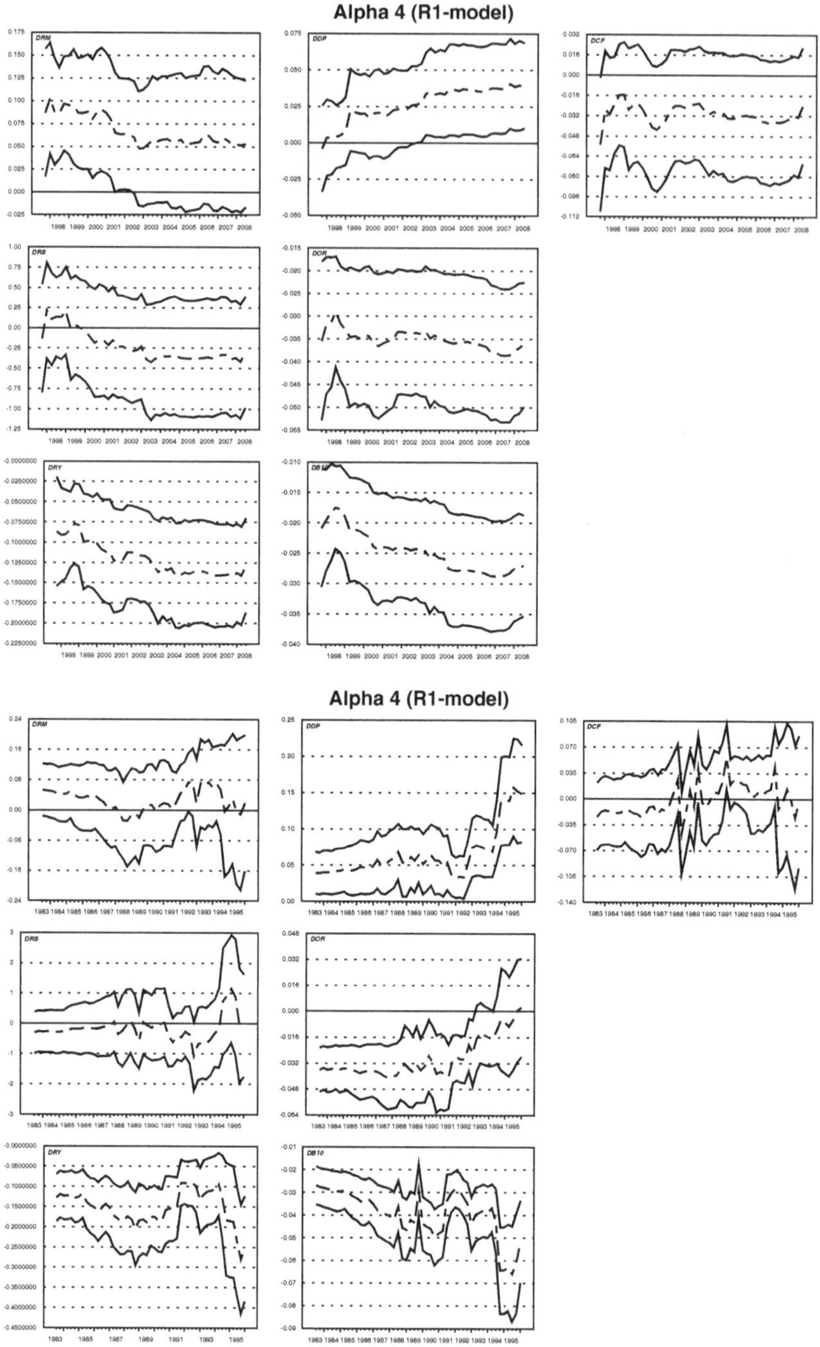

Fig. B.81 South Korea quarterly data: recursively calculated αs of the fourth cointegration relation (forward, base sample 1983:03 to 1997:04, depicted above; backward, base sample 2008:03 to 1996:01, depicted below)

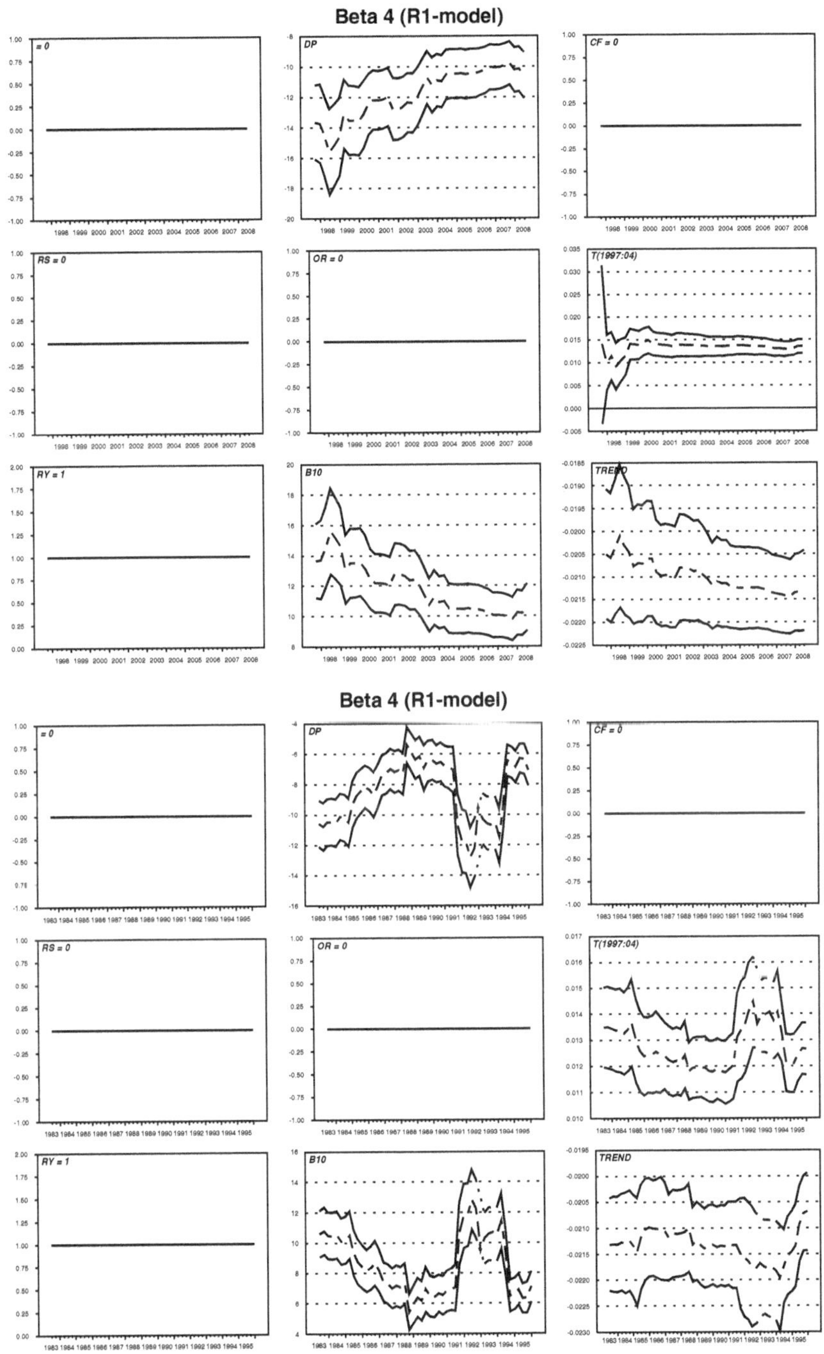

Fig. B.82 South Korea quarterly data: recursively calculated βs of the fourth cointegration relation (forward, base sample 1983:03 to 1997:04, depicted above; backward, base sample 2008:03 to 1996:01, depicted below)

B.7 Thailand: Quarterly Data

B.7.1 Data Sources (Table B.25)

Table B.25 Thailand quarterly data: data sources

m	Variable	Nominal money M3, NSA[a]
	Datastream name	M3 *and* MONEY SUPPLY: M3 (BROAD MONEY)
	Datastream Mnemonic	THQ59MC.A *and* THM3....A
	Data source	IMF IFS *and* Bank of Thailand
s	Variable	Nominal stock market level, NSA
	Datastream name	THAILAND-DS Market
	Datastream Mnemonic	TOTMKTH(RI)
	Data source	Datastream
y	Variable	Nominal gross domestic product, NSA[b]
	Datastream name	GDP *and* MANUFACTURING PRODUCTION INDEX
	Datastream Mnemonic	THI99B..A *and* THIPMAN.H
	Data source	IMF IFS *and* Bank of Thailand
p	Variable	Consumer price index, NSA
	Datastream name	CPI
	Datastream Mnemonic	THCONPRCF[c]
	Data source	Bureau of Trade and Economic Indices, Ministry of Commerce
or	Variable	Short-term interest rate, NSA
	Datastream name	TH MONEY MARKET RATE (FEDERAL FUNDS)
	Datastream Mnemonic	THI60B..[c]
	Data source	IMF IFS
*b*10	Variable	Long-term interest rate, NSA
	Datastream name	GOVERNMENT BOND YIELD - 10 YEARS
	Datastream Mnemonic	THGBOND10[c]
	Data source	Main Economic Indicators, Copyright OECD
cf	Variable	Capital flows, NSA
	Time series name	External Counterpart of Money
	Data source	Constructed by author (see Appendix A), original data series from IMF BoP database

[a]The time series for nominal money stock is based on two time series because the first ends early (2006) and the second starts late (1997). It is constructed by starting with information from the IMF and applying growth rates from the BoT time series from 1997 onwards.
[b]The time series for nominal GDP is based on two time series because information on quarterly GDP data is only published from 1993 onwards. To cover a longer time frame growth rates of the manufacturing production index are applied for earlier years.
[c]Since quarterly data for this time series is constructed as the average value of the quarter, the values of the last month in the quarter of monthly data are applied instead.

B.7.2 Graphs of the Cointegrating Relations of the Unrestricted Model (Fig. B.83)

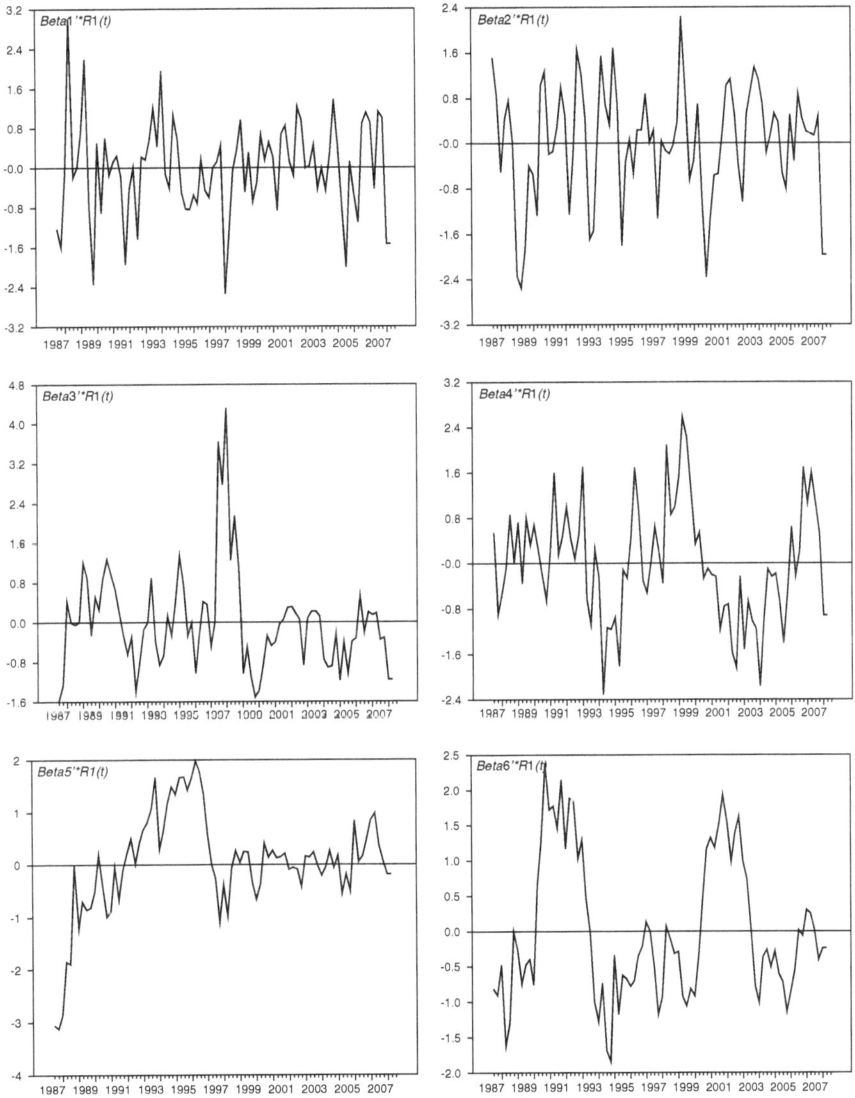

Fig. B.83 Thailand quarterly data: the cointegration relations ($\beta_1, \ldots, \beta_6$) of the unrestricted model

B.7.3 Forward and Backward Recursive Tests for Parameter Constancy of the Unidentified System with Rank $r = 3$ Imposed (Figs. B.84, B.85, B.86, and B.87)

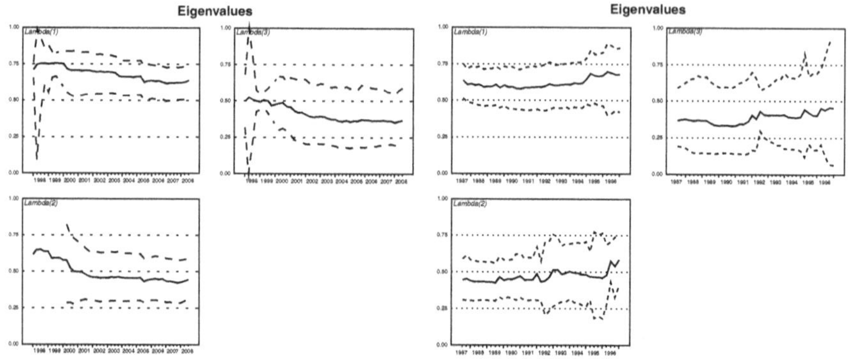

Fig. B.84 Thailand quarterly data: recursively calculated eigenvalues λ_i (forward, base sample 1987:03 to 1998:01, depicted left; backward, base sample 2008:03 to 1997:01, depicted right)

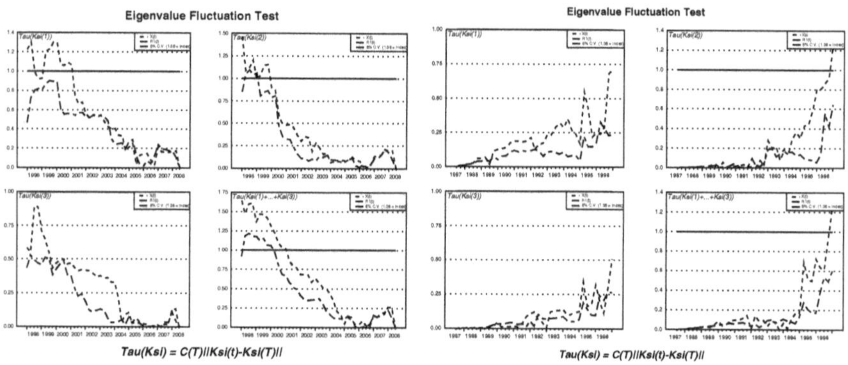

Fig. B.85 Thailand quarterly data: recursively calculated eigenvalue fluctuation test (forward, base sample 1987:03 to 1998:01, depicted left; backward, base sample 2008:03 to 1997:01, depicted right)

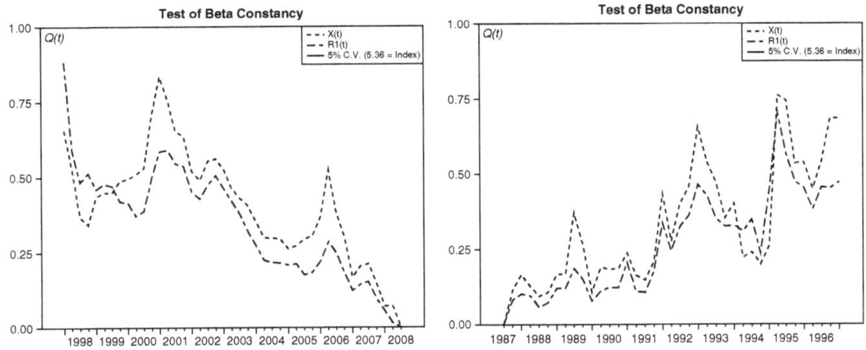

Fig. B.86 Thailand quarterly data: recursively calculated test of β constancy (forward, base sample 1987:03 to 1998:01, depicted left; backward, base sample 2008:03 to 1997:01, depicted right)

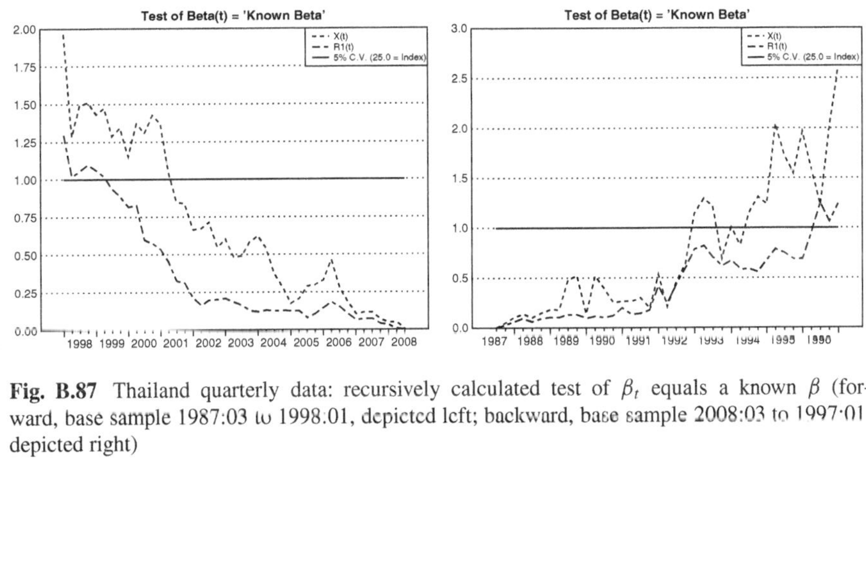

Fig. B.87 Thailand quarterly data: recursively calculated test of β_t equals a known β (forward, base sample 1987:03 to 1998:01, depicted left; backward, base sample 2008:03 to 1997:01, depicted right)

B.7.4 The Partitioned Unrestricted Π-Matrices (Table B.26)

Table B.26 Thailand quarterly data: the partitioned unrestricted Π-matrices based on 4 cointegrating vectors (t-values in brackets)

β'								
	m_r	s_r	y_r	Δp	or	cf	$D_s 9001$	*Trend*
Beta(1)	−0.027	0.012	−0.248	1.000	0.482	0.100	−0.004	0.006
Beta(2)	0.031	−0.030	0.175	1.000	−0.821	0.430	0.001	−0.003
Beta(3)	−0.039	−0.012	0.093	−0.238	1.000	−0.291	−0.000	−0.000

α			
	Alpha(1)	Alpha(2)	Alpha(3)
Δm_r	0.271 [1.434]	0.351 [1.766]	0.083 [0.608]
Δs_r	**−8.746** [−4.019]	2.540 [1.109]	−1.657 [−1.047]
Δy_r	**1.754** [4.183]	**−1.738** [−3.937]	**−1.303** [−4.274]
$\Delta^2 p$	**−0.607** [−7.099]	**−0.426** [−4.734]	**0.041** [0.664]
Δor	**−0.183** [−2.343]	0.080 [0.977]	**−0.194** [−3.408]
Δcf	**−0.360** [−1.975]	**−0.501** [−2.607]	**0.459** [3.456]

B.7.5 Rank Conditions of the Identified Long-Run Structure

Checking formal identification of the restrictions imposed by:

H_1'							
0	0	1	0	0	0	0	0
0	1	0	0	0	0	0	0
0	0	0	0	0	0	1	0
0	0	0	0	0	0	0	1

H_2'							
0	0	0	1	0	0	0	0
0	1	0	0	0	0	0	0
0	0	0	0	0	0	1	0
0	0	0	0	0	0	0	1
0	0	0	0	0	1	0	0

H_3'							
0	0	0	0	1	0	0	0

The set of restrictions imposed by $H_1, \ldots H_3$ are formally identifying if for all i and $k = 1, \ldots, r-1$ and any set of indices $1 \leq i_1 < \cdots < i_k \leq r$ not containing i it holds that

$$R(i.i_1, \ldots, i_k) = rank\left(R_i' \left[H_{i_1} \cdots H_{i_k}\right]\right) \geq k$$

where $R_i = H_{1\perp}$ for all i. The conditions are summarized in Table B.27:

Table B.27 Thailand quarterly data: rank conditions of the identified long-run structure

Rank Conditions			
$R(i.j)$		$R(i.jk)$	
(1.2):	2	(1.23):	3
(1.3):	1		
(2.1):	1	(2.13):	2
(2.3):	1		
(3.1):	4	(3.12):	6
(3.2):	5		

B.7.6 Graphs of the Cointegrating Relations of the Identified Long-Run Structure (Fig. B.88)

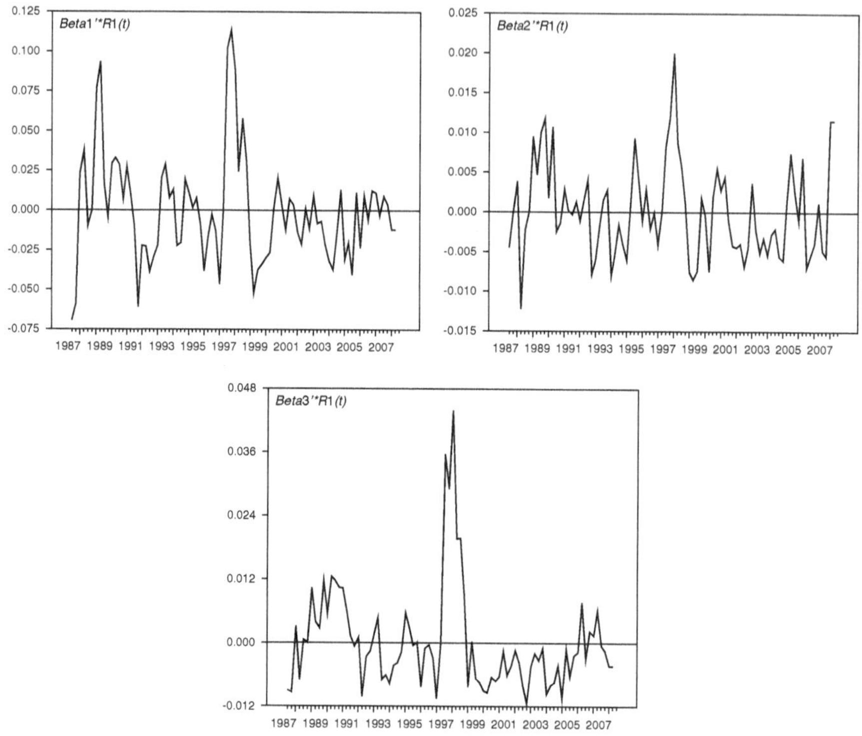

Fig. B.88 Thailand quarterly data: the cointegration relations ($\beta_1, \ldots, \beta_3$) of the restricted model

B.7.7 Tests for Parameter Constancy of the Identified Long-Run Structure (Figs. B.89, B.90, B.91, B.92, B.93, and B.94)

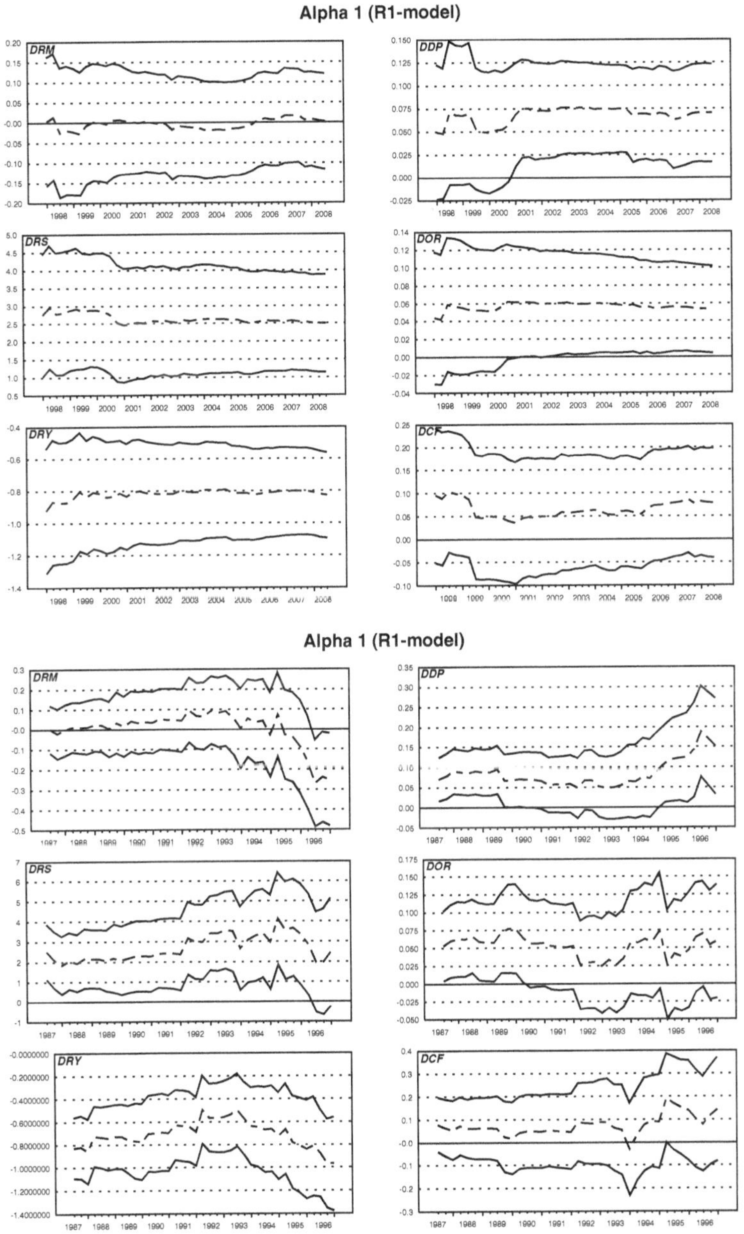

Fig. B.89 Thailand quarterly data: recursively calculated αs of the first cointegration relation (forward, base sample 1987:03 to 1998:01, depicted above; backward, base sample 2008:03 to 1997:01, depicted below)

Beta 1 (R1-model)

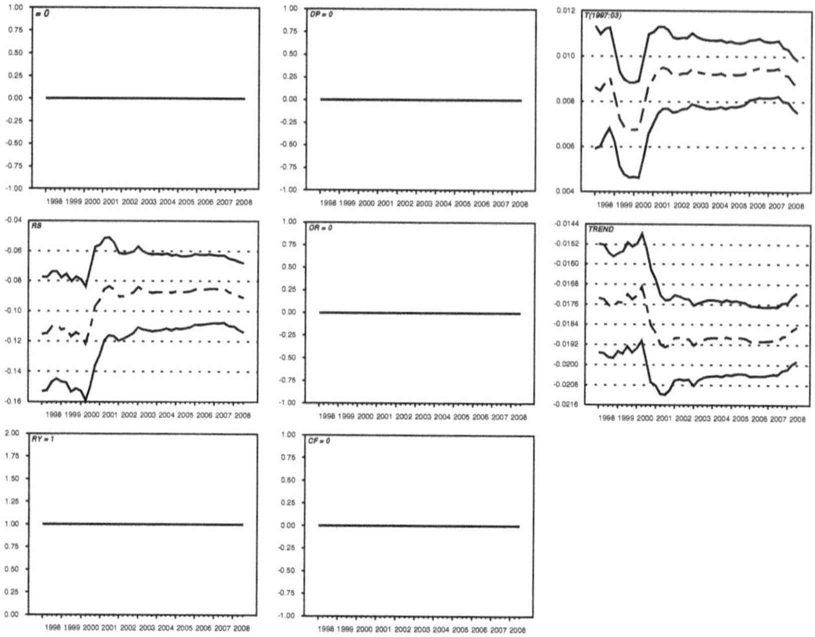

Beta 1 (R1-model)

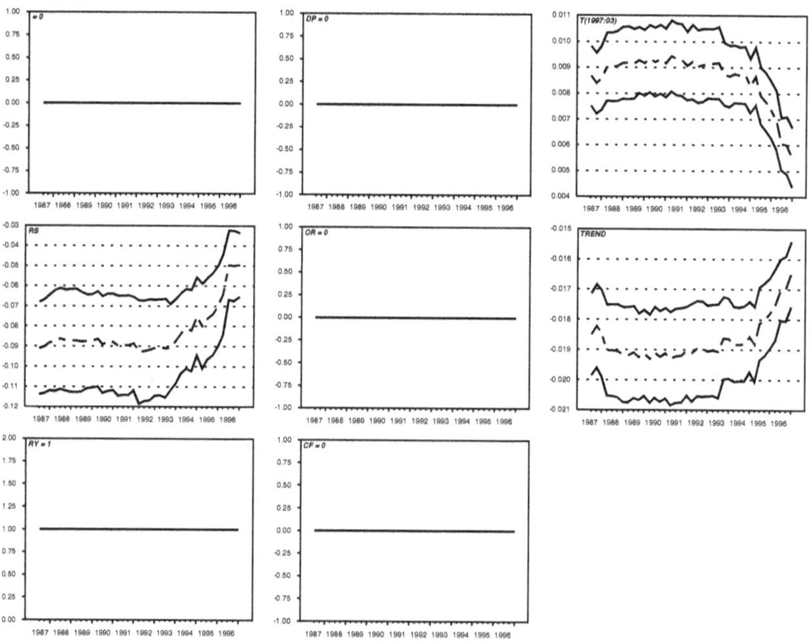

Fig. B.90 Thailand quarterly data: recursively calculated βs of the first cointegration relation (forward, base sample 1987:03 to 1998:01, depicted above; backward, base sample 2008:03 to 1997:01, depicted below)

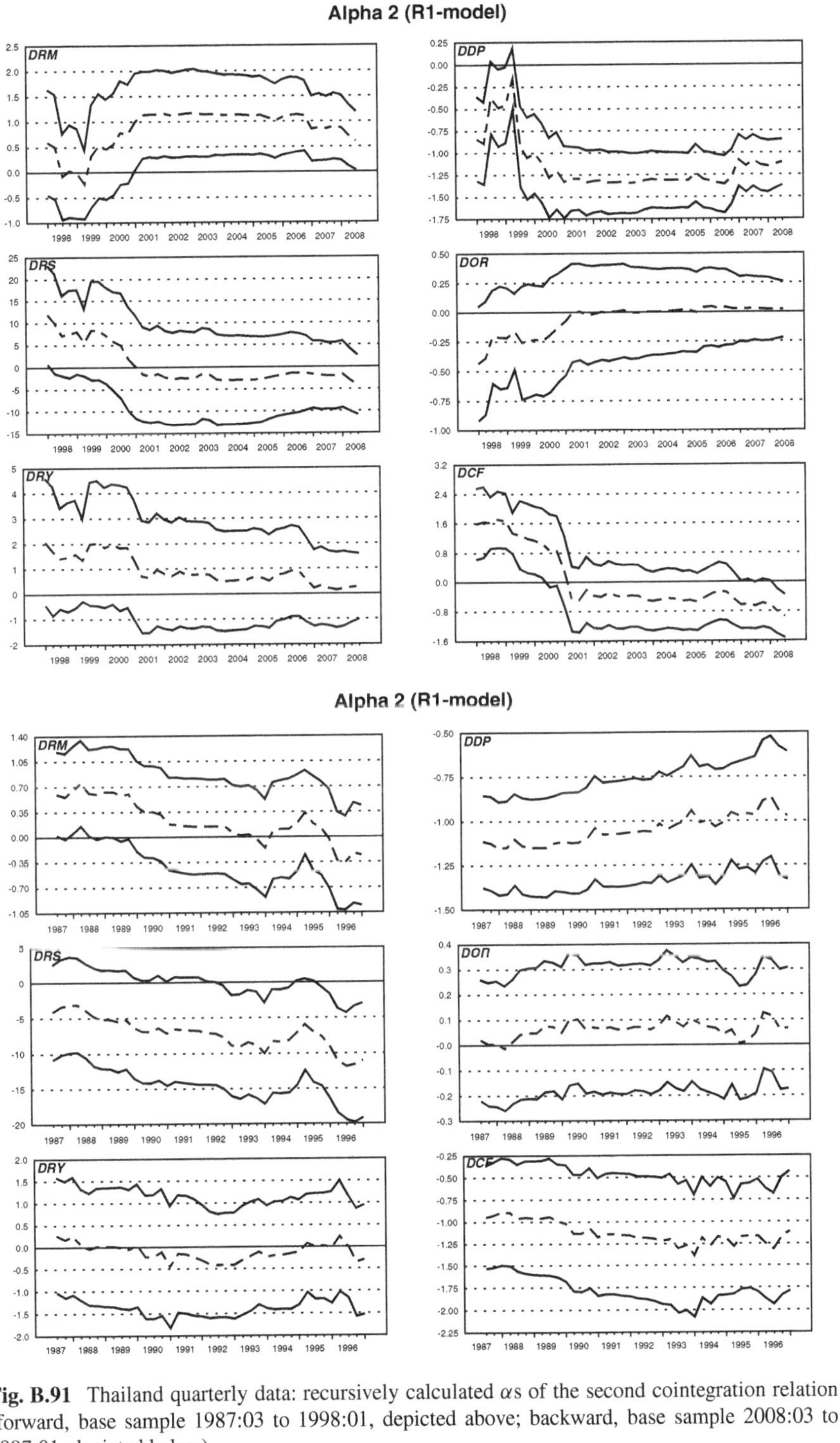

Fig. B.91 Thailand quarterly data: recursively calculated αs of the second cointegration relation (forward, base sample 1987:03 to 1998:01, depicted above; backward, base sample 2008:03 to 1997:01, depicted below)

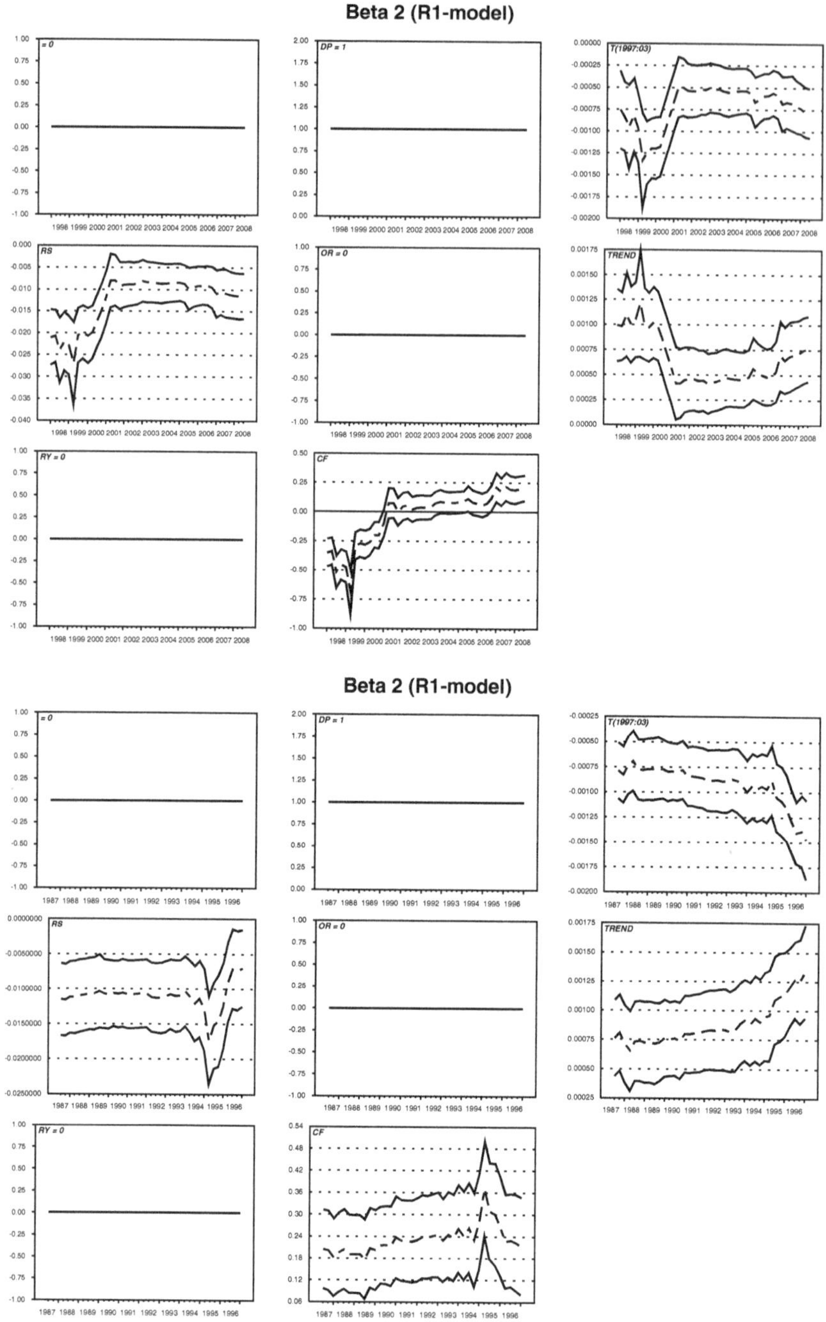

Fig. B.92 Thailand quarterly data: recursively calculated βs of the second cointegration relation (forward, base sample 1987:03 to 1998:01, depicted above; backward, base sample 2008:03 to 1997:01, depicted below)

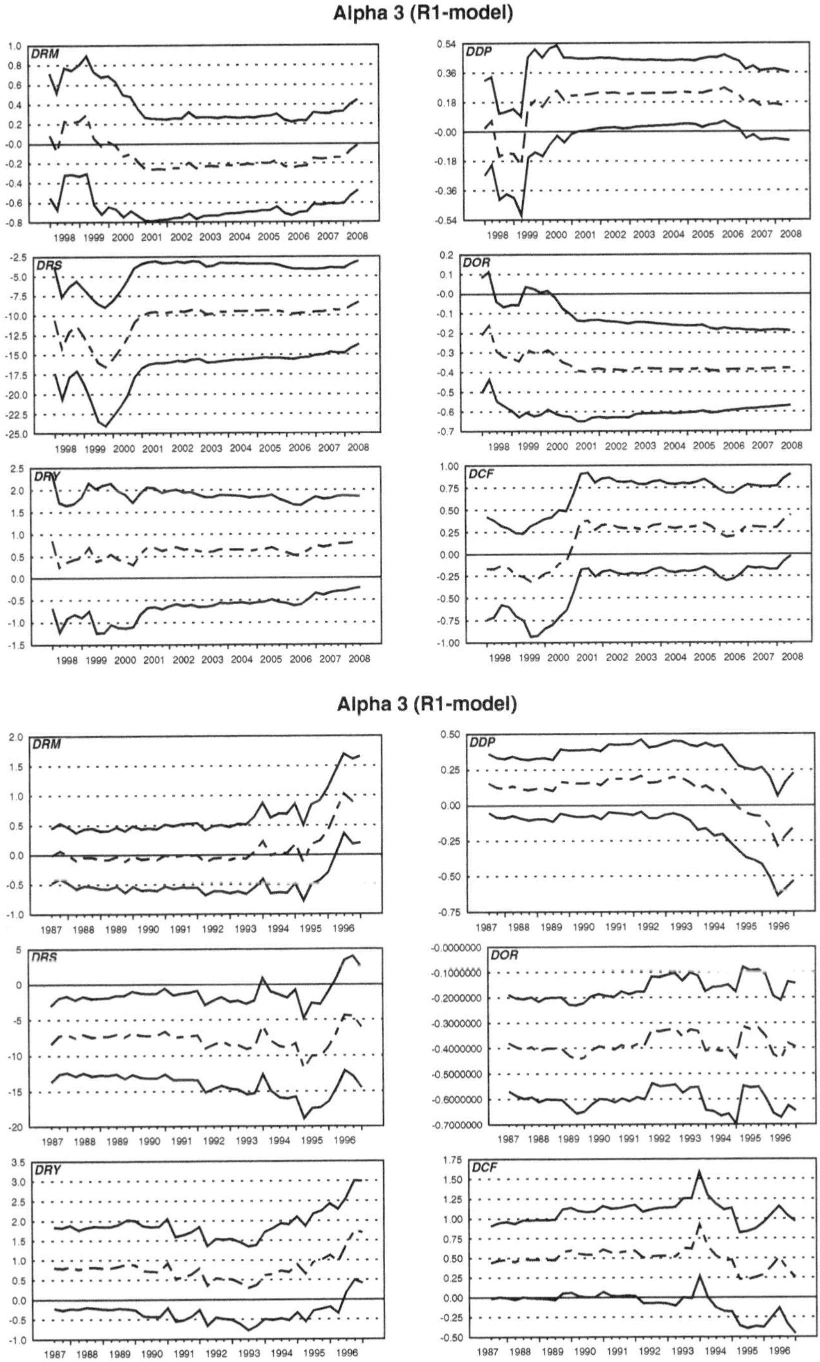

Fig. B.93 Thailand quarterly data: recursively calculated αs of the third cointegration relation (forward, base sample 1987:03 to 1998:01, depicted above; backward, base sample 2008:03 to 1997:01, depicted below)

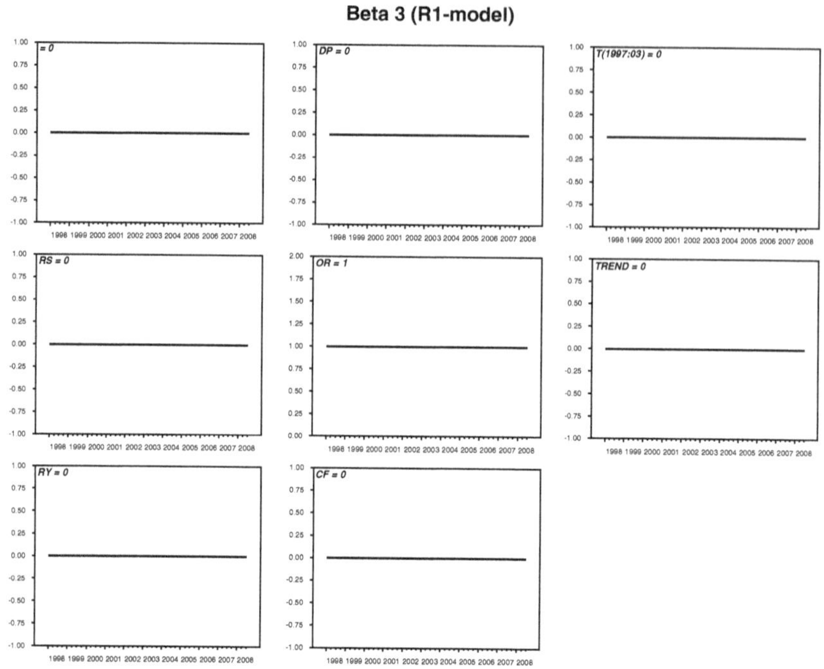

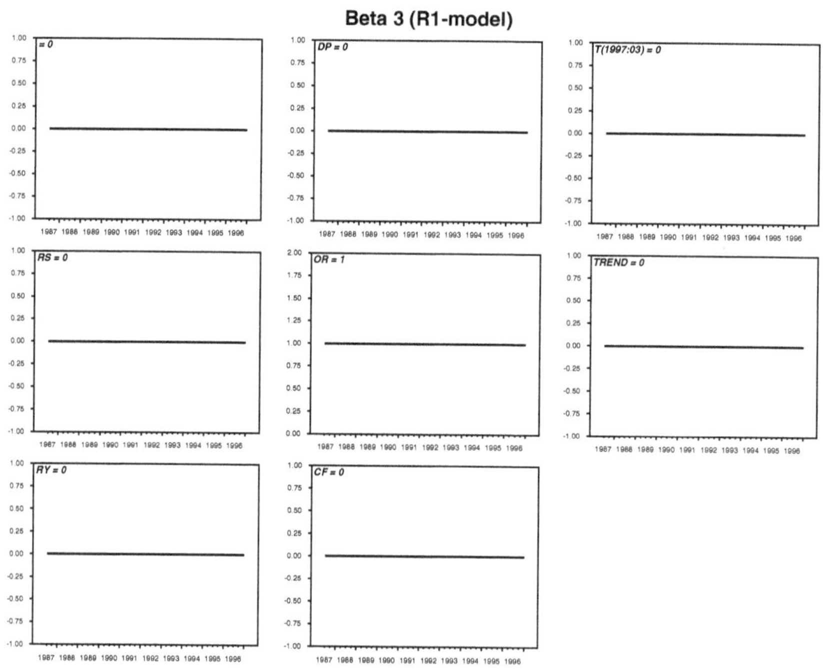

Fig. B.94 Thailand quarterly data: recursively calculated βs of the third cointegration relation (forward, base sample 1987:03 to 1998:01, depicted above; backward, base sample 2008:03 to 1997:01, depicted below)

B.7.8 The Identified Long-Run Structure with Weak Exogeneity Imposed (Table B.28)

Table B.28 Thailand quarterly data: the identified long-run structure with weak exogeneity imposed on real money (t-values in brackets)

	β'							
	m_r	s_r	y_r	Δp	or	cf	D_s9703	*Trend*
Beta(1)	0.000 [NA]	**−0.091** [−7.804]	**1.000** [NA]	0.000 [NA]	0.000 [NA]	0.000 [NA]	**0.009** [14.591]	**−0.018** [−26.636]
Beta(2)	0.000 [NA]	**−0.011** [−4.178]	0.000 [NA]	**1.000** [NA]	0.000 [NA]	**0.194** [3.455]	**−0.001** [−5.753]	**0.001** [4.775]
Beta(3)	0.000 [NA]	0.000 [NA]	0.000 [NA]	0.000 [NA]	**1.000** [NA]	0.000 [NA]	0.000 [NA]	0.000 [NA]

	α		
	Alpha(1)	Alpha(2)	Alpha(3)
Δm_r	0.000 [0.000]	0.000 [0.000]	0.000 [0.000]
Δs_r	**2.478** [3.625]	**−7.140** [−2.139]	**−8.269** [−3.132]
Δy_r	**−0.837** [−6.156]	0.140 [0.210]	0.827 [1.574]
$\Delta^2 p$	**0.068** [2.228]	**−0.967** [−6.511]	0.153 [1.303]
Δor	**0.054** [2.101]	0.097 [0.783]	**−0.378** [−3.845]
Δcf	0.075 [1.246]	**−1.134** [−3.854]	0.436 [1.872]

B.7.9 The Long-Run Impact of the Common Trends with Weak Exogeneity Imposed (Table B.29)

Table B.29 Thailand quarterly data: the long-run impact matrix with weak exogeneity imposed on real money (t-values in brackets)

	The Long-Run Impact Matrix, C					
	$\hat{\epsilon}_{m_r}$	$\hat{\epsilon}_{s_r}$	$\hat{\epsilon}_{y_r}$	$\hat{\epsilon}_{\Delta p}$	$\hat{\epsilon}_{or}$	$\hat{\epsilon}_{cf}$
m_r	**1.445** [4.643]	0.003 [0.177]	0.004 [0.041]	−0.071 [−0.147]	−0.033 [−0.042]	0.041 [0.351]
s_r	3.527 [1.047]	**0.708** [4.211]	0.410 [0.396]	−6.551 [−1.253]	**−17.615** [−2.083]	−0.332 [−0.264]
y_r	0.320 [1.047]	**0.064** [4.211]	0.037 [0.396]	−0.595 [−1.253]	−1.599 [−2.083]	−0.030 [−0.264]
Δp	**0.097** [2.417]	**0.007** [3.641]	−0.002 [−0.142]	0.048 [0.779]	**−0.270** [−2.693]	**−0.110** [−7.383]
or	0.000 [NA]	0.000 [NA]	0.000 [NA]	0.000 [NA]	0.000 [NA]	0.000 [NA]
cf	**−0.293** [−2.593]	0.004 [0.631]	0.033 [0.942]	**−0.627** [−3.577]	0.371 [1.309]	**0.549** [12.974]

B.8 Brazil: Quarterly Data

B.8.1 Data Sources (Table B.30)

Table B.30 Brazil quarterly data: data sources

m	Variable	Nominal money M2, NSA
	Datastream name	MONEY SUPPLY - M2 (EP)
	Datastream Mnemonic	BRM2....A
	Data source	Banco Central do Brasil
s	Variable	Nominal stock market level, NSA
	Datastream name	BRAZIL-DS Market - TOT RETURN IND
	Datastream Mnemonic	TOTMKBR(RI)
	Data source	Datastream
y	Variable	Nominal gross domestic product, NSA
	Datastream name	GDP
	Datastream Mnemonic	BRGDP...A
	Data source	Instituto Brasileiro de Geografia e Estatística
p	Variable	Consumer price index, NSA
	Datastream name	NATIONAL CPI OR INPC
	Datastream Mnemonic	BRCPINATF[a]
	Data source	Instituto Brasileiro de Geografia e Estatística
or	Variable	Short-term interest rate, NSA
	Datastream name	MONEY MARKET RATE OR CDI (% PER MONTH)
	Datastream Mnemonic	BRCDI%..
	Data source	Banco Central do Brasil
cf	Variable	Capital flows, NSA
	Time series name	External Counterpart of Money
	Data source	Constructed by author (see Appendix A), original data series from IMF BoP database

[a] Since quarterly data for this time series is constructed as the average value of the quarter, the values of the last month in the quarter of monthly data are applied instead.

B.8.2 *Graphs of the Cointegrating Relations of the Unrestricted Model (Fig. B.95)*

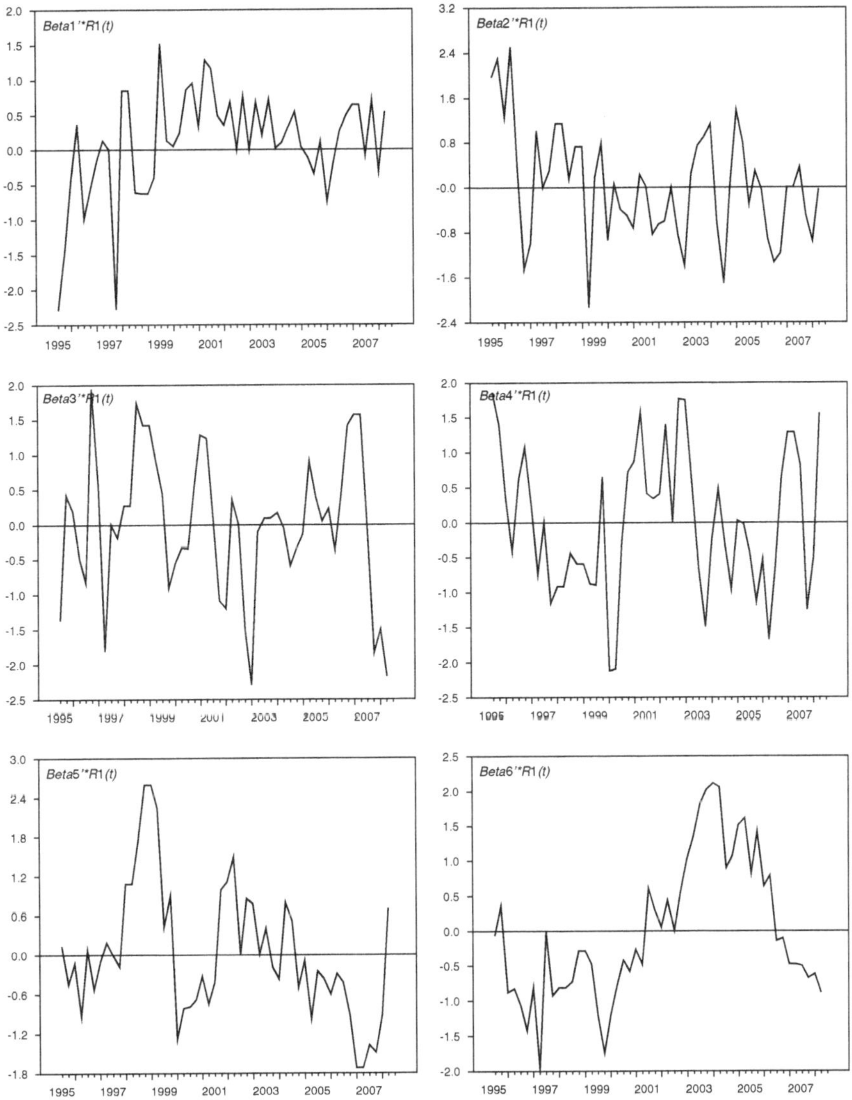

Fig. B.95 Brazil quarterly data: the cointegration relations ($\beta_1, \ldots, \beta_6$) of the unrestricted model

B.8.3 Forward and Backward Recursive Tests for Parameter Constancy of the Unidentified System with Rank r = 3 Imposed (Figs. B.96, B.97, B.98, and B.99)

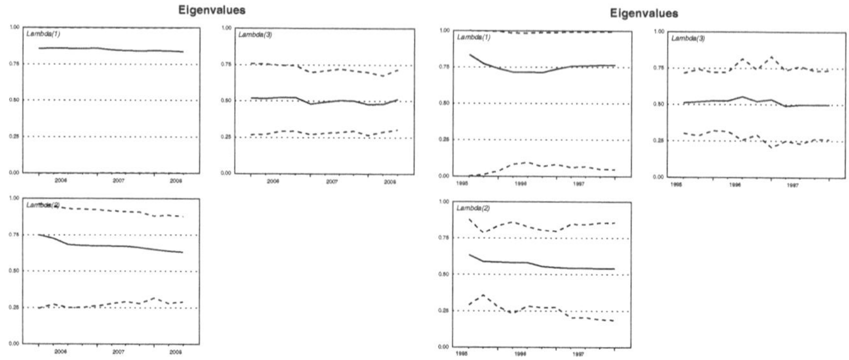

Fig. B.96 Brazil quarterly data: recursively calculated eigenvalues λ_i (forward, base sample 1995:03 to 2006:01, depicted left; backward, base sample 2008:03 to 1998:01, depicted right)

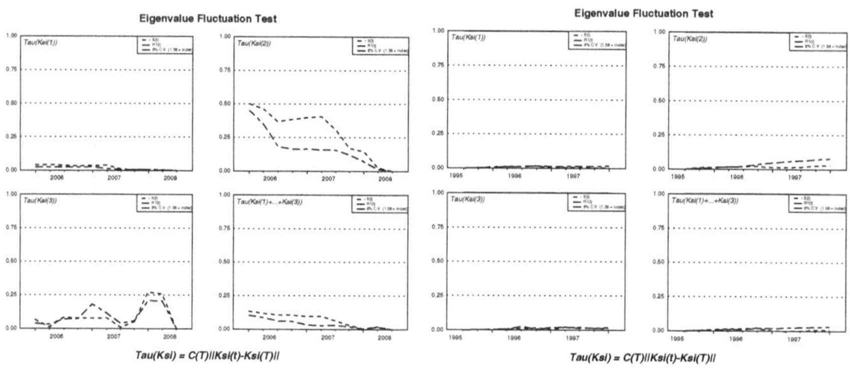

Fig. B.97 Brazil quarterly data: recursively calculated eigenvalue fluctuation test (forward, base sample 1995:03 to 2006:01, depicted left; backward, base sample 2008:03 to 1998:01, depicted right)

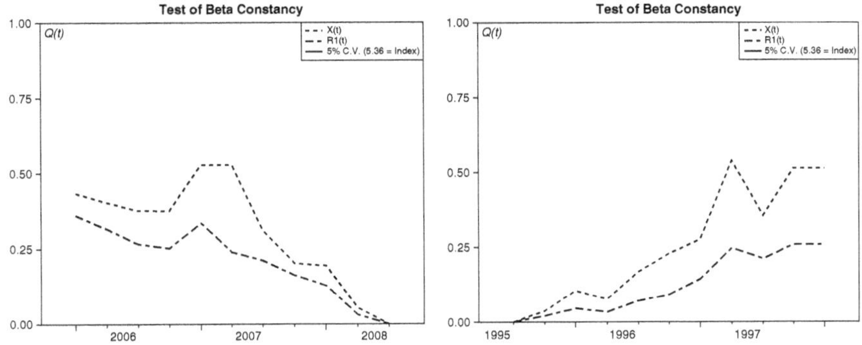

Fig. B.98 Brazil quarterly data: recursively calculated test of β constancy (forward, base sample 1995:03 to 2006:01, depicted left; backward, base sample 2008:03 to 1998:01, depicted right)

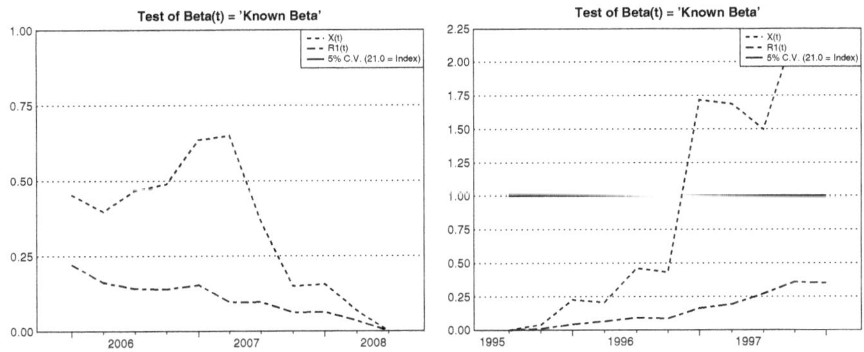

Fig. B.99 Brazil quarterly data: recursively calculated test of β_t equals a known β (forward, base sample 1995:03 to 2006:01, depicted left; backward, base sample 2008:03 to 1998:01, depicted right)

B.8.4 The Partitioned Unrestricted Π-Matrices (Table B.31)

Table B.31 Brazil quarterly data: the partitioned unrestricted Π-matrices based on 3 cointegrating vectors (t-values in brackets)

	β'							
	m_r	s_r	y_r	Δp	or	cf	D_s9001	*Trend*
Beta(1)	−0.107	0.040	0.169	0.034	1.000	−0.272	−0.001	
Beta(2)	0.216	−0.024	−0.623	0.003	−0.190	1.000	0.002	
Beta(3)	−0.118	−0.096	1.000	−0.797	0.448	0.487	−0.004	

	α		
	Alpha(1)	Alpha(2)	Alpha(3)
Δm_r	0.138 [0.903]	−0.256 [−1.860]	−0.136 [−0.942]
Δs_r	0.651 [0.727]	−0.686 [−0.852]	**3.105** [3.677]
Δy_r	−0.230 [−1.699]	**0.257** [2.115]	**−0.470** [−3.690]
$\Delta^2 p$	−0.067 [−0.948]	−0.100 [−1.561]	**0.259** [3.867]
Δor	**−0.419** [−13.836]	**−0.094** [−3.457]	**−0.082** [−2.878]
Δcf	**0.917** [7.402]	**−0.707** [−6.348]	0.095 [0.810]

B.8.5 Rank Conditions of the Identified Long-Run Structure

Checking formal identification of the restrictions imposed by:

H_1'						
1	0	0	0	0	0	0
0	1	0	0	0	0	0
0	0	0	0	0	1	0

H_2'						
0	0	0	0	1	0	0
0	0	0	0	0	1	0

H_3'						
0	0	0	0	0	0	1
1	0	0	0	0	0	0
0	0	1	0	0	0	0
0	0	0	0	1	0	0

The set of restrictions imposed by $H_1, \ldots H_3$ are formally identifying if for all i and $k = 1, \ldots, r-1$ and any set of indices $1 \leq i_1 < \cdots < i_k \leq r$ not containing i it holds that

$$R(i.i_1, \ldots, i_k) = rank\left(R_i'\left[H_{i_1} \cdots H_{i_k}\right]\right) \geq k$$

where $R_i = H_{1\perp}$ for all i. The conditions are summarized in Table B.32:

Table B.32 Brazil quarterly data: rank conditions of the identified long-run structure

Rank Conditions			
$R(i.j)$		$R(i.jk)$	
(1.2):	1	(1.23):	3
(1.3):	3		
(2.1):	2	(2.13):	4
(2.3):	3		
(3.1):	2	(3.12):	2
(3.2):	1		

B.8.6 Graphs of the Cointegrating Relations of the Identified Long-Run Structure (Fig. B.100)

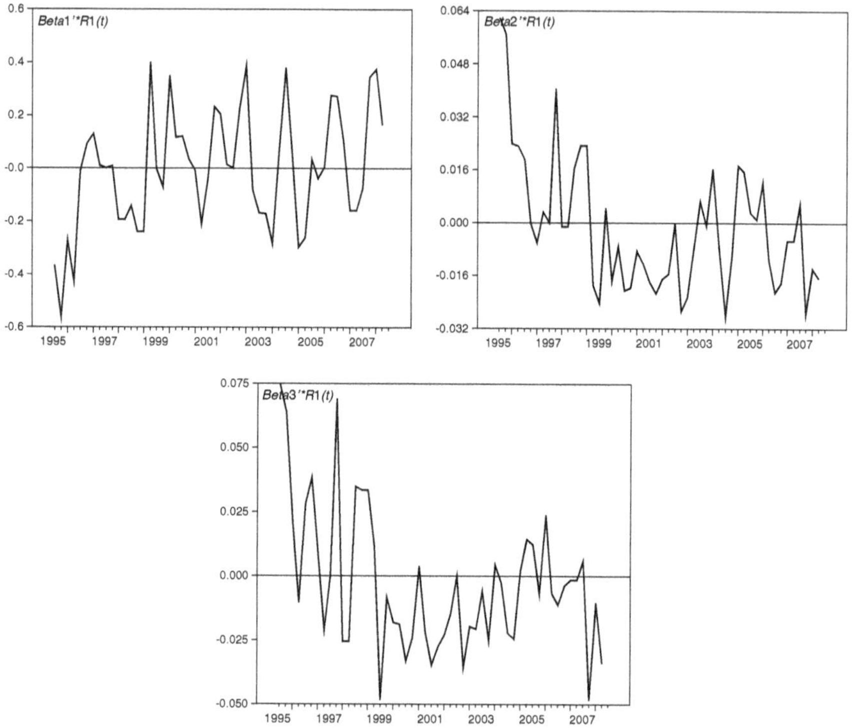

Fig. B.100 Brazil quarterly data: the cointegration relations ($\beta_1, \ldots, \beta_3$) of the restricted model

B.8.7 Tests for Parameter Constancy of the Identified Long-Run Structure (Figs. B.101,B.102, B.103,B.104,B.105, and B.106)

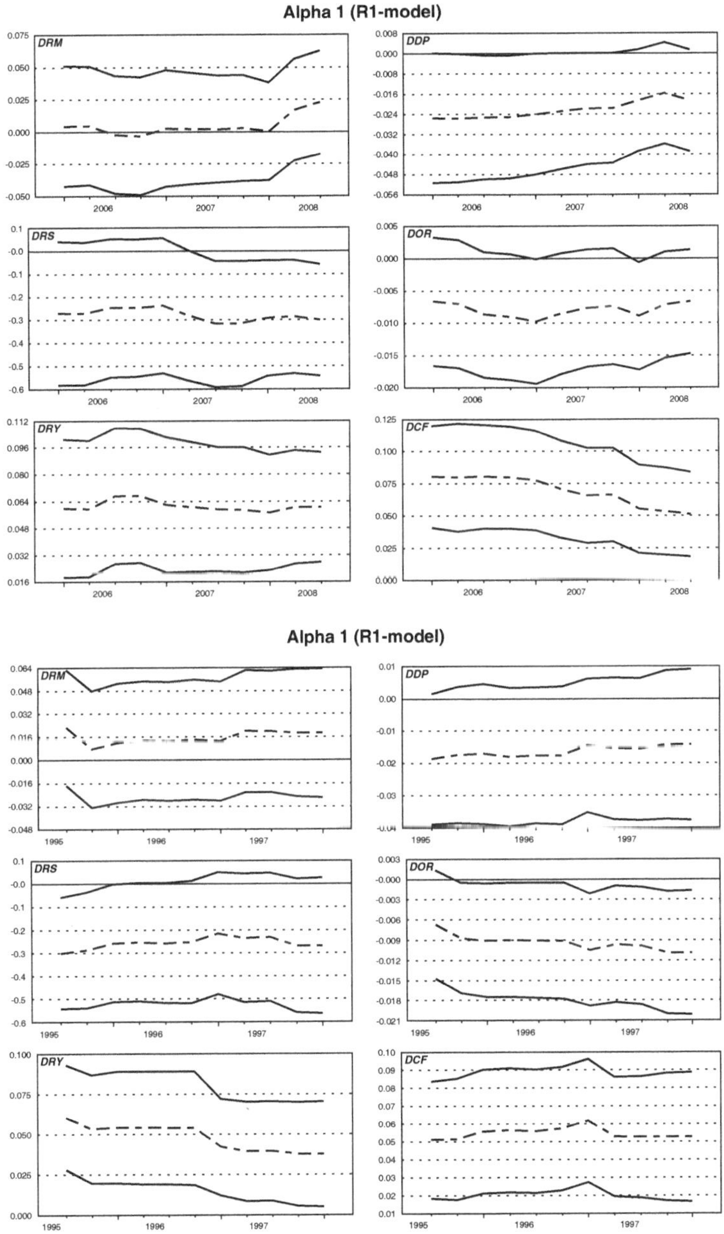

Fig. B.101 Brazil quarterly data: recursively calculated αs of the first cointegration relation (forward, base sample 1995:03 to 2006:01, depicted above; backward, base sample 2008:03 to 1998:01, depicted below)

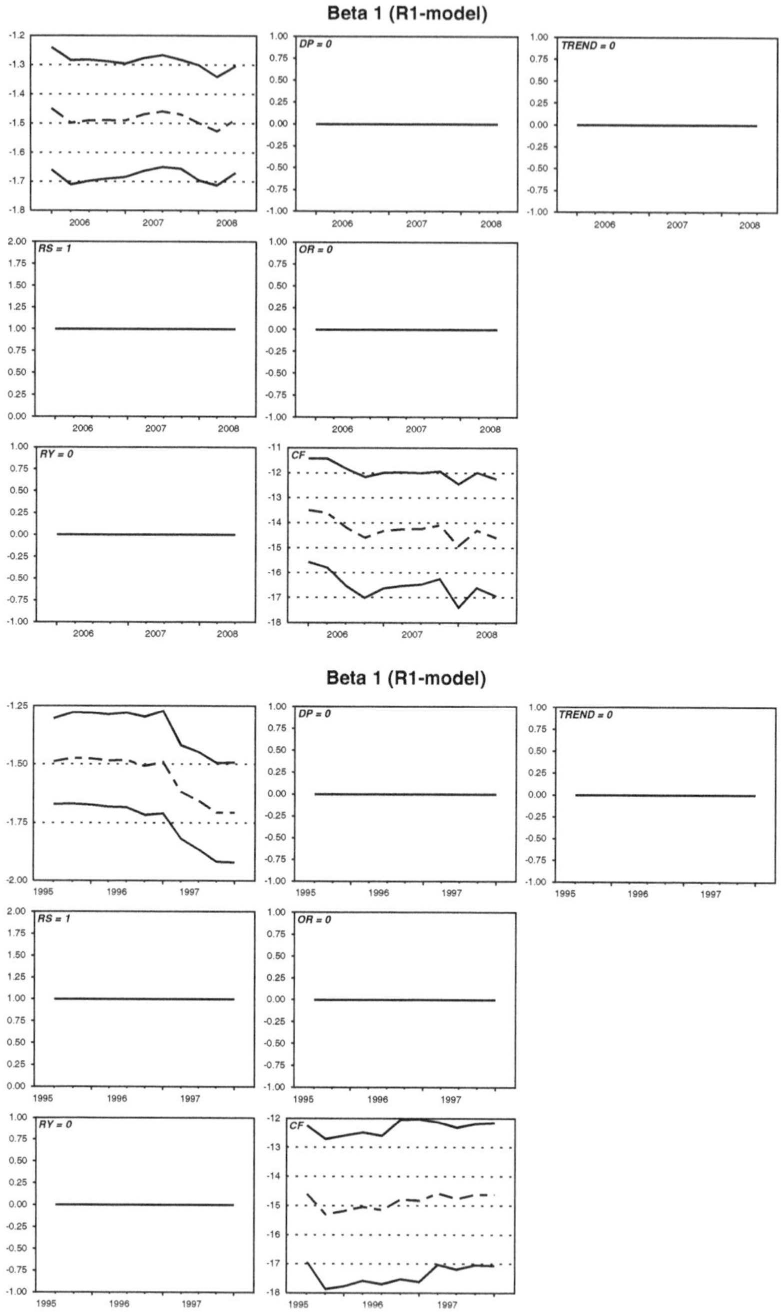

Fig. B.102 Brazil quarterly data: recursively calculated βs of the first cointegration relation (forward, base sample 1995:03 to 2006:01, depicted above; backward, base sample 2008:03 to 1998:01, depicted below)

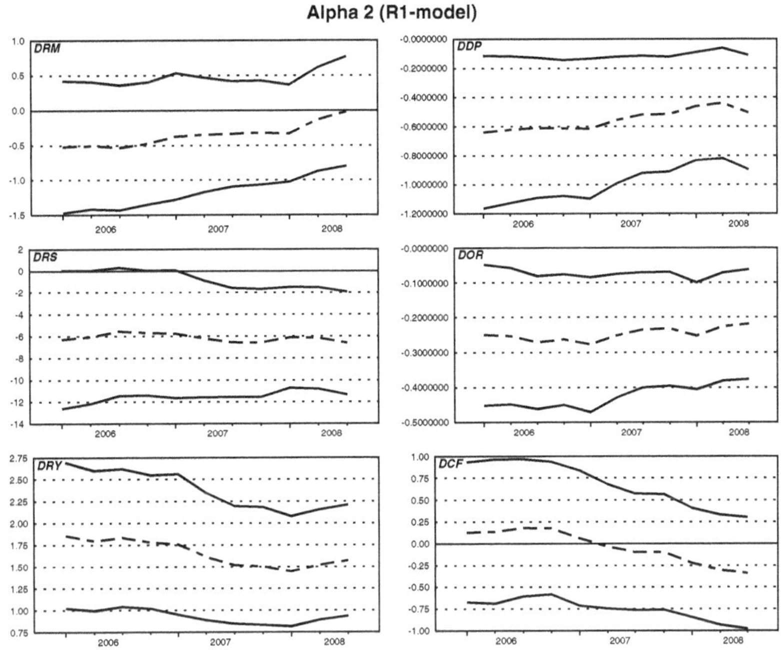

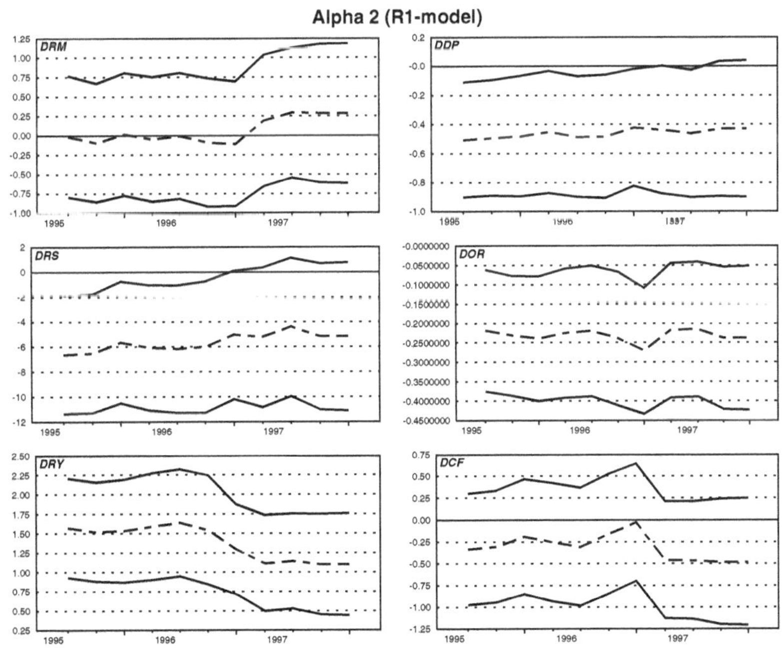

Fig. B.103 Brazil quarterly data: recursively calculated αs of the second cointegration relation (forward, base sample 1995:03 to 2006:01, depicted above; backward, base sample 2008:03 to 1998:01, depicted below)

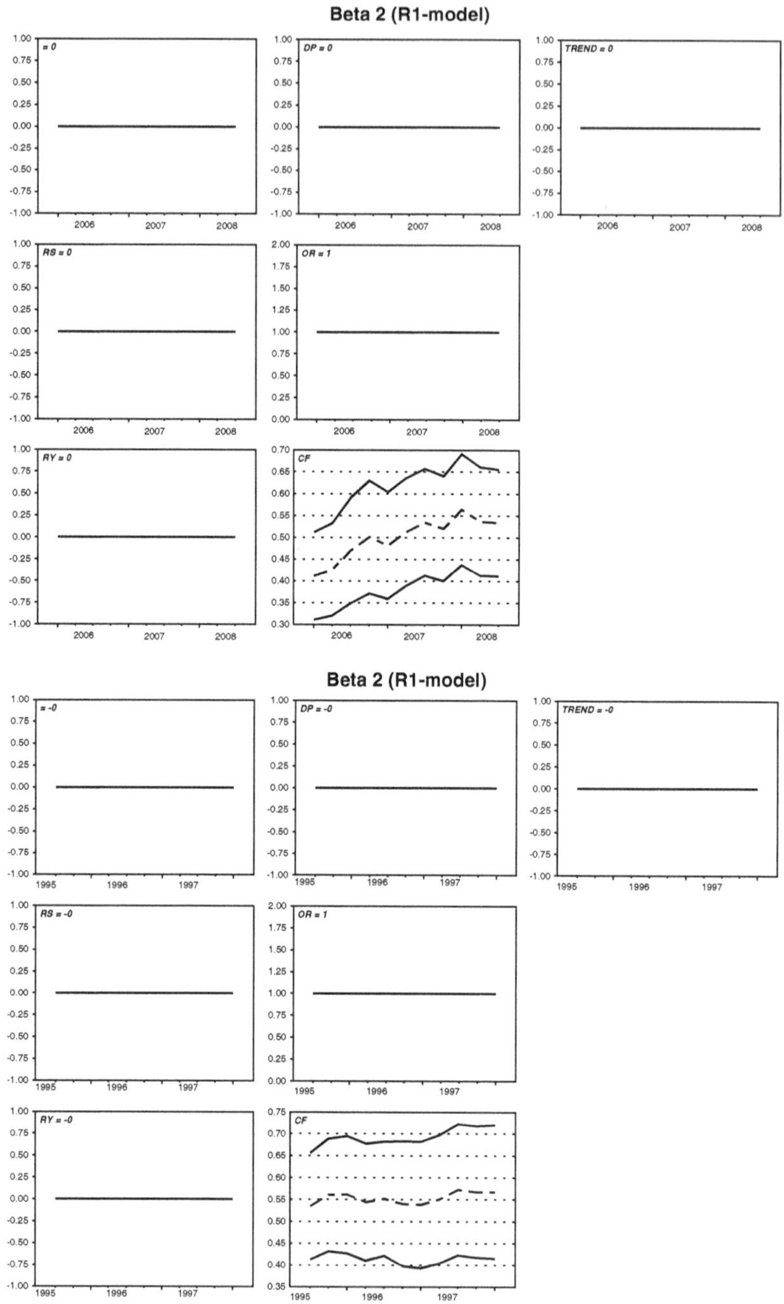

Fig. B.104 Brazil quarterly data: recursively calculated βs of the second cointegration relation (forward, base sample 1995:03 to 2006:01, depicted above; backward, base sample 2008:03 to 1998:01, depicted below)

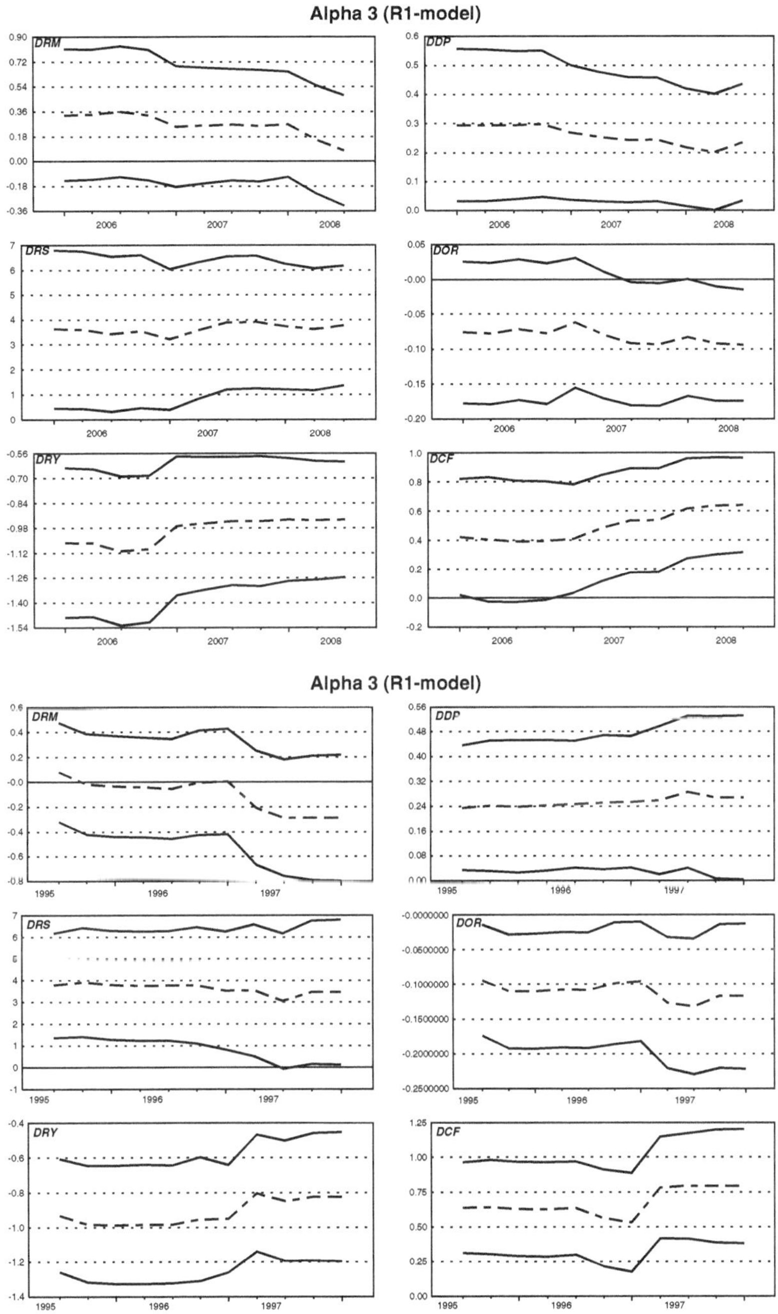

Fig. B.105 Brazil quarterly data: recursively calculated αs of the third cointegration relation (forward, base sample 1995:03 to 2006:01, depicted above; backward, base sample 2008:03 to 1998:01, depicted below)

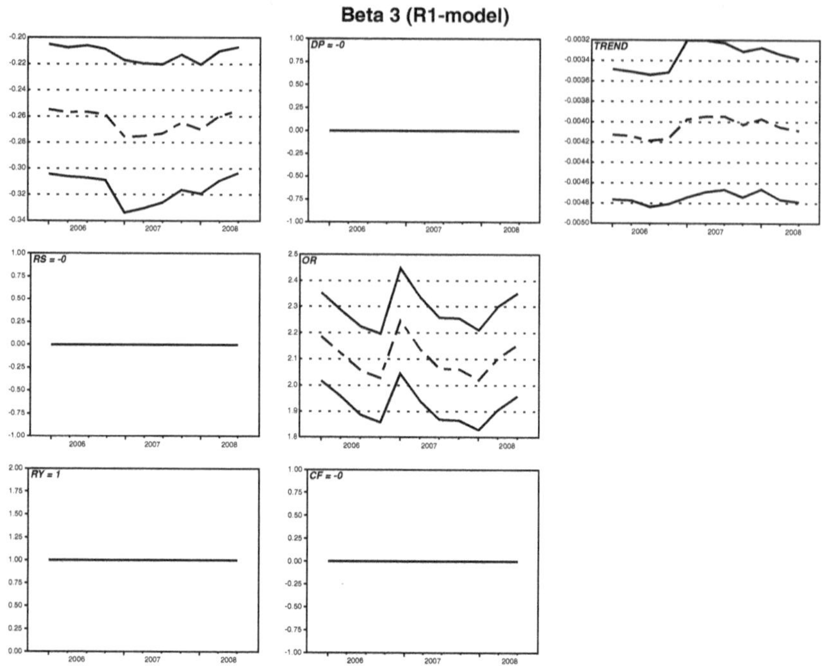

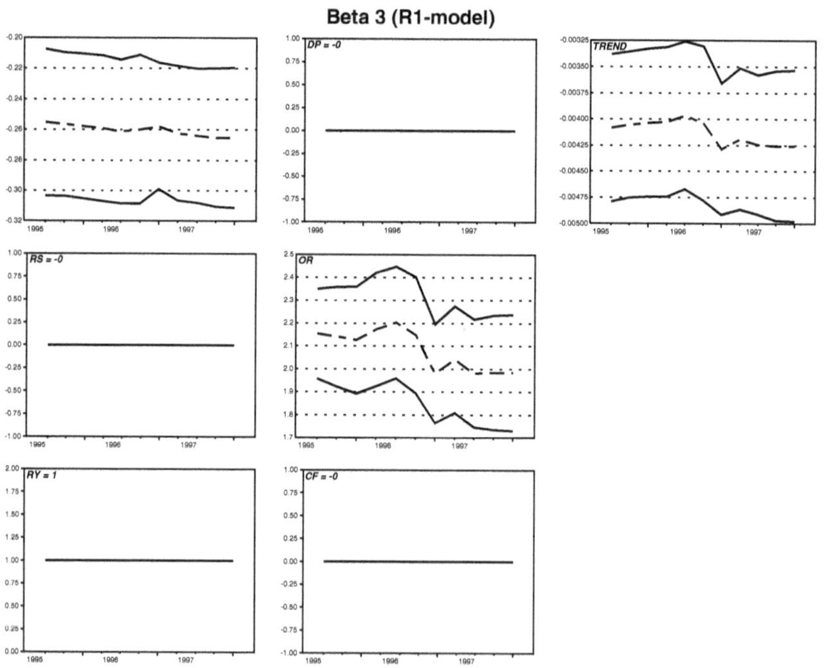

Fig. B.106 Brazil quarterly data: recursively calculated βs of the third cointegration relation (forward, base sample 1995:03 to 2006:01, depicted above; backward, base sample 2008:03 to 1998:01, depicted below)

Appendix C
Impact of Macro Variables on Each Other: Summary Tables

The tables in this appendix provide an extensive overview of the effect of the included macro variables on each other in the long and short run. It is constructed to cover all aspects of the empirical analysis, including long-run effects and equilibria (columns *a* to *e*) as well as short-run dynamics (columns *f* to *j*).

Columns *a* and *b* show which cumulated shocks to the variables have a significant positive or negative long-run effect on the respective variable, respectively. Columns *c* to *e* describe the long-run cointegration relations, which can be interpreted as economic equilibria between the variables. Columns *c* and *d* show, to which of the variables the respective variable is related in the long run and shows dynamic adjustment behavior in the short run. Column *e*, on the other hand, shows cointegration relations, in which the respective variable is present but the respective variable does not react to disequilibria.[1]

Short-run dynamics are divided into adjustment to the equilibrium errors of the cointegration relations and significant effects of lagged variables. More precisely, on the one hand, column *f* documents the cointegration relations, to which the respective variable shows error-correction behavior. Columns *g* and *h*, on the other hand, demonstrate, to which disequilibrium errors the respective variable reacts without being part of the cointegration relation. Finally, columns *i* and *j* describe positive and negative significant effects of lagged values of the variables. These are derived from applying the full information maximum likelihood estimator in simultaneous equation modeling.

[1] To enhance readability of the table the coefficients to the parameters of the cointegration relations are left out. The idea here is to gain understanding of significant relationships between the variables. A more detailed view of the cointegration relations is presented in the respective country analyses.

Table C.1 Impact of macro variables on real money

	Long run					Short run				
	Common trends		Cointegration			Adjustment to cointegration relations			Effects of lagged variables	
Country	Positive impact of cumulated shocks to variable	Negative impact of cumulated shocks to variable	Positively related to	Negatively related to	Part of but not reacting to it	Equilibrium correcting to deviations from CI relation	Pushed positively by deviations from CI relation	Pushed negatively by deviations from CI relation	Positive significant effect	Negative significant effect
	a	*b*	*c*	*d*	*e*	*f*	*g*	*h*	*i*	*j*
USA	Real money				$y_r - m_r - s_r - trend$				Real money	Real stocks
					$\Delta p - (m_r - y_r)$				Short rate	
Euro area	Real money				$b10 - m_r$			$s_r - (y_r - trend)$	Real stocks	Short rate
										Bond rate
Japan		Real stocks		Real stocks		$m_r + s_r + \Delta p$		$y_r - s_r + or$		Real money
		Bond rate		Inflation				$b10 - \Delta p$		Inflation
										Capital flows
UK	Real money	Short rate			$cf + m_r - s_r$		$\Delta p - y_r + or - b10$	$or - s_r - y_r$	Real money	
Australia	Real money		Real stocks			$m_r - s_r - y_r + trend$			Real output	Bond rate
	Real output		Real output							

(*continued*)

Table C.1 (Continued)

	Long run					Short run				
	Common trends		Cointegration			Adjustment to cointegration relations			Effects of lagged variables	
Country	Positive impact of cumulated shocks to variable	Negative impact of cumulated shocks to variable	Positively related to	Negatively related to	Part of but not reacting to it	Equilibrium correcting to deviations from CI relation	Pushed positively by deviations from CI relation	Pushed negatively by deviations from CI relation	Positive significant effect	Negative significant effect
	a	*b*	*c*	*d*	*e*	*f*	*g*	*h*	*i*	*j*
South Korea	Real money		Real stocks	Term spread		$m_r - s_r - y_r + (b10 - or)$	$s_r - m_r + y_r - cf - trend$		Real output	Short rate
	Short rate		Real output			$\Delta p - (m_r - trend)$				Capital flows
	Capital flows		Inflation							
Thailand	Real money						$\Delta p - s_r + cf$		Real money	
Brazil					$s_r - m_r - cf$				Real money Inflation Capital flows	

Table C.2 Impact of macro variables on real economic activity

	Long run					Short run				
	Common trends		Cointegration			Adjustment to cointegration relations			Effects of lagged variables	
Country	Positive impact of cumulated shocks to variable	Negative impact of cumulated shocks to variable	Positively related to	Negatively related to	Part of but not reacting to it	Equilibrium correcting to deviations from CI relation	Pushed positively by deviations from CI relation	Pushed negatively by deviations from CI relation	Positive significant effect	Negative significant effect
	a	*b*	*c*	*d*	*e*	*f*	*g*	*h*	*i*	*j*
US	Real money		Real money		$\Delta p-(m_r-y_r)$	$y_r-m_r-s_r-trend$			Real output	
	Real stocks		Real stocks							
Euro area	Real stocks		Real stocks			$s_r-(y_r-trend)$			Short rate	Real output
										Capital flows
Japan	Real stocks	Real money	Real stocks	Short rate		y_r-s_r+or	$m_r+s_r+\Delta p$			Real money
	Real output	Inflation					$b10-\Delta p$			Inflation
		Short rate								
UK	Real output	Short rate			$or-s_r-y_r$					
					$\Delta p-y_r+or-b10$					
Australia	Real output			Real bond rate	$m_r-s_r-y_r+trend$	$y_r+(b10-\Delta p)$			Real output	

(continued)

Table C.2 (Continued)

	Long run					Short run				
	Common trends		Cointegration			Adjustment to cointegration relations			Effects of lagged variables	
Country	Positive impact of cumulated shocks to variable	Negative impact of cumulated shocks to variable	Positively related to	Negatively related to	Part of but not reacting to it	Equilibrium correcting to deviations from CI relation	Pushed positively by deviations from CI relation	Pushed negatively by deviations from CI relation	Positive significant effect	Negative significant effect
	a	*b*	*c*	*d*	*e*	*f*	*g*	*h*	*i*	*j*
South Korea	Real output			Real bond rate	$s_r - m_r + y_r - cf - trend$	$y_r + (b10 - \Delta p) - trend$		$\Delta p - (m_r - trend)$	Real stocks	Short rate
					$m_r - s_r - y_r + (b10 - or)$				Real output	
Thailand	Real stocks		Real stocks			$y_r - s_r - trend$			Real money	Real stocks
									Inflation	
Brazil	Real stocks		Real money	Short rate		$y_r - m_r + or - trend$	$s_r - m_r - cf$		Real money	
	Real output						$or + cf$			

Table C.3 Impact of macro variables on the inflation rate

	Long run				Short run					
	Common trends			Cointegration	Adjustment to cointegration relations				Effects of lagged variables	
Country	Positive impact of cumulated shocks to variable	Negative impact of cumulated shocks to variable	Positively related to	Negatively related to	Part of but not reacting to it	Equilibrium correcting to deviations from CI relation	Pushed positively by deviations from CI relation	Pushed negatively by deviations from CI relation	Positive significant effect	Negative significant effect
	a	*b*	*c*	*d*	*e*	*f*	*g*	*h*	*i*	*j*
USA	Real money		Excess liquidity		$b10-\Delta p-or$	$\Delta p-(m_r-y_r)$	$y_r-m_r-s_r-trend$ cf		Bond rate	
Euro area				Inflation		Δp		$s_r-(y_r-trend)$		Inflation
Japan	Inflation		Bond rate		$m_r+s_r+\Delta p$	$b10-\Delta p$	y_r-s_r+or		Real money	Bond rate
	Bond rate									
UK	Real output	Short rate	Real output	Short rate		$\Delta p-y_r+or-b10$	$or-s_r-y_r$		Inflation	
	Bond rate		Bond rate							
Australia	Real output		Real output			$y_r+(b10-\Delta p)$			Real money	
	Inflation		Bond rate							
	Bond rate									

(continued)

Table C.3 (Continued)

	Long run					Short run				
	Common trends		Cointegration			Adjustment to cointegration relations			Effects of lagged variables	
Country	Positive impact of cumulated shocks to variable	Negative impact of cumulated shocks to variable	Positively related to	Negatively related to	Part of but not reacting to it	Equilibrium correcting to deviations from CI relation	Pushed positively by deviations from CI relation	Pushed negatively by deviations from CI relation	Positive significant effect	Negative significant effect
	a	*b*	*c*	*d*	*e*	*f*	*g*	*h*	*i*	*j*
South Korea	Real money		Real money			$\Delta p - (m_r - trend)$			Short rate	
	Short rate		Real output			$y_r + (b10 - \Delta p) - trend$				
	Capital flows		Bond rate							
Thailand	Real money	Short rate	Real stocks	Capital flows		$\Delta p - s_r + cf$	$y_r - sr - trend$		Short rate	Inflation
	Real stocks	Capital flows								
Brazil	Inflation						$y_r - m_r + or - trend$	$or + cf$	Real money	Inflation

Table C.4 Impact of macro variables on the overnight rate

	Long run				Short run					
	Common trends		Cointegration		Adjustment to cointegration relations				Effects of lagged variables	
Country	Positive impact of cumulated shocks to variable	Negative impact of cumulated shocks to variable	Positively related to	Negatively related to	Part of but not reacting to it	Equilibrium correcting to deviations from CI relation	Pushed positively by deviations from CI relation	Pushed negatively by deviations from CI relation	Positive significant effect	Negative significant effect
	a	*b*	*c*	*d*	*e*	*f*	*g*	*h*	*i*	*j*
USA	Real output		Bond rate	Inflation		$b10-\Delta p-or$	$y_r-m_r-s_r-trend$		Real output	
	Short rate						$\Delta p-(m_r-y_r)$			
	Bond rate									
Euro area	Real stocks		Real stocks			$or-s_r$	$b10-m_r$	$s_r-(y_r-trend)$		Real output
								Δp		Short rate
								cf		
Japan	Inflation				y_r-s_r+or		$m_r+s_r+\Delta p$		Real output	Inflation
	Short rate								Short rate	
									Bond rate	
UK	Real stocks	Short rate	Real stocks		$\Delta p-y_r+or-b10$	$or-s_r-y_r$				
	Real output		Real output							
Australia	Real stocks								Inflation	
	Real output								Bond rate	
	Short rate									

(continued)

Table C.4 (Continued)

	Long run					Short run				
	Common trends		Cointegration			Adjustment to cointegration relations			Effects of lagged variables	
Country	Positive impact of cumulated shocks to variable	Negative impact of cumulated shocks to variable	Positively related to	Negatively related to	Part of but not reacting to it	Equilibrium correcting to deviations from CI relation	Pushed positively by deviations from CI relation	Pushed negatively by deviations from CI relation	Positive significant effect	Negative significant effect
	a	*b*	*c*	*d*	*e*	*f*	*g*	*h*	*i*	*j*
South Korea	Real money	Real stocks	Real money	Real stocks		$m_r - s_r - y_r + (b10 - or)$	$s_r - m_r + y_r - cf - trend$	$\Delta p - (m_r - trend)$	Inflation	
	Short rate	Real output	Bond rate	Real output				$y_r + (b10 - \Delta p) - trend$	Capital flows	
		Capital flows								
Thailand				Short rate		or	$y_r - sr - trend$			
Brazil	Real money		Real money	Capital flows		$or + cf$			Real money	Real stocks
				Real output		$y_r - m_r + or - trend$			Real output	
									Inflation	

References

Abdullah DA, Hayworth SC (1993) Macroeconometrics of stock price fluctuations. Q J Bus Econ 32(1):50–67

Abreu D, Brunnermeier MK (2003) Bubbles and crashes. Econometrica 71(1):173–204

Adalid R, Detken C (2007) Liquidity shocks and asset price boom/bust cycles. ECB working paper series (732)

Adrian T, Shin HS (2007) Liquidity, monetary policy and financial cycles. Current issues in economics and finance (September 2007)

Agrawalla RK, Tuteja SK (2008) Share prices and macroeconomic variables in India: An approach to investigate the relationship between stock markets and economic growth. J Manag Res 8(3):136–146

Aizenman J, Lee J (2005) International reserves: Precautionary versus mercantilist views, theory and evidence. NBER working paper series (11366)

Allen F, Gale D (2000) Bubbles and crises. Econ J 110(January):236–255

Allen F, Gale D (2002) Liquidity, asset prices and systemic risk. In: CGFS Conference vol. 2, Part 1, October 2002

Altug S, Labadie P (1995) Dynamic choice and asset markets. Academic

Amihud Y (2002) Illiquidity and stock returns: Cross-section and time-series effects. J Financ Market 5:31–56

Amihud Y, Mendelson H, Pedersen LH (2005) Liquidity and asset prices. Foundations Trends Finance 1(4):269–303

Anderton R, di Mauro F, Moneta F (2004) Understanding the impact of the external dimension on the euro area: Trade, capital flows and other international macroeconomic linkages. ECB occasional paper series (12)

Angelini E, Marcellino M (2007) Econometric analyses with backdated data – unified Germany and the euro area. ECB working paper series (752)

Assenmacher-Wesche K, Gerlach S (2008) Ensuring financial stability: Financial structure and the impact of monetary policy on asset prices. University of Zurich Institute for Empirical Research in Economics working paper series (361)

Baba Y, Hendry DF, Starr RM (1992) The demand for m1 in the U.S.A., 1960–1988. Rev Econ Stud 59(1):25–61

Bagliano FC, Morana C (2009) International macroeconomic dynamics: A factor vector autoregressive approach. Elsevier Econ Model 26(2):432–444

Baks K, Kramer C (1999) Global liquidity and asset prices: Measurement, implications, and spillovers. IMF working paper (168)

Bakshi GS, Chen Z (1996) Inflation, asset prices, and the term structure of interest rates in monetary economics. Rev Financ Stud 9(1):241–275

Ball L, Cecchetti SG (1990) Inflation and uncertainty at short and long horizons. Brookings Paper Econ Activ (1):215–254

Bank of England (2003) Monetary & financial statistics - UK monetary aggregates: Main definitional changes, july 2003, p. 6
Bank of England (2006) Monetary and financial statistics: monetary and financial statistics division - Handbooks in Central Banking No. 25. Bank of England
Bank of Japan (2008) Guide to Japan's money stock statistics
Barbosa Filho NH (2001) International liquidity and growth in Brazil. CEPA working paper (4)
BCA Research (2007) Special report: Too much liquidity? BCA research global investment strategy (January 12, 2007)
Becker S (2007) Globale liquidititätsschwemme und vermögenspreisinflation. Deutsche Bank Research, Aktuelle Themen (391)
Be Duc L, Mayerlen F, Sola P (2008) The monetary presentation of the euro area balance of payments. ECB occasional paper series (96)
Belke A, Cui Y (2009) US-Euro area monetary policy interdependence - new evidence from taylor rule based vecms. Ruhr economic papers (0085)
Belke A, Polleit T (2006) (how) do stock market returns react to monetary policy? An ardl cointegration analysis for Germany. Kredit Kapital 39(3):335–365
Belke A, Polleit T (2007) How the ECB and the US fed set interest rates. Appl Econ 39:2197–2209
Belke A, Polleit T (2009) Monetary economics in globalised financial markets. Springer
Belke A, Rees A (2009) The importance of global shocks for national policymakers - rising challenges for central banks. Discussion Papers of DIW Berlin (922)
Belke A, Orth W, Setzer R (2008) Sowing the seeds for the subprime crisis: Does global liquidity matter for housing and other asset prices? Int Econ Econ Pol 5(4):403–424
Belke A, Bordon IG, Hendricks TW (2009) Global liquidity and commodity prices. Ruhr economic papers (102)
Benassy JP (2007) Money, interest, and policy: dynamic general equilibrium in a non-ricardian world. MIT
Berk JM (1998) The information content of the yield curve for monetary policy: A survey. Economist 146(2):303–320
Bernanke B, Gertler M (1999) Monetary policy and asset price volatility. Federal Reserve Bank of Kansas City, Economic Review Fourth Quarter:17–51
Bernanke BS (2002) Asset-price "bubbles" and monetary policy. In: Before the New York Chapter of the National Association for Business Economics, New York
Bernanke BS (2005) The global saving glut and the U.S. current account deficit. In: Remarks by Governor Ben S. Bernanke at the Sandridge Lecture, Virginia Association of Economics, Richmond, Virginia, March 10, 2005
Bernanke BS (2006) Monetary aggregates and monetary policy at the federal reserve: A historical perspective. In: Speech at the Fourth ECB Central Banking Conference, Frankfurt, Germany, November 10, 2006
Bernanke BS, Kuttner KN (2005) What explains the stock market's reaction to federal reserve policy? J Finance 60(3):1221–1257
Beyer A, Doornik JA, Hendry DF (2001) Constructing historical euro-zone data. Econ J 111(February):102–121
Bini Smaghi L (2007) Global capital and national monetary policies. In: Speech at the European Economic and Financial Centre, London, 18 January 2007
BIS (2004) IV monetary policy in the advanced industrial economies. 74th Annual Report of the Bank for International Settlements pp 61–80
Blanchard O (2009) Macroeconomics, 5th edn. Prentice Hall
Blanchard OJ, Riggi M (2009) Why are the 2000s so different from the 1970s? a structural interpretation of changes in the macroeconomic effects of oil prices. NBER working paper series (15467)
Bodurtha JN, Cho DC, Senbet LW (1989) Economic forces and the stock market: An international perspective. Global Finance J 1(1):21–46
Bordo M, Eichengreen B, Klingebiel D, Martinez-Peria MS (2001) Is the crisis problem growing more severe? Econ Policy 16(32):51–82

Bordo MD, Wheelock DC (2004) Monetary policy and asset prices: A look back at past U.S. stock market booms. NBER working paper series (10704)
Borio C, Lowe P (2003) Imbalances or "bubbles"? implications for monetary and financial stability. In: Hunter WC, Kaufman GG, Pomerleando M (eds) Asset price bubbles: The implications for monetary, regulatory, and international policies. Cambridge, pp 247–270
Borio C, Kennedy N, Prowse S (1994) Exploring aggregate asset price fluctuations across countries. BIS economic papers (40)
Borja DV, Goyeau D (2005) International liquidity, monetary spillovers and asset prices. ASIA-LINK Programme, Euro-Philipines Network in Banking & Finance Enhancing Teaching and Research
Boschi M, Girardi A (2007) Euro inflation: Long-run determinants and short-run dynamics. Appl Financ Econ 17(1):9–24
Boyle GW (1990) Money demand and the stock market in a general equilibrium model with variable velocity. J Polit Econ 98(5):1039–1053
Boyson NM, Stahel CW, Stulz RM (2008) Hedge fund contagion and liquidity. NBER working paper series (14068)
Bracke T, Fidora M (2008) Global liquidity glut or global savings glut? a structural var approach. ECB working paper series (911)
Brand C, Reimers HE, Seitz F (2003) Forecasting real gdp: What role for narrow money? ECB working paper series (254)
Brüggemann R, Lütkepohl H (2006) A small monetary system for the euro area based on German data. J Appl Econometrics 21:683–702
Browne F, Cronin D (2007) Commodity prices, money and inflation. ECB working paper series (738)
Bruggeman A (2007) Can excess liquidity signal an asset price boom? National Bank of Belgium working paper research (117)
Bruggeman A, Donati P, Warne A (2003) Is the demand for euro area m3 stable? ECB working paper series (255)
Brunner K (1961) Some major problems in monetary theory. Am Econ Rev 51(2):47–56
Brunner K, Meltzer AH (1968) Liquidity traps for money, bank credit, and interest rates. J Polit Econ 76(1):1–37
Brunnermeier M, Nagel S (2004) Hedge funds and the technology bubble. J Finance 59(5): 2013–2040
Brunnermeier M, Pedersen LH (2004) Predatory trading. NBER working paper series (10755)
Brunnermeier MK, Pedersen LH (2007) Market liquidity and funding liquidity. NBER working paper series (12939)
Deutsche Bundesbank D (1999) Taylor-zins und monetary conditions index. Deutsche Bundesbank Monatsbericht (April 1999):47–63
Deutsche Bundesbank D (2006) Bestimmungsgründe der zinsstruktur - ansätze zur kombination arbitragefreier modelle und monetärer makroökonomik. Deutsche Bundesbank Monatsbericht (April 2006):15–29
Deutsche Bundesbank D (2007) Der zusammenhang zwischen monetärer entwicklung und immobilienmarkt. Deutsche Bundesbank Monatsbericht (Juli 2007):15–27
Caballero RJ (1997) Aggregate investment. NBER working paper series (6264)
Campbell JY, Shiller RJ (1988) Stock prices, earnings, and expected dividends. J Finance 43(3):661–676
Campbell JY, Shiller RJ (2001) Valuation ratios and the long-run stock market outlook: An update. Cowles Foundation Discussion Paper (1295)
Campbell JY, Vuolteenaho T (2004) Inflation illusion and stock prices. Am Econ Rev 94(2):19–23
Campbell JY, Lo AW, MacKinlay AC (1997) The econometrics of financial markets. Princeton University Press
Carpenter SB, Lange J (2003) Money demand and equity markets. Finance and Economics Discussion Series (3)
Carstensen K (2004) Is European money demand still stable? Kiel working paper (1179)

Caruana J (2003) Banking provisions and asset price bubbles. In: Hunter WC, Kaufman GG, Pomerleando M (eds) Asset price bubbles: The implications for monetary, regulatory, and international policies. Cambridge, pp 537–546

Caruso M (2006) Stock market fluctuations and money demand in Italy, 1913-2003. Economic Notes by Banca Monte dei Paschi di Siena SpA 35(1):1–47

Cassola N, Morana C (2002) Monetary policy and the stock market in the euro area. ECB working paper series (119)

Catarineu-Rabell E, Jackson P, Tsomocos DP (2003) Procyclicality and the new basel accord: Banks' choice of loan rating system. Bank of England working paper (181)

Cecchetti S, Genberg H, Lipsky J, Wadhwani S (2000) Asset prices and central bank policy. Geneva Report on the World Economy (2)

Cerra V, Saxena SC (2007) Growth dynamics: the myth of economic recovery. BIS working papers (226)

Chaudhuri K, Smiles S (2004) Stock market and aggregate economic activity: Evidence from Australia. Appl Financ Econ 14(2):121–129

Chen NF, Roll R, Ross SA (1986) Economic forces and the stock market. J Bus 59(3):383–403

Chen SS (2007) Does monetary policy have asymmetric effects on stock returns? J Money Credit Banking 39(2-3):667–688

Cheng AC (1995) The UK stock market and economic factors: A new approach. J Bus Finance Account 22(1):129–142

Cheng ACS (1996) Economic factors and stock markets: Empirical evidence from the UK and the US. Int J Finance Econ 1:287–302

Cheung YW, Ng LK (1998) International evidence on the stock market and aggregate economic activity. J Empir Finance 5(3):281–296

Chordia T, Sarkar A, Subrahmanyam A (2001) Common determinants of bond and stock market liquidity: The impact of financial crises, monetary policy, and mutual fund flows. Federal Reserve Bank of New York Staff Report (141)

Choudhry T (1996) Real stock prices and the long-run money demand function: Evidence from Canada and the USA. J Int Money Finance 15(1):1–17

Christiano LJ (1991) Modeling the liquidity effect of a money shock. Fed Reserv Bank Minneapolis Q Rev 15(1)

Christiano LJ, Eichenbaum M (1992) Liquidity effects and the monetary transmission mechanism. Am Econ Rev 82(2):346–353

Christiano LJ, Eichenbaum M (1995) Liquidity effects, monetary policy, and the business cycle. J Money Credit Bank 27(4):1113–1136

Ciccarelli M, Mojon B (2005) Global inflation. ECB working paper series (537)

Clerc L (2007) Understanding asset prices: Determinants and policy implications. Banque de France Notes D'Études et De Recherche (168)

Coenen G, Vega JL (1999) The demand for m3 in the euro area. ECB working paper series (6)

Cohen RB, Polk C, Vuolteenaho T (2005) Money illusion in the stock market: The modigliani-cohn hypothesis. Q J Econ 120(2):639–668

Congdon T (2005) Money and asset prices in boom and bust. The Institute of Economic Affairs

Conover CM, Jensen GR, Johnson RR (1999) Monetary environments and international stock returns. J Bank Finance 23(9):1357–1381

Cooper RVL (1974) Efficient capital markets and the quantity theory of money. J Finance 29(3):887–908

Cox JC, Ingersoll JE, Ross SA (1985) A theory of the term structure of interest rates. Econometrica 53(2):385–407

Darrat AF (1987) Money and stock prices in West Germany and the United Kingdom: Is the stock market efficient? Q J Bus Econ 26(1):20–35

Dennis JG (2006) CATS in RATS. Cointegration analysis of time series, vol version 2. Estima

Dennis JG, Hansen H, Johansen S, Juselius K (2005) CATS in RATS, vol version 2. Estima

De Santis RA, Fevero CA, Roffia B (2008) Euro area money demand and international portfolio allocation. ECB working paper series (926)

Detken C, Smets F (2004) Asset price booms and monetary policy. ECB working paper series (364)
Dhakal D, Kandil M, Sharma SC (1993) Causality between the money supply and share prices: A var investigation. Q J Bus Econ 32(3):52–74
Disyatat P (2005) Inflation targeting, asset prices and financial imbalances: Conceptualizing the debate. BIS working papers (168)
Donnery S (2003) Money supply in Ireland. Central Bank and Financial Services Authority of Ireland, Quarterly Bulletin Autumn 2003:73–95
Doornik JA (2007) PcGive, vol version 12. Oxmetrics
Doornik JA, Hansen H (2008) An omnibus test for univariate and multivariate normality. Oxf Bull Econ Stat 70(s1):927–939
Doornik JA, Hendry DF (2006a) Empirical Econometric Modelling - PcGive 11: Volume I, vol version 11. Timberlake Consultants Ltd
Doornik JA, Hendry DF (2006b) Modelling Dynamic Systems - PcGive 11: Volume II, vol version 11. Timberlake Consultants Ltd
Döpke J, Hartmann D, Pierdzioch C (2006a) Forecasting stock market volatility with macroeconomic variables in real time. Deutsche Bundesbank - Discussion Paper Series 2: Banking and Financial Studies (01/2006)
Döpke J, Hartmann D, Pierdzioch C (2006b) Real-time macroeconomic data and ex ante predictability of stock returns. Deutsche Bundesbank - Discussion Paper Series 1: Economic Studies (10/2006)
Dupor B, Conley T (2004) The fed response to equity prices and inflation. Am Econ Rev 94(2): 24–28
Durham JB (2003) Does monetary policy affect stock prices and treasury yields? an error correction and simultaneous equation approach. Finance and Economics Discussion Series
ECB (1999a) Euro area monetary aggregates and their role in the eurosystem's monetary policy strategy. ECB Monthly Bulletin (February 1999):29–45
ECB (1999b) The stability-oriented monetary policy strategy of the eurosystem. ECB Monthly Bulletin January 1999(February 1999):39–49
ECB (2001a) Die neue basler eigenkapitalvereinbarung aus der sicht der ezb. EZB-Monatsbericht May 2001 pp 65–84
ECB (2001b) Framework and tools of monetary analysis. ECB Monthly Bulletin May 2001:41–58
ECB (2003) Monetary presentation of the euro area balance of payments. ECB Monthly Bulletin June 2003, Box 1:15–16
ECB (2004) The Monetary Policy of the ECB. European Central Bank
ECB (2005a) Asset price bubbles and monetary policy. ECB Monthly Bulletin April 2005:47–60
ECB (2005b) External capital flows and domestic monetary dynamics in the euro area. ECB Monthly Bulletin February 2005, Box 2:20–24
ECB (2005c) Recent developments in mfi net external assets. ECB Monthly Bulletin July 2005, Box 2:18–27
ECB (2006a) Measuring world growth: Do weights matter? ECB Monthly Bulletin June 2006, Box 1:13–15
ECB (2006b) Worldwide trends in monetary aggregates: Some conceptual issues. ECB Monthly Bulletin November 2006, Box 3:27–29
ECB (2007) Mfi net external assets and their impact on monetary developments. ECB Annual Report Box 1:34–39
ECB (2008a) The ecb's definition of euro area monetary aggregates. ECB
ECB (2008b) The external dimension of monetary analysis. ECB Monthly Bulletin August 2008:71–84
ECB (2008c) The monetary presentation of the euro area b.o.p. ECB Monthly Bulletin February 2008:1–4
Ehrmann M, Fratzscher M (2004) Taking stock: Monetary policy transmission to equity markets. J Money Credit Bank 36(4):719–737

Ely DP, Robinson KJ (1992) Stock returns and inflation: Further tests of the role of the central bank. J Macroecon 14(3):525–543
Engle RF, Granger CWJ (1987) Co-integration and error correction: Representation, estimation, and testing. Econometrica 55(2):251–276
English JR (2001) Applied equity analysis: stock valuation techniques for Wall Street professionals. McGraw-Hill
Ericsson NR (1998) Empirical modeling of money demand. Empir Econ 23(3):295–315
Estrella A (2001) The cyclical behavior of optimal bank capital. J Bank Finance 28(6):1469–1498
Estrella A, Mishkin FS (1995) Predicting U.S. recessions: Financial variables as leading indicators. NBER working paper series (5379)
Evans MD, Hnatkovska V (2005) International capital flows returns and world financial integration. NBER working paper series (11701)
Fagan G, Henry J (1998) Long run money demand in the eu: Evidence for area-wide aggregates. Empir Econ 23(3):483–506
Fama EF (1970) Efficient capital markets: A review of theory and empirical work. J Finance 25(2):383–417
Fama EF (1981) Stock returns, real activity, inflation, and money. Am Econ Rev 71(4):545–565
Farmer RE (2009) Confidence, crashes and animal spirits. NBER working paper series (14846)
Feldstein M (1980) Inflation and the stock market. Am Econ Rev 70(5):839–847
Ferguson RW (2005) Asset prices and monetary liquidity. In: Remarks by Vice Chairman Roger W. Ferguson, Jr. to the Seventh Deutsche Bundesbank Spring Conference, Berlin, Germany, May 27, 2005
Filardo A (2004) Monetary policy and asset price bubbles: Calibrating the monetary policy tradeoffs. BIS working paper (155)
Financial Markets Center (2005) Causes and consequences of the buildup in global liquidity. Capital Flows Monitor
Financial Markets Center (2006) Another year awash in liquidity. Capital Flows Monitor
Fisher I (1896) Appreciation and Interest. American Economic Association, Reprinted by Princeton University Press
Fisher I (1912) Elementary principles of economics. Macmillan
Fisher I (1928) The money illusion. Adelphi
Fisher I (1930) The theory of interest. Macmillan
Flannery MJ, Protopapadakis AA (2002) Macroeconomic factors do influence aggregate stock returns. Rev Financ Stud 15(3):751–782
Friedman BM (1993) The role of judgment and discretion in the conduct of monetary policy: Consequences of changing financial markets. In: Changing Capital Markets: Implications for Monetary Policy, The Federal Reserve Bank of Kansas City, pp 151–196
Friedman BM, Kuttner KN (1992) Money, income, prices, and interest rates. Am Econ Rev 82(3):472–492
Friedman M (1988) Money and the stock market. J Polit Econ 96(2):221–245
Fuerst TS (1992) Liquidity, loanable funds, and real activity. J Monetary Econ 29:3–24
Galí J (1992) How well does the is-lm model fit postwar U.S. data? Q J Econom 107(2):709–738
Ganjarerndee S (2001) Thailand. In: Kim YH (ed) Government Bond Market Development in Asia, Asian Development Bank, pp 642–684
Garratt A, Lee K, Pesaran MH, Shin Y (2003) A long run structural macroeconometric model of the uk. Econ J 113(487):412–455
Giese JV, Tuxen CK (2007) Global liquidity and asset prices in a cointegrated var. Preliminary Draft
Giese JV, Tuxen CK (2008) Has excess global liquidity fueled asset prices? evidence from i (1) and i (2) cointegrated var models. Working Paper
Girardi A, Paesani P (2004) Net foreign assets in the euro area: A cointegration analysis. Università degli Studi di Roma "La Sapienza" (76)
Goodhart CAE (1995) Price stability and financial fragility. In: Sawamoto K, Taguchi H, Nakajima Z (eds) Financial stability in a changing environment, St. Martin's Press

Gordon DB, Leeper EM (1994) The dynamic impacts of monetary policy: An exercise in tentative identification. J Polit Econ 102(6):1228–1247
Gordon MJ (1962) The Investment, Financing, and Valuation of the Corporation. Richard D. Irwin, Inc.
Gouteron S, Szpiro D (2005) Excès de liquidité monétaire et prix des actifs. Banque de France (131)
Graham B, Dodd D, Cottle CS (1962) Security analysis, 4th edn. McGraw-Hill
Granger CWJ (1981) Some properties of time series data and their use in econometric model specification. J Econometrics 16(1):121–130
Granger CWJ (1986) Developments in the study of cointegrated economic variables. Oxf Bull Econ Stat 48(3):213–228
Greene WH (2003) Econometric analysis, 5th edn. Prentice Hall
Greenspan A (1999) Testimony of chairman alan greenspan. The Federal Reserve's semiannual report on monetary policy, July 22, 1999
Greenspan A (2002) Economic volatility. In: At a symposium sponsored by the Federal Reserve Bank of Kansas City, Jackson Hole, Wyoming, August 30, 2002
Greiber C, Lemke W (2005) Money demand and macroeconomic uncertainty. Deutsche Bundesbank Discussion Paper, Series 1: Economic Studies (26/2005)
Greiber C, Setzer R (2007) Money and housing – evidence for the euro area and the us. Deutsche Bundesbank Discussion Paper, Series 1: Economic Studies (12/2007)
Gros D (2006a) Foreign investment in the us (i): Disappearing in a black hole? CEPS working document (242)
Gros D (2006b) Foreign investment in the us (ii): Being taken to the cleaners? CEPS working document (243)
Gudmundsson M (2008) Financial globalisation: Key trends and implications for the transmission mechanism of monetary policy. BIS Papers (39):7–29
Hamburger MJ, Kochin LA (1972) Money and stock prices: The channels of influence. J Finance 27(2):231–249
Hashemzadeh N, Taylor P (1988) Stock prices, money supply, and interest rates: the question of causality. Appl Econ 20(12):1603–1611
Hau H, Rey H (2004) Can portfolio rebalancing explain the dynamics of equity returns, equity flows, and exchange rates? Am Econ Rev 94(2):126–133
Heise M, Schneider R, Milleker DF, Broyer C (2005) Global liquidity glut: Problem or growth driver? Economic Research Allianz Group Dresdner Bank working paper (47)
Helbling T, Terrones M (2003) Real and financial effects of bursting asset price bubbles. IMF World Economic Outlook pp 61–94
Hendry DF, Juselius K (1999) Explaining cointegration analysis: Part i. Working Paper
Hendry DF, Juselius K (2000) Explaining cointegration analysis: Part ii. Discussion Papers Institute of Economics University of Copenhagen (00-20)
Hendry DF, Mizon GE (1993) Evaluating econometric models by encompassing the var. In: Phillips P (ed) Models, methods and applications of econometrics: Essays in Honor of A.R. Bergstrom. MIT, Cambridge, Mass
Homa KE, Jaffee DM (1971) The supply of money and common stock prices. J Finance 26(5):1045–1066
Homer S, Sylla R (2005) A History of Interest Rates, 4th edn. Wiley
Hoover KD, Johansen S, Juselius K (2008) Allowing the data to speak freely: The macroeconometrics of the cointegrated vector autoregression. Am Econ Rev Papers Proc 98(2):251–255
Hördahl P, Packer F (2007) Understanding asset prices: An overview. BIS Papers (34)
Huang J, Wang J (2008) Market liquidity, asset prices and welfare. NBER Working Paper Series (14058)
Humpe A, Macmillan P (2009) Can macroeconomic variables explain long-term stock market movements? a comparison of the US and Japan. Appl Financ Econ 19:111–119
IMF (1993) Balance of Payments Manual. International Monetary Fund
IMF (1999) Global liquidity. World Economic Outlook - Box 44, pp 118–121

IMF (2000) Asset prices and the business cycle. IMF World Economic Outlook, pp 77–112
IMF (2008) Selected issues in balance of payments and international investment position analysis – alternative presentations of balance of payments data. Balance of Payments and International Investment Position Manual, Sixth Edition (BPM6) – December 2008, Pre-Publication Draft pp 333–337
Inoguchi M (2007) Influence of ADB bond issues and US bonds on Asian government bonds. Asian Econ J 21(4):387–404
Issing O (2004) Financial integration, asset prices and monetary policy. In: Dinner speech at the Symposium concluding two years of the ECB-CFS research network on "Capital Markets and Financial Integration in Europe", May 10, 2004
Issing O (2007) Einführung in die Geldtheorie. Verlag Franz Vahlen GmbH
Ito T (2003) Looking forward on monetary and supervision policies to protect against bubbles. In: Hunter WC, Kaufman GG, Pomerleando M (eds) Asset price bubbles: The implications for monetary, regulatory, and international policies. Cambridge, pp 547–552
Jara A, Tovar CE (2008) Monetary and financial stability implications of capital flows in Latin America and The Caribbean. BIS papers (43)
Johansen S (1995) Likelihood-Based inference in cointegrated vector autoregressive models. Oxford University Press
Johansen S (2002) A small sample correction of the test for cointegration rank in the vector autoregressive model. Econometrica 70(5):1929–1961
Johansen S (2005) Interpretation of cointegrating coefficients in the cointegrated vector autoregressive model. Oxf Bull Econ Stat 67(1):93–104
Johansen S (2007) Correlation, regression, and cointegration of nonstationary economic time series. Discussion Papers Department of Economics University of Copenhagen (07-25)
Johansen S (2009) Cointegration. overview and development. Forthcoming Handbook of Financial Econometrics
Johansen S, Juselius K (1992) Testing structural hypotheses in a multivariate cointegration analysis of the PPP and the UIP for UK. J Econometrics 53(1/2/3):211–256
Johansen S, Juselius K (1994) Identification of the long-run and the short-run structure: An application to the islm model. J Econometrics 63(1):7–36
Johansen S, Juselius K (2001) Controlling inflation in a cointegrated vector autoregressive model with an application to us data. Working Paper ECO (2001/2)
Juselius K (1996) An empirical analysis of the changing role of the German bundesbank after 1983. Oxf Bull Econ Stat 58(4):791–819
Juselius K (1998) Changing monetary transmission mechanisms within the eu. Empir Econ 23:455–481
Juselius K (1999) Models and relations in economics and econometrics. J Econ Meth 6(2):259–290
Juselius K (2001) European integration and monetary transmission mechanisms: The case of Italy. J Appl Econometrics 16(3):341–358
Juselius K (2006) The cointegrated VAR model: methodology and applications, 2nd edn. Oxford University Press
Juselius K, MacDonald R (2004) International parity relationships between Germany and the United States: A joint modelling approach. FRU working papers (2004/08)
Juselius K, Toro J (2005) Monetary transmission mechanisms in Spain: The effect of monetization, financial deregulation, and the ems. J Int Money Finance 24(3):509–531
Kent C, Lowe P (1997) Asset-price bubbles and monetary policy. Reserve Bank of Australia Research Discussion Paper (9709)
Keran MW (1971) Expectations, money, and stock market. Federal Reserve Bank of St Louis Rev 53(1):16–31
Keynes JM (1936) The general theory of employment, interest and money. Macmillan Cambridge University Press
King M (2003) No money, no inflation - the role of money in the economy. In: Mizen P (ed) Central Banking, monetary theory and practice: Essays in honour of Charles Goodhart, vol 1. Edward Elgar Publishing, pp 62–89

King M (2006) Speech in ashford, kent. In: At a Dinner for Kent Business Contacts in conjunction with the Kent Messenger Group/Kent Business, on Monday 16 January 2006
Kiyotaki N, Moore J (1997) Credit cycles. J Polit Econ 105(2):211–248
Knight M (2006) Money, credit and asset prices: (re-)learning to read their message. In: Speech for the ECB Colloquium, Otmar Issing's Festschrift "Monetary policy: A journey from theory to practice", Frankfurt, 16–17 March 2006
Kohn DL (2008) Monetary policy and asset prices revisited. In: Speech at the Cato Institute's 26th Annual Monetary Policy Conference, Washington, D.C., November 19, 2008
Kongsted HC (2005) Testing the nominal-to-real transformation. J Econometrics 124(2):205–225
Kroszner RS (2003) Asset price bubbles, information, and public policy. In: Hunter WC, Kaufman GG, Pomerleando M (eds) Asset price bubbles: The Implications for monetary, regulatory, and international policies. Cambridge, pp 3–13
Kuttner KN (2001) Monetary policy surprises and interest rates: Evidence from the fed funds futures market. J Monetary Econ 47:523–544
Kuttner KN, Mosser PC (2002) The monetary transmission mechanism: Some answers and further questions. FRBNY Econ Policy Rev May 2002:15–26
Kwon CS, Shin TS (1999) Cointegration and causality between macroeconomic variables and stock market returns. Global Finance J 10(1):71–81
Lane PR, Milesi-Ferretti GM (2006) The external wealth of nations mark ii: Revised and extended estimates of foreign assets and liabilities, 1970-2004. IIIS Discussion Paper (126)
Lane PR, Milesi-Ferretti GM (2008) Where did all the borrowing go? a forensic analysis of the U.S. external position. IMF working paper 08/28
Laopodis NT (2006) Dynamic interactions among the stock market, federal funds rate, inflation, and economic activity. Financ Rev 41(4):513–545
Lastrapes WD (1998) International evidence on equity prices, interest rates and money. J Int Money Finance 17(3):377–406
Lee BS (1992) Causal relations among stock returns, interest rates, real activity, and inflation. J Finance 47(4):1591–1603
Lee KY (2008) Causal relationship between stock returns and inflation. Appl Econ Lett 15(2): 125–129
Lowe P (2002) Credit risk measurement and procyclicality. BIS working paper (116)
Lütkepohl H (1994) Interpretation of cointegrating relations. Econometric Rev 13:391–394
Marshall DA (1992) Inflation and asset returns in a monetary economy. J Finance 47(4):1315–1342
Mauro P (2000) Stock returns and output growth in emerging and advanced economies. IMF working paper 00/89
Maysami RC, Koh TS (2000) A vector error correction model of the Singapore stock market. Int Rev Econ Finance 9(1):79–96
McKibbin WJ, Sachs JD (1991) Global linkages: Macroeconomic interdependence and cooperation in the World Economy. The Brookings Institution
McKinsey Global Institute (2008) Mapping global capital markets: Fourth annual report. McKinsey Global Institute
McKinsey Global Institute (2009) Global capital markets: Entering a new era. McKinsey Global Institute
Meltzer AH (1995) Monetary, credit and (other) transmission processes: A monetarist perspective. J Econ Perspect 9(4):49–72
Mishkin F (2009) Not all bubbles present a risk to the economy. Financial Times
Mishkin FS (1995) Symposium on the monetary transmission mechanism. J Econ Perspect 9(4): 3–10
Mishkin FS (1996) The channels of monetary transmission: Lessons for monetary policy. NBER working paper series (5464)
Mishkin FS (1999) Lessons from the asian crisis. J Int Money Finance 18(4):709–723
Mishkin FS (2001) The transmission mechanism and the role of asset prices in monetary policy. NBER working paper series (8617)
Münchau W (2009) A polite discourse on bankers and bubbles. Financial Times

Modigliani F (1971) Monetary policy and consumption: Linkages via interest rate and wealth effects in the fmp model. In: Consumer Spending Money and Monetary Policy: The Linkages, 5, The Federal Reserve Bank of Boston

Modigliani F, Cohn RA (1979) Inflation, rational valuation and the market. Financial Analysts J 35(2):24–44

Moller Christensen A, Bohn Nielsen H (2003) Has us monetary policy followed the taylor rule? a cointegration analysis 1988-2002. Working paper

Montgomery J (1999) Analyzing global liquidity. Morgan Stanley Dean Witter Global Investment Research

Moreno R (2003) Comments on "asset price bubbles" and prudential regulation. In: Hunter WC, Kaufman GG, Pomerleando M (eds) Asset Price Bubbles: The Implications for Monetary, Regulatory, and International Policies. Cambridge, pp 523–527

Mukherjee TK, Naka A (1995) Dynamic relations between macroeconomic variables and the Japanese stock market: An application of a vector error correction model. J Financ Res 18(2):223–237

Muscatelli VA, Spinelli F (2000) The long-run stability of the demand for money: Italy 1861-1996. J Monetary Econ 45(3):717–739

Mussa M (2003) Asset prices and monetary policy. In: Hunter WC, Kaufman GG, Pomerleando M (eds) Asset price bubbles: The implications for monetary, regulatory, and international policies. Cambridge, pp 41–50

Nasseh A, Strauss J (2000) Stock prices and domestic and international macroeconomic activity: A cointegration approach. Q Rev Econ Finance 40(2):229–245

Nautz D (2008) Volatility transmission in the european money market. N Am J Econ Finance 19(1):23–39

Neri S (2004) Monetary policy and stock prices: Theory and evidence. Bank of Italy, research department working paper (513)

Nielsen B, Rahbek A (2000) Similarity issues in cointegration analysis. Oxf Bull Econ Stat 62(1):5–22

Noland M (2005) South Korea's experience with international capital flows. NBER working paper series (11381)

Ohanian LE, Stockman AC (1995) Theoretical issues of liquidity effects. Federal Reserve Bank of St Louis Rev (May/June 1995):3–25

Okun AM (1971) The mirage of steady inflation. Brookings Paper Econ Activ (2):485–498

Pagan AR, Robertson JC (1995) Resolving the liquidity effect. Federal Reserve Bank of St Louis Rev (May/June 1995):33–54

Papademos L (2007) The effects of globalisation on inflation, liquidity and monetary policy. In: Speech at a conference on the "International Dimensions of Monetary Policy", S'Agaró, Girona, 11 June 2007

Pearce DK, Roley VV (1983) The reaction of stock prices to unanticipated changes in money: A note. J Finance 38(4):1323–1333

Pepper G (1994) Money, Credit and Asset Prices. St. Martin's Press

Pepper G, Oliver MJ (2006) The liquidity theory of asset prices. Wiley

Pesando JE (1974) The supply of money and common stock prices: Further observations on the econometric evidence. J Finance 29(3):909–921

Pesaran MH, Shin Y, Smith RJ (2001) Bounds testing approaches to the analysis of level relationships. J Appl Econometrics 16(3):289–326

Pilbeam K (2005) Finance and Financial Markets, 2nd edn. Palgrave Macmillan

Polleit T, Gerdesmeier D (2005) Measures of excess liquidity. HfB – working paper series (65)

Pollock AJ (2009) Why not negative interest rates? J Am Enterprise Institute

Poole W (1970) Optimal choice of monetary policy instruments in a simple stochastic macro model. Q J Econ 84(2):197–216

Rahbek A, Hansen E, Dennis JG (2002) Arch innovations and their impact on cointegration rank testing. Revised version of preprint no12, 1998, Department of Theoretical Statistics, University of Copenhagen, Working paper No 22, Centre for Analytical Finance

Rajan RG (2005) Has financial development made the world riskier? NBER working paper series (11728)
Rajan RG (2006) Monetary policy and incentives. In: Bank of Spain Conference on Central Banks in the 21st Century, June 8, 2006
Rao BB (2007) Estimating short and long-run relationships: A guide for the applied economist. Appl Econ 39:1613–1625
Rapach DE (2001) Macro shocks and real stock prices. J Econ Bus 53(1):5–26
Ratanapakorn O, Sharma SC (2007) Dynamic analysis between the us stock returns and the macroeconomic variables. Appl Financ Econ 17(5):369–377
Rees A (2009) Die weltweite liquiditätsschwemme. UniCredit Markets & Investment Banking
Reimers HE (2002) Analysing divisia aggregates for the euro area. Discussion paper 13/02 Economic Research Centre of the Deutsche Bundesbank
Reinhart CM, Rogoff KS (2004) Serial default and the "paradox" of rich-to-poor capital flows. Am Econ Rev 94(2):53–58
Reinhart CM, Rogoff KS (2008) Banking crises: An equal opportunity menace. NBER working paper series (14587)
Reinhart CM, Rogoff KS (2009) The aftermath of financial crises. NBER working paper series (14656)
Reserve Bank of Australia Bulletin (2002) Statement on monetary policy. Statements on Monetary Policy (August 2002)
Rüffer R, Stracca L (2006) What is global excess liquidity, and does it matter? ECB working paper series (696)
Rigobon R, Sack B (2004) The impact of monetary policy on asset prices. J Monetary Econ 51(8):1553–1575
Rogalski RJ, Vinso JD (1977) Stock returns, money supply and the direction of causality. J Finance 32(4):1017–1030
Rogoff K (2006) Impact of globalization on monetary policy. In: Symposium sponsored by the Federal Reserve Bank of Kansas City on "The New Economic Geography: Effects and Policy Implications," Jackson Hole, Wyoming, August 24–26, 2006
Romer D (1996) Advanced macroeconomics. McGraw-Hill
Ross SA (1976) The arbitrage pricing theory of capital asset pricing. J Econ Theory 13(3):341–360
Ross SA (1987) The interrelations of finance and economics: Theoretical perspectives. Am Econ Rev 77(2):29–34
Rozeff MS (1974) Money and stock prices: Market efficiency and the lag in effect of monetary policy. J Financ Econ 1(3):245–302
Rozeff MS (1975) The money supply and the stock market. Financial Analysts J 31(5):18–26, 76
Sachs G (2006) Global liquidity and asset prices. Global Economics Weekly (06/05, February 8, 2006)
Sarno L, Taylor MP (1999) Moral hazard, asset price bubbles, capital flows, and the east asian crisis: the first tests. J Int Money Finance 18(4):637–657
Schwartz AJ (2002) Asset price inflation and monetary policy. NBER working paper series (9321)
Schwert GW (1990) Stock returns and real activity: A century of evidence. J Finance 45(4): 1237–1257
Sellin P (2001) Monetary policy and the stock market: Theory and empirical evidence. J Econ Surv 15(4):491–541
Semmler W (2006) Asset prices, booms and recessions: financial economics from a dynamic perspective, 2nd edn. Springer
Serletis A (2006) Money and the economy. World Scientific Publishing
Serletis A (2007) The demand for money, 2nd edn. Springer
Shenton LR, Bowman K (1977) A bivariate model for the distribution of $\sqrt{b_1}$ and $b2$. J Am Stat Assoc 72(357):206–211
Shiller RJ (2007) Low interest rates and high asset prices: An interpretation in terms of changing popular economic models. NBER working paper series (13558)

Sims CA, Stock JH, Watson MW (1990) Inference in linear time series models with some unit roots. Econometrica 58(1):113–144

Singh A, Weisse BA (1998) Emerging stock markets, portfolio capital flows and long-term economic growth: Micro and macroeconomic perspectives. World Development - Elsevier 26(4):607–622

Smets F (1997) Financial asset prices and monetary policy: Theory and evidence. BIS working papers (47)

Sousa J, Zaghini A (2004) Monetary policy shocks in the euro area and global liquidity spillovers. ECB working paper series (309)

Sprinkel BW (1964) Money and stock prices. Richard D. Irwin, Inc.

Sprinkel BW (1971) Money and markets - a monetarist view. Richard D. Irwin, Inc.

Sriram SS, Adams C (1999) Survey of literature on demand for money: Theoretical and empirical work with special reference to error-correction models. IMF working paper 99/64

Standard & Poor's (2009) Australia all ordinaries index by sector

Stark J (2007) The external dimension of monetary analysis. In: Dinner speech on the occasion of the ECB workshop on "The external dimension of monetary analysis", Frankfurt am Main, 12 December 2007

Stracca L (2001) Does liquidity matter? properties of a synthetic divisia monetary aggregate in the euro area. ECB working papers (79)

Sutthirat J (2006) Impacts of news on stock's return volatility under different economic conditions: Evidence from stock exchange of thailand. J Econ Chiang Mai Universität pp 44–59

Taboga M (2008) Macro-finance vars and bond risk premia: A caveat. Munich Personal RePEc Archive Paper (11585)

Taylor JB (1981) On the relation between the variability of inflation and the average inflation rate. Elsevier - Carnegie-Rochester Conference Series on Public Policy 15:57–85

Taylor JB (1993) Discretion versus policy rules in practice. Carnegie-Rochester Conference Series on Public Policy 39:195–214

Taylor JB (1995) The monetary transmission mechanism: An empirical framework. J Econ Perspect 9(4):11–26

Taylor MP, Sarno L (1997) Capital flows to development countries: Lang- and short-term determinants. World Bank Econ Rev 11(10):451–470

The Bank of Korea (1995) Current economic and financial movements. Q Econ Rev

The Economist (1997) On the trail of the mutant inflation monster. Economist 345(8037):77–78

The Economist (2005) The great thrift shift. a survey of the world economy. Economist pp 3–5

The Economist (2007) Only human - a special report on central banks and the world economy. Economist

The Economist (2009a) Googling the future. Economist

The Economist (2009b) Greed-and fear. a special report on the future of finance. Economist

Tobin J (1969) A general equilibrium approach to monetary theory. J Money Credit Bank 1(1): 15–29

Tobin J (1991) Money still counts. Wall Street J 73(16 December 1991):A14

Trichet JC (2003) Asset price bubbles and their implications for monetary policy and financial stability. In: Hunter WC, Kaufman GG, Pomerleando M (eds) Asset price bubbles: The implications for monetary, regulatory, and international policies. Cambridge, pp 15–22

Trichet JC (2005) Asset price bubbles and monetary policy. In: Mas lecture, The Monetary Authority of Singapore

Walter P (2003) Understanding the impact of external trade and international capital flows on euro area monetary growth and Austria's contribution from 1999 to 2002: The monetary presentation of the balance of payments. In: Focus on Austria, vol 3/2003, Oesterreichische Nationalbank, pp 76–94

Warnock FE, Warnock V (2006) International capital flows and U.S. interest rates. NBER working paper series (12560)

Wheatley J (2009) Brazil sets 2% tax on capital inflows. Financial Times

White WR (2006) Is price stability enough? BIS working papers 205

Williams N (1999) Global liquidity: Strong but peaking? Goldman Sachs Global Economic and Strategy Weekly
van Wincoop E, Tille C (2007) International capital flows. NBER working paper series (12856)
Wong WK, Khan H, Du J (2006) Do money and interest rates matter for stock prices? An econometric study of Singapore and USA. Singapore Econ Rev 51(1):31–51
WSJ (2009) Cleveland fed inflation model finds favorable results. Wall Street J

Index

Kolibri 360 GmbH
Ferdinand-Jühlke-Straße 7
99095 Erfurt, Deutschland
produktsicherheit@kolibri360.de